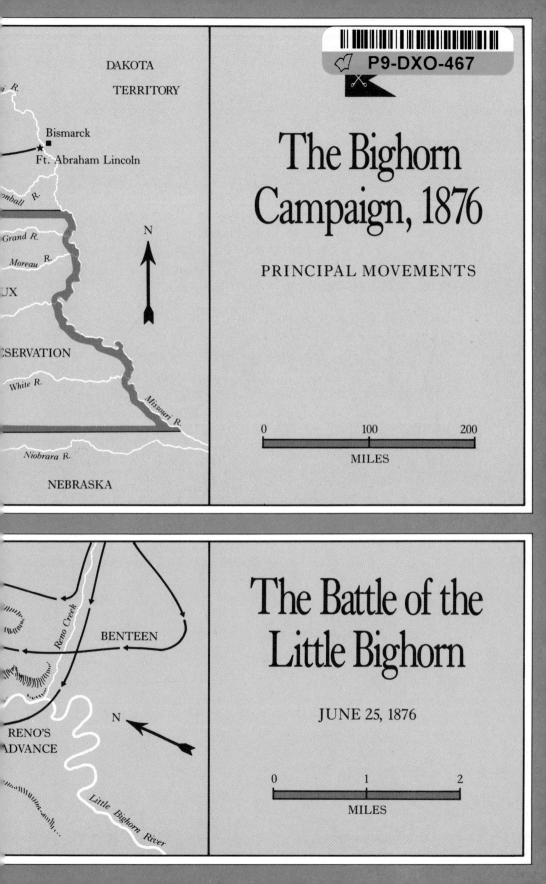

DAKOTA
TERRITORY

Bismarck
Ft. Abraham Lincoln

_i R._

onball R.

Grand R.

Moreau R.

UX

SERVATION

White R.

Missouri R.

N

Niobrara R.

NEBRASKA

P9-DXO-467

The Bighorn Campaign, 1876

PRINCIPAL MOVEMENTS

0   100   200

MILES

Reno Creek

BENTEEN

N

RENO'S
ADVANCE

Little Bighorn River

The Battle of the Little Bighorn

JUNE 25, 1876

0   1   2

MILES

Other Books by Evan S. Connell

The Anatomy Lesson and Other Stories
Mrs. Bridge
The Patriot
Notes from a Bottle Found on the Beach at Carmel
At the Crossroads
The Diary of a Rapist
Mr. Bridge
Points for a Compass Rose
The Connoisseur
Double Honeymoon
A Long Desire
The White Lantern
Saint Augustine's Pigeon

EVAN S. CONNELL

Son of the Morning Star

NORTH POINT PRESS · SAN FRANCISCO · 1984

TO CURT GENTRY

We do not see our hand in what happens,
so we call certain events melancholy accidents . . .
                                         Stanley Cavell

Son of the Morning Star

Lt. James Bradley led a detachment of Crow Indian scouts up the Bighorn Valley during the summer of 1876. In his journal he records that early Monday morning, June 26, they saw the tracks of four ponies. Assuming the riders must be Sioux, they followed these tracks to the river and came upon one of the ponies, along with some equipment which evidently had been thrown away. An examination of the equipment disclosed, much to his surprise, that it belonged to some Crows from his own command who had been assigned to General Custer's regiment a few days earlier.

While puzzling over this circumstance, Bradley discovered three men on the opposite side of the river. They were about two miles away and appeared to be watching. He instructed his scouts to signal with blankets that he was friendly, which they did, but for a long time there was no response. Then the distant men built a fire, messages were exchanged by smoke signal, and they were persuaded to come closer.

They were indeed Crow scouts: Hairy Moccasin, Goes Ahead, White Man Runs Him. They would not cross the river, but they were willing to talk.

Bradley did not want to believe the story they told, yet he had a feeling it was true. In his journal he states that he could only hope they were exaggerating, "that in the terror of the three fugitives from the fatal field their account of the disaster was somewhat overdrawn."

The news deeply affected his own scouts. One by one they went aside and sat down, rocking to and fro, weeping and chanting. Apart from relatives and friends of the slain soldiers, he later wrote, "there were none in this whole horrified nation of forty millions of people to whom the tidings brought greater grief."

Bradley at once rode back to his commandant, General Alfred Terry, and repeated what the Crows had said. Terry, accompanied by Colonel John Gibbon and surrounded by aides, did not join in the chorus of disbelief but sat on his horse with a thoughtful expression, "biting his lower lip and looking at me as though he by no means shared in the wholesale skepticism of the flippant members of his staff."

The column then resumed its march and shortly after noon crossed into the valley of the Little Bighorn.

A white scout named "Muggins" Taylor—described as a gambler and professional hunter—was directed to look around. When he came back he reported the smoke of a large fire up ahead. Col. Gibbon thought this was good news because it meant one of two things: Custer had taken the Indian village or the Indians themselves were burning it.

General Terry offered $200 to anybody who could reach Custer. Taylor and another scout named Bostwick decided to try. Both returned in a little while saying nobody could get through.

Horsemen materialized on a ridge and through field glasses it could be seen that several of them wore blue uniforms, meaning they must belong to Custer's regiment—possibly his Arikara scouts. Lt. Charles Roe led a troop of cavalry forward. Roe advanced cautiously, uncertain whether he was approaching Arikaras or Sioux. He dispatched a sergeant to find out. Advance, tie a handkerchief to your gun, wave it, and we will see what happens, said Roe. But just then a party of at least sixty United States cavalrymen—or what resembled cavalry, proceeding by twos, with a guidon flying—rode into view. A second cavalry unit then merged with the first and Lt. Roe understood that they were hostile Indians dressed in Army clothing. With this frightful masque to contemplate it seems odd that he did not rescind his order to wave a handkerchief at them, but he did not: "I immediately ordered the sergeant to move forward, saying that we would support him. . . ."

The obedient sergeant commandeered two enlisted men and these guinea pigs galloped ahead while Roe and the others followed. Very soon a familiar noise could be heard: Pop! Pop! Pop! Pop!

Neither the intrepid sergeant nor his companions were hit, but the plateau was by now carpeted with Indians and Lt. Roe thought it wise to retreat.

Until this withdrawal, most of the troops with Gibbon and Terry thought the disciplined blue-clad riders must belong to Custer. Only a few remained suspicious. Although the riders maintained cavalry formation, Lt. John

McBlain noted, "there was an indefinable something in their movements that did not appear altogether natural." Capt. Henry Freeman bet a cigar they were hostile, despite rumors that two of them had been seen shaking hands with Roe, and in his journal Freeman commented somewhat dryly that he had won a cigar.

While discussing the day's events around a campfire most infantrymen predicted more unpleasant news, whereas the cavalrymen—emotionally related to Custer's Seventh—argued that if indeed there had been a fight Custer must have been victorious. "So obstinate is human nature," Bradley wrote, "that there were actually men in the command who lay down to sleep that night in the firm conviction, notwithstanding all the disclosures of the day, that there was not an Indian in our front. . . . They could explain ingeniously every circumstance that had a contrary look, and to argue with them was worse than useless."

Tuesday morning not an Indian could be seen.

Farther up the valley, on a hillside east of the river, lay a number of pale unidentifiable objects which were assumed to be dead buffalo. Several dark objects among these carcasses were thought to be buffalo skins left behind when the Indians fled. Bradley crossed the river to investigate.

Not long after his departure the column reached the site of an Indian encampment so recently deserted that the fire beds had not cooled. A few skulking dogs loped away when the army approached. Debris littered the ground: shotguns, axes, blankets, soup bowls, horn spoons, brass kettles, hammers, coffee mills, chunks of meat, antique pistols, a grindstone, tin cups, a small bellows, saddles and buffalo robes, along with such incongruous items as photographs, letters, and china dishes. Wounded horses from Custer's regiment and various pieces of army equipment also were discovered in the village, and from an upright pole dangled three human heads bound together with wires—all three so badly burned they could not be identified.

Gibbon's surgeon, Dr. Holmes Paulding, noticed Lt. James Porter's buckskin shirt. "Poor fellow," Dr. Paulding wrote in his diary, "there was a hole under the right shoulder & blood over the rest—Found 'Yates, 7th Cav' marked on a pair of gloves—under-clothing of Jack Sturgis, with his spurs, and traces of other old friends of that gallant regiment. There were immense fresh trails of lodge poles leading toward the ravines & bluffs and along all of them packs, travoises, lodge poles & utensils dropped or hastily cut loose. . . ."

Several lodges had not been dismantled. Terry's soldiers at first thought this was because the hostiles had been in a hurry to escape; but inside each of these lodges lay one or more dead warriors, each handsomely dressed and—as was the burial custom—wearing moccasins with ceremonially beaded soles.

About this time Lt. Bradley returned from the other side of the river to say that the dark objects on the hillside thought to be buffalo skins were, in fact, dead horses. What had been mistaken for skinned buffalo carcasses were the naked bodies of Custer's men. Bradley had counted 197 dead soldiers. This news paralyzed the advancing army. A mule packer in Roe's company, Pvt. William H. White, said that for a quarter of an hour there was very little talking.

The column then proceeded through the valley in an attempt to learn what had happened.

As the troops marched south they noticed occasional clusters of arrows standing up like cactus. Before long they understood that each cluster would mean another dead cavalryman.

Moving figures could be discerned on a hilltop some distance ahead—rushing around in such excitement that they were assumed to be Indians—and with them a herd of ponies. A detachment of soldiers guided by Muggins Taylor went forward.

After a while Terry's army caught up with this unit and found the officer in charge talking with emissaries from the hill, who turned out to be Lts. Luther Hare and George Wallace of a Seventh Cavalry battalion commanded by Major Marcus Reno. It developed that Reno's battalion had been surrounded by Sioux and Cheyennes for two days, Sunday and Monday, until late Monday afternoon when the Indians dismantled their portable village and moved south toward the Bighorn mountains. What had appeared from the distance to be a pony herd was the Seventh Cavalry mule train.

Reno's messengers were thankful that Terry and Gibbon had arrived, but they were puzzled because they thought this column was led by General Custer. They said there had been no word from him since he divided the command and rode off with five companies early Sunday afternoon. They were stunned to hear that everybody who went with Custer was dead, and they had trouble realizing that their two-day ordeal was a peripheral fight.

Fifty-two of Reno's men were wounded, which gave Dr. Paulding plenty of work. In a letter to his mother some time afterward he sounds bemused by the resilience of the survivors. Although Custer's death shocked them, he wrote, they got over it quickly and became rather cheerful.

Captain Walter Clifford of the Seventh Infantry rode up into the hills for an elevated view of Reno's defensive position and there he happened to see an Indian pony with a shattered leg—the leg swinging hideously each time the little animal moved. Flies swarmed on the wound. The pony came hobbling over and rested its head against the flank of Clifford's horse. Clifford pulled away because nothing could be done, but when he looked around he saw the pony trying to follow. He rode back and again the pony approached, "this time laying his head on my horse's rump, looking straight at me, as if pleading for help." Clifford held his pistol against the pony's head and fired. "Lightning could not have finished him sooner."

On his way down Capt. Clifford studied the west bank of the Little Bighorn. Reno's men had fled to the hilltop after losing a skirmish at the upper end of the valley and had plunged from this embankment into the river. He estimated its height at about ten feet. They landed in water four or five feet deep and after crossing the stream they climbed hills that were too steep for a direct ascent. "The marvel is that with such a multitude of Indians around them so many escaped. The retreat was a mad race to a place of safety."

Preparations were begun to carry Reno's wounded troopers to the mouth of the Little Bighorn where the steamer *Far West* was waiting, moored to a cottonwood tree. Pvt. White was one of the men assigned to collect material for litters and he reports that at first they cut saplings, but then realized it would be easier to obtain poles by tearing apart Sioux burial lodges. Besides, this would give them a chance to hunt for souvenirs. White and others in this detail were fascinated by what they saw. Dr. Paulding wanted a pair of beaded moccasins laced on the feet of a dead warrior. He tugged at them, "but they were a tight fit, since his flesh was swollen, and the skin slipped when he took hold of a leg. Notwithstanding he was a doctor, the offensive odor and the repugnant situation in general caused him to quit his undertaking. Those bodies had been lying there through two days and nights of the warm weather of the 25th, 26th, and 27th of June."

The journal of Dr. Paulding fails to mention this incident.

White himself picked up half a dozen pairs of moccasins and a mirror studded with brass tacks. He also found a gunnysack full of letters which must have been taken from a stagecoach or a post office, and somebody's account book containing a list of about twenty names together with amounts charged against them. On several pages of this book were Indian drawings presumably made by whoever had stolen it, but these drawings did not interest him. He gave the letters and the account book to a Chicago journalist who was traveling with the army. The book has now disappeared. A number of journalists accompanied the army, but just two from Chicago: Charles Diehl of the *Times* and "Phocion" Howard of the *Tribune*. One of them must have carried it off.

Except for the tack-studded mirror—which, in photographs, suggests a medieval Viking artifact—White lost his Sioux memorabilia when some person or persons unknown ran away with a bag containing the moccasins. He told an interviewer many years afterward that he suspected a cavalryman from the Seventh.

The day after his excursion to the village White spent a while wandering through the valley where Reno's men started the fight. All of the bodies he saw had been horribly gashed. Entrails protruded. Heads, feet, arms, legs, and hands were chopped off. He noted just one exception—a trooper lying almost hidden beneath the belly of a horse. This man had not been found by the Indians and before dying of his wounds he must have gone mad with thirst because he had thrust his head between the animal's hind legs and opened a haunch with his knife. The knife lay on the ground beside his right hand. His left hand clutched a tin cup in which there were a few ounces of clotted blood.

In 1920 ex-Private William Slaper described what he saw in the valley to historian E. A. Brininstool: "Corporal Henry Scollen of M Troop was found badly mutilated, with his right leg severed from his body. Jim Turley's body was found with his hunting knife driven to the hilt in one eye. . . ."

Scollen felt some deep apprehension. On June 24 his bunkmate, Pvt. Daniel Newell, went for a dip in Rosebud Creek and when he returned to camp he noticed Scollen writing in a diary. "If anything happens to me," Scollen said, "notify my sister Mary, who lives in Gardiner, Massachusetts. My name is Henry Cody. . . ." This was the second time within a few days that he had told Newell his true name.

He was killed during the retreat from the valley. Newell saw him go down and heard him say "Good-bye, boys!"

His horse got away and later was caught by a soldier from another company. In a saddlebag was his prayerbook, *The Key of Heaven*, which Newell mailed to his sister. She wrote back wanting to know if her brother had been disfigured. Newell lied, assuring her that he was not. "I would have given most anything if I could have recovered his diary," Newell remarked in 1930, "but I suppose the squaws got that when they stripped his body. Poor boy."

An engineering officer of Gibbon's command, Lt. Edward McClernand, jotted down a few reflections while passing through the valley. He noted that this region had been scouted the previous April, at which time some Crow guides—well aware of Sioux nearby—had left an ideograph for their enemies to find: an empty breadbox decorated with charcoal drawings. These pictures informed the Sioux that they were going to be wiped out, and the Crows stuffed grass in the cracks of the box to indicate that this would happen in summer. Considering the great amount of territory scouted by Gibbon's patrols, McClernand wrote, it was strange that this breadbox should have been left just a short distance from the actual site of the battle.

Here on the valley floor, at the south end of the Sioux-Cheyenne encampment, the battle may have been resolved before Custer himself fired a shot. In 1883 an Unkpapa Sioux woman told of being here when Reno charged. She thought the man who led the attacking troops must have been drunk or insane: "He had the camp at his mercy, and could have killed us all or driven us away. . . ."

Instead, Reno's men dismounted and formed a skirmish line. Then they began to retreat. They ran very fast, she said, dropping guns and cartridges. She was disgusted by the conduct of these whites, saying they must have been seized with panic worse than that which seized her own people.

Things looked different from the troopers' point of view. They saw hundreds of Sioux galloping from the Unkpapa village—stretched out flat on their ponies or clinging to the far side. Bullets began pattering into the earth. Pvt. William Morris said so many bullets hit the ground that he got dust in his eyes. Sgt. John Ryan remembered that when the order to dismount was given they were in a prairie dog town and the men employed these little cones of earth as breastworks. Ryan says nothing else about such a defensive posture, but he and every other soldier knew that a prairie dog mound would not deflect a bullet or an arrow.

Most of the warriors rode back and forth yelping and firing at the prone troopers, but some turned the west end of the line intending to surround them, and when this happened Reno's battalion withdrew toward a stand of cottonwoods beside the river.

Trees offered more protection than prairie dog hillocks and several military analysts believe Reno should have stayed there instead of doing what he did. They point out that his battalion so near the village would have engaged a great many warriors, thus allowing Custer's plan to unfold. Other strategists think he had no choice but to break away, recross the river, and establish a defensive position on the bluff. Sgt. Ryan, whose opinion was formed while Sioux bullets zipped past his head, clearly favored getting out. He observed to his company commander, Capt. Thomas French, that some Indians had managed to get completely behind them. "Oh, no," Capt. French said, "those are General Custer's men." At that moment, according to Ryan, a bullet struck Pvt. George Lorentz in the back of the neck. The bullet dropped out of Lorentz's mouth and he fell to the ground.

Just then Major Reno rode up and shouted, "Any of you men who wish to make your escape, follow me!"

Pvt. Morris thought Lorentz had been hit in the stomach. Whatever happened, Lorentz was dying. Morris dragged him to a tree and propped him up.

"Go on," Lorentz said, "you cannot do me any good."

Morris protested. Lorentz again told him to leave.

"All right, if you say so," Morris answered and tried to mount his horse but the animal was terrified and he could not get a foot in the stirrup. By now everybody else was gone. Morris danced around while the horse reared and struggled. Finally he lunged at it, grabbed the pommel, and hauled himself up. The horse went running through the brush: "I on my stomach across the saddle. . . . The Indians were closing in. Two Indians got so close to me that I thought they were going to lasso me. . . ."

Lt. Wallace said that when he rode out of the cottonwoods he saw hostiles everywhere. Reno's troops were in a column of fours and the Indians would give way to let them pass, then start firing, and if any man did not use his pistol the Indians would come very near.

Another trooper interviewed long afterward said they howled "like incarnate fiends." Although forty-five years had elapsed, he said, he never would forget a Sioux riding so close that he could have touched the Indian with a saber.

Pvt. James Wilber escaped from the valley unhurt, but on the second day of the battle he was wounded and left partly paralyzed. He remembered that during this retreat a big Sioux galloped alongside and tried to pull him from the saddle. The Sioux had been hit in the shoulder, "and with every jerk he made at me the blood gushed from the wound and stained my shirt and trousers. He was a determined devil and hung on to me until we almost reached the river."

Reno's skirmish line had been supported by Arikara scouts—usually called Rees. Among them was Red Bear, whose story appears in *The Arikara Narrative* which was compiled with the help of interpreters and published in 1920.

Red Bear decided to pull out when it became apparent that the bluecoats could not stop the Sioux, but he had not ridden very far when his horse stumbled and fell. It scrambled up and galloped toward the river while he chased it through the trees and wild rose bushes. Finally a dead limb snagged the bridle. The limb broke off and dragged behind, which stopped the horse, but just then a Dakota Sioux came riding up. The bottom of the Dakota's face was painted red and the top was yellow. Red Bear shot him. The Dakota fell to the ground. By this time, Red Bear said, all he could hear was gunfire and the shrill eagle-bone whistles of the Sioux. He ran to the Little Bighorn, saw his horse swimming around, and jumped in. He caught the mane of his horse and together they reached the opposite side, but as he was climbing out he saw the Dakota horse—a dark bay with a white streak on the forehead. It wore a necklace of deer hooves and he heard the necklace clattering while the Dakota horse swam across the river. Then he saw Bobtailed Bull's big pinto which came plunging through the brush snorting with fright—"the tail and mane floating in the wind." The reins were flying, Red Bear said, and the rawhide saddle was bloody.

Weeks later this pinto showed up at the Arikara village near Fort Berthold, three hundred miles from the Little Bighorn. The Arikaras composed a song about it.

Red Bear saw Major Reno with a handkerchief tied around his head: ". . . his mouth and beard white with foam, which dripped down, and his eyes were wild and rolling."

Quite a lot of testimony indicates that Reno did lose control and that a good many soldiers were scared witless. The Sioux ignored some of these terrified men, leaving them to be dragged off their horses and killed by boys. An eighteen-year-old Cheyenne named Wooden Leg said he and his friends jeered the bluecoats, telling them they should not even try to fight, they should get more Crows and Shoshones to help them. He and another Cheyenne rode beside one soldier who was so frightened that instead of killing him they lashed him with pony whips.

Reno was a West Point graduate with combat experience in the Civil War, so it is not likely that his eyes rolled desperately and he foamed at the mouth. But he was excited, of this there is not much doubt. One officer present at the time said Reno ordered the men to mount and dismount three times in quick succession. As for the handkerchief, it was either red or white and he had tied it around his head because he had lost his straw hat. Under the circumstances this insignificant detail might be considered remotely symbolic. Soldiers do not like to see their commandant lose his helmet.

That he should wear a straw hat while charging an enemy camp sounds eccentric, but Reno was not the only member of his battalion thus equipped. It was hot—two months later Gibbon's men would report 111 degrees in the shade, 116 degrees inside a tent—and a shrewd Yankee merchant on the Yellowstone turned a neat profit selling straw hats for twenty-five cents. There is no record of how many he sold, but it must have been a sight when Reno charged the village.

Although correspondent John F. Finerty was not at the Little Bighorn he had met the major and described him as a short, stout man "with a determined

visage, his face showing intimate acquaintance with the sun and the wind."
Arikara scouts, who knew him better than Finerty ever did, compressed his
nature and his appearance into a single phrase: Man With the Dark Face.

Just when the Arikaras began to call him that is uncertain, possibly after he
got into an argument with a scout named High Bear. Reno misunderstood a
figure of speech, taking it as an insult, and threatened to shoot High Bear—
who responded by drawing a knife. Another scout, invoking Custer's name,
jumped between them and managed to prevent a bloody settlement. From
then on, if not earlier, the Rees had no trouble identifying that dark face.

How well or how badly Major Reno directed his troops is still, after all this
time, a subject of querulous dispute among Little Bighorn buffs. He himself
felt so maligned and traduced by subsequent criticism that he demanded a
Court of Inquiry, and by order of President Hayes this court convened at
Chicago's Palmer House on January 13, 1879. The investigation lasted almost a month. Some thirteen hundred pages of testimony were recorded.

Among the officers who testified was Reno's chief of scouts, Lt. Hare, who
said that if they had continued their advance the column would have been
demolished in five minutes.

Sgt. Culbertson testified: "If the skirmish had not been retired, or had
been held out for three minutes longer, I don't think any one would have
gotten off the line."

Lt. DeRudio saw no indication of cowardice: "When he halted and dismounted I said, 'Good for you,' because I saw that if we had gone five hundred
yards farther we would have been butchered."

Capt. Moylan said: "In my judgment if he had continued to charge down
the valley he would have been there yet." Nobody insisted the retreat was a
triumph, Moylan went on, and as for himself, he preferred life on the hilltop
to death somewhere else. This observation moved the Court Recorder, Lt.
Jesse Lee, to ask if the captain did not think it more honorable for a soldier to
die fighting than to sit dishonored on a hill—a question Moylan resented.

Reno testified that although he knew nothing of the local topography it
later developed that if they had charged another three hundred yards the
entire command would have plunged into a ditch several feet deep and ten
yards wide. Indians were concealed in this ditch and he thought most of his
men would have been shot from the saddle even before they got to it. As for
getting out—impossible.

Lt. Varnum said the ground appeared to be open prairie. He did not see
any ditch.

Reno was asked about his relationship with Custer. He replied that he felt
no animosity, he and the general got on well enough. But the implication of

this was unmistakable, so he added that even if his own brothers had been riding with Custer he could not have done any more than he did.

His response did not satisfy Lt. Lee:

"The question is, did you go into that fight with feelings of confidence or distrust?"

Reno again responded that he and the general got along all right: "My feelings toward Gen. Custer were friendly."

"I insist that the question shall be answered," said Lee.

"Well, sir, I had known General Custer a long time," Reno said, "and I had no confidence in his ability as a soldier."

Reno's counsel was a civilian named Lyman Gilbert and after all witnesses had been examined he addressed the Court on Reno's behalf. Speaking of the retreat, Gilbert asked rhetorically: "Was he justified in doing so?"

Gilbert pointed out that the Indians, rather than confronting the battalion as might be expected, began separating in an attempt to surround it—thus leaving their camp exposed to direct attack. This circumstance illustrated their strength. If they had been afraid, said Gilbert, undoubtedly they would have resisted any approach to the village: "but when they gave way, and invited an attack that if successful would have destroyed their homes, they declared to the commanding officer that they were not only able to protect themselves, but were able to destroy his command." And it must follow, therefore, that when Reno signaled a retreat he acted wisely.

During a recess in this trial Captain Frederick Benteen was asked by a Chicago *Times* reporter why there seemed to be so much trouble with Indians. Benteen answered that larceny by agents of the Indian Bureau was responsible. There had been, he said, "enormous pilfering and stealing." Agents whose annual salary was $1,500 were saving as much as $15,000 annually. Treat the Indians honestly and there should be no problem.

Charles Campbell, who served in the Third Infantry and later as a government agent in Oklahoma, had this to say—not at Reno's trial but long afterward: "The Indian agent has for years been the butt of the paragraphist and cartoonist, held up to public view as a grafter, if not a persistent robber. . . . As a rule they were a set of underpaid officials who had assumed the duties at the call of the various religious denominations to which they belonged, at much sacrifice of comfort and ease, not only to themselves but as well to their families, to help bear the white man's burden. It is not possible to conceive that they would foment disorder or endanger the lives of those dear to them, by acts that would foster rebellion. . . ." Campbell may have been correct about the situation in Oklahoma, but there was hanky-panky elsewhere. For example, it is known that a Baltimore contractor who supplied flour to the

Sioux arranged with an agent to defraud the Indians by using three sacks. From Baltimore to Cheyenne came the flour, at which point the inspector stamped each sack "100 pounds," whereupon one hundred pounds of flour was distributed and three sacks retained as evidence that three hundred pounds had been delivered.

Things were different in Canada. Bishop Henry Whipple pointed out that on the northern side of the boundary lived "the same greedy, dominant Anglo-Saxon race, and the same heathen." Yet the Canadians escaped massacre and warfare. There was no single reason for this, but above all the Canadian government kept its word. As Benteen implied, Canadian bureaucrats had sense enough to treat the natives honestly.

When asked how the Sioux felt about being forcibly transported from one reservation to another, he suggested that one act with a little consideration for an Indian's feelings, just as with other people. "I am a southerner, and I have noticed that you may take a negro far away from home, but he will always have an inclination to return. The same feeling actuates the salmon. . . ."

The Court eventually decided that Reno had been opposed by such overwhelming force that any deeper penetration into the hostile village would have brought about the annihilation of his command. While his subordinates may in some instances have accomplished more for the safety of all concerned, "there was nothing in his conduct which requires animadversion from this Court." Such a verdict suggests that his decision to retreat was based on a rational understanding of the situation. Perhaps this is true. To a degree undoubtedly it is true. But after they had withdrawn into the cottonwoods near the river he began talking with Custer's favorite Indian scout, Bloody Knife. He was trying to find out what the hostiles might do, when a bullet struck Bloody Knife in the head and spattered his brains on Reno's face. Some historians believe the shock of this left him psychologically paralyzed. Perhaps. But Reno saw gobbets of blood during the Civil War and may well have been spattered numerous times. Accordingly, one may speculate. At the time of this grotesque incident Bloody Knife was wearing, along with his distinctive clam shell–bear claw necklace, a black neckerchief with blue stars which Custer had given him. He was, therefore, emblematic of command; and when he collapsed it may be that Reno perceived the future. All one can say with certainty is that the major was shocked. How deeply and for how long, nobody knows.

He lost his straw hat in the timber, he said, although he did not say just when. Quite possibly he threw it away at this moment. A blood-soaked shirt or trousers may be endured but a bloody hat hangs close to the face.

Major Reno's conduct—whether he behaved rationally or was too frightened to think—has been argued for a century. He had a good Civil War record, twice decorated for gallantry, but this was his first experience with Indians, who did not behave at all like Confederates. Boiling dust, an alien landscape, arrows thumping into flesh—it made less sense than a premeditated cavalry charge in Virginia.

Four horses bolted out of formation, carrying their desperate riders toward the Sioux. Two of these men regained control and got back. The other two— Pvts. George Smith and James Turley—rode on into the Unkpapa village where they were caught, dragged from the saddle, stabbed, beaten, chopped up. A nephew of Sitting Bull, Henry Oscar One Bull, saw the horses break out of line and when interviewed many years later he remarked with satisfaction: "These soldiers didn't last long." Pvt. Morris thought Turley was killed someplace else, but there seems to be little doubt that the Unkpapa villagers got Smith. The head of a white man—possibly Smith—was found on the abandoned site of the village. Whoever he was, he had been dragged at the end of a rope until he fell apart.

Henry One Bull said the bluecoats were confused; some jumped off their horses and scampered toward the cottonwoods beside the river, turning around and shooting while they ran. He rode up behind one of them, knocked him down with a stone-headed club and held him under water until he quit struggling.

Black Elk, an Oglala, claimed to have been thirteen years old at the time. He looked like a child because he was not very robust, but already he had experienced a vision and had performed a number of valorous deeds, so by the white man's count he might have been older. He talked about the dust raised by the ponies' hooves, the smoke, the cries, the gunfire, the shriek of eagle-bone whistles, the women singing to encourage their husbands and sons, and he remembered big American horses galloping through the dust with empty saddles. "Those wasichus had come to kill our fathers and mothers and us," he said, using a Sioux term which implies an unwelcome or disagreeable persistence, "and it was our country."

He and several other boys surrounded a soldier who was hiding in a clump of bulberry bushes. The soldier tried to escape, crawling this way and that, while the boys ran around shooting arrows at him. Black Elk said it was like hunting a rabbit. They knew they hit him at least once because he yelped. After a while they set fire to the grass, which brought him out of the bushes, and some warriors killed him.

Black Elk himself scalped a soldier who was still alive. It was hard work because the soldier's hair was short and the knife was dull. The soldier ground his teeth and made such a fuss that Black Elk had to shoot him in the head.

After finishing the job he wanted his mother to know about the scalp so he rode over to a crowd of women and children who had gathered on a hill to watch the fight, and when his mother saw the trophy she uttered a shrill tremolo in his honor.

To Reno's soldiers trapped in the cottonwoods a valley swarming with naked, yipping, barking, fantastically painted aborigines must have resembled a nineteenth-century illustration of Dante's Hell; and what should have been a disciplined withdrawal from this position turned into a rout with Major Reno himself leading the way, deserting those who were unable to follow or who did not understand what was happening. It has been alleged that after emptying his revolver he became so distraught that he tossed it aside, although this was never proved.

His eagerness to escape from the valley might be traced to an unpleasant Civil War experience. In the spring of 1865 his regiment was chasing a Confederate guerrilla known as the Gray Ghost—John Singleton Mosby—chasing him with very little success until one day they came upon Mosby chatting with a few men in the village of Hamilton. Delighted by such good luck, Reno spurred forward and the Gray Ghost fled in panic up the road to Middlebury. Then from the woods alongside Middlebury Road came a fusillade of bullets. Twenty-one of Reno's men dropped from the saddle.

Now, the major might not have been brilliant, yet neither was he stupid, so it is a fair assumption that he did not forget the Gray Ghost's murderous trap. Eleven years later in the Little Bighorn Valley he had once again charged an apparently vulnerable enemy, only to be surprised by the response. A sudden recollection of that mistake in Virginia might have sucked his courage. Or, as Napoleon is supposed to have said: Show me a man who makes the same mistake twice and I will show you a fool.

During this retreat from the cottonwoods to the bluffs across the river the Indians very often shot at the cavalrymen's horses, which at first sounds illogical, considering how highly the Indians valued horses. But a horse is a big target and if it went down, or was crippled, the rider had no chance to escape. This inference was drawn by General Terry's command while marching through the valley because his troops noticed that the body of a cavalryman almost always lay beside the carcass of a horse.

Squaws, children, and old men rushed out of the village as soon as the bluecoats fled—stripping, robbing, mutilating, killing those who still twitched. Bloody Knife's head was cut off, perhaps by one of Inkpaduta's Santee Sioux because the Santees were the only tribe that habitually practiced decapitation instead of scalping.

There is another possibility. By some accounts two young Unkpapa sisters were the first to see Bloody Knife's corpse. They did not know who he was, but from his clothing they knew he had been a scout for the soldiers, and his graying hair was parted on the side, which identified him as a Ree instead of a Crow—whose men usually cut their hair short in front and combed the rest into a ruff or pompadour. So the girls cut off the bullet-smashed head of this middle-aged Ree and went back to camp with it swinging between them like a ball, each sister holding one of the dusty braids. In the village they mounted their trophy on a stick.

Bloody Knife was well known to adult Sioux. Although his mother was Ree his father had been Sioux, and the first fifteen or sixteen years of his life were spent among his father's people. Those years were difficult, perhaps because of his mixed blood. At times the Sioux and the Rees got along all right—if they felt like trading—but ordinarily they did not, and the Sioux spoke of the Rees with contempt as Corn Eaters.

Sahnish was what the Rees called themselves. Mandan neighbors along the upper Missouri called them Panis because they were related to the Skidi Pawnees. But the name by which they were best known was Arikara—antlers—because in the old days they arranged their hair around two bones projecting from the head like horns or antlers.

Early in the nineteenth century when Lewis and Clark visited the Rees they were friendly. "But owing to the system of trade," said the artist George Catlin who saw them a generation later, "they have been inflicted with abuses, for which they are harboring the most inveterate feelings toward the whole civilized race." Joshua Pilcher, who managed a fur-trading post in 1823, said they were notorious for treachery and barbarity and had murdered more people than all the other tribes combined.

The Sioux also behaved with great friendliness at first, from the days of their meeting with Lewis and Clark until some time after the California gold rush. One forty-niner remarked that without their help in fending off the Pawnees, Cheyennes, and Arapahoes no white man could have gotten through without an army. As to just when and why the Sioux began to feel differently, there is no simple answer. Senator Thomas Hart Benton blamed the War Department, telling his colleagues in Washington that the brass hats dispatched "school-house officers and pot-house soldiers to treat the Indians as beasts and dogs."

Whatever the causes, American response to aboriginal treachery and barbarity was devastating, although inadvertent. On June 20, 1837, the steamboat *St. Peter's* unloaded at Fort Clark, delivering goods the Indians cherished along with something unexpected. A Mandan stole a blanket contaminated by smallpox, which started the plague in that area, and upriver at Fort

Union the Indians refused to disperse, even after being warned away from the boat by whites who now understood the danger. They refused to leave because they assumed that once more they were about to be swindled. Jacob Halsey, in charge of the Fort Union depot, thought the best thing to do was to vaccinate everybody and he is said to have been surprised when a number of his subjects began vomiting, bleeding, and dying. Halsey himself caught the pox. He got over it, but his Indian wife did not.

Five opportunistic Assiniboin, thinking to benefit from the chaos at Fort Union, nimbly scaled the palisade and stole two horses. They were chased and caught by a detachment of soldiers who persuaded them to give up the horses, so the incident ended with no trouble—except that one of the soldiers happened to be infected and the Assiniboin horse thieves innocently took the disease home. Eight hundred of their people died.

From the Assiniboin it spread to the Cree. Seven thousand Cree died. Then it reached the Blackfoot.

How many Indians from the Missouri tribes died of smallpox within the next few years can hardly be estimated. Possibly one hundred thousand. Some who recovered from the plague committed suicide after seeing their faces in a mirror. Vacant lodges stood on every hilltop. Starving people wandered aimlessly back and forth. "No sound but the raven's croak or the wolf's howl breaks the solemn stillness. . . ."

Audubon met what was left of the Rees in 1843. He characterized them as alert, lanky, and dwelling in filth. When a warrior wanted to shake hands with him Audubon obliged but found the touch disgusting. Their squaws, he thought, were immoral, which may be a narrow Protestant judgment; but at that time the Rees were incestuous—brother with sister, daughter with father, son-in-law with mother-in-law—and chronicles of the period indicate that a great many were sick with venereal disease. A young Philadelphian who met them in 1858 described them as sullen and insolent with villainous countenances. "Sore and inflamed eyes are very common among them, owing to their filthy habits. . . ."

Whatever the physical or moral state of this tribe, the Sioux felt superior, which could explain Bloody Knife's wretched childhood. He was taunted, abused, humiliated. Gall, later to become one of the most famous Sioux warriors, especially disliked him. In 1856 Bloody Knife's mother left the Unkpapa camp for a visit with her own people who lived farther east, perhaps as a way of resolving the unhappy situation. She took her sons, leaving a husband and probably a daughter, and it appears that she did not return.

Four years later Bloody Knife decided to visit the Unkpapas, presumably to see his father and say hello to what few childhood friends he did have in the old village. This idea nearly cost his life. Once a traveler reached an Indian camp he was, by custom, safe. But this proscription did not apply when Bloody Knife showed up; he was spat upon, stripped, cursed, mocked, beaten with musket ramrods and ceremonial coup sticks. Why he was so despised is not clear. His Ree blood alone does not justify such treatment.

A couple of years after this experience his two brothers, who were on a hunting trip, fell into the hands of a Sioux war party led by Gall. Their bodies were quartered and left for the wolves. So it is no mystery why Bloody Knife offered to guide bluecoat armies against the Sioux.

Fort Stevenson records give his height as 5′7″, eyes brown, hair black, complexion copper, date of enlistment May 1, 1868.

Chicago *Inter Ocean* correspondent William Eleroy Curtis described his features as not fundamentally Indian but Spanish or Cuban: "His mouth and nose are small, the latter a smooth aquiline, and his lips are superbly cut, but wear, in repose, a sort of cynical curl, an index sign of his character. . . ." He could not be seduced, as many Indians were, by trinkets or cheap finery. He affected no ornament, Curtis said, except a small steel horseshoe hooked to his cartridge belt, "the significance of which I have never been able to discover."

He is said to have been impertinent toward whites. He did not hesitate to ridicule them, even ridiculing General Custer's marksmanship. Custer seems to have been amused by such insolence and occasionally rewarded him like a king rewarding the court jester. Two months before the Little Bighorn while he was in Washington he ordered a silver medal with Bloody Knife's name engraved on it.

The instinctive hatred felt by the Sioux toward this half-Sioux, along with whatever they disliked about him as an individual, was further augmented by his defection to white invaders. They observed him guiding Custer through the sacred Black Hills in 1874 and two years later they splashed his brains on Major Reno.

Among those adults in the Unkpapa village who remembered him was the mother of the two girls who brought back his head. Although the head must have been in poor shape, and she had not seen it for some time, she recognized it at once because Bloody Knife was her brother. According to David Humphreys Miller, who interviewed a good many witnesses and participants in the battle, this woman exclaimed: "Gall has killed him at last!" Other accounts do not mention Gall. Nor have any historians bothered to record the feelings of the Unkpapa sisters, or tell us what they said when they realized they had brought home the head of their uncle.

It appears that this battered trophy was scalped because two Ree scouts,

Young Hawk and Forked Horn, went to the deserted village looking for something to eat after the battle and there they met a soldier from Gibbon's command who was carrying a scalp on a stick. This soldier asked if the scalp was Dakota, meaning Sioux. Young Hawk and Forked Horn studied the gray hair and told him who it was. They also told him to throw it away. "No," he said, "if it is Bloody Knife's scalp, I will keep it for my father knew him and I will show it to him."

Bloody Knife's widow, She Owl, arrived at Fort Berthold on April 14, 1879. Upon being sworn to the truth, She Owl declared before agent Thomas Ellis that she had been married to Bloody Knife for ten years, had not received the wages owed him at the time of his death, was "the sole and only legal representative of said Bloody Knife," and would like to get the money. Two years later, almost five years after her husband's head was cut off at the Little Bighorn while he was serving the United States, the government allotted said widow, She Owl, $91.66.

Custer's favorite white scout, "Lonesome Charley" Reynolds, also died in the valley with Reno.

Nobody knew much about Lonesome Charley except that he had spent quite a while in Dakota Territory and that he used to be in partnership with a man named Deitrick who sold firewood to steamboats. Once he told Custer's wife, Elizabeth, that he was born a gentleman, but this disclosure seemed to embarrass him and he quickly diverted the conversation. When he was first introduced to her he was too shy to meet her gaze. He was not picturesque, she said, as most scouts were. His eyes were large and dark blue.

Inter Ocean correspondent Curtis described him as short and stocky, "one of God Almighty's gentlemen . . . with a shrinking blue eye." He was a little taller than Bloody Knife, but stoop-shouldered. He lived by himself, absolutely alone, without even a dog for company. His voice was as soft as a woman's and Curtis said he did not smoke, curse, or drink. He was not, however, a zealous prohibitionist because interpreter Fred Gerard testified during the Reno inquiry that as they trotted toward the hostile village Charley asked for a drink of whisky, saying he had never felt so depressed and discouraged in his life. Gerard must have felt the same because he himself took a drink before handing over the flask.

One person who knew Charley said his eyes were "restless gray," and there were some who questioned his experience: "For whom did he scout before the Custer battle?" asked photographer D. F. Barry. But all agreed that he was a modest, private man with a subdued voice.

Since those days much of the mystery has dissolved. Scholars learned that Lonesome Charley was born in Warren County, Illinois on March 20, 1842.

His comment to Elizabeth about a genteel heritage was more or less correct; his father was a respectable physician and the family has been traced back to colonial Virginia. He attended Abingdon College and might have lived out a sedate existence if his father had not moved west. Dr. Reynolds chose a Kansas town called Pardee, near Atchison, and from there young Charley took off. In the spring of 1860 he struck out for Pike's Peak where a man could fill a gunnysack with gold, but the emigrant train with which he traveled was attacked and looted, probably by Cheyennes. A few survivors made it to Fort Kearny and here Charley went into business with a crusty old trapper named Green who lived on an island in the Platte. One day they saw the corpse of an Indian woman in a tree, which was not unusual, but old man Green climbed the tree, shook her down, and used her for wolf bait. This was a bit much for Charley, who decided to move along. It was now 1861, the Civil War had erupted, and he joined a regiment of Kansas volunteers. Little has been learned about his wartime service except that he was in the Missouri-Kansas border fighting and worked as an escort along the Santa Fe Trail.

After the war he and a Mr. Wamsley decided to establish themselves as traders, but on Rabbit Ears Creek in southwestern Kansas a band of Cheyennes broke up the partnership by killing Wamsley and capturing the goods. Charley managed to squeeze into an abandoned dugout which probably had been constructed by a trapper and from this hole the Cheyennes were unable to evict him. They hung around, perhaps waiting until thirst forced him to surface, but during the night he crept away, somehow got to Trinidad, and from there to Santa Fe where he fell in love with a Mexican girl. This romance withered. Charley never said much about it.

By 1866 he was a buffalo hunter, drifting north, working along the Republican in eastern Colorado and southern Nebraska. Here again he almost lost his scalp, so for reasons of security he moved to Jack Morrow's ranch on the Platte.

In the spring of 1867 an army officer at Fort McPherson disagreed with him about something and when the quarrel ended the officer had just one arm.

Charley kept drifting. By 1869 he had entered the wild upper Missouri region where he worked as a hunter and guide. Thus he met Custer.

How he died at the Little Bighorn has been disputed. It appears that he was more or less alone, as usual. By one account fifty-eight shells were counted near his body, but this sounds like fiction. Gerard saw him whipping his horse in a desperate effort to escape, which was no reflection on his courage. Everybody was trying to make it across the river. Gerard said Charley's route was blocked by Indians who must have shot his horse because after he fell he seemed to be pinned under the animal. Because of the dust and gunsmoke and excitement and because of concern with his own prospects that was all Gerard saw.

Charley had a seriously infected, suppurating thumb—described in contemporary journals as a "felon"—which troubled him so much that one of the regimental surgeons, Dr. Henry Porter, advised him to stay behind. Nevertheless, he was determined to go, and because Dr. Porter could not cure his thumb Charley approached Custer's orderly, John Burkman, who concocted a poultice of wet hardtack. On the morning of June 25 he still wore this bulky poultice, but when Burkman saw his body it was gone, which meant that he probably peeled it off when the shooting started.

A year after the fight not much could be found of him. Mr. P. W. Norris, who was a close friend, as well as being Superintendent of Yellowstone National Park, wanted to locate his remains and provide a decent burial. Norris and "Yellowstone Jack" Baronette reached the site on July 5, and following a map drawn by Gerard they came upon the skeleton of a horse, shreds of Charley's hat, a few little bones, and tufts of auburn hair. The skull was missing. Norris wrapped the debris in a handkerchief. Then he and Yellowstone Jack rode away, chased by a party of hostiles who had been watching them from Reno Hill. Norris later wrote that he kept some of the hair, but most of it he distributed "in the earnest but fruitless effort to find his birthplace. . . ." Norris may have buried the relics in his own family plot in Norris, Michigan.

A nephew, Charles Edwin Reynolds, wrote to historian Brininstool in 1925 that the first news they had of the Custer battle came from Chicago newspapers. "I have never forgotten, although then a small boy, the look of agony on father's face as his eye ran down the casualty list and he reached the name of Charley Reynolds."

Lt. Donald McIntosh died not far from Charley. Pvt. Theodore Goldin saw a mob of about sixty Indians attacking McIntosh. "I noticed that his lariat was dragging on the ground, once in a while catching in the tall grass or sage brush and then breaking loose and the picket pin bounding high in the air. . . ."

The Bismarck *Tribune* wrote: "McIntosh, though a half-breed, was a gentleman of culture and esteemed by all who knew him. He leaves a family at Lincoln. . . ." Thus far the *Trib* may be right. His father was Canadian, his mother probably an Indian of the Six Nations. That "Tosh," as the soldiers called him, was a gentleman of culture may be accepted on faith. Photographs are deceptive, but this angular male with an invisible smile and a long nose does not look like an oaf or a lout. That he was esteemed by all who knew him is an expression of courtesy we extend, unless there is massive contradictory evidence. That he left a "family" at Lincoln might be argued. The *Army and Navy Journal*, which handled money from a relief fund established for the benefit of widows and children, allocated $510 to "Mrs. Donald McIntosh," but no children are listed.

The *Trib* becomes less reliable when describing his death, which is presented as though a reporter witnessed it: "He was pulled from his horse, tortured and finally murdered at the pleasure of the red devils." The *Trib* also has McIntosh armed with a saber, which is untrue. As for being pulled from his horse, this is possible although by no means certain. Indians interviewed years after the battle mentioned "one of the littler chiefs" who tried to remount his horse and stuck his boot all the way through the stirrup. The animal bolted, dragging this officer. This might possibly have been McIntosh. But there is no evidence that the Sioux caught him alive, tortured and disposed of him at their pleasure.

In the grass beside a severely mutilated corpse whose features had been pounded into a gelatinous glob a sergeant-major from Gibbon's command noticed an unusual gutta-percha button. Lt. Francis Gibson of H Company was able to identify it. He remembered that his sister gave some of these buttons to her husband just before the regiment left Fort Lincoln. Her husband was Tosh McIntosh.

Not much remained of McIntosh when the slain officers were disinterred and shipped east for reburial in 1877. Ex-Private Roman Rutten wrote to ex-Sergeant John Ryan long afterward that he had talked with the man who prepared McIntosh for shipment to Arlington. There were only a few bones in a cast iron box, the skull smashed by a tomahawk. "I suppose you have one of Anhauses & Bushes pictures of the fight," Rutten continued, alluding to the horrifying Anheuser-Busch lithograph which still hangs in thousands of saloons from one corner of America to another. "I have a grand one."

Capt. Benteen wrote to Mrs. Benteen: "I am inclined to think that had McIntosh divested himself of that slow poking way which was his peculiar characteristic, he might have been left in the land of the living."

He must have been homelier than one might suspect from his photograph because it is said that when Lt. George Wallace, who was not very handsome, reported for duty at Fort Rice he went immediately to pay his respects to the senior lieutenant: McIntosh. It was evening when Wallace arrived so he went to the McIntosh home. Mrs. McIntosh opened the door. "My God," she exclaimed, throwing up her hands, "you are the first man I ever saw that is uglier than my husband."

Reno's adjutant, Benjamin Hubert "Benny" Hodgson, was one of several doomed men who predicted the future. Before the fight he remarked that if he was wounded or dismounted he intended to grab somebody's stirrup and be dragged to safety. So it happened. While Reno's disorganized unit was trying to get across the river a bullet went through Hodgson's leg and killed his horse. He called for help. Somebody came splashing by, he clutched a stirrup and was towed across. But his prescience dissolved before the end, or else he could not believe what he foresaw. On the opposite bank, temporarily safe, he was struck by another bullet and killed.

It is not clear whose stirrup he grabbed—at least four troopers from Reno's battalion claimed this honor—nor is it clear who served him last. Pvt. Thomas Coleman of McDougall's B Company kept a most extraordinary journal. Coleman reports on the twenty-seventh:

> . . . this Morning after sunrise i went oaver the Battlefield on this side of the river and the first person i saw was Lieut. B. H. Hodgson of my Company he was shot twise with Ball and once with arrow Several other Boddies lay close by I buried the Lieut on a nice Knowl oaverlooking the River with a Cedar tree at his head he was a Brave officer and a true gentleman. . . .

Capt. McDougall subsequently declared under oath that he himself, assisted by Pvts. Ryan and Moon, buried Hodgson on the night of the twenty-sixth after sewing him up in blankets and a poncho. Most historians trust McDougall, whereas Coleman is thought to be imaginative or at times confused—although his journal never lacks flavor.

During Reno's famous retreat from the valley a number of men found their path of escape blocked, so they hid among the cottonwoods and thick brush near the river. Lt. Charles DeRudio was one of these. His account, which appeared in the New York *Herald*, is regarded with bleak suspicion. Walter Camp, for instance: "There is a story written in the first person under the name of Lieut. DeRudio, but it was written by Major Brisbin, of the 2nd Cavalry. DeRudio told me this himself, and cautioned me not to take all of it seriously, saying that Brisbin 'colored' it a good deal."

DeRudio's cautionary advice seems justified because there is no doubt that Major Brisbin exhibited a talent for creative writing, as may be seen from the optimism of his magnum opus, *The Beef Bonanza: Or, How to Get Rich on the Plains*. Here we learn that a $100,000 investment would easily double within five years, besides paying a handsome annual dividend. Or let us say the investor prefers sheep to cattle: "The time will come when we will have both shepherds and shepherdesses on the plains when the patriarch, as of old, with his sons, daughters, and sons' wives and daughters will follow the herds,

crook in hand. Any large family can become rich by following the herds."
Dairy farming, too, will flourish: "In the West the mild air and thousands of
pure gushing streams furnish multitudes of natural butter-and-cheese
ranches. The melting snows not only keep the waters cool, but the snow, air,
and cool nights make the milk houses a paradise. . . ."

We hear Major Brisbin's voice again in the so-called DeRudio narrative.
The narrator, concealed in a ravine, listens to "the silvery, but to me diabolical
voices of several squaws" who are scalping an unfortunate soldier. "Two of
the ladies were cutting away, while two others performed a sort of war dance.
. . ." This must be the major at work. Truth, no matter how startling, customarily rings with a distinctive note, rather like the high hard ring of a silver
coin dropped on a table, but this clinks like a potmetal counterfeit.

Brisbin was known among the troops as "Grasshopper Jim" because he
often talked about the agricultural possibilities of Montana. One might suppose he would be nicknamed Alfalfa Jim or Winter Wheat Jim, but he probably talked a good deal about the grasshoppers which encrusted these northern
plains and frequently annihilated crops. They were described as "exceedingly rapacious" by the Chief Engineer for the Department of Dakota, Captain William Ludlow, who said they would arrive in giant clusters and looked
like a fall of snowflakes while descending through the last rays of the sun.
Being an engineer, Ludlow undertook to calculate their numbers. One day
when the insects were not especially thick he counted how many there were
on a twelve-inch by twelve-inch plot of earth and found twenty-five, which
meant at least a million per acre. The famous scout Luther North, en route to
Nebraska in 1874, saw the land devastated—trees stripped, fields empty.
People in the town of Columbus had tried to save their gardens by covering
them with blankets and sheets but the voracious creatures devoured the cloth
before eating the vegetables and flowers and eating the paint off the houses.

Anyway, a band of Sioux approached the place where DeRudio–Brisbin
and Pvt. Thomas O'Neill had hidden themselves. Both troopers fired: "The
private's eye was true, and his carbine trusty, for Mr. Indian dropped his rein,
threw up his paws and laid down on the grass to sleep his long sleep. The
gentleman I greeted rode a short distance and then did likewise."

According to the *Trib*, DeRudio finally escaped because some beavers dove
into the Little Bighorn. "DeRudio followed them, got out of sight, and after
hiding twelve hours or more. . . ."

Beavers? Why would he follow beavers? The *Trib* does not elaborate.

Well, after creeping from bush to bush for nearly two days the droll narrator and Pvt. O'Neill manage to wade the river and scale the heights to join
what remained of Reno's decimated battalion. Capt. Benteen later com-

mented that DeRudio had a romantic, thrilling story made up by the time he reached safety, so it appears that Grasshopper Jim embroidered what was already a fancy tale.

As for Pvt. O'Neill, "he is a cool, level headed fellow, and tells it plainly and the same way all the time—which is a big thing towards convincing one of the truth. . . ."

Deadeye Dick O'Neill's report of this encounter does sound less fabricated. In addition to problems with enraged Sioux, he found himself troubled by a nosebleed. A nosebleed! Here we have an unhorsed cavalryman tucked into a patch of dusty underbrush. At any instant he might be seen, in which event he will quickly resemble a porcupine, yet he is concerned about a bloody nose. At the start of the fight, he tells us, he tripped, fell, and bumped his nose. "Not being able to give it attention at the time . . ." the blood had trickled down his throat and almost choked him. It must be true. Nobody who was trying to fake a story would pause to insert this ridiculous diversion.

With them on the first day were interpreter Fred Gerard and a mixed-blood Pikuni scout named Billy Jackson. Gerard was French, although born in St. Louis. He married a Ree squaw and eventually sold advertising for Pillsbury Mills—which may sound implausible but is nonetheless a fact. Before obtaining this excellent position with the milling company he had worked as an Indian trader, during which time he learned Arikara and Sioux and occasionally spent a brutal Dakota winter huddled with prospective clients in ravines along the upper Missouri.

He and Billy Jackson were mounted, but DeRudio and O'Neill had lost their horses, a circumstance which made this uncommon quartet extremely vulnerable. In case of discovery the horsemen might escape, but not if they tried to carry passengers. Therefore a plan was worked out. If the Sioux should find them the equestrians would gallop off, expecting to be chased, while the pedestrians would duck into the shrubbery and hope for a miracle. It was not an altogether satisfactory plan but they had few alternatives. They were further imperiled by the fact that Gerard was riding a stallion and Billy Jackson was riding a mare. These animals began to act very badly, Gerard says, "putting us in danger of being discovered by the noise they made. We finally improved the situation by tying their heads together."

All day Sunday the fugitives kept quiet and about ten o'clock that night started moving upstream. They passed a number of bodies. In the hazy moonlight they recognized McIntosh—which sounds a little surprising because Gibbon's men could not identify him. But of course Gibbon did not get there until Tuesday.

At one point O'Neill asked Gerard to enter the stream on horseback to find out how deep it was. Gerard refused. O'Neill then waded in, or jumped off the bank, and almost disappeared. Obviously this was not a good place to cross, but all four were thirsty so before climbing out O'Neill filled his hat and passed it up to the others. No doubt this was logical. If you are thirsty and find water, you drink. Nevertheless it is preposterous. If these men were seen they would be shot, yet O'Neill stood there dipping his hat in the stream, carefully handing it up to his friends.

Farther along the water rippled, indicating shallows, and here Gerard removed his expensive gold watch. "Oh, Powerful One, Day Maker!" he muttered in Sioux while holding aloft the watch, "And you, people of the depths, this I sacrifice to you. Help us, I pray you, to cross safely here!"

"What were you saying?" DeRudio asked. "What was that splash?"

They entered the stream cautiously, feeling for the bottom, but it was so shallow that the horses' knees did not even get wet. Billy Jackson said he had to bite his lip to keep from laughing when he thought about Gerard's watch.

Not long afterward a party of Sioux heard them. Gerard and Jackson galloped away, as agreed, while DeRudio and O'Neill wriggled into some bushes. Darkness saved all four.

They remained hidden the next day—DeRudio and O'Neill together, Gerard and Jackson separately. That night they met again on Reno's hilltop. None of them had eaten since Sunday morning and Gerard, at least, felt ravenous. He was offered cold coffee and biscuit. His stomach objected. Then he tried to chew a piece of salt pork but fell asleep with the pork still in his mouth and did not open his eyes for ten hours.

One of Reno's white scouts, George Herendeen, also was trapped in the valley but managed to hide in a willow thicket not far from the black interpreter, Isaiah Dorman, who had been caught. Herendeen could do nothing to help. "I saw Indians shooting at Isaiah and squaws pounding him with stone hammers. His legs below the knees were shot full of bullets. . . ." By another account, Dorman's ankles and shins were scored with buckshot.

More significant than the choice of weapon is the fact that they wanted him to suffer. They wanted all of the bluecoats and everybody who accompanied the bluecoats to pay for this attack, but Isaiah Dorman became a special target. Nearly every description of his death emphasizes that the Indians killed him slowly. He had a coffee pot and a cup—although why he carried a coffee pot into battle is not explained—and as he lay dying among the prairie dog mounds they filled the cup with his blood. Rees who found his body mentioned a "kettle" full of blood, but that might be a questionable translation. Near him the Rees discovered one of their own: stripped, sliced open, a willow branch stuffed into his chest with the leafy part extruding.

A Sioux chief talked about Isaiah's death without animosity, almost indifferently. "We passed a black man in a soldier's uniform and we had him. He turned on his horse and shot an Indian right through the heart. Then the Indians fired at this one man and riddled his horse with bullets. His horse fell over on his back and the black man could not get up. I saw him as I rode by."

Pvt. Slaper told Brininstool that Isaiah was "badly cut and slashed, while unmentionable atrocities had been committed." Custer's orderly, John Burkman, was more direct. Dorman had a dozen arrows in his breast and "a picket pin through his balls."

Stanley Vestal observed that he was well liked by the Indians. Vestal, who was not present at the Little Bighorn, talked to various participants long after the battle and subsequently produced a story of Isaiah's death which sounds incredible. We are told that Sitting Bull came upon Isaiah grievously wounded. "The Negro asked for water, and Sitting Bull took his cup of polished black buffalo horn, got some water, and gave him to drink." Well, just such a tender scene occurs in an 1896 book for boys, *Fifty Famous Stories Retold*. Here we learn of a seventeenth-century battle between Swedes and Danes in which the Swedes are defeated. A Danish soldier is about to drink from his flask when he hears a voice nearby: "O Sir! give me a drink, for I am dying." It was the voice of a wounded Swede. The Dane compassionately "knelt down by the side of his fallen foe, and pressed the flask to his lips. . . ."

Pvt. Roman Rutten, unlike Vestal, did fight at the Little Bighorn and his report of Isaiah's last stand rings true. Rutten was on a horse that hated the odor of Indians so his immediate problem was how to stay in the saddle. During a wild ride he passed Isaiah, whose horse had been shot. The black man was on one knee, firing carefully with a non-regulation sporting rifle. He looked up and shouted, "Good-bye, Rutten!"

That the black white man, wasicun sapa, was well liked by Indians seems to be a fact. They called him Teat, among other names, possibly because Isaiah sounds rather like azinpi—their word for it. Or perhaps his black skin reminded them of the buffalo cow's smooth black nipple. There are no photographs of him and only two descriptions, both from hostiles. Both said he was very black and very big. A pictograph of Reno's retreat shows a black man in army uniform flat on the ground beside a prostrate white horse. For some inexplicable reason he has an abnormally thick right thumb.

Where he came from and what drew him to the unexplored Dakotas is not known. He may have been a runaway slave or a freedman, because there is no record of him until after the Civil War. Several male slaves belonging to the D'Orman family of Louisiana and/or Alabama during the 1840s are said to have escaped and one of them reputedly was named Isaiah. He first appears on November 11, 1865, when he was hired by the War Department as a courier at $100 a month, which was good pay. He traveled from Fort Wadsworth to Fort Rice and back again every month, afoot, with a sleeping bag on his shoulder and the mail wrapped in waterproof cloth. Wadsworth and Rice were almost one hundred miles apart and each trip took five days. He may not have been able to afford a horse, or he may have thought a horse would deteriorate in such rough country. Whatever the reason, he walked, and the government paid him well because at any moment some discontented or ambitious Indian might lift a courier's scalp.

He did this off and on for about two years, then vanished. He showed up intermittently during the next four years, working as a woodcutter for Durfee & Peck, but most of that time he spent with the Sioux. It is known that he married a Santee squaw and probably he did become friendly with Sitting Bull.

In 1871 the Army hired him to guide the Northern Pacific Railroad survey team, and for the ensuing five years he worked as an interpreter at Fort Rice. Custer demanded his services at the last moment in the fatal year:

> Hq Middle District
> Dept. Dak Ft. A. Lincoln
> D. T.
> May 14, 1876

Special Order
No. 2
IV The Commanding Officer Ft. Rice, D.T. will order Isaiah Dorman
Post Interpreter to proceed to this post and report for duty. . . .

Regimental Quartermaster H. I. Nowlan's official report concerning persons and articles hired and employed—*Expedition in the Field on the March between Fort Abraham Lincoln and the Yellowstone River, M.T.*—notes that Isaiah Dorman was owed $62.50 for services rendered during June. Three years later a certain Isaac McNutt tried to collect this money. McNutt worked as a handyman around Fort Rice and had known Dorman, but he could produce nothing to substantiate his claim. There were no other claimants. And because Isaiah's next of kin—his Santee wife—could not be located, the Treasury Department retained his wages. Perhaps by now the file has been closed, but it is hard to tell what goes on behind government doors so Isaiah's wages might still be accumulating interest.

Considering that he married an Indian and felt comfortable among them, and they with him, their savage treatment of him seems odd. The explanation is simple: They thought he had betrayed them by working for bluecoats and a traitor deserves no respect.

So much for Isaiah.

Together with Herendeen, DeRudio, O'Neill and several other whites, a number of Ree scouts looked for hiding places among the cottonwoods and willow thickets. One of these—Young Hawk—decided after a while that death would be preferable to such humiliation. He took off his government coat and blouse, hugged his horse and said, "I love you." Then he stood up and began shooting. The Sioux fired at him but missed. Young Hawk ducked back into the bushes, crawled a little distance and again jumped up. Once again the Sioux bullets missed, and not long after that they went riding downstream to attack Custer. Young Hawk, finding himself alive, concluded that his valiant death could be postponed, maybe for quite some time, and headed for the American flag on the hilltop.

Life at the top was better, if not much. Thirty-two of Reno's command were dead, ten or eleven wounded.

According to plan, Custer would strike the north end of the camp, or the flank, while Reno attacked from the south. Now the lower jaw of this primitive trap had been bent out of shape and the upper jaw was nowhere in sight.

Major Reno was said to be "in an excited condition" on the hilltop, according to testimony from Lt. Winfield Edgerly at the Chicago Court of Inquiry, and was alleged to have fired his revolver at some Indians a thousand yards away—or about nine hundred yards out of range.

Untrue, responded the major: "I did not fire my pistol . . ."

Whether he did or did not, he failed to give the impression that he was in control of himself or of his men. It is therefore a little surprising that 235 of these men—about eighty percent of the survivors—later petitioned the President and House of Representatives:

We the enlisted men the survivors of the battle on the Heights of Little Horn River, on the 25th and 26th of June, 1876, of the 7th Regiment of Cavalry who subscribe our names to this petition, most earnestly solicit . . . that the vacancies among the Commissioned Officers of our Regiment, made by the slaughter of our brave, heroic, and now lamented Lieutenant Colonel George A. Custer, and the other noble dead Commissioned Officers of our Regiment who fell close by him on the bloody field, daring the savage demons to the last, be filled by the Officers of the Regiment only. That Major M. A. Reno, be our Lieutenant Colonel vice Custer, killed; Captain F. W. Benteen our Major vice Reno, promoted. . . .

This being a formal petition, Custer is referred to as Lieutenant Colonel instead of General. Although he had reached the rank of Major General during the Civil War his appointment was brevet, meaning temporary. In 1866 when the Army was reorganized he had been appointed Lieutenant Colonel of the Seventh and was so designated in official communications. Socially speaking, however, he remained General Custer because it was customary to address an officer by the highest rank he had achieved.

The petition continued, explaining that the men understood such promotions would violate established military procedure, but begged to solicit a deviation from the usual rule in recognition of their belief that only the actions of Reno and Benteen had saved them all from death.

Shadows creep across this document. Major E. S. Luce, former superintendent of the Custer Battlefield National Monument, noted various irregularities: signatures of men known to have been illiterate, signatures of men on detached service, signatures of three men whose names could not be found on any regimental roster, etc. In 1954 Major Luce submitted a photostat of the petition and some other documentary material to the FBI, requesting an analysis of the handwriting. The FBI answered that no definite conclusion could be reached because of the limited amount of comparable handwriting. Nevertheless, "variations were noted in the signatures listed below and the corresponding known signatures which suggest in all probability that the signatures on the petition are forgeries."

The FBI listed seventy-nine dubious signatures, and in the opinion of Major Luce these closely resembled the handwriting of Joseph McCurry, first sergeant of Benteen's H Company. Therefore it has been argued that Benteen concocted this petition, persuaded and/or coerced many enlisted men into signing it, and instructed his devoted sergeant to pad the document with seventy-nine more. This may sound unlikely. Indeed it does sound unlikely. But devoted subordinates do sometimes fiddle with records, as Americans learn once in a while to their astonishment and dismay.

Whether or not the petition was loaded, it accomplished nothing. General Sherman replied:

> The judicious and skillful conduct of Major Reno and Captain Benteen is appreciated, but the promotions caused by General Custer's death have been made by the President and confirmed by the Senate; therefore this petition cannot be granted.

Sherman's brisk, courteous response implies no lack of faith in Reno, but many officers were less politic. Brigadier C. A. Woodruff, who had been a lieutenant in Gibbon's column, corresponded with historian Cyrus Brady in 1904 and had this to say: "I conversed with most of the officers of that command at one time or another, while in the field, and nearly all were very pronounced in their severe criticism of Reno. . . ."

Major Reno was not the only one to break down. Benteen stated that upon reaching the crest of the bluff he observed Myles Moylan, "the gallantly-mustached captain of Troop A blubbering like a whipped urchin, tears coursing down his cheeks."

Benteen took command, at least temporarily.

Although Reno's behavior will be argued as long as the Little Bighorn is remembered, there has not been much controversy about this moon-faced pipe-smoking Southerner. Some, but not much. A Chicago *Times* reporter wrote of Benteen: "He has a very juvenile face and head, set on a most masculine body. To look at him casually, he might be mistaken for an overgrown drummer boy. . . ."

In not a single photograph does he look formidable, not even very military. He appears placid, gentle, benevolent, with feminine lips and prematurely white hair. Only after contemplating that orotund face for a while does one begin to perceive something rather less accommodating. Embedded in that fleshy face are the expressionless agate eyes of a killer. One might compare them to the eyes of John Wesley Hardin or Billy the Kid. Now, this sinister absence of expression could be nothing more than a result of myopia, a condition afflicting him after the Oklahoma winter campaign of 1868–9 when he lent his protective goggles to a regimental surgeon. Still, in Civil War photographs he has almost that same look.

His family background suggests affluence. During the eighteenth century the Benteens emigrated from Holland, settling in Baltimore, and were so conservative that the American Revolution could not shake their loyalty to the Crown. They became music publishers—Stephen Foster was a client.

Sometime in the 1830s Frederick's father moved to Virginia where he owned two slaves, according to the 1840 census, and he could afford to enroll Fred at a private academy. Yet all of this is rather misleading. The elder Benteen painted houses and worked as a storekeeper selling glass, hardware, and paint. As for owning slaves, in Virginia at that time it was not unusual. In 1849 he moved to St. Louis, perhaps drawn by the wake of the California gold rush, and in St. Louis young Fred went to work as might be expected, painting houses and signs.

When the Civil War erupted Fred sympathized with the Union, which is surprising if one considers the family's southern heritage. A natural assumption would be that he detested slavery, but apparently he felt more troubled by the idea of southern politicians manipulating the war to their personal advantage. In 1897 he told a reporter from the Atlanta *Journal* that slavery was not the issue, and he went on to say that he never had known an abolitionist in the Union army.

Another factor must have been a young lady from Philadelphia, Catherine Norman, a vehement Unionist whom he would later marry.

Whatever the intellectual persuasion, he seems to have been emotionally moved by a federal defeat at Wilson's Creek near Springfield. He might have participated in this fight; he might only have observed it. He later claimed to have been a spectator, which is improbable. The battle took place in a wooded area twelve miles from town and nobody with any brains strolls into the woods with a picnic basket to watch a battle. He almost certainly fought with the Union, perhaps as a civilian. Charles K. Mills, who thoroughly studied the incident, thought Benteen might have joined a column which broke and ran and he ran with them. Later, to excuse the shame of this, he claimed he was not involved. If such a scenario is correct it might be the only time in his life that Benteen ran from a fight. His record is studded with citations for gallantry.

What seems beyond dispute is that he felt shocked by the cowardly retreat of Union troops.

On September 1, 1861, he accepted a lieutenancy in Bowen's Battalion, which subsequently evolved into the Tenth Missouri. This treasonous act enraged his father, who disinherited him and prayed aloud that a relative loyal to the South would kill him. The elder Benteen allegedly remarked: "I hope the first God damned bullet gets you!"

This intransigent old loyalist went to work on a Mississippi steamboat called the *Fair Play* which supplied the Confederacy. On August 18, 1862, it was captured by a Union flotilla that included two companies of Bowen's Missourians—among them Capt. Frederick Benteen. The civilian crew of the *Fair Play* was taken to Helena, Arkansas, and there released—all except chief engineer T. C. Benteen, who was locked up for the duration.

The immediate question, then, is why Benteen the elder was not turned loose.

The Judge Advocate at Helena and the Provost Marshal both were good friends of Benteen the younger, which establishes a most unusual coincidence. Mills, who has preserved the features of this articulate and complex individual as meticulously as they are apt to be preserved after such a long time, believes that Fred Benteen secretly conspired with federal authorities to guarantee his father's safety for the rest of the war. In custody the old man would be safe.

Young Fred served the North with considerable distinction. The list of skirmishes, full-scale engagements, sieges, raids, and captures in which he participated requires several inches of type in his biography. Bolivar, Pea Ridge, Batesville, Kickapoo Bottom, Milliken's Bend, Pleasant Hill, Little Osage, Montevallo, Greenville, Selma, Columbus, etc. Cited for gallant and meritorious service. Steadily promoted. Recommended for brevet rank of brigadier general on June 6, 1865—although this recommendation was not accepted. Then came the Indian fights. Saline, Washita, Little Bighorn, Nez Perce campaign.

From the beginning of his association with the Seventh Cavalry he mistrusted and disliked Custer. He was five years older and no man enjoys subservience to his junior, but Benteen's antipathy was nourished by something else. He greatly admired a Third Cavalry commandant whose division was assigned to Custer in 1864. This historically insignificant change of command meant a lot to Benteen. From then on he resented the prominent young general.

They met on January 29, 1867, at Fort Riley. Benteen was disgusted by Custer's pretense. At various times he had gotten to know a number of generals, he said, but never before was he subjected to such bragging.

Custer invited him back for a little dime-ante poker the next day. Five or six officers sat in on this amiable gathering. For a while, as Benteen later wrote to the celebrated photographer D. F. Barry, "Custer clawed everything in sight." Elizabeth stood behind him with her hands resting on his shoulders or "in his bosom"—by which Benteen evidently meant that she slipped a hand through the buttons of his tunic. She watched her husband rake in the chips and gently reprimanded him, saying, "Now you must give them their money back. . . ."

Not long after she went to bed two of the gamblers dropped out and Custer proposed raising the ante to $2.50. The survivors played until dawn, at which time Benteen had to quit because he was Officer of the Day. On several occasions, he wrote to Barry, Custer left the table and visited his wife, "to get the sinews of war to prosecute the game, and when Reveille sounded, I had all the money. . . ."

Not only did Benteen have everything on the table, he pocketed an IOU for $150 from Captain Weir.

This poker game, after he had been at Fort Riley just three days, did not win him any new friends. Nobody likes a winner. Besides, Weir was a close friend of the general—a member of the so-called Custer Gang.

Nor could he get along with Major Reno. Benteen attributed this to an argument at a post trader's establishment where, for some reason that is not now clear, he called Reno a son of a bitch and slapped his face. In regard to this, and quite a few other disputes, professor Edgar Stewart has described Benteen's preeminent characteristic as "jealousy of and hostility to almost everybody and everything." Such a comment makes him easy to remember, but of course it is an oversimplification; one or two vivid strokes with a pen do not delineate a man.

General E. A. Garlington, in those days a Seventh Cavalry lieutenant, called him proud and vain, not a steady drinker but one who occasionally started hoisting a cup and did not quit for several days, during which time "he became abusive & insulting to those whom he disliked or disapproved of. He was much liked by most of the officers in the regiment and they took care of him in such periods."

The cause of these drinking bouts seems to be related to his wife, Catherine, who was not very strong and who did not belong on a frontier. He called her Kate or Kittie, logical diminutives. He also called her Pinkie and Goose, names that might be simply affectionate or could have originated during some private moment. However, he very often referred to her as Frabbie, Frabbel, Frabbelina, and at least once as Frabbelina of Gay Street—which is, to say the least, uncommon. It might be the name of a dramatic or fictional character from the time of their courtship.

She lost four of their five children "following the music of the cavalry trumpet," as Benteen expressed it. All four died of spinal meningitis—a disease from which he himself suffered, so he said. If indeed he was afflicted with the tubercular variety, as opposed to influenzal meningitis, he could have transmitted the disease. And if this was so, as Mills points out—if Benteen knew that he himself had caused the deaths of those four children—it must be regarded as an important clue to his personality.

In 1887 he was court-martialed for unmilitary behavior of various sorts.

Charge 1st: Drunk on duty, in violation of the thirty-eighth Article of
    War.
Specification 1st: In this, that Major Frederick W. Benteen, Ninth Cav-
    alry, when in command of the Post of Fort Du Chesne, Utah, was
    found drunk. That at Fort Du Chesne, Utah, on or about the 25th
    (twenty-fifth) day of September, 1886.

Specifications 2nd, 3rd, 4th, 5th and 6th were identical, only the dates
changed. While in command of Fort Du Chesne he was found drunk on or
about September 27, October 10, November 10, November 11, November
12. November must have been a difficult month.

Charge 2nd: Conduct unbecoming an officer and a gentleman.
Specification: In this, that Major Frederick W. Benteen, 9th U.S. Cav-
    alry, did, when in command of the post of Fort Du Chesne, Utah,
    conduct himself in a scandalous manner, in the post trader's store—
    using obscene and profane language; taking off his clothes, to quar-
    rel with citizens, and exposing his person. This, to the dishonor
    and disrepute of the military service, at Fort Du Chesne, Utah, on
    or about the eleventh day of November, 1886.

To each charge Benteen pleaded not guilty.
His trial began February 2, 1887.
Mr. S. D. Cotton, Citizen, being duly sworn, testified that on the infamous
eleventh of November he and Mr. L. Johnson walked into the sutler's store
and encountered Colonel Benteen—his brevet rank at the time. Colonel Benteen had been drinking freely, said Mr. Cotton, and got into a quarrel with
Mr. Johnson, using some pretty hard language. Nevertheless, Benteen insisted upon buying drinks for these two citizens. Mr. Johnson then attempted
to return the compliment and tossed out a dollar, whereupon Benteen said,
"I believe you denied being a Mormon, Mr. Johnson." To which Mr. Johnson
replied that he was mistaken.

"You are a God damned liar," Benteen said, "you did deny it to me. Some
think I came here to fight Indians, but I came here to fight Mormons."

Furthermore, according to Mr. Cotton's testimony, Colonel Benteen said,
"I'll make the Star-Spangled Banner float over all your heads before I get
through with you."

The two citizens then walked out of the sutler's establishment.

About an hour later Benteen located them and tried to apologize, but it did not go very well. "I think you are both God damned Mormons," he said, "and the Mormons are a set of God damned sons of bitches."

This enraged Mr. Cotton, who got ready to fight. He took off his overcoat and called Benteen a liar—at which Benteen peeled down to his shirt, threw off his suspenders, rolled up his sleeves, and was ready to go when a lieutenant managed to separate them.

"He kept on abusing me," Mr. Cotton testified, "calling me all the God damned sons of bitches he could lay his tongue to, until I left. I realized of course that he was very drunk, or he would not talk to me that way, for he had always treated me as well as any gentleman I could wish to meet, but he was very drunk then. I saw him that afternoon, but did not speak to him—they was taking him home."

The Court asked about the state of the accused man's clothing during this altercation.

"He had his cap off," Mr. Cotton answered, "his coat off down to his shirt sleeves, and his breeches down half way over his hips. He was staggering around as drunk as a man could be and stand on his pegs."

Mr. L. Johnson then came before the Court. Being duly sworn, he testified that his name was Lycurgus Johnson, resident of Ashley, Uintah County, Utah, whose occupation was "varied."

Did he know the accused? Yes.

Had he seen the accused at the trader's store on or about November 11? Yes.

Being asked to state anything unusual that occurred on this date, he verified the testimony of his friend Mr. Cotton, including the remark about the Star-Spangled Banner. He stated also that he had observed Benteen later in the day. "I see them taking him home. I don't know whether it was home, it was in a direction southeast."

J. W. Vanderhoof, Citizen, carpenter, and resident of Sidney, Nebraska, testified for the prosecution that he had observed the accused staggering about, "using language that no gentleman would use, unless under the influence of liquor." Mr. Vanderhoof testified that citizens who entered the trader's establishment were ordered by the accused to "hit the breeze." He told the Court that the accused had gotten into an argument with Mr. Isaac Cummins who, upon being ordered to leave, stepped behind a coal stove. The accused discovered him, said Vanderhoof, "and pointed a finger to him, and said, 'There stands the son of a bitch behind the stove.' He said, 'Boys,' speaking to no one specially, 'give me a revolver and I'll make the son of a bitch of a Mormon pull his freight.'"

Mr. William Theiss, Citizen, resident of Fort Du Chesne, who gave his occupation as "roustabout," also testified for the prosecution.

Did he recognize the accused? Yes.

Did he see the accused on or about November 11? Yes. "I seen him down at the place where I am employed. At that time I was cooking for the Post Trader. The place where I saw him was down at the cook-house."

Being asked to relate the circumstances, Mr. Theiss stated that shortly after five o'clock Major Benteen arrived for supper. He was intoxicated.

Did the witness hold any conversation with the accused?

Yes, the accused asked the witness his name. Upon being told "William Theiss," the accused continued to ask the same question. "I answered him three or four times. He was almost through his supper, then he fell from his chair, whether it was done by accident, I don't know. For supper, I gave him eggs. They were boiled soft, and they run down his beard."

After the accused fell off his chair, inquired the Court, what did the accused do?

Mr. Theiss stated that the accused "broke part of his pants open. I presume it was by accident as this was the first I saw of it. He fell on the floor and as I say before, the front part of his pants unbuttoned, or broke open. He did not get right up. He laid there for a matter of two or three minutes. . . ."

How did the witness happen to observe the disordered condition of the pants of the accused?

Mr. Theiss replied that it would be natural to observe this.

Did the accused at any time improperly expose any part of his person?

"Not that I know of. No sir."

A transcript of the Court-Martial notes that the accused declined to cross-examine this witness.

The Court also heard testimony from a certain Mrs. Bailey who was chatting with several other ladies in Colonel Benteen's tent when he approached in an intoxicated condition, addressing her as follows:

"Your husband must have a hell of a time with you."

Mrs. Bailey responded by asking what he meant. He next made some reference to her eyes—his words were repeated differently by different witnesses—after which there seems to be no doubt about what he did. He stepped outside and pissed on the tent very close to where the ladies were sitting.

"We all heard it," testified Captain J. A. Olmstead.

Miss Violet Norman was called to testify on behalf of the accused. Being asked if she recognized the accused, she replied that she did. He was her uncle.

Being directly questioned by the accused as to his condition at the time of the reputed insult to Mrs. Bailey, Miss Norman answered: "You had been drinking some, was rather talkative, but was not in my opinion drunk."

Being asked to give her recollection of the incident, she stated to the Court: "Colonel Benteen was joking with Mrs. Bailey about her eyes, and I remember his having said to her that any woman with such eyes must be a holy terror. I think that was the only thing said about the matter, and was said in pleasantry, and taken as such by Mrs. Bailey, for they had been joking and were joking for some time after that."

Did Colonel Benteen escort Mrs. Bailey to and from supper?

"He did."

What were the relations between Mrs. Bailey and the accused?

"They were very pleasant. Mrs. Bailey came out almost every day to walk with me, and we were very frequently joined by Colonel Benteen, and I never saw anything that was contrary."

At the time of the alleged insult did anything occur which would offend the taste of the most fastidious person?

"There was nothing of the kind."

The testimony of Miss Violet Norman was read aloud by the Judge Advocate and Miss Norman pronounced it correctly recorded.

The most eloquent defense of the accused seems to have come from Benteen himself in the form of a lengthy document entitled *Exhibit H: Being further statements of F. W. Benteen, submitted in writing*. Much of it is dull, but now and then—aggrieved by all these slanderous insinuations—he responds with fairly senatorial wrath. In regard to Captain Olmstead:

> Why gentlemen, this man Olmstead broods over fancies until he believes them to be facts, and then he propagates them as facts. This is well known in the 9th Cavalry, and such a man's testimony cannot, is not allowed to be impeached by this Court. This officer is not prejudiced against me, but when asked whether he is, says, no, and then proceeds to inject all the virus that his little syringe will hold by dragging in an occurrence as antique as the spring of 1884, which, if the facts were told by disinterested witnesses, would redound to my credit—and he was known as "a Benteen man!" Thank God, gentlemen, there are not many such, or I could truly say save me from my friends! I should think it an insult for a man like that to take my part, for he has not a single idea of his own; they are all reflected.

Benteen is not through with Olmstead. He summarizes a conversation alleged to have taken place between himself and a Mr. Lorenzo Hatch during

which he, Benteen, told Olmstead to keep his damned nose out of the business. "Gentlemen, I neither referred to his nose—or his 'damned nose,' but I
can inform him of one thing that I will pull it for him if I ever hear of his
meddling with anything that concerns me or mine again. This man is a dangerous man, and I regret that I did not find it out sooner."

Concerning the charge of drunkenness on a particular day, Benteen remembers it well. He was in the sutler's tent, "and though I had drank some
during the afternoon, principally ginger ale, I had caught cold, my spine
being bent, so that I could not stand erect, and on going towards home, I
called Lieut. Styer's attention to the fact, asking him if I did not appear somewhat as the man in Joe Jefferson's Rip Van Winkle, who is carrying the Keg
up to the skittle players in the Catskills?"

As for those damaging witnesses S. D. Cotton and Lycurgus Johnson, they
are not worthy of belief. Benteen knows them. A pity the Court does not.
"I've heard enough more of them to make one's hair stand on end, and one of
the stories was that Johnson let his poor old mother drown, as she was an
incumbrance, but had ample time to save the horses while crossing a swollen
river."

Oh yes, he continues, admonishing those who must decide his fate: "I
know too well that subtle poison has been diligently and assiduously poured
into the ears of the members of this Court by my detractors . . ."

And in a rolling summation which opens with the first shot fired at Fort
Sumter he explains how he came to be where he is. To a Southerner whose
father and family "were Calhounists of the Ultra stamp, where States Rights
and Nullification were among the earliest remembered words," it became no
easy matter to answer the Union call—to rush with fixed bayonet upon
brother, father, home, friends, and companions: "Such, gentlemen, was the
predicament I was in, living in Missouri when the 'Rally round the Flag!' was
being sounded in clarion tones by the loyal people of the country."

The fruit of the Civil War he called "a harvest of barren regrets," although
the Union prevailed. Afterward he felt obligated to provide a home for his
widowed sister and her three infant daughters, as well as a home for the widow
and three children of his brother who had fallen from a scaffolding in 1882.
His aged Yankee-hating father, too, depended on him.

So he wrote in 1887, reminding the Court that those small children now
were grown, with children of their own:

> . . . and their little children clamor to rest on the knees of their soldier
> uncle, and every night from their little bedsides the prayers of those
> prattlers are offered up to the Divine Being to protect, care for and bless

their dear old soldier uncle, and that their childish wishes will be heeded in due time, by our Maker, the Great Grand Master, I verily believe with them. I truly know that there is nothing so dear to all their childish hearts, as the wish to be just such a man as they think their dear old uncle to be.

To no avail, this majestic defense.

The Court did not find him guilty of indecent exposure, nor of drunkenness on three of the specified days; but of substantial drunkenness, as well as conduct unbecoming an officer and gentleman, he was guilty.

AND THE COURT DOES THEREFORE SENTENCE HIM, MAJOR FREDERICK W. BENTEEN, 9TH U.S. CAVALRY, TO BE DISMISSED FROM THE UNITED STATES MILITARY SERVICE.

A document superscribed "Headquarters Department of the Platte," dated March 11, 1887, states that the proceedings, findings, and sentence have been approved and are forwarded to the president with a recommendation that if, in view of Major Benteen's past record, clemency should be extended to him, he should be somehow disciplined "for his insubordinate and disrespectful language, and his unsoldierlike conduct, as shown in these proceedings, indicating, as they do, that he is sadly in need of such discipline." Signed: George Crook, Brigadier General.

Crook's respectful hint that clemency be extended was echoed by his superior and former West Point roommate, Little Phil Sheridan.

President Cleveland took their word for it. Benteen was suspended from rank and duty for one year at half pay. He served this penitential year in Atlanta where he had been stationed at the conclusion of the Civil War and where he had decided to live.

On April 27, 1888, he reported for duty at Fort Niobara, Nebraska, but three days later he applied for a medical discharge. The Army granted his request because of a bad back, defective vision, and "frequent micturition"— all attributed to injuries during his period of service.

After getting out of the Army he retired to Atlanta where he lived in reasonable comfort with his wife and their son, dividing his time between a farm and a cottage in town, writing a few memoirs, enjoying the friendship of such luminaries as Joel Chandler Harris. He himself was something of a celebrity, though regarded as little more than a carpetbagger by the Atlanta nobility. He did not mind talking to reporters but he would not discuss the great battle. The Atlanta *Journal* commented that there was nothing he disliked more than publicity "and if it were left to him none of his valorous deeds would be handed down to posterity."

In 1890, despite his scandalous behavior at Fort Du Chesne, he was awarded the brevet rank of brigadier for gallant and meritorious service in two battles, one as thoroughly forgotten as the other is famous: Canyon Creek and the Little Bighorn. Eight years later, on June 17, he was paralyzed by a stroke. Five days after that he died. Among the pallbearers were the mayor of Atlanta, the governor of Georgia, and a vice-president of Coca-Cola.

In 1902 he was exhumed and reburied at Arlington.

Once he wrote to a former Seventh Cavalry private with whom he had served at the Little Bighorn: "I've been a loser in a way, all my life by rubbing a bit against the angles—or hair—of folks, instead of going with their whims; but I couldn't go otherwise—'twould be against the grain of myself."

The same undoubtedly could be said for Reno, and for the Seventh Cavalry commandant himself. All three rubbed against the hair because they could not do otherwise. So it happened that the Seventh's three ranking officers created a triangle with Custer at the apex while his subordinates held themselves apart at the lower corners.

Why Major Reno and Captain Benteen did not get along is puzzling. Their mutual antipathy lacked the virulence that inflamed their relationships with Custer, but in spite of all they had in common they could not, or would not, march in step.

One thing the captain might have resented was the fact that Reno attended West Point while he himself did not; and he probably knew about Reno's miserable West Point record, which must have added to the contempt he felt. Reno was scheduled to graduate with the class of 1855 but twice derailed himself with excessive demerits and did not make it until 1857. During those six years he picked up 1,031 demerits, an Academy record. At the opposite extreme, a few cadets have graduated without a single black mark, the most illustrious being—as one might guess—Robert E. Lee, class of '29.

Reno got demerits easily, almost deliberately. A button on his tunic was unfastened. A trace of lint clung to the bore of his rifle. He arrived at formation several seconds late. He carved his initials on a tree. While on guard duty he decided to sing. By normal standards such crimes are not heinous, but Reno was in the Army, where normal standards do not prevail. Accordingly he was busted, saved from permanent expulsion once by the grace of Secretary of War Jefferson Davis who himself had accumulated 137 demerits during his fourth year as a cadet. Busted again, barely saved by a reduction of charges, Reno emerged from the nest twentieth in a fledgling class of thirty-eight. This was not good, but during his career with the Seventh he must have reflected that it was better than the record of his commanding officer. George Armstrong Custer, class of '61, graduated last.

Reno's record also was superior to that of his closest friend at West Point, James McNeill Whistler, who piled up demerits with heroic aplomb and concluded one examination by defining silicon as a gas. Whistler reputedly said to Reno some years afterward that if silicon indeed had been a gas he probably would have stayed in the Army and become a major general; and Reno said yes, but then nobody would ever have heard of his mother. That must have been one of the cleverest things Reno ever said. Unlike Custer and Benteen—with their very different styles—he seems humorless. There is no levity in that dark face.

From the start, almost from the day he entered West Point, he radiates an aura of misfortune. It never diminishes. During the Civil War when he led a charge against Fitzhugh Lee near the Rappahannock his horse went down, pinning him underneath. He was cited for gallantry and recommended for brevet promotion from captain to major, but the gods always poisoned their gifts to Reno: the accident resulted in a severe hernia.

After the war he was sent to West Point as an instructor. This ought to have been good news, considering various alternatives, but at West Point—after eight years as a cavalry officer—he was assigned to teach infantry tactics.

Thus far it sounds like bad luck, but henceforth Reno seems increasingly responsible for the necklace of tin cans he wore. He protested the infantry assignment by writing to Superintendent George Washington Cullum. Cullum thought this presumptuous and requested the War Department to relieve Captain Reno of his duties at West Point. He therefore was ordered to New Orleans. Again he protested by writing to the Adjutant General, which further blemished his reputation as an obedient soldier.

In 1866, convinced that he deserved promotion and that the way to accomplish this was to let important people get a look at him, he visited the capital. Nothing happened. He invoked the aid of a senator. Then he wrote a letter to President Johnson. As a result, having antagonized various parties, including the Secretary of War, he was shipped to Fort Vancouver, Washington Territory—about as far from the throne as a soldier could be sent in those days.

During the summer of 1869 he was finally promoted to major in the regular army and assigned to the Seventh Cavalry at Fort Leavenworth. So to the Kansas prairie he went with his wife and son. There the gods offered him to Custer.

Five years later, while he was afield in Montana, a courier delivered a telegram containing the news that his wife had unexpectedly died. Reno turned over the unit to his senior captain and rode all night to Fort Benton where he sent a telegram requesting permission to attend his wife's funeral.

Headquarters replied: "While fully sympathizing with your affliction, the Department Commander feels it is imperative to decline to grant you leave. You must return to your command."

His wife came from a wealthy family, but they despised him and saw to it that he never got a dime.

In 1876 after the Little Bighorn defeat he returned to Fort Lincoln, but presently was given command of a wretched stronghold thirty miles south of Fargo called Fort Abercrombie. Here he ran afoul of a captain's wife, Mrs. Emeline Bell. Her reputation was not good. Perhaps she was maligned; today it is impossible to know. Reno himself—justifiably or not—compared her to a spoiled egg.

How intimate they were is a matter of academic dispute. That he slid closer to her than he should have while the captain was absent is beyond doubt. That he accomplished much, if anything, seems very questionable. Whatever did or did not happen, his behavior caused gossip. He might have eased out of this delicate situation except for the presence of an Episcopal missionary and longtime friend of the Bells, Reverend Richard Wainwright, who lodged at the captain's house. It appears that Wainwright was outraged by what he heard and persuaded the captain to file charges of immoral conduct. This being done, Reno was ordered to relinquish command of Fort Abercrombie and deliver himself up to his superiors at St. Paul, there to stand trial.

Under provisions of Article of War 61, it was specified that in disregard of his honor and duty Reno did visit the quarters of Captain Bell "and then and there take improper and insulting liberties with the wife of the said Captain Bell, by taking both her hands in his own, and attempting to draw her person up close to his own. This to the scandal and disgrace of the military service, at Fort Abercrombie, D.T., on or about the 18th day of December, 1876."

Three or four days later, no doubt convinced that he had made a little progress, Captain Bell being yet away from the fort, Reno slipped an arm around Mrs. Bell's waist.

"This to the scandal and disgrace. . . ."

On Christmas he was not invited to a party given by Mrs. Bell. He was the only officer who did not get an invitation, and he was overheard exclaiming to Mr. John Haselhurst, post trader: "This means war! Mrs. Bell has thrown down the gauntlet, and I will take it up. Perhaps these people do not know the power of a commanding officer." By which it was understood that he had in mind "to revenge himself upon the said Mrs. Bell for her failure to invite him to the social gathering aforesaid."

Five days after that, rounding out a disastrous year, he forbade Reverend Wainwright to hold religious services on the post. When the missionary demanded an explanation Reno told him a member of the garrison had objected. But instead of leaving it there Reno went on to suggest that Wainwright and Mrs. Bell were taking advantage of the captain's absence. And on the very last day of 1876 he did "maliciously attempt and endeavor to annoy and humiliate the wife of Captain James M. Bell" by refusing to permit her to play the organ. Evidently he had arranged some sort of truce with the preacher because religious services were authorized and she was engaged to play; but at the last moment he sent a note forbidding her participation. Reverend Wainwright could preach, but if Mrs. Bell played the organ he would put a stop to it. All of this very much to the scandal and disgrace of the military.

And there were charges concerning his behavior at Fort Lincoln, upon which he was not tried. There, acccording to the addendum, on or about September 26, when said post was exposed and liable to attack from Sioux Indians, he, Major Marcus A. Reno, did become drunk. And did, by malicious and insulting comments, provoke a rough-and-tumble fistfight with first Lt. John A. Manley, Twentieth Infantry, during which struggle the combatants rolled around on the floor of the officers' club room "in the slops and filth covered by spittle and the spilling of liquor over said floor," in the presence of civilians and junior officers, to the disgrace of all.

He did furthermore attempt to provoke a duel with first Lt. Charles A. Varnum, causing pistols to be sent for, and upon being threatened with arrest he responded: "Who in hell are you?" or words to that effect.

These allegations, plus two or three others, were forwarded to Colonel Samuel Sturgis, *de jure* commandant of the Seventh. Sturgis had not led his regiment against the Indians because he was stationed temporarily in St. Louis as Superintendent of the Mounted Recruiting Service. Thus it was Lt. Col. Custer who led the troops that summer.

Sturgis forwarded these complaints about Reno as he was required to do, but he was also expected to evaluate them, and he refused to approve them: "They appear now with a bad grace, and do not carry with them the idea that they proceed from conscientious motives. I was not at Ft. Lincoln at the time of the alleged occurrences; but am credibly informed that the occasion was the return of the Regt. from the field and the 'opening' of the Club room at Lincoln—and that the debauchery was pretty general. . . ."

Even so, it was another tin can around Reno's neck.

A lucky man might have eluded the charges filed by Captain Bell, either through the liquidity of his tongue or the glow of his guiding star, but Marcus Reno was not lucky. His star flickered. The St. Paul court recommended that he be dismissed from the Army. President Hayes, taking into account Reno's twenty years of meritorious service, reduced this punishment to suspension without pay for two years.

It did not take him long to get in trouble again. Restored to active duty, stationed at Fort Meade near the Black Hills, he felt himself overcome with passion for Col. Sturgis' daughter—twenty-year-old Ella. By this time Reno was a paunchy, middle-aged alcoholic, so it is not likely that the choleric colonel enjoyed the sight of him beaming at Ella. Then too, young Jack Sturgis, the colonel's son, was killed at the Little Bighorn and a great many people considered Reno responsible for the disaster. Sturgis himself blamed Custer. Nevertheless, Reno must have been associated in Sturgis' mind with the death of his son. Under the very best circumstances he probably did not care for the presence of the dark-faced major.

On the evening of August 3, having been invited to supper at the home of post trader W. S. Fanshawe, Reno got drunk—"disgustingly drunk" according to Mrs. Fanshawe. So drunk that he got the hiccups, she later said, and she feared he might become ill.

On the evening of August 8 in the billiard room of the Officers' Club he got drunk, knocked some money out of the bartender's hand, punched a hole through a window with a chair, and fell down three times on the way home.

October 25 was another big evening in the billiard room. He lost approximately $300 playing against Lt. William Nicholson, after which they got into a fight. Reno hit Nicholson with a cue, which broke. Nicholson grabbed Reno by the throat and flung him to the floor. Lt. James Pettit intervened, threatening them both with arrest.

Col. Sturgis ordered Reno confined to quarters until this very serious matter could be resolved. He was permitted to leave his quarters only for exercise.

Then came the dreadful night of November 10.

While circling the parade ground on his evening constitutional Reno walked by the colonel's house. He observed a light in the parlor. He approached. He raised himself on a ledge, he looked in the window, and he discovered sweet Ella—presumably alone. He tapped on the glass. Ella jumped. He then perceived that she was not alone—Mrs. Sturgis also was in the parlor—and Ella cried out in manifest alarm: "Mama, it is Major Reno!"

Mrs. Sturgis called to her husband who was upstairs in bed, or almost in bed, and moments later the colonel flew out of the house with his suspenders flapping, brandishing a cane. Reno decided this would not be an appropriate moment to explain the situation. He retreated to his quarters. There he was soon confronted by the regimental adjutant who demanded to know what he had been doing at the colonel's house.

Next morning he wrote an apologetic note to Mrs. Sturgis. He understood that his troubles were now compounded, because he kept a draft of this note, which has a few words misspelled:

> November 11th, 1879. whatever others may say or think I do not wish to be misunderstood by you, and I write this that you may appreciate what motives actuated me when I stopped to look through your window. It has been my habit since in arrest to walk on favorable nights on the pathway in front of Officers quarters to or three times for exercise. On the evening in question I saw your daughter in Complete toilet through the window, and it was such a picture that I said to myself. Can there be any harm in looking upon it. no one will know it and in my loneiless and thoughs of the past, I felt myself impatient to resist the temptation. . . . I sincerely ask your pardon for all that does not seem to you as innocent, for I do assure you if not guiltless the fault was in the judgment and not heart of course I would like you to show this to "E."

It was not enough. At least it failed to mollify the exasperated colonel because Reno found himself saddled with another charge: that he did, "in the darkness and at a late hour in the evening, surreptitiously enter the side grounds adjoining the private residence or quarters of his commanding officer, Col. S. D. Sturgis, 7th Cavalry, and did peer into . . ." etc.

They brought him to the rail again, charged with conduct unbecoming an officer and gentleman.

On November 28 he stood before a General Court-Martial. The presiding officer was Col. William Henry Wood who had once disciplined him at West Point. Another member of this Court was a good friend of Sturgis. Another was Lt. Col. Elmer Otis whom Reno had known as a cadet, which should have been reassuring. Unfortunately they did not like each other, and in a fit of temper Reno had once told Otis that instead of attending the Academy he should have gone to cooking school.

In regard to the Fanshawe supper, Reno testified that he was not the only one drinking. In fact, he said, five people had shared that bottle. Furthermore, nobody except Mrs. Fanshawe considered his behavior disgusting.

As for that rowdy evening at the club, "all the witnesses agree that it was a frolic; that the chair was thrown or tossed when I was sober. . . . Is there anything here to attach disorderly conduct to?"

Concerning the business with Lt. Nicholson—he brought that on himself by repeated insults. "I struck him under great provocation with a billiard cue. Can there be anything criminal in that? Could I, as an officer and gentleman, have acted otherwise?"

And about peeking into the Sturgis parlor, it was an act of pure admiration. He would rather cut off his right arm than disturb one single hair of sweet Ella's head.

He might have escaped with cursory punishment had it not been for this final indiscretion, because there was testimony in his favor. But that unhappy swarthy face at the window had alarmed Col. Sturgis' daughter more than words could tell. Lt. Baldwin Spilman, witness for the prosecution, testified that he saw Reno walk away from the Sturgis home that night and he saw Ella very soon thereafter, her features "considerably distorted."

Ella herself claimed that the face at the window had left her "paralyzed." She had been so frightened, she told the Court, that she could hardly speak. Major Reno looked excited, pale, and desperate. Their eyes met "for at least six seconds," and her first impression was that she was going to be shot.

Benteen was called to the stand. Although he felt contemptuous of Reno he testified on Reno's behalf. He had read the note of apology to Mrs. Sturgis before it was sent and he considered it an honest explanation of the major's otherwise inexplicable behavior. The major was, he believed, "dead in love with the young lady."

The Court found Reno guilty as charged, only modifying the language somewhat, and recommended dismissal from service. Despite this verdict, five of the seven judges urged clemency. General Terry thought the sentence excessive and joined the petition for clemency. Sherman, higher up, gave a similar opinion. But this time President Hayes did not feel magnanimous.

After twenty-three years in uniform, Reno was dishonorably discharged.

Then it was steeply downhill. He had no idea what to do. He could not get a job. He borrowed money from his son. He moved to Washington where he met a government clerk named Isabella Ray and in January of 1884 they got married. After a few months she left him. Finally the Bureau of Pensions hired him as an examiner.

He thought people might like to know about the Little Bighorn so he advised the New York *Weekly Press* that he still had his diary—"written on the battlefield lying in the grass within scent of the dead horses"—and he wondered if the editor might be interested in a contribution. When the editor said yes, Reno mailed him an account of the fight. It was rejected.

In Nashville his son married a whisky heiress, Miss Ittie Kinney, but Reno did not attend the wedding. He explained that he was too busy, which was untrue. He could not afford train fare to Nashville.

Such indigence must have been corrosive because according to one biographer—who does not provide much documentation—he was a descendant of Philippe François Renault, who accompanied Lafayette to America in 1777. This distinguished ancestor was rewarded by the United States with tracts of land said to have been worth four hundred million dollars by the nineteenth century, but litigation prevented Reno from tasting this marvelous pie. Another biographer states that he was a descendant of French Huguenots named Reynaud who fled to Virginia in the early eighteenth century, and no reference is made to prodigious wealth. Four hundred million or not, his first wife unquestionably was rich, while he himself could not buy a ticket to Nashville.

His star glittered darkly until the end. He developed cancer of the tongue and died after an operation at Providence Hospital. On March 29, 1889, the Washington *Evening Star* took notice:

RENO — in this city,
died, Marcus A. Reno,
late Major and Brevet
Lt. Col., U. S. Army.

General Custer's widow, who lived into her nineties, held him responsible for what happened at the Little Bighorn. In 1926 she was invited to Montana for the fiftieth anniversary, at which time a monument to the hapless major would be unveiled. She answered with a letter of dismay, urging that no memorial "to so great a coward as Major Reno" be situated on the field. "In writing this," she continued, "I feel almost my husband's hand taking the pen away from me. . . . I *long* for a memorial to our heroes on the battlefield of the Little Big Horn but not to *single out* for honor, the one coward of the regiment."

If she was the last to forgive, Major General Thomas Rosser, who had been Custer's roommate at West Point, surely was among the first to condemn. Only two days after the astounding headlines, a letter from him was published by the St. Paul *Pioneer-Press*: "I feel that Custer would have succeeded had Reno, with all the reserve of seven companies, passed through and joined Custer after the first repulse. . . . As a soldier I would sooner today lie in the grave of Gen. Custer and his gallant comrades alone in that distant wilderness, that when the 'last trumpet' sounds I could rise to judgment from my post of duty, than to live in the place of the survivors of the siege on the hills."

Everybody had an opinion.

On March 8, 1879, the *Army and Navy Journal* reprinted a letter from the *National Republican* by a member of the First Cavalry, which said in part:

"My estimate of Reno and Custer is this: The former was brave but not rash, and Custer was both. Through rashness Custer and the '3rd Cavalry Division' got surrounded at Trevillian Station in 1864, and it was a brave but not a rash man who cut him out. I mean Wesley Merritt, who commanded the 1st Cavalry, of which Marcus Reno's regiment . . . formed a part. It was Custer's rashness that got him into the scrape at the Little Big Horn in 1876, and it would require a larger force than Reno had at his command to cut him out."

Another critic thought the assault failed because of Reno's timidity, "because the Sioux shook their blankets at him."

Years after the major's death a great-nephew, Charles Reno, asked that the official charges against him be reexamined. This was done, and the Judge Advocate General's office concluded that he had been improperly dismissed, which was perhaps the only bit of decent luck Reno ever had.

On September 9, 1967, a unique ceremony began at the First Christian Church in Billings, Montana. Major Reno's casket, followed by the traditional riderless horse, was escorted by units of the Montana National Guard from the church to the battlefield sixty miles southeast. There the honors were presented: an eleven-gun salute—signifying his Civil War brevet rank of Brigadier General—and three rifle volleys across his new grave. Elizabeth would have been disgusted. Although the bones of many troopers lie on the field, the only man to be buried with such pomp at the Custer National Cemetery was the one she could not abide.

Now this man with the dark face rests a few steps due north of the flagpole, his rank posthumously restored, while the posthumous squabble about his cowardice goes on and on.

That he was at least temporarily unsettled or incapacitated is admitted by all scholars, amateur or professional, and there are some who look upon this troubled man with the utmost virulence. Quite often those who most flagrantly despise him are career soldiers, which at first sounds like a paradox, but of course is natural. Captain R. G. Carter, for instance, himself a veteran Indian fighter of the celebrated Fourth Cavalry, made this comment: "Reno showed the white feather from the start, and his entire conduct was that of a white-livered, yellow-streaked coward. He was terrorized and panic stricken. . . . He should have been tried and cashiered for the part he took in 'Custer's Last Fight.' If ever there was a pusillanimous poltroon in the army whose name should be handed down to future generations as an arrant coward, Marcus A. Reno is the man."

Lt. Edward Mathey testified during the Chicago inquiry that he had heard many discussions of the fight and many opinions offered, but one expression in particular he could not forget. He did not identify the speaker, but he heard somebody say: "If we had not been commanded by a coward we would all have been killed."

A religious magazine, the *Northwestern Christian Advocate*, assigned the blame not exactly to cowardice: "What, then, was the explanation of his conduct at the Battle of the Little Big Horn? . . . HE WAS DRUNK."

This is another disputed charge. Whisky was indeed dispensed from traders' boats on the Yellowstone, along with champagne cider and such commonplace produce as butter, eggs, vegetables, pickles, lemons, licorice root, tinned salmon, chewing tobacco, shoelaces, thread, needles, etc. Out of cider and bourbon a drink was invented, christened Rosebud to honor this desolate region, and drunks were exiled to the prairie until they got over it, which probably did not take long, considering the possibility of Sioux warriors whooping over the nearest ridge.

James Coleman set up shop in a tent at General Terry's base camp, a wall of canned goods separating officers and men. Prices were the same on either side: whisky one dollar a pint, although if a soldier wanted his three-pint canteen filled to the brim with old tanglefoot he needed an OK from the captain. An Arikara named Red Star said Coleman's tent was black with thirsty soldiers, "like a swarm of flies."

So it would have been easy enough for Major Reno to fill his canteen and numerous other containers before leaving the Yellowstone. Indeed it would be unusual for a man who enjoyed drinking as much as he did to pass up the opportunity, especially when he knew that within a week he might lose his scalp.

The ingenuity of soldiers when confronted with the problem of transporting alcohol cannot be overestimated. The most unlikely receptacles were found. Officers, more or less exempt from personal inspection, might drape a loaded goatskin across the saddle, but enlisted men were obliged to be circumspect. During the Civil War, for instance, they discovered that a rifle barrel would hold several jolts. Ulysses Grant, despite his rank, is said to have benefited from this.

Indian scouts later said that some pack mules carried a little keg on either side. Curly—reputed to be the one survivor of Custer's immediate command—told his grandson that during the march up Rosebud Creek he was sent with a message to the rear of the column and there he noticed soldiers tapping the kegs. He saw these same mules after crossing the divide, just before the attack. He said Custer halted the regiment until the mules arrived. Then the kegs were unplugged and the soldiers filed past, each man with a cup. White Man Runs Him told the same story, according to his son-in-law Robert Yellowtail: "We scouts joined in; before long my finger tips and lips tingled and felt numb. Our interpreter Mitch Bouyer, explained that the whisky was to make the soldiers brave."

Lt. E. S. Godfrey said Reno took along a half-gallon keg and refused to share it. Godfrey's assertion cannot be verified but it is pretty well established that Reno carried a flask obtained from some trader and was observed holding this flask in a horizontal position with his lips conjoined to the orifice. Lt. DeRudio came across him chatting with interpreter Gerard in the middle of the Little Bighorn where they had paused to water their horses. The major was swigging at a flask when DeRudio splashed by. "What are you trying to do?" Reno asked. "Drown me before I am killed?"

Gerard said that after the skirmish line collapsed he saw Reno pull out a bottle of whisky and drink everything in it.

During the Chicago inquiry Reno admitted having a flask, but declared that he did not take a nip until long after the retreat from the valley when his battalion was marooned on the bluff. He insisted further that his one-pint flask was not emptied until three days later at the site of Custer's last stand. Burying the dead was very disagreeable, he said, and he shared his pint with Captain French.

The most damaging statement came from a civilian mule packer, John Frett, who got into an argument with Reno on the hilltop. Frett claimed that he had been verbally abused, quoting the major, to wit: "God damn you. . . ." In addition, said Frett, he had been physically struck in the face by the hand of the major, during which altercation the major staggered, while he, Frett, was splashed with liquor from the major's flask. Further, the major leveled a carbine at him, saying, "I will shoot you." And in this testimony Mr. Frett was supported by another civilian mule packer, Mr. B. F. Churchill.

Benteen did not think the major was overloaded. He saw no indication of staggering or stammering and doubted if there was enough whisky on the hilltop for anybody to get drunk. If he had known Reno was carrying some whisky, he said, he would have asked for a drink himself.

"I was close to him," said Pvt. Daniel Newell, "and if he had been the least bit drunk I would have known it."

Custer's orderly, John Burkman, had been detailed to the pack train on that fatal day. This hurt his feelings. So devoutly did he worship the general that he might have chosen death at Custer's side to life on Reno Hill. In any event, on the night of the twenty-fifth he was assigned to guard Major Reno's tent. "He had a keg," Burkman said many years afterward, "and he was drinkin' considerable."

Burkman lived to be eighty-eight—an illiterate, gnarled, bad-tempered, childish curmudgeon with white eyebrows and a white beard, "hugging jealously to himself the precious heritage of memories." Nothing else mattered to old John, and for this reason, as well as the increasing cloudiness of senility, he may have fabricated or twisted the truth.

The contradictions cannot be resolved. All one might say with certainty is that the *Northwestern Christian Advocate* overstated the case, although Major Reno probably was not as dry as the Montana bluff.

A month later he must have been ninety proof because the Little Bighorn survivors drank copiously when they again fell into the embrace of Yellowstone traders, and according to records kept by Leighton & Jordan no member of this devastated regiment bought more booze than the man with the dark face.

The names of very few enlisted men show up on L&J's accounts, maybe because they paid cash, so it is possible that some of them outdrank Reno, but among the fourteen surviving officers nobody compares with him. During the first three weeks of August he bought seven gallons and two demijohns of whisky, which comes to about ten quarts a week. Lt. Edwin P. Eckerson took second place—far behind Reno—with three gallons. This may indicate just how deeply the major was shocked, because an officer who customarily swallowed such an amount would not be on active duty.

Eckerson's gallon-a-week is formidable, and becomes particularly interesting when one learns that he was not in the fight. He was on detached service at Fort Lincoln and he joined the troops on the Yellowstone after the battle. Now, there could be a number of explanations for Eckerson drinking. Perhaps he had quarreled with his wife. But he was the second lieutenant of a company wiped out at the Little Bighorn and if he had not been assigned to duty at Fort Lincoln he would have been a dead hero.

Behind Reno and Eckerson on the Leighton & Jordan register one finds Capt. Myles Moylan and Lt. George Wallace with two gallons apiece. Wallace bought his two gallons in a single day, along with some fishing tackle, so he may have been hosting a party.

During this period Benteen did not buy any whisky. At least if he did, he did not charge it. This fact, too, says something because he liked to drink; but what his apparent abstinence means, if anything, is not clear.

Quite a few Indians thought the soldiers were drunk. The Cheyenne warrior Wooden Leg said that while wandering around Custer Hill he picked up two metal bottles partly filled with liquid. He tasted both bottles and offered them to other Indians, none of whom knew what the liquid was until a Sioux identified it as whisky. Wooden Leg insisted that several bottles were found on the hillside. Another Cheyenne, Bobtail Horse, pointed out to Dr. Thomas Marquis the exact spot where he found a canteen half full of whisky. In those days Bobtail Horse did not understand whisky so he drank it like water and got sick.

Wooden Leg's name, faintly absurd in English, does not mean he had a peg leg. It was his uncle's name—Kum-mok-quiv-vi-ok-ta—implying that he could walk all day without getting tired, whose legs therefore must be made of wood instead of flesh. The boy who later became known as Wooden Leg admired this uncle, followed him everywhere, and told his father that was what he himself would like to be called. When he was about seventeen he helped to kill a Crow horse thief and in recognition of this act his father decided the time had come. So there was a feast and the boy received his favorite uncle's name.

His story about the whisky flasks may have been contrived—he is said to have retracted it—and except for rumors there is not much to suggest a drunken regiment. If any troopers did swallow a little porcupine juice before entering the valley it could not have been enough to disable them. Given the circumstances—approaching this enormous village of very dangerous Sioux and Cheyennes—whatever they drank must have tasted like herb tea. Reno, for example, may have taken a drink while pausing in mid-stream to water his horse, but his angry response to being splashed by DeRudio's horse indicates that he was stone sober.

How many barking, yelping Unkpapas galloped out of Sitting Bull's camp to stop Reno's charge can only be estimated. The major himself guessed that when he withdrew from the valley there were at least six hundred warriors on his left, with many more streaming from the lodges. Some historians believe that perhaps a thousand Sioux chased him up the hill while several thousand more rode around looking for other bluecoats. Col. W. A. Graham interviewed a number of veterans long afterward at a retirement home in Washington and one old trooper, Sgt. Fremont Kipp, said: "You take a stick and stir up a big ant hill; stir it up good and get the ants excited and mad. Then try to count 'em."

Reno was less concerned with the numerical strength, position, tactics, or weapons of the Sioux than with getting out alive. "I mounted my command and charged through the Reds in a solid body," he wrote. "As we cut our way through them the fighting was hand to hand and it was instant death to him who fell from his saddle. . . . Our horses were on the dead run with, in many instances, two or three men on one animal. . . ."

The surviving cavalrymen formed a ragged circle around a trough or crease in the hilltop and threw up barriers of pack saddles, blankets, breadboxes, sacks of bacon, oats, hay—whatever might deflect an arrow or a bullet. They scrabbled at the hard ground with forks, jackknives, spoons, coffee cups, mess kits and sticks, meanwhile wondering and asking aloud why Custer did not return. At the conclusion of the 1879 Chicago inquiry the Judge Advocate General stated in his report to Secretary of War George McCrary that the feeling among Reno's troops was of anger at General Custer for having placed them in such a position.

The excitement, danger, and strangeness of the situation twisted their responses. When the first breadbox was dumped on the line one of Benteen's troops immediately flung himself down behind it, but no sooner was he neatly hidden than a bullet ripped through the box and killed him. Quite a few troopers laughed. Lt. Godfrey wrapped himself in bedding, although he knew this was useless, and found himself wondering if sagebrush would stop bullets. A trooper of M Company, after narrowly missing death when a bullet smashed the stock of his carbine, glared at the Indians and shouted, "Damn you! You'll have to shoot better than that. . . ."

Many of these enlisted men did not know how to use their weapons. Some had not once fired a carbine. Now—trapped, isolated, terrified, bewildered—they riddled the earth and the sky. Godfrey watched one recruit take aim and squeeze the trigger like a veteran. The muzzle of the gun dipped and the recruit flinched, obviously expecting a loud report, but nothing happened because he had forgotten to cock it.

Late that afternoon they began to hear an unfamiliar noise: *Zing*! instead of *Zip*!

"When a zing-g-g sound came," Lt. Varnum wrote to Graham, "that made you take notice." What this meant was that Custer's battalion had been destroyed and the Indians now were using 7th Cavalry carbines. Thousands of arrows struck Custer's troops, yet nobody on Reno Hill mentioned arrows. Evidently the Indians used bows and arrows against Custer because they did not have much else; later, equipped with modern U.S. guns, very few resorted to arrows.

Godfrey said the ping-ping overhead was more frightening than the swish-thud of bullets burrowing into the ground; and although it was foolish to duck, they could not prevent their bodies from twitching. Varnum remarked that Benteen was the only man he ever saw who did not try to dodge bullets. Benteen seemed oblivious to danger; he walked around checking on his troops, deliberately inviting fire, but was hurt just once when a bullet nicked his thumb.

Years later Benteen described the siege: "I state but the facts when I say that we had a fairly warm time with those red men. . . ."

The day was cloudy, Lt. Wallace remembered: "The sun went down as a red ball. . . ."

That night the valley was scored by intermittent flashes of heat lightning which illuminated the hostile encampment, yet even in darkness the pattern of the great village could be distinguished by the light of thousands of camp-fires. Some of Reno's men slept, others must have spent the night awake, horrified and fascinated, as they listened to the barking dogs and the howls of dancing savages.

The troops on the hilltop assumed these Indians were celebrating, but much of the noise was a lament for their dead. Howls of joy did mingle with the dolorous concert and jubilant dances erupted as warriors visited one demonstration after another, reciting their exploits and being hailed accordingly; but the mourning period among these tribes was four days and there could be no formal celebration until the stricken relatives consented. Sioux fighting men cropped their hair as a sign of grief. Cheyennes untied their long braids. Women of both tribes gashed themselves with shards of flint and many of them amputated part of a finger.

Custer was appalled by this practice of self-mortification. The amputation of fingers especially disgusted him. In his autobiography, *My Life on the Plains*, he wrote that they would chop off the first joint without regard for the principles of surgery, often using a dull knife. As a result, when the flesh healed it withdrew and left almost an inch of bone exposed, a condition he found "most revolting."

Large fires visible from the hilltop were not victory bonfires as the soldiers thought. The Sioux—although not the Cheyennes—cremated some of their dead and these towers of flame were burial lodges; and what the soldiers heard very often was a dirge, accompanied by improvised kill-songs. At that time the Indians did not realize they had fought Custer. They had defeated a blue-coat army, that was all they knew. Later, when they found out, they sang about him.

David Humpreys Miller transcribed one such kill-song:

Long Hair has never returned,
So his woman is crying, crying,
Looking over this way, she cries.

Long Hair, horses I had none.
You brought me many and I thank you.
You make me laugh!

Long Hair, guns I had none.
You brought me many . . .

The shrieks and wails—whether of elation or sorrow—were easily heard on the heights across the river, and shadows capering like demons around innumerable fires lured imaginative soldiers to the edge of madness. Pvt. James Pym believed he saw renegade whites circling the rifle pits and shouting insults, challenging the troopers to come out. He thought these renegades carried the little swallowtail company flags called guidons, and when Reno's bugler blew calls they would be exactly repeated—meaning there must be a white bugler with the Indians. Other men saw columns of soldiers approaching and distinctly heard the commands of officers. Guns were fired to guide these rescuers and a trumpeter blew "Stable" call. They wondered aloud about the identity of these troops. Godfrey said every opinion was ratified with a cheer. Somebody thought it must be Crook's army so one of the packers jumped on a horse and galloped around the hill shouting: "Don't be discouraged, boys! Crook is coming!"

Two surgeons, James DeWolf and Henry Porter, had accompanied Reno's battalion into the valley. DeWolf was killed while scrambling up the bluff. Followed by his orderly, Pvt. Elihu Clear, he thought he could make better time by following a ravine two or three hundred yards north of the one used by most of the men during the retreat. Today, looking down this brush-choked ravine from the top of Reno Hill, it is difficult to imagine why DeWolf chose it; but he did, and there they caught him. Nearby troopers saw an Indian take his scalp.

He seems to have been congenitally unfortunate, rather like Major Reno. During the Civil War he volunteered for the Union army and by the age of seventeen he had been shot, discharged, and pensioned. In 1865 he somehow managed to enlist as a regular and became a hospital steward, meanwhile attending Harvard medical school. Although he obtained an M.D. from Harvard he could not pass the Army Medical Board examination and was discharged for the second time in 1875. He then contracted to serve the Army as a private physician in the Department of Dakota.

He wrote constantly to his wife after leaving Fort Lincoln. He enjoyed the march and was anticipating a pleasant time in the field. He had brought along rubber leggings and a coat in the event of rain, and in his valise was a quart of whisky. An enlisted man had been assigned to set up his tent, make his bed, saddle his horse, and otherwise relieve him of diurnal chores. "Reno who commands my wing I cannot like but suppose acquaintance will improve perhaps when we understand each other," he wrote, adding that he did like the adjutant, Benny Hodgson. "Well darling," he concludes, "my letters may be far between after this but I shall write every opportunity and will try & keep a memoranda of the incidents."

Three days out he admonishes her not to worry because he is perfectly safe. He doubts they will see an Indian all summer, but he carries a revolver and a carbine, just in case. The regiment had an easy march that day and he thinks he will like General Custer who appears "very Fashionable and Nobby" in a buckskin suit.

On May 22 he reports that he sees quite a lot of Reno, who is often left in command because Terry and Custer like to ride a mile or so ahead. Only a few troopers have fallen sick, though it is wet and dreary. "I had a nice sponge bath tonight and changed all my clothes & feel nice & took a nasty pill. well darling as I have to get up at 2½ or 3 AM tomorrow I must retire & it is getting chilly as I have taken off my flannel. . . ."

Next day they marched only eight miles. For dinner there was soup and roasted antelope rib. "The band has just struck up dont you wish you was along it is nice when the weather is fair and the marches short but my nose and ears are nearly burned off I am trying Glycerine & alum. . . . no Indians yet or signs. . . ."

A note dated the twenty-seventh mentions that they have reached the badlands: "The days are getting pretty hot & the horses get stuck up with wild cactus & then dont they bound. . . ."

June 1. When he awoke at 3 A.M. the ground was white. All day it snowed. He found a stretcher to use as a bedstead, built a fire at the entrance to his tent, and felt cozy except for ashes and smoke blowing in.

June 2. Still bivouacked, unable to move because of snow squalls: "I suppose when you get this we will be near ready to turn back hoping so darling I expect we shall be in by Aug 15 or 20 night darling from your loving husband."

June 8. Camped beside the Powder, he writes again that his nose and ears are about to fall off and laughing is impossible, but he feels fine. The troops are enjoying venison steak, beans, bacon, biscuits with butter, apple pudding, and coffee. He expects to get home soon.

June 21. At the mouth of Rosebud Creek: "I think it is very clear that we shall not see an Indian this summer the Post Trader or John Smith has opened his whisky &c & of course you all know what will follow. . . . it is believed that the Indians have scattered & gone back to their Reservations. Yesterday I went out with Dr. Porter Lt Harrington & Hodgson pistol shooting and came out second best Porter was best so you see some of the cavalry cannot shoot very well. . . . Rosebud Creek takes its name by being profusely bordered by the wild Roses like those of Warner. I send you one in this letter. . . . well darling I must close this as the Boat moves down the River some little distance & the mail closes tonight . . . your loving Hub   J M DeWolf."

There seems to be only one photograph of him: a bald young man with dark, patient eyes and a drooping mustache. He looks as though he has just received bad news.

His body was not mutilated, probably because he lay close to the Reno line of defense. His diary, which was picked up by Dr. Porter, contains one entry of unusual significance. Some days earlier, before the Sioux had been located, General Terry dispatched Reno on a scouting sortie with a horse-drawn Gatling gun for protection. Dr. DeWolf accompanied Reno and, as usual, kept a record of events. He notes that at one point the Gatling overturned, injuring three men. Later, just before the Seventh rode away from Terry's command for the last time, Custer was offered the use of several Gatlings but rejected them. Just why he declined this clumsy, frightening artillery will never be known. He said the guns would impede his march, which was true; but DeWolf's diary reveals that not only were they awkward, they were dangerous.

As for the other surgeon, Dr. Porter, he managed to scramble out of the valley, and the first thing he said to Reno on the hilltop was: "Major, the men were pretty well demoralized, weren't they?"

"No," Reno answered, "that was a charge, Sir."

Not only did Dr. Porter survive this uncommon charge, he survived two days on the hilltop, and he lived a long time after. He spent his last years traveling about the world in a gentlemanly manner and he died at the Hotel Metropole in Agra, India, where he had gone to view the Taj.

On a bluff overlooking the Little Bighorn, clad in a white linen duster, he worked heroically throughout the night, operating by touch because the light of a candle or even the quick flare of a match invited a murderous shower. Despite what he was doing, aware that nobody else could do it, Dr. Porter grew discontented with his role. He felt that he should contribute more to the defense. Several times he snatched up a rifle and started for the firing line, turning back only because his patients loudly objected.

That anybody could work under these conditions sounds preposterous, but frontier surgeons acquired skills not taught in medical school. They learned, for instance, to distinguish the arrows of each tribe by their structural characteristics and dimensions. This knowledge might be enough to save a man's life. By measuring how much of the shaft was exposed a surgeon could tell how deeply the head was buried, and by feeling the bowstring notch he could determine the angle of the blade. Thus, even in darkness, he knew what to expect.

The most difficult wounds to treat were caused not by bullets or flint arrowheads but arrowheads cut from the white man's sheet iron. These iron triangles very often bent or "clinched" when they struck bone, making extraction brutally painful. Surgeons of that era used a technique devised by Dr. J. H. Bill which consisted of inserting a looped wire and manipulating it until the loop engaged the arrowhead, whereupon the shaft and the head together could—with luck—be pulled out. This seldom happened unless the victim was treated promptly because the animal tendons that bound the head to the shaft would soften and loosen. Besides, many Indians deliberately weakened the binding so that even if a soldier or homesteader managed to withdraw the shaft the blade would remain inside.

Either way, lucky or not, in a field hospital with no chloroform the removal of an arrow must have been excruciating.

Abdominal wounds usually were fatal, whether or not the blade could be withdrawn. This fact being known to Indians, they frequently aimed at a soldier's bellybutton, and it is said that experienced frontiersmen sometimes would wrap a blanket around their middle in hopes of stopping the point or at least diminishing the impact. Dr. Bill went so far as to recommend that soldiers be equipped with an abdominal cuirass. These wounds were deadly because of peritonitis. Still, it might not have been a bad way to go. An 1885 publication from the U.S. Government Printing Office entitled *The Soldier's Handbook*, authored by a loyal bureaucrat, Mr. N. Hershler, who sounds like the natural ancestor of today's Foggy Bottom flacks, contrives to make peritonitis sound almost pleasant, no worse than radiation sickness: ". . . the person lives a day or two, with perfect clearness of intellect, and often not suffering greatly."

June 26, their second day in purgatory, broke cloudy with a few spatters of rain. Troopers scurried around setting up kettles, buckets, stretching lengths of canvas, holding out tin cups—anything to catch water. But the clouds evaporated, the sun blazed on the hilltop, and Indians down below were setting grass fires either to conceal their movements or to prevent soldiers from approaching the river.

Some of Reno's men were willing to face whatever must be faced; others began to wilt. One man who disintegrated had to be tied up like a hog.

Some got so thirsty that they punched holes in tins of fruit and sucked the juice—a forbidden practice because nobody knew how long the siege might last and everything must be conserved. Pvt. Peter Thompson said the offers by wounded men were pitiful. Ten dollars for one drink of water. Fifteen dollars for a canteen, twenty for a canteen—as though it was an auction. "A man by the name of McVey, to whom I handed the canteen that he might drink seemed determined to keep it in his possession. I jerked it from his grasp and passed it on to the next. With a cry of rage he drew his revolver from beneath his overcoat and taking aim at me he told me to skip. . . ."

McVey later was shot in the stomach. He begged continuously for water, offering seventy-five dollars for a drink, and finally got it. The water trickled through the hole in his stomach, said Pvt. Daniel Newell, "but he laid back and died in peace."

Pvts. James Tanner and Henry Voight were buried that morning. Tanner had been hit outside the line. Four men dashed out, rolled him in a blanket, and brought him back, but he soon died. Voight was trying to lead a horse that had been shot in the head when his own brains were scattered. These two privates were laid in one grave and covered with dirt, their names penciled on a board pried from a breadbox.

F. C. Mann, a mule packer, was seen aiming his carbine. He held the position steadily, as a good marksman does, but he neglected to pull the trigger. At last somebody went to investigate and found a hole in his temple.

Chief mule packer J. C. Wagoner also got a bullet in the skull. He kicked and flopped around, evidently done for; but it had been a long-distance shot, the bullet was nearly spent, and he surprised everybody by sitting up.

Sgt. Charles White had brought a glass of jelly in one of his saddlebags and he walked around giving each wounded soldier a taste of jelly, though he himself was shot in the elbow.

An esthetic problem developed. Dead horses were beginning to stink and whenever a bullet punctured a bloated carcass everybody close by would be splashed with putrefying flesh. Glistening carrion beetles arrived to sample this prodigious feast. Tiny white maggots squirmed blindly in the corruption. Vultures hung lazily overhead. But worst of all was the dehydration. Scout George Herendeen told of men with swollen tongues, of some who could hardly talk. They would try to eat crackers or hardtack but could not raise enough saliva. "Several tried grass, but it stuck to their lips, and no one could spit or speak plainly. The wounded were reported dying from want of water. . . ."

Now and then a black feathered head rising cautiously above a bush would be blown apart by a fusillade—although usually it was a feathered coup stick or a mat of buffalo hair draped on a gun barrel. Reno's inexperienced men also wasted ammunition trying to kill a buckskin suit stuffed with grass which the Indians tied to a pony.

Pvt. Coleman occasionally got the dates mixed in his marvelous journal, but that should be overlooked in such a dramatic story:

> . . . the indians oapened a Murderous fire on us with their long range Winchester Rife and one of our men got Killed and two baddley wounded we had now been 22 hours without water and we were Suffering verry Much for the want of it espessially the wounded it was almost impossible for a Man to goe to the River without getting Killed. . . .

In 1877 a number of forked sticks were found on distant slopes and it is believed these sticks were used by Indian sharpshooters to cradle their guns, a trick they learned from watching professional buffalo hunters.

Several ambitious braves wriggled to within a few yards of the line. How anybody, even a skillfully camouflaged Indian, could have crept almost to the skirmish line without being detected is hard to imagine because there is not much ground cover on Reno Hill, not near the top. A century ago the brush might have grown higher and thicker; still it is surprising. Some Indians got close enough to throw clods of dirt at the soldiers and a Sans Arc named Long Robe counted coup on a man he killed—an act of bravado which cost his own life. Reno mentions it in an official report: "When I say the stick was only ten or twelve feet long, some idea of the desperate and reckless fighting of these people may be understood."

Long Robe and an Unkpapa named Hawk Man may have been the only Indians killed during this two-day siege, although in 1923 ex-Private Edwin Pickard told a journalist that he had watched a hand-to-hand struggle between an unidentified sergeant and a big Sioux. The sergeant grabbed the Indian's scalplock, forced his head back and sank his teeth into the warrior's throat. They rolled around and around, the sergeant chewing away like a bulldog until he managed to chew open an artery. Then he broke the Indian's neck.

There is no corroborative evidence of hand-to-hand fighting on the hilltop and very few historians think much of Pickard's story. Whether or not it happens to be true, there is no doubt that the proximity of the Indians was alarming. They got so close that Benteen was afraid a sudden rush might breach the defense. He therefore told Reno that a squad must be assembled to charge the nearest hostiles and drive them back. Reno hesitated.

Reno's uncertainty or timidity seems beyond dispute. Lt. Godfrey, having discussed this critical situation with Captain Weir, noted in his diary: "We both thought that to Col. Benteen we must look for the wisdom to deliver us . . . as it was evident that Col. Reno carried no vigor or decision, and his personal behavior gave no confidence in him."

Godfrey was present when Benteen recommended the charge. He heard Benteen say with obvious annoyance: "You've got to do something here pretty quick; this won't do, you must drive them back."

Reno at last consented.

Benteen collected a few volunteers, planted himself in front and braced them with a speech that might have sounded natural in 1876 but today sounds ludicrous: "All ready now, men. Now's your time. Give them hell. Hip, hip, here we go!"

Off they went with a loud hurrah, "every man, but one who lay in his pit crying like a child."

Hip, hip, hurrah! Every man Jack—except that coward. It is straight from the pages of a Victorian adventure book.

This weeping trooper was not alone. Others behaved badly. Some acquired nicknames they would never lose. "Crackerbox Dan" spent two days behind a crackerbox. "Aparejo Mickie"—possibly a reference to Capt. Myles Moylan—hid behind a pack saddle. And according to John Burkman, young Billy Blake pretended to be hurt so he would not have to fight. They were good soldiers, Burkman adds, but the panic in the valley had emptied their heads.

Pvt. Peter Thompson saw a man from A Company lying motionless, face down, apparently dead. Two soldiers dragging a piece of canvas with which they meant to build a shelter for the wounded told him to get out of the way. He did not move. One of them kicked him and he struggled to his feet insisting that he was sick. "A more miserable looking wretch it would be difficult to find," says Thompson. "The man was almost frightened to death. He walked a few steps and fell to the ground heedless to the heat of the sun or anything else going on around him."

Lt. Edgerly wrote to his wife that a D Company trooper, Pvt. Patrick Golden, did everything he was supposed to on the first day, but that night after the firing stopped he asked a sergeant if the Indians would return. The sergeant guessed they would return in the morning. Golden then began to cry, and he said, "Tom, if they come back they will kill me."

There are two other accounts of Golden's behavior, very different, but Edgerly's is considered the most reliable. Next morning, he said, when he and Pvt. Steins came to a large rifle pit, with Golden alone in the middle of it, Steins asked: "Paddy, whose hole is this?" Golden didn't know, and because everybody else was hiding in a pit Edgerly and Steins threw themselves down next to him, one on either side. Moments later a bullet streaked through the crest of the pit, showering them with dirt, and struck Golden. He groaned once, Edgerly wrote, "pushed with his right foot, and was dead."

Other men fought bravely at first, like Golden, but after a while grew timid. Others, for reasons known only to themselves, behaved just the opposite.

Benteen's berserk charge turned out to be a spectacular success. The closest warriors fled from these savage bluecoats, not one of whom was injured. But then, just as they got back to the pits, a bullet hit the weeping coward between the eyes. Presumably he was hit by an Indian bullet, although some enraged member of Benteen's squad may have murdered him.

The captain's view of this absurd charge—which he called "the Chinese act"—is neither idealistic nor heroic. He was a pragmatic man. He understood the psychological effect of noise so he instructed his volunteers to shout. And the astonished warriors fell head over heels in their efforts to escape.

Not long afterward Benteen was inspecting the line when a sergeant raised his head and a bullet knocked off his hat.

"Damn you," Benteen said, "I told you to keep down."

The sergeant grinned and said, "Why don't you keep down, Captain?"

Benteen, who referred to his wife as "Mother," said: "Oh, I'm all right. Mother sewed some good medicine in my blouse before I left home, so they won't get me."

Enlisted men usually become exasperated when an officer exposes himself to the enemy because it draws fire, but again and again we are told by troopers who served with Benteen on the hill that his conviction of immortality reassured them. Although the day was hot he never rested. Back and forth he went giving advice, examining bulwarks, encouraging the troops. His shirt tail had worked out of his pants and hung over his rump like a flag while he tramped around saying, "This is a groundhog case, men. It is live or die. We must fight it out."

On the afternoon of the twenty-sixth quite a few Indians dressed up in Seventh Cavalry coats taken from Custer's dead, some wore military hats, and at least one carried a guidon, so the renegade whites seen by Pvt. Pym were not altogether imaginary. In spite of such macabre evidence before their eyes the trapped men did not suspect what had happened. From the rifle pits they gazed at Sioux warriors wearing blue uniforms with yellow cavalry piping, they looked at the flag, and they asked each other why Custer had abandoned them.

During this afternoon a file of mounted Indians paused in the valley to contemplate the men on Reno Hill, and among their horses was a golden buckskin with distinctive white patches. The identity of these Indians has not been learned but several troopers who had been with the Seventh for a long time said this buckskin pony belonged to the Oglala war chief Crazy Horse, whose presence suggested that a final assault was near. Whoever they were, they dismounted and settled themselves in a circle for a smoke. It is said that they flashed signals with mirrors and gestured with feathered lances.

Lances would indicate Cheyennes rather than Sioux, nevertheless it is conceivable that the man on the golden buckskin was Crazy Horse.

Many Indians eventually came to regard this Oglala as their greatest chief, more important than Red Cloud or Sitting Bull. He was known as a man who walked through the village without speaking or noticing anybody. Sioux loved to dance and sing but he never joined a dance, not even the Sun Dance, and nobody ever heard him sing. He was small, with a narrow face, and his eyes looked beyond things.

Journalists liked to portray him as being utterly reckless in battle, but an Oglala who rode with him said this was not true. At critical moments Crazy Horse would dismount before shooting: "He is the only Indian I ever knew who did that often. He wanted to be sure that he hit what he aimed at. . . . He didn't like to start a battle unless he had it all planned out in his head and knew he was going to win." This is what distinguished him from his younger brother, Little Hawk. Old men of the tribe thought Little Hawk would become greater than Crazy Horse, but Little Hawk was impetuous. He crossed the Platte on a raiding expedition and never came back. Some time later Crazy Horse went looking for his brother's body, which he found and buried.

He never boasted about what he did, nor would he take part in the lamentation that traditionally followed the death of a friend or relative. When he was a boy the adults often discovered him standing in the shadows listening to their conversation, and when he grew up he continued to listen. He attended very few councils. Even then he would not speak. He always listened.

His father was an Oglala holy man. His mother came from a different tribe. Most scholars think she was a Brulé, a sister of Chief Spotted Tail, although Dr. V. T. McGillycuddy said she was a Miniconjou of the Cheyenne River Sioux whose chief was Touch the Clouds. In either case, emigrants on the Oregon Trail frequently noticed a fair-skinned boy among the Sioux near Fort Laramie and thought he must be a captive white child.

At this time nearly all of the plains Indians were restless. One ugly experience with whites created the next. Some of the Blackfoot had been stealing various items from Fort McKenzie—and may also have stolen horses—so the manager, Francis Chardon, resolved to punish them. He greeted one party with a cannon blast. It has been alleged that Chardon's welcome killed about thirty Blackfoot, which probably is an exaggeration. The most detailed and reliable account seems to be that of a trader, Charles Larpenteur, known as Lumpy Neck because of a goiter. He was not present, but he talked to a Fort McKenzie clerk and was informed that these Indians had murdered an employee—"a negro by the name of Reese." This murder, not petty theft, caused Chardon to concoct his disastrous plan.

Whatever the motive, Chardon enlisted one Alexander Harvey "who, wishing no better fun, agreed to take an important part." Harvey carried a bowie knife or dirk, the French word for which is *dague*. An old man named Berger also was enlisted, evidently because Chardon decided to let three Blackfoot chiefs into the stockade where they would be assassinated, after which the gates would swing open and the cannon would blast the crowd outside. Any survivors would of course run away, leaving the ground covered with buffalo robes, jewelry, beaded moccasins—everything they had brought to trade. Chardon's plan did not work because the Blackfoot leaders inside the stockade suspected treachery. Two of them escaped, the other went down with a bullet in one leg. The cannon was quickly fired, killing three, not thirty, but wounding two others. Harvey rushed out of the fort and stabbed these wounded Indians. "I was told he then licked the blood off the dagy and afterward made the squaws of the fort dance the scalp dance around the scalps. . . ."

The Blackfoot stopped trading at McKenzie and moved across the boundary into Canada, but they returned to attack the fort. They may have burned it. After so much time the reports are contradictory. One way or another, what had been a mutually profitable and agreeable relationship was destroyed.

In Canada things were different. The Hudson's Bay Company, part of a smoothly functioning empire, understood how to live with Indians whereas the newly arrived, impatient, disorganized, aggressive Americans did not. They streamed westward, lacerating the earth. George Bent, a half-breed son of trader William Bent, mentions emigrant trains several miles long, the huge freight wagons with white canvas tops resembling ships at sea. Indians who watched these creaking trains approach every season—growing longer and longer—could foresee the result. Cottonwood groves where they had camped for generations began to diminish. Grass in the valleys was eaten down to the ground.

With the 1849 gold rush came cholera. The Sioux and Cheyennes, closest to the emigrant road, suffered most, but the epidemic spread northward to the Blackfeet, southward into Kiowa and Comanche territory. Bent visited empty villages where he saw teepees full of bodies.

In the summer of 1853 a longtime trader and recently appointed Indian agent, Thomas "Broken Hand" Fitzpatrick, traveled among the Cheyennes, Arapahoes, and Sioux: "They are in abject want of food half the year, and their reliance for that scanty supply, in the rapid decrease of the buffalo, is fast disappearing. . . . Their women are pinched with want and their children constantly crying out with hunger. . . ."

One year after that, when the boy who would become Crazy Horse was twelve or thirteen years old, a Mormon's cow wandered close to a Sioux camp just east of Fort Laramie and a Miniconjou named High Forehead could not resist temptation. Whether he wanted the hide or hungered for a steak is the subject of learned disagreement, and Bent describes the animal as a lame ox straying near the road. George Hyde, a cautious scholar, says a Mormon was "leading a lame or worn-out ox" when it was shot, and he considers the Indian's behavior "purely provocative." William Bordeaux, whose grandfather owned a nearby trading post, and who got the story of this incident from a great-aunt named Tripe, says that an emigrant party "left a crippled ox by the wayside." Historian Donald J. Berthrong thinks High Forehead meant to kill the Mormon but hit the beast instead.

In any case, Sioux tribal elders offered to pay reasonable damages—say ten dollars or a cow, maybe two cows. The facts are lost in a spiral of dust. What does seem clear is that a belligerent Irish lieutenant fresh from West Point, John Grattan, set out to arrest High Forehead. This was both illegal and stupid. It violated a provision of the 1851 Laramie treaty which stipulated that reds and whites should punish their own malefactors, and it was stupid to send Grattan because the Sioux detested him. He was a familiar type: the apple-green egoist. On various occasions he had strutted around the post thrusting a fist at Indians, calling them cowards, warning them to look out.

Beyond doubt Grattan wanted and expected trouble when he left the fort to go after High Forehead. "When I give the order," he told his men, "you may fire as you damned please."

His posse included a sergeant, a corporal, twenty-seven luckless troopers, and a frightened interpreter named Auguste Lucien who was at least half drunk and who rode around shouting that all the Sioux were going to be killed and he, Auguste—pronounced Wa-Use by the Indians—he himself, Auguste, was going to eat their hearts.

J. P. Dunn in *Massacres of the Mountains* says this wild bunch consisted of just nineteen men. No matter. The crucial element was Grattan's artillery: a twelve-pound fieldpiece and a mountain howitzer.

Precisely what happened will never be learned. There seems to have been a conference during which Wa-Use shouted additional insults, the soldiers leveled their guns, the Indians thought they were about to fire, a shot was heard by men watching from the flat roof of Bordeaux's trading post, more shots, Grattan let fly with the heavy stuff. William Bordeaux was told by great-aunt Tripe that the hired man, Dominic Bray, rode up a nearby knoll after the first shots were heard. Bray returned "at great speed" to report that the Sioux encampment was boiling. The trader himself and several other men, some of whom were married to squaws, hurried to the camp but arrived too late.

Grattan's conference with the Sioux may have fallen apart because of an outrageous misunderstanding. He may have responded to some remark as an Indian would by exclaiming "Hownh! Hownh!"—meaning yes, all right, I agree—but the troopers thought he cried "Now! Now!" and promptly opened fire. It sounds like a vaudeville skit. It sounds implausible, yet this is why there was no J Company in Custer's regiment. J, when spoken, may be misunderstood as A, and if clumsily written it looks like I.

Well, when things quieted down the drunk interpreter and every whiteskin except one lay dead. Pvt. John Cuddy either escaped and managed to hide among some wild rose bushes or he was protected by Indians who had wisely avoided the confrontation. William Bordeaux said his great-uncle, Swift Bear, found Cuddy in the bushes—bleeding so much that he had tried to plug the wounds with sagebrush. Swift Bear carried him to the trading post. Later he was carried to Fort Laramie where he died. As for Grattan, the Sioux terminated his visit with extreme prejudice in the form of twenty-four arrows, one arrow passing completely through his skull. His face must have been pounded to mush with rocks or clubs because he could be identified only by his pocket watch.

The single Indian casualty was a Brulé chief named Whirling Bear—Brave Bear, Conquering Bear, Bear That Scatters Enemies. He was shot in the back, presumably by Grattan or the drunk interpreter.

As a result of all this the Sioux came near slaughtering everybody at Bordeaux's trading post, but finally were bought off. Still enraged, they plundered an American Fur Company depot. Then, having had some experience with whites, they loaded their mortally wounded chief on a travois and fled north. Whirling Bear soon died. His ceremonially wrapped body was placed on a scaffold beside the Niobara River close to the mouth of the Snake.

Grattan's soldiers were buried on a plateau in extremely shallow graves, so shallow that a caravan of Mormons en route to the promised land about a month later observed cadaverous heads peeping through the sod.

Eastern newspapers reported the treacherous massacre of a gallant young West Point lieutenant with all his men and the public responded, as always, by clamoring for revenge. Nor did it take long for the bad judgment of Grattan and that of his superior who had authorized the arrest of High Forehead to be magically transformed. Their foolishness became a cunning redskin plot. The lame ox had been shot neither for its hide nor its succulent ribs but in order to lure these brave soldiers out of the fort.

An Army inspector arrived. He recorded the testimony of witnesses, which testimony was forwarded, along with the inspector's conclusion: "The time has now fully arrived for teaching these barbarians . . . how to appreciate and respect the power, the justice, the generosity, and magnanimity of the United States."

What this meant was that two generations of delicate but peaceful coexistence would be replaced by a generation of savagery.

Arapahoes and Cheyennes who had nothing to do with Grattan's folly remained where they were, encamped near Fort Laramie. Although they had not participated, they were affected. The Cheyenne agent reported that on his next visit they behaved with great insolence—"the sauciest Indians I have ever seen." They galloped around the corral, they fired shots overhead, they demanded that no more emigrants travel the Platte road, they wanted $4,000 cash, they wanted the rest of their government annuity in guns and cartridges, "and one thousand white women for wives."

Well!

Crazy Horse—Curly as he was then known—had been so shocked by the explosive meeting at Fort Laramie that when his people fled north he left them somewhere along the way. He spent three days on a hilltop without food or sleep, hoping for supernatural guidance. He wedged pebbles between his toes and put rocks under his back so that he could stay awake while meditating upon this experience with whites. At last, weak and dizzy, he thought he saw his horse approach, carrying on its back a warrior who flourished no scalps, whose unbound hair hung below his waist and who wore a smooth brown pebble behind one ear. The warrior's body had been decorated with hail spots and a streak of lightning descended from his forehead to his chin. Bullets and arrows attacked him but fell away without touching him. A storm broke, yet he passed through unharmed. People clutched at him, trying to restrain him, but he rode through them with a red-backed hawk flying above his head.

Curly did not reveal this manifestation to anybody until he was sixteen and ready to become a warrior. From then on he painted white hail spots on his body and a red lightning bolt down one cheek before going into battle. He tied a brown pebble behind one ear, wore the red-backed hawk on his head, and threw a handful of dust—perhaps symbolic of the storm—across himself and his pony. Except for moccasins and breechcloth he rode naked.

When he was about eighteen he participated in a fight against some Arapahoes trapped on a rocky knoll. Several times he charged them. He killed two but unwisely scalped them, either forgetting or ignoring the fact that the warrior in his vision kept no scalps, and because in this respect he had violated the message of his presiding spirit an arrow struck him in the leg. His bravery against these Arapahoes was celebrated and in recognition of what he had done he received his father's name: Crazy Horse. His father, the Oglala holy man, thereafter called himself Worm.

So runs the most creditable account of how Crazy Horse acquired that name.

It has been said also that while taking a steam bath with his father and a war chief named Hump he grew dizzy and saw the apparition. When he told the older men about it they said he had seen a vision of himself.

Then there is a popular legend that during his birth a wild pony galloped by his mother's lodge.

If the first story is correct, as many historians believe, one might reasonably ask how his father got the name Crazy Horse. And once upon a time, no doubt, that question could have been answered.

A few years after the fight with Arapahoes a medicine man named Chips created a charm for the young warrior: a small white stone suspended from a thong. This thong probably was slung across one shoulder so that the magic stone nestled under his left arm. The charm was devised in 1862 or 1863 and after he began wearing it he was never again wounded, although a number of ponies were killed beneath him—strangely duplicating the luck of his blue-jacketed Doppelgänger, Custer.

About this time one of Red Cloud's nieces, Black Buffalo Woman, was married to a violent man whose name usually is translated No Water or No Face. He is said to have been a jealous husband; but young Crazy Horse, whose eyes looked beyond things, ignored such inconsequential matters.

Stories of his involvement with the wife of No Water/No Face have been told so many times that it becomes a palimpsest: erased, scraped, revised until the original truth cannot be perceived. William Bordeaux, whose information came from elderly relatives, said that Crazy Horse eloped with No Water's wife as a way of getting even for some intra-tribal dispute. The infuriated husband caught up with them and fired a shot which grazed the cheek of Crazy Horse. The two men began wrestling but were separated by the famous seven-foot warrior, Touch the Clouds. At last, to avoid further trouble, Crazy Horse relinquished his prize.

Or he might have fallen in love with her when she was single, because it is said that while he was on a raiding expedition in Crow territory she got married—perhaps at the urging of Red Cloud. When Crazy Horse returned and found out about this he went into his mother's lodge and did not emerge for several days. Then he visited Crow territory again, alone, and when he got back he flung two Crow scalps to the dogs.

He took no more scalps for the rest of his life. When he was a youth wild with excitement he scalped two Arapahoes, and two Crows for some reason that cannot logically be understood. This is the consensus of scholars. However, Captain John Bourke of Crook's Third Cavalry states that he himself owned a shirt trimmed with scalps which had been the property of Crazy Horse. How many trophies dangled from it, Bourke does not say. This shirt—presumably the same—used to be on exhibit at the Fort Robinson museum. Perhaps it did belong to the famous Oglala, although such vanity would not have been characteristic.

At any rate, he was unable to forget Black Buffalo Woman. Finally, when she had three children, he showed how much he cared for her by giving a feast, whereupon she deposited her children with relatives, told her husband good-bye, and moved in with Crazy Horse. This was permissible. A Sioux woman could change her mind about husbands, and just as in other societies the jilted husband was expected to behave decently. No Water did not. He entered the lodge of the newlyweds while they were eating and he shot his rival in the jaw. The bullet was meant to catch Crazy Horse between the eyes, and a second bullet might have followed except for the presence of Touch the Clouds.

No Water was rebuked for this assault because it was he, not Crazy Horse, who had violated Sioux tribal structure. He was therefore expected to apologize by offering a gift of ponies, which he did. His gift was accepted, so the feud should have ended. It did not. One day Crazy Horse attacked No Water. As a result, he himself was disgraced.

Some very old Oglalas who had known the chief were interviewed by Eleanor Hinman in 1930. The account given by He Dog of this fight in the lodge and of what followed is the most detailed that exists. He Dog, narrating the story through interpreter John Colhoff, said that Crazy Horse and Black Buffalo Woman were seated by the fire in a friend's lodge when No Water rushed in and cried: "I have come!" Crazy Horse jumped up, reaching for a knife. No Water shot him beneath the left nostril. The bullet broke his upper jaw and he collapsed into the fire. No Water then left the tent and told his companions that he had killed Crazy Horse.

No Water had been riding a fast mule when he came looking for revenge, but he did not ride away when he learned that his bullet had only wounded Crazy Horse. He disappeared. Friends of Crazy Horse tried to find him because they wanted to kill him. When they could not find him they killed his mule.

After things had calmed down No Water sent Crazy Horse two very good ponies: a roan and a bay.

They avoided each other until one day near the mouth of the Bighorn where both of them were hunting buffalo. No Water jumped on a buckskin belonging to somebody else and rode off as fast as he could. Crazy Horse chased him all the way to the Yellowstone. After such a narrow escape No Water went south to the Red Cloud agency and stayed there with the Indians who loafed around. That was where he stayed during the war with the soldiers.

Black Buffalo Woman had a fourth child, a light-haired girl, and He Dog said many people believed this child was the daughter of Crazy Horse, "but it was never known for certain."

So, one way or another, the fight between these two dangerous men concluded. Black Buffalo Woman may have gathered her children and returned to her husband; at least it is known she and Crazy Horse separated. As for Crazy Horse himself, the passion he felt may have given way to self-disgust. All in all it had been a messy business.

When he was about twenty-six he married Black Shawl or Black Robe, not with much enthusiasm. His parents might have arranged it. They lived together and had a daughter. Then Black Shawl developed tuberculosis, which was a common disease, and after that she stayed at her parents' lodge, gradually declining.

The baby died of cholera while Crazy Horse was once again harrassing the Crows. When he got back and learned about this he fell apart. The Oglala camp had moved during his absence and the infant's body had been left on a scaffold now seventy miles away. He rode off to find it. A frontier character named Frank Grouard who lived with the Oglalas for several years claimed to have accompanied Crazy Horse on this pilgrimage. Grouard is not dependable—at least his biography is not—so the account must be read with suspicion; but Grouard said that Crazy Horse mounted the scaffold, lay down beside his daughter's body, which was wrapped in a buffalo robe, and remained there for three days. It sounds like Juana la Loca, the mad queen of Spain, who opened her young husband's coffin and tore apart the shroud to kiss his feet.

After the death of this little girl he became indifferent to his own life, taking unreasonable chances, and frequently left the village without revealing what he meant to do. During this period quite a few solitary miners panning the Black Hills for gold were found dead but not scalped, each with an arrow driven into the ground beside the corpse. Any wandering Sioux might have killed these men and disdained their scalps, but the presence of that symbolic arrow implies an unusual mind.

He always was strange, Black Elk said, and he grew more strange. People would see him outside the village, alone and cold. "Once my father found him out alone like that, and he said to my father: 'Uncle, you have noticed me the way I act. But do not worry; there are caves and holes for me to live in, and out here the spirits may help me. I am making plans for the good of my people.' He was always a queer man. . . ."

Ten or twelve years after his marriage to Black Shawl he married a French-Cheyenne girl, Nellie Laravie. Except for No Water's wife he does not seem to have pursued women; instead, he seems merely to have accepted them, yielding to their presence.

His sister told about seeing a woman enter his lodge and speak to Black Shawl, who was sewing a robe. The side of the lodge had been rolled up because of the heat, which made it possible to listen and watch. Crazy Horse returned while they were talking. The unfamiliar woman met him at the entrance, saying: "I am Joe Laravie's daughter so I am part white. I have heard about your great deeds, for my father has told us about you and your victory over Long Hair. He says that you are worthy to be the mate of any woman and though I realize that you already have a wife I pick this day to offer myself to you for your second mate. I have taken the matter up with your wife and she has consented. . . ."

He replied that he thought she was sincere, "so bring your belongings and be one of my family."

As he grew older his odd ways became more apparent. He would not smoke a pipe unless each smoker tamped down the tobacco with a thumb—not with a finger, it had to be a thumb. Much of what he did, no matter how peculiar, can be explained. Some things cannot.

Captain Bourke, who was introduced to him by Frank Grouard in 1877, described him as 5'8" tall, lithe and sinewy, with a scar on his face—which must have resulted from No Water's bullet. Bourke judged him to be about thirty years old, though in fact he was close to forty. According to an Oglala calendar he was born the year Left Hand Big Nose was killed by Shoshones, which is to say, 1839. "He had made hundreds of friends by his charity towards the poor, as it was a point of honor with him never to keep anything for himself, excepting weapons of war. I never heard an Indian mention his name save in terms of respect."

Grouard states that he was light-complexioned, with sandy hair, and did not have the customary high cheekbones of an Indian.

Short Buffalo agreed with Grouard's description. The chief was neither tall nor short, not thin yet not broad. His hair and skin were light. He wore an Iroquois shell necklace, but Short Buffalo did not know or chose not to say where Crazy Horse got this distinctive ornament. He also liked to wear a scarlet blanket plucked from a wagon train in 1867. His features were unlike those of most Indians. His face was narrow with a high, sharp nose. "He had black eyes that hardly ever looked straight at a man. . . ."

General Miles called him the embodiment of ferocity, "a fierce restless warrior" who had become the recognized leader of the Oglalas by the time he was twenty-six.

There are no authenticated photographs of him. It was said that he did not want to lose himself inside the white man's box. Dr. Valentine McGillycuddy tried several times to get a picture, but Crazy Horse resisted. "My friend," he would answer, "why should you wish to shorten my life by taking from me my shadow?"

D. F. Barry was convinced that no photographer caught the elusive chief. He himself photographed Low Dog at Fort Buford in 1881, a picture sometimes misrepresented as being Crazy Horse; and he caught the chief's brother, Wild Horse, who resembled him, but Wild Horse seems to be as close as Barry got.

An 1874 photo credited to Major Wilhelm of the Eighth Infantry shows a dark-skinned man wearing a huge feather bonnet. From the statements of those who knew Crazy Horse, or at least had seen him, Wilhelm's chief must be somebody else—perhaps Flat Iron. An ostentatious bonnet, like the scalp-trimmed shirt, would not be characteristic. Besides, at the time Major Wilhelm supposedly took this picture his regiment was stationed in Arizona. Wilhelm did not reach Crazy Horse territory until 1890.

In the W. H. Over collection at the University of South Dakota there is a photograph of a remote, angular, light-skinned Sioux with an averted look of distant intensity. This was taken by S. J. Morrow in 1876 or 1877 and has been labeled Crazy Horse. Colonel Graham says Morrow himself labeled it and the photo may be authentic. Other scholars think this might be a portrait of Crazy in the Lodge.

John Selover took a picture labeled " 'Crazy Horse' and son" which is remarkably unconvincing for various reasons, such as the fact that Selover's chief must be ten or fifteen years older than Crazy Horse was at the time of his death.

Short Buffalo told Eleanor Hinman about two photographs of a man on horseback which he, Short Buffalo, considered authentic. And he said: "I have seen a third photograph that I am sure was he, because it showed him on the pinto horse he rode in the Custer fight. I could not possibly make a mistake about that horse, and nobody rode it but Crazy Horse. The man who owns these pictures got them from soldiers who used to be at Fort Robinson. He has quite a collection of pictures of chiefs. I think he lives out in California now, near the National Park there. I do not remember his name."

In August of 1876, two months after the Little Bighorn, when the Cheyennes and Sioux thought it was time to split up, Sitting Bull led many of his people to Canada where they would be safe from American vengeance, while others slipped away to agencies in order to obtain food from gullible wasichus; but the strange Oglala refused to leave the land that always had been his home, yet he would not register at an agency, and he spoke with contempt of Indians who negotiated the sale of the Black Hills, saying, "One does not sell the earth upon which the people walk."

Red Cloud near the end of his life would be accused of "obtuse and unsubduable Indianism." The same must be said of Crazy Horse.

Misinterpretation, deliberate or unintentional, brought about his death in 1877. Frank Grouard told General Crook that Crazy Horse would ride north *against the whites* during the Nez Perce campaign, although the message should have been that he would ride north to *assist the whites*. Col. Graham thinks this was an honest mistake, "a classic example of erroneous interpretation." However, Dr. McGillycuddy called it "a purposeful misinterpretation of his words by Frank Grouard, who had once been a friend of Crazy Horse but was now his enemy and feared him."

The trader Louis Bordeaux was present at an earlier conference when Crazy Horse and Lt. Philo Clark talked about the Nez Perces. On this occasion, too, Grouard interpreted. Clark asked if Crazy Horse would help fight the Nez Perces. Crazy Horse replied that under certain conditions, which were then enumerated, he and his Oglalas would fight until not one Nez Perce was left; but Grouard told Clark the Oglalas would fight until not a soldier was left. Clark then turned to Louis Bordeaux and asked if this was indeed what Crazy had said. Bordeaux said it was not, and gave his own translation, but was interrupted by Grouard, who called him a liar.

Whether the interpretation was malicious or accidental, Crook resolved to arrest Crazy Horse. He was escorted to Fort Robinson where he realized that the whites meant to imprison him. He pulled a knife. Little Big Man grabbed his arm. Moments later Private William Gentles speared him with a bayonet.

He may not have been surprised. Eleanor Hinman interviewed an Oglala woman named Carrie Slow Bear in 1930. Hinman asked this woman if she knew why Crazy Horse refused to visit Washington. Carrie Slow Bear replied that at first Crazy Horse had been willing to go, but then he thought something would be done to him because another Indian said the whites planned to kill him, either in Washington or at Fort Robinson. Hinman asked who had told him so. Carrie Slow Bear said: "Little Big Man told him that."

Major H. R. Lemly, then a Ninth Infantry lieutenant at Fort Robinson, claimed that Little Big Man was a paid spy employed by the whites—which, if true, makes him a double agent. But with which faction did Little Big Man truly feel allied? Or was he indifferent?

Regarding the death of Crazy Horse, Dr. McGillycuddy would not equivocate: "A combination of treachery, jealousy and unreliable reports simply resulted in a 'frame-up' and he was railroaded to his death." McGillycuddy went on to say that it was just as well, because he would have gone to the Dry Tortugas as a prisoner for life. McGillycuddy's opinion is substantiated by at least two other men who were present. Lemly wrote: "Already it had been planned to imprison the chief in Fort Marion, at St. Augustine, Florida. He was to have been taken in an ambulance at midnight, with a troop of cavalry for an escort, to Fort Laramie, thence by the Deadwood stagecoach to Cheyenne and by trains east and south." The Spotted Tail agent, Capt. Jesse Lee, said he was told by a Third Cavalry captain that his troop had been detailed to escort the chief from the guardhouse at midnight, "push on rapidly to the railroad, and from there he was to be sent a prisoner to the Dry Tortugas, Florida."

General James Allison, editor of the *Journal of the Military Service Institution*, studied this mysterious business at some length. He absolved Grouard of malice, accusing him only of incompetence, but denounced Washington officials: "There is little doubt that certain 'higher authorities' . . . found appetite keener and sleep sweeter through the knowledge that Crazy Horse had, through hook or crook, become a 'good Indian' and would give no further trouble. A simple, easy and reasonable solution was to state that he had been killed in an attempt to escape from the guardhouse, and let it go at that!"

Crazy Horse made a speech just before he died, a rather long speech. After being bayoneted he had been carried to the post adjutant's office. His blanket was spread on the floor and there for several hours he lay unconscious, bleeding internally. When he awoke he lifted himself on one elbow. According to interpreter Baptiste Pourière, the chief said he had not been hostile to whites. Buffalo supplied his people with food and clothing and they preferred to chase buffalo rather than live idly at the agencies, arguing with each other and sometimes starving. But the Gray Fox—Crook—came in midwinter and destroyed their village. Then came Long Hair in the same way. When the Indians first saw Long Hair they wanted to escape but could not, so they were obliged to fight. They fought because the government would not let them alone. Then, said Crazy Horse, he decided to live in peace on the Red Cloud agency. And at this point he interjected a seemingly irrelevant comment, saying he had taken a half-breed wife. Why did he make such a remark? Perhaps it related to his expressed desire to live amicably with whites—Nellie being half-white. All the same, it is a curious thing for a dying man to mention. He then reiterated that all he ever wanted was to be left alone, and had come to the agency to talk, but white men had tried to imprison him and a soldier had run a bayonet into him. This concluded the speech. Very weakly he began his death-song.

Indians outside the adjutant's office heard him singing and almost at once his parents begged to be admitted. Lemly refused, saying he had no authority to let them in, but after Crazy Horse was dead he permitted them to enter. He described them as a wrinkled little old couple. He said they bent over the body of their son, crooning to it, "and fondled it as if he had been a broken doll, and they strangely-withered pygmies or children."

Excerpts from the diary of agent Jesse Lee seem to indicate that he had no part in the plot to murder Crazy Horse, if there was a plot.

Thursday, Sept. 6, 1877.
No one can imagine my feelings this morning. I often ask myself, "Was it treachery or not?" To the Indian mind how will it appear? My part in this transaction is to me a source of torture. Started Touch-the-Clouds and Swift Bear to Spotted Tail agency in the ambulance . . . had a long talk with Gen. Bradley. He did most of the talking. I felt so miserable that I could scarcely say anything. . . .

Saturday, Sept. 8th, 1877.
Everything is quiet and I think will remain so. Crazy Horse's body was brought to this agency and put on a little platform, Indian fashion, on the hill overlooking the post, not half a mile away. Whenever I go out of my quarters I see the red blanket in which his body is wrapped, and thus is recalled to my mind and heart Crazy Horse's pathetic and tragic end.

Wednesday, Sept. 12, 1877.
I think it was yesterday that I received word from Crazy Horse's father and mother, who were mourning in Indian fashion beside the body of their son, from daylight to dark, that the cattle at night would not disturb his body. They asked me to have a skeleton fence put around his body. So Jack Atkinson and I loaded a spring wagon with a few posts and some rough planks and went up there, and in an hour made a fence. . . .

George Hyde, acerbic and patient biographer of the Teton Sioux, sounds baffled by the attention devoted to this renowned chief, whom he considered to be morose, sullen, and rather limited. Says Mr. Hyde, the Crazy Horse cult is amazing. "It was evidently started among the Oglalas at Pine Ridge . . . aided by some white admirers of the Oglala fighting chief. They depict Crazy Horse as the kind of being never seen on earth: a genius in war, yet a lover of peace; a statesman, who apparently never thought of the interests of any human being outside his own camp; a dreamer, a mystic, and a kind of Sioux Christ, who was betrayed in the end by his own disciples—Little Big Man, Touch-the-Clouds, Big Road, Jumping Shield, and the rest." And he continues rhetorically: "One is inclined to ask, what is it all about?" Whatever it was about, this quite possibly was the laconic individual, intimidating even to those who knew him all his life, who rode a golden buckskin and settled himself on the valley floor to smoke a pipe and contemplate the bluecoats trapped on the bluff.

From their viewpoint high above, Reno's beleaguered men presently observed something as providential as it was unexpected: The tribes dismantled their enormous village and began moving south. Terry and Gibbon were approaching—such is the usual explanation for the departure of these Indians. No doubt there would have been a second battle of the Little Bighorn if the hostiles had stayed where they were, yet they may have left for a different reason. Sitting Bull allegedly wished to spare the lives of Reno's men and an Oglala messenger named Knife Chief rode around the bluff notifying everybody.

If Sitting Bull did indeed call off the attack it was not because of any affection for whites, whom he hated with abiding and impenetrable rancor, but because he understood how vindictive they could be. If all the soldiers were slaughtered the whites would insist upon another battle, and another, and another, whereas they might quit molesting Indians if these soldiers were permitted to escape. The story may or may not be true, but what seems rather well documented is the fact that Reno's men would have been allowed to withdraw. If they had retreated in the direction from which they had come they would not have been pursued. According to David Humphreys Miller, all of the Indians he interviewed were convinced they had shown the soldiers how foolish it was to attack the village, "and most of them felt the survivors should be allowed to warn other troops out of the area."

Only one thing is certain. Later that afternoon the lodges were packed on travois and a brightly colored horde began to move.

Reno's officers studied this movement through field glasses. The entire camp—Unkpapa, Brulé, Miniconjou, Two Kettle, Santee, Oglala, Sans Arcs, Blackfeet, Cheyenne—all of the tribes were flowing southward "with savage dignity" toward the Bighorn Mountains. Thousands of ponies and travois poles lifted a vast cloud of dust. "The length of the column was fully equal to that of a large division of the Cavalry Corps of the Army of the Potomac," said Reno. Some troopers thought it was five miles long. Benteen estimated it at three miles long and half a mile wide: "They had an advance guard, and platoons formed, and were in as regular military order as a corps or division."

One member of H Company, Charles Windolph, recalled many years later: "The heavy smoke seemed to lift for a few moments, and there in the valley below we caught glimpses of thousands of Indians on foot and horseback, with their pony herds and travois, dogs and pack animals, and all the trappings of a great camp, slowly moving southward. It was like some Biblical exodus; the Israelites moving into Egypt; a mighty tribe on the march." Lt. Edgerly felt less poetic: "I thought before the ponies commenced to move that it was like a lot of brown underbrush; it was the largest number of quadrupeds I ever saw in my life. . . . It looked as though a heavy carpet was being moved over the ground."

Capt. Thomas French, who owned a .50 caliber Springfield, and Sgt. John Ryan, who had a fifteen-pound Sharp's equipped with a telescopic sight, spoke the last lines of the Little Bighorn drama. From the hilltop they took long-distance pot shots at the vanishing horde. They did not hit a thing, so far as anybody knows, but this defiant epilogue probably gave the exhausted troops some satisfaction.

Interpreter Fred Gerard, trapped in the valley, got a fearfully close look at the spectacle observed by Reno's men through field glasses; Gerard was close enough to see wounded braves on travois, dead men lashed to the backs of ponies, and he could hear the squaws wailing.

When this reddish-brown traveling carpet passed almost out of sight Reno's soldiers ventured down to the river where they drank and filled their canteens. Nobody felt like celebrating, and that night they stayed on the hilltop, moving only a little to get away from the stench. The departure of the Indians could be a massive feint to draw them out of position; or, they reasoned, the ponies might need more grass, which meant that after the village was relocated the warriors would come back.

Major Reno addressed a message to General Terry on the morning of June 27: "I have had a most terrific engagement with the hostile Indians. They left their camp last evening at sundown moving due south in the direction of the Big Horn Mountains. I am very much crippled and cannot possibly pursue. Lieutenants McIntosh and Hodgson and Dr. DeWolf are among the killed. I have many wounded and many horses and mules shot. I have lost both my own horses. I have not seen or heard from Custer. . . ."

That same morning—just about the time Gerard awoke from his long nap with a mouthful of unswallowed salt pork—Reno's troops saw another dust cloud far to the north. They studied it anxiously, wondering if more Indians had come to join the party, but at last decided the dust was raised by General Crook. This does not seem to make sense. They had been expecting Terry to arrive from that direction whereas Crook was thought to be somewhere to the south or southeast. But as they looked through field glasses at the approaching cavalry they did not see any gray horses. Lt. Algernon Smith's E Company, which rode with Custer, had been mounted entirely on gray horses. Therefore, if Smith's gray horse company was not part of this column it must not be Custer, and without doubt Custer would have met Terry somewhere down the valley. After all, that was the plan. So, if this could not be the re-united Terry-Custer army, it must be Crook.

Cheer after cheer went up for General Crook as Terry and Gibbon approached.

Lt. Godfrey remembered a scout arriving with a note dated June 26, addressed to Custer. This scout had been detached on his mission before Terry learned of the disaster and had spent all night trying to sneak around the village.

Next came Lt. Bradley.

Godfrey said to him: "Where is Custer?"

Bradley answered: "I don't know, but I suppose he was killed, as we counted 197 dead bodies. I don't suppose any escaped."

Benteen asked the same question of General Terry.

Terry replied: "To the best of my knowledge and belief he lies on this ridge about four miles below here with all of his command killed."

Benteen said: "I can hardly believe it. I think he is somewhere down the Bighorn grazing his horses. At the battle of the Washita he went off and left part of his command, and I think he would do it again."

Terry answered that he was mistaken. He told Benteen to go look.

Benteen returned from this trip very pale and disturbed. An officer who accompanied him reported that while they stood looking down at the general's naked body Benteen said, "There he is, God damn him, he will never fight anymore."

Nobody knew exactly where Custer went after he divided the regiment early Sunday afternoon, and in the years since then only a little more has been learned. For a while he paralleled Reno's course toward the Unkpapa village, then led his five companies into the hills east of the Little Bighorn. He planned to ride northward until he could sweep down on the far end of the encampment. This much has always been clear, but even today his precise route is not known. The usual assumption is that he kept his troops out of sight until they reached the point where they were discovered, surrounded, and butchered. But before reaching this point he may have tried to split the huge camp in half. At least there is evidence to suggest that he attacked the center, was repulsed, and only then continued northward to the fatal site.

The bearer of the last message, John Martin, told Walter Camp in 1910 that he was with Custer very close to the Little Bighorn and after being detached from the battalion he looked back: "and I saw him and his command right down on the flat within a few hundred yards of the river, retreating from it."

Three days later Reno's men found the prints of metal-shod horses in a gully close to the water. These prints could have been made after the battle when victorious warriors rode around on captured Seventh Cavalry horses. Yet the testimony of several Indian participants seems to corroborate the idea of an attempted crossing; and the Crow scout, White Man Runs Him, agreed. White Man said that after dividing the regiment Custer sent him up a knoll. "Go and look and see where I can make a success," Custer signaled. White Man did as he was told and suggested a place to cross the river. Custer's battalion followed him: "We went down to the Little Horn until we came to a little coulee, and were moving towards the enemy's camp. We wanted to cross the river at that place. The Sioux fired at us. We then went up the hill to the ridge. . . ."

One of Gibbon's scouts, Tom LeForge, was told by a Sioux that Custer's guide and interpreter—Minton or Michelet "Mitch" Bouyer—died at the edge of the river. The Sioux found him there after the battle, alive, his back broken. He asked them to kill him, which they did. A Sioux then took his vest before shoving his body into the stream. LeForge said this vest, "made of the skin of a spotted calf," was picked up near the water. He was a half-breed, his father being French, his mother a Santee Sioux, so the Indians knew him as Two Bodies and very often they had tried to kill him. Sitting Bull offered one hundred ponies for his head.

An Arapaho—one of six who had been camping with the Sioux and Cheyennes—said Mitch Bouyer and a man with a bugle crossed the Little Bighorn and hid in some underbrush on the west bank where they were caught and killed. The Arapaho, too, mentioned Bouyer's distinctive calfskin vest; but he said Custer already was trapped on the slope when these men tried to escape.

Bouyer may have gone down just as the Sioux and the Arapaho said, but Custer's whereabouts at the time is a different problem. Besides, they might have been wrong. Gibbon stated that Bouyer's corpse was found among the troops who died with Custer—several hundred yards from the Little Big- horn. "He was the protégé and pupil of the celebrated guide Jim Bridger. . . ."

Now the age of technology has produced, together with innumerable gad- gets of questionable merit, a handy instrument called the metal detector, and the metal detector has pointed out shells and other artifacts—binoculars, canteens, spurs, pocket knives, brass buttons, trumpets, horseshoes, buck- les, spoons, harmonicas—in quite a few places. Which is to say, the route of the doomed battalion can be approximately if not absolutely reconstructed. Of particular interest is the presence of a great many empty cartridges very close to the river in Medicine Tail coulee. Here, too, after the battle, some- body found an enlisted man's pants hanging on a tree stump. And about five years later Hairy Moccasin was told by a Sioux that one soldier rode into their village—undoubtedly because his horse bolted. The identity of this unfor- tunate cannot be established, but it may have been Sgt. James Bustard of I Company. Whoever he was, he did not emerge from the village.

Everything considered, there must have been a skirmish very near the water. Perhaps Custer ordered a full assault down Medicine Tail coulee but had to withdraw. Or possibly, as some tacticians believe, one company at the rear may have ventured down this ravine. Other students of the business think Custer divided his five companies—creating two battalions—and sent two companies down Medicine Tail while the other three continued along the ridge.

Lt. Godfrey in 1891 thought Custer never approached the Little Bighorn: "The numerous bodies found scattered between the river and the ridge were supposed to be the first victims of the fight. I am now satisfied that these were men who either survived those on the ridge or attempted to escape the mas- sacre."

By whatever path, he reached the head of this wandering village where he encountered a horde of Cheyennes. That he met them in this position was no accident. They were leading the other tribes, and for a reason which can be traced back fifty years.

Early in the nineteenth century under James Monroe an Indian program began to take shape. God alone could guess how many millions of square miles of useless land unrolled beyond the frontier, therefore boost all eastern redskins west. Let them join their wild western cousins, leaving the United States to civilized people. Such was the government philosophy. So, having "touched the pen" to make everything legal, thereby ceding property they never knew they owned, except that they had lived on it as long as anybody could remember, these aborigines were nudged westward.

But still, no matter what assurances they were given before touching the pen, the boundary of white civilization seeped toward them.

This program accelerated when Jackson got into the White House. He had fought Indians in Tennessee and he nourished few doubts. His attitude grew out of the frontier conviction that no redskin had any rights a white man was under moral or legal obligation to respect—an attitude which would prevail for at least a century. "I suggest the propriety of setting apart an ample district west of the Mississippi . . ." he wrote in his first address to Congress. There went the Cherokees, Choctaws, Chickasaws, and Creeks. Escorted to their new home by troops, several thousand died en route.

By the end of Jackson's reign at least ninety thousand had been resettled and it was assumed they would copy the life of Indians accustomed to the plains. There should be no shortage of buffalo, and the government would keep an eye on things through the Bureau of Indian Affairs.

The Seminoles, who were supposed to leave, backed into their Florida swamps and for six years confounded the majesty of the United States. Here and there a few would be captured by offering to discuss the situation under a white flag, at which time they could be overpowered and shipped west; nevertheless it proved to be an expensive, inconclusive and exasperating struggle which cost the lives of fifteen hundred soldiers and at last the Army gave up, having managed to execute or deport most of the Seminoles, leaving a few hundred in the swamps.

Eighteen forty-two saw the first westbound emigrant train pull out of Independence, Missouri, on what would become known as the Oregon Trail— eighteen wagons carrying one hundred whites. Next year ten times as many whites would follow this trail through Indian territory.

By 1848 California was in American hands, which meant that the intermediate Great Plains dividing the states no longer could be ignored, and with the '49 gold rush came not only more palefaces than an Indian could imagine but alcohol, guns, cholera, smallpox, venereal disease, and the ineradicable debris characteristic of industrial nations. The tribes grew increasingly restive. Even the monstrous buffalo herds tried to avoid this white plague.

In 1851 a council of plains Indians met with American politicians at Horse Creek thirty-five miles east of Fort Laramie. Ten thousand Indians showed up. Ponies darkened the hills. On September 6 nearly a thousand Sioux rode in column behind an American flag. Cheyennes gave a similarly peaceful demonstration. Numerous dogs were boiled and served. Old enemies vowed friendship. Everybody danced. This council, which lasted almost three weeks, had been designed by Anglos to insure the safety of emigrant trains. If the Indians would quit molesting emigrants and if they would stop wandering around, thereby enabling the government to monitor their activities and punish them for transgressions—if, that is to say, they would make an effort to live like civilized people—they would be rewarded with all sorts of commodities. To the Anglos it seemed a logical, reasonable approach to the hazardous condition of life on the plains.

Nez Perces were not invited to Fort Laramie because they lived too far west, but they would later feel the pinch, and Chief Joseph's comment on white logic deftly summarizes the response of most Indians. One might as well expect rivers to run backward as expect free men to live in a coop, he said, and he asked who had authorized white men to keep Indians in one place while the whites might travel as they pleased. To such an extraordinary question, of course, there could be no answer. The Sioux, Cheyennes, and every other tribe on the continent were of Joseph's mind; they thought they might live wherever they chose—a posture guaranteed to infuriate bureaucrats who believed quite rightly that wandering Indians would disrupt the system. The Sioux and Cheyennes, being numerous and particularly obdurate, were especially annoying.

In 1868 the government arranged a treaty with the Sioux, setting apart for them a huge tract of land comprising the western half of what is now South Dakota:

> . . . commencing on the east bank of the Missouri, where the 46th parallel of north latitude crosses the same, thence along the low water mark down the said east bank to a point opposite where the northern line of the state of Nebraska strikes the river, then west across said river and along the northern line of Nebraska to the 104th degree of longitude west from Greenwich, thence north on said meridian. . . .

This area was reserved to them for all time. Six years later, though, General Custer found gold in the Black Hills, "with the inevitable resulting inroads of covetous settlers," as Col. T. M. Coughlan explained the business in 1934. Because of these prospectors, often attended by families and followed by merchants, the Sioux and their Cheyenne allies grew more belligerent. "Toward the close of 1875 the Indian unrest alarmed the Indian Department. The War Department was authorized by the President to chastise some of the warlike tribes. . . ."

To accomplish this, General Sheridan drew up a plan. Three armies would converge upon the savages.

General George Crook would move north from Fort Fetterman in eastern Wyoming.

Colonel John Gibbon would move east from Montana.

General Alfred Terry, with Custer in command of the Seventh, would move west from Dakota Territory.

Crook probably was the most astute and experienced Indian fighter in the Army, known as a mean opponent, worse than a badger in a barrel. Capt. Charles King, who served under him, said he had fought all the tribes on the western slope of the Rockies and most of those on the eastern side. "Pitt River Indians sent an arrow through him in 1857, and since the day he took command against the Apaches in Arizona no white man's scalp would bring the price his would, even in the most impoverished tribe on the continent."

Indians knew Crook not only by reputation but by his singular appearance. Studio photographs show an erect, handsome, middle-aged officer in a proper military suit with brass buttons, a World War II haircut, and crinkly eyes that betoken a life spent outdoors as well as an amiable disposition. In fact, he was not so amiable. His adjutant, Capt. Bourke, called him reticent and taciturn, brusque to the point of severity. At work he did not resemble the man in studio pictures. His beard forked beneath his jaw as though parted by a breeze and he sometimes wrapped these halves in twine or braided them—perhaps to keep them out of the soup. With a nose like a knife and his split beard he looks undeniably imperial, much like Lucas Cranach's portrait of Augustus, Grand Duke of Saxony. Those who knew the general said he could exist on slippery elm bark and acorns.

He left Fort Fetterman on March 1, 1876, to round up and intimidate a wandering band of Sioux in southeastern Montana. Nobody anticipated much trouble. This would be little more than an excursion, a prelude to the full-dress summer campaign. On the banks of the Powder his advance column under Col. J. J. Reynolds pitched into a village thought to be that of Crazy Horse. The inhabitants fled, Reynolds captured the pony herd and a gratifying amount of property. According to Bourke this village was provided with just about everything a savage could desire, "and much besides that a white man would not disdain to class among the comforts of life." Among these comforts were elk skins and buffalo robes "wondrously embroidered with porcupine quills," fur couches, brilliantly painted valises made from pony hide, trunks for kitchen utensils. Bourke also mentions feathered war bonnets long enough to touch the ground. Concerning food, so much venison and buffalo meat that no adequate idea could be given; he estimated not less than one thousand pounds. There was ammunition enough for a regiment along with powder, pig-lead, and moulds for casting bullets.

Only three of Reynolds' men were killed during this attack, though another was fatally wounded. The village had been seized, the enemy dispersed, all seemed well, but Reynolds panicked. Bourke says he "concluded suddenly to withdraw." So abrupt was this withdrawal that the dead troopers were left behind, together with an injured man—Pvt. Lorenzo Ayers—who would soon be chopped to pieces. At least that is the paleface version of how Ayers died.

Stanley Vestal talked with an old Indian who thought this story about Ayers might have gotten started because of a trick some Cheyennes played on a Sioux. After the battle these Cheyennes were roasting pieces of meat when a Sioux named Little Shield came up and stood beside the fire warming himself. Little Shield was hungry, and because he did not know how to speak Cheyenne he helped himself to a piece of meat. The Cheyennes watched him do this. Then they began talking among themselves. After Little Shield had swallowed the meat one of the Cheyennes told him in sign language that they had found a fat soldier and cut him up and what Little Shield had just eaten was soldier meat. The Cheyennes looked very serious. Little Shield was horrified. He did not know much about Cheyennes and thought maybe they were cannibals. So just because of this joke, Vestal was told, a lot of Sioux thought the Cheyennes had cut up a soldier and finally the whites heard about it.

Anyway, before withdrawing from the village Reynolds set it afire and, as might be expected, teepees stuffed with ammunition did not merely burn. They exploded, says Bourke, launching eighteen-foot lodge poles into the atmosphere like skyrockets: "It was a great wonder to me that some of our party did not receive serious injuries. . . ."

That night the dispossessed natives recaptured most of their ponies and rode off, leaving Crook with not much to do except march back to Fort Fetterman where he reported a victory over Crazy Horse. If a surprise assault at dawn may be so designated, this was a victory, but the Indians were not Oglala Sioux led by Crazy Horse; they were Sioux-Cheyennes under the joint leadership of He Dog and Old Bear. It appears that Crook's scout, Frank Grouard, recognized several of He Dog's ponies, and because He Dog ordinarily accompanied Crazy Horse, Grouard thought the celebrated chief must be present. In fact, He Dog had left Crazy Horse, explaining that there were children who could not escape the soldiers, and many frightened women, so he had decided to obey the government by going to the Red Cloud agency. Old Bear, a Cheyenne, was doing the same. By other accounts, the Cheyennes had just left the agency—which would explain all the gunpowder, pig-lead, and bullets.

George Hyde, after talking to an old Cheyenne woman in 1912, became convinced this was indeed the village of Crazy Horse, augmented by forty Cheyenne lodges. When the Indians scattered, she told him, Crazy Horse was seen running up a steep hillside with a child clinging to his back. Hyde is the one important scholar who believes it.

Sioux and Cheyennes both were in the village, this has been established. One other thing is certain: destroying so much food was uncommonly stupid, even for the Army, because Crook's troops had almost nothing to eat. Bourke states that as a result of this victory Crook aborted the expedition: "We had no beef, as our herd had been run off on account of the failure to guard it; we were out of supplies, although we had destroyed enough to last a regiment for a couple of months; we were encumbered with sick, wounded, and cripples with frozen limbs, because we had not had sense enough to save the furs and robes in the village; and the enemy was thoroughly aroused, and would be on the *qui vive* for all that we did." At the first bivouac, named Camp Inhospitality, they could not even feed the wounded. "Here and there would be found a soldier, or officer, or scout who had carried a handful of cracker-crumbs in his saddlebags, another who had had the good sense to pick up a piece of buffalo meat. . . ."

Reynolds would be court-martialed ten months later, as much for stupidity as cowardice. The Court suspended him from rank and command for a year, but Grant remitted the sentence and six months after that the colonel retired.

As for the hungry, burned-out, freezing Indians, they traveled three days to the village of Crazy Horse where they were given food and shelter. If they had been somewhat inclined to cooperate with the Great Father who lived beyond the sunrise in Never-Never Land, this incendiary strike changed their disposition.

Crazy Horse agreed to a military alliance with the refugees and they decided to enlist the support of Sitting Bull's Unkpapas who were encamped several days' travel northeast. Here the destitute people were again welcomed, as they knew they would be, for it was inconceivable to Indians that those who had plenty should fail to provide for those who had nothing. Wooden Leg said that when they reached Sitting Bull's camp the Unkpapa squaws already had pots boiling. They were given all the meat they wanted, and more. A herald rode through camp describing the wretched condition of these guests, so everybody brought presents. A ten-year-old Unkpapa girl gave Wooden Leg a buffalo robe. "Whoever needed any kind of clothing got it immediately. They flooded us with gifts of everything needful. Crowds of their men and women were going among us to find out and supply our wants."

Unkpapa, Uncpapa, Hunkpapa—however this euphonious name is spelled it means something, just as Oglala, Brulé, and other Indian names have meaning. Unkpapa signifies an edge or a border, and it identified this tribe which traditionally camped at the village entrance. In other words: They Camp by Themselves.

Oglala is difficult to translate. There was a derogatory gesture among these people—flicking the fingers—which might be likened to throwing dirt, and long ago when they resolved to separate from their Brulé relatives the Oglalas expressed their feelings with this gesture. According to Hyde, "we have always known that the name *Oglala* means scattered, divided." He thinks it could have originated during the eighteenth century when the Oglalas attempted, like the Miniconjoux, to raise crops and were therefore spoken of contemptuously as dust-scatterers. Which is to say, somebody was finger-flicking the Oglalas, not vice versa. Maybe everybody did it, just as today a certain insulting gesture is commonplace. But the word might have meant wanderer, and because on one government treaty it has been spelled *O'Gallalla* there are those who suspect these Indians must be Irish.

Tom LeForge said finger-flicking was used also to identify Bannocks, whose lodges were not well kept. One signified Bannock by creating a teepee with the fingers, followed by that terrible gesture. Bad Lodge people. Worthless Lodge people.

The Brulé tribe was caught in a prairie fire sometime around 1763 and several people burned to death. Most escaped by running through the flames and jumping into a lake, but their legs were seared, which caused the tribe to become known by this characteristic disfigurement. Prince Paul of Würtemberg, who visited the American West three times, encountered them in 1823 and understood the tribal name to be Cu Brulé, Burnt Buttocks.

Miniconjoux signifies those who planted crops beside water. This band at one time had settled among the fortified village of corn-eating Rees along the Missouri and tried to imitate the Ree pattern of life. After a while they gave up because agriculture did not suit them, but apparently they kept at it longer than the Oglalas, long enough to be called Miniconjoux.

Wahpeton Sioux lived among trees, Wahpeton meaning a village in the leaves.

The usual English translation of Oo-hen-on-pa—Two Kettle—might be more properly rendered as Two Cookings, because the chief of this band liked to brag that his hunters could supply meat enough for two meals.

The Blackfeet, Sihasapa, may have gotten their name because they wore black moccasins; although James McLaughlin, who was for many years the agent at Devil's Lake and Standing Rock, believes the name originated with a family that arrived in camp wearing worn-out moccasins, their feet blackened because they had walked across a burnt prairie. These people were distinct from the Blackfoot, Siksika, who lived farther north and west, ranging into Canada, and who were related to the eastern Algonquins. As to why the Siksika were so-called, maybe their moccasins were discolored by ashes and soot because they often camped on fire-blackened ground.

Those without bows, Sans Arcs, got this name after some family or clan found itself disarmed—which was the fault of an hermaphrodite. Or the fault of those who listened to him/her/it. These not-quite-people lived out their existence among the Indians much as they do elsewhere, in terrible isolation: the year 1839 is recorded on an Unkpapa pictographic calendar as Winkte Peji wan ici kte—the year an hermaphrodite committed suicide. Nevertheless they had a certain status not granted to them in Anglo-European society; they were thought to possess great powers of divination and therefore would be consulted on important business. So it happened that once upon a time an hermaphrodite advised his fellow tribesmen to place their weapons on a hilltop while he consulted the future. Most unwisely they did, and a hostile war party showed up. Other Sioux considered the resultant massacre to be very funny, and ever since then the foolish people have been called Sans Arcs.

As for the generic word Sioux, Ralph Andrist calls it an etymological monstrosity: "a truncation of Nadouessioux, which in turn is a French form of the Chippewa Nadoue-is-iw, meaning little snake. . . ." In other words, an enemy. Dakota, a word meaning allies, is what they called themselves. More precisely—because the Yankton, Teton, and Santee Sioux all spoke different dialects—they should be referred to as Nakota, Lakota, and Dakota.

So much for etymology.

After deliberating with Sitting Bull, who thought the best way to negotiate with whites was to avoid them, the burned-out Cheyennes and Oglalas joined the Unkpapas. All three tribes then drifted in a northwesterly direction, meanwhile gathering strength from the Blackfeet, Sans Arcs, and from Lame Deer's Miniconjoux. It had been agreed that the Cheyennes should travel at the head of this column, farthest from any pursuing bluecoats—which explains why Custer met them at the north end of the serpentine village—and the powerful Unkpapas under Sitting Bull would guard the rear. Thus, when Reno charged the tail of the village he had the misfortune to encounter these Unkpapas.

In this manner, following game herds, a restless and wary conglutination of aborigines moved from one valley to the next.

Meanwhile, back at Fort Fetterman after his dubious success, General Crook was reorganizing. On May 29 he again started north. Now, cooperating with General Terry and Colonel Gibbon, he was after Sitting Bull, and this time his baptized troops knew what to expect.

On June 17 in southern Montana about twenty miles above the present Wyoming state line he ran into a force of at least one thousand warriors—Cheyennes, Oglalas, Sans Arcs, Miniconjoux, Blackfeet, Unkpapas—who knew where to find him and who had made a fast night march from their camp just east of the ridge which separates the valleys of the Little Bighorn and Rosebud. This unusual maneuver seems to have been the result of a conference among several chiefs who felt that Crook's army was a threat. These normally independent fighting men probably traveled in a disciplined column with the flanks patrolled by warrior societies whose job was to keep ambitious braves from sneaking ahead and ruining the surprise. Wooden Leg remembered it differently. Years later he said the chiefs had decided to let these soldiers alone but a great many young men, along with a few older ones, slipped out of camp and rode across the divide looking for a fight.

However it came about, by dawn an immense throng of warriors had assembled in the Rosebud Valley. Here they watered their ponies and got dressed. Each man wanted to look his best when entering a battle from which he might not emerge, so each brought to the field a particular graphic idea. A Cheyenne named Black Sun, for instance, wore nothing but moccasins, a blanket around his loins, and the stuffed skin of a weasel on his head. He was mortally hit. He died several hours later and the Cheyennes put his body in a hillside cave.

Jack Red Cloud, son of the famous chief, wore his father's trail bonnet—which he should not have done—and borrowed his father's Winchester. He was just eighteen, clearly too young to be such a warrior as the bonnet proclaimed. Crook's Indian allies went after him. They shot his pony and Jack Red Cloud then failed to do what a warrior should: instead of first removing the bridle he tried to escape. Not that a bridle was important; what mattered was to demonstrate courage and composure. Three Crows chased him. They lashed him with whips. One of them snatched the bonnet from his head. They took his father's gun, which was a present from the United States government with *Red Cloud* engraved on it. By this time Jack Red Cloud was crying. He begged the Crows either to kill him or stop humiliating him. They hooted with laughter.

Such embarrassing scenes alternated with moments of intense beauty. Chief Washakie, the great Shoshone, rode naked to the waist, wearing a bonnet with so many feathers that they swept the earth.

The canyon was in bloom. It is said that the odor of blossoming crabapple, roses, and wild plum mingled sweetly with the dust and acrid smoke of black powder. Gunfire reverberating from the rocky walls echoed the rhythmic pounding of horses' hooves, dislodging thousands of petals which drifted down like keepsakes among the desperate men. The fight lasted several hours. At times they battled hand-to-hand.

Ex-trooper Phineas Towne wrote to Cyrus Brady:

I don't think I had gone more than ten yards when I was surrounded by about twenty or more of the most murderous looking Indians I ever saw. You can talk of seeing devils; here they were in full form, painted in the most terrifying manner, some with their war bonnets adorned with horns of steers and buffalo. It was enough to strike terror to anyone's heart.

I knew that my time had come, I knew that I would be taken prisoner. I fought, but it was fighting against terrible odds. There I was down in that ravine, alone and in the midst of a lot of murderous savages.

Taking my carbine from me and throwing a lariat over my head and tightening it about my feet, I was helpless. This was all done in an instant, while I struggled and fought in vain, until I was struck on the head with something which rendered me unconscious and caused me to fall. As I went down a bullet struck me in the body.

I think that when the bullet struck me I regained my consciousness, because I realized I was being dragged at a lively pace over the ground by a pony at the other end of the lariat. It was, I think, the intention of the Indians either to drag me to death at the heels of the pony or after getting me away to torture me in some other manner.

They captured one other comrade of mine by the name of Bennett, of L Troop, Third Cavalry, and completely cut him in pieces. His remains were buried in a grain sack.

After I was dragged in this manner for some distance, my captors were charged by one of the troops of cavalry, and to save themselves from capture abandoned me. . . .

Military analysts today evaluate the Rosebud either as a stand-off or something of a defeat for Crook—undoubtedly his least successful Indian fight. Numerically it might be regarded as a success because just nine troopers and one Shoshone scout were killed while the hostiles lost thirty or forty. Crazy Horse said thirty-six. These numbers might have been much less favorable to General Crook if the concatenation of forces that annihilated Custer had been fully assembled, but two redoubtable war chiefs—Gall and Crow King—were absent.

Bourke claimed it as a victory. He said they chased the enemy seven miles and controlled the field, which is true. Otherwise very little was accomplished. They had nothing but the remnants of the four days' rations with which they had started, so all they could do was return to the wagons.

In any case, statistics seldom tell the story. Consider one dead Shoshone scout. A negligible loss, hardly worth the ink on a government ledger. His name has been forgotten. He was not even a warrior, just a boy. He had asked Chief Washakie's permission to visit a spring or tributary of the Rosebud in order to paint his face. He was almost ready to fight—"his medicine song was half done," says Bourke, when a Sioux or Cheyenne found him, shot him through the back and stripped the top of his head "from the nape of the neck to the forehead, leaving his entire skull ghastly and white. It was the boy's first battle. . . ." Plenty Coups, chief of the Crows, said this boy was not a Shoshone but a Cree who had lived with the Crows for so many years that they thought of him as one of their own. Whatever his identity, he and nine dead bluecoats were buried late at night in a deep trench beside the creek. These ten bodies—counting trooper Bennett's pieces in the grain sack—were covered with stones and earth, then a bonfire was kindled on top and kept burning all night. Next morning General Crook marched the entire command across the site to obliterate every trace of the excavation, for it was thought the savages might dig up and lacerate the cadavers.

During the retreat the Crows scored one last coup. They heard a voice begging for water, "Mini! Mini!" and they discovered a blind Cheyenne warrior hidden among the rocks. He had been led to this place or had wandered there. When he heard the Crows talking among themselves he mistook the language for Sioux and called out. The Crows responded by chopping off his arms and legs.

Many strange sights were seen, Chief Plenty Coups remarked. He himself met a soldier riding very fast with both arms hanging down like strips of bloody meat. The chief did not know who he was, but from the description this must have been a Third Cavalry trooper, Elmer Snow, who escaped with two badly crippled arms.

Bvt. Col. Guy Henry took a bullet in the head which pierced both cheekbones, smashed his nose, and destroyed one eye, according to journalist John F. Finerty. Nevertheless he somehow remained upright in the saddle with blood gushing from his mouth while he tried to encourage the troops. He was spurring his horse forward to lead a charge when he fainted and toppled to the ground. Finerty saw him later, more or less alive, with a blood-saturated cloth shielding his face from a cloud of flies, and tried to cheer him up.

"It is nothing," the colonel replied. "For this we are soldiers."

Brady's version is slightly less poetic: "It's all right, Jack, it's what we're here for."

Nobody thought he could last the night, and as Col. Henry listened to the mass grave being dug he might have thought the same. If so, he refused to admit it. Capt. Anson Mills, learning that he had been shot, went to visit and inquired if he were badly hurt.

"The doctors have just told me that I must die," said Col. Henry, "but I will not."

They carried him out of the valley feet first on a mule litter, but the poles were too short and occasionally the second mule's head bumped Henry's head. Then they turned him around, which was more comfortable, although at any instant the front mule might kick his brains out.

Capt. Azor Nickerson states that during the retreat one of the litter poles struck a boulder on a mountainside and pitched Col. Henry into some rocks twenty feet below. When they reached him he was unable to speak. They wiped off the fresh blood and dirt and gave him a sip of water. And just how was he feeling? "Bully!" whispered the half-dead colonel. He insisted he never had felt better and he thanked them all for being so kind.

Plenty Coups thought this was no way to carry a wounded man. A travois would not cause such pain. "I should have liked to tell the soldiers how to handle their chief, but they did not ask me. . . ."

The colonel's personal account of being shot in the head and his subsequent agony is depreciated to the extent that it sounds ludicrous. The bullet stung, as though he had been slapped, and he did not realize he fell to the ground like a shotgunned mallard—he thought he dismounted and lay down. He must have been dimly conscious because he could remember Sioux warriors charging by, and had it not been for the valiant Shoshone Chief Washakie fighting above his prostrate body he would have been finished off and scalped.

Concerning the trip back, he mentions a detail Finerty missed: a mule did kick him in the face. This by itself would eliminate quite a few men. Not Col. Henry.

Because the Sioux might resume hostilities at any time General Crook ordered a fast retreat. The mules were flogged into a trot and he concedes that he found this motion unpleasant. Indeed, he admits, death would have been preferable.

Nights were so cold that ice formed. He welcomed the low temperature because he did not bleed as much.

While crossing the Tongue River he was nearly washed overboard.

At the Goose Creek base camp they set up a tent to protect him from the sun and put a mattress under him, which he considered a luxury.

During the next two hundred miles his escort managed to shoot a few little birds. These were boiled and the broth poured down his throat. Now and then he got a teaspoonful of brandy.

They reached the North Platte across from Fort Fetterman just as the fer-

ryboat cable snapped. Henry calls this a disappointment. Within sight of
houses and beds they would be obliged to camp once more. But an officer
from Fetterman crossed the Platte in a skiff and told the colonel they would
try to get him to the fort if he would take the chance of capsizing. By this time
Henry was totally blind and probably had not much more than a pint of blood
in his body. If the skiff capsized he would drown. He said he was willing to
take the chance. With the officer cradling Henry in his arms, two enlisted men
paddling, they got across. He was now three hundred miles beyond the frontier. A week later he had survived a jolting field ambulance trip to Medicine
Bow where the Union Pacific stopped. He got there on July 4 when everybody
in town was drunk, yelling, firing guns. A bullet zipped through his tent.
Next day they loaded him aboard a train bound for civilization.

At Fort Russell the surgeons went to work, probing his wounds every day,
but even they could not kill him.

After two months, having regained the use of one eye, he traveled to California to recuperate and in less than a year he was back on duty at Fort Laramie. So we are told by one historian, although another insists he toured Europe and did not return to active service until the fall of '79. In either case—
ten months or three years—the colonel was a sinewy bird.

He himself found nothing remarkable about this experience. He had suffered, yes. He almost died, yes. But he was a warrior. He kept his feelings to
himself.

He said the reason the Indians did not renew their attack when General
Crook withdrew from the Rosebud was—"as we learned afterwards"—that
they were concerned about the approaching army of Terry and Custer.

Crook bivouacked on Goose Creek after this indecisive, bloody battle and
it sounds like a pleasant interlude not merely for the general but for his troops:
big game hunting—deer, elk, bear, mountain sheep—and superb fishing. In
one day Capt. Anson Mills and two enlisted men caught 146 trout. Crook
himself caught seventy in a single afternoon. Major Noyes did not return
from a fishing trip when expected and it was feared that he might have
drowned or been attacked by a bear or some other wild animal; but he was
discovered asleep under a tree, exhausted by his great haul of fish. Bourke
estimates that Crook and his men took more than fifteen thousand trout in
three weeks: "and I am convinced that my figures are far below the truth.
. . ." He says that his notebooks for this period resemble the chronicle of a
sporting club.

If not hunting or fishing the troopers might amuse themselves with foot
races or games of checkers and whist. Artistic soldiers passed the time sketching. Intellectuals discussed Macaulay and Shakespeare, while those who

were not so intellectual speculated on the private life of one teamster—the fabulous Calamity Jane.

On June 23 a lieutenant arrived from Fort Fetterman with news of the outside world. Especially interesting to Crook was the fact that one of his Civil War subordinates, Rutherford Hayes, had been nominated for the presidency. Crook thought well of Hayes and seemed pleased by the nomination. Still, he would rather have learned something about General Terry and Colonel Gibbon. They were on the march, he knew, but that was just about all he knew: ". . . and much comment, not unmixed with uneasiness, was occasioned thereby."

Two days later Capt. Mills, who had traveled to the northern peaks of the Bighorns on a reconnoitering expedition, observed smoke in the far northwest. Almost certainly this smoke arose from grass fires set by the Indians when they counterattacked Reno, and although Mills had no way of knowing this he suspected there had been a fight. When he got back to camp on the night of June 25 he reported what he had seen.

Bourke writes that the failure to hear from either Terry or Gibbon distressed Crook more than he would admit: "he feared for the worst, obliged to give ear to all the wild stories brought in by couriers. . . ."

Gibbon, whom the Indians called No Hipbone because of a Civil War injury, had assembled his column from three forts and a field camp in western Montana, collecting as many troops as could be spared without imperiling the lives of settlers. He set out for the rendezvous with twenty-seven officers, 409 enlisted men, and a party of Crow scouts. According to Sheridan's master plan he would meet Terry and Custer somewhere along the Yellowstone—above the hostile Sioux—while Crook would threaten them from below.

Because he had a long way to travel and his units were dispersed, and the snow was deep, Colonel Gibbon started in mid-March: south to the Yellowstone, then eastward.

En route his men discovered and tore apart a number of Indian burials. Chief of scouts Bradley recorded in his journal that on Sunday, May 21, he investigated certain reddish objects which were thought to be quarters of freshly butchered meat suspended from poles, but turned out to be moldy Sioux corpses wrapped in red blankets. The scaffolds on which they were placed had partly fallen, leaving the bodies half-dangling. Bradley asked the squaw man Tom LeForge—whose name he spelled LeForgey, maybe because that was how LeForge pronounced it—he asked LeForge to open one of these macabre bundles. It contained all that was left of a middle-aged warrior who had been dead about two years. "His effects had been buried with him, and among them was a small package of letters, a soldier's hymn book, and a picture-history of his life. The book had belonged to a soldier of some regiment of Iowa volunteers. . . . There was also a paper signed 'Fannie Kelly, captive white woman,' whose reading touched us all to the heart and made us wish the savage was again alive that we might wreak upon him some of the indignation we felt."

The captive had written that the Indians were kind to her, but she was "compelled to do their bidding."

Bradley digests this suggestive yet ambiguous remark, growing turgid with Christian rage: "May the military operations that are now in progress result in so complete an overthrow of the hell-hounds called Sioux. . . ."

He must have been the first white man to read Mrs. Kelly's letter, which she wrote almost eleven years earlier, sometime during the last few months of 1864. She had been born in Canada but her father emigrated to the American frontier so Fanny grew up and got married in Kansas. At the age of nineteen she started for Idaho with her husband Josiah, their adopted daughter, a friend named Wakefield, and two black servants who had once been Cherokee slaves. A few days on the road they were joined by a Methodist preacher, then by another little family and a Mr. Taylor.

On July 12, west of Fort Laramie, the landscape blossomed with two or three hundred Oglala Sioux painted for war. The chief, Ottawa—Silver Horn—slapped himself on the chest, saying to Josiah Kelly: "Good Indian, me." Ottawa gestured at the others, saying: "Heap good Indian, hunt buffalo and deer."

Nobody believed this but they had no choice. Indians and emigrants shook hands. Everybody grinned and nodded. The Indians thought they would like to trade one of their ponies for Josiah Kelly's racehorse, so he traded. They wanted flour, but after being given flour they poured it on the ground, keeping only the sack. They wanted clothes, which they got. Now, more certain of themselves, one reached for Kelly's gun, which he would not surrender.

Ottawa signaled that the emigrants might move on. Ahead lay a dark, rocky glen. Kelly refused to enter it.

The Sioux then demanded a feast.

Wakefield was getting provisions from a wagon, Kelly had wandered some distance away to gather firewood, and the preacher was distributing sugar when the Oglalas quit playing games. Fanny Kelly said she never would forget the face of Mr. Taylor when a bullet struck his forehead: "He looked at me as he fell backward. . . ."

One of the black servants dropped at her feet, writhing with arrows, and Sioux leaped into the wagons where they began to open boxes. After stealing whatever they wanted the Indians set the wagons afire and rode off, taking

Mrs. Kelly and her infant daughter. She did not know if her husband was dead or alive.

She must have picked up the Sioux language quickly because almost at once she realized what her captors thought about the inescapable war that was developing. The country across which they traveled was scarred by innumerable paths. Generation after generation of Indians followed the game herds—travois poles scoring the earth—and the invasion of this land was felt with deep bitterness. When trees were chopped down, when buffalo were slaughtered, when a train chugged across the horizon—all such signs of permanent possession by whites excited in these people a deadly hostility. The land was all they had. Should they give it up, then they must die or submit to the laws of white men. So they killed, robbed, and harrassed the foreigners.

General Alfred Sully was trailing these Indians. When he got close they turned back to fight. She said her feelings at this time—when she heard rifle shots and the boom of a cannon—her feelings were indescribable. She believed the soldiers would overtake Ottawa's village. But after a while the warriors brought back trophies, "reeking scalps, soldiers' uniforms covered with blood. . . ." One Indian showed her a letter taken from a dead soldier in which he wrote that the topographical engineer had been killed but Sully's men caught two of the red devils, cut off their heads and displayed them on poles. Despite this letter and other such examples of white savagery—several Oglalas died after eating poisoned crackers—she remained a frontier woman who spoke with contempt of the "sugar-plum and rose-water policy" endorsed by peace advocates.

An Oglala boy died along the way. They wrapped his body in curtains that had once draped the windows of her home in Kansas. They placed him on a scaffold with a red blanket and a few items for use in the land of the white buffalo, and continued traveling.

On the high plains a band of Unkpapas became her temporary custodians because these Oglalas wanted their government allowance and they reasoned, quite correctly from the American point of view, that it would be undiplomatic to present themselves at the agency with a white captive.

Her last days among these people obliged her to witness a massacre. Settlers on a Yellowstone flatboat made the mistake of camping ashore. None survived. The scalps included that of a woman with beautiful chestnut hair about four feet long, but the brave who took this prize did not join the celebration that night. She asked why he was not dancing, so he went into his lodge and came out with a blood-soaked dress. He explained that he had been thinking. It seemed to Mrs. Kelly that he was confused by a sense of remorse, because he had been taught it was honorable to kill women and children.

In late November, following negotiations with officers at Fort Sully, she was turned over to some Blackfeet who would escort her to the fort. Along the way they crossed a formation of sandy ridges where she noticed seashells. She asked how shells came to be on these summits and was told that a great sea rolled over the face of this country. Only one man escaped. He sailed around with his family until the flood receded. Then he became the father of all Indians.

Officers at Fort Sully had been led to think the Blackfeet would release her in exchange for presents—by which stratagem several Blackfeet would be able to get inside the stockade. Once inside they could prevent the gates from being closed while a war party which was hiding nearby would ride down from the hills. Thus everybody in the fort could be murdered. It was a good plan, and except for Mrs. Kelly it would have worked. By this time, however, she understood Sioux pretty well and during the negotiations she managed to warn the gullible white men. Fort Sully was not strong. In the opinion of almost everybody stationed there during the winter of 1864–5 the thing that saved them was an almost illegible note Mrs. Kelly had written with a soft lead bullet on a page torn from a business ledger.

On December 12 the Blackfeet delivered her. They must have felt cheated when the gates quickly closed.

Her husband was alive. When their wagon train was attacked it had been almost sunset and in the falling darkness he escaped. So they were reunited, but she found him dramatically changed. His hair was beginning to turn gray although they had been separated just five months.

On the night she was captured she had somehow been able to hide her daughter, telling the child to lie still, that they were only a few miles from help and that next day the soldiers from Fort Laramie would find her. The child eventually was found dead, three arrows in her body, and scalped. After having been told of this Mrs. Kelly reflected upon it with the sentiment of an era long gone, with a prose style whose complexity indicates a much higher level of public education in those days:

> Surely He who numbers the sparrows and feeds the ravens was not un-
> mindful of her in that awful hour, but allowed the heavenly kingdom, to
> which her trembling soul was about to take its flight, to sweeten, with a
> glimpse of its beatific glory, the bitterness of death, even as the martyr
> Stephen, seeing the bliss above, could not be conscious of the torture
> below.

Lt. Bradley mentioned in his journal that after finding a paper signed by Fanny Kelly on a Sioux burial scaffold he thought the name sounded familiar.

For a long time he puzzled over this. At last it occurred to him: "I had some-where read an account of her ransom a few years ago, followed afterward by an announcement that she had written and published a book of her experi-ences." He does not say what she wrote on the scrap of paper, but it probably had nothing to do with the scheme to overrun Fort Sully or he would have commented. The message must have been one of several that she left along the way or entrusted to Indians who appeared sympathetic and who fre-quently visited the settlements.

Why the Indian kept this note instead of delivering it to a white who could read English and would perhaps give him a reward is a mystery. Other letters, just as incomprehensible to Indians who kept them, turned up in various hostile villages; and journalists at the 1867 Medicine Lodge peace conference observed Cheyenne squaws collecting discarded envelopes—hiding envel-opes in their clothing or riding off with a handful. Paleface calligraphy at-tracted them, but why? Maybe they thought if they looked at the writing long enough they would be able to communicate as the whites did.

Whatever his particular reason, a middle-aged Sioux, dead two years when LeForge tore apart his scaffold, had kept Mrs. Kelly's message.

Lt. Bradley concentrates on the sinister phrase "compelled to do their bid-ding." He cannot get over it. He repeats it with an exclamation. "Alas," he goes on, "how many poor captive women have suffered this to them worse fate than death!"

She was not sexually abused. Not by Oglalas, Unkpapas, or Blackfeet. They ordered her about with harshness and cruelty, "yet I had never suffered from any of them the slightest personal or unchaste insult. Let me bear testi-mony to this redeeming feature in their treatment of me."

These were the Sioux—independent, implacable. General Crook had as-saulted them twice with superior force and both times drew back. Now, irri-tated and baffled, he camped alongside Goose Creek in the afternoon shade of the Bighorns while he waited for news.

Three columns had been ordered to converge on these people like the tal-ons of a carnivorous bird on a pigeon. Although Crook was disabled, the other talons were moving. From Fort Lincoln in Dakota Territory came Terry and Custer, alert for signs of the enemy, looking up the Yellowstone for Gibbon's scouts. Down the north bank of the Yellowstone came Gibbon, preceded by Lt. Bradley, Tom LeForge, and twenty-three apprehensive Crows who knew all too much about the Sioux.

On May 23, two days after Bradley discovered Mrs. Kelly's letter on a scaffold, three men drifted out of Gibbon's camp to do a little hunting. They were ambushed in a ravine and killed. Dr. Paulding's autopsy, dispassionate and professional, illustrates the abruptness of death on this frontier. Pvt. Augustine Stoeker gave up the ghost because two bullets passed through the left side of the lower jaw and exited on the opposite, carrying away most of his tongue; a third bullet caught him on the "right frontal eminence," exiting close to the right ear; two knives were driven into his brain, "one above & behind & one below left ear & left sticking in body"; a fourth bullet through the head exited behind, creating an orifice "from which brain escaped." Lesser injuries might not have been fatal: "bullets through both elbow joints. . . ."

Pvt. Henry Rahmeir—Paulding spells it Rehmeyer: "Skull mashed in with butt of gun or a rock. Left ear lobe cut off. . . ."

Teamster Quinn—Paulding spells it Quin: "Bullet behind mastoid process downward into neck, 2 tomahawk fractures. . . ."

Dr. Paulding here makes a slight mistake. The Sioux did not have tomahawks; Quinn's head was fractured with an ax or a hatchet. As for Paulding's eccentric orthography, it was habitual; indeed, he had problems writing his own name—often transposing letters so that occasionally he wrote "Pauldnig." One might feel suspicious of a doctor with such a visual or mental disturbance, but there seems to be no indication that it affected his work.

The journal of Capt. Henry Freeman also mentions this incident, if rather casually. After noting that these three men left camp without permission he goes on to say that a trader named Chestnut came downriver from Bozeman. "He asks 8¢ for potatoes, 1.00 for butter & Eggs. Don't want any at that price. Want eggs bad enough but can't afford it. Had two letters from Sallie. Indians were reported to be crossing the river. . . ."

Somebody named Thompson bought all of the beer on Mr. Chestnut's boat—eight gallons—and that night gave a party in his tent.

As for the reckless hunters, they were stitched into blankets and buried in a single grave while a band of Sioux observed the ceremony from across the Yellowstone. "Stoker lies to the south, next to the tree," Paulding wrote. "Quin, wrapped in 2 blankets, in the center Rehmeyer to the north, wrapped in a blanket & covered also with a green blanket put on the body by Show-His-Face, the Crow chief to testify his grief. . . ."

Paulding notes on May 28 that Col. Gibbon seems in bad shape, much alarmed by the proximity of Indians. "He is trembling & frightened so it is pitiable to see him—If I am to be under the command of such imbecile damned fools I think I'll get out of it as soon as possible." Col. Gibbon was not the only one with a stomach full of butterflies. Bradley reported that his Crow scouts were mortally afraid. There is no reason to doubt Bradley's appraisal, yet this remark could be misleading. As Linderman points out, the Crows frequently were at war with surrounding tribes of Sioux, Cheyennes,

Arapahoes, and Blackfeet, and the mere fact that they could survive when outnumbered and encircled was an eloquent proclamation of bravery.

June 5 is very warm. After making camp they roll up the sides of the tents and loiter in the shade, reading newspapers or books, writing letters, playing cards, talking, dozing. Bradley describes an agreeable prelude to supper when nutmeg, lemon, sugar, Angostura bitters, champagne cider, and *spiritus frumenti* are brought out to make toddies and cocktails.

> In the dusk of evening, when most of the officers were gathered in front of some of the tents, a chorus of cavalrymen not far away burst forth with a round of merry camp songs, that came pleasantly to the ear and suspended for a time the conversation upon battles we haven't fought and victories we haven't won. And when "taps" imposed silence upon the enlisted men, the officers, who enjoyed larger liberties, took up the suspended harmony and woke the night air with many a song of sentiment and jollity. We have a number of very sweet singers in our company. . . .
> It is hard to realize when about the camp that we are an invading army, liable at any moment to be engaged in deadly conflict with a cruel foe.

In this leisurely manner, intermittently punctuated by moments of wild activity, the Montana column wound eastward preceded by Crow scouts examining the earth and remote bluffs for any sign of Sioux and looking downstream for another bluecoat army.

Colonel Gibbon is not quite what one expects of a West Point soldier. He seems less narrowly focused, at times digressing like a scholar educated in the liberal arts. Some days before the rendezvous with General Terry a party of horsemen was reported coming down Rosebud Creek on the opposite side of the Yellowstone, and because they must be from Terry's command Gibbon ordered two Crows to deliver a message. He watched them get ready for this cold, dangerous swim by smearing themselves with red paint. "I had the curiosity to inquire the object of this, and was surprised to learn that it was to protect them against the attack of *alligators*. As the alligator is an animal unknown to the waters of this region, the fact referred to is a curious evidence of the southern origin of the Crows. . . ." Although it is not definitely established where these people came from, Gibbon probably was correct. Linderman, who knew them well, states that they often mentioned alligators and sea monsters despite the fact that they were plains Indians, which led him also to believe that the tribe at one time lived much farther south.

Linguistically, they belong to the large Siouan group and are thus related to the Hidatsas, from whom they separated—according to tradition—during an argument over the stomach of a buffalo. Supposedly this happened about the end of the seventeenth century. The Crows, all in a snit, moved toward the Black Hills, which they apparently liked, but were driven into Montana by the more numerous Sioux and Cheyennes.

Absaroka they called themselves—*Absanokee* it was originally pronounced—which has been translated as Sparrowhawk People, but may signify Chosen People, this latter being a universal conceit. Lt. Bradley insists that the correct spelling is *Up-sah-ro-ku*. He says the meaning has been lost. The medicine woman Pretty Shield agreed, saying that she did not know what it meant and never had met any man or woman who did. Dr. W. J. McGee, director of the Bureau of American Ethnology, said it meant something like "great warrior people," and that the Crows, after they came to know and respect white soldiers, applied this self-congratulatory name to the whites as a way of complimenting them. The final word, so to speak, comes from tribal historian Joseph Medicine Crow, who says *Absaroka* is now an obsolete expression.

Why they became known as Crows is not clear. In the Hidatsa dialect of North Dakota, *Abisa* means large-beaked, *roka* means its children, so once upon a time some Crow may have pointed to a corvine bird while trying to interpret the tribal name.

They were lighter in color than Sioux, which made them less frightening. *Beaux hommes* they were called by Chevalier de la Verendrye and his companions, who met them in the mid-eighteenth century. This judgment was repeated a century later by Capt. William Raynolds who described them as nicely formed, of medium height, sporting buffalo hide caps trimmed into points, "imparting a decidedly regal appearance." Raynolds also mentions how they gloried in long hair, letting it hang down to their knees and saturating it with gum until the hair formed a solid mass which they enhanced with dots of white paint. More than any other Indians they were noted for the prodigious length of their hair. George Catlin saw many Crows whose hair swept the ground when they walked, "giving exceeding grace and beauty to their movements." Every morning they oiled it with bear grease, which he thought might account for the luxuriant growth.

General Crook's army met these exotic allies in northern Wyoming. Adjutant Bourke felt that in stature, dress, and demeanor they were preferable to the enemy Sioux. He too remarked on their light skin, which he thought might be attributed to living in a cool mountainous atmosphere.

Lt. Edward Maguire, who was an engineer with Terry, first saw them on the Yellowstone when the two columns joined. "A very handsome set of men . . . extremely good-natured." Maguire thought they looked more aggressive than did the Rees, and he found their language quite musical, "not unlike Spanish."

Terry had left Fort Abraham Lincoln with a band of Ree scouts, three and one-half infantry companies, the entire Seventh Cavalry, a battery of Gatling guns, a wagon train, and a beef herd. The exact number of officers and men is disputed. Major George Gillespie, Chief Engineer of the Military Division of the Missouri, stated in his 1876 annual report that there were 30 Indian scouts, 45 officers, and 906 enlisted men. Gillespie, though, did not accompany this task force whereas the lieutenant did. Maguire lists 45 scouts, guides, and interpreters; 50 officers; 968 men; 190 civilian employees; and 1,694 animals—which sounds as though he walked the length of the column with a tablet. Whatever the facts, this was a formidable aggregation. It should scatter the hostiles like dust in a windstorm.

Pvt. Henry Bailey wrote to his mother a couple of weeks before leaving Fort Lincoln that they intended to wallop the medicine man. He would think he was in a hornet's nest, wrote Bailey, when the Seventh got after him. And to an unidentified correspondent he wrote that although they did not know where they were going he thought it was somewhere up around the Bighorn and Powder Rivers. "Old Sitting Bull has sent word that if we come up there, he will have all our scalps, but I think the old boy is mistaken; he has got a bad crowd to fool with and had better keep quiet." Bailey was the blacksmith of Capt. Myles Keogh's company which was wiped out.

Pvt. Coleman had better luck. He served with Capt. Thomas McDougall's company which guarded the pack train and lost only two men. In October, after a safe return, he transcribed his journal into a three-by-five-inch leather-bound notebook addressed to his sister:

> I am going to send you an account of our Compain against the Siews this summer I have cept this Diary for future Reference We left Fort Lincoln on the 17th of May on a Compaigne against the Siux. . . .

How many Gatling guns lurched and bumped across the prairie is uncertain. Probably three. Sgt. John Ryan of M Company listed two Gatlings, one twenty-four pound brass Napoleon cannon, and a Rodman—this being a small cannon with a rifled barrel. While en route they were reinforced by a company of the Sixth Infantry and another Gatling. So there may have been five mechanical weapons. Ryan's narrative was published by the Hardin *Tribune* in 1923, forty-seven years after the event. In at least a few details it is demonstrably inaccurate. The black interpreter's name, for example, was not Izar but Isaiah.

Regarding the big brass cannon, it has been listed elsewhere as a twelve-pounder. The size, though, is not important. What matters is that some heavy artillery did reach the Yellowstone and must have been dragged up the Little Bighorn because—according to the testimony of a former Confederate soldier named Huston who joined the Sioux—scouts hurried into Sitting Bull's camp reporting the approach of "two bang guns." Whether the imminent arrival of this artillery persuaded the Indians to leave the valley is not known. There is no doubt that many warriors wanted to continue the fight but Sitting Bull concluded the signs were no longer auspicious. Two-bang guns, or two bang-guns, might have seemed inauspicious. Still, his warriors had just broken the back of the most powerful offensive unit on the frontier: Custer's gung-ho regiment—32 officers and 718 enlisted men, more or less.

Bismarck *Tribune* correspondent Mark Kellogg noted in his first dispatch that 1207 men left Fort Lincoln, counting soldiers, Ree scouts, civilian mule packers, herdsmen, teamsters, wheelwrights, guides, et al. Kellogg's figures for these components do not total 1207, but very few things about this expedition do add up.

Somewhere between Fort Lincoln and the Yellowstone, according to *The Arikara Narrative*, Custer and a scout rode so far ahead that they were out of sight. When the column reached a fork in the trail nobody knew which way they had gone. Custer's "negro servant, Isa" was asked. This might have been Isaiah Dorman, although it is strange that he would be called Custer's servant. Isa/Isaiah knew no more than anybody else, nevertheless he was asked which way to go and unwisely he recommended one of the forks.

He guessed wrong.

Custer was furious when he learned the army had been misdirected. An Arikara coming down out of the hills told of seeing the black man on his knees in front of Custer, weeping and pleading for mercy while the general cursed him. And the next day, as punishment, Isa had to walk.

This may or may not have occurred. Such a grotesque incident ought to crop up in a good many journals, especially those kept by men who despised Custer, but only the Arikara scout Red Star mentions it. Assuming it did happen, how would Custer have treated a white who misdirected the army? Custer probably would not have driven a white man to his knees, not in public. However, he did sometimes use the lash and it is at least possible that a white would have been ceremonially lashed instead of being forced to walk. Hundreds of soldiers walked all the way from Fort Lincoln and hundreds of Gibbon's men walked all over Montana, so in that respect such punishment would be a tap on the wrist.

Maybe the incident, if it occurred, had nothing to do with color. The general's rage was spasmodic and unpredictable. During an 1874 trip through the Black Hills he got mad at Bloody Knife, yanked out a revolver and began shooting. Whether he meant to kill Bloody Knife or only scare him, we do not know. Neither did Bloody Knife, who jumped behind a tree. This affair, too, could be interpreted as racial except that fair-skinned blue-eyed Lonesome Charley also jumped behind a tree. On one occasion Tom Custer overslept, so the general set fire to the grass outside his tent. Another time he entered the tent while brother Tom was enjoying a leisurely breakfast and kicked over the table. Subordinates walked softly around him.

What does one make of such a man? Says Mr. Van de Water, who did not think highly of the general, his strange personality can no more be determined now than one may fix the taste of wine by examining an empty bottle.

What other commandant would have included a sixteen-piece band mounted on white horses? A recruit named Jacob Horner said that while traveling through rugged territory Custer ordered the musicians to dismount, clamber up a rocky hillside, and perform.

Custer wanted his band on the battlefield—wherever it might be—but Terry would not consent, so Chief Musician Felix Vinatiori and his instrumentalists dismounted for the last time at the confluence of the Powder and the Yellowstone where a supply depot had been established. Here, at this desolate seam in the universe where two sluggish rivers joined, a party of enlisted men, officers, and Vinatiori's Germanic musicians—Pvts. Arndt, Bammbach, Einenberger, Emerich, Griesner, Jungsbluth, Kneubuchler, Rudolph, a few Englishmen, and one Bernard O'Neill—waved good-bye to the fighting Seventh and to the band's white horses which Custer had annexed.

Jacob Horner was one of those recruits who walked all the way from Fort Lincoln. He and the others may have looked forward to an exciting battle with the Sioux, or at least pretended to, but they were tired and their feet hurt and it is not likely they objected when they were assigned to guard General Terry's depot. Horner drew picket duty on the hills and there he stayed from June 11 until July 4 when the *Far West* barged downstream with a cargo of wounded soldiers and a tale that scarcely anybody could believe.

Horner was Alsatian, the son of a baker who must not have thought much of America because he returned to Europe after six years. Jacob did like this country, at least he wanted to see more of it than he saw as a child. He came back alone when he was fifteen, worked along the Atlantic seaboard, and by 1875 had become a meat cutter in New Orleans. However, the Gulf climate oppressed him so he started up the Mississippi, stopping at a plantation to butcher cattle. A dog began to follow him around. Some children threw rocks at the dog. Jacob got mad and hit a boy who ran away screaming because Jacob's hands were red with cattle blood. In the Southern tradition, therefore, a mob gathered to lynch the foreigner and Jacob spent the next few days hiding in a swamp.

In St. Louis he resumed his sanguine trade and he contemplated recruiting posters which described wonderful times out west.

On April 7, 1876, he presented himself at Jefferson Barracks. The government found him a trifle short but allowed him to stand on tiptoe. The surgeon who inspected him asked about a scar running the length of his left arm. He explained that in Alsace a streak of lightning had entered the chimney of his parents' home, flashed through the bedroom, and seared him. It never had bothered him, he said, and because he could flex that arm about as well as the other one the Army signed him up.

He was assigned to K Company, Seventh Cavalry, and quickly found himself en route to Fort Snelling, Minnesota, where he became a working soldier on April 18, although there had been no time for basic training. A few days later his unit headed west. On May 1 they reached Fort Lincoln. Two weeks later they started for the Little Bighorn. So he came to the junction of the Powder and the Yellowstone and there he walked the hills.

Three or four Ree scouts stopped at the depot not long after the Little Bighorn battle. They asked for a piece of canvas. They drew pictures on the canvas but nobody could understand what the pictures meant.

On July 4 the horseless Teutonic band assembled to celebrate American independence while Pvt. Jacob Horner took his place in ranks, prepared to fire a three-volley salute. They got off one volley, which was answered by a steamboat whistle. They put down their guns and ran to the river bank. They saw the *Far West* approaching with hay strewn all over the deck and wounded men lying on blankets.

Custer had expected to command the entire Fort Lincoln army, not just the cavalry, but he had annoyed Ulysses Grant. It seems that any professional soldier would be more prudent. Not Custer. He testified against Grant's Secretary of War, William Belknap, who had been accused of accepting bribes—specifically $24,450 for awarding the Fort Sill sutler's rights to one John Evans—and he let it be known that he did not think much of the president's brother, Orvil, whose palm had been crossed with silver more than once.

Grant, personally incorruptible but quite touchy, retaliated by forbidding Custer to join the campaign against the Sioux and it was only through the intercession of generals Terry and Sheridan, who wanted him in the field, that Grant relented.

It is said that while imploring Terry to intercede, Custer with tears in his eyes actually got down on his knees.

G. A. C. on his knees. We imagine him as reckless, brave, arrogant, foolish, heartless, but not supplicating. He never begged. He never wept. It would be easier to visualize Patton kneeling on the carpet in front of Eisenhower. Now, after a century, with this dashing cavalier embedded like a fossil in American folklore, such a tableau sounds repugnant and absurd, yet the excruciating moment was witnessed by Terry's brother-in-law, Colonel Robert Hughes.

On May 6, following military protocol, Custer addressed President Grant via the Adjutant General, Division of the Missouri:

> I have seen your order transmitted thro' the General of the Army, directing that I be not permitted to accompany the expedition about to move against hostile Indians. As my entire regiment forms a part of the proposed expedition and as I am the senior officer of the regiment on duty in this department, I respectfully but most earnestly request that while not allowed to go in command of the expedition, I may be permitted to serve with my regiment in the field. I appeal to you as a soldier to spare me the humiliation of seeing my regiment march to meet the enemy and I to not share its dangers.
>
> Signed: G. A. Custer
Brevet Maj. Gen. U.S.A.

To this petition General Terry added a respectful postscript, stating that while he had no desire to question the president's orders he felt that Custer's services in the field would be valuable.

Sheridan at division headquarters in Chicago forwarded these supplications to Brigadier E. D. Townsend in Washington with his own endorsement, which reads in part:

> . . . On a previous occasion in eighteen sixty-eight (1868) I asked executive clemency for Colonel Custer to enable him to accompany his regiment against the Indians, and I sincerely hope if granted this time it will have sufficient effect to prevent him from again attempting to throw discredit on his profession and his brother officers.

Sherman quickly telegraphed Terry:

The dispatch of General Sheridan enclosing yours of yesterday touching General Custer's urgent request to go under your command with his regiment, has been submitted to the President who sends me word that if you want General Custer along he withdraws his objections. Advise Custer to be prudent not to take along any newspaper men who always work mischief, and to abstain from any personalities in the future. Tell him I want him to confine his whole mind to his legitimate office. . . .

Why he was esteemed as an Indian fighter is puzzling. None of his frontier campaigns demonstrated particular skill or insight. Not that they were botched, just that his strategy could not be called brilliant. During an attack on a Cheyenne village in 1868 his regiment escaped possible annihilation because of a superb feint for which he usually receives credit, but this maneuver may have been suggested by his chief of scouts, Ben Clark. Custer's most evident assets seem to have been relentless courage and vitality.

He could be likened more to an actor than to a playwright. Invariably he gives the impression of a man on stage performing as he has been instructed to perform, delivering lines composed by somebody else. Throughout the Civil War his smashing victories were plotted by other men. Gregg was in command at Gettysburg, Torbert at Cedarville, Merritt at Winchester, Sheridan at Yellow Tavern, Crook at Sailor's Creek. In a tight situation his response was instantaneous and predictable: he charged. This response to challenge was not something he learned; he reacted as instinctively as a Miura fighting bull. When he was a schoolboy he once drove his fist through a window at a classmate outside who was making faces at him. Such uncontrolled violence quite often will carry the day, although not necessarily. At Trevillian Station, for instance, he moved too fast, lost his personal baggage, and nearly lost the brigade.

Even now, after a hundred years, his name alone will start an argument. More significant men of his time can be discussed without passion because they are inextricably woven into a tapestry of the past, but this hotspur refuses to die. He stands forever on that dusty Montana slope.

As values change, so does one's evaluation of the past and one's impression of long gone actors. New myths replace the old. During the nineteenth century G. A. C. was vastly admired. Today his image has fallen face down in mud and his middle initial, which stands for Armstrong, could mean Anathema. Paul Hutton, writing in *The Western Historical Quarterly*, observed that as America's concept of the frontier evolved from that of a desert resisting civilization to that of a refuge from civilized decadence, so did Americans begin to look differently at the men and women who participated in settling that distant territory. "Thus, from a symbol of courage and sacrifice in the winning of the West, Custer's image was gradually altered into a symbol of the arrogance and brutality displayed in the white exploitation. . . . The only constant factor in this reversed legend is a remarkable disregard for historical fact."

That he was vigorous and gallant never has been denied, even by those who detested him, and he seems to have been fortuitously noticed by his superiors. During the Civil War he advanced with extraordinary speed: brigadier at twenty-three—one of our youngest general officers. And by the time he galloped across the plains he was a national totem. How odd that this consummate thespian's greatest role was a flop. One feels obligated to ask why.

On July 7, 1876, the New York *Herald* published an interview with an officer in Philadelphia who, as the saying goes, did not care to have his name mentioned. This man knew the young general, whom he compared to a thermometer, and his diagnosis may be correct: "The truth about Custer is, that he was a pet soldier, who had risen not above his merit, but higher than men of equal merit. He fought with Phil Sheridan, and through the patronage of Sheridan he rose; but while Sheridan liked his valor and dash he never trusted his judgment. He was to Sheridan what Murat was to Napoleon. While Sheridan is always cool, Custer was always aflame. Rising to high command early in life, he lost the repose necessary to success in high command."

His rapid promotion is surprising because at West Point he unfurled less like a flower than a weed, graduating thirty-fourth in a class of thirty-four. He accumulated 726 demerits—known as "skins"—which placed him comfortably ahead of, or behind, Cadet George Watt who graduated next-to-last with 695 skins. Patrick Henry O'Rorke, the top graduate, who might have become famous, was killed at Gettysburg.

Delinquency records are preserved in West Point archives, so cadet Custer's illegitimate activities together with his demerits may be scrutinized, e.g.:

Sept. 29, 1857: Trifling in ranks march'g. from parade	3
Dec. 19, 1857: Highly unmilitary & trifling conduct throwing stones on post, 3:30 & 4 P.M.	4
Dec. 19, 1857: Calling Corporal in a boisterous tone of voice 3 P.M.	3
Feb. 21, 1858: Unauthorized articles in ventilator	3
Mar. 8, 1858: Cooking utensils in chimney	3
Apr. 3, 1858: Hair out of uniform at gd. mtg.	2
May 14, 1858: Gazing about in ranks at gd. mtg.	2

July 26, 1858: Rubbish behind tent   3
Jan. 26, 1859: Late at parade   1
Jan. 27, 1859: Late at form't. of Comp'y at M.H. at dinner   1
Jan. 27, 1859: Late at supper r.c.   1
Jan. 30, 1859: Late at bkfst. r.c.   1
Feb. 5, 1859: Laughing & talking in Drawg. Acad'y. on 4th   2
Feb. 17, 1859: Throwing snow balls on stoop of bks. 1:30 &
   2 P.M.   3
Mar. 18, 1859: Throwing bread in M.H. at dinner (on 17th)   2
Apr. 22, 1859: Making boisterous noise in sink 7 & 8 P.M.   3
Nov. 19, 1859: Idle, laughing & talking in Draw'g Acad'y. (on
   15th)   3
Feb. 17, 1860: Wall defaced with pencil marks 9½ & 10 A.M.   4
Mar. 19, 1860: Room grossly out of order, bed down & floor
   not swept 9½ & 10 A.M.   4
Mar. 19, 1860: Bread, butter, potatoes, plates, knives, and
   forks in qrs. 9½ & 10 A.M.   3
July 4, 1860: Swinging arms marching from dinner   1
Feb. 3, 1861: Long beard at inspection (Par. 173, Army
   Regs.)   2
Mar. 10, 1861: Long hair at insp. (Par. 173, Army Regs.)   2
Apr. 3, 1861: Throw'g. snowballs in vicinity of bks. 4 & 5 P.M.
   (Par. 194, Army Regs.)   3
June 4, 1861: Sitting at window in shirt sleeves, with feet in
   window sill 11 A.M. (Camp Police Regs.)   2
June 15, 1861: Unauthorized ornament on coat march'g off
   guard   2
June 22, 1861: Too much furniture in tent at morn'g insp.   1
June 23, 1861: Swing'g. arms march'g. from pub. of Delin-
   quencies   1
June 27, 1861: Swing'g. arms march'g. from pub. of Delin-
   quencies   1

He was as profane, libidinous, and alcoholic as the average cadet, possibly more so. Beyond doubt he was contrary and eccentric. One of his roommates later recalled his absolute indifference to everything: "It was all right with him whether he knew his lesson or not; he did not allow it to trouble him." West Point never had been afflicted with a less promising pupil, remarked one biographer, and Custer himself observed that his days at the Academy might be studied by future cadets as an example to be avoided.

Nobody has yet managed to explain his remarkable ascent. As a lieutenant at Bull Run he was cited for bravery, and by August of that year—two months out of West Point—he was an aide to Brigadier General Philip Kearny.

In the spring of 1862, while serving under General William F. "Baldy" Smith, he ascended quite literally. Professor T. S. C. Lowe, a balloonist, had been employed by the Union to spy on Confederate forces near Richmond, but Lowe reported "clouds of dust," "new earthworks," "a large encampment," and "great activity." Smith therefore directed Custer to take a notebook, pencil, compass, and field glasses, hop into the basket, go up, and see what he could see. This order was received, Custer admits, "with no little trepidation; for although I had chosen the mounted service from preference alone, yet I had a choice as to the character of the mount, and the proposed ride was far more elevated than I had ever desired or contemplated."

There is a photograph of him—it could hardly be anybody else—standing like a mannequin in the gondola, which is elegantly decorated with big stars and vertical stripes. It appears to be thirty or forty feet up and is being restrained by a ground crew hanging on to ropes. The thing was tethered near Baldy Smith's headquarters "like a wild and untamable animal" which Custer approached reluctantly:

Previous to this time I had never even examined a balloon except from a distance. Being interested in their construction, I was about to institute a thorough examination of all its parts, when the aeronaut announced that all was ready. He inquired whether I desired to go up alone, or he should accompany me. My desire, if frankly expressed, would have been not to go up at all; but if I was to go, company was certainly desirable. With an attempt at indifference, I intimated that he might go along. The basket in which we were to be transported was about two feet high, four feet long, and slightly over half as wide, resembling in every respect an ordinary willow basket of the same dimensions, minus the handles. This basket was attached to the cords of the balloon. Stepping inside, my assistant, after giving directions to the men holding the four ropes, told me to take my place in the basket. I complied, and before being fully aware that such was the fact found that we were leaving *terra firma*, and noiselessly, almost imperceptibly, were ascending toward the clouds. The assistant was standing upright, supporting himself by the iron band placed for that purpose about two feet above the top of the basket. I was urged to stand up also. My confidence in balloons at that time was not sufficient, however, to justify such a course, so I remained seated in the bottom of the basket, with a firm hold upon either side. I first turned my attention to the manner in which the basket had been constructed. To me it seemed fragile indeed, and not intended to support a tithe of the weight then imposed upon it. The interstices in the sides and bottom seemed immense, and the further we receded from the earth the larger they seemed to become, until I almost imagined one might tumble

through. I interrogated my companion as to whether the basket was
actually and certainly safe. He responded affirmatively; at the same
time, as if to confirm his assertion, he began jumping up and down. . . .

The balloon reached an altitude of about one thousand feet by which time
Custer had somewhat regained his confidence. To his right he could see the
York River flowing into Chesapeake Bay, to his left the James, and between
them the theater of operations for two great armies. With field glasses—
whenever the balloon momentarily stabilized—he could distinguish the outlines of earthworks, tents, and heavy guns "peering sullenly through the em-
brasures."

He himself was observed. Soldiers gathered around their entrenchments,
staring up at the gigantic balloon. Why didn't they shoot at him? They knew
he was spying, he was within artillery range, and improvised platforms could
have elevated the trajectory of cannon balls. Yet they did nothing except
gawk, as though transfixed by the apparition.

Baldy Smith thought the survey useful and ordered him aloft almost every
day until the Confederates retreated.

In May of the same year during the struggle for Richmond he was noticed
by General McClellan. It had become imperative to cross the Chickahominy,
but the bridge was gone and the Confederates held the opposite bank. Mc-
Clellan's chief engineer needed to know if the stream could be forded so he
turned to Custer who jumped in and waded across—a large, slow target. If
one rebel had been alert he would have caught a bullet in the chest. He knew
this, yet it is said that he leaped into the stream without pausing to remove his
tunic. In 1876 General McClellan wrote to his widow: "He was reported to
me as having accomplished an act of desperate gallantry. . . . I sent for him
at once, and, after thanking him, asked what I could do for him. He seemed
to attach no importance to what he had done, and desired nothing. Whereupon I asked him if he would like to come upon my staff as Captain. He gladly
accepted, and remained with me until I was relieved of my command."

During that ferocious summer he killed a man—probably his first. At
White Oak Swamp his regiment under the command of Colonel Averill hit
and broke the enemy position. Custer began chasing an officer mounted on a
thoroughbred. In a letter to his sister Lydia Ann he confided that it was the
most exciting sport he had ever known: "I selected him as my game. . . ."
They jumped a rail fence and Custer became increasingly excited. He yelled
at the rebel to surrender but got no response, so he fired. Nothing happened.
He fired again. The Confederate reeled in the saddle, hung on for a moment,
and fell to the ground. Custer rode past him in search of other game and some
time later saw the riderless horse, which he recognized by a red morocco

breast strap. "I have him yet and intend to keep him. The saddle, which I also retain, is a splendid one, covered with black morocco and ornamented with silver nails."

A lieutenant who witnessed the shooting said the Confederate officer got to his feet, turned around, threw up both hands and died with blood gushing from his mouth. Custer wrote to Lydia: "It was his own fault; I told him twice to surrender. . . ."

Who this affluent rebel was, who rode to war with such sumptuous equipment, nobody knows.

Not only did Custer pick up an expensive, ornate saddle and a thoroughbred, he got the victim's unusual double-edged sword—its blade engraved in Spanish: *No me saques sin razon; no me envaines sin honor.* That is, draw me not without reason nor sheathe me without honor. Because the engraving is in Spanish this blade always is described as Toledo steel; but after going over it with a jeweler's loupe the eminent Custer historian, Lawrence Frost, could find nothing to verify this. Indeed, close to the hilt were a few nearly obliterated letters which he read as Solingen—the name of a German sword-smith. The blade is about three inches longer and half an inch wider than the standard cavalry weapon and weighs very nearly twice as much, indicating that the Confederate must have been a big, powerful man. Custer himself stood less than six feet and was thin, but the fact that he carried and used this sword seems to substantiate the legend of his physical strength. However, the size of it is less interesting than his occasional habit of buckling it on while reenacting the enemy's death.

He liked swords and apparently collected them with the innocent pleasure of those who collect cognac bottles or postage stamps. One of these weapons, which Mr. Frost acquired, has an unusually short blade with an ivory-channeled grip, the pommel consisting of a gold-plated lion's head "with ruby-like eyes." It probably was made in England and might have belonged to one of his ancestors. Then there is a militia officer's sword with a mother-of-pearl grip and a brass pommel in the shape of a knight's helmet. It dates from the mid-nineteenth century and was manufactured in Chicopee, Massachusetts, but that is all Mr. Frost could find out.

Frederick Van de Water discerned a "precocious ruthlessness" in Custer's harsh cheekbones and raptorial profile. No flexibility, no hint of a contemplative nature. This was the face of the archetypal swordsman, with deep-laired challenging eyes above a rapaciously curved nose. Several of G. A. C.'s associates no doubt would concur. One, identified only as a gentleman who accompanied him through the Black Hills, noted that he had a tenacious memory and paid close attention to detail, but what he assimilated served only his memory, not his mind: "He was no philosopher; he could reel off facts from his mind better than he could analyze or mass them. He was not a student, nor a deep thinker. He loved to take part in events rather than to brood over them."

His Civil War orderly, Joseph Fought, writing about their experiences in 1863, recalled a determined leader who was at the same time curiously diffident. Soon after the battle of Aldie, Custer approached with a paper in his hand. "I have been made a Brigadier General," he said.

Fought replied: "The deuce you have."

"Yes," Custer said, and he read the paper aloud.

Fought shook hands with him.

"How am I going to get something to show my rank?" Custer asked.

"Well," Fought said, "the rebels have just gone through here and have robbed and threatened everybody. But I will see what I can do."

Late that night, according to the orderly's memoirs: "I found an old Jew and in his place he had a box of things belonging to a uniform and some stars. I bought two, then went back and found the Captain in his room at Headquarters. He was glad to have the stars—but who would sew them on? And where could we get a needle and thread? I scratched around and got them, and sewed them on, one on each corner of his collar."

Fought also mentions Custer leading a charge against a rebel force outnumbering his own five-to-one. Such recklessness appears suicidal, like the mad charges of Indian warriors who called to each other that it was a good day to die. He seems to have been similarly fatalistic.

"I have never prayed as others do," he once wrote to his wife. "Yet, on the eve of every battle in which I have been engaged, I have never omitted to pray inwardly, devoutly. Never have I failed to commend myself to God's keeping, asking Him to forgive my past sins, and to watch over me while in danger. . . . After having done so all anxiety for myself, here or hereafter, is dispelled. I feel that my destiny is in the hands of the Almighty. This belief, more than any other fact or reason, makes me brave and fearless as I am."

During the battle near White House Station, Virginia, an enlisted man was shot through the heart. "He was even then in the death-struggle, but I could not bear the thought of his being struck again, so rushed forward, and picking him up, bore him to a place of safety. . . ."

Maybe this absolute lack of regard for his own skin contributed to his quick climb up the ladder; such impetuous acts as leaping into the Chickahominy and darting beyond the line to rescue a dying soldier could not be ignored. These might not be qualities required of a senior commandant, but on lower levels an officer is judged personally by his men and they will be influenced by his deportment.

While he served on McClellan's staff his natural exuberance blossomed into what could only be called flamboyance. The Army at that time was less totalitarian—or at least less standardized—than it is now, particularly in the matter of clothing. At West Point a cadet wearing unauthorized gear would be skinned, but a private on active duty might not even be reprimanded. Officers in the field enjoyed still more freedom. Custer took advantage of this. He began to wear a tightly fitted hussar jacket, gold lace on his pants, and rebel boots. One staff member likened him to a circus rider. Fought recalled him wearing a dark blue sailor shirt that he got from a gunboat on the James, a bright red tie, a velveteen jacket with gold loops on the sleeve, and a Confederate hat.

About this hat there remains some question. During the battle for Aldie his wild charge took him so deep inside Confederate ranks that he was lucky to get out and he attributed his escape to the fact that they mistook him for one of their own, not because he wore a rebel hat but because it looked like one. Whatever he had on his head, it was not a regulation Federal hat. He wore it because his pale skin burned easily and a regulation hat did not give enough protection, so it was practical, but he did like the rakish set of it above those reddish-gold curls dripping almost to his shoulders.

He insisted that his costume, especially the cherry necktie, had a purpose. He wanted the troops to recognize him, to know that he was with them, not cowering behind the lines. And of the manifold accusations slung around his neck, timidity never was one. He rode in front—always—and at Gettysburg more than one-fourth of the luckless wretches who followed him were killed or wounded. Another time he led four hundred volunteers on a saber charge against an entire Confederate division and lost eighty-six men: it was theatrical, audacious, and it stopped the rebel advance, which was the intent, but military analysts believe that cautious defensive maneuvering would have accomplished the same thing at less cost.

Like Crazy Horse, he almost always escaped unhurt. In a skirmish near Brandy Station he was cut by shrapnel. Otherwise he charged through the Civil War with nothing worse than a touch of influenza or poison oak.

Between assaults on the enemy he continued his assault on Elizabeth "Libbie" Bacon of Monroe, Michigan, whom he had first seen when he was ten years old. A neighbor said he got occasional jobs working for the Bacon family in order to hang around Libbie. "He was not received in her home. He was of good character but the family just couldn't see him." The reason being that her father was a judge, his father was a blacksmith. "They were quite ordinary people, no intellectual interests, very little schooling."

During October of 1861 he spent a while in Monroe on leave and there occurred perhaps the most traumatic day of his life. His behavior so embarrassed everyone concerned that just what happened will never be clear, but there is no doubt that he had been drinking and that he lurched past the house of Judge Daniel Bacon—reeling, staggering, vomiting, falling on his ear, etc. Somehow, possibly crawling, he got back to his sister's house where he disintegrated and finally awoke to see Lydia on her knees praying for his deliverance from old Demon Rum.

Whether he was appalled by Lydia on her knees, or the remembrance of what he had done, or perhaps understood that he did not have the stomach for booze—whatever the reason he never again took a drink, not even wine with supper. When asked what he would like to drink he would use the circumlocution "Aldernay," which is a breed of cattle named for an island in the English Channel. In other words, he would take a glass of milk.

At this same time he renounced profanity, but here he was less successful. From that day on he swore very seldom, only once in a while, and without vigor, which was uncharacteristic.

Whether Lydia lectured him about gambling is not known. Probably she did. By instinct he was a gambler so it was impossible for him to quit entirely, but he tried. His struggle sounds like a textbook exercise in Protestant sin and redemption. In December of 1869 he gave Elizabeth a New Year's Resolution in writing that he would cease and desist, as long as he was married, to play cards or any other game of chance for money. This was eight years after Lydia shamed and scolded him, which means he was still at it. By 1871 he was momentarily on top of the devil, having spent two hours inside a casino without feeling the urge. "You often said I could never give it up. But I have always said I could give up anything—except you."

After much discreet, circuitous correspondence he managed to persuade Elizabeth's father that he was not a bad sort and that his intentions were honorable. She was allowed to communicate with him:

"Oh, I scarce know how to write to a gentleman. . . ."

The wedding approaches. She writes to cousin Rebecca Richmond: "I am going to Detroit to have my dresses made, and my underclothes made on the machine. I am sending to New York for my silks. . . ."

She asks Custer to wear his parade uniform for the ceremony.

She plans her wedding gown: pea-green silk looped with yellow military braid. Green silk veil. She will hold a bouquet of red roses tied with a yellow cord. She will not require a personal maid after they are married, but will need a colored housekeeper.

February 9, 1864. A few minutes after 6 P.M. they were united in Monroe's First Presbyterian Church by Reverend Erasmus J. Boyd assisted by Reverend D. C. Mattoon. Custer dressed to the eyebrows. Gold braid. Gold buttons. Gold epaulets. Blue frock coat. Lightning-rod pants. Cousin Rebecca wrote to her sister that Libbie wore "rich white rep silk with deep points and extensive trail, bertha of point lace. Veil floated back from a bunch of orange blossoms fixed above the brow." Why she gave up the pea-green for traditional white is not explained.

The ceremony passed off to everyone's satisfaction, after which the couple departed for Cleveland en route to New York, thence to Washington and military headquarters on the Rapidan. Wedding gifts were left on display and Rebecca itemized them as meticulously as a pawnbroker: "Silver Dinner Service from the 1st Vermont Cavalry, Silver Tea Sett, 7 pieces, 7th Michigan Cavalry. Silver card-case, card receiver, syrup cup, sugar spoons, berry spoons, thimble (gold-lined), napkin-ring. Two white silk fans, sandal wood. Mrs. Browning's Poems; 'Whispers to a Bride'; 'Female Poets.' Knit breakfast shawl; Mosaic chess-stand of Grand Rapids Marble. . . ."

From Howlett's Hill, New York, the bride wrote to her father that while visiting relatives they danced in the kitchen: ". . . I had to sit right down on the floor to laugh to see Uncle Ben and Aunt Eliza dance their old-fashioned way, it was too amusing to see them bounding up and down."

On the train to Washington she met General Grant. Richard Henry Dana, who met Grant on another occasion, noted "a slightly seedy look." Colonel Charles Wainwright described him as "stumpy, slouchy & Western-looking—very ordinary." Elizabeth thought him ordinary yet not unattractive, with sandy hair and greenish-blue eyes, and most considerate. He went out on the platform to smoke his cigar because he did not want to offend her.

In Baltimore the newlyweds attended a show where "the great comedian Clarke" sent the bridegroom into laughing fits, and Libbie remarked in a note to her mother that she felt like a red-cheeked Dutch milkmaid beside the city girls. She enjoyed old General Sickles: "He does not use his cork leg but goes on crutches. He is very agreeable, especially to the ladies."

Then there is Abe Lincoln:

> . . . the gloomiest, most painfully careworn looking man I ever saw. We have sat in a box opposite him at the theatre several times, and reports of his careworn face are not at all exaggerated. . . . He—the President—shook hands with me, as with everyone, and I felt quite satisfied and was passing on, but it seems I was to be honored by his Highness. At mention of my name he took my hand again very cordially and said, "So this is the young woman whose husband goes into a charge with a whoop and a shout. Well, I'm told he won't do so any more."
>
> I replied I hoped he would. "Oh," said the prince of jokers, "then you want to be a widow, I see." He laughed. . . .

War separates them, but Custer writes almost every day: "When I think of the sacrifices you have made for me, the troubles and trials you have endured to make me happy, the debt of gratitude you have placed me under, my heart almost fails me to think I have only the devotion of my life to offer you in return. . . . Loving so fine a being truly and devotedly as I do, it seems impossible that I ever should or could be very wicked." Elizabeth responds to this and other such declarations. "Swept along as I am in the current of your eventful life I can still stop to realize that your history is simply marvelous. Every event seems to fit into every other event like the blocks in a child's puzzle. Does it not seem strange to you?"

In the spring of 1864 he continued his bravura performance during the so-called Wilderness Campaign, leaving one-third of his men *hors de combat*. Yet, just as his regiment earlier had stopped a division, now his brigade mortally slashed General Jeb Stuart's Confederates. Stuart himself died with a bullet in the stomach.

On and on goes the slaughter. Custer brushes his teeth with salt, treats his wavy hair with oil of cinnamon, compulsively washes his hands.

Elizabeth writes to her parents from Washington about ambulances passing with flag-draped coffins, government hearses, wounded soldiers in the streets. She mentions that during one battle he lost everything except his toothbrush, which must mean that he habitually carried it in a pocket. "He brushes his teeth *after every meal*. I always laugh at him for it, and for washing his hands so frequently."

She is terrified that he will be killed. She passes the afternoon with a box of watercolors: "If you had come in to-day you would have found your little wife in a common, rather short dress—no hoops—and hair tucked up, busy painting. I cant sit at my easel with hoops on so I become rather primitive in style."

One day she meets her bridegroom at Harper's Ferry and next day from camp he writes: "My dear little Army Crow—following me around. . . ."

She describes to the folks at home a Virginia mansion where they are billeted. "Mother, if once you had colored servants you would never want any other. Mrs. Glass used to have 19, now she has but two, and has to do without many things we think indispensable. It is so pleasant here. . . ."

Her husband leads a cavalry charge while she waits at the mansion: "I have a lovely little horse. . . . I jumped a ditch with it yesterday."

The butchering continues. Not many Civil War officers worried about losses if an objective was gained. On June 3, 1864, at Cold Harbor the Union leadership sacrificed seven thousand men in a few hours. Sherman remarked in a letter to Elizabeth years afterward that the object of war is to produce results, a statement which cannot be argued. Even so, Custer lost more men during the Civil War than almost any other commandant. Wherever he met the enemy he advanced like a fighting cock.

The impression he gave of himself, somewhat deliberately, was that of a preposterous figure, very nearly comic—which he was, and which he was not. Behind the pranks and the outrageous costume rode a killer. Ordered by Grant and Sheridan to execute guerrillas without trial, he obeyed with no regret. At Front Royal, Virginia, on September 23, 1864, Federals caught six of Mosby's Rangers. Mosby—the Gray Ghost who came close to killing Reno on the Middlebury road a few months later.

Somebody shot four of Mosby's men while the band played "The Dead March." The other two—Carter and Overby—were hanged, and to Overby's dangling corpse a note was pinned:

Such is the Fate of All Mosby's Gang
Hung in Retaliation for the Death
of Lieut. McMaster, 2nd U. S. Cav.

Jay Monaghan in a heavily documented if rather cloying biography of Custer implies that the Federal unit responsible for executing these men was commanded by Col. Peter Stagg. In either case, Mosby thought Custer did it.

Three weeks after the execution a seventh butternut guerrilla was strung up by Brigadier William Powell.

Mosby sent word of these atrocities to Robert E. Lee, adding that he meant to hang an equal number of Custer's men. Lee endorsed the savage decision: "Respectfully referred to the honorable Secretary of War. . . . I have directed Colonel Mosby, through his adjutant, to hang an equal number. . . ."

To which the honorable Secretary, J. A. Seddon, added that General Lee's directive was "cordially approved."

Thus, at Rectortown, Virginia, twenty-seven prisoners from Custer's brigade were told to draw slips of paper from a hat. The seven losers were then escorted toward Berryville on Winchester Turnpike because Mosby wanted to hang them as close as possible to Custer's headquarters. It was a black, rainy night. Along the road one prisoner escaped, allegedly because both he and the guard were Masons. Five of the other six being properly dispatched, a miscalculation was observed: The lynching party had not brought enough rope. A logical solution was to shoot the last victim, so a ranger drew his pistol and fired; the hammer snapped but nothing else happened and a moment later the Yankee bounded out of sight.

Why this prisoner had not been tied up is curious, especially since one man already had escaped. It sounds as though the executioners found their job distasteful and gave the doomed men every chance. Monaghan believes two others got away or survived by feigning death. Whatever the exact truth, Mosby pinned a note to one of the dangling bodies:

These men have been hung in retaliation
for an equal number of Colonel Mosby's men,
hung by order of Gen'l Custer at Fort Royal.
Measure for measure.

In October of 1864 young General Custer commanded a division for the first time, his opponent being his former West Point roommate, Thomas "Tex" Rosser.

Custer charged. The Confederate line broke. Rosser's supply train, ambulances, and private wardrobe wagon were captured. Custer thought it would be amusing to try on Rosser's uniforms, which did not fit, as he knew they would not, because Rosser was a large man.

Soon a message arrived:

Dear Fanny,
You may have made me take a few steps back to-day, but I'll be even with you to-morrow. Please accept my good-wishes & this little gift—a pair of your drawers captured at Trevillian St.

Tex

After shipping Rosser's gold-laced Confederate gray coat to Elizabeth, Custer replied:

Dear Friend,
Thanks for setting me up in so many new things, but would you please direct your tailor to make the coat-tails of your next uniform a trifle shorter.

Best Regards,
G.A.C.

This relationship is as easy to understand as it is astonishing: two professional soldiers—good friends—attempting to destroy each other. Back and forth they fought. If one felt obliged to retreat he abandoned the field with courtly grace.

Union troops managed to round up a Confederate beef herd, but Rosser counterattacked so nimbly that Custer himself had to cut a switch and join the cattle drive. And in a letter to Elizabeth he chortles over the fact that he has captured a raccoon and a squirrel from his roommate's menagerie. It sounds less like the Civil War than a tactical game at West Point.

The Confederate general Joseph Kershaw, waiting at Custer's headquarters to surrender on April 6, 1865, noted his arrival. "A spare, lithe, sinewy figure; bright, dark, quick-moving blue eyes; florid complexion, light, wavy curls, high cheek-bones, firm-set teeth—a jaunty close-fitting cavalry jacket, large top-boots, Spanish spurs, golden aiguillettes . . . a quick nervous movement, an air telling of the habit of command—announced the redoubtable Custer. . . ."

He worked longer and harder than normal men. He could demand almost anything of his body and it would respond. His chief of staff, Colonel Edward Whitaker, observed him one night just before the war ended; he was sitting upright on a log with a coffee cup in one hand and his eyes closed, fast asleep.

In Wilmer McLean's home at Appomattox when the papers were signed— Lee ensconced like an emperor behind a marble-topped table in the center of the room, Grant in a rumpled uniform at a little pine table—as soon as their signatures declared an end to those tumultuous years the ambience changed. The rebel Fitzhugh Lee, another of Custer's classmates, walked up to him outside McLean's home; they embraced and fell to the ground, wrestling like schoolboys.

Mementos of Appomattox were sold and for two ten-dollar gold coins Sheridan bought the pine table which he gave to Custer, telling him it was a present for Elizabeth. Custer rode away with this important table balanced upside down on his head.

Jefferson Davis once remarked lightly while chatting with a great-granddaughter of Benjamin Franklin: "War between North and South? My dear Madam, inconceivable! Two friendly nations, rather, living side by side. . . ." Now this indivisible nation was again stitched together, yet it remained an uncomfortable alliance—the suture could very nearly be traced on a map—and Ulysses Grant directed Sheridan to do something about the restless Southwest. Little Phil ordered four thousand troops under Major General Wesley Merritt to San Antonio, another four thousand under Custer to Houston.

Elizabeth went along. It was a tedious trip, first by rail, then by steamboat down the Mississippi to New Orleans, up the Red River to Alexandria, overland to their destination. The last segment of this journey being especially boring, jolting, and at times oppressive, Custer arranged for his wife's comfort by ordering a spring wagon to be rain-proofed, embellished with curtains, and drawn by a team of four matched grays. The seats were altered so she might lie down if she felt tired. There was a pocket for her shawl, books, and needlework. Some congenial soldier fitted a canteen with a leather jacket and stitched *Lady Custer* into it with the yellow silk used by saddlers. One result of such solicitude was that Elizabeth became known to enlisted men as the Queen of Sheba.

Custer did not know this part of the South. In a letter to his father-in-law from Alexandria he wrote that it reminded him less of Virginia than of Uncle Tom's cabin. He saw a Negress whose back was scarred by five hundred lashes and he reflected that if the war accomplished nothing else it had at least abolished this evil. Yet he himself resorted to the lash. Congress prohibited flogging as a disciplinary measure on August 5, 1861, but Custer seems to have felt that this proscription did not apply to G. A. C. He announced twenty-five lashes and a shaved head for a man who was caught stealing fruit, and he served up the same punishment for equally trivial crimes on other occasions.

> Headquarters
> Second Cavalry Division
> September 14th, 1865.

Captain Davidson, *Commanding Provost Guard*:
You will at once shave the head and lash G. Darr, Company D, Twelfth Illinois Cavalry, and H. Cure, First Iowa . . .

Two soldiers half-starved during the interminable march to Houston got forty lashes apiece for butchering a calf, and Lt. Thomas Cogley wrote in *History of the Seventh Indiana Cavalry Volunteers* that the illegal order was carried out despite the protests of subordinate officers: "This outrage won for Custer the lasting hatred of every decent man in the command."

An Iowa veteran, commenting twenty years afterward, said that during the Civil War he had camped in Missouri snow a foot deep, found himself frozen to the earth in Arkansas mud, wrestled vermin in Southern trenches, and been doubled up with cramps, but not until he rode through Texas in peacetime with General Custer did he face true hardship. He said that when they started westward from Alexandria the men were instructed to report in ranks with their coats buttoned, and to carry a carbine, revolver, seventy rounds of ammunition, and a saber. "The temperature was about 120 degrees, and there wasn't a rebel in the land. When the division reached a narrow bridge that had to be crossed in single file, Custer and staff stood on either side the line with sabers drawn, and where a soldier overcome with heat had fastened his carbine, revolver or sword to the saddle, they clipped it off and let it fall into the stream. The arms were charged to the soldier. . . . Many a poor fellow I have seen with head shaved to the scalp, tied to a wagon wheel and whipped like a dog, for stealing a piece of fresh meat or a peach from an orchard by the wayside."

G.A.C. himself rode unencumbered by equipment and frequently changed horses. The troops often saw him prancing ahead on a fresh, powerful mount.

Emmet West wrote in *History and Reminiscences of the Second Wisconsin Cavalry* that he did not think it strange the men hated Custer. "I can compare his inhuman treatment of the men under him that summer to nothing I saw or experienced in four years' service, but the inhuman treatment of the Union prisoners at Cahaba by Col. Jones."

The food on this trip could have been improved. Reports speak of hairy hog jowls, maggots, bread like stone. Some cavalrymen preferred the raw corn allocated to their horses. Officers ate reasonably well, at least by comparison, and the general's table was decently supplied—often through his own efforts with a rifle or shotgun. He would halt the entire column if he spotted a covey of quail.

There was no reason to occupy this territory, said Emmet West, because there were no armed rebels. Men sickened and died, everybody suffered, nothing was accomplished. "It was simply a great picnic excursion for General Custer. . . ."

Elizabeth in her renovated spring wagon was aware of these ragged, sullen troops and she did not want to be an inconvenience. Every morning Custer delayed the march until she was ready. She worried about this; four thousand men might be held up while she looked for a hairpin.

Overnight a heavy dew accumulated in east Texas. "My husband lifted me out of the wagon, when reveillé sounded, into the tent, and by the light of a tallow candle I had my bath and got into my clothes. . . . Then, to keep my shoes from being soaked with the wet grass, I was carried to the dining-tent, and lifted upon my horse afterward."

The division was stationed for a while at Hempstead, fifty miles northwest of Houston, and the local gentry sometimes invited him to go hunting—invitations he happily accepted. Each hunter brought his own pack of hounds, a spectacle which delighted Custer. He was entranced to learn that despite the multitude of dogs and horns each animal would respond to the horn of its master. So he bought himself a horn and practiced, and five dogs which had been presented to him would arrange themselves "in an admiring and sym-

pathetic semicircle," according to Elizabeth, "accompanying all his practic-
ing by tuning their voices until they reached the same key." One member of
the Hempstead pack was a greyhound named Byron, "a most lordly dog," she
remarks. "The tribute that a woman pays to beauty in any form, I gave to
Byron, but I never cared much for him. A greyhound's heart could be put
into a thimble. Byron cared for the general as much as his cold soul could care
for any one. . . ."

The general who would order an enlisted man lashed for a negligible of-
fense could be uncommonly solicitous of a dog. They were given a female
pointer named Ginnie and one morning they learned she had given birth to
seven pups under the Negro quarters at the rear of the house. Custer thought
this was not a good place for Ginnie to nurse them, but instead of directing an
orderly to move the pups he himself crawled under the house, which was set
on low pilings, and tenderly handed them out one at a time. Ginnie's bed was
in the hall, but Custer decided this was inadequate. He placed the mother and
seven pups on his marital bed. And Elizabeth reports in *Tenting on the Plains*
that one night he paced the bedroom for hours with a sick puppy in his arms.

On October 30 the command moved to Austin where it remained until
mustered out of service. Occasionally the troops would be asked to help local
authorities enforce the law, otherwise they had nothing to do. Almost every
day the general took his lady for a ride through the countryside. Frequently
they would be accompanied by a regimental band and they would pause for
lunch on some hilltop. Atop Mt. Bonnell, which Elizabeth misnamed "Brun-
nel," they enjoyed the view while listening to such popular numbers as the
"Anvil Chorus." She remarks that the music "descended through the valley
grandly."

Once they visited the state insane asylum with a band which could play
music appropriate for dancing. There, she says, "we watched with wonder
the quadrille of an insane eight."

His favorite excursion was to the Texas State School for the Deaf. Elizabeth writes in *Tenting* that he stared at the supple fingers and wrists of the
deaf children, "and as their instructor spelt the passions of love, hatred, remorse and reverence on his fingers, one little girl represented them by singu-
larly graceful gestures, charming him, and filling his eyes with tears. . . ."

J. P. Dunn states in *Massacres of the Mountains* that Indians and deaf-
mutes who have been brought together experimentally are able to communicate through ideographic signs, from which Dunn concludes that certain
signs must be the natural expression of thought and thus might be a more
natural method of communication than vocal language. For instance, peace
or friendship is made clear by an open hand to show that one does not hold a

weapon—which quite probably is how the custom of shaking hands originated. One may characterize a white man by pulling a finger across the forehead to mark the brim of a European hat. Who could mistake the significance
of a finger twirled beside the head?

What Custer learned from his visits to the school for deaf children and how
well he utilized the knowledge when he dealt with Indians can only be conjectured, but he seems to have become fairly good at this mute speech. Not long
after being stationed in Texas he used his hands to address a council of Sioux,
Apache, and Cheyenne chiefs in Kansas and his oration was understood. And
the Arikara scout Red Star, who got to know him later in Dakota Territory,
thought he expressed himself pretty well.

At the end of 1865 when the army of occupation was dismantled and the
troops began leaving Texas a great many soldiers bade good-bye to this paradoxical man without regret. Emmet West departed happily on foot, walking
a hundred miles to the town of Brenham where mechanical transportation
was available to points north and east. Custer did not accompany these
marchers so they did not have to walk all the way to Brenham four abreast,
"and for slight offenses have heads shaved and receive twenty-five lashes. We
never saw more of Custer nor had any desire to."

If the general perceived this hatred he did not allude to it. Men being
released from service always were glad to go home and that was that. On
Christmas Day, 1865, he wore a Santa Claus suit while distributing gifts to
members of his staff.

Before long he, too, had been mustered out of the Volunteer Army, ex-
changing his $8,000 major general's pay for the $2,000 of a Regular Army
captain. This reduction in pay and prestige must have caused him to reflect
upon the years ahead; already he was twenty-six. He decided to look around
Washington and New York for possible employment as a civilian. Elizabeth
would go back to Michigan until he made up his mind about their future.

Benteen wrote that after the general's departure from Texas "stupendous
frauds" were uncovered in contracts he had authorized for grain, hay, etc.
These swindles were revealed by a man Custer did not like, who did not like
him, and who was soon to become his immediate superior: Lt. Col. Samuel
Sturgis. According to Benteen, Sturgis notified whoever was responsible for
supervising such contracts and they were annulled, but that did not end the
business. Custer found out what Sturgis had done and began laying plans for
revenge.

The virulent antipathy of these officers for one another was sensed by enlisted men—dividing sympathies, poisoning their spirit, weakening the
pride that should have held them together. Although the Seventh Cavalry

had not yet come into existence, quite a few men who served with Custer in Texas would later be assigned to that regiment, and most historians believe this bitter legacy contributed to the debacle in Montana.

While scouring Washington for employment he learned that he might obtain a post as Foreign Minister. It is not clear just who made this promise, how definite it was, or to which nation he might be sent, but without doubt he regarded it as a possibility. Meantime, with Elizabeth in Michigan, he had to amuse himself. He attended musicales and plays, visited an art gallery to view the scandalous "Oriental Princess"—which he thought a superb piece of work, although shocking—and in the company of several West Point friends he flirted with whores, calling them Nymphes du Pavé.

He wrote to Elizabeth about attending a masked ball dressed as the Devil: "My costume was rich and elegant. Cape and coat, black velvet with gold lace. Pants the same, reaching only to the thighs. Red silk tights with not even drawers underneath. Red velvet cape with two upright red feathers, for horns. Black shoes with pointed toes upturned. Handsome belt. Mask, black silk." He loved masquerade, on stage or in the street. Theatrical tragedy made his eyes water. At comedies he all but lost control: "Last night I saw Joseph Jefferson. . . . You know how I fairly squeal when laughter becomes impossible. I laughed till my sides ached. Oh, he was splendid."

In New York he met celebrities: "A very distinguished breakfast was arranged. . . . Among those who had accepted invitations were Bancroft, the historian; Wm. Cullen Bryant . . ."

Meanwhile he had been offered a commission as Major General of Caballeros by Porfirio Díaz and Benito Juárez, who thought he might be just the hombre to oust Maximilian. Custer became enthusiastic. It sounded exciting. The pay was $16,000 a year in gold. He was to recruit and lead a force of mercenaries, salaries to be paid by the Mexican nationals. Grant sent a letter to the Mexican ambassador in Washington, Don Matías Romero: "This will introduce to your acquaintance Gen'l Custer, who rendered such distinguished service as a cavalry officer. . . ."

He requested a one-year leave of absence in order to become a south-of-the-border soldier of fortune, but President Johnson did not approve. Permission denied.

This was disappointing. However, on July 28, 1866, he was commissioned lieutenant colonel of the newly created Seventh Cavalry with headquarters at Fort Riley, Kansas. He thought he might do better. He wrote to the president, asking for a commission as full colonel, not necessarily of the Seventh. He did not even insist on a cavalry unit; the one proviso attached to his request was that he should be assigned to a white regiment.

He could be friendly with individual blacks, browns, reds, or yellows, but he held a visceral conviction that as a race the white race was what mattered: "I am in favor of elevating the negro to the extent of his capacity and intelligence, and of our doing everything in our power to advance the race morally and mentally as well as physically, also socially. But I am opposed to making this advance by correspondingly debasing any portion of the white race. As to trusting the negro of the Southern States with the most sacred and responsible privilege—the right of suffrage—I should as soon think of elevating an Indian Chief to the Popedom of Rome."

Benteen wrote to photographer D. F. Barry in 1895 that Virginians had no love for Custer, not because of any Civil War success in Virginia but because—and here Benteen grows evasive: "You, Barry, would be—well, horrified, if I'd tell you what I've learned here from an old Va. classmate. . . ."

Another letter became explicit:

It was notorious throughout the Cav. Corps Army of the Potomac that Gen. Custer used to sleep with his cook, who was one of the blackest, most monkeyish looking African woman ever turned out. (The Latin maxim *de gustibus non est disputandum* comes in here)—only it shows monstrous poor taste in the General; only a trifle of economy I suppose with him—and everyone who knew him, knew that he was penurious to the fullest extent of its meaning. This mixing with Africans was carried out on his campaign with the 7th Cav. in Dakota.

Such things wouldn't be thought of by the many knowing them, provided Mrs. Custer—who was aware of many of his derelictions in this regard, and others—did not attempt to throw such a gorgeous mantle of saintliness around him—and at the same time cause so much mud to be thrown on the character of his betters.

Historian Robert Utley represents Capt. Benteen as a man afflicted with "monumental vindictiveness and cancerous bitterness toward almost all his old comrades." This may be an exaggeration, but not much, and life with Custer no doubt exacerbated whatever vindictiveness came naturally to this capable, moon-faced officer who could bite like a copperhead.

As the general and his lady both unconsciously testify in their memoirs— to say nothing of Benteen—stereotypes prevailed. Elizabeth wrote that black infantrymen who guarded Fort Riley during the Seventh Cavalry's absence were "boisterous, undisciplined creatures" who used the parade ground for a playground, "turning hand-springs all over the sprouting grass. . . ."

Capt. Stephen Jocelyn, stationed at Fort Du Chesne, observed that black trumpeters were easy to teach, "and several of the colored troops from the Ninth Cavalry had the usual excellent negro ear for music."

Speech patterns differed. To a white veteran a new soldier was a "recruit";

to a black veteran he was a "young soldier." And it is said that blacks customarily repeated the word "sir" three times when responding to an order: "Yes sir, Captain sir, it shall be done, sir."

Despite such differences, according to Erwin Thompson in his study of the Tenth Cavalry at Fort Davis, blacks and whites got along all right. Other scholars doubt this. Peter Olch concludes that black units "were the targets of searing racial prejudice from within and outside the army." Secretary of War Belknap, after visiting racially mixed posts, remarked on the good conduct and splendid military aspect of all the troops—which quite probably was so. There is hardly a soldier on earth, regardless of color, dumb enough to start a fight when the Secretary of War is present.

Journalist Theodore Davis said they were enthusiastic Indian fighters who seemed to enjoy the sport and won the respect of everybody who watched them in the field. Eighteen of them earned the Congressional Medal of Honor.

Col. Richard Dodge said that Indians did not like to fight black troops and never scalped them, but he could not find out why. All he ever got by way of explanation was: "Buffalo soldier no good, heap bad medicine."

Just how they acquired this nickname is disputed. According to an 1872 letter from an Army wife: "because their heads are so much like the matted cushion that is between the horns of the buffalo." However the name originated, they were not offended by it. Thompson reports that they felt proud to be called buffalo soldiers.

In any event, after Custer was denied permission to operate as a mercenary in Mexico, and his petition for a full colonelcy being rejected, he joined the bright new all-Caucasoid Seventh at Fort Riley; but no sooner had he and Elizabeth unpacked than he was directed, along with every other officer, to face an examining board in Washington. For senior officers this turned out to be little more than a bureaucratic formality enlivened with jokes. General Gibbs, who seems to have been responsible for assembling the regiment, was asked: "When is a lady not a lady?" The correct answer—which he may or may not have known—was: "When she is a little sulky." Junior officers, at least those without much experience, did not get off so easily. Elizabeth, who heard about it afterward, thought the examinations "terribly severe."

While waiting for her husband to return from this examination she busied herself around their new home at Fort Riley, and she wrote letters—immensely detailed letters to relatives and friends. To cousin Rebecca in Grand Rapids she described this fort at the end of the world, the look of the land, the barracks, the nearby town of Junction City where she went to market. The quarters seemed to her almost luxurious.

Our house has a large parlor, my bedroom back of it and dressing room next to that at the end of the hall. We have a back entry and Eliza's room at the rear. Four chambers upstairs. Anna's the front room with a dressing room off from it. Tom's is at the head of the stairs. . . . I have bought Autie a lovely black cane seated & backed arm chair, for him when he returns. I have an oak and green carpet—a green & black tablecloth on a round table and albums, card basket, book rack, & on it; another round table we use for a writing table. Our chairs are quite comfortable and the wood fire in the place makes the room very cheerful. I have lace curtains like mothers and put up like hers. My easel stands by one of the windows and I am just finishing a picture for Autie when he returns, of a bulldog smoking a pipe. . . . Prince Qusosoff nephew of the Saar of Russia (the small dictionary dont say Sar so I cant spell it.) has been on a buffalo hunt. He visited us and so we found his highness the Prince quite like other dutchy boys. . . . We have a set of table croquet and we play nearly every evening. It is so fascinating I know you and Mary would like it. The table is about eight foot long and the wire wickets are placed in the same order as in field croquet. We use marbles for balls. Its charm is that gentlemen like it. It is like billiards I think. We have company all the time. . . .

Just beyond Fort Riley, which was a point of departure for Colorado and the distant coast, lay wind-scoured, dust-whipped plains alive with coyotes, buffalo, and wildly painted Indians. Unfamiliar animals, swirling dust, savages, a tempestuous wind that obliged ladies to sew lead weights in the hems of their skirts, sparks showering from a grindstone, the abrasive scream of sabers being whetted—Elizabeth would remember such things as long as she lived.

Major T. I. McKenny, Inspector General of the Department of Kansas, had been predicting trouble on this frontier. Guard the trains and the mail against Indian attacks, he advised. Stop vigilantes who could not distinguish one tribe from another and who would kill anything resembling an Indian. Only a few more murders would unite these militant people. McKenny had less influence than a chipmunk in a forest fire. He and those who argued as he did were overwhelmed by an indignant, righteous majority.

The *Nebraska City Press* reasoned that for the common good it might be wise to cleanse the plains: "exterminate the whole fraternity of redskins."

The Montana *Post* agreed: "It is high time the sickly sentimentalism about humane treatment and conciliatory measures should be consigned to novel writers, and if the Indians continue their barbarities, wipe them out."

Brigadier General Patrick Connor told Major General Grenville Dodge: "They must be hunted like wolves."

Then, on the morning of December 21, 1866, Captain William Fetterman led eighty men out of Fort Phil Kearny at the base of the Bighorn Mountains in Wyoming. His command did not number precisely eighty. Dunn says eighty-four. Marquis, eighty-three. Other historians list eighty-one. No matter. Capt. Fetterman had been ordered to rescue a train of woodcutters under attack by Red Cloud's Oglalas. Before setting out he was twice warned by the post commandant, Col. Henry Carrington, that he should do nothing except escort the wood train to the fort. Frances Grummond—soon to be a widow—states in her memoir that these instructions "were distinctly and peremptorily given within my hearing."

As Fetterman marched out the gate Col. Carrington jumped up on the sentry walk and ordered the column to halt. He then repeated his instructions quite specifically: "Under no circumstances must you cross Lodge Trail Ridge." These words, Mrs. Grummond says, were heard by everybody.

A few minutes later Carrington realized that Fetterman had not taken along a surgeon, so one was dispatched. This surgeon presently returned to the fort because Fetterman already had crossed Lodge Trail Ridge and it was now impossible to join him.

Fetterman's march ended on a knoll beside U.S. 87 a few miles below Sheridan—less than a hundred miles from Custer's blind alley. Today a rough stone barricade encloses the site. A flagpole stands beside a cairn emblazoned with a bronze shield and a summary of the disaster. One farmhouse can be seen about a mile up the road, otherwise there is nothing to look at except a line of telephone poles. Not many people use the old highway, traffic cruises along I-90 some distance east. Very few tourists leave the freeway to commune with the shade of this arrogant officer who, like Lt. Grattan twelve years earlier, thought a handful of bluecoats could ride straight through the Sioux nation. The black iron gate to this memorial frequently hangs open.

Lt. Fetterman was sucked to death by a stratagem antedating the Punic wars. He met a weak party of Oglalas just out of reach. Naturally he chased them. He almost caught them. A few yards farther—a few more yards. It is said that young Crazy Horse was among these decoys.

Meanwhile, the woodcutters got back safely.

Fetterman could not have been very bright because two weeks earlier the Sioux just about bagged him in a similar ambush. From that experience he learned nothing. He entered the trap again. Why? Because he was new to the frontier, because of constitutional arrogance, perhaps because he had been educated at West Point to assume that one American soldier could handle a dozen savages. And he might possibly have been enraged by the decoys shouting in English: "You sons of bitches!"

Dunn, whose ponderous history of these sanguine days appeared in 1886, claims that many years after the fight he was shown an oak war club bristling with spikes—still clotted with blood, hair, and dried brains—which the Oglalas used on Fetterman's troops. He does not excuse Fetterman, but at the same time he has no very high opinion of Col. Carrington, whom he labels a dress-parade officer. Carrington should not have been assigned to the frontier, says Dunn, he should have been teaching school: "He built a very nice fort, but every attack made on him and his men, during the building, was a surprise. There is nothing to indicate that he ever knew whether there were a thousand or only a hundred Indians within a mile of the fort. He seems to have disapproved of Indians. Perhaps he would have ostracized them socially, if he could have had his way."

Two experienced civilians, James Wheatley and Isaac Fisher, had joined the party in order to try out their new sixteen-shot Henry repeating rifles. These men especially infuriated the Sioux, probably because they punctured a good many of Red Cloud's finest before being dropped. Identification was tentative because their faces were reduced to pudding, and one of them— scholars disagree as to which—had been spitted with 105 arrows.

Except for these two, and a few soldiers gathered around them, it was no battle. Carrington said during a speech at the unveiling of the monument in 1908 that all firing stopped in less than twenty-one minutes. Why he should have paid such attention to his watch under the circumstances is a mystery, but that is what he said. Maybe Dunn was right, he should have been a schoolmaster. He said also that when the firing stopped he assumed, as did his subordinates, that Fetterman had killed or repulsed the Indians—just as the men with Terry and Gibbon assumed from a pall of smoke ahead that Custer was burning the hostile villages. "We could not imagine the real facts. . . ."

Another parallel turned up in the legend of one survivor, the only living thing on the ghastly field. At the Little Bighorn this was Myles Keogh's horse, Comanche. Here it was a badly wounded gray horse from C Company, Dapple Dave.

Sixty-seven bodies were counted after the Sioux disappeared. The rest were found next morning. Fetterman and Capt. Frederick Brown lay side by side, and because each had a bullet hole in the temple it was thought they had blown each other's brains out. After an autopsy, however, the post surgeon concluded that Fetterman had been slashed to death and the hole in his temple probably was a *coup de grace*. Brown, who may have committed suicide, sounds ferocious. So eager was he for a chance to fight and kill savages that he slept in uniform. He had received orders transferring him to Fort Laramie but said he must get a scalp, and joined Fetterman's column without authorization.

John Guthrie was one of the first troopers on the scene. He noted his impressions in a convulsive, agitated style. He wrote that the command lay on the old Holiday coach road near Stoney Creek ford just over a mile from the fort—which is not quite accurate, the true distance being at least twice that far.

The fate of Colonel Fetterman command all my comrades of the detail could see, the Indians on the bluff, the silver flashed with the glorious sunshine, flashed in the hair of the skulking Indians carrying away the clothing of the butchered, with arrows sticking in them, and a number of wolves, hyenas and coyotes hanging about to feast on the flesh of the dead men's bodies. The dead bodies of our friends at the massacre lay out all night and were not touched or disturbed in any way again, and the cavalry horse of Co. C 2nd, those ferocious and devourers of bodies, did not even touch. Another rather peculiar feature in connection with those massacres is that it is thought by some that those wild animals that eat the dead bodies of the Indians are not so apt to disturb the white victims, and this is accounted for by the fact that salt generally permeates the whole system of the white race, and at least seems to protect to some extent even after death, from the practice of wild animals. Twenty four hours after death Dr. Report at Fort detailed we start to load the dead on the ammunition, all of the Fetterman boys huddled together on the small hill and rock some small trees nearly shot away on the old coach road, near the battle field or Massacre Hill, ammunition boxes we packed them, my comrades on top of the boxes terrible cuts left by the Indians, could not tell Cavalry from the Infantry, all dead bodies stripped naked, crushed skulls, with war clubs ears and noses and legs had been cut off, scalps torn away and the bodies pierced with bullets and arrows, wrist feet and ankles leaving each attached by a tendon. We loaded the officers first. Col. Fetterman of the 27th Infantry, Captain Brown of the 18th Infantry and bugler Footer of Co. C 2nd Cavalry were all huddled together near the rocks, Footer's skull crushed in, his body on top of the officers. . . . Sargeant Baker of Co. C 2nd Cavalry, a gunnie sack over his head not scalped, little finger cut off for a gold ring; Lee Bontee the guide found in the brush near by the rest called Little Goose Creek, body full of arrows which had to be broken off to load him. . . . Some had crosses cut on their breasts, faces to the sky, some crosses cut on the back, face to the ground, a mark cut that we could not find out. We walked on top of their internals and did not know it in the high grass. Picked them up, that is their internals, did not know the soldier they belonged to, so you see the cavalry man got an infantry man's gutts and an infantry man got a cavalry man's gutts. . . .

Only one man, bugler Adolph Metzger, had not been touched. His bugle was so badly dented that he must have gone down swinging it like a club, and for some reason the Indians covered his body with a buffalo robe.

Years later an Oglala named Fire Thunder, who had been sixteen at the time, described with eloquent simplicity the Indian trap. He said that after finding a good place to fight they hid in gullies along both sides of the ridge and sent a few men ahead to coax the soldiers out. After a long wait they heard a shot, which meant soldiers were coming, so they held the nostrils of their ponies to keep them from whinnying at the sight of the American horses. Pretty soon the Oglala decoys came into view. Some were on foot, leading their ponies to make the soldiers think the ponies were tired. Soldiers chased them. The air filled with bullets. But all at once there were more arrows than bullets—so many arrows that they looked like grasshoppers falling on the soldiers.

The American horses got loose, Fire Thunder said. Several Indians went after them. He himself did not because he was after wasichus. There was a dog with the soldiers which ran howling up the road toward the fort, but died full of arrows. Horses, dead soldiers, wounded Indians were scattered across the hill "and their blood was frozen, for a storm had come up and it was very cold and getting colder all the time." Then the Indians picked up their wounded and went away. The ground felt solid underfoot because of the cold. That night there was a blizzard.

Colonel Carrington's official report, dated January 3, 1867, confirms trooper Guthrie's unique essay, although Carrington wrote in a dispassionate style typical of government documents:

> The road on the little ridge where the final stand took place was strewn with arrows, arrowheads, scalp poles, and broken shafts of spears.
>
> The arrows that were spent harmlessly from all directions show that the command was suddenly overwhelmed, surrounded, and cut off while in retreat. Not an officer or man survived. A few bodies were found at the north end of the divide over which the road runs just beyond Lodge Trail Ridge.
>
> Nearly all were heaped near four rocks at the point nearest the fort, these rocks inclosing a space about 6 feet square, having been the last refuge for defense. Here were also a few unexpended rounds of Spencer cartridge.
>
> Fetterman and Brown had each a revolver shot in the left temple. . . .
>
> I give some of the facts as to my men, whose bodies I found just at dark, resolved to bring all in, viz:
>
> MUTILATIONS
> Eyes torn out and laid on the rocks.
> Noses cut off.
> Ears cut off.
> Chins hewn off.
> Teeth chopped out.

Joints of fingers cut off.
Brains taken out and placed on rocks, with members of the body.
Entrails taken out and exposed.
Hands cut off.
Feet cut off.
Arms taken out from socket.
Private parts severed . . .

Carrington observes at the end of this catalogue that while his report does not approximate the whole truth, he believes he has said enough. It has been, he remarks, a hard but absolute duty.

Custer noted in *My Life on the Plains* that news of the Fetterman tragedy was met "with universal horror, and awakened a bitter feeling toward the savage perpetrators. The government was implored to inaugurate measures looking to their prompt punishment. This feeling seemed to be shared by all classes."

In his book Custer reproduced a telegram from Sherman to Grant, dated one week after the slaughter, which says in part: "We must act with vindictive earnestness against the Sioux, even to their extermination, men, women, and children. Nothing less will reach the root of the case." If one word of this extraordinary telegram is altered it reads like a message from Eichmann to Hitler.

Three months later, in March of 1867, a government aroused by the Fetterman calamity dispatched Major General Winfield Scott Hancock, erstwhile Thunderbolt of the Grand Army of the Potomac, on a punitive expedition. His target was not Red Cloud's triumphant Oglala horde which—at least for the moment—ruled Wyoming; Hancock went after their allies, the less numerous but more accessible Cheyennes who had been terrorizing homesteaders and obstructing work on the Kansas-Pacific Railroad.

Led by fifteen Delaware scouts plus three frontiersmen—among them Wild Bill Hickok fashionably attired in a jacket of many colors and a ten-gallon hat, his luxuriant mustachios flowing in the prairie breeze—a caval-cade of fourteen hundred soldiers which included Custer's Seventh, the Thirty-seventh Infantry, a battery of the Fourth Artillery, and a pontoon train, accompanied by Mr. Theodore Davis of *Harper's New Monthly Magazine* and Mr. Henry M. Stanley reporting for the New York *Herald*—this creaking armada set forth to pursue, intimidate, and, if necessary, chastise the wily redskins. Custer, who combined pleasure with business whenever possible, took along five of his favorite hounds: Rover, Lu, Sharp, Rattler, and Fanny.

The origin of that resonant word *Cheyenne* was not clear to people of the nineteenth century. Most thought it derived from the French word for dog, *chien*, specifically the female *chienne*, because early French traders discovered this tribe eating dogs; and from that gastronomic practice came the expression dog-soldier for a Cheyenne fighting man.

Cheyennes did eat dogs, but so did quite a few Indians. Journalist Stanley once attended a Brulé feast hosted by Spotted Tail at which a variety of succulent wild meat was displayed: lumps of buffalo, antelope hind quarters, venison, duck, goose, turkey, all of it wonderfully garnished with beans, rice, corn, and herbs. The *pièces de résistance*, though, were three plump puppies "of a dropsical appearance, the hair merely scorched, which had been roasted entire, intestines and all." Stanley felt obliged to sample a puppy, which he describes as brownish in color, resembling porpoise meat, and reflects that if he had been able to overcome his prejudice he might have enjoyed it. Fanny Kelly during her five months as an Oglala captive decided it must have religious significance. Buffalo and venison tasted so much better that she could find no other explanation for eating dogs. Catlin agreed, calling it a truly religious ceremony during which the Indian honors a guest by sacrificing this most faithful companion: "I have seen the master take from the bowl the head of his victim and talk of its former affection and fidelity with tears in his eyes." Venison or buffalo meat, by contrast, must be offered to any guest and signified nothing beyond daily nourishment. Wooden Leg, who had eaten dog meat on numerous occasions, detested it. He thought it tasted like wolf. The smell of an old wolf or an old dog boiling in the pot sickened him, he said, and boiling pups smelled almost as bad.

As for dog-soldier, the origin of that term remains in doubt. The name might come from the fact that they were tribal police, supervising a village very much as quadruped dogs supervised village life and raised an alarm if strangers approached. Tom LeForge, who lived twenty years with the Crows, did not speculate on the name itself, but he had unkind words for historians who painted dog-soldiers in violent hues. They were, he said, just cops, "the immediate directors of conduct," and a feature of every plains Indian tribe, not to be confused with Cheyenne fraternal organizations such as Crazy Dog Warriors or Elk Warriors, or the Kit Fox and Red Stick fraternities among the Crows. But this felicitous expression—dog-soldier—struck the fancy of certain writers "as implying the utmost of wild ferocity, so the orderly home policemen had attributed to them, especially, many of the gory deeds done by the Indians who resisted the movement of emigrants across the plains."

If the genesis of dog-soldier remains obscure, that of Cheyenne is not. Today's philologists, more knowledgeable than those of Custer's era, believe it derives from Sha-hi-ye-na—red talkers—signifying those who spoke an alien language. That is what the Sioux called them, although the Cheyennes referred to themselves as Tsistsistas, meaning people who were alike or similarly bred. In a word: Us. But the name which most graphically evokes them is Kite Indians, because they usually could be seen only from a distance, their lodges as small as kites in the sky.

Whatever they were called, however they were named, these people separated into Northern and Southern Cheyennes in 1825 or 1826 when several bands drifted south. Those who remained in the north grew increasingly like the Sioux, so that forty years later—which is to say, just about the time General Hancock marched ponderously across Kansas—the half-breed George Bent, a southerner, found his northern relatives wearing strange clothes and using unfamiliar words. Southern Cheyennes wore cloth blankets, cloth leggings, and other items manufactured by whites, but those associated with the Sioux were still dressed in buffalo robes. Northern Cheyennes wrapped their braids in strips of painted buckskin and wore feathers with the ends oddly cropped. To a southerner they looked wild.

During Bent's visit nine Crow horse thieves made off with some ponies. Cheyenne avengers hit the trail. Four Crows were caught and killed. Their scalps were then cut in half, providing eight trophies to celebrate. Northern Cheyennes were great scalp dancers, Bent says, men and women both: "For three long weeks the scalps of those unfortunate Crow men were danced through all the camps, almost without a pause, and the beating of the drums made such a racket that the buffalo herds left our vicinity. The Indians used to say that buffalo were terribly afraid of the sound of the drums, though, queerly enough, they did not mind singing. . . ."

That General Hancock with his wagon train, pontoons, and journalists should so much as contemplate overhauling a few nimble and wary Kite Indians, northern or southern, was of course absurd. However, Cheyenne marauders had alarmed the frontier and something must be done. Congress at this time wished to negotiate, which displeased the generals. In the euphemistic language favored by military men, General Sherman advised Hancock on March 14, 1867, that Congressional sentiment "prevents our adopting preventive measures."

The harsh contour of Hancock's caravan was softened by that sweet affection for nature which was so much a part of nineteenth-century life, military or civilian. Theodore Davis reports on a menagerie acquired here and there by the troops: wolf pups, coyote pups, eagle chicks "with abnormal appetites," and several half-grown pronghorn antelope that trotted alongside the column. These young antelope became very fond of Custer. He loved animals, which is common enough, but he seems to have exuded this feeling more powerfully than other men. Audubon and Catlin agree, says Davis, that the American antelope cannot be tamed; but whenever the Seventh dismounted to pitch camp these antelope would locate Custer, "and quite ignoring the presence of strangers . . . would paw his hand precisely as a pet dog might have done in mute request to be fondled"—a performance which caused grave surprise among visiting Indians.

It is a prairie idyl with all the naive charm of a Landseer painting, but General Hancock and his affectionate cavalry commander had come to western Kansas on serious business.

At the top of a long list of Indian grievances was the buffalo slaughter. Two herds, each so vast that no reasonable estimate was possible, had darkened the plains, one above and one below the Platte. Frémont, who traveled through this region in 1842, found himself surrounded—the herd extending for several miles behind him and forward as far as he could see.

Francis Parkman saw them in 1846. Working on a history of LaSalle he reflected that the French explorer, too, must have observed a wondrous spectacle, ". . . the memory of which can quicken the pulse and stir the blood after the lapse of years: far and near, the prairie was alive with buffalo; now like black specks dotting the distant swells; now trampling by in ponderous columns or filing in long lines, morning, noon, and night, to drink at the river—wading, plunging, and snorting in the water—climbing the muddy shores and staring with wild eyes at the passing canoes."

Twenty-five years later not much had changed. Col. Dodge notes that during spring migration the buffalo sometimes would move north in a single column perhaps fifty miles wide, of unknown length. At other times they traveled in parallel columns, all marching at the same pace, blackening the earth. On one occasion when he was engulfed by a migrating herd he climbed Pawnee Rock to get out of the way and saw the prairie covered with buffalo for ten miles in every direction.

Then came the gun-bearing palefaces.

A professional hunter named Robert Wright said that he traveled through an almost continuous herd for two hundred miles along the Arkansas River. If the creatures became alarmed and stampeded, "they made a roar like thunder and the ground seemed to tremble. . . . Charles Rath and I shipped over two-hundred thousand buffalo hides the first winter the Atchison, Topeka and Santa Fe Railroad reached Dodge City and I think there were at least as many more shipped from there, besides two hundred cars of hind-quarters and two cars of buffalo tongues. Often have I shot them from the walls of my corral, for my hogs to feed upon."

Eight million—give or take a million or so—were shot for their hides during a period of three years. Col. Dodge wrote that a land which used to vibrate with life had become a putrid desert. The high plains stank with rotten meat. By 1874 he saw more hunters than animals: "Every approach of the herd to water was met by rifle bullets. . . ."

Foreigners joined the sport. The London *Times* ran ads for a trip to Fort Wallace in western Kansas. Cost: fifty guineas. Lords, ladies, and celebrated grenadiers showed up. If galloping around on horseback seemed a bit arduous the sportsman could be driven to the herd in a comfortable spring wagon, or shoot from the window of a railway carriage on the Kansas-Pacific.

Enterprising Yankees turned a profit by collecting bones, which brought five dollars a ton. Porous bones were shipped east to be ground up as fertilizer; solid bones could be whittled into decorative trinkets—buttons, letter openers, pendants. And because a bone was a bone, Indian skeletons occasionally joined the heap: an Arapaho femur made quite an attractive knife handle, a skull suitable for reduction into ladies' combs brought $1.25.

It is said that at the beginning of the twentieth century one buffalo wandered across the prairie not far from a small town in Wyoming. The townspeople hitched up their wagons and rode out to have a look. They drove around the creature and stopped, the wagons forming a circle with the buffalo inside. For a long time they stared at this legendary animal. Then, because they could not imagine what else to do, somebody shot it.

A few years later the buffalo was almost extinct. A brief item in a 1932 *North Dakota Historical Quarterly* announces that once again the mighty bison are visible against distant hills:

A buffalo bull, cow and calf, stand in their case as silent reminder of the herds that once thundered across the North Dakota scene.

The exhibit has been arranged by Russell Reid, superintendent of the historical society. A painted background, done by Clell G. Gannon, Bismarck, shows a herd grazing in the distance.

Purchased from a buffalo ranch in Montana and converted into stuffed exhibits . . .

The herds were not being decimated in 1867 when General Hancock trundled into view, yet here and there itinerant hunters were setting up shop and the Indians did not like it. *Pte*, the buffalo, provided just about everything they needed, right down to his tail which made a splendid fly whisk. Fresh meat, tallow, warm robes, leggings, bow strings, bone needles, battle shields and coracles from his tough hide, axes and hoes from his shoulder blades, sledge runners from his ribs, glue from his boiled hooves, red paint from his blood, fuel from his dung, ladles from his horns, hair to stuff pillows, and so on. They even used his long black beard to ornament their clothes. Therefore they addressed him as Uncle, this useful monster, and followed him across the seasons.

Furthermore, his many nephews found him easy to kill. Durable and obstinate he might be, but simple to predict—the cows especially. Father Pierre Jean De Smet watched an Assiniboin approach a herd, conceal himself, and imitate the bleat of a calf, at which all of the females hurried toward him. He shot one. The others ran away. The Assiniboin reloaded his rifle and resumed crying. The females stopped. They looked around. As though enchanted they hurried again toward this noise. He shot another, which supplied all the meat he wanted, but he assured Father De Smet that he could have gone right on crying like a baby and killing them.

James McLaughlin, the agent at Standing Rock from 1881 until 1895, once organized a hunt for his famished dependents—the last big buffalo hunt. Indians shot approximately five thousand animals, a massacre he describes as "awful but not wanton." He never had known an Indian to kill a game animal that was not needed, McLaughlin said, although most whites would kill, kill, kill, kill until nothing moved.

The testimony of this experienced, sophisticated agent should be heard with respect; but of course there is more to the truth than one man's deposition. Fifty years ahead of McLaughlin came that peripatetic artist and inquisitive traveler George Catlin. Just before Catlin reached Fort Pierre an immense buffalo herd had been discovered on the opposite side of the Missouri. Several hundred Sioux forded the river at noon, returning to the fort about sundown with fourteen hundred tongues which they exchanged for a few gallons of whisky. Catlin refers to the hunt as a profligate waste of these animals. "Not a skin or a pound of the meat (except the tongues) was brought in. . . . A fair exhibition of the improvident character of the Indian and his recklessness in catering to his appetite, so long as inducements are held out to him for its gratification."

Historian George Hyde never saw the frontier. Most of what he knew about Indians was acquired at the Omaha Public Library despite the handicap of deafness and wretched eyesight—vision so poor that instead of depending on his eyes to guide him to the library he found it easier to memorize the route. Nevertheless his ponderous history of the Teton Sioux is a standard reference, and Mr. Hyde has this to say:

> Some believing souls who have listened to the tales of modern Sioux tell us that the Indian was the first conservationist, that he killed only as much game as was required to feed his family, was very careful not to destroy timber, and had, indeed, established all the rules and regulations of the United States Conservation Service centuries before that office was established. In truth, most of the Sioux of early times were born wasters. They hunted game out of a district and moved on to fresh hunting grounds; they destroyed great numbers of cottonwood trees, cutting off the bark to feed to their horses in winter; and they had a custom of firing the prairies in autumn to insure an early growth of new grass in the spring, caring nothing that the prairie fires they set swept across the country for one hundred miles, burning belts of timber, killing animals, and doing other damage.

These fires must have been spectacular. Many explorers, trappers, and soldiers have noted them. Across the bluffs, where grass was thin, the flames would creep slowly, so feebly that a man could step over them. Animals stayed where they were until it almost licked their noses. At night, according to Catlin, flames could be seen miles away climbing the perpendicular sides of cliffs, "sparkling chains of liquid fire hanging suspended in graceful festoons from the skies." But when it reached the bottomland and fed on thick grass eight feet high the pretty fire became a roaring red hurricane that quickly left the country black and desolate.

How many buffalo vanished in such holocausts—whether the fire started by accident or was set deliberately by Indians or by whites—cannot even be guessed. Historians as a rule do better on specific, localized incidents than when attempting to reconstruct an incomprehensible calamity. Hyde, for instance, could detail a buffalo slaughter by Oglalas at Pawnee Fork because a train of Mormon emigrants watched it. These Oglala gourmets helped themselves to a few choice cuts from the butchered herd while abandoning tons of perfectly good meat, although at the same time they were furious about white travelers dining on buffalo steak.

Fanny Kelly, unlike George Hyde, experienced life not only on the frontier but well beyond it during her five months as an Oglala captive. They killed for sport, she said, killing much more than they needed: "Each man selects the part of the animal he has killed that best suits his own taste, and leaves the rest to decay or be eaten by wolves, thus wasting their own game, and often suffering privation in consequence."

Nor was it only the Sioux. Ex-trooper Phineas Towne wrote to Brady: "I have seen the Crow Indians shoot buffalo and let them lie where they fell, not even undertaking to remove the hide. . . ."

General Hugh Scott knew and loved the West. Oklahoma in 1888 was "a wonderful primeval country," the creeks around Fort Sill bordered by elm, oak, cottonwood, pecan, hackberry, and walnut. The U.S. Army at this time was methodically chopping down trees for use as fuel because it was expensive to haul coal sixty-seven miles from the nearest railroad. Scott, upon being appointed quartermaster, refused to accept pecan or walnut wood, and he notes with pride that many fine trees survived which otherwise would have gone up in smoke. And having changed the course of the insensate U.S. Army—not altogether but at least a little—Scott prohibited Indian women from chopping down trees in order to collect nuts, "a wasteful habit which had arisen from their migratory lives with the buffalo; here to-day and gone to-morrow, probably never to see that part of the country again, the women knew no reason for conservation, which comes later in the history of peoples. We are only coming to it now ourselves."

At present anybody who visits Chaco Canyon in northwestern New Mexico can observe the result of wasteful habit. Juniper, ponderosa, and piñon pine once were as numerous as buffalo on the plains, but the prehistoric Indians who built and inhabited those mud-brick apartments stripped the land. Now, after almost a millennium, the forest has not returned. From a bleak horizon the sun ascends like a balloon. Beneath it Chaco lies cracked and empty: a broken pot. Greasewood, sage, and saltbush mottle the dusty alkaline floor. Lizards flicker silently across Chaco's crumbling walls.

Twelfth-century Indians saw little reason to preserve the trees and nineteenth-century Indians could not conceive of an end to the buffalo, though they became enraged by the sight of yellow-eyed invaders butchering Uncle Pte who provided so many necessities and luxuries. They were further enraged by the destruction of ancestral scaffolds. Theodore Davis noted in *Harper's*: "When the contracts are let for the supply of wood needed at the different Government posts the contractor and his men repair to some favorably-located grove, and proceed to cut and haul the wood to the fort. It is not difficult to imagine that the Indians object to this, and proceed at once to attack the men. . . ."

That Indians should be angered by this does not sound implausible, yet they themselves showed no respect for the dead of other tribes. Parkman said the desecration of burial scaffolds was common: "I have myself known an instance in which five corpses of Sioux Indians, placed in trees, after the practice of the Western bands of that people, were thrown down and kicked into fragments by a war party of Crows, who then held the muzzles of their rifles against the skulls and blew them to pieces."

So it would seem—if Indians violated sepulchres and squandered natural resources—they ought not to complain about white behavior. Nevertheless they did, expressing their rage indiscriminately. A gandy dancer at the end of the Kansas Pacific or some pedestrian homesteader might lose his life, his hair, and his clothes merely because he was born with a disgusting white skin.

Thus it came about that in windblown outer Kansas on April 12 an assembly of fourteen Cheyenne tribal leaders heard General Hancock deliver a menacing and abusive speech, the evident purpose of which was to impress upon them, in Stanley's words, "the necessity of keeping to the strict letter of their treaties."

This conference took place at night. Usually the Cheyennes did not discuss such matters at night but their arrival had been delayed three days by a storm and the general was anxious to talk, so they gathered around a bonfire near his tent. Wearing necklaces, medallions, copper and silver brassards, heavy brass rings dangling from slits in their ears, scalp locks decorated with silver disks, they listened while Hancock's speech was translated, murmuring their disbelief just once—when he assured them he would punish any whites who mistreated Indians.

Next day, to emphasize his determination, Hancock moved up Pawnee Fork toward the Indian camp. Three years earlier Col. John Chivington had led a force of Colorado militia against Black Kettle's peaceful village on Sand Creek southeast of Denver. Chivington attacked without warning, although the Cheyennes had been assured by the Commissioner of Indian Affairs that they would not be molested. Now the Cheyennes who had listened to General Hancock saw a very similar column approaching and decided it would be foolish to hang around. Women and children fled without even dismantling the lodges, and once they had a good start the warriors followed. They were all gone before Hancock quite realized it. Surprised and angered by this development, the Thunderbolt of the Potomac planted artillery around some 250 vacant wigwams and ordered Custer to round up the fugitives.

The Cheyennes escaped, not because of inept leadership but simply because they could move across familiar territory faster than the bluecoats. Custer had been on the frontier long enough to understand this. Neither the elite Seventh nor anybody else would overtake those savages; all he could do was trail them a while before returning to General Hancock. That being so, one might as well enjoy the ride. In an article for a sportsman's journal, *Turf, Field and Farm*, which was published in September of 1867 he described for his readers the thrill of a buffalo hunt without mentioning that on this particular April day he was supposed to be hunting Cheyennes. "I left the column, and galloped in advance for a few miles, taking with me but one attendant. . . ."

With him also went Rover, Lu, Sharp, Rattler, and Fanny, who very soon picked up a scent. Custer galloped after them on his fast thoroughbred Custis Lee, outdistancing the orderly.

After a while he realized that what he was doing might be foolish. He called off the dogs and was about to turn back when he saw a buffalo bull the size of his horse—an irresistible challenge. Three miles farther he overtook it. As he galloped alongside, preparing to shoot, the beast swung toward him, the horse pulled away, Custer's finger instinctively tightened on the trigger, and Custis Lee fell dead with a bullet through the brain. The hunter himself catapulted forward and hit the ground almost in front of the buffalo. He knew what had happened but had been so stunned that he could not move. The buffalo peered at him, shook its head and trotted off. Custer got up, and with a pair of field glasses slung around his neck, trailed by the dogs, he started walking back in what he hoped was the right direction. If he did not meet the column he could look forward to a wandering band of hostiles or death by starvation.

He was not the first white man to appreciate the immense emptiness of that land. Coronado marched across Kansas in 1542 and from chronicles of this expedition it is easy to see how an individual, or an army, could be digested. Indeed, the Spaniards sound almost mystified. Pedro de Castañeda rhetorically asks how such an army, accompanied by five hundred cows, five thousand sheep, and fifteen hundred Indian allies—how could such a horde march across the plains without leaving a trace? The land is like a bowl, "so that when a man sits down the horizon surrounds him. . . ."

Francisco Vásquez de Coronado, the Captain General himself, wrote that they could see no landmarks—not a tree, not a shrub, not an elevation; and with nothing to guide them, no natural feature to prevent them from marching in circles, they held a straight line by the expedient of having an archer shoot an arrow directly ahead, toward which they marched, then another, then another.

Catlin, exploring these plains early in the nineteenth century, rode through meadows of grass so deep that he stood up in the stirrups to see over the top.

Custer may have walked for an hour before noticing a dust cloud, which necessarily meant buffalo, Indians, or the Seventh. He provided at least three versions of his rescue. *Turf, Field and Farm* is the least dramatic. Here he simply recognizes the cavalry, sits down, and waits. In a letter to his wife he spoke of seeing the wagons. But for the admiration of his public in *My Life on the Plains*—which Captain Benteen chose to call *My Lie on the Plains*—he describes hiding in a gully with the dogs nestled around him until at last, through field glasses, he is able to make out a guidon with the stars and stripes fluttering above the riders. Hurrah!

Once again he had been lucky.

Luck may be just luck, as everybody knows, yet more often it is the result of ability, instinct, or knowledge. A less agile man might have broken a leg when he hit the ground, in which case he probably would have died there. A less courageous man under the horns of a buffalo might have communicated his fright and been gored. Somebody less acutely tuned to survival might have walked the wrong direction. But Custer believed in luck, which may not be irrelevant.

Meanwhile, back at Pawnee Fork, General Hancock assiduously guarded an empty camp. He tried to prevent looting, which was impossible. Acquisitive soldiers slithered around the pickets, crept into the lodges and helped themselves to tomahawks, calumets, robes, war clubs, dog skins, moccasins, knives, dolls, arrows, and live puppies.

Custer finally sent word that the Cheyennes had been attacking stagecoach depots and upon receipt of this news Hancock resolved to burn the village, despite being warned that it might make a bad situation worse. Stanley, as a journalist, could not help being delighted. He reports with obvious enthusiasm that the wigwam poles caught fire like tinder and the smoke from burning hides obscured the sky. "Flakes of fire were borne on the breeze to different parts of the prairie, setting the prairie grass on fire. With lightning speed the fire rolled on, and consumed an immense area of grass, while the black smoke slowly sailed skyward. Every green thing, and every dead thing that reared its head above the earth, was consumed, while the buffalo, the antelope, and the wolf fled in dismay. . . ."

Hancock felt obliged to do this, Stanley explains, because Cheyennes had disemboweled, scalped, and burned the bodies of three men employed at the Fossil Creek depot.

Custer's first dispatch had indeed led Hancock to believe Cheyennes were responsible for this atrocity, but in a subsequent dispatch Custer wrote that neither he himself nor his Delaware scouts had found proof—which left General Hancock in a sticky position. He cleared himself as best he could. He explained to General Sherman that Indians from the now smouldering Cheyenne village might possibly have murdered these men at the stage depot, even though it could not be proved.

Ten days after Hancock's holocaust at Pawnee Fork the vermilion-mad Kiowa chief Satanta—a corruption of Set-t'á-iñt-e, meaning White Bear— showed up at Fort Larned where another peace council had been scheduled. He was a thick, muscular individual with brilliant eyes and red paint smeared all over his face, and for the occasion he chose to wear a United States Army officer's coat complete with epaulettes, with little brass bells attached to his leggings. This spectacular apparition lived in a bright red lodge and when he rode off to war, which he did rather often, he painted not only his face but his entire body red. With obsessive consistency he carried a red shield. He may also have painted his war pony red, right down to the hooves. He was adored by Kiowa squaws and it is probable that every paleface female who saw him was either horrified or hypnotized. Stanley remarks that he had a great name for recklessness and daring from the Rio Grande to the Republican.

About three years before this Fort Larned conference Satanta had been visited by a missionary named H. T. Ketcham who found him to be amiable, energetic, and intelligent, although somewhat ostentatious. At lunchtime he would order a carpet spread in his lodge and the repast would be served on painted boards which he had decorated with tacks. "He has a brass French horn," notes Mr. Ketcham, "which he blew vigorously when meals were ready." He sounds like a splendid host, as engaging and sociable as a good many Caucasian chiefs, but in neither case does this preclude acts of funda- mental violence. During an 1866 raid Satanta captured a certain Mrs. Box. She held a baby in her arms. The infant wails exasperated him so he crushed the baby's head against a tree. Eventually he was imprisoned, as were a great many defiant Indians; and being unable to tolerate such treatment he dove headfirst from a second-floor window of the prison hospital at Huntsville, Texas.

General Hancock's address to this wild Kiowa could not have been very different from his address to the Cheyennes. Whatever he said did not make much of an impression because a month later Satanta raided Fort Dodge, stampeding most of the animals. "He had the politeness, however, to raise his plumed hat to the garrison of the fort," Mr. Davis reports, "although he dis- courteously shook his coat-tails at them as he rode away with the captured stock."

General Sherman, whose photographs now and then give him the aspect of a vulture with scrofula, came visiting that summer and correctly analyzed the situation. He wrote to President Grant that the poor, proud Indians felt tempted beyond endurance by the sight of grazing herds and flocks, and in order to steal they occasionally would kill. "We in turn cannot discriminate—all look alike and to get the rascals, we are forced to include all."

In October yet another conference took place, this time along Medicine Lodge Creek in southern Kansas just above the Oklahoma border, and it inaugurated a new policy. No longer would the government be satisfied to acquire Indian land; now the government had decided to alter a centuries-old pattern of life—to make the savage live in a box, wear shoes, turn a furrow, and otherwise emulate wasichu farmers.

Stanley showed up at Medicine Lodge, presumably dressed as he was during the Hancock expedition in a blue felt cap, voluminous cloak, and rawhide boots embellished with enormous Mexican spurs. Satanta also appeared. He recognized Stanley, which could not have been difficult, and greeted him with a monstrous red embrace, seeming to indicate that he preferred newspapermen to generals.

Stanley sounds like a changeling. While on tour with Hancock he offered a chauvinistic defense of government policy: "Are our countrymen to be murdered and scalped without retaliating? Are delicate women to be carried away by the remorseless savage to his wigwam, to be sold to vile bondage and for other purposes for which we have no name? The people of the West pause with anxious hearts for an answer!" Somewhat later these remorseless savages became "wronged children of the soil."

He developed a unique ability to materialize simultaneously in various places—"a sort of ubiquity," says Thomas Isern, that allowed him to pop up here while being there. He could write from Fort Sedgwick for the New York *Tribune* while describing a theatrical performance in Omaha for the St. Louis *Missouri Democrat*.

His presence at Fort Sedgwick must be questioned because it is known that he did attend the theater in Omaha: he hurled a bouquet at the feet of Miss Annie Ward, who kicked it aside, after which he got into a fistfight with a local editor. Apparently he did not look like much. Peace Commissioner Samuel Tappan said he resembled the breaking up of a hard winter, which probably explains Miss Ward's cruel rebuff—although it is said that she subsequently modified her behavior long enough to clean out his wallet. Artist J. D. Howland called him "the most abjectly forlorn creature imaginable."

The Medicine Lodge conference seems to have been a brilliant affair. Uniformed generals accentuated the roguish individuality of Indians and of certain wasichu civilians—Commissioner John "Black Whiskers" Sanborn, for instance, resplendent in a purple suit; or the Cheyenne interpreter Margaret Adams, of Arapaho and French-Canadian parentage, thrice married, an ostrich feather adorning her chapeau and a scarlet satin dress provocatively visible beneath the hem of her cloak. She is said to have attended every meeting drunk.

General William "White Whiskers" Harney, the ranking officer, physically huge and ceremoniously erect, would have made quite a show by himself. With a great masculine head topped by an epicene little cap of the sort college sophomores used to wear, he could be mistaken for a gingerbread general. He is said to have been a splendid athlete, a very fast runner.

There was fastidious General Terry, described in one account as "calmly dumb," in another as "intrepid."

There, too, was General C. C. Augur of the hound dog gaze and mutton-chop whiskers, puffing a thin cigar, known for his organizational and planning ability.

Commissioner Tappan whittled a stick. Journalists observed that throughout this protracted and significant conference he whittled. He did so because he was a down-home whittler, and if that is what a man is, that is what he must do. Being a Peace Commissioner makes no difference. Consulting with wild Indians makes no difference. Tappan whittled his way through one speech after another and apparently he did not do much else. The Indians must have been confounded. These wasichus were beyond understanding.

The chiefs looked their best. Red ochre enlivened their faces, their cheeks displayed symbolic signs. They broke out the war bonnets and several of them put on Mexican serapes. Others tidied up by spreading their blankets on anthills—which quite naturally enraged the ants who came swarming to the surface and ate the lice nestled in the blankets. Then, of course, it was easy enough to shake out the ants and put on a clean blanket.

Black Kettle was present, sporting a long blue robe and a dragoon's hat.

Satanta carried his bugle—French horn, trumpet, whatever it was—on a rawhide thong slung around his neck.

Se-tan-gya or Satank, the spidery Kiowa with a similar name, wore a medal embossed with the head of President Buchanan. At the time of the conference he was sixty-seven years old. Today he glares from the National Archives album with one eye like a drill, the other a slit. Beneath a thin Mongolian mustache his lips are compressed like a man tasting a bitter seed.

Ten Bears, an amiable Comanche some years older than Satank, his ancient face creased like the Staked Plains where he lived, wore gold-rimmed spectacles that gave him a peculiar resemblance to Benjamin Franklin.

Also in camp were at least five thousand lesser Comanches, Kiowas, Arapahoes, and Cheyennes, any number of them fantastically painted, any one of whom would cause an urban white man to blink. They wore medals and silver crosses, feathered bonnets, brightly beaded moccasins. Many wore clothing stripped from the bodies of slain troopers. Little bells dangling from the bridles of their ponies tinkled musically.

Journalists noted that after Missouri Senator John B. Henderson finished embracing various Indians his nose was yellow, one cheek retained a red streak, and the other cheek had several green tattoos. No color photos exist, but a black-and-white picture reveals a middle-aged man with a grizzled beard, plenty of forehead, and frazzled hair. The pupils of his eyes are distinctly enlarged, giving him a dazed look, as though he could not believe it.

October in southern Kansas. Elms alongside Medicine Lodge Creek rustled in the cool breeze, turning red and gold, but there had been no frost. Persimmon trees were bright orange. What a grand time and place for a meeting.

Disregarding oratorical protestations of friendship, whether calculated or sincere, and no doubt much garbled by translation, a desperate hunger for peace seems indicated by certain details. Captain Albert Barnitz, who had charge of a cavalry squadron, wrote in his journal on October 17: "This evening an Arrapahoe, whom I have never noticed before brought and presented me a pair of moccasins. . . ."

Satanta addressed the government functionaries. He spoke for a long time, as usual. Stanley, quite fascinated by this hulking and extremely dangerous Kiowa, listened with close attention. Being unable to understand the language, he transcribed a bit of Satanta's speech phonetically: "Anitate y ben antema, usebah ghis elek men a yu tah durpua cabelah inst ma den y cat ah damht ahu echan arabeuy shtabelunyau . . ."

Here, too, Stanley met the chief's agent—more properly, the Kiowa agent—Colonel Jesse Leavenworth, son of the man who built the famous fort: "Colonel Leavenworth is now a cripple, and his beard is silvered with age. He has an astute look, and is devoted to red tapeism. His coat pockets are always full of official documents, and the ends of said papers can be seen sticking out an inch or so, and on each and all will be found legally inscribed, 'Leavenworth, Indian Agent.' " This bizarre figure—this incompetent, idealistic bureaucrat—had graduated from West Point but did not belong in the Army. During the Civil War he was dismissed from service. Later the Kiowas accused him of graft, perhaps without justification, and at last he shuffled uncertainly off stage, official documents sticking out of his pockets like souvenir programs of a play that failed.

Three vast heaps of gifts had been assembled at Medicine Lodge, provided by the Great Father in Washington for his troubled red children: one to be distributed among Kiowas and Comanches, another for Arapahoes and Apaches, a third for Cheyennes. There were baskets of glass beads, knives, trinkets beyond counting, and 3,423 surplus bugles purchased by Commissioner Sanborn. There were quite a few Civil War uniforms—dress coats, pants, boots, campaign hats—which the Indians remodeled according to their taste. A Union soldier's hat, for instance, looked better if the crown was cut out, the rim decorated with feathers and streaks of paint. Pants were more comfortable without a seat. As for boots, the bottom part that clutched the foot was useless so it was cut off and discarded, but the upper part could be transformed into moccasin soles. And food—more food than these Indians could imagine. Such was the harvest of food that when the conference ended and everybody went home they could not load so much food on their ponies, and because the white men did not carry the surplus back east it was left to rot.

Nothing more pleased the beneficiaries than kegs of black powder, percussion caps, lead, paper cartridges, and guns. Because these items were valued above all else, they were distributed last. Impetuous young braves could scarcely wait. The first pistol exploded but the brave who fired it seemed less concerned about his bloody hand than the ruined gun. Two more pistols exploded, whereupon the Indians began to mutter because they thought the whites were cheating them again, and Stanley wrote that the manufacturer— Union Arms—should be investigated by Congress. But then some Colt revolvers were issued. Indians knew the Colt. They had used Colt revolvers many times and knew they were good.

This issuance of weapons disturbed a few officials, especially the Peace Commissioners, who wondered if such gifts might not be used inappropriately, but military members of the commission argued that guns were needed for hunting. General Terry in particular favored the distribution of weapons.

Before starting home with his presents old Satank visited the dignitaries. He touched his Buchanan medal and said, either in Comanche or Kiowa: "Look at this medal I wear. By wearing this, I have been made poor. Before, I was rich in horses and lodges. Today I am the poorest of all. When you gave me this silver medal on my neck, you made me poor." He went on to say that his people thanked the Great Spirit that such wrongs were about to end. Do what is best for us, he said. Teach us which road to travel. "And now the time has come that I must go. You may never see me more, but remember Satank. . . ." They never did see him again. On June 8, 1871, handcuffed and guarded by cavalry because of his part in a Kiowa-Comanche raid during which several teamsters were killed, Satank was en route to prison when he decided enough was enough. A Caddo rode by the government wagon train and Satank asked him to deliver a message: "Tell my people I am dead. I died the first day out of Fort Sill. My bones will be lying beside the road. I wish my people to gather them up and take them home." Down the road a mile or two he shouted: "I will not go beyond that tree!" He got loose—it is said he tore the flesh from his hands while pulling them through the manacles. He whipped out a butcher knife concealed in his blanket, stabbed one guard, seized a carbine, and was just getting into action when other guards shot him down. For about an hour he refused to die. He was at least seventy years old, so it is not hard to guess how difficult he must have been some decades earlier.

William Connelley wrote in 1928 for the Kansas State Historical Society that the government collected flour, coffee, sugar—Comanches loved sugar, dumping half a cup in each cup of coffee—"dried fruits in quantities sufficient for an Army campaign," and a herd of cattle for these Indians. "To feed what Indians? The very Indians that had been murdering settlers, scalping women and children, killing workers on the railroads, burning houses and stage stations, attacking forts, and laying waste to the frontier all summer. . . . Knowing all the outrages these Indians had committed on the border settlements, the commission still received them as 'good Indians' and made treaties with them. Their treachery was not once mentioned. It is fortunate that their mirth never shows in their faces and that they laugh deep down in their abdomens." Concerning ammunition: "The Indians had used up their entire supply along the frontier killing settlers and ranchmen and railroad workmen, and it was good of the Great Father to load them up for another campaign. . . ."

General Hancock did not attend this conference. By then he had retreated to departmental headquarters at Fort Leavenworth, leaving Custer in charge of the outposts. Whether his cumbrous expedition succeeded or failed depended on one's point of view. Peace Commissioner Sanborn addressed Secretary of the Interior Orville Browning: "The operations of General Hancock have been so disastrous to the public interests, and at the same time seem to me to be so inhuman . . ." Black Whiskers went on to say that for a mighty nation to prosecute a war against a few nomads was a disgusting spectacle, "an injustice unparalleled, a national crime most revolting, that must, sooner or later, bring down upon us or our posterity the judgment of Heaven." Superintendent of Indian Affairs Thomas Murphy advised the new commissioner, Nathaniel Taylor, in Washington: "General Hancock's expedition, I regret to say, has resulted in no good, but, on the contrary, has been productive of much evil."

Homesteaders who had endured the rage of Indians felt less sympathetic. The Topeka *Weekly Leader* did not equivocate: "a set of miserable, dirty, lousy, blanketed, thieving, lying, sneaking, murdering, graceless, faithless, gut-eating skunks as the Lord ever permitted to infect the earth, and whose immediate and final extermination all men, except Indian agents and traders, should pray for. . . ."

Sherman hoped to avoid this, but he thought there could be no peace until the Indians were removed, one way or another. He informed Secretary of War Stanton that if as few as fifty Indians were allowed to remain between the Arkansas and the Platte it would be necessary to guard every stage depot, every train, every man laying tracks. He advised clearing the field and it made little difference whether they were coaxed out by Indian commissioners or killed.

Custer did his part by trotting around western Kansas, although hostile redskins proved difficult to find, much less engage, because they would not stand up and fight like Confederates. They did what they often did when harassed: like an amoeba each band would divide, divide, and divide again, and again, and once again, leaving a less and less distinct trail, with the result that his blue-jacketed cavaliers never could catch anybody to punish. He did not even glimpse a village of white Cheyenne lodges like a cluster of kites beyond some faraway ridge.

Between October 1, 1866 and October 1, 1867 more than five hundred members of the Seventh Cavalry elected to take the Grand Bounce, which is to say they deserted.

Capt. Barnitz, addressing his wife somewhat testily from Fort Hays during the summer of 1867, wrote that Custer had set up several tents for the comfort of Elizabeth and a friend named Anna Darrah—a Michigan grocer's daughter who liked to go adventuring—"and has had bowers and screens of evergreens erected, and triumphal arches, and I know not what else. He has a large square Hospital tent, among other things—nearly as large as the little chapel at Fort Riley—and so the ladies will be very comfortable, I have no doubt. . . ." Before he could finish this letter Barnitz heard a fusillade from the picket line. Fourteen troopers had skipped. "So they go! If Genl Custer remains long in command, I fear that recruiting will have to go on rapidly to keep the regiment replenished."

Custer did not entirely blame these disgruntled soldiers. Then, as now, government food was the subject of ridicule and a persistent root of discontent. Bureaucratic corruption at Fort Leavenworth produced shipments of maggot-infested hardtack—some of the bread delivered to Fort Hays was six years old—and at least once a shipment of rocks invoiced as food. Elizabeth, accompanying her husband on an inspection, noticed a flat stone cleverly packed between layers of bacon. And the situation would get worse. A member of the Eighth Cavalry wrote that his 1890 field rations were twenty-seven years old—the packing date still legible on the box. "The hardtack had a green mould on it, but we just wiped it off. . . ." Soldiers ordinarily marinated this ancient hardtack before trying to eat it. Or it could be fried and sprinkled with brown sugar.

Lunch might be Cincinnati Chicken, otherwise known as bacon, together with salt pork—perhaps eaten raw after being dipped in vinegar—and Angel Cake, this last being another bakery product almost guaranteed to chip a tooth. As for coffee, a trooper was issued green beans and what he brewed was nobody else's concern. Usually he roasted the beans in his mess kit, pounded them with a rock or the butt of his revolver, and emptied the scorched debris into a can of muddy creek water. Pulverizing beans with a revolver was easier than using a rock, but many officers looked upon this practice as a crime.

"Bad provisions were a fruitful cause of bad health," Custer noted. "Inactivity led to restlessness & dissatisfaction. Scurvy made its appearance, and cholera attacked neighboring stations. For all these evils desertion became the most popular antidote."

He had rejected inedible food, sending it back to Leavenworth with a crisp suggestion that the commissary shape up, and he organized hunting parties to supply fresh meat. And although he himself makes no mention of it, correspondent Davis wrote for *Harper's* that officers of the Seventh "one and all, depleted their purses to procure from sutlers and others the anti-scorbutic food for which the soldiers were suffering." Nevertheless, troopers galloped relentlessly toward the sunset. In 1867, according to the Adjutant General's report to the Fortieth Congress, the desertion rate from Custer's Seventh reached fifty-two percent.

His was not the only regiment to evaporate. In that year 14,068 men discharged themselves from the U.S. Army. In 1868, for some unknown reason, the number dropped to 7,893. And for the next two years it declined before starting up again. Between 1867 and 1891 almost one-third of the recruits decided they had made a dreadful mistake.

The preferred season for changing employment was spring. It was easier to travel when the snow began to melt, and anybody could get a job because the mines reopened and work resumed on the trans-continental railroad. Deserters therefore came to be known as snowbirds because so many enlisted with the idea of soldiering only through the winter. Of course there was always a chance of being caught, not only by the military, but by citizens eager to collect the thirty-dollar reward.

The low desertion rate among blacks has puzzled historians. In 1867, for example, twenty-five percent of the army simply vanished, but of these magicians only 570 were black. Nobody knows why. Regardless of color, men endured the same food and were paid alike. It has been suggested that they could not so easily merge with frontier communities and for most of them a soldier's uniform represented a social step forward. The only thing certain is that very few buffalo soldiers missed roll call.

Punishment for desertion varied according to circumstance, the humor of the day, and the commandant. One soldier bagged by citizen bounty hunters near Fort Dodge killed himself rather than submit to Army justice.

Prior to the Civil War a deserter could expect flogging and dishonorable discharge, but in 1861 the whip was dropped in favor of relatively humane punishment such as tattooing. At the discretion of the post commandant, however, he might be branded like a steer. Sgt. John Ryan recalled one such example which he described in 1909 for his hometown paper, the Newton, Massachusetts *Town Crier*:

> The several deserters were laid on their left side with the right hip exposed, and the letter "D" was branded on them with a heated iron an inch or more in diameter. Immediately after the branding, the guards fell in and marched the men around the garrison. The soldiers' quarters occupied two sides of it, the officers' quarters the third, and the quartermaster's and commissary's stores the other. This procession consisted of a detachment of soldiers with arms reversed, and the fort musicians playing the "Rogue's March," ahead of the prisoners, and in the rear a detachment with charged bayonets. Behind the deserters were a couple of colored men kicking them. They started from the guard house, marched around one side of the square, and were proceeding in front of the officers' quarters when the commanding officer of the district, Colonel English, who was seated on the piazza, stepped up, held up his hand and commanded them to halt. He inquired by whose authority the prisoners were treated in such manner and received the reply that it was the

order of the post commander, Joel H. Elliott. Colonel English ordered the kicking part of the program to cease, and the procession continued. . . . Major Elliott later was placed under arrest on account of the affair, but still later, when another expedition was formed, he was placed in command of it. As he was killed on that expedition it was the last heard of the case. Lieut. Gardner, of Co. B, 38th U.S. Colored Infantry, was the officer in charge of the punishment of the deserters, and did the branding.

Unofficially, illegally, the whip remained in use—splitting the hide of enlisted men when a commandant felt so disposed. Occasionally it was used to instruct civilians.

At Fort Sedgwick a certain Mr. Hendriks who unwisely bought a bottle of whisky at the request of two soldiers was seized and delivered to the guardhouse. Next day, on the authority of habeas corpus and without trial, he got one hundred lashes. The lieutenant in charge, thinking it prudent to absolve himself, informed the sergeant that, although he would like to see this rogue punished, he was not ordering it. The sergeant, complying with the lieutenant's manifest desire, ordered Mr. Hendriks stripped nearly to his shoes and tied to a cross. Soldiers with plaited thongs stood on either side like Roman centurions and at a signal they went to work. They raised their arms ". . . and, swinging the ropes over their shoulders, the one on the right brought the hissing lash full on the naked hips of the man, who sprang convulsively upward as if shot." Mr. Hendriks soon began to leak blood, which trickled down his legs, and at each new stroke the nearby spectators were splashed. Halfway through this ritual the victim's body assumed a livid color "and the skin hung in strips and flakes."

Together with the branding iron and lash, or in lieu of them, was that restraint which always dangles in a moonless niche of the mind: the ball and chain, known to nineteenth-century soldiers as Uncle Sam's watch and chain. The ball weighed anywhere from ten to twenty-five pounds. The chain, usually about six feet in length, was attached to the ankle by an iron band and so painful was the shackling process that shrieks could be heard for a mile or two on the quiet prairie. Occasionally a sympathetic blacksmith would use a soft lead rivet instead of an iron rivet, which allowed the prisoner to remove the chain at night and put it on before morning inspection; but of course any blacksmith who did this was risking his own liberty.

If a commanding officer wished, he could have a man hung by the thumbs, toes just touching the floor like a cartoon figure in a dungeon.

A man could be horizontally crucified—spread-eagled on the ground. Stanley described a Thirtieth Infantry soldier pinned to the earth under a swarm of buffalo gnats. For two hours the man screamed, cried, and begged to be released.

Then there was bucking-and-gagging, which was practiced in various forms and sounds like a fraternity initiation stunt but could easily be fatal. The malefactor was trussed like a pig with a stick tied between his teeth or a rag crammed into his mouth. Pvt. David Spotts, who served with the Kansas Volunteers, happened to notice a man seated alone on the company parade ground and upon investigating he found J. A. Studabecker bucked and gagged. "I spoke to him but he was unconscious, and his eyes were wide open and staring. I hurried up to Capt. Finch . . . we hurried and took the gag out of his mouth and unloosed him so he could breathe, but it took some vigorous rubbing to bring him to." Studabecker had lent his knife to a soldier who wanted to slice a stolen ham. What happened to the thief is not recorded.

Ryan was confronted by a soldier named Lawton who tried to brain him with a club. Ryan knocked him out with a saber blow. The tumult brought Lt. McIntosh who ordered Lawton and another soldier bucked and gagged. The bucking in this case consisted of tying their arms and feet together in such a way that they were seated but could not move without falling over. Each man had a stick in his mouth. They fell asleep in this position, after which Lt. McIntosh—who seems to have been fairly lenient by the standards of the day—released them from bondage and dumped them in the guard-house pending court-martial.

Custer was not so lenient. He sounds unusually strict, although there is no reason to suppose he was the Army's worst martinet. While he might under-stand the bitterness of enlisted men and empathize with them to some degree, he would not tolerate ragged behavior any more than he could afford to over-look serious offenses; and certain measures he introduced to preserve the architecture of his regiment would earn him a legacy of hatred. At Fort Hays he constructed a remarkable guardhouse. On a knoll behind camp he ordered a circular pit to be dug, twenty or thirty feet deep and about twenty feet in diameter. Logs were placed like rafters across the top, covered with hay and then with dirt. There was an open square in the middle, and a ladder. Pris-oners were kept in guarded tents during the day but at night they went into this hole, which often got so crowded that nobody could lie down.

Punishment at Fort McPherson sometimes consisted of tying a man's legs together and throwing him into the Platte. When he clawed his way ashore he would be tossed back like an unsatisfactory fish, again and again and again, until he almost drowned.

In Dakota Territory, exasperated by whisky in the barracks, he ordered miscreants to carry the barrel. That is, to wear an empty vinegar barrel, carrying it by straps over the shoulders so that only the man's head and feet protruded. This sounds amusing, but Custer's victims might wear a barrel for ten days.

A drunken regiment could not be permitted, as nobody would deny, yet it is easy to understand why men at these isolated posts smuggled whisky into camp. Except for interludes of terror, life on the majestic western plains alternated between tedium and ennui. One might pluck out "La Paloma" and "Susan James" and "Little Annie Roonie" on the banjo, or harmonize on the subject of Jeannie's light brown hair until moisture seeped into the eye and one's throat constricted, but it was not enough. Sunday could be a welcome respite, even if there was nothing to do, but next came Monday, Tuesday, Wednesday, the jackass captain, and a spring wagon full of garbage.

Prohibition was difficult to enforce. The Fort Yates surgeon noted that as a result of prohibition the men had begun drinking extracts of vanilla, cinnamon, peppermint, ginger, lemon, Worcestershire sauce, red pepper sauce, bay rum, cologne, and various quack nostrums loaded with alcohol. Mrs. Fanny McGillycuddy, wife of the Fort Robinson doctor, wrote in her diary at the end of December, 1876: "Outfit all drunk."

A telegraph operator at Camp Brown, Wyoming, wrote to an influential friend:

> . . . I want to get out of the Army honorable but if I can't get out otherwise I will give the cursed outfit the "Grand bounce." I can not endure them much longer. None but a menial Cur Could stand the usage of a soldier of the Army of today in America. The Majority of the Officers are "dead-beats" and the soldiers Escaped Convicts and the lowest of Gods Creation. I do not want any thing to do with them at all, I will not scringe at the look of the bigoted fools (the officers) and the man that Considers himself as good as them, they make it pretty hot for him. . . .

Frontier duty probably was worse than any account of it because the suicide rate among Army recruits during this period was almost eight percent— three times the suicide rate of British soldiers. Vicious punishment, loneliness, boredom, booze, fleas, maggoty bread, tarantulas, mosquitos, blizzards, deserts, psychotic sergeants, incomprehensible lieutenants and captains and majors and colonels, yipping savages anxious to part your hair— there were easier ways to go.

Mosquitos got so thick along the upper Missouri that soldiers walked around dressed in balloon-like wire helmets draped with netting. Every evening they rose above Big Muddy like the locusts above Egypt, and although the thermometer might register ninety degrees it was necessary to sleep under blankets, wearing gloves and a head shield: "Take off your glove to button your collar closer, or adjust your net, and your hand is a swollen and unseemly thing."

In lieu of this accursed life one might as well skip off to work on the railroad. If one did not quite have courage enough to desert, the least one could do was start a fight. Troopers stationed near a town would get ready for their occasional hours of freedom by putting on iron knuckles made from horseshoe nails: "drinking jewelry." And should there be no town—in that case any sort of excitement was better than none. Men at Fort Yuma provoked fights between colonies of red and black ants. The way to do this was to punch a hole in each nest and insert cans which had held peaches or some other sweet. Very soon the cans filled up with ants which could then be poured into a basin where, says Captain Bourke, furious combat began at once, and he observes with the impartiality of a scientist that red ants were more courageous. One red ant would assault two or even three black ants. "If the rumpus lasted for any length of time, queens would appear, as if to superintend what was going on. At least, that was our impression. . . ."

Lack of virtuous women made a miserable situation worse. Any unattached female in the neighborhood of a fort was apt to be diseased. Opposite Fort Lincoln on the east bank of the Missouri stood a number of Hog Ranches. Elizabeth and other matrons were intensely conscious of these establishments and during the great spring flood of '75 they watched through field glasses, perhaps with grim delight, as the turbulent river swamped My Lady's Bower and the Dew Drop Inn.

Dancing helps to pass the time, but very seldom was there anybody to dance with except another soldier. This they did. They took turns impersonating—each tobacco-stained, stubble-faced, reeking beauty identified by a handkerchief pinned to his sleeve.

Now and again they danced with regimental laundresses, which might not sound appealing, but among those honest laundresses were some engaging creatures who did not limit themselves to the trade. At Fort Kearny a laundress known as Colored Susan was accused of baking and selling pies made from government flour, and of selling "ardent spirits"—however that should be interpreted. General Tasker H. Bliss—which sounds like the name of a fictional character—General Bliss said post surgeons in those days had little to do except "confine laundresses and treat the clap."

Laundresses turned up in a variety of shapes, colors, and dispositions. At Fort Concho, Texas, three were discharged because of "utter worthlessness, drunkness and lewdness." At Camp McDermit, Nevada, a certain Mrs. Cavanaugh threatened a lieutenant with a butcher knife because he had suspended her husband by the thumbs. At Fort Bascom in the moody southwest a Latin laundress vowed to cut out a soldier's tongue if he told one more lie about her—which he did—and she caught him in a drunken sleep and sliced off the tip of it.

Then there was Mrs. Nash, who joined the Seventh in Kentucky and followed the regiment north to Fort Lincoln. Invariably she wore a veil, or a shawl pinned beneath her chin, and she is described as being rather peculiar looking. John Burkman, Custer's orderly, said she was a good laundress, a good nurse, and a good midwife, always in demand to "chase the rabbit" when a woman was expecting. Her next-to-last husband, a quartermaster clerk named Clifton, was known as a jolly fellow until he got married. After the ceremony, however, Clifton seldom laughed and a few days before his term of enlistment expired he deserted.

Her last husband was a private named Noonan. They lived together in obvious bliss on Suds Row east of the Fort Lincoln parade grounds, but while he was away on a scouting expedition she sickened and died. Just before graduating to a better world she asked her friends to bury her without the usual cleaning and dressing. They refused. They would not hear of such a thing. Lo and behold, when two of them set about this mournful task they perceived that the much-married laundress, seamstress, nurse, baker of delicious pies, and popular midwife was not female. Burkman and several other troopers were gathering flowers on the prairie so Elizabeth could make a funeral wreath when a laundress hurried out of the Noonan quarters with this extraordinary bit of information. Said Burkman: "We was flabbergasted."

Pvt. Noonan did not say much when he got back, but he turned pale and he twitched. He quit playing poker with the boys, he took long walks alone, he began to lose weight. One day when he entered the blacksmith shop a trooper remarked, "Say, you and Mrs. Noonan never had no children, did you?"

The *Army and Navy Journal*, which often incorporated material scavenged from other periodicals, reprinted from the Bismarck *Tribune*:

> Corporal Noonan, of the 7th Cavalry, whose "wife" died some weeks ago, committed suicide in one of the stables of the lower garrison. It was reported some days ago that he had deserted, but no one this side of the river had seen him. It now appears that the man had kept himself out of the way as well as he could for several days. His comrades had given him a sort of cold shake since the return of the regiment from the chase after the Sioux, and this, and the shame that fell on him in the discovery of his wife's sex, undermined his desire for existence, and he crawled away lonely and forsaken and blew out the life that promised nothing but infamy and disgrace. The suicide was committed with a pistol, and

Noonan shot himself through the heart. The affair created almost as intense excitement at the post as did the announcement of the death of Mrs. Noonan, but there was a sigh of relief on the corporate lips of the 7th Cavalry when its members heard that Noonan by his own hand had relieved the regiment of the odium which the man's presence cast upon them.

The gossipy *Journal* went on to say that Pvt. Noonan had continued to insist right up until the end, despite certain protruding evidence, that the light of his life was female. The *Journal* also transmitted this tidbit: "There is no explanation of the unnatural union except that the supposed Mexican woman was worth $10,000 and was able to buy her husband's silence."

So, despite the monotonous drama of frontier life there might be startling intermissions.

One August night a big gray wolf loped into Fort Larned, slowing down just enough to bite a sentinel. It then ran into the hospital, bit a patient, dragged another out of bed, ran through the hall of a nearby home, pounced on a dog, and then leaped up on Col. Wyncoop's porch to taste a visiting lieutenant, John Thompson. The bite of a hydrophobic wolf was fatal. Everybody knew this. Dodge says that Indians who were barely scratched by the teeth of a mad wolf would give away their property and wait to die, although for some reason the bite of a rabid skunk did not affect them. Lt. Thompson recovered. Benteen, who was there, attributes this to the fact that the wolf bit through his clothing, which absorbed the virus. However, Benteen adds, "It scared Thompson 'pissless' as we say. . . ."

Mad wolves were not uncommon. The queer thing about the Fort Larned wolf was that it showed up in August. Usually they went mad in February or March.

Then there was the crazed Viennese—"a richly dressed person"—who arrived at Fort Lincoln with the idea of buying land. This by itself was odd, but he displayed "strange freaks" while discussing his project, so he was watched. On his second day at the fort he announced that he was going to Yellowstone Park—six hundred miles as the raven flies—and off he walked in a westerly direction. This fact being reported to Custer, the general ordered him brought back. The stranger protested, when overtaken, explaining that he had planned to return in a few days. Nevertheless, Custer's posse cut short his trip and it was felt expedient to learn what might be in his satchel. He was carrying more than $1,200 in cash. Documents identified him as Mr. Emil Kluky, although cards in his wallet gave the name as Joseph Kluky, No. 26 Wohlzeilestrasse, Vienna. Eventually it was learned that he had been corresponding with a loan and land agent, Henry Reimann, Broad Street, New York City. "A telegram concerning his condition was sent to the latter address, but no reply has yet been received. . . ."

Mr. Kluky may have been unbalanced before he entered Dakota Territory or he might have become deranged by the western horizon. Even a man of unusual equanimity could feel its power. Capt. John Bourke, for instance, was a tough soldier who stood with both feet flat on the sod. Once he found himself billeted at latitude 42° 49′ 8″ North, longitude 105° 27′ 3″ West, "on the south side of the North Platte River at its junction with La Prele (or Rush) Creek." In other words: Fort Fetterman. Although this could not be Paradise, Captain Bourke looked around and listened:

> The sharp boom of the evening gun signalled the descent of the sun; slowly the golden tints of the clouds changed to bronze, to carmine, to a dull red; this last turned into a pale yellow blending imperceptibly into the darkness of night, relieved by myriads of sparkling stars.
>
> The atmosphere in its purity gave free passage to every beam of light, or re-echoed the slightest sounds. Only the crunching of feet trampling the crisp, crystalline snow, or the barking of some shadow-scared hound, relieved the stillness. It was night in Wyoming and Winter had begun.

Quite obviously the frontier could reward a man of Bourke's sensibilities, but he was an uncommon sort: At the age of eight he studied Latin, Greek, and Gaelic, and as he wrote about military life he concerned himself with more than military business. Trudging alongside a pack train in Arizona, his mind floats to the siege of Granada "whither Isabella the Catholic ordered the removal of her Court to the newly-erected city of the Holy Faith and brought together more than 15,000 mules. . . ." He contemplates the braying of mules, to which many soldiers objected. Yet, says Bourke, "the objection strikes me as frivolous and untenable. The mule's song may be just a particle monotonous and the nasal pitch he commonly employs, somewhat harsh for cultivated ears, but the question of pitch is a question of taste, and the mule's taste may be better than our own; or, if worse, this is the land of liberty, and the mule is free to enjoy himself as he pleases."

Early in '76, marching through fearful Montana cold on half-rations, the mercury thermometer *hors de combat*, he pulled out his notebooks and wrote until the ink bottle cracked, after which he continued with a pencil. He was unable to quit; his mind would not rest. His field notes alone take up eight feet of shelf space.

Most soldiers, less reflective than Captain Bourke, did not look or listen so acutely. Instead, they devoted themselves to the prompt gratification of three or four elementary appetites, and being stationed on the frontier they found themselves frustrated. The West did not provide what they needed. Make-believe fandangos, transvestite laundresses, hydrophobic wolves, ant-fights, crazed foreigners, pretty sunsets—this was not enough. The West was not dull, it was stupendously dull, and when not dull it was murderous. A man could get killed without realizing it. There were unbelievable flash floods, weird snakes, and God Himself did not know what else, along with Indians descending as swiftly as the funnel of a tornado.

On the Oregon Trail a French trapper complained to Parkman about this place and the way he had chosen to earn a living. It was not easy, *mon vieux*. Arapahoes recently had murdered two of his associates—stabbed one in the back, shot the other with his own rifle. But of course if one trapped beaver in the mountains or otherwise poked about the raw edge of the world that was the treatment one must expect.

Catlin's friend, Baptiste, explained the business similarly: "I am enlist for tree year in de Fur Comp in St. Louis—for a bounty, vous comprenez, ha?—eighty dollars. . . . If it not pour de dam Riccaree, et de dam Pieds noirs, de Blackfoot Injun, I am make very much money. But I am rob—rob—rob too much, I suppose five time. I am been free trappare seven year, et I am rob five time. Take all de horse. Take my gun. Take all my clothes. Take all de bevare, et I come back on foot."

To these leathery individuals, or to soldiers or homesteaders who might glance up just in time to recognize sudden death—to these people an Arapaho, for instance, was neither more nor less than a redskin, as primitive and dangerous as a grizzly. But to the eastern citizen, protected by a variety of barriers, this was not true. Capt. Charles King noted that those most sympathetic to aborigines were New Englanders, and his explanation was direct: The farther from them a citizen lived, the better he liked them. Each state had in turn elbowed them westward, "and by the time the struggling aborigine was at the safe distance of two or three states away, was virtuously ready to preach fierce denunciation of the people who simply did as it had done."

Having been educated by the novels of James Fenimore Cooper, said Col. Dodge, easterners are quick to believe everything good but nothing bad about the noble savage. Westerners, however, as they scan the horizon, cannot help looking upon their untamed neighbors with deep suspicion. When easterners are able to contrast the pictures drawn by such romantics as Cooper—chivalrous warriors, beautiful maidens, counterparts of fairy-tale knights and damsels—with the Indian as he is, "I fear they will turn from him with loathing and disgust."

Journalist Finerty was more succinct: "I detest the race. . . ."

Capt. Barnitz wrote to his wife Jennie on July 1, 1867, that folks back in Ohio might think it amusing to be told the nation was at war, but it was not very laughable to come across some poor fellow whose body had been filled with revenge arrows.

Barnitz was not specific but he probably referred to an adventurous Eton graduate named Frederick Wyllyams who had joined the American army. Sgt. Wyllyams was killed, possibly by the famous warrior Roman Nose, during a skirmish on the morning of June 26 when a party of Arapaho, Sioux, and Cheyenne horse thieves assaulted Fort Wallace. These Indians—executing an obviously pre-arranged maneuver—galloped off but suddenly turned, "and came literally *sailing* in, uttering their peculiar Hi!-Hi!-Hi! and terminating it with the war-whoop—their ponies, gaily decked with feathers and scalp-locks, tossing their proud little heads high in the air, and looking wildly from side to side. . . ."

Wyllyams' corpse was photographed by another Englishman, Dr. William Bell, almost as soon as the raiders were out of sight.

Dr. Bell, a member of the Ethnological Society of Great Britain, had come to America only that spring, and so anxious was he to observe wild Indians that he accompanied a railroad survey through western Kansas. These surveyors were escorted by G Company, Seventh Cavalry, commanded by Barnitz; thus Dr. Bell met a fellow countryman and very soon got a chance to photograph the handiwork of the people he wanted to study. Considering how Sgt. Wyllyams was mutilated it seems faintly degenerate that Dr. Bell would take a picture of his new friend. The reason, Barnitz explains, was to reveal the nature of these savages to peace advocates in Washington.

The photograph suggests an early Renaissance painting of St. Sebastian, or the crucified Christ, or a figure exhumed from the ash at Herculaneum. Sgt. Wyllyams lies on his back, naked. Five arrows penetrate the stiffly sculptured alabaster form, each protruding like a javelin. No longer a man, he has become symbolic of mankind's past. The Indians sliced him from breast to groin, opening him up like an ox in a butchershop, and slashed his throat so deeply that his head nearly rolled off. In spite of this and everything else they did to him he appears to be grinning through his black beard.

"I shall minutely describe this horrid sight," Dr. Bell wrote, "not for the sake of creating a sensation, but because it is characteristic of a mode of warfare soon—thank God! to be abolished; and because the mutilations have, as we shall presently see, most of them some meaning, apart from brutality and a desire to inspire fear." After noting that a piece of the sergeant's scalp lay near him, although the larger part was gone, and a bullet had passed through his head, and a tomahawk blow above the left eye had rendered the brain visible, and the nose was slit, he points out that an arm had been cut to the bone and both legs were gashed from the hip to the knee.

Dr. Bell then proceeds to summarize the relevant signs: drawing a finger across one arm to symbolize Cheyenne, seizing the nose to indicate Arapaho, cut throat signifying Sioux.

> If we now turn to the body of poor Sergeant Wylyams, we shall have no difficulty in recognizing some meaning in the wounds. The muscles of the right arm, hacked to the bone, speak of the Cheyennes, or "Cut arms;" the nose slit denotes the "Smeller tribe" or Arapahoes; and the throat cut bears witness that the Sioux were also present. There were, therefore, amongst the warriors Cheyennes, Arapahoes, and Sioux. It was not till some time afterwards that I knew positively what these signs meant, and I have not yet discovered what tribe was indicated by the incisions down the thighs, and the laceration of the calves of the legs, in oblique parallel gashes. The arrows also varied in make and colour according to the tribe; and it was evident, from the number of different devices, that warriors from several tribes had each purposely left one in the dead man's body.

Today's ethnologists may dispute fine points of Dr. Bell's analysis, but essentially he knew what he was talking about. It is agreed that pretending to gash an arm or a finger meant Cheyenne. How this originated is uncertain, possibly because Cheyenne women gashed themselves to express grief. Or the sign might have evolved from their habit of cutting off the limbs of dead enemies. During Crook's battle on Rosebud Creek they were seen to chop off the arms of soldiers at the elbow and ride away brandishing these trophies. Another explanation is that the barred feathers of wild turkeys were used on Cheyenne arrows, and one designated such a feather by pulling the right index finger across the left as though striping it.

Dr. Bell also was correct about the cut throat meaning Sioux. In the patois of early French traders they were *coupes-gorges*, maybe because they decapitated enemies—although by the time of the Little Bighorn only the Santee Sioux retained this custom.

Most tribes could be identified by a simple gesture. Touching the left breast meant Northern Arapaho because they were known as good-hearted people. Rubbing the right side of the nose meant Southern Arapaho, although nobody is quite sure why. A finger held like a stick or a bone horizontally beneath the nose meant Nez Perce. The index finger traveling sinuously forward meant Snake. Flapping the hands at shoulder level meant Crow. The sign for Kiowa was more complex: a cupped hand passed around the right side of the face in a circular motion indicated the Kiowa habit of cutting hair only on the right side.

Most Indians thought the Kiowas invented sign-talk because they were by far the most proficient, just as those tribes farthest from Kiowa territory were the least proficient. More probably the Kiowas were adept because they lived at a geographical crossroads: Comanches, Lipans, and Tonkaways to the south, Great Plains tribes to the north. Kiowas served as intermediaries, whether the cause might be trade or war, and out of necessity they amplified this mute language, but did not invent it. Sign-talk developed wherever there was no alternative, and by the time of the white invasion it had become a subtle, rapid substitute for speech. Colonel Dodge gives as one example the word "coffee," represented by five hand signals which could be executed almost as fast as the word is pronounced. Dodge also mentions an Arapaho who was so incompetent that he needed an interpreter to conduct business with a Cheyenne.

Some gestures, of course, were easily read. For instance, split fingers darting from the mouth was a condemnation too vile to be misunderstood. Such pantomime spoke as eloquently as the lacerations reported by Dr. Bell.

Wyllyams had a distinctive tattoo on his chest: a unicorn, a lion, and a coat of arms flanked by British flags. This tattoo—which is to say, an oval patch of skin bearing this design—later turned up in a Cheyenne village. Any interesting piece of skin might be kept, even the hairy armpit. Dodge once saw the entire upper half of a human skin, from face to crotch: "It was thickly covered with hair, had been carefully cured, and peculiar value was set upon it as 'big medicine'." Usually the scalp alone was kept, no doubt because it represented a defeated enemy's head.

Scalping never became popular west of the Rockies. Now and then a Westerner would lose his hair, yet this may have been the result of copying eastern tradition or the result of Indians imitating their white-skinned cousins who, as many witnesses have testified, could be enthusiastic collectors. Indeed, territorial governments often encouraged it by paying a bounty. Apache scalps would bring as much as $250 in Arizona, and because it was hard to tell one glossy black hank from another the American bounty hunters might ease across the Sonora line to supplement their income with Mexican hair.

How it all began, nobody will ever know because the earliest instance far antedates written history. Anthropologists studying the skull of Ethiopia's Bodo man—a predecessor of Homo sapiens—removed some encrusted rock and deduced that the flesh had been stripped from the head with stone tools. This was done after the creature's death; that much could be determined, but not the purpose.

The first historical record occurs in Herodotus, writing in the fifth century B.C. He says that Parthians took the hair of slain enemies with which to enhance their weapons and clothing: "It is apparent that they use a sharp and very keen dagger by which they make a circle of flesh above the eye level. . . ."

A couple of generations later Xenophon notes that after some of his men were killed while en route to the Mediterranean the hair was taken from their heads.

The Byzantine historian Procopius refers to Count Belisarius being much concerned about the behavior of certain auxiliary soldiers. After first torturing a captive these wild tribesmen "by making a series of short slashes about the victim's skull below the line of the ears, removed the entire upper skin portion of the skull. This they treated with oils and stuffed with padding, making a most grisly trophy. . . ."

Genghis Khan in the thirteenth century, although he did not take scalps, discovered that plaited human hair was less suceptible to rain and cold than rope or leather. Accordingly, human hair gathered from the skulls of his victims was used to operate catapults and siege engines.

Spaniards in the New World soon learned that Caribbean natives took heads and hair, and presently it came to the notice of Captain Alvarado that Guatemalans were skinning the heads of captured conquistadors. Spanish captains exploring Chihuahua and Sonora in northern Mexico also found this practice among tribesmen who were, very probably, predecessors of the Yaqui and Apache. And it is recorded that during the sixteenth century when Jacques Cartier met the famous chief Donnacona along the St. Lawrence River he asked why Indians took scalps, and was told they did so because their enemies did.

By this time, clearly, a tradition had been established in the western wilderness. Whether the idea migrated north from Mexico, evolved independently, or perhaps had existed in the Americas ever since a party of Asiatic hunters crossed the Bering Strait, is a matter of argument. In any case it was an artistic process, as correspondent Finerty observed, "and, when neatly done, may be termed a satanic accomplishment."

The procedure alone was not fatal, although very few victims survived, which may be explained by the fact that most of them had been thoroughly banged up otherwise. Still, a few cases have been documented. The Bozeman *Times* carried a story on July 16, 1876, about one Herman Ganzio who was attacked when he wandered ahead of his companions in the Black Hills. A bullet punctured his left leg, another hit his left shoulder, and down he went. Moments later an Indian was kneeling on his back. Ganzio was struck with a club or the butt of a gun, he did not know which: "All I knew was that I was being scalped; my hair was held tight. . . ." A reporter described the top of Ganzio's head as one large mass of sores. Surgeons had shaved off what remained of his hair in an effort to prevent infection, "but the pear-shaped patch made by the scalping knife is thus made all the more distinct."

Delos G. Sandbertson was an infantryman with Custer during the 1868 attack on Black Kettle's village in Oklahoma. He survived, but spent the next six months in a hospital. Upon being released and discharged from service he permitted an inquisitive journalist to inspect his poll—"the still red and tender spot from which the scalp was jerked"—and he told his story:

Just in the gray of morning, the firing commenced on both sides, and we had it all our own way for a few minutes, the cursed snakes being much confused, and not knowing what was up. At length they rallied, and we could hear Black Kettle shouting and ordering. The vermin got into holes and behind rocks—anywhere they could find a place, and began to fight with a will. We fired whenever we could see a top-knot, and shot squaws—there were lots of them—just as quick as Indians. We just went in for wiping out the whole gang.

When it was full daylight, we all gave a big yell and charged right down into camp. The lodges were all standing yet, and lots of Indians in them. As we run through the alleys, a big red jumped out at me from behind a tent, and before I could shorten up enough to run him through with my bayonet, a squaw grabbed me around the legs and twisted me down. The camp was then full of men fighting, and everybody seemed yelling as loud as he could. When I fell, I went over backward, dropping my gun, and I had just got part way up again, the squaw yanked me by the hair, when the Indian clubbed my gun and struck me across the neck. He might just as well have run me through, but he wasn't used to the bayonet, or didn't think. The blow stunned me; it didn't hurt me the least, but gave me a numb feeling all over. I couldn't have got to my feet then if all alone, while the squaw kept screeching and pulling my hair out by the handful.

I heard some of our boys shouting close by, and the squaw started and ran—one of the boys killing her not three rods off. The Indian stepped one foot on my chest, and with his hand gathered up the hair near the crown of my head. He wasn't very tender about it, but jerked my head this way and that, and pinched like Satan. My eyes were partially open, and I could see the beadwork and trimming on his leggings. Suddenly I felt the awfulest biting, cutting flesh go on round my head, and then it seemed to me just as if my whole head had been jerked clean off. I never felt such pain in all my life; why, it was like pulling your brains right out. I didn't know any more for two or three days, and then I came to to find that I had the sorest head of any human being that ever lived. If the boys killed the viper, they didn't get back my scalp; perhaps it got lost in the snow. I was shipped down to Laramie after a bit, and all the nursing I got hain't made the hair grow out on this spot yet.

The most celebrated scalpee was Mr. William Thompson who rode into trouble on a railroad handcar in central Nebraska. He and five other men set out from the Plum Creek depot to fix a broken telegraph line on August 6,

1867. They were ambushed by a party of Cheyennes from Turkey Leg's camp. Thompson started to run. A bullet went through his arm. He kept running. A mounted Cheyenne overtook him, clubbed him to the ground, stabbed him in the neck, "and making a twirl round his fingers with my hair, he commenced sawing and hacking away at my scalp."

Unlike Sandbertson, Thompson remained conscious throughout the procedure, but he neglects to mention the noise of his scalp being ripped off—a distinctive sound, according to some who lived to describe it—a peculiar popping, evidently similar to the noise of bubbles or blisters popping.

Well, when the job was finished the Indian hopped on his pony and trotted away, but either lost or discarded the prize. There is reason to think it was deliberately tossed aside. John Stands in Timber, himself a Cheyenne, said that his people regarded white scalps with contempt or disgust. Whites would be scalped, but instead of flourishing such a paltry hank a warrior might throw it in the bushes.

Another explanation may be considered. LeForge states that on several occasions he noticed scalpers behave strangely. They appeared to be nervous. Twice he saw a brave pause during the operation in order to vomit. The Cheyenne who lifted Thompson's scalp might have had similar feelings and wanted no reminder.

Thompson and those with him were not foolish, as Ganzio had been foolish for exploring a dangerous region alone; they were just unlucky. If they had started out to fix the telegraph line an hour later they could have repaired it and gone back to Plum Creek with no trouble. The Cheyennes who caught them were returning from an excursion into Pawnee country when they observed the handcar approaching and decided to wreck it. They piled logs on the tracks and hid themselves and when the car passed by they jumped up, yelling and shooting. So the white men began pumping the handles faster and faster in an effort to escape from the Indians.

This happened seventeen years before John Stands in Timber was born, but he heard all about it. He said that a man named Sleeping Rabbit suggested to the others after they had wrecked the handcar that maybe they could wreck a train by bending the tracks. "Then," Sleeping Rabbit pointed out, "we could see what is in the cars."

A train arrived just about dark so the Cheyennes began yipping and shooting, and just like the handcar the train went faster, puffing and making noise until the engine hopped off the tracks. Right away a man came running up from the back of the train. He was carrying a light and he was shouting. At that time the Cheyennes did not understand English, but one of them whose name was Wolf Tooth remembered a word this white man shouted and he used to say he was the first Cheyenne who could speak any of the white man's words. He thought maybe it meant "Indian," and years afterward he repeated this word to John Stands in Timber, who had to laugh because it did not mean at all what Wolf Tooth thought.

So, after killing the white men on this train they broke into one of the cars and found hatchets. Then they went around chopping open the other cars to see what was inside. They packed what they wanted on their ponies and rode back to camp. Wolf Tooth got a hatchet and something made of shiny metal that came in a box. He did not know what this thing was although he thought it must be valuable, but nobody could tell him how to use it so he threw it away.

Next morning they went back to the train. Several boys had gone with them into Pawnee territory and now these boys had lots of fun. They would tie a bolt of calico to a pony's tail and hit him with a quirt. The pony would look around to see why they were hitting him and would see this cloth and get scared and run away with the calico bouncing and unrolling and streaming way out behind.

Such was the story told by Cheyennes.

Wasichu accounts do not coincide exactly with the Cheyenne version, but almost. They did wreck a train that night, either by pulling apart the tracks or by constructing a barricade. They murdered the engineer and fireman. The brakeman and the conductor jumped out of the caboose and ran away. The train carried whisky, tobacco, flour, saddles, and a considerable amount of plumage for frontier ladies. The Indians got drunk, dressed up in velvet and calico and silk and spent the night staggering around a bonfire. About dawn they set the boxcars afire and threw the bodies of the engineer and fireman into the flames. Thompson, who had been lying motionless since the handcar was wrecked, decided this was the time to escape. After recovering his scalp he crawled and lurched along the tracks to the Willow Island depot where another train took him to Omaha. Just how long Thompson was obliged to sit around the Willow Island depot with his scalp at his side is not clear, but it must have been a while because the immolated bodies of the engineer and fireman accompanied him to Omaha.

Correspondent Stanley was in Omaha when this train arrived. At least he wrote as if he were present and his report sounds authentic. He says that a general rush was made to the baggage car because of rumors that the bodies had been burnt and everybody wanted to look. Two boxes, approximately twelve by thirty inches, contained all that was left. For the benefit of the public one box was opened. There "surrounded by cotton, lay a charred trunk about two feet in length, resembling a half-burnt log. . . ."

Horrified spectators soon learned about another fascinating specimen aboard the Union Pacific: Mr. Thompson, three-fourths alive, his scalp riding in a bucket of water. People flocked from everywhere, Stanley reports, "to view the gory baldness which had come upon him so suddenly." Thompson was quite weak, which is not surprising, what with a bullet hole through one arm, a knife wound in the neck, and the top of his head gone.

A local surgeon, Dr. R. C. Moore, stitched the scalp into place but the operation did not succeed. A photograph taken after his recovery shows a full-bearded man seated in a chair wearing a stunned, shocked look and a coat that is too large, as though the experience had caused him to shrivel. The top of his skull does look peculiar. Ordinarily, it is said, he wore a black skull cap. He was British and he later went home, taking his scalp, which by this time had been tanned. For some unexplained reason he subsequently mailed it to Dr. Moore who gave it to the Omaha Public Library where it was displayed in a jar of alcohol as recently as 1967. Stanley, who peeked in the bucket when the Union Pacific reached Omaha, said the patch of skin was about nine inches long and four inches wide, "somewhat resembling a drowned rat, as it floated, curled up, on the water."

Nine inches by four, indicating a rectangle, is a surprise. One thinks of scalps as being circular, but many were not. Just as each tribe marked its arrows in a distinctive way, so each had a particular style of scalping: dia-mond-shaped, triangular, square, oval. Sgt. Ryan observed in his memoirs that when the scalped body of a trooper was found the Indian scouts knew immediately which tribe was responsible.

Custer denounces the custom as "barbarous" in *My Life on the Plains*, yet he shows an uncommon interest in the procedure, especially in the seasoning and embellishment. Most of those he saw were three or four inches across, stretched within a hoop by a network of thread. When cured, "the dried fleshy portion of the scalp is ornamented in bright colors, according to the taste of the captor, sometimes the addition of beads of bright and varied colors being made to heighten the effect. In other instances the hair is dyed, either to a beautiful yellow or golden, or to crimson." It is, he concludes, horrible evi-dence of past depredations, and one cannot help sensing beneath his disgust the temptation to cure and decorate a few.

Custer's attitudes—like those of Colonel Dodge, of Captains King and Barnitz, of Godfrey and Gerard and Lonesome Charley and Mitch Bouyer and Pvt. Coleman and Mrs. Kelly and of other adventurous people who re-fused to spend their lives behind fences—his thoughts and feelings evolved not from assorted newspaper stories but from his own experiences. He was employed by the United States to control Indians, to fight them if necessary, so he looked upon them not through urban spectacles but as they appeared to him in the field. They were, as a rule, enemies. If not actively hostile, they might be. Yet he felt an affinity for them. He liked their courage and passionate independence; and what seeps through his book like a stain is a feeling of regret that he could not share that uninhibited pattern of life. As a West Point cadet in 1858 he wrote a boring, prophetic, ingenuous little essay sentimentally titled "The Red Man" in which he laments the imminent destruction of the red man's home of peace and plenty. He speaks of the Indian's "dauntless brow" and "manly limbs," and regrets that already these red men have been scattered "by the fury of the tempest." Gone are familiar forests in the shade of which Indians could stretch their weary limbs, swept away by the woodsman's ax. "We behold him now on the verge of extinction, standing on his last foothold, clutching his bloodstained rifle, resolved to die amidst the horrors of slaughter, and soon he will be talked of as a noble race who once existed but have now passed away."

After some rough experience, however, he did not write sentimentally about Indians and he was annoyed by those who did. He felt sorry Cooper's Indians were not real Indians, but they were not. That was all there was to it.

Stripped of the beautiful romance with which we have been so long willing to envelope him, transferred from the inviting pages of the novelist to the localities where we are compelled to meet with him, in his native village, on the war path, and when raiding upon our frontier settlements and lines of travel, the Indian forfeits his claim to the appellation of the "*noble* red man." We see him as he is, and, so far as all knowledge goes, as he ever has been, a *savage* in every sense of the word; not worse, perhaps, than his white brother would be similarly born and bred, but one whose cruel and ferocious nature far exceeds that of any wild beast of the desert. That this is true no one who had been brought into intimate contact with the wild tribes will deny.

This absolute, irrefutable conviction—that he was leading a regiment of civilized humans against bestial enemies—should explain the rigidity of Custer's command. If his unit was to survive it must above all else be disciplined, which of course is true. Yet he had been a compulsive disciplinarian five years earlier when his troops fought civilized Virginians.

Whatever the cause, his unrelenting grip alienated officers as well as enlisted men. "Things are becoming very unpleasant here," Captain Barnitz wrote to Jennie from Fort Hays. "General Custer is very injudicious in his administration, and spares no effort to render himself generally obnoxious. I have utterly lost all the little confidence I ever had in his ability as an officer. . . ."

Barnitz sounds more and more like Benteen.

Six enlisted men went to the Fort Hays post exchange to buy tinned fruit. This was not against orders but they neglected to get permission, which meant that technically they were absent without leave for about forty-five minutes. Custer symbolically scalped them. A line was drawn across the top of each man's head, from the nose to the occipital bone. On one side of this line the hair was left untouched, the other side was shaved. They were then paraded through camp, Barnitz notes in his journal, to the mortification and disgust of every decent officer.

Such disciplinary methods no doubt were effective in certain cases—it is hard to imagine anybody else buying tinned fruit without authorization—but the ultimate results might be questioned. Barnitz mentions in one letter to his wife that since the Seventh Cavalry was organized twelve hundred men had deserted.

Custer left Fort Hays on June 1, 1867, with a wagon train and 350 troops "to hunt out & chastise the Cheyennes, and that portion of the Sioux who are their allies, between the Smoky Hill & the Platte."

On this expedition thirty-five men deserted, including a party of thirteen who left camp boldly, arrogantly, as though challenging him to stop them. It seems incredible that men who had served any time at all in the Seventh would make such a mistake. He sent a detail after this insolent group with orders to bring them back dead or alive. The regiment had been losing about fifty soldiers a month, which was bad enough, but this exodus deep in hostile territory was the most flagrant and ominous revolt. If these men got away with it there was no telling what the rest might do. Enough desertion would imperil the lives of those who remained and a gravely weakened unit could end up as Cheyenne pemmican. So he took "severe and summary measures."

Of those thirteen, seven escaped. Six were brought back alive, three of them shot while resisting arrest. One of those three, Pvt. Charles Johnson, died at Fort Wallace. According to some witnesses he was on his knees begging for mercy when the general's posse gunned him down. This incident eventually would cause trouble, but for the moment Custer seems to have been well satisfied because no other snowbirds took wing.

From the Platte he led his squadron southwest, following the south fork of the Republican into Colorado, turned northwest—still hunting will-o'-the-wisp Indians—then looped down to Fort Wallace beside the Smoky Hill in western Kansas. Here, by his own account, he found the garrison suffering from hunger, cholera, and scurvy. Marauding Cheyennes had cut the supply line from Kansas City to Denver. The Butterfield Overland stage was disconnected—relay stations and dugouts had been abandoned. More important, he learned of trouble at Fort Hays: a flash flood, emergency evacuation of personnel, telegraph lines down. The situation at Fort Hays alarmed him because that was where he had left Elizabeth, so he commandeered three officers and seventy-two men and went galloping off to see her.

By this time Jennie Barnitz also was billeted at Fort Hays and she, like just about everybody else, was keeping a journal. "Oh! what a night," she wrote on June 7. The air smelled of electricity. Chain lightning hissed and burst like rockets. "At about 3 O'C a m Gen Smith came to our tent and screamed, 'For God's sake Barnitz get up, we are under water.' I was obliged to look for my things got dressed soon. With one shoe & one of Alberts boots, & took my watch jewelry & money and went out. . . . The ladies were out half dressed, with hair over their shoulders, & to add to the terror of the scene, drowning men went floating past us shrieking for help. . . ."

Elizabeth recalled that just after creeping out of her tent a stroke of lightning illuminated the creek, which had risen thirty-five feet. Usually it was a trickle at the bottom of a gulch, now it overflowed the banks. Tree branches were bending in the current: "the whole arc above us seemed aflame. We were aghast at what the brilliant light revealed. Between the bluffs that rose gradually from the stream, and the place where we were on its banks, a wide newly made river spread over land that had been perfectly dry. . . ." One drowning man was caught by a tree. She saw his face during explosions of light, features pinched with suffering, eyes bulging.

In the midst of this scene, which must have looked like a sixteenth-century representation of humanity's penultimate moments, Rover the foxhound and a white bulldog named Turk broke their shackles and began to fight. They were longtime enemies. Their war had been savage and bloody. They wallowed in the muck, each trying to bury its fangs in the other's throat while lightning sizzled and the terrible flood deepened—which might, of course, be interpreted as a parable of nations or taken for what it was: a dogfight in the rain.

By daybreak the rain had stopped but the camp was an island. About mid-morning when the water began to recede a hideous spectacle emerged: a drowned soldier embedded in the mud bank. He had been waving for help. Elizabeth says they could scarcely avoid looking at the bloated corpse with one arm stretched out for assistance.

Jennie Barnitz reports Elizabeth saying with patrician equanimity during the worst of this flood: "Well, we will all go down together. I am glad the Gen doesn't know of it."

In her memoirs Elizabeth cheerfully admits to being a coward. She presents herself as a nineteenth-century Michigan honeysuckle. Nothing delights her more than being rescued by a gallant male—preferably her husband—from some awful threat such as a tarantula in the wagon. She shrieks and trembles. Masculine bystanders clutch their ribs. What could be more satisfactory! Yet now, when in fact she might be drowned—when the husband who protects her is far away—she becomes magically self-assured. One thing she was not told. If the water had risen much higher every woman at Fort Hays would have been lashed to a Gatling gun, which was the heaviest equipment in camp.

General Miles blamed the vast herds of buffalo for these terrifying flash floods. They had trampled the ground until it was impervious to water, he said, which explained the abrupt rise of streams and the quick inundation of low land.

Custer had been on the prairie long enough to respect the situation; very anxiously he pushed down the road, and along the way he met a wagon train escorted by Capt. Benteen which was hauling supplies to Fort Wallace. And at this point a curious discrepancy develops. Unknown to anybody, the supply train was carrying cholera to Fort Wallace, yet Custer would write in *My Life* that the plague already had erupted at Fort Wallace. The officer in charge of this garrison told him, he said, that unless better rations could be obtained it would be impossible to check the epidemic. As a matter of fact, the officer in charge said no such thing for a very good reason: there was no epidemic. There would be soon enough, but Custer seems to have advanced the date by several days, even as he exaggerated the food shortage and the incidence of scurvy, to justify his trip east. He selected about a hundred of his best men, he would later explain, so he could force his way through to Fort Harker, from which point these desperately needed rations might be conducted back to Fort Wallace.

Where and when the cholera plague began its devastating journey westward is not known, but the principal carrier seems to have been the Thirty-eighth Infantry, which was afflicted at Fort Leavenworth just before being transferred to Fort Union, New Mexico. Why a diseased regiment was ordered to travel across inhabited country could be explained only by an accomplished bureaucrat, but the Thirty-eighth moved west, infecting everything in its path.

The plague hit Fort Wallace when Benteen's supply train arrived, a few days after Custer left. Barnitz wrote to Jennie on July 28: "We are becoming very fashionable out here! We are having the cholera just like other people, and are beginning to feel quite as important as city folks! Only think, seven dead men in an evening. . . . Yes, seven dead men in an evening, and more the following day. . . ."

Anyway, Custer helped himself to provisions from Benteen's train and hurried along. Then at Castle Rock station he met two mail coaches, and because one or the other might have a letter from his wife he searched them. Later he defended this illegal act by insisting that he was looking for military orders.

By now the troopers who followed him were groggy with fatigue, the column was strung out, and he could not locate his mare Fanchon. He therefore detailed a sergeant with six men to poke up the stragglers, shoot exhausted horses so the Indians could not use them, and bring the mare forward. The sergeant's squad was attacked by fifty or sixty Cheyennes while carrying out these orders. Two enlisted men were cut off. The other four and the sergeant overtook the column at Downer's station where Custer had paused long enough to eat. News of the attack did not trouble him. The captain in charge at Downer's mentioned in a letter to his parents that Custer finished lunch and rode on without a word.

Through Custer's eyes this incident can hardly be noticed. He states in his autobiography that while stopping to rest the horses for a few minutes it came to his attention that twenty-five or thirty Indians had attacked a small party of soldiers who lagged behind. "As there was a detachment of infantry guarding the station, and time being important, we pushed on. . . ."

Barnitz wrote about Custer's blistering trip to Fort Hays: "They do say that he just squandered that cavalry along the road!—that whenever a horse gave out or a man took sick, or became faint from sunstroke, that man or horse or both remained by the road side until the arrival of Lo, the poor Cheyenne, who acts as public scavenger on these highways, and there was an end of the matter!—I do not credit the rumor however—though the occasional arrival in camp of a broken down and riderless horse, with blood upon the saddle, gives some credence. . . . "

Lo, the poor Cheyenne, or Lo, the poor Sioux—or Comanche, Ute, Arapaho, Kiowa, Apache, or whatever—often turns up in frontier diaries, occasionally as the pronoun Lo without specific identification. Every trooper understood it as a sardonic play on the naïve humanism of Alexander Pope:

Lo, the poor Indian! whose untutor'd mind
Sees God in clouds . . .

Custer, desperately worried about his wife, or at least very anxious to enjoy himself with her, did not find her at Fort Hays so he rode sixty miles in a mule-drawn ambulance to the next post, Fort Harker, accompanied by brother Tom and Lt. Cooke.

At Harker the deprived husband learned that his honeysuckle was in good health but had been escorted still farther east to Fort Riley. He therefore boarded the Kansas-Pacific and continued his trip.

Elizabeth thought it marvelous that he would travel such a long way just to be with her. "There was in that summer of 1867 one long, perfect day," she wrote at the end of *Tenting on the Plains*. "It was mine, and—blessed be our memory, which preserves to us the joys as well as the sadness of life!—it is still mine, for time and for eternity." The U.S. government, however, looked upon this romantic journey from a militaristic point of view, being more concerned with its effects upon his regiment and the campaign to pacify western Kansas. On July 28 the gallant husband was arrested, pending court-martial. For an enlisted man in those days a court-martial was not the event it is today; more than thirteen thousand courts-martial occurred in a single year—approximately one for every two men in service, but for a ranking officer to be tried was unusual.

Two months after his arrest Custer's trial began. On eight charges he was found guilty. The evidence and judicial procedure were reviewed by the Washington Bureau of Military Justice, which reported to War Secretary Lorenzo Thomas.

> Bvt. Maj.-Gen'l G.A. Custer, Lt.-Col. 7th U.S. Cavalry, was tried in Sept. & Oct. last by Gen'l Court-Martial convened at Ft. Leavenworth, Kansas, by order of the General-in-Chief, under the following Charges:
>   I. Absent without leave from his Command
>   Finding: *Guilty*
>   In that Accused did, at or near Ft. Wallace, Kans., on or about July 15th last, absent himself from his Command without proper authority . . .

Among other things, he was found guilty of ordering deserters shot on the spot, one of the most virulent witnesses being his implacable enemy Benteen, who testified about the Platte River incident with very little reluctance: "It was like a buffalo hunt. The dismounted deserters were shot down, while begging for their lives, by General Custer's executioners: Major Elliot, Lieutenant Tom Custer, and the executioner-in-chief, Lieutenant Cooke. . . . Three of the deserters were brought in badly wounded, and screaming in extreme agony. General Custer rode up to them, pistol in hand, and told them if they didn't stop making so much fuss he would shoot them to death."

The mortally wounded snowbird, Pvt. Charles Johnson, had been shot twice with a pistol. According to another fugitive, Clement Willis, they gave up their arms when ordered to do so and were then told to leave. But as soon as they began to run the officers opened fire.

Dr. I. T. Coates, Acting Assistant Surgeon, testified during the court-martial that Johnson had a flesh wound in the left side but was shot also in the head: "the ball entering the left temple and coming out below, under the jaw, and passing down into his lungs, the same ball entering again at the upper part of the chest." The trajectory of this bullet was questioned because it implied that whoever shot Johnson had been above him—either standing above him or on horseback. In other words, it smacked of assassination.

The Court pursued this matter.

Q: How near should you judge him to have been to the person who fired the shot?

A: From the power of the ball he must have been within twenty-five yards at least, and perhaps much nearer.

The Court asked if the bullet would or would not have gone straight through Johnson's head, rather than passing downward into the lungs, if the person firing the shot had been at a distance of twenty-five yards. Dr. Coates replied that the bullet might have taken the course it did, and, begging the Court's permission, explained: ". . . it is recorded in medical history of a ball having struck the breast bone, and to have been found lodged in the testicles. I know of one instance of a ball striking what is known as the 'Adams Apple' and passing clear around the neck and was taken out at the very same place."

The surgeon's testimony may have been construed in Custer's favor—implying at least the chance of a capricious long-distance shot rather than short-range execution—but if so, it was not enough.

Sentence: To be suspended from rank & Command for one (1) year, and to forfeit his pay proper for the same time.

Custer officially received this news on the Fort Leavenworth parade ground, November 25, mounted like a conquistador on a coal-black stallion, backed up by his regiment in dress uniform. He wore a blue tunic with gold epaulettes and tassels and stripes, yellow-striped gray trousers, white kid gloves. A saber dangled at his side. On his head stood a high polished helmet with an eagle insignia topped by a scarlet plume. There he posed, stiff as a mannequin, this mustached hero with the chiseled face, electric blue eyes, long yellow hair—a magazine illustrator's dream.

It is said that he listened impassively to the charges. He thought they were unjustified. He thought he should have been acquitted. As a matter of fact he was once again lucky. Had he not been who he was he would have been dishonorably discharged. General Grant observed that the Court "in awarding so lenient a sentence" must have taken into account his previous record.

He manages to glide past this unpleasant episode in the story of his life: "It not being my privilege to serve with the regiment. . . . I remained at Fort Leavenworth some time longer, and later in the summer repaired to my home in Michigan, there amid the society of friends to enjoy the cool breezes of Erie until the time came which would require me to go west." Thirty-five pages later, to make certain his readers understand, he pats the court-martial into shape: "I will briefly remark in parenthesis . . . it had apparently been deemed necessary that my connection with certain events and transactions, every one of which has been fully referred to heretofore, should be submitted to an official examination in order to determine if each and every one of my acts had been performed with due regard to the customs of war in like cases. To enter into a review of the proceedings which followed, would be to introduce into these pages matters of too personal a character to interest the general reader."

Two months after that unjustified reprimand on the Fort Leavenworth parade grounds he got a telegram from Little Phil Sheridan, stating that on or about October 1 his regiment would move against hostile Indians in what is now Oklahoma:

> Generals Sherman, Sully, and myself, and nearly all the officers of your regiment, have asked for you, and I hope the applications will be successful. Can you come at once?

He did not wait for Sheridan's petition to be approved; one day after receiving this telegram he was on a train to Fort Hays accompanied by two staghounds and a pointer.

The hostiles Little Phil had in mind were Black Kettle's Cheyennes, at that time wintering along the Washita River just east of the Texas panhandle. Four years earlier while encamped at Sand Creek a few miles northwest of Fort Lyon, Colorado, this peripatetic village had been visited by a former Methodist preacher, Col. John Chivington, leading two regiments of Colorado militia and four mountain howitzers—an early morning surprise that provoked a Congressional inquiry.

At the treaty of Fort Wise in 1861 the Commissioner of Indian Affairs had presented Black Kettle with an American flag and told him that if it flew above his lodge the village would be safe. Not unreasonably, therefore, when Chivington's militia swept toward him, he wished to make sure this flag was not overlooked. It is said to have been a large garrison flag and George Bent states that he saw Black Kettle holding it up at the end of a long pole.

When Chivington organized this attack, using the First and Third Cavalry, several junior officers protested that the Cheyennes had been given assurances of safety. Chivington—a big, thick, violent man whose obsidian eyes glare out of every photograph—grew furious. He threatened these dissidents, shoved a fist at Lt. Joseph Cramer, and roared: "I have come to kill Indians, and believe it is right and honorable to use any means under God's heaven to kill Indians!" He was also heard to say, according to one J. M. Coombs: "Scalps are what we are after. . . . I long to be wading in gore!"

Although the mad preacher plotted and directed this assault, he was not alone. Most people on the frontier felt more or less the same. In particular the troops of his Third Cavalry, made up of hundred-day volunteers, were anxious for a fight because their term of enlistment was just about over and they had not accomplished much. They had attacked one small band—killing six warriors, a boy, and three squaws—but in Denver they were contemptuously called the Bloodless Third.

At daybreak on November 29, 1864, Col. Chivington saluted Black Kettle's village.

When Congress got around to investigating this matter there was quite a lot of testimony. A militiaman who inspected the bodies of several murdered children said one had been slashed with some unspecified sharp instrument, presumably a cavalry saber, and another's ears were gone. A lieutenant of the New Mexico volunteers heard a Colorado trooper say he had a squaw's heart on a stick. An unnamed lieutenant was observed scalping three women and five children who had been captured alive.

Robert Bent, another of trader William Bent's sons, watched a soldier attack a squaw whose leg was broken. When he approached with a saber she lifted an arm to protect herself: ". . . he struck, breaking her arm. She rolled over, and raised her other arm; he struck, breaking that, and then left her without killing her." Thirty or forty squaws who had attempted to hide in a depression or hole in the river bank sent out a little girl with a white flag, but the child walked only a few steps before a trooper cut her down. Bent states that he saw a pregnant squaw sliced open, the foetus at her side. "I saw the body of White Antelope with the privates cut off, and I heard a soldier say he was going to make a tobacco pouch out of them." White Antelope may have been wearing a medal given to him by President Lincoln. If so, it worked no greater magic than Black Kettle's flag.

Cpl. Amos Miksch, E Company, First Colorado Cavalry, testified that on the morning after the battle he saw a boy, still alive, in a trench filled with the bodies of slaughtered adults: "I saw a major in the 3d regiment take out his pistol and blow off the top of his head. I saw some men unjointing fingers to get rings off, and cutting off ears to get silver ornaments. I saw a party with the same major take up bodies that had been buried in the night to scalp them and take off ornaments. I saw a squaw with her head smashed in before she was killed. Next morning, after they were dead and stiff, these men pulled out the bodies of the squaws and pulled them open in an indecent manner. . . . It was the 3d Colorado men who did these things."

Major Scott Anthony reported the murder of a child about three years old: "I saw one man get off his horse at a distance of about seventy-five yards and draw up his rifle and fire. He missed the child. Another man came up and said, 'Let me try the son of a bitch. I can hit him.' He got down off his horse, kneeled down, and fired at the little child, but he missed him. A third man came up, and made a similar remark, and fired, and the little fellow dropped."

Lt. James Connor testified that while going over the battlefield he did not find a single Indian corpse, regardless of age or sex, that had not been scalped. Soldiers mutilated bodies "in the most horrible manner—men, women, and children's privates cut out, &c; I heard one man say he had cut out a woman's private parts and had them for exhibition. . . . I also heard of numerous instances in which men had cut out the private parts of females and stretched them over the saddle-bows and wore them over their hats while riding in the ranks."

By way of rebuttal, on the fifty-ninth day of this inquiry surgeon Caleb Burdsal testified that he had been treating wounded soldiers in a Cheyenne lodge when a trooper came to the entrance with five or six Caucasian scalps.

Dr. Burdsal was cross-examined. What reason had he to think these scalps came from the heads of white persons?

He replied that he was convinced by the color of the hair: blond, sandy brown, but none very black.

Might they not have faded or been altered by age from their original color?

Dr. Burdsal thought not. "My impression is that one or two of them were not more than ten days off the head."

He was asked how he could determine this.

"The skin and flesh attached to the hair appeared to be yet quite moist."

William Breakenridge, best known as a deputy sheriff of Tombstone, was a young soldier at the time of Chivington's raid. His testimony corroborated Dr. Burdsal. "There were a lot of scalps of white men and women, some very fresh, found in the teepees. . . ."

Chivington himself talked about a white scalp in one of the lodges, and although it never was displayed as proof of Cheyenne barbarity it reproduced itself until Denver citizens knew beyond doubt that his men had found dozens of auburn and blond trophies. Worse yet, they saw a blanket woven of human hair—hair from the heads of white women. Everybody knew this to be a fact. Still worse, according to an editor of the *Rocky Mountain News*, William Byers, the troops found a white woman's skin stretched across an Indian saddle.

However such stories evolved, they expressed the fear and rage of Colorado citizens.

About three weeks after Chivington's assault on the village his militiamen trotted triumphantly through Denver, led by the venomous ex-preacher holding a captive eagle tethered to a pole. According to the *News*: "Headed by the First Regiment band, and by Colonels Chivington and Shoup, Lieut. Col. Bowen and Major Sayre, the rank and file of the 'bloody Thirdsters' made a most imposing procession, extending, with the transportation trains, from the upper end of Ferry street, through Latimer, G and Blake, almost back to Ferry street again. As the 'bold sojer boys' passed along, the sidewalks and corner stands were thronged with citizens saluting their old friends."

Sensitive souls might quiver. The *News* did not. Testimony delivered to the Thirty-eighth Congress included a long editorial: "Among the brilliant feats of arms in Indian warfare, the recent campaign of our Colorado volunteers will stand in history with few rivals, and none to exceed it. . . . Among the killed were *all* the Cheyenne chiefs, Black Kettle, White Antelope, Little Robe, Left Hand, Knock Knee, One Eye, and another, name unknown. Not a single prominent man of the tribe remains, and the tribe itself is almost annihilated. . . . Colorado soldiers have again covered themselves with glory."

Col. Chivington thought his troops fought well: "I, at daylight this morning, attacked a Cheyenne village of one hundred and thirty lodges, from nine hundred to one thousand warriors strong. We killed Chiefs Black Kettle, White Antelope and Little Robe. . . ." In fact, there were eighty or ninety lodges containing fewer than five hundred people, two-thirds of them women and children. White Antelope was killed, Black Kettle and Little Robe survived.

Not long after the bloody Thirdsters came to town another sanguine performance took place on stage at the Apollo theater: one hundred Cheyenne scalps were displayed. Helen Hunt Jackson, who did not attend the Apollo that evening, claims the audience "applauded rapturously."

That a string of scalps was exhibited on stage seems fairly certain, although nobody—Madame Jackson nor anybody else—has preserved the details of this atavistic tableau, such as the date, the featured program, nor what remarks might have been provided by Chivington or one of his Thirdsters when the scalps were introduced. It is also reasonably certain that frantic applause greeted the spectacle because quite a few members of the Apollo audience had lost relatives and neighbors to aboriginal scalping knives. If the audience did applaud it surely validates the comment of a visiting Britisher that America might be the only nation in history to have slipped from a primitive estate into decadence without ever knowing civilization.

Elizabeth Tallman, interviewed in 1936 for *The Colorado Magazine*, had this to say:

> I was in Denver when Col. Chivington started for Sand Creek. John M. Tallman, later to be my husband, belonged to the Third Regiment, part of which was in the battle. I have some rings made of a white woman's hair, taken off the bodies of dead Indians. Had you been living at that time, as we were, in a constant state of fear and anxiety, almost daily seeing the bodies of friends or acquaintances that had been mutilated by the Indians, you would have found no censure in your heart for Col. Chivington's act.

J. P. Dunn, a judicious nineteenth-century scholar who very often sounds critical of government policy, called Chivington's mad raid justified. Today such an evaluation must be doubted, or at least disputed, but at the time Dunn was writing and meditating there were learned arguments about whether or not the red savage possessed a soul.

Montana Congressman James Cavanaugh spoke for most Americans of that period: "I have never seen in my life a good Indian . . . except when I have seen a dead Indian."

General Sheridan boiled it down. After listening to the Penateka-Comanche chief Tosawi—Silver Brooch—allude to himself as a good Indian, Little Phil observed: "The only good Indians I ever saw were dead." And the collective American unconscious gradually reduced Sheridan's remark to that celebrated epigram: The only good Indian is a dead Indian.

Like Napoleon, Sheridan was uncommonly short: five feet, five inches. He is said to have had such a lumpy skull that his hats did not fit, an allegation which cannot be verified from photos. With black almond eyes and a dangling mustache he resembles those ancient portraits of Mongol emperors, although one staff officer called him "thick-set & common Irish-looking"—adding that Sheridan combed his hair "in the Bowery soap-lock style." Historian Stephen Ambrose characterized him as an obstinate little man, "given to intense rages, mad with battle lust during an engagement, quick to censure and slow to forgive, bursting with energy, forever demanding the impossible of his men."

Custer stood half-a-head taller, women found him exciting, and unlike Sheridan he seldom cherished a grudge; otherwise they must have been much alike. Custer might erupt at any instant, he loved to fight and was quick to blame. He could be sarcastic and impossibly demanding. They understood each other, these two. Sheridan perceived in the audacious young cavalryman a sympathetic spirit, one who was not reluctant to discipline troops and who thought the best way to handle dangerous redskins was to crush them.

Little Phil was supported by his boss, William Tecumseh Sherman—himself no shrinking violet. He wrote to Sheridan on October 15 that it was up to the Indians themselves to decide whether or not they would be exterminated:

> As brave men and as the soldiers of a government which has exhausted its peace efforts, we, in the performance of a most unpleasant duty, accept the war begun by our enemies, and hereby resolve to make its end final. If it results in the utter annihilation of these Indians it is but the result of what they have been warned again and again, and for which they seem fully prepared. I will say nothing and do nothing to restrain our troops from doing what they deem proper on the spot, and will allow no mere vague general charges of cruelty and inhumanity to tie their hands, but will use all the powers confided to me to the end that these Indians, the enemies of our race and of our civilization, shall not again be able to begin and carry on their barbarous warfare on any kind of a pretext that they may choose to allege. . . . You may now go ahead in your own way and I will back you with my whole authority, and stand between you and any efforts that may be attempted in your rear to restrain your purpose or check your troops.

Sand Creek would have been more than enough for Crazy Horse or Sitting Bull, but lack of familiarity with such professional warriors as Sherman, Sheridan, and Custer—or possibly some humanistic view of the universe—

caused Black Kettle to persist in his ingenuous way. He continued to believe that reds and whites could share the land on equal terms. Thus, in the autumn of 1868 while Little Phil was arranging to finish what the Colorado preacher had started, Black Kettle from his headquarters on the Washita was engaged in a long-distance conference with yet another paleface, General W. B. Hazen.

A white woman named Clara Blynn and her infant son Willie had been captured by Cheyennes and Arapahoes. They were still alive, that much the Army knew, although it was not known whether they were captives of the Cheyennes, Arapahoes, or of the neighboring Kiowas. They had been offered for ransom and General Hazen was trying to negotiate their release when Sheridan squashed the idea: "After having her husband & friends murdered, and her own person subjected to the fearful bestiality of perhaps the whole tribe, it is mock humanity to secure what is left of her for the consideration of 5 ponies."

Mrs. Blynn viewed the situation differently. A message from her, addressed to KIND FRIEND, was delivered by an emissary about three weeks before the Seventh Cavalry descended. Variations of this letter exist, each represented as authentic, and the woman's name often is spelled Blinn. No matter. Her anxiety cannot be misinterpreted.

> Whoever you may be, if you will only buy us from the Indians with ponies or any thing, and let me come and stay with you until I can get word to my friends, they will pay you well; and I will work for you also, and do all I can for you.
>
> If it is not too far to this village, and you are not afraid to come, I pray you will try.
>
> The Indians tell me, as near as I can understand, they expect traders to come, to whom they will sell us. Can you find out by the bearer, and let me know if they are white men? If they are Mexicans, I am afraid they will sell us into slavery in Mexico.
>
> If you can do nothing for me, write, for God's sake! to W. T. Harrington, Ottawa, Franklin County, Kansas—my father. Tell him we are with the Kiowahs, or Cheyennes; and they say when the white men make peace we can go home.
>
> Tell him to write to the Governor of Kansas about it, and for them to make peace. Send this to him, please.
>
> We were taken on October 9th, on the Arkansas, below Fort Lyon. My name is Mrs. Clara Blynn. My little boy, Willie Blynn, is two years old.
>
> Do all you can for me. Write to the Peace Commissioners to make peace this fall. For our sake do all you can, and God will bless you for it!

If you can let me hear from you, let me know what you think about it. Write to my father. Send him this. Good-by!

Mrs. R.F. Blynn

P.S.—I am as well as can be expected, but my baby, my darling, darling little Willie, is very weak. O, God, help him! Save him, kind friend, even if you can not save me. Again, good-by.

If Custer knew about this frantic plea it made no difference. He was a soldier following orders. No doubt he hoped to save the woman, but his concern was tactical: the destruction of an enemy stronghold. To threaten these people by a display of strength would be insufficient; he meant to smash them. Captain Barnitz had written to Jennie a month earlier that no mercy would be shown. A trooper who fell into enemy hands must expect torture and death; a redskin caught by the Seventh should not expect to live long.

Custer decided to surround Black Kettle's village by splitting the regiment, pretty much as he would do eight years later in Montana.

An assortment of dogs had followed the men from camp and about half an hour before the attack he ordered them killed because they might howl or bark, thereby alerting the Indians. One of these condemned creatures was a mongrel named Bob, which Sgt. Ryan called harmless as a kitten. Most of the dogs were muzzled with ropes and then strangled or stabbed but somebody drove a picket pin into Bob's head. Several days afterward Bob rejoined the regiment, which sounds incredible, but Ryan says it was so. Bob lived another two years, probably suffering terrible headaches. He accompanied the Seventh from Fort Hays to Kansas City on an express train when the regiment was ordered south to intimidate the Ku Klux Klan and on this trip he committed suicide. A soldier known as "Telegraph Smith" got drunk and became so abusive that little Bob jumped out a window. ". . . and thus ended his career," says Ryan, although any dog that could survive a picket pin through the head should have no trouble jumping off a train.

Anyway, Custer's order meant death for two of his own dogs, possibly more, but exempted at least one—a favorite staghound named Blucher.

In absolute silence and darkness—forbidden to talk much above a whisper, to walk around, even to stamp the chill out of their feet—his troopers waited for dawn. And suddenly the morning star emerged from a ground fog, rising with such brilliance that at first the astonished men mistook it for a rocket. How they could mistake a planet for a rocket is hard to understand, if only because one does not associate Indians with rockets. Nevertheless they did.

The Sioux had devised a method of signaling at night with arrows. Moist gunpowder would be smeared on an arrowhead and lighted, and a degree of meaning could be expressed by various flights—a graphic form of Morse code. These Indians along the Washita were Cheyenne, but a recollection of Sioux fireworks might account for the misapprehension.

Or possibly some troopers remembered Cheyenne fireworks. In Kansas they had contrived an exploding arrow which was made by fitting a percussion cap to the blade, encasing this arrangement in a cotton sack filled with gunpowder. Upon impact the blade would split the percussion cap, which would ignite the gunpowder, which would start a little fire. It did not always work, but they did manage to burn a number of stage depots with this gadget.

Or perhaps the Cheyennes were known to buy rockets from traders.

However this misapprehension should be explained, Custer's men and the commandant himself were stupefied: "Slowly and majestically it continued to rise above the crest of the hill, first appearing as a small brilliant flaming globe of bright golden hue. As it ascended still higher it seemed to increase in size, to move more slowly, while its colors rapidly changed from one to the other, exhibiting in turn the most beautiful combinations of prismatic tints. There seemed to be not the shadow of a doubt that we were discovered."

Very probably they would have been discovered if the Cheyenne sentry Double Wolf had been on his toes instead of his back; but the night was cold and bluecoat armies far away. Double Wolf retreated to his cozy lodge where he fell asleep, which was foolish because that afternoon two Kiowas had paused at the village with news of a broad trail made by shod horses. Cheyennes laughed at this report; they could not believe the army would be after them in such weather. One Kiowa was anxious to move along but his companion wanted to stay because the Cheyennes were having a dance that night, so the Kiowas stayed to dance while Custer's men crept closer; and Double Wolf, stiff with cold, took a nap.

Elizabeth, in *Following the Guidon*, did her best to evoke this frigid night: "Excitement kept the ardent soldiers warm, and when the band put their cold lips to the still colder metal, and struck up 'Garryowen,' the soldiers' hearts were bursting with enthusiasm and joy at the glory that awaited them." Very few combat soldiers of the cynical twentieth century would describe their feelings as Elizabeth did, yet it seems to be true that when the band opened up with Custer's theme song his benumbed troops charged violently and perhaps even enthusiastically toward the village, firing as fast as they could at the tall white lodges. Elizabeth, safe at home, had imagined the scene or was repeating what she had been told; but Lt. Francis Gibson was there, and he too mentioned this patriotic fervor: "At last the inspiring strains of this rollicking tune broke forth, filling the early morning air with joyous music. . . . On rushed these surging cavalcades from all directions, a mass of Uncle Sam's cavalry thirsty for glory. . . ."

The wild assault earned Custer a new name. From that day on he was called—among other things—*Ouchess*, Creeping Panther.

In Dakota Territory five years later the Arikaras christened him Son of the Morning Star, or Child of the Stars. At least that is how he might have received the name. Maybe the Crow scout White Man Runs Him, who also was known as Son of the Morning Star, conferred this—his own name—upon Custer. Whether a Ree or a Crow first called him that, Son of the Morning Star must be regarded as a child of Dakota Territory; but symbolically it seems right to say he was born at dawn in Oklahoma beneath the bright soft light of Venus. No matter how he got the name, he liked to be called Son of the Morning Star. Without doubt he liked it better than several names the troopers called him: Hard Ass, Iron Butt, Ringlets.

During this charge Alexander Hamilton's grandson, Captain Louis Hamilton, took a bullet through the heart, probably from the rifle of a warrior named Cranky Man. Most accounts place Hamilton alone at the head of his company. In *My Life* Custer implies that he and the captain were riding side by side, although he wrote to Hamilton's mother that they had just separated. According to an officer who saw what happened, Hamilton jerked convulsively, "stiffened in his stirrups and was thus carried a corpse for a distance of several yards, when he fell from his horse. . . ." He was twenty-four years old, the youngest captain in the regular army. He is said to have been ambitious, energetic, capable, and popular.

His tunic, later presented to the Oklahoma Historical Society by his brother, shows one bullet hole, not in front but in back, above the right shoulder blade. And because of this odd fact it has been suggested that a cavalryman meant to shoot Custer but accidentally killed Hamilton. While this is possible, there is no evidence to support such a theory. The correct explanation may be that Hamilton was riding with his tunic open, the bullet went through his body and punctured the back of his coat when it emerged. The warrior who killed him was on foot—a detail mentioned by George Bent who was told by Red Shin and Medicine Elk Pipe that Cranky Man rushed out of his lodge and shot the officer later identified as Hamilton. So it must follow that the bullet angled upward, which is substantiated by surgeon Henry Lippincott's report: "Ball entered about five inches below left nipple, and emerged near inferior angle of right scapula."

Hamilton enjoyed sketching and obviously was good at it: the Oklahoma Historical Society owns a pen-and-ink drawing of some politician or government agent in a plug hat which brings to mind the relentless caricatures of Daumier. He liked to do impressions of his comrades in the Seventh, but after everybody had laughed at them he tore them up, "thus taking away the sting of ridicule," Elizabeth says, "which constant sight of the caricature might produce." One can hardly imagine such refinement today.

During the Hancock expedition he got acquainted with journalist Theodore Davis and after Davis went back east they corresponded. From camp near Fort Dodge about a month before he was killed Hamilton wrote that a grand winter campaign was being organized. He then made a disparaging remark about General Sully but asked Davis not to publicize it for fear of hurting the general's feelings. And he commented on the sympathy for Indians which was being expressed by government Peace Commissioners and by certain newspapers: "I only wish some of the most enthusiastic of their admirers both male and female could have been the recipients of the 'Noble Red' kindnesses instead of the unfortunate settlers on the Saline and Solomon. One of the women brought into Fort Harker was ravished by twenty-three of the villains. . . . Comstock was one of the first victims to the savages. He and a scout named Grover had visited the camp of 'Black Kettle' a Cheyenne chief then supposed to be friendly and were leaving it when they were followed and shot. Grover feigned death and escaped. . . ."

Barnitz was luckier than Hamilton. He and a Cheyenne fought a picturesque duel—Barnitz galloping back and forth while the Indian jumped from side to side. Each man knew that a miscalculation could mean death. They fired simultaneously. The Cheyenne—probably Chief Magpie—tossed up both hands and collapsed. Years later Magpie remembered dueling with a big officer on a brown horse, which correctly describes Barnitz.

The captain himself took a bullet in the stomach at such close range that the blaze of the Indian's gun scorched his overcoat. Long afterward he wrote that because he was leaning forward the rifle ball struck a rib and glanced downward, smashed the next rib, took a piece out of the rib below, where it was deflected, passing entirely through his body and out the muscles near the spine. He rode another two hundred yards, dismounted and lay down, holding the reins of his horse. After a while he was found, placed on a buffalo robe, and carried to a field hospital where two surgeons—both suffering from snow-blindness—thought he was mortally wounded. He believed them, dictating a message to Jennie: "Tell Mrs. B that I don't regret the wound so much as I do leaving her. It has been so long since we met, that the expectations of the happiness we would enjoy upon our reunion is more than I can bear. . . ."

To everyone's astonishment he gradually recovered. On Christmas Eve from Camp Supply he wrote to Jennie that a mass of tissue about the size of a fist had protruded from the anterior opening and resembled the balls of sausage one finds in butcher shops. Dr. Sternberg removed it "with a curious instrument of recent invention."

The Barnitz case fascinated Dr. Sternberg, who described his procedure in the Surgeon General's Circular No. 3, 1871: "I commenced the operation with a wire ecraseur, but before it was completed the loop of wire broke. . . ." So interested was Dr. Sternberg that he presented this mass of tissue, known as "omentum," to the Army Medical Museum in Washington where it was publicly displayed in a jar of formaldehyde.

Sternberg and his assistant, Dr. Lippincott, were more or less correct about the injury being mortal. Barnitz lived a long time, dying in 1912 at the age of seventy-seven, but an autopsy showed that death had been caused by a growth around this 1868 bullet wound. The autopsy also disclosed a shred of his Army overcoat which he had been wearing outside-in, so to speak, ever since the battle of the Washita.

The big round bullet that brought him down came from a muzzle-loading Lancaster rifle, possibly one of many weapons given to the Cheyennes by the government at the Medicine Lodge peace council. Barnitz himself had been at Medicine Lodge and was amazed: "Indians signed treaty. Presents distributed—among other things 65 new revolvers!—and hundreds of new butcher knives!"

Eight years later Major Reno wrote his official report of the Custer business while on the banks of the Yellowstone, concluding with these lines: "The harrowing sight of the dead bodies crowning the height on which Custer fell, and which will remain vividly in my memory until death, is too recent for me not to ask the good people of this country whether a policy that sets opposing parties in the field armed, clothed and equipped by one and the same government should not be abolished."

A century later it is obvious that Major Reno's question has not yet been answered.

Along with Capt. Barnitz, the irascible Benteen almost lost his life during that furious charge through Black Kettle's village. A young Cheyenne, apparently about fourteen years old, dashed out of the chief's lodge, hopped on a pony, and tried to escape. Benteen galloped after him, signaling as clearly as possible under the circumstances that if he would surrender he would not be hurt. The boy responded by wheeling his pony and firing—the bullet sang past Benteen's ear. Twice more the young Cheyenne fired. The second or third shot dropped Benteen's horse and sent him tumbling in the snow. Once again the Cheyenne charged. Enough was enough. Benteen killed him.

This aggressive young man usually is identified as Black Kettle's son, but in fact he was a nephew named Blue Horse and he was older than he looked. According to George Bent, who married Black Kettle's niece and who therefore should know, Blue Horse was about twenty-one when he made the mistake of challenging the plump, grandfatherly soldier.

A casualty of some consequence from the general's point of view was his favorite staghound Blucher. Foolish Blucher. Confused by so much excitement, unable to distinguish friends from enemies, Blucher decided to join the Indians and got an arrow through the ribs. Months afterward, says Custer, "I discovered his remains on the ground near where the overcoats had been deposited on that eventful morning."

The fight in the village lasted only a few minutes, although several hours were required to finish off isolated warriors who hid in gullies and underbrush. Custer's tally listed 103 fighting men killed. In truth, only 11 could be so classified: Chief Black Kettle, Chief Little Rock, Cranky Man, Blue Horse, Bear Tongue, Red Teeth, Blind Bear, Little Heart, Red Bird, Tall Bear, White Bear. The other 92 were squaws, children, old men. A New York *Tribune* story by an unidentified witness compared the devastated camp to a slaughter pen littered with the bodies of animals and Indians smeared with mud, lying one on top of another in holes and ditches. It sounds as though Black Kettle's village lay in the path of Genghis Khan.

When things quieted down a bit Custer sent details of men to round up any loose ponies. Sgt. Ryan was assigned to one of these squads. In his 1909 memoir he tells of very nearly being killed on the way back from this excursion. As he rode around the foot of a bluff he came upon a dismounted warrior. They were so close that Ryan's first impulse was to ride over the man—which he did—and manage to shoot him at the same time. But now Ryan's horse, with spurs jammed halfway through its body, was difficult to hold and ran some distance before it could be checked. "I wanted very much to scalp that Indian," Ryan said, and having finally regained control of the animal he turned back. The enemy was still alive. The sergeant put two more bullets in him. Just then another blanketed individual appeared, who turned out to be not a Cheyenne warrior but Pvt. Eagan of Ryan's own company, and from his home state of Massachusetts:

> I asked Eagan if he would hold my horse, and I dismounted, turned the Indian over on his face, put my left foot on his neck and raised his scalp. I held it up to Eagan saying, "John, here is the first scalp for M troop." I secured the rifle, which was a heavy muzzle-loading buffalo gun made at Lancaster, Pennsylvania, and of the style issued to the Indians for hunting purposes. I also took a 44-calibre Remington revolver and a sheath knife, but did not bother with trinkets which he had. I believe some of these articles are in my collection at my home at the present time.

Hanging the scalp at the sabre hook of my waist belt, I started to find our command, and on the way noticed that the skirt of my overcoat was covered with blood. So I threw the scalp away, and upon arriving at camp reported my experience to the company commander, Lieutenant Owen Hale. He asked me what I did with the scalp, and I told him. He smiled and said that I should have kept it, as it was considered an honor on that occasion. I called Lieutenant Hale's attention to the condition of my $14 overcoat, and he asked me how I felt about that time. I told him I felt like the Irishman who belonged to one of the New York regiments in my brigade, known as Meagher's Irish Brigade. The man's brother was killed in front of Petersburg on June 16, 1864, and he felt so bad about it that the next day he got behind a stump and killed 10 Confederates. His captain asked him how he felt about it, and he said that he did not know as it would help poor Tom any, but he felt a little relieved about the heart. That was the way I felt.

A Kiowa named Hagone, or Silverhorn, painted the Washita battle on a strip of muslin which now hangs in the Southwest Museum in Highland Park, California. An oval cluster of Indians dominates the center of Hagone's representation. The muslin everywhere is speckled with flying arrows, U-shaped horseshoe tracks, decorated teepees, and coup sticks. Rigidly synchronized American troops descend from the upper right corner like a phalanx of chorus girls, all of the soldiers pointing their rifles in the same direction. They wear blue pants and pale green blouses and every soldier has yellow hair—which probably does not refer to General Custer but to the fact that it is just about impossible to tell white men apart.

This was Custer's one significant victory on the plains; it enraged and disheartened not only the Southern Cheyennes but several other tribes.

As soon as the field had been secured he totted up the loot: 573 buffalo robes, 241 saddles, 47 rifles, 35 revolvers, 90 bullet molds, 75 spears, 12 shields, 35 quivers, numerous hatchets, lariats, bridles, 300 pounds of tobacco, and so forth. Included were several bags of flour labeled "Department of the Interior," evidence that these Indians were present at Medicine Lodge. He chose an unusually fine white teepee as a personal souvenir, then ordered Lt. Godfrey to burn the others and all of the property: robes, saddles, quivers, bows, shields, food, leggings embellished with scalps—whatever could be incinerated.

Godfrey thought it a waste, but complied. "I began the destruction at the upper end of the village, tearing down teepees and piling several together on the teepee poles, set fire to them. . . ."

Funnels of reeking black smoke drifted across the stream.

"One man brought to me that which I learned was a bridal gown, a 'one piece dress,' adorned all over with bead work and elks' teeth on antelope skins as soft as the finest broadcloth. I started to show it to the General and ask to keep it, but as I passed a big fire, I thought, 'What's the use, "orders is orders" ' and threw it in the blaze. I have never ceased to regret that destruction."

Custer turned to the herd of mules and ponies. Officers and scouts were allowed to keep any they wanted, after which fifty-three captive women and children were instructed through interpreter Romero—known inevitably as Romeo—to choose mounts so they would not have to walk sixty or seventy miles to the base camp. Custer next detailed Lt. Godfrey with four companies to kill the remaining animals because he did not want the Cheyennes to recover them and it would have been difficult or impossible to drive such a herd. Godfrey's executioners at first tried to cut their throats, but this turned out to be surprisingly difficult because they could not abide the odor of white men and struggled desperately whenever a soldier approached. After a while, says Godfrey, his men were getting tired, so he sent for reinforcements and the creatures were shot. Even with extra men it took some time because there were about eight hundred ponies and mules, and when the job was done the snowy Oklahoma field bloomed with dark flowers.

Crook followed this procedure after capturing the village governed by Old Bear and He Dog, but for some reason his men had less trouble controlling the Indian ponies and were able to kill them with axes and knives. Bourke, after explaining the necessity of this act, sounds quite distressed: "It was pathetic to hear the dismal trumpeting (I can find no other word to express my meaning) of the dying creatures, as the breath of life rushed through severed windpipes. The Indians in the bluffs recognized the cry, and were aware of what we were doing. . . ."

Mackenzie did the same thing to the Comanche-Kiowa-Cheyenne pony herd in September of 1874. Guided by Kit Carson, Mackenzie surprised the Indians on the headwaters of the Red River, chased them out of camp, burned their homes, and littered several acres of ground with the carcasses of fourteen hundred ponies. The strategy was merciless and effective. Let nothing survive.

Accounts of Chief Black Kettle's death do not exactly coincide, but almost. It appears that he jumped on a pony, drew up his wife in front of him, and started across the river but did not get very far. He was shot in the back. His wife—her name awkwardly rendered into English as Medicine Woman Later—was shot dead beside him.

Years afterward an old woman called Moving Behind talked about the fight and about going to look for Black Kettle. The chief and his wife lay under water, she said. Four men—Roll Down, Scabby, Afraid of Beaver, Clown—dragged their bodies up on the bank. Clown spread a blanket. Black Kettle and his wife were placed on this blanket. By then it was getting late so Moving Behind and the others went away. They rode westward, passing the bodies of men, women, and children. They would stop to look at the bodies and mention their names. They rode up the Washita until they got to the camp of a man named Crooked Wrist. "There were some of my relatives there, and they told me to remain, that I was welcome. . . ."

Another Indian account states that Black Kettle and his squaw lay overnight in the icy stream. Survivors did not find them until the next day.

Chief Magpie said Black Kettle's body was submerged except for the face. With the help of a few squaws he carried it along the pony trail and up a sandy knoll. There he left the women, who were discussing whether to bury Black Kettle on the knoll or on higher ground.

The chief was sixty-seven when a trooper shot him. He was a Sutai—the correct plural of which is Sutaio—one of those people from the northeast who brought the Sun Dance to the Cheyennes, who spoke the same language but a different dialect.

Little Phil, anxious to monitor the progress of this campaign, had made a long trip from field headquarters at Fort Hays to Custer's base camp on the north fork of the Canadian. He arrived a couple of days before the regiment set out.

On Sunday morning, November 29, two of Custer's scouts returned: a scruffy eccentric known as California Joe, and his partner Jack Corbin. In camp at that time was a journalist euphoniously christened DeBenneville Randolph Keim who described Joe as a veteran pioneer with long knotty hair and flaming red whiskers. Both men had slept on the ground so their appearance might be excused, but Joe was abnormally filthy. His whiskers and hair were matted with dry grass, leaves, and dust. A bandanna around his neck is said to have resembled a warrior's breechclout.

Sheridan asked what had brought them back so soon. Had they run away?

Joe used a strip of gunnysack for a handkerchief and his nose must have been dripping because Keim says he wiped it on the gunnysack before delivering Custer's dispatch.

Sheridan quickly read the news, after which he sent them back to Custer with a message:

The Battle of the Washita River is the most complete & successful of all our private battles, and was fought in such unfavorable weather & circumstances as to reflect the highest credit on Yourself & Regt.

Along with this note Sheridan included a copy of his official report, which Custer instructed Adjutant W. W. Cooke to read aloud:

> Hd.-Qrs., Dept. of the Mo.
> In the Field, Depot on N. Can
> At Junction of Beaver Creek
> Ind. Terr., Nov. 29th, 1868
>
> Gen'l Field Orders No. 6:
>
> The Maj-Gen'l Cmdg. announces to this Command the defeat, by the 7th Regt. of Cavalry, of a large force of Cheyenne Indians under the celebrated Chief Black Kettle, reinforced by the Arapahoes under Little-Raven & the Kiowas under Satanta, on the morning of the 27th inst., on the Washita River, near the Antelope Hills, Indian Territory, resulting in a loss to the savages of 103 warriors. . . .

On December 1, after being told that the victorious regiment was approaching, Sheridan got dressed up.

Custer, equally conscious of this occasion, brought the Seventh to a halt and rearranged everybody before marching into view. He put his wild Osage guides in front, their plaited scalp locks trailing streams of feathers and freshly acquired Cheyenne silver ornaments. They carried rawhide shields, rifles, spears, and bows. Keim, who observed this dramatic parade, saw bloody scalps dangling from the spears and said that even the Osage ponies were trimmed with scalps and with strips of red and blue Cheyenne blankets. Prominent among these braves was Trotter—Koom-la-Manche—displaying a scalp which he claimed to have lifted from the head of Black Kettle after a terrific fight. According to what Chief Magpie said later, this was untrue. Black Kettle was not scalped, nor did Koom-la-Manche fight him.

Behind the Osage guides rode the white scouts, notably Corbin and California Joe. Custer seems to have regarded Joe as a drunken buffoon, although useful. Asleep or awake he wore a huge sombrero, he carried a long breechloading Springfield musket, and as Custer wrote in *My Life on the Plains*, he always rode a mule "in whose speed and endurance he had every confidence." Custer knew almost nothing else about him.

Joe's name was Moses Embree Milner. He was a Kentuckian who ran away from home, worked as a scout and/or packer for Kearny during the Mexican War and prospected for gold in California. Along came Nancy Emma Watts, age thirteen. They got married and had four children but domestic life just about asphyxiated Joe. After getting Nancy Emma and the kids settled on a ranch in Oregon he resumed doing what he loved—adventuring. On October 29, 1876, at Fort Robinson he was shot in the back by one Thomas Newcomb who worked in the post butcher shop and with whom he had quarreled. Their disagreement evidently had been settled because they shook hands, but about 5 P.M. while Joe stood on the banks of the White River talking with some friends Newcomb slipped up to the quartermaster's corral, steadied a Winchester on a wagon wheel and sent Joe across the great divide. Dr. Valentine T. McGillycuddy wrote to historian Brininstool in 1922 that authorities in eastern Nebraska were notified but nobody seemed to care. "Four days elapsing, and no one appearing, we were obliged to turn Newcomb loose . . . he is now living in Gardner, Montana, as a hunting guide."

Dr. McGillycuddy put a red cedar headboard on Joe's grave, but many years later the Fort Robinson cemetery was relocated and the last visible trace of California Joe—that red cedar board—seems to have been discarded. He was a friend of Wild Bill Hickok and had said publicly that a bunch of gamblers arranged Hickok's death, an injudicious remark which may have brought about his own death.

In any case, right behind Joe and his partner rode Lt. Silas Pepoon's civilian scouts, followed by the regimental band. Lt. Pepoon sounds as unsavory as Newcomb. He was later accused of cheating at cards and scheduled for a court-martial. It is said that he begged the accusing officers to withdraw their charges. When they would not, he killed himself.

Next came the famous young general in fringed buckskin, astride a dancing black stallion.

Then the woebegone captives: fifty-three orphans and widows bundled up in blankets and robes until only their eyes could be seen. Keim says the women looked straight ahead, never glancing right or left. They thought they were going to be shot.

Enlisted men and supplies brought up the rear.

At an appropriate moment Custer spurred forward to greet his boss while the band struck up "Garry Owen." A warm sun beamed down. The snow began to melt. That night the Osages held a scalp dance and General Sheridan admired Custer's souvenir lodge.

It sounds like the end of a perfect campaign, but the men of the Seventh were in an ugly mood because a detachment of eighteen troopers commanded by Major Joel Elliott had failed to return. They were last seen riding downstream after some fleeing Cheyennes. At first, because of the excitement, nobody worried. Hours went by. Not until late afternoon did Custer send out a search party, which found nothing.

Why he neglected to scour the area has never been adequately explained, unless we accept his explanation in *My Life*: "As it was now lacking but an hour of night, we had to make an effort to get rid of the Indians, who still loitered in strong force on the hills. . . ."

Sgt. Ryan's memoir, written almost half a century afterward, implies that

Custer did order an immediate search but increasing numbers of Indians prevented it; and Ryan comments ominously that had they known Elliott was dead there would have been no Indian prisoners. Whatever the situation and Custer's response, the mysterious fate of Major Elliott was a touchy issue in 1868 and has remained so with historians ever since.

For almost two weeks nobody knew what happened.

Early in December, accompanied by Sheridan, ten companies of the Nineteenth Kansas Volunteers, and journalist DeBenneville Keim, Custer's Seventh marched out of Camp Supply to polish off the red menace. "If we can get in one or two more good blows," Sheridan observed, "there will be no more Indian troubles in my department."

The route was almost identical. Sheridan wanted to see the Washita battlefield, partly from curiosity, but also because they wanted to know what had become of Elliott. It was a bitter cold march. They crossed the Canadian River on December 10 with the temperature at eighteen below zero.

Keim recorded what they saw as they approached: "The sunlight glistening upon the heavy frost, which had not yet disappeared from the trees and long grass of the lowlands, lent the only charm to the landscape. The barren hills, the wild and silent valley, the leafless and lifeless vegetation, formed the picture of desolation. . . . The foot prints of the charging squadrons could be followed in one extended front through the tangled brush."

When they got closer they disturbed a host of flesh-eating animals and birds. Wolves and coyotes trotted ahead of the army, pausing often to look back, and settled on the hills to wait. Ravens and crows, gorged with meat, flapped away heavily.

Where Cheyenne lodges had stood there were now circles. Corpses lay on the charred earth, many of them tied up in blankets. Several had been placed in the forks of trees, others hidden beneath stacks of brush. Black Kettle's body could not be found. It was assumed that he, along with other important men, had been carried to a remote canyon for burial, an assumption which proved more or less correct. Not quite seventy years later—July 13, 1934— some WPA laborers who were lengthening a bridge over the Washita accidentally uncovered a skeleton dressed in Black Kettle's jewelry. For this reason, and because the skeleton lay close to the sandy knoll where Magpie had left him with the squaws, it seems probable that this was the chief. His bones were donated to a local newspaper, the *Cheyenne Star*, which displayed them in a window.

From a hillside Custer explained to Sheridan the strategy he had used, pointing out avenues of attack and recreating the action, while search parties continued down the valley looking for Elliott.

Near a dry tributary east of the Washita one naked body was discovered, the skull so battered that part of the brain had emerged. Two hundred yards farther lay the rest of the troops, frozen as solidly as stone, Keim reports. All of them lay face down, bristling with arrows. Several were beheaded. An early account in *Chronicles of Oklahoma* says each man's throat "had the appearance of having been cut. This was caused by the Indians having cut out the thyroid cartilege." But why the Indians did this was not explained.

Dr. Lippincott examined these frozen cadavers. File F, 421, Old Military Records, National Archives, is gruesome and clinically precise:

Carrick, William, Corporal "H" Troop: Bullet hole in right parietal bone, both feet cut off, throat cut, left arm broken. Penis cut off.

Downey, Thomas, Private "I" Troop: Arrow hole in region of stomach, thorax cut open, and right shoulder cut by tomahawk.

Myers, Carson, Private "M" Troop: Several bullet holes in head, scalped, nineteen bullet holes in body, penis cut off, and throat cut.

Unknown: Head, right hand, and penis cut off, three bullet and nine arrow holes in back.

In a confidential report Custer added a few particulars to the surgeon's catalogue, including the fact that the stock of a Lancaster rifle protruded from the side of one victim. The rifle had been broken, the wooden stock jammed about eight inches into the body.

As for Elliott, he had two bullet holes in the skull and one in the left cheek. His right hand was cut off, his penis chopped off. There was a deep gash in the right groin, gashes in the calves of both legs. The little finger of his left hand was missing. His throat had been slashed.

Elliott just did survive the Civil War. In June of 1864 at White's Station, Mississippi, he was shot through the lungs and left on the field, presumably dead. Six months later he returned to active duty with the Seventh Indiana Cavalry. In 1866 he was mustered out, but when the Army reorganized he again volunteered, and because of an exceptional score on the mental tests he was commissioned a major. He is said to have been aggressive, whether battling Confederates or Indians, and this intemperance begot his disastrous charge. A cautious officer would not have gone plunging down the Washita through unfamiliar territory with less than twenty men.

Which Indians he was chasing cannot be learned. Quite a few women and children tried to escape by wading downstream—which sounds illogical, especially in freezing water, but soldiers rode along the bluffs and by wading close to the river bank these women and children were nearly hidden. Below the village, at a horseshoe bend where the water ran deep, they were obliged to come out. Here, possibly, they were noticed and Elliott rode toward them.

His last stand has been reconstructed from scattered evidence and from what the victorious Indians said.

What happened was just about what happened eight years later in Montana: More hostiles showed up than the wasichus expected. Downstream from Black Kettle's village were a great many Comanches, Kiowas, Apaches, and Arapahoes—a nearly contiguous village of perhaps six thousand people camped along the Washita for about twelve miles. Custer did not know this because he was so eager to attack the Cheyennes. Almost certainly he knew Black Kettle's village was not the only one in the area but he ignored the others. When he surrounded the Cheyennes he thought he had surrounded all the Indians who mattered. Major Elliott must have thought the same, and by the time he learned differently it was too late: Upriver came a swarm of warriors attracted by the shooting. The first to arrive probably were Arapahoes led by Powder Face and Left Hand.

Elliott ordered his men to dismount, turn the horses loose, and lie down in a thicket of grass with their feet together, facing outward like the spokes of a wagon wheel. This was not a good idea. They were obliged to remain where they were, they could hardly see through the grass, and the place where he chose to make a stand was overlooked by high banks on the opposite side of the stream. Here the Indians concealed themselves and picked off the immobilized troopers.

Indian testimony suggests that Elliott's men were terrified. They lay flat on their bellies and fired their weapons without taking aim. They lasted about an hour. During this time they managed to kill one warrior: an Arapaho named Tobacco. He carried a flat war club and any man who carried such a club felt obligated to perform an outstanding feat. It is thought that Tobacco, anxious to count coup before anybody else, rushed among the soldiers a little too soon.

Elliott probably was killed by a warrior named Big Cow—a corpulent, thick-lipped individual who looks surly and rather dangerous, if one may judge from photographs, like a beer-drinking truck driver who would as soon be left alone.

When Elliott rode off in pursuit of the escaping Cheyennes he turned in the saddle, waved to Lt. Owen Hale, and delivered a line which sounds theatrical: "Here goes for a brevet or a coffin!" Whether this exit line occurred to him spontaneously or whether he had rehearsed it is not known, but it does recall similar epigrams. Colonel Bennet Riley, for instance, told Jefferson Davis that he would win a yellow sash or six feet of Mexican soil. Brigadier William J. Worth called to Zachary Taylor at Monterrey that he would have a grade or a grave. Navy Lt. William Barker Cushing was heard to say when he went off to sink the Confederate *Albemarle*: "Another stripe or a coffin." No doubt such sentiments have echoed across battlefields from Philippi to Guadalcanal and beyond. Indeed, bullets scarcely had stopped thumping into Seventh Cavalry troopers at the Little Bighorn when a patriotic citizen declared by way of the New York *Herald* that two thousand men were prepared to avenge the hero's death: "They would win patents of loyalty in the lava beds, or they would stay there with Custer." The reference to lava beds is curious because no lava is visible in the Little Bighorn Valley. The *Herald* patriot might have been thinking about Oregon and northern California where the Modocs fought in 1873.

Anyway, it is said that during the gestation of *Remembrance of Things Past* the author gradually became convinced of a frightening psychological truth: Contrary to popular belief, people do not learn by experience. Instead, they respond to a particular stimulus in a predictable way, and this repeatedly. Again, again, again, and again this undeviating, compulsive response may be observed. A brevet or a coffin. A yellow sash or six feet of Mexican soil. A grade or a grave. Again, again, again, and again, generation after generation, the dismal message reappears like writing on the wall.

Custer himself seems to validate this shocking insight. The slaughter of Elliott's command may be traced to inadequate reconnaissance, a fact more or less acknowledged, though Custer never admitted it. Lt. Godfrey, having observed two Indians riding in circles—their method of signaling alarm— rode to the peak of a ridge, looked downstream, and was astonished to see a multitude of teepees. He also observed a host of mounted warriors riding upstream. Custer, being informed of this, exclaimed: "What's that?" Yet Custer had made the same mistake during the Civil War when he assaulted Wade Hampton's division without first scouting the area. If he had done so he would have learned that another Confederate army under Fitzhugh Lee was nearby.

Neither of these mistakes taught the Son of the Morning Star anything. At least they did not affect his tactics. Eight years after losing Major Elliott he became excited by the spectacle of another village crawling with savages beside another tortuous stream and he responded predictably. Instead of remembering the past, he charged.

Not true, according to certain biographers. Robert Ege argues that at the Little Bighorn this natural instinct of Custer was subjugated for perhaps the first time: "He chose to conduct a 'reconnaissance-in-force.' It was his plan to advance cautiously. . . ."

This is possible, but nobody knows what Custer had in mind. He confided nothing.

Benteen summarized the Elliott fiasco in a letter to William DeGress of St. Louis with whom he had served in the Tenth Missouri during the Civil War; and apparently without asking permission, DeGress handed along this letter to the St. Louis *Democrat*, where it was published. Benteen wrote that Major Elliott's detachment was found in a circle, the bodies stripped as naked as when they were born. Heads were crushed. Several had the Adam's apple cut out. Nearly all were mangled "in a way delicacy forbids me to mention." The letter included a slanderous evaluation of Custer. While Elliott fought for his life just two miles away, Benteen wrote, the commandant was taking inventory of captured equipment and demonstrating his skill with a rifle. Eight hundred animals having been scheduled for execution: "Our Chief exhibits his close sharp-shooting and terrifies the crowd of frightened, captured squaws and papooses by dropping the straggling ponies in death near them. Ah! he is a clever marksman. Not even do the poor dogs of the Indians escape his eye and aim as they drop dead or limp howling away. . . ."

Some unidentified friend or enemy of Custer sent him a copy of the *Democrat*, which arrived in January while the regiment was pushing through Oklahoma in search of more Cheyennes. Custer thought it failed to give an unbiased account of the Washita victory and ordered his bugler to sound "Officers' Call." Benteen showed up late. He saw Custer striding back and forth in a Sibley tent whacking his boot with a rawhide quirt. Somebody had belittled the Washita fight, the general announced to his assembled subordinates while displaying the newspaper, and if he found out who was responsible he meant to cowhide that party.

Benteen asked to see the paper. After reading a few lines he stepped outside and twirled the cylinder of his revolver. He then stepped back inside and said, "I guess I am the man you are after, and I am ready for the whipping promised."

Lt. John Weston, who was present, said Custer seemed dumbfounded. He turned red and began to stammer, as he often did. He said: "Colonel Benteen, I'll see you again, sir!" He then dismissed the officers.

By virtually every report this is just about what happened, although how it is interpreted depends on the scholar's bias. Anti-Custerites see the arrogant general faced down by the indomitable Benteen. Custer partisans believe he resolved the business satisfactorily.

This latter position is a little difficult to understand and is best explained by Col. Charles Bates, who wrote that for Custer to have pressed the issue would play directly into Benteen's hand: "Pride in the regiment was stronger than mere personal pride, and he would do nothing to injure its efficiency. Perhaps he was quick-tempered and impulsive when he called his officers together and uttered his threat (which no one would expect to be taken literally) but in the end he showed his presence of mind and self-control."

Or maybe he felt responsible for Elliott's death, and although he could not admit this to the assembled officers, neither could he lift the quirt.

So far as Benteen was concerned, the business lay unfinished. He rounded up journalist Keim for a witness and went back to settle it. During a second confrontation, if his view is to be accepted, the general "wilted like a whipped cur."

Keim told Sheridan about the incident and Sheridan had a talk with the flamboyant young general.

Had this ugly scene concluded with Benteen puncturing Custer's heart the drama of 1876 might have been much less dramatic. There is little doubt that Benteen was ready to kill. Whatever his defects of character, and there were some, nobody ever accused him of bluffing. One stroke with that rawhide quirt would have rung down the curtain, and Custer's evasive response to the challenge indicates how well he understood this.

In addition to Elliott, Mrs. Blynn and her son turned up. She had been en route to the Pacific coast with her husband when their wagon train was surrounded for three days—until soldiers from Fort Lyon drove the Indians away. Despite Sheridan's belief that her husband and friends had been murdered, nobody was killed. Just how she and her infant son were abducted is not clear, and it is surprising that the Indians were able to carry her off because this convoy included eleven armed men, ten of whom were not even wounded.

Nor is it clear whether the bodies of the woman and child lay on the site of Black Kettle's village or downstream. Capt. George Jenness of the Nineteenth Kansas volunteers placed them very close to the riverbank where Black Kettle himself was killed. Sheridan and Custer, who did not see the bodies until later, insisted they had been recovered from a deserted Kiowa camp five miles away. Comanche-Kiowa agent A. G. Boone said they were at least ten miles away. Custer, identifying her as "a young and beautiful white woman," reported that she had been shot in the forehead. He said her scalp was taken and her skull badly crushed. "The child also bore numerous marks of violence."

Kiowas did not murder Mrs. Blynn, insisted General W. B. Hazen, who was so angered by one of Custer's magazine articles that he published a long rebuttal. "The whole story of this unfortunate woman and her child, has been told me a dozen times by as many different Indians both before and after the battle, each corroborating the story of the others, and I was on the point of rescuing her and in correspondence with her when the battle took place."

Hazen sounds convincing, and Satanta's daughter told W. S. Nye many years afterward that on the day of the fight the Kiowas were encamped fifty miles downstream. Nevertheless, Satanta got credit. Sheridan and Custer both said the Kiowas were guilty and Satanta was the Kiowa chief. Ergo, he himself split the woman's skull.

Fanny Kelly, restored to civilization four years earlier, did not hesitate to write as an eyewitness: "The heart of Mrs. Blynn must have beat wildly, mingling with hope and dread, when she heard the noise and firing, and saw the United States soldiers charging upon her captors. Springing forward, she exclaimed: 'Willie, Willie, saved at last!' but the words were scarce on her lips, ere the tomahawk of the revengeful Satanta was buried in her brain; and in another instant little Willie was in the grasp of the monster. . . ."

Mrs. Blynn had not been tomahawked; she was shot twice in the head with a rifle held so close that gunpowder scorched her face. Members of the detail which found her body said a piece of cornbread was hidden in her bosom, as though she might have been planning to escape when she was shot. Willie, reduced to a skeleton, did not show "numerous marks," only a bruised cheek. How the starving boy died is not known; he might have been picked up by the feet and slung against a tree.

There were rumors that Mrs. Blynn was shot accidentally by a soldier. Jesse Leavenworth testified at a Senate hearing in February of 1869 that she was hit while running toward the troops, but he could produce nothing to substantiate this and another agent contradicted his assertion by pointing out that she had been scalped. Leavenworth may have believed what he said or he may have been trying to shelter the Kiowas, whose guardian he was.

Another rumor concerned a so-called captive white child eviscerated by these frenzied savages. A Seventh Cavalry trooper named T. P. Lyon is known to have talked about it and he may have been the source of Keim's fictitious, rabble-rousing tale: "In the midst of the conflict, the bullets falling around in a perfect shower, a squaw, with demoniac fury, knife in hand, as if looking for an object upon which to revenge the loss of the day, fell upon an innocent captive child, and, with one terrible gash, completely disemboweled it—the warm, smoking entrails falling upon the snow. . . ."

Scout Ben Clark talked about this incident, but he told it plainly—as Benteen remarked about Pvt. O'Neill's harrowing escape from the Little Bighorn Valley—which is a big thing towards convincing one of the truth. He said some Indians were hiding behind a pile of dirt near the river. Soldiers kept shooting at them and killed all except one squaw and her child. Then, Clark said, "I saw a terrible example of a Cheyenne mother's despair. A squaw arose from behind the barricade holding a baby at arm's length. In the other hand was a long knife. The sharpshooters mistook the child for a white captive and yelled, 'Kill that squaw. She's murdering a white child.' Before a gun could be fired the mother with one stroke of the knife, disemboweled the child, drove the knife to the hilt in her own breast, and was dead. A trooper poked his carbine over the embankment and shot her through the head but it was a needless cruelty."

If Clark's version is true—and it does sound more factual than Keim's horror story—it bloodily discloses the aboriginal fear of whites. Better die than be captured by Americans. Black Elk, an Oglala Sioux, told his biographer that when he was a child his mother used to frighten him by saying: "If you are not good the Wasichus will get you."

Custer's wasichus wiped out Black Kettle's village, but as often happens one way or another the victims got revenge. In this case, Fort Sill medical records show that during January and February of 1869 a number of Seventh Cavalry officers took the mercury cure for venereal disease. Among those visiting the clinic, it has been alleged, were the general and his brother Tom. This is possible, although there seems to be no documentary evidence. In 1977 the available records were studied by Dr. D. E. Beckman, who found nothing to indicate that either of the Custers was infected. Elizabeth and the general wanted to have children but never did, which might be explained if she had contracted gonorrhea from him. Other explanations, of course, may be just as plausible.

That he noticed the Cheyenne women who survived his assault is undeniable. One of the prisoners was a girl about seventeen years old named Me-o-tzi—Mo-nah-se-tah as it sometimes is spelled—the daughter of a slain chief, Little Rock. He describes her as "exceedingly comely . . . her well-shaped head was crowned with a luxuriant growth of the most beautiful silken tresses, rivalling in color the blackness of the raven and extending, when allowed to fall loosely over her shoulders, to below her waist."

Her name he translates as "The young grass that shoots in the spring."

He was told that she had been married to an affluent brave who paid Little Rock eleven ponies—which was at least three times the usual price for an attractive girl. Despite this compliment, Me-o-tzi was not pleased with her husband. She would not render unto him that wifely obedience and menial service which was expected, nor did time soften her recalcitrant heart, and one day she shot her husband in the knee with a pistol, thereby permanently disabling him. Me-o-tzi was then divorced. Little Rock gave back the eleven ponies and his difficult daughter returned to the family lodge.

All of this Custer was told, and there is no reason to disbelieve it. Somewhat harder to accept is his statement that soon after the battle he unwittingly became Me-o-tzi's second husband. Her hand was placed in his, while the sister of Chief Black Kettle pronounced what he took to be a sort of benediction: "I, in my ignorance . . . remembering how sensitive and suspicious the Indian nature was, and that any seeming act of inattention or disrespect on my part might be misunderstood, I stood a passive participant in the strange ceremony then being enacted."

His men had just killed this girl's father and more than a hundred members of the tribe. Now the sister of Black Kettle offers him a lovely present. The question is: Why? Before a battle, if one army feels intimidated, the chief's daughter might be offered in marriage. Anything to avoid a disastrous conflict. But afterward, without much to lose, there is no reason to propitiate the enemy.

Benteen's version of this affair, as might be expected, does not coincide with the general's. Twenty-eight years after the event Benteen wrote to ex-Private Theodore Goldin:

> Of course you have heard of an informal invitation from Custer for officers desiring to avail themselves of the services of a captured squaw, to come to the squaw round-up corral and select one! (?) Custer took first choice and lived with her during winter and spring of 1868 and '69.
>
> To crown the marriage (?) the squaw "calved" at site of the present Fort Sill. The issue was, however, a simon-pure Cheyenne baby, the seed having been sown before we came down on their fold at Washita.
>
> The husband presented himself at same camp, but "Custer's woman" gave him the marble heart in the finest of shapes.
>
> She was senior wife (present) of the two-starred big chief, with lots of "chuck-away" in the lodge, and wagon upon wagon-full outside!
>
> "Go away, you poor one-blanketed Indian man! You must swappy for some older squaw to keep your lodge-fire going and your back warm. Custer heap good!"

Benteen often is accused of malicious distortion, but what can be verified is that Me-o-tzi had a baby in early January, 1869. The Cheyennes later insisted Custer was the father, although this is impossible because the first time he saw Me-o-tzi was, as Benteen correctly stated, in November of 1868. Elizabeth saw the baby and perceived no resemblance to her husband: ". . . it was a cunning little bundle of brown velvet, with the same bright, bead-like eyes as the rest."

Me-o-tzi had a second baby, prematurely, in 1869. So goes another version. This was Custer's child, with creamy skin and yellow streaks in its hair, named Yellow Bird or Yellow Swallow—which was a not uncommon name.

Mrs. Kelly during her five months among the Oglalas saw quite a few children with light complexions, "the offspring of fort marriages," and one of Chief Ottawa's daughters was named Yellow Bird.

That Custer liked Me-o-tzi—that he liked her very much—never has been denied. Whether he acted upon his feelings is the mystery. Tom Custer described this pistol-packing Cheyenne divorcee in the idiom of the day as just another Sally-Ann, and remarked that she was "a great favorite with the entire Command"—a phrase easy to misconstrue. Benteen, frankly contemptuous, wrote that the general "winks at being cuckolded by his kid-brother," adding that this relieved the general of blanket duty. And in a letter to Goldin, dated St. Valentine's Day, 1896, he repeats old gossip from Camp Supply to the effect that the post surgeon had watched Custer and Me-o-tzi fornicating.

Such malignant stories persist like the odor of a swamp, and they are curious because Cheyennes were noted among plains tribes—at least by the Indians themselves—for the chastity of their women. Furthermore, Me-o-tzi was high caste; her father had been an important chief, second only to Black Kettle.

In any event, she and two other squaws were delegated to accompany Custer's task force around Oklahoma. Sheridan meant to subdue all of the Cheyennes—as well as Arapahoes, Kiowas, and Comanches—either by persuasion or bullets, and Custer took these women along because they knew the territory. That is, the older women did. Me-o-tzi at seventeen would not have been particularly helpful.

Led by Osage and Kaw scouts, perhaps directed by these Cheyenne women, he located an encampment of two neighboring villages whose chiefs were Medicine Arrow and Little Robe. But instead of charging to the tune of "Garry Owen" he advanced with his orderly and interpreter Romero. Considering recent events this sounds suicidal. He got away with it. Medicine Arrow invited him to a conference and Custer rode jauntily through the hostile village with nobody except his adjutant, Lt. W. W. Cooke.

In Medicine Arrow's lodge he was offered a pipe.

After having smoked for the appropriate length of time—an unpleasant obligation because he did not smoke—he assured both chiefs of his good intentions. He said, evidently through sign language, that he had not come to make war. Medicine Arrow was skeptical. He called the general a treacherous man and said if Custer again broke his word by making war on the Cheyennes he and all of his soldiers would be destroyed. To emphasize this he tapped the ashes of the pipe on Custer's boots.

David Humphreys Miller credits a chief named Brave Bear with this insult: "I took the dead ashes from the pipe and spilled them on the boots of the soldier-chief. . . ."

George Bent, who married Black Kettle's niece Mo-he-by-vah, and whose information probably is correct, states that the ashes were dumped by Rock Forehead—which was another name for Medicine Arrow. By either name, this chief guarded the Cheyenne sacred arrows and in his lodge the conference took place.

These four carefully worked stone-headed arrows were bequeathed to the Cheyennes by a diety or spirit known in English as the Culture Hero, and they represented one of the tribe's two most powerful charms—the other being a sacred buffalo hat which customarily remained with the northern branch of the tribe.

John Stands in Timber, being a Northern Cheyenne, did not know much about the arrows, but he described and explained the hat bundle. He saw it many times in the lodge of the keeper. It hung above a bed of willow sticks which had been painted red, white, and yellow. So much cloth had been attached to the bundle over the years that it had grown to the size of a man. Inside the bundle was a buffalo-hide sack containing the hat itself, a number of less significant items which he did not enumerate, and five enemy scalps representing five enemy tribes: Crow, Ute, Shoshone, Pawnee, Blackfeet. This bundle, like the sacred arrows, was very seldom unwrapped. Stands in Timber said it had been opened in 1934 as a favor to General Hugh Scott, and again in 1959 because some people mistrusted the keeper. He himself was one of fourteen witnesses when it was opened on July 12, 1959. The scalps were safe. The hat was safe. "It looked the same as pictures taken of it for Scott—with horns and a beaded head band."

The sacred arrows of the southern tribe—not unwrapped for the benefit of General Custer—were kept in a strip of fur cut from a coyote's back. Two of the shafts were painted red, symbolizing procurement of food. The other two were black, symbolizing victory in war. Custer may or may not have noticed them; he does not allude to them in his book. They were suspended from a forked stick and he was offered a seat beneath them, which implies that he was on trial, though he himself considered it a place of honor because he sat at the chief's right hand. In fact, this seat was considered the place of dishonor.

An Indian held the stem of the pipe while Custer smoked. He said it was "the medicine man," the second-ranking dignitary in the lodge. According to Bent, it was the chief himself, Rock Forehead, who held the stem, and who warned Custer that if he failed to speak the truth he and his command would be killed. After the ceremonial smoking was finished, Rock Forehead loosened the ashes with a stick and poured them on the general's toes to give him bad luck. So says Bent.

The identity of the Indian who held the pipe and dirtied Custer's boots is less important than the gravity of this warning. Custer himself does not mention the incident, although of course he might choose to ignore such an insult. It may or may not have occurred. As Professor Stewart points out, the story could have been fabricated eight years later by Cheyenne medicine men hoping to credit themselves for that legendary victory in Montana.

With the Cheyennes subdued, at least temporarily, the Seventh returned to Kansas and spent the summer of '69 encamped near Fort Hays. Now and then a squadron would be dispatched to scout the neighborhood for trouble, but nothing serious was reported. Custer's first biographer, Frederick Whittaker, thinks this may have been one of the happiest periods of his life, although it is just as possible that he felt bored. He could endure anything except idleness. Frederic Van de Water, who wrote a very different sort of biography with seldom a kind word for the general, likened him to Antaeus, invigorated by contact with the earth: "He was one of the healthiest, most vital men who ever lived, almost immune to hunger and thirst, heat and cold, sleepiness and fatigue."

In rural Kansas he had little to do except entertain tenderfoot dignitaries, most of whom wanted to shoot a buffalo. So there were hunting parties to organize, familiar questions to answer, compliments to accept as though he had not heard them before. Now and then he would gamble at cards or he would read. Few novelists interested him, but he did enjoy Dickens and once remarked that he felt like Macawber waiting for something to turn up. He preferred history to fiction. That he should study Napoleon's campaigns is to be expected; Elizabeth used to watch him mark the paths of armies in an atlas, using a different kind of pencil for each. But along with Napoleon a curiously mixed company of men comes wandering through *My Life*: Diodorus, Osceola, Thomas Jefferson, Alexander, Hanno, Columbus, Thorwald Ericsson, Theopompus.

In October the Seventh returned to winter quarters at Fort Leavenworth where he had even less to do. Earlier he had written a series of articles for a sportsman's journal under the pseudonym "Nomad," and now he wrote a few more.

"The Hunt on the Plains," which appeared in a November issue of *Turf, Field and Farm*, tells about "nine ardent lovers of sport" who set out from Detroit in a Pullman car, bound for the Seventh Cavalry camp at Fort Hays. "The party headed by Hon. K. C. Barker, consisted of Hon. W. G. Beckwith, the genial and popular President of the Michigan State Agricultural Society; General R. L. Howard . . ." et al.

It concludes with a sentimental and instructive example of Custer's poetry. One of his dogs, Maida, had been killed by a soldier.

Poor Maida, in life the firmest friend,
The first to welcome, foremost to defend;
Whose honest heart is still your master's own,
Who labors, fights, lives, breathes for him alone.
But who with me shall hold thy former place,
Thine image what new friendship can efface.
 Best of thy kind adieu!
The frantic deed which laid thee low
 This heart shall ever rue.

What happened to the perpetrator of this frantic deed, he does not reveal.

He loved animals, including those he killed and stuffed, but dogs and horses were his favorites, and the dogs most clearly returned his affection. Elizabeth reports that whenever he took a nap the dogs would lie down as close to him as possible. "I have seen them stretched at his back and curled around his head, while the nose and paws of one rested on his breast."

There may have been no living creature below the order of Mankind that he did not love, or at least tolerate. He once kept a field mouse in an empty inkwell on his desk. Occasionally he would dip a finger into the inkwell. Then the mouse would scurry up his finger and up his arm and wriggle through the famous curls to the top of his head. Elizabeth hated this mouse. The sight of it clinging to those curls, which she adored, must have been insufferable. Finally, to placate her, he took the mouse outside and released it but the creature would not go away.

During this aimless, idle period of his life, if one believes Capt. Benteen, everybody knew he was "criminally intimate with a married woman," the wife of an officer stationed at Fort Leavenworth. Not only that, avows the disgusted captain, General Custer hung around saloons patronized by whores and tried insistently to beat Jayhawker Jenison's faro game: "These facts all being known to Mrs. Custer, rendered her—if she had any heart (?) a broken-hearted woman. From knowing her as well as I do, I only remark that she was about as cold-blooded a woman as I ever knew, in which respect the pair were admirably mated."

It is probable that Custer felt enormously relieved when summoned to Washington in December of 1870. The Army was being reorganized.

Once again he thought about getting out. He had just turned thirty, young enough for a second career.

While waiting to see what the government would do, and trying to make up his own mind, he visited New York. He wrote passionately to Elizabeth, interminable letters stuffed with trivia:

> What would you think of a Bunkey grown so corpulent about the waist he cannot keep his pants up without suspenders? . . . I have bought some new musical selections: "Champagne Charlie," the "Letter Song" sung by Aimee in "Perichole" and "Lui Dit," Persigni in "La Grande Duchesse.". . . Pongee parasols are the style, some with colored border, some with small ruffles at the edge. Chignons are unpopular. The prevailing style is to wear the hair in two braids in the morning, and in the afternoon tuck these up, the ends concealed with little curls. . . .

He enjoyed trailing street nymphs and told Elizabeth that one young blonde had walked past his hotel several times, obviously trying to get his attention. Twice he followed her. She turned around to look directly at him. He declined these offers but he nibbled at the idea. He found out where she lived—"opposite Mr. Belmont's." He watched her enter the house and he loitered outside until she came to a window.

His restless energy burns through every page of every letter to Elizabeth. "General Torbert has invited me to visit him at his Delaware home. He says he will take my halter off and turn me loose in a peach orchard."

On September 3, 1871, he assumed command of a two-company post at Elizabethtown, Kentucky, a few miles south of Louisville, and while waiting for his wife to arrive he lived in a boarding house. Any number of ladies fluttered around, each one anxious to show him the local attraction, Mammoth Cave, but he would not visit the cave without Elizabeth.

His soldiers had little to do except harass moonshiners and frustrate the Ku Klux Klan. Custer again was bored. Elizabeth herself found their new home wearisome: "the stillest, dullest place." Not a sound all day long except the sheriff in the courthouse calling "Hear ye!" as each case opened. She wrote to her aunt Eliza Sabin that this part of Kentucky was very poor, "the people low and uneducated." Three or four of them would ride the same horse. Everything was old. Buildings. People. Animals. The boarding house dog was sweet sixteen and could scarcely walk. The liveliest citizen in the neighborhood was a pig. She had not been accustomed to such tedium, not since marrying Custer. They found the wealthy, cultivated Kentuckians agreeable enough, but life remained somnolent. She describes a mechanical contraption consisting of a series of wooden paddles strung on a rope. This device was meant to keep flies away from the supper table. The boards moved and clattered because a Negro boy pulled the rope, and with a ripple of wit she adds: ". . . so we dine to music."

For several months during this period Custer was absent. Just what he did has never been learned, but early in 1872 he functioned as a guide or escort for the young Grand Duke Alexis who had been sent to the United States on a goodwill visit by his father, Czar Alexander II. The tour—via private train—included a Nebraska buffalo hunt, during which he seems to have been coached by Custer, and a swing through the Old South, which inspired the boosters of Mammoth Cave to recommend it.

Custer responded by telegraph:

His Imperial Highness the Grand Duke Alexis and suite will arrive in Louisville at 2 o'clock AM Tuesday. The Ducal party desires to visit Mammoth Cave. . . .

The Duke liked Custer and Libbie and invited them to accompany him to New Orleans, which they did. She observes that the nineteen-year-old nobleman showed more interest in music and girls than in the scenery. When they got to New Orleans the Duke honored them with a suite adjoining his own. But all too soon Alexis went on his way.

The Custers made a quick trip to Michigan where his kid sister Maggie was getting married to Lt. James Calhoun. Then they returned to Elizabethtown and the oppressive southern summer.

He played games with neighborhood children and played chess with Judge Quince Johnson. He served on a military board assigned to buy cavalry horses—a pleasant assignment that took him through the Lexington bluegrass country—and he attended various social events. What the disenfranchised people thought about him has not been recorded, but with the local aristocracy he seems to have been popular. It is said that a cake sale was almost postponed because he was otherwise engaged.

Wherever he went he was followed by a pack of dogs. His orderly, John Burkman, mentions eighty hounds—which must be an exaggeration. Burkman exercised them, chained in pairs, and he said they behaved all right unless they caught sight of a Kentucky dog, after which nobody could hold them. They chewed up several of Elizabethtown's finest, including an excellent bird dog, along with at least one cat and a pig. As a result of these attacks, according to one biographer, the citizens petitioned for his removal. If so, the complaint was destroyed or lost. The Hardin County Historical Society in Elizabethtown has no record of it.

He continued writing for *Turf, Field and Farm* and he began a serial account of the Hancock campaign for *Galaxy*, but his heart was elsewhere.

Some thirty years earlier the frontier trader and historian Josiah Gregg had published a ruminative essay which begins: "I have striven in vain to reconcile myself to the even tenor of civilized life in the United States; and have sought in its amusements and its society a substitute for those high excitements which have attached me so strongly to Prairie life. . . ." It might have come from the quill of Nomad.

His period of exile concluded in the spring of 1873 when the dispersed Seventh was ordered to reunite at Memphis, proceed from there by steamer to Cairo, Illinois, from there by rail to Yankton, Dakota Territory, and proceed from there as a mounted cavalry regiment to Fort Rice—its ultimate mission to protect surveyors for the Northern Pacific Railroad, and by a display of strength to persuade the Sioux that whether they liked the idea or not an iron horse soon would come hooting and chuffing through this land.

The first whites to explore these northern plains were trappers, and Crow Indians who observed them in canoes named them Beta-awka-wahcha—Sits on the Water—although after a while the Crows joined the Cheyennes in calling them Veho or Mastachuda, which means Yellow Eyes. LeForge points out that Mah-ish-ta-schee-da, as he spells it, if literally translated would be Eyes Yellow, because the first three syllables mean "eyes" while the last two designate that color. He speculates that early trappers might have been suffering from jaundice, hence the generic name. Or perhaps an eye of any color except deep brown or black would seem yellowish.

Although the Sioux ordinarily referred to these queer-eyed foreigners as wasichu or wasicun, they might be called Dog Faces because of their disgusting whiskers, or Crooked Feet because their toes slewed out, or Flop Ears because Mormon emigrants habitually twisted the ears of disobedient children. Whatever they were called, they smelled like two porcupines.

In 1867, while Custer chased Kite Indians around Kansas, an extraordinary French nobleman—Baron Philippe Régis de Trobriand—was appointed commander of the Middle District in the Department of Dakota, and a journal he kept during two and a half years at Fort Stevenson tells quite a lot about military life in that region. Baron de Trobriand's journal and that of Pvt. Coleman could scarcely be more different, which is to be expected, for one recorded the West through the spectacles of an erudite European with a long view of human history, while the other was more naturally and necessarily concerned with immediate matters such as his own preservation. Yet they are equally instructive.

De Trobriand reached America in 1841 as a privileged tourist, visited a number of cities, contributed articles to *Le Courrier des Etats Unis*, and returned to Europe where in 1843 he married a New York girl, Mary Mason Jones. From Paris he went to Venice where he passed three years studying music, painting, and history with members of the exiled Bourbon family.

In New York again he started a literary magazine, *La Revue du Nouveau Monde*, featuring such illustrious authors as Lamartine, De Vigny, and Gautier, but *La Revue* folded within a year, as do most literary ventures.

Back to France for a while, then once more to America, now as an editor of *Le Courrier* for which he wrote a gossip column until the Civil War erupted. On April 18, 1861, he watched the Sixth Massachusetts regiment marching through New York, a sight that recalled his childhood "when the French battalions defiled before the starry epaulets of my father . . ." so he became an American citizen and joined the Lafayette Guard. He fought at Fredericksburg, Chancellorsville, and Gettysburg, and was promoted to major general, the only Frenchman other than Lafayette to achieve this rank.

After the war he again returned to France where he wrote *Quatre Ans de Campagne a l'Armée du Potomac*, but in the midst of this work he learned that he had been appointed a colonel in the regular army and should report for duty. He requested a leave on account of the Civil War memoirs and his request was granted. Colonel de Trobriand then joined his regiment, the Thirty-first Infantry, at Fort Stevenson.

Lucille Kane, who translated his journal, observes that he came to the American West not only as a soldier but as an artist and writer who could appreciate the grandeur of this country, its immensity, its loneliness, and therefore his journal is as much a record of the region's impact on a sensitive man as it is a narrative of military life. He writes of the burning wind, of dry summer storms, of snow, "and always of the great plains rolling away to nowhere."

For ten years he served on the frontier. From Dakota Territory he was sent to Montana, Utah, Wyoming, and at last to Louisiana. In 1879 he retired, living thereafter as one might expect a man of such varied appetites to live:

summer in Paris or on Long Island, winter in New Orleans—where he died in 1897. Madame Kane remarks that de Trobriand was a man who contributed richly to the diverse culture of which this nation is so proud.

Two hours before midnight on the final day of 1867 he meditates. Very soon this year will close:

> . . . and will join in the abyss of the past some millions of other years of which only a few thousand have left on us their distinct marks and of which scarcely forty—a nothing—have their place in my memory. I have neither family nor friends around me to bid it goodby. For me no clock will strike the twelve strokes of midnight at its passing. No familiar sound, no family celebration will mark the portentous moment when 1868 succeeds 1867.
>
> As I take leave of the dying year and welcome its successor, I am alone in a log house in the heart of the deserts of the American continent, dreaming of my dear absent ones, and looking back on bygone days. And what a variety of places and experiences are in the succession of those first few days of the year!

He remembers January 1, 1840, at Tours, by the sickbed of his father who died ten days afterward. In 1841 he was a young man enjoying Paris. In 1842, New York. Back and forth, one world succeeding the next, years of gold and silk, music, painting, society.

1853: Chateau de la Fourgeraie, the country gentleman.

1855: New York journalist. His children are growing up.

1862: In a tent near Washington he awaits the enemy.

1863: Fredericksburg.

1865: Petersburg.

1866: New York.

1867: Brest.

1868: Dakota.

"But what do I know?" he asks. "After all that, in comparison to what I should still be able to learn, if life were not too short and if one did not forget with the years half of what is learned. The little Greek that I knew I have forgotten. . . . I should have forgotten Italian while studying Spanish if I had not stopped myself in time. And now I am learning Sioux. . . ."

The last instants of 1867 evaporate while he sits behind a crude desk in this uncivilized territory:

> Where is the most intense realm of the heart, the soul, the faculties? In passion or in reason? Everything is logical in this world. Age of passions

first; the age of reason next. He who has not gone through these phases has only half lived. The person who has had only passions knows but one side of life; he who has had only reason is no better off; and he who upsets the natural order of the two periods has been nothing but a fool from beginning to end.

At least, I need not reproach myself on this score, and I have not done things out of season. . . .

And I should see you again as I saw you, and I should love you again as I loved you, you of whom I try in vain to say nothing here, although my thoughts are all filled with you—you who brighten my past when I look back, a past which is bright because of you and which would be dark without you—you who appear to me still young and beautiful and charming as in other days. . . .

Next morning he observes that the Dakota sky is "uncordial," though the sun attempted to come out. "Like a good prince it showed itself for a few minutes. . . ."

The day ended gloomily.

On January 5 the weather was terrible, wind sang lugubriously down the stovepipe. And the weather got worse. At reveille his servant leaped inside like a white statue.

"Where the devil did you come from?" he asked.

"From my room," said the orderly, whose room was just thirty feet away. "And I thought I'd never find the door. The building is half buried. . . ."

De Trobriand peeked into the kitchen, which reminded him of an opera setting—a grotto with needles of ice hanging from the roof.

Another day he reports that although the sun has come out and the air remains calm the thermometer registered five below zero. The sun tried to put on a good face but it was the colorless face of a convalescent. It arose very late in the southeast, traveled a short arc across the sky with languid resignation, and declined early in the southwest. He expresses surprise at the absence of polar bears.

Apart from such uncordial weather there were the savages. News arrived from Fort Berthold on April 11 that Sitting Bull's Unkpapas had persuaded the Blackfeet and Miniconjoux to form an alliance. This news was not good. De Trobriand mentions that a few years before—by which he must mean the early 1860s—Sitting Bull had been wounded in a skirmish with army troops, whereupon Bloody Knife jumped off his horse and was about to cut Sitting Bull's throat when the commanding officer forbade him to do so. The result, says de Trobriand, was that Sitting Bull escaped, recovered, "and since then, bent on vengeance, he has always done us every harm in his power and is the spirit or arm of all the coups attempted or accomplished against us. It is he in particular who inspires the others with his hate. . . ."

Like every other white who encountered the Unkpapa medicine man, this highly sophisticated European was fascinated. He notes that Sitting Bull is about forty years old and rather inclined to fat. "His fierceness is masked by a good-natured manner and a conversation abounding in good humor. To judge by appearances one would believe him to be the most harmless of red-skins. In reality, he is a ferocious beast who seems to be laughing when he is showing his teeth."

Sitting Bull. Sitting Bull.

In English this name sounds a little absurd, and to whites of the nineteenth century it was still more so; they alluded to him as Slightly Recumbent Gentleman Cow.

Exact translation from the Sioux is impossible, but his name may be better understood if one realizes how plains Indians respected and honored the bull buffalo. Whites considered this animal to be exceptionally stupid. Col. Dodge states without equivocation that the buffalo is the dullest creature of which he has any knowledge. A herd of buffalo would graze complacently while every member was shot down. He himself shot two cows and thirteen calves while the survivors grazed and watched. He and others in his party had to shout and wave their hats to drive the herd away so the dead animals could be butchered.

Indians, however, regarded buffalo as the wisest and most powerful of creatures, nearest to the omnipresent Spirit. Furthermore, if one says in English that somebody is sitting it means he is seated, balanced on the haunches; but the Sioux expression has an additional sense, not equivalent to but approximating the English words *situate* and *locate* and *reside*.

Thus, from an Indian point of view, the name Sitting Bull signified a wise and powerful being who had taken up residence among them.

As a boy, he was called Slow, Hunkesni, because of his deliberate manner, and it has been alleged that his parents thought him ordinary, perhaps even a bit slow in the head. Most biographies state that he was known also as Jumping Badger; but Stanley Vestal, after talking with many Indians who knew him, said that none of them nor any member of Sitting Bull's family could remember him being called Jumping Badger. In any event, Slow he was called, and Slow would suffice until he distinguished himself.

When he was fourteen he touched a slain Crow with a coup stick. To touch a dead enemy with a stick may not sound impressive, but nineteenth-century Sioux thought otherwise: in honor of this deed his father provided a feast and bestowed his own name upon the boy.

That is one explanation of how he acquired the name, although some scholars think he chose it himself because of the buffalo's wisdom and strength. Others think he saw a cloud resembling a seated buffalo.

If he did acquire the name from his father, which seems probable, one must ask how the father got that name.

It is said that the elder Sitting Bull occasionally could understand the language of animals and once on a hunting trip he was able to interpret the noises made by a bull. This bull was talking about the four ages of man: infancy, youth, maturity, old age. These ages were identified by metaphor, transmogrified from Dakota into English as Sitting Bull, Jumping Bull, Bull Standing with Cow, Lone Bull. The hunter knew that the buffalo was offering these names to him, so he chose one. He chose the first, which was the most important because it had been spoken first. Years later, after his son touched an enemy, he knew it was time to give the boy this name; and from then on the father called himself by the less important name of Jumping Bull.

Hereditary nomenclature was not unusual, even if whites prefer to think of Indians acquiring their names in dreams and visions. Little Big Man, for instance, was so-called to differentiate him from his father, Big Man. The Sioux form of Big Man is Chasa—an abbreviation of Wichasa—Tonga. Literally: Man Big. Chikala, which means Little, was added to designate the son.

Thus: Old Man Afraid of His Horse, Young Man Afraid, etc.

The patriarch of this Man Afraid family was an Oglala chief born about 1815 whose descendants, like the offspring of other illustrious chieftains, evidently decided to polish up his name. He got that name, they said, not because he feared his horse but because he was such a redoubtable fighter. The mere sight of his horse was enough to make enemies tremble. In other words, a more accurate translation would be They Are Afraid of His Horse. Preposterous, according to that irascible scholar George Hyde. It is a story swallowed like a goldfish by gullible historians. In fact, the name has been traced back to about 1760 when the Sioux first acquired horses and had trouble managing them. Indians were quick to invent humorous nicknames; they were much more apt to do this than to bestow upon somebody an exalted title, so it is not hard to guess how this famous name originated. Dunn provides yet another version. The great chief's name actually meant that he feared losing his horses. So valuable were they that during an attack by Shoshones he abandoned his family in order to save the pony herd.

As for Red Cloud, he might have been named after a meteorite which roared across Sioux territory the night of September 20, 1822, and colored the clouds spectacularly—a phenomenon recorded in a Sioux pictographic calendar and noted also by white men at Fort Snelling near the mouth of the Minnesota River. Or Red Cloud could have been a family name for several generations.

If twentieth-century Oglalas ever knew the origin of this famous name they have forgotten it, says Hyde, because they have offered at least a dozen stories on the subject. In one appealing legend, thousands of Oglala warriors sat on the hills wrapped in scarlet blankets so that from a distance they resembled a red cloud. Hyde calls this nonsense, pointing out that Red Cloud carried the name when he was a young man without followers, and by 1866 when he did have thousands of followers the Oglalas had not traded with whites for some time and owned very few blankets. Furthermore, Mr. Hyde continues as if he had just enjoyed a refreshing sip of vinegar, a lot of Indian children were named after that meteorite: "The word *makhpiya* may be translated either as cloud or sky; thus when the Sioux say blue cloud, they mean blue sky. In this instance the word may refer to the meteorite itself. Inkpaduta had twin sons born at that time, and he seems to have named them for this event. One was called Roaring Cloud, the other Fire Cloud."

All of which leaves Indian nomenclature much in doubt. Only now and then is the origin of a name beyond dispute. For example, it seems fairly clear that the Cheyenne miracle man, Walks Above the Earth, became famous as Crazy Mule because, like a Christian ascetic indifferent to earthly conceit, he rode a mule instead of a horse and one day when he rode into a Sioux village somebody said, "Here comes that crazy Cheyenne on his mule." Right away he was Crazy Cheyenne on a Mule, and pretty soon Crazy Mule.

Wooden Leg knew this magician. Once he saw Crazy Mule stand with his back against a tree and ask four Cheyennes to shoot him. All right, they said. One after another they walked up close and each fired a bullet into his body. Then he took off his moccasins and poured out four bullets. Wooden Leg had this to say: "He was known as a man whose mind was at all times on spiritual things, who gave little or no thought to ordinary earthly matters."

What held true for Crazy Mule could not be said of Sitting Bull, known to Unkpapas as a man of both worlds—earthly and spiritual. Unlike the famous magician, Sitting Bull grew up not as a remote mystic but as a participant in village life. There were those who resented the immense authority he acquired, while others disliked him for private reasons, but it is said that most Unkpapas found him to be affectionate and considerate. He had a powerful, resonant voice and became well known as a singer, often composing songs instead of merely repeating familiar chants.

He became a celebrated warrior. He was among the braves who returned from Crow territory with a harvest of ears, scalps, genitals, fingers, and the hand of a warrior tied to a stick by the thumb. Frank Grouard, who lived several years among the Sioux, claimed that during a Sun Dance he heard Sitting Bull recount sixty-three battle coups.

He became one of only two sash-wearers in the Strong Hearts warrior society, a distinction that entitled him to wear a buffalo horn bonnet covered with crow feathers, his mark of office being a strip of wool long enough to drag the ground. This trailing sash was more than decorative: when a sash-wearer took a stand in battle he pinned it to the earth with a lance, signifying that he would never retreat.

Bellicose Cheyennes did the same. Their sash was a strip of buffalo hide about eight feet in length, ornamented with brightly dyed porcupine quills. From the end of it dangled a picket pin attached to a dog-rope. After a warrior had driven this pin into the ground he must fight all enemies or die where he stood unless a comrade pulled up the pin and ceremonially lashed him with a quirt. Which is to say, the warrior was so brave that he would not retreat unless whipped like a dog.

This symbolic act of pinning one's self to the earth must date back several hundred years to a time when plains Indians fought on foot, before they knew about horses, because it would be suicide for any warrior, no matter how brave, to immobilize himself in front of a mounted enemy.

Sitting Bull must have performed the sash dance on various occasions and one way or another he survived this rococo display of courage. Like Crazy Horse and Custer, he was seldom hurt. His only debilitating wound occurred in 1865 on a horse-stealing expedition against the Crows when he was shot in the left foot. This was a freak injury—the bullet merely creased the sole. His foot was treated with some kind of balm obtained from the neighboring Rees but it did not heal properly. The sole contracted and from then on he limped.

About 1870 a Yankton Sioux showed up at Fort Buford with an old Thirty-first Infantry roster. On the blank side of each page was a picture drawn by an

Indian. Altogether there were thirty-seven drawings, mostly in brown and black inks. They illustrated the activities of a mighty warrior and in one corner of each page, like a Japanese signature, sat the totemic bull. Twenty-three pictures showed him slaughtering men, women, children, soldiers, teamsters, scouts, Indians, mail couriers—anybody who got in the way. He was as impartial as death itself, comments historian Dunn. The next twelve pictures showed him collecting horses, "a pursuit in which he displayed good taste. . . . He may fairly be considered one of the ablest horse-thieves the country ever produced." In the last two pictures he led his warrior fraternity, the Strong Hearts, against two Crow villages.

The Yankton who brought this pictorial history to Fort Buford had stolen it from Sitting Bull and wanted to sell it. Eventually he did so. He got $1.50 worth of supplies. What happened to him after that is not known. Perhaps he lived long and happily and boasted to his grandchildren about stealing the famous medicine man's picture book, but one should not bet on it.

Bearcoat Nelson Miles encountered the old warrior a few months after the Little Bighorn. They had a brief conference. Miles had been ordered to lead the Unkpapas to a reservation; Sitting Bull wanted all Yellow Eyes out of Sioux territory. The conference, or confrontation, resolved nothing. They met again the next day but again they could not agree, so they started fighting. The Unkpapas set fire to the prairie, which they very often did when annoyed; General Miles retaliated with artillery.

After two days, having been chased forty miles, the Sioux once again talked it over with Bearcoat and many of them agreed to do as he insisted. Sitting Bull, Gall, Pretty Bear, and others refused. Miles chased these incorrigibles a while longer but at last gave up, saying they had been driven so far north they were no longer a threat. He had nearly accomplished what he set out to do and it seemed impossible to accomplish much more. So these two obdurate leaders parted, but Miles got a close look at the infamous Unkpapa. He saw a sturdily built man almost six feet tall with a big head and a big nose, whose pale brown skin was scarred by smallpox, a man whose gestures were deliberate and reserved, who did not speak without considering what to say. "At first he was courteous, but evidently void of any genuine respect for the white race. Although the feeling was disguised, his manner indicated his animosity. . . ."

Miles infuriated Sitting Bull by revealing that he knew where the Sioux intended to hunt buffalo, a bit of information acquired from agency Indians. To the Unkpapa chieftain this represented betrayal. He no longer disguised his rage: "His whole manner appeared more like that of a wild beast than a human being; his face assumed a furious expression; his jaws closed tightly; his lips were compressed, and you could see his eyes glistening with the fire of savage hatred." He told Miles that there never was a white man who did not hate Indians and there never was an Indian who did not hate whites. As for himself, God Almighty had made him an Indian, not an agency Indian either—not one of those cracker-and-molasses chiefs—and he did not intend to be one.

He was about as consistent and inflexible as a man could be. His hatred of whites long antedated that epic meeting with Custer's Seventh. Nine years earlier at Fort Union he said he had killed and robbed so many whites that he could not expect peace. He wanted nothing to do with those who carried water on their shoulders and hauled manure. He asked if whites considered him to be a poor man, but provided the answer himself: "You are fools to make yourselves slaves to a piece of bacon fat, some hardtack, and a little sugar and coffee."

Several months after confronting Bearcoat Miles he led his shabby, belea-guered followers across the international boundary into Canada and there he camped, waiting to see what would happen. The Canadian government wished he would go home, although it refused to extradite him, and the U.S. government attempted in various ways to entice him across the border. He was, after all, the mystic leader of the Sioux. If he could be jailed the Indian problem might be solved.

Correspondent Finerty met him in Canada: ". . . an Indian mounted on a cream-colored pony, and holding in his hand an eagle's wing, which did duty for a fan . . . stared solidly, for a minute or so, at me. His hair, parted in the ordinary Sioux fashion, was without a plume. His broad face, with a promi-nent hooked nose and wide jaws, was destitute of paint. His fierce, half-blood-shot eyes gleamed from under brows which displayed large perceptive or-gans, and, as he sat there on his horse regarding me with a look which seemed blended of curiosity and insolence, I did not need to be told that he was Sitting Bull."

A frontier artist named DeCost Smith described him as "recalcitrant," which was hardly an overstatement. Smith, who became acquainted with a number of previously wild Indians, once visited two Apaches immured in the old "cheesebox fort" on Governors' Island in New York harbor. These Apaches had not the slightest idea why they were buried alive in such a place, nor how long they would be held. They asked Smith these questions "and many more I could not answer." He had been told by government officials that the Apaches were locked up because they would not give in—would not submit to authority. They were therefore considered to be unrepentant pris-oners of war, as guilty as old Red Cloud of obtuse and unsubduable Indian-ism. Consequently, the United States chose this method of breaking their spirit.

Neither would Sitting Bull submit. He denied the authority of the United States and his flight to Canada indicates that he understood perfectly how Americans responded to such an attitude.

In 1880 a delegation of these Canadian refugees—not including the slightly recumbent gentleman cow—ventured across the line for a visit with Bear-coat. They were not yet ready to give up, but they were contemplating the idea and they wanted to hear his words. Miles notes in his recollections that they were deeply interested in various activities south of the border, such as bridge-building and long-range rifle practice, but they seemed especially impressed by the telegraph and telephone. He decided to work on this. He had blankets draped across the windows of the telegraph office in order that they might see the spark leap from the key to the contact point. This was shrewd, because after watching the spark for a while they agreed among themselves that it exceeded the best medicine of the Sioux.

Miles then demonstrated the frightful power of the telephone. Half of the visitors were escorted to a house some distance away, a phone was cranked up, and they were instructed to talk to each other. When they recognized the voices of distant friends speaking the Dakota language, he says, "huge drops of perspiration coursed down their bronze faces and with trembling hands they laid the instrument down." These were men who had endured the torture of the Sun Dance and had been ready to give their lives at the Little Bighorn, but after this horrifying experience they became urgent advocates of peace.

At a later date Sitting Bull, too, met the instrument. He was hooked up to a Mrs. Parkin, who was twenty-five miles away at Cannonball River. She was a mixed-blood who spoke fluent Sioux, but Sitting Bull reasoned that the telephone understood only English, so when Mrs. Parkin answered the call he exclaimed, "Hello, hello! You bet, you bet!" which exhausted most of his English. And when he realized that he could speak Dakota with this woman such a long way off he, like his contemporaries, was gravely shocked.

Capt. John Bourke learned quite a lot about Indians during sixteen years as a member of Crook's staff and he thought the wars could have been shortened, possibly even avoided, if hostiles had been confronted by a regiment of magicians and jugglers. Along with Miles and other experienced frontiersmen, Bourke did not hesitate to make the most unscrupulous use of wasichu magic. He once took an old electric battery to a Sioux camp. He put a silver dollar in a pan of water, attached his battery, and told the medicine men he would give five dollars to any one of them who could lift the silver dollar out of the water—providing he took hold of the brass battery handle with one hand. A huge crowd of Sioux assembled. Bourke estimates the number at one thousand. And, he says, "they conceived a deep reverence for me, as they had seen the most famous of their medicine men attempt to do this and fail, being almost thrown into convulsions in the attempt." At last a very powerful Indian tried it. He seized the handle and grabbed the dollar. "The electricity went through him like a shot, and he kicked the battery all to pieces. He wanted to try it again and we patched the battery up, and he finally succeeded in getting the dollar, owing to the weakness of the broken battery." Bourke adds laconically that the big Indian was almost twisted out of shape.

While employing such dirty tricks on behalf of the government he remained careful not to discredit the native magicians; he did not ridicule their power, merely insisting that his own was greater.

He once took a professional sleight-of-hand artist to a Sun Dance. This magician walked up to one of the chiefs, "and without warning gave him a slap on the cheek, nearly knocking him over. Then with his other hand he got hold of the other cheek and apparently pulled a twenty-dollar gold piece out of it, while the rest of the Indians looked on with open-mouthed wonder. He went up to another chief, who rejoiced in the title of Little Big Man, and grabbing him by the nose pulled a twenty-dollar gold piece out of his nose, much to the chief's surprise. I saw him a number of times afterward, and when he thought I was not looking would pull his blanket up over his nose and feel the end of it. . . ."

In 1881 Sitting Bull crossed the border. He may have been disheartened by wasichu black magic, but probably he surrendered because the alternative for those few Unkpapas who still followed him was starvation. He did not want to come back. Speaking of the United States he remarked: "The country there is poisoned with blood. . . ."

Another fierce Unkpapa—Crow King—also held out until 1881. Together with Black Moon and Gall he had led the fighting men. When at last Crow King admitted it was all over he capitulated totally. After giving up his weapons he asked a Chicago *Times* correspondent for two dollars so he could buy dolls for his daughters.

The blind old Santee, Inkpaduta—Scarlet Point, named for a homicidal career—had died two years earlier in Canada, which they called the Grandmother Land. Whether he would have buried the hatchet anyplace other than in some white man's head is questionable. He is said to have hated whites more fanatically than any other Indian.

Sitting Bull may have been induced to surrender by a trader at Leighton & Jordan's Woody Mountain store, Gus Hedderich. They were friends and Hedderich probably convinced him there was no way out. It is said, too, that he became despondent when he learned that his favorite daughter Minnestema, Sleeping Water, had run off with a man he despised.

A scout named E. H. Allison negotiated with various hostile bands, and when interviewed in 1912 he stated that during the winter of 1881 he had succeeded in luring away nearly all of the Unkpapas, leaving just forty-three families in Canada. He was about to consult with the medicine man himself when General Terry concluded this was unnecessary because Sitting Bull now had very few followers, "and his power for evil being entirely destroyed, it was a matter of indifference to our government if he himself never came in. . . ."

Capt. Walter Clifford was detailed to escort Sitting Bull from the international boundary to Fort Buford at the confluence of the Yellowstone and the Missouri. By this time only the sturdiest Sioux were alive. In a country that just recently had supported numberless deer, buffalo, and antelope, Clifford wrote in his account of this depressing assignment, "now not a solitary hoof-track can be seen. Another winter and there would not have been enough of them left to make a decent surrender." Of Sitting Bull he wrote: "The one hitherto unyielding spirit that has kept up an unceasing warfare for 19 years, is broken at last."

Almost. Not quite. Sitting Bull clung to his dream beyond all reasonable hope. Even after they had crossed the boundary on that final march he tried to persuade his people to break away. "We will cross the Missouri River at Wolf Point, cross the Yellowstone, and go up the Tongue River into the mountains," he told them. "There we can find plenty of game and hide from our enemies." He did not know that while he was in Canada this region had been settled.

Clifford said many of the people following him had only one garment. Some were naked. What little clothing they did have was dropping off their bodies.

In this condition Sitting Bull with 186 Unkpapas was escorted to Fort Buford. There, on July 20, at eleven in the morning, the obstinate fugitive behaved as usual. Instead of handing his rifle to the American major who conducted this bittersweet ceremony, he gave it to his six-year-old son, telling him to give it to the major; and he made a speech during which he said that he wished to be remembered as the last of his tribe to surrender his weapon.

With this the Indian trouble ended. Not literally, not until the last shot at Wounded Knee. But when Sitting Bull admitted defeat the intermittent warfare stopped. Count Hermann Keyserling, speaking of America, remarked that no gods had been born of this nation's marriage with man. There was Manitou, whose ghost continues to hover on the plains; but Manitou was not strong enough to become the soul of a continent—as did Osiris, Allah, and Jahve. When Sitting Bull gave up his rifle he surrendered the only god ever known to America.

The government assembled a fleet of steamboats to transport his ragged Unkpapas downstream. His power for evil might have dissipated, as Allison thought, or else the government did not want him prowling around the edge of civilization where he might once again work his dreadful magic.

Down the turbulent Big Muddy they went, the old demagogue aboard the *General Sherman*.

Just across from Bismarck stood Fort Lincoln where friends and relatives of Custer's dead cavalrymen still lived, and these emigrating Sioux could perceive such bitterness in the air that one Indian on the leading boat displayed a white flag. Yet, in accordance with the laws of human behavior, the farther downstream they traveled the less hostility they encountered, and when the tiny armada reached Standing Rock near the present border of South Dakota these Indians were welcomed as celebrities. Men, women, and children crowded aboard the *General Sherman* to shake hands with Sitting Bull. Judson Elliott Walker, who was just then finishing a book on Custer's campaigns, had to stand on a chair to catch a glimpse of the medicine man and reports that he was wearing "green wire goggles." No details are provided, so green wire goggles must have been a familiar sight in those days.

Sitting Bull mobbed by fans while wearing green wire goggles. It sounds like Hollywood.

Most of the Indians disembarked at Standing Rock. Sitting Bull himself went ashore to have lunch at the Merchants' Hotel "by special invitation of Mr. Marsh, the popular landlord." Then he probably camped with his people for a short time in the ominous shadow of Fort Yates, after which he was shipped farther downstream to Fort Randall on the Nebraska border. A missionary named Mary Clementine Collins who got to know him quite well— well enough that rumors spiraled around them—Miss Collins thought Sitting Bull and a few other important men ought to be segregated. It was not a time for false sentiment, she observed. Nobody wanted another Indian war.

Just before he left camp to board the *Sherman* for his trip to Fort Randall he pulled a knife. He offered the knife, together with an ax or a hatchet, to Captain Stowe who was in charge of transporting him, telling the captain that by these signs he surrendered. And he dropped to the ground while urging the captain to kill him, torture him, do anything, if only the people who had followed him could be treated kindly.

The reason for this shameless melodrama seems to be that he felt his prestige slipping. The whites had found his great rival Gall to be more tractable and went about subtly promoting Gall in the eyes of the Sioux. Furthermore, they had given command of the camp to Sitting Bull's old and powerless uncle, Four Horns. So it is thought that he posed as a sacrificial hero by flinging himself at Captain Stowe's boots, hoping thus to regain the allegiance of his despondent, bedraggled, weary followers.

The Indians he had hoped to impress merely laughed at him. He had made a fool of himself. He was pushed aboard the *General Sherman* with the butt ends of soldiers' muskets.

In 1882 the government decided he was no longer a threat and shipped him back upstream aboard the packet boat *W. J. Behan*, captained by Grant Marsh, ex-skipper of the *Far West*. On this trip Marsh noted "an amusing peculiarity" of Indians accustomed to the equilibrium of prairie life: They could not walk up a staircase. Invariably, he said, they would stumble and fall and were able to reach the top only by crawling. This peculiarity must have been noted by a great many whites yet nobody else thought it remarkable enough to mention, like the green wire goggles. If Sitting Bull went up a staircase on hands and knees Captain Marsh thoughtfully ignored the spectacle. At least he avoided any reference to it in his book.

Crowds materialized wherever the *W. J. Behan* docked. At Chamberlain and again at Pierre so many spectators gathered to stare at the famous Unkpapa that his escort—a company of the Fifteenth Infantry—almost lost control.

The government thought these wild Sioux should become farmers. That the tribe had no agricultural tradition was irrelevant; twelve acres of arable dirt near Standing Rock were assigned to Sitting Bull's band and he was instructed to report for work like everybody else.

He used a hoe awkwardly and was not a nice character, said agent James McLaughlin, who did not like him in the least. McLaughlin described him as stockily built, with an evil face and shifty eyes, and said he would take whatever looked good to him, whether it was a woman or property of another sort. McLaughlin's animosity is so frank and persistent that one cannot help wondering if even now something between them remains undetected. He called Sitting Bull avaricious, crafty, mendacious, and ambitious:

> He had no single quality that would serve to draw his people to him, yet he was by far the most influential man of his nation for many years,— neither Gall, Spotted Tail, nor Red Cloud, all greater men in every sense, exerting the power he did. I never knew him to display a single trait that might command admiration or respect, and I knew him well in the later years of his life. But he maintained his prestige by the acuteness of his mind and his knowledge of human nature.

It is hardly possible to imagine Sitting Bull chopping weeds or planting grain under the supervision of a government agent. One sees him as he used to be, as he was in 1876 when excited warriors under his tutelage shocked the United States silly.

News of the Little Bighorn calamity was at first discredited. Americans could not believe that Sitting Bull had defeated General Custer. A few days later, when there was no doubt, they refused to admit that an uneducated savage could have defeated a West Point graduate. Therefore such a genius must be white—perhaps a disguised renegade. So it was alleged that a mysterious swarthy youth from the Great Plains, nicknamed "Bison," had attended West Point and there absorbed the military science that laid General Custer low.

In late summer of 1876 an unidentified Army officer publicly asked this question. Evidently he thought there might be substance to rumors that Sitting Bull had graduated from the Academy, could read French, and was familiar with Napoleon's tactics. Could the dark, hairy cadet known as Bison have been, in fact, this omnipotent Sioux?

Bison was alleged to have graduated in the upper third of his class. He kept to himself, never was known to smile or laugh. Just after graduation he got drunk in the village of Buttermilk Falls near West Point and started a fight, which caused the Army to withhold his commission. He then disappeared, but later turned up in Galveston, Texas, where he fought some outlaws; aboard a California steamer where he got into a brawl with the ship's officers; and near the mouth of the Colorado River where it empties into the Gulf of California.

This last reputed sighting of Bison sounds very odd. It occurred in 1858, about ten years after he graduated from West Point. Lt. Joseph C. Ives of the Topographical Engineer Corps was surveying the Colorado when a party of Mojave Indians approached. At first they talked in Spanish. Then their leader asked in English: "Ives, do you know me?"

Lt. Ives replied that he did not, and asked the Indian where he had learned to speak English.

"Never mind that," the Mojave chief said. "But do you know me, Ives?"

Whereupon he disclosed his identity, saying they had been cadets together, and were it not for his presence the Mojaves would have killed the surveyors. "I have made them understand that after you have left and gone back trade will spring up," he said, "and we can then do better by trading or robbing the boats loaded with goods and supplies of all kinds."

Shortly after this the Mojaves went away.

Bison also was reported to have fought a detachment of soldiers led by a Capt. Lyon on some island in the Colorado, and to have raided settlements in Arizona.

The nameless officer who asked about Bison must have conducted an investigation because he is quoted in Fletcher Johnson's 1891 biography of Sitting Bull: "It may be, and we think it probable . . . that this Indian chief may have gone as far North as the Black Hills, and may be even the veritable Sitting Bull, for to the close observer, Sitting Bull has shown as much skill and judgment as any educated civilized soldier could have done."

Another West Point officer, also unnamed, who knew Bison as a cadet, claimed to have met him during the summer of 1852 in New Mexico where he had joined the Gila Apaches. Bison told this officer that he would not forget or forgive West Point authorities for withholding his commission because of the trouble at Buttermilk Falls. And there seems to have been more to this Buttermilk Falls episode than a fistfight. Bison was seeing a village girl, reputed to be very pretty, by the name of Effie Conklin. Nowadays a girl may not be easy to ruin, but in the nineteenth century this very often happened, and it appears that Bison, having promised to marry Effie Conklin, ruined her.

All of which sounds improbable, but in fact just such a cadet did arrive at West Point in 1844. Col. James B. Fry of the Adjutant General's Department reported that despite the cadet's youth he was fully grown,

> having a large head covered with bushy, uncombed hair; a square face; low, rectangular forehead; small, deep-set, piercing eyes; straight, short nose and heavy jaw; a bull neck rising out of broad and massive shoulders; a long body tapering downward to the hips, and short, stout arms and legs. He was as suggestive of the American bison as a man could be. As uncultivated as he was uncouth, he was yet gifted with more than ordinary talent, and not only passed the examination for admission as a cadet, but remained at the Academy the entire term of four years, and mastered every course of instruction. In character, however, he was from first to last a wild animal.

Col. Fry goes on to state that he was nicknamed Bison and that the Academy failed to tame his savage nature. For assaulting an officer he was deprived of furlough, which increased his ferocity. He terrified people in the neighboring village, and he ruined a young woman whose name Col. Fry does not choose to reveal.

So the bizarre story had a root, even if Bison was not Sitting Bull, which he was not, because this extraordinary Sioux never watched a sunrise east of Dakota Territory until long after the Little Bighorn.

As for the swarthy cadet, a citizen of Huntsville, Missouri, addressed a letter studded with facts to the St. Louis *Republican*. The cadet's name was McLean. He was raised in Randolph County, Missouri, "of highly respectable parentage," and was a nephew of the United States senator from Illinois, John McLean. He graduated from West Point in the same class with Stonewall Jackson and was killed by Indians near Tubac, Arizona, about 1870:

> . . . Lieut. Hall of the Fifth Cavalry, who was with Crook in Arizona, and now with him, and who is well acquainted with Bison's relatives here, confirms the statements received by his relatives of his death and the manner of his death. Of Bison I suppose it may be said that his greatest fault was that of having an ungovernable temper, which he knew, and which no doubt led him to pass his life beyond the confines of civilization. It was through the influence of Senator Benton that he received the appointment as a cadet to West Point, though his father, Charles McLean, was a zealous Whig. As to who Sitting Bull is, the writer of this does not know. But certain it is that he is not Bison.

In 1878 the Chicago printing firm of Knight & Leonard published a thirteen-page pamphlet, *The Works of Sitting Bull in the Original French and Latin, with Translations Diligently Compared*, to which was appended an eleven-page supplement, *The Works of Sitting Bull, Part II*. An unsigned editorial preface states that because of the medicine man's surprising military success it is commonly believed he must have been educated at some institution of high learning, a belief sure to be enhanced by the accompanying works.

Included in the pamphlet are some letters given to this anonymous editor by "an army officer lately arrived from the West." How this officer came by them is a rather twisted tale. One letter, in French, was addressed to James Du Frene, a French-Canadian guide who lived at a trading post or near an army post. When Sitting Bull's courier reached this post Du Frene happened to be escorting a party of English tourists around the Yellowstone, so Du Frene's son accepted the letter. In red sealing wax was impressed the figure of a seated bull. Du Frene *fils* naturally felt obliged to open it.

Camp at the Assiniboin River,
September 29th, 1877

Mr. Dear Friend: I thus salute you, with all the compliments which one can offer in circumstances like mine. You will see by the enclosed missive that Chief Joseph and the Nez Perces have friendly relations with myself in regard to certain important interests. I therefore entreat you to send this letter. . .

Du Frene the son thereupon opened the enclosed missive addressed to Chief Joseph. Finding it written in an incomprehensible language, and worried that Sitting Bull might be trying to form a military alliance with Joseph, young Du Frene turned over both letters to the army officer—who promptly turned them over to General Crook. General Crook, however, did not think they amounted to much and let the officer keep them.

So it came about, according to the anonymous editor of this pamphlet, that Sitting Bull's letters were placed at his disposal by the officer lately arrived from the West.

Young Du Frene's anxiety about renewed warfare was grossly misplaced. Indeed, a translation of the letter to Joseph reveals that Sitting Bull's message to the great Nez Perce proposed something altogether different. After a respectful salutation to Joseph, and a paragraph concerning their mutual burden as leaders of the Red cause, Sitting Bull asks rhetorically what they should do. What should be their course? "I lately came here—here into British territory—with my full forces and in unbroken strength; and here it was my purpose to remain. . . ." Alas, British authorities toward whom he always had felt most affectionate were preparing to turn him over to the enemy Americans. Further warfare would be impossible, considering the inequality of resources. Wild game upon which they depended was diminishing. The women and children of his warriors were hungry and in need of clothes.

> Such being the state of affairs, and the enemy also sending us commissioners to treat of peace, it seems to me we should do well to accept such terms as may be offered us. This is my counsel to you, Joseph. The Great Spirit himself seems now to desire that you and I should return to the civilized mode of life in which, as youths, we were educated. Still I cannot deny that the prospect of the change gives me much pain. Hear, therefore, the thoughts which in this state of mind, I have, with pen long disused, set down:

> *Sapphic Poem*
> The Time for use of warlike arms is past:
> Our savage valor finds its goal at last.
> To the long wanderings of our wearied feet
> No place is open for a safe retreat;
> For now upon me, pressed with sullen frown,
> The British Lion sits unjustly down . . .

A letter from the Commissioner of Indian Affairs to the Recorder of the Order of Indian Wars, dated November 7, 1925, in response to a request for information about Sitting Bull, concludes with an opinion that the work cited was not that of Sitting Bull, but of "a clever writer." The identity of this writer has not been determined, although it probably was a member of Crook's staff, R. D. Clarke, whose name appears on the 1878 copyright. Clarke's motive— assuming it was Clarke—is unknown. The chance of making a few dollars from this hoax seems insufficient, considering that he had jeopardized his military career.

Quite a few people thought Sitting Bull was a blue-eyed half-breed named Charlie Jacobs, born in Canada near old Ft. Garry, converted to Catholicism by Father De Smet. He learned French at St. John's College, thus enabling him to analyze Napoleon's tactics. A French-language biography of Napoleon was seen in his teepee. When he—Charlie Sitting Bull Jacobs—retreated to Canada after the Little Bighorn he told a police officer that he was a Fort Garry native. When asked what he remembered about it he gave several names, including that of another half-breed named James Ross who became Chief Justice of the Riel-Lepine government in 1869. In fact, he said, he and Ross grew up together. He also told Canadian police that his father, Henry Jacobs, had been employed by Father Proulx as an interpreter on Manitoulin Island. Nothing about this Charlie Jacobs can be substantiated and one is left to wonder how the story originated, although the psychological necessity is obvious, just as it was with the fable of Bison. Americans needed to believe that the man who defeated Custer must have graduated from an eminent academy such as West Point or St. John's.

Careful scholars now are convinced that Sitting Bull was a full-blooded Sioux, born alongside a tributary of the Missouri in South Dakota—perhaps Willow Creek—between 1830 and 1837. During the course of his life he was called by various names, some complimentary, others less so. He might have been addressed simply as Bull or Bison, but it is doubtful that anybody ever called him Charlie.

He did know Father De Smet and several other missionaries. None of them converted him, although he seems to have been impressed by ecclesiastic ornaments and by what he was told about the faraway pope. Somewhere he obtained a big cameo ring of a curly-headed youth which he wore on the middle finger of his left hand, probably because he had seen pictures of bishops wearing huge rings. That this prepossessing symbol ought to have been displayed on the third finger of the right hand was unimportant, or else he never noticed. The artist DeCost Smith said that on formal occasions he would pose with this extravagant cameo at the fourth button of his waistcoat; and however implausible it sounds, he may actually have ordered a buffalo robe sent to the pope.

Concerning his linguistic accomplishments, he spoke no French and very little English. He might have understood both languages better than anybody suspected, but all he ever said was "Hello," "You bet!," "Seeda Boo"—meaning his name, and "How ma' tci?"—which could mean either "How much?" or "How are you? Can I borrow a match?"

Smith encountered him for the first time at the Martin & Williams store in

Standing Rock. A clerk, Louis Primeau, asked if he knew who the Indian was, and because photographs of the famous man were tacked up all over the territory Smith answered, "Yes, it's Sitting Bull." At the sound of these syllables the blanketed Indian clutched Smith's hand and exclaimed, "Seeda Boo, you bet!"

He loved to shake hands. Nothing left him more puzzled and aggrieved than a white man who declined the offer. That he should feel baffled when a white man refused to shake hands is easy to understand because he had picked up the habit from them. Thomas Henry Tibbles got to know Indians so well that he was one of only two white men admitted to the Omaha Soldier Lodge—the other being General Crook—and Tibbles remarked that Indians, who never shake hands among themselves, consider this act to be one of the funniest things in the world. Nevertheless, having learned that whites express friendship by seizing each other, they happily do the same.

Sitting Bull was always anxious to make a good impression, according to Smith. "Up to a very short time before his death, when he was thought to hate all white men, he still showed evidence of this. It may have been self-conceit, but in his way I think Sitting Bull was a lover of humanity." Smith also thought most photographers misrepresented him, perhaps deliberately. By focus, by lighting, and by posing him a certain way the photographer could exaggerate his nose and give his eyes a murderous glint. The reason for doing so was that such portraits gratified the public expectation.

His intelligence seems to have gone unrecognized by most nineteenth-century whites. A pamphlet accompanying the 1889 Boston Cyclorama, after providing him with "a restless, discontented disposition," states that he is fifty-four years old, muscular, and five feet, eight inches tall—which is nearly four inches less than the estimate given by General Miles. But of course Miles was looking at an undefeated chieftain, not a subjugated entertainer. "He is not an intellectual man. He is very vain of his notoriety. . . ."

Agent McLaughlin, having noted Sitting Bull's acute mind and knowledge of human nature, contradicts himself somewhat by describing the chief as "an Indian of very mediocre ability, rather dull, and much the inferior of Gall and others of his lieutenants in intelligence. I cannot understand how he held such sway over or controlled men so eminently his superiors in every respect, unless it was by his sheer obstinacy and stubborn tenacity. He is pompous, vain, and boastful. . . ."

Capt. Clifford thought his appearance misleading. "Sitting Bull does not strike one at first sight as an intellectual man but a little study reveals deep character in every line of his face." Clifford added that he seemed to be about fifty years old and had the expression of a miser.

There is much agreement that he was vain.

What is now Fargo, North Dakota, was then a camp full of civil engineers, mostly single, or at least alone in the forsaken place; but some had brought families, and the wife of one of these engineers recalled Sitting Bull's visit to their camp. He and eight or ten other Sioux were on their way to visit the Great Father in Washington. They had started this long trip dressed as usual but during a stop at Bismarck two or three of the Sioux changed into cast-off Army uniforms, which they wore beneath their blankets. Sitting Bull scoffed at them, yet according to the interpreter who accompanied this group he began to feel uneasy. In fact, he would not be presented to officials of the Northern Pacific Railroad unless he could find more suitable clothes. White man clothes being what he wanted, the people in camp put together an outfit. What they collected sounds as though they tried to make him ridiculous, although this does not seem to have been their intention. They did the best they could.

The pants were too short, so in order to close the gap between shoes and cuffs he was given a pair of white stockings belonging to the Negro cook, Aunt Venny. And to keep the stockings from drooping Aunt Venny fastened them to his pants with safety pins. He was given a white flannel shirt and a coat that was too narrow. Aunt Venny fixed the coat by ripping out the center seam and widening it with a vertical strip cut from a red blanket. Then they found a black stovepipe hat.

These clothes satisfied him. He agreed to meet the Northern Pacific dignitaries.

He wandered around camp, strolling into whatever tents attracted him to inspect the property of white people, and the engineer's wife said that in her tent he noticed a small hand-mirror. He squatted on the floor to look at himself, which caused her to reflect that the man in her tent was about as different from the Sitting Bull known to the War Department as it is possible to conceive. Still, there was as much reality to one as to the other.

He took the mirror. He thrust it someplace inside his blanket and left the tent. After a while he came back with a white plume he wore when dressed for battle. He plucked a quill from this plume and gave it to the woman's infant daughter. The tip had been stained crimson and he explained, presumably through sign language, that this was the blood of Wah-ton-set, an Arikara chief.

She saw him again in Bismarck a long time afterward, surrounded by Easterners to whom he was selling his autograph for twenty-five cents, and she noticed a pretty girl whisper into his ear. He responded by grinning and shaking his head, which is fairly convincing proof that he did understand several English words. The girl pressed something into his hand, no doubt a coin. ". . . and with another grin to the crowd the grimy, dirty, smoke-scented old heathen bent down his head and kissed her."

The price of his autograph varied. Occasionally he would demand two dollars, although it is said that he never charged a woman. When he performed with Buffalo Bill's Wild West extravaganza the going rate for his autograph was one dollar, and during the four months he was on tour he earned a tidy amount.

Who taught him to write his name is a mystery. Canadian missionaries, perhaps, or the trader Gus Hedderich. Burdick states that Sitting Bull learned by copying what Hedderich wrote, "and a comparison of the hand-writing of Hedderich and that of Sitting Bull, which appears in many books, leaves no doubt. . . ." Well, maybe. Judson Elliott Walker copied his signature on tracing paper and a photographic reproduction of this tracing shows an awkward, trembling hand quite unlike that of a professional clerk-trader such as Hedderich.

According to Hanson he spelled it "Seitting Bull"—which makes no sense, considering that his teacher or teachers must have spoken English. One conceivable explanation for this peculiar orthography might be that he was taught by a semi-literate Southerner who spelled phonetically, because in various parts of the South the letter *i* becomes two letters: *e* and *i*. Pin, for example, becomes Pe'in. Sitting, therefore, would become Se'itting. However this came about, Hanson remarks that the unusual spelling increased the value of his autograph—as it should. Perhaps he wrote like a Confederate sometimes, but not invariably, as may be seen from Walker's tracing.

Another facsimile, reproduced in Norman Wood's *Lives of Famous Indian Chiefs*, which probably was made a year or so after the Walker tracing, shows how Sitting Bull's penmanship changed. Here the capitals are elaborate, both *t*'s have been crossed with one sophisticated sweep high above the vertical strokes, and the overall impression is that of a confident scribe. Indeed, the signature is almost arrogant.

Without doubt he got plenty of practice. Excepting the President of the United States and a spatter of popular entertainers, no autograph was more treasured than his. "A striking scene was that observed in 1883 . . ." we are told by Mr. Wood. This scene consisted of the medicine man "on a windy eminence" hawking his signature, surrounded by a gaggle of brass hats including Little Phil Sheridan, various senators, financiers, railroad officials, Teutonic professors, and British noblemen.

Apparently he took drawing lessons from some wasichu with academic training. In 1881 he painted himself killing a Crow warrior—always a favorite subject—but this time the animal he rides is not that free-floating rocking-horse customarily drawn by native artists. The big, solid, voluptuously rounded rump and erect head of the animal halfway suggest a Bellini equestrian, and probably resulted from instruction by a German artist/correspondent named Rudolph Cronau.

In 1884 this singular Indian was exhibited at the Philadelphia YMCA. He attracted a smaller crowd than had been anticipated because a local newspaper printed atrocity stories which were attributed directly or indirectly to him, causing righteous citizens to boycott the show. This enraged the agent who had organized the show, and naturally the agent blamed the star, abusing him with "severe and blasphemous language"—which he would not have dared to do a few years earlier—proving once again that we live in a mad world.

Many things attributed to Sitting Bull may be untrue, but one thing is beyond dispute: he liked women. He liked women enormously. He was married at least three times, possibly eight or nine times. One wife died soon after marriage. Later he was married to She That Had Four Robes and She That Was Seen by the Nation. This much seems well established. How many children he and his wives produced is a matter of conjecture, perhaps ten or fifteen, among which—he claimed—were three sets of twins. Walker, who first saw him aboard the *General Sherman*, observed that although he shook hands with everybody he paid special attention to ladies. His voice ordinarily was guttural, deep, and melodious, but when he spoke to a female of any race it grew soft and ingratiating.

A feminine element very often radiates from sexually powerful males and in the case of Sitting Bull this was so unmistakable that one journalist, fascinated by the oval face between long braids, spoke of his "manhood and womanliness."

The Indians themselves—those who liked him, although many did not—compared him to a bull elk, amorous and bold.

During the years of his internment, or semi-captivity, most whites found him to be dignified yet not rigid. The wife of one post trader described him as the nicest Indian in the neighborhood, saying that he always treated her with consideration and did not loiter outside their house at mealtime as quite a few Indians did. Other whites, with few exceptions, agreed that he did not beg. Buffalo Bill disagreed, referring to him as "an inveterate beggar," and seemed convinced that his refusal to speak English was more a matter of stubbornness than of ignorance.

After a quarrel with Red Cloud concerning the best way to survive in a land crawling with acquisitive Yellow Eyes, Sitting Bull refused to accept anything from the government and from then on seldom appeared at trading posts. If he did arrive to conduct a little business his visit was apt to be remembered. One time at the Poplar Creek store he climbed over the counter, shoved the clerk aside and pretended to be a white man—criticizing the furs and buffalo robes offered by Indians, praising the manufactured goods on the shelves. On this occasion, however, he picked the wrong man to bully; the clerk held a lighted match above an open keg of gunpowder, which caused Sitting Bull and his friends to hurry out the door grumbling.

Notwithstanding the opinion of DeCost Smith that the perverse old medicine man loved humanity, the consensus must be that he never did and never could love whites, at least en masse. And it seems fairly certain that those of his people who had been seduced by offers to buy Indian land filled him with disgust. At a Sioux council meeting he proposed that they get a scale and sell the earth at so much per pound.

From his refuge in Canada after the Little Bighorn he denied the charges flung across the border by outraged Americans. "They tell me I murdered Custer," he said. "It is a lie. . . . He was a fool and rode to his death."

From the moment of Custer's arrival in Dakota Territory the explosive chronicle of his life seems preordained. In July of 1873 somewhere along the Yellowstone he shot an antelope whose carcass dripped blood on a package of doughnuts he meant to have for lunch. He noted the incident briefly in a letter to Elizabeth—he thought nothing of it—yet the queer misfortune reverberates like an Etruscan augury.

The purpose of the Yellowstone expedition was to protect surveyors for the Northern Pacific Railroad, who would not have lasted three days by themselves. An auxiliary purpose was scientific, and among those in the column was a taxidermist, Mr. C. W. Bennet. From him Custer took lessons. After a full day on horseback Custer would study the art, often until late at night while everybody else lay exhausted, and he became—by his own estimate—

rather good at it. He prepared various trophies including the heads of several antelope, the head and skin of a bear, and a complete elk.

G. A. C. in a tent beside the Yellowstone, sleeves rolled to the elbow, supervised by Mr. Bennet, while half a dozen dogs sleep just outside and a summer moon floats on the shallow river—the image evokes a forgotten era: Wordsworth idyls, Burne-Jones ladies, cameo brooches, pressed flowers, mossy ruins, parasols, hoop skirts, muttonchops.

The elk was his *chef d'oeuvre*. At first he planned to mount only the head as a present for Elizabeth but he got so absorbed in the work that he could not stop, and because an elk would require a room of its own he shipped it to the Detroit Audubon Club. He did, however, prepare a handsome specimen for his wife—a buffalo head "beautifully haired and with symmetrical horns."

The elk nearly killed two of his dogs. In a Nomad article for *Turf, Field and Farm* he tells us that after he shot the huge beast it plunged into the river. Then a death struggle occurred while he stood on the bank and watched. He insisted that he trembled for the lives of his dogs.

Custer trembling? Inconceivable.

And why did he remain on the bank? Why not wade into the river far enough to get another shot at the elk?

Dr. Charles Hofling, a psychiatrist, is persuaded that Custer had a water phobia: "Insofar as entering the water often has the unconscious significance of a return to the mother's womb, Custer's dread of the water can be construed as a dread of his own passive tendencies." Well, if such a phobia existed it must have developed after he leaped into the Chickahominy because there is not the slightest hint that he trembled or even paused on the bank of that river.

As to the Yellowstone incident, how much is imaginary? We have only his statement that he scarcely knew what he was doing or where he was: "I called wildly to the dogs to come away—almost beseeched them as if they were human, and understood my every word. 'You'll all be killed! you'll all be killed! was my oft-repeated exclamation. . . ." What a dramatic, touching moment. He identifies three of these dogs as Maida, Blucher, and Cardigan, and informs his readers that they are gathered around his camp stool even as he writes. Cardigan might have been present, but Custer himself wrote in *My Life* that Blucher was killed during the Washita fight by an arrow through the ribs, while poor Maida was dropped by an awkward soldier during that Kansas hunt on the plains.

What should be made of such a story? Perhaps, as the wise chief Plenty Coups observed, there are things in life we do not understand and when we meet them all we can do is let them alone.

The Yellowstone panorama excited him. He compared the winding progress of the column to the shifting spectacle seen through a kaleidoscope. Not even Bierstadt could represent such a land. He would do his assigned duty, he would guard the railroad surveyors, but what attracted him was the wild life: blacktail deer, foxes, buffalo, geese, prairie chickens, ducks, white wolves. These scuttling, burrowing, flying, prowling inhabitants of the Yellowstone wilderness fascinated him as he was fascinated by any sort of life beyond the painted shacks of civilization.

He picked up fossils and he collected animals, including a porcupine which he snagged by tossing a blanket over it. This porcupine along with a wildcat eventually would be shipped to Central Park via Adams' Express, there to join a cinnamon bear previously forwarded, either because he assumed the park would like to have them or he thought it good politics. He might be out of sight, but he did not forget or neglect urban centers of power. Not only in the field would his career be evaluated, his future decided. People would talk about this Montana porcupine, this wildcat, this bear. They would know who sent these gifts.

He advised Elizabeth that Fred Grant, the President's son, might be in her neighborhood. She should do everything possible to make his visit pleasant. Meet him at the depot with a carriage. "Have his father's picture hung in the parlor. . . ."

Major General David Stanley, who commanded the Yellowstone expedition, wrote to Mrs. Stanley soon after leaving Fort Rice that he had not had any trouble with Custer and would try to avoid any, "but I have seen enough of him to convince me that he is a cold-blooded, untruthful and unprincipled man. He is universally despised by all the officers of his regiment excepting his relatives and one or two sycophants."

Stanley himself was no plum. A squat, humorless, alcoholic Welshman, he sounds like the antithesis of Custer, who was lean as a wolf, enjoyed jokes immensely—the more boisterous the better—and had not swallowed a drop of the grape since that humiliating scene in Monroe twelve years earlier. If two such disparate commandants could get along it would be astonishing, and indeed they did not. Their mutually distasteful alliance was stretched, warped, cracked, and precariously glued together while the surveyors crept forward. On July 1 the bilious C. O. told Custer that he never had dealt with a more troublesome subordinate.

One thing General Stanley grew to hate was Custer's stove. Sheridan, who disliked Army food, engaged a black woman to cook for him during the Civil War and Custer at some point evidently felt entitled to the same privilege.

First there was Eliza, then Aunt Mary or Marie, and where Custer went there went his cook, and with the cook went a cast iron stove. Stanley's dissatisfaction began to focus on this piece of equipment. For some absolutely unknown reason the stove came to represent everything he despised about Custer.

On July 7, drunk and discontented, General Stanley expropriated one of Custer's three headquarters wagons, which meant Custer would be obliged to jettison a variety of non-military items, including the hated stove. In addition to written orders, he seems to have been told verbally to dump the stove.

The next day Custer addressed a note to Stanley's adjutant, informing him that he had complied, which was partly true. No longer did the stove occupy space in a headquarters wagon, that much was true; but Captain French had managed to wedge it into one of his own wagons. Stanley discovered this. Either he observed Aunt Mary at work or he heard about the stove in French's wagon, because he summoned Custer and placed him under arrest. There had been previous trouble. Custer had lent a government horse to a civilian employee, there had been insolent language, etc. But it was the stove—the cast iron private kitchen stove—that Stanley could not abide. Six times he ordered Custer to get rid of it. Six times. The explanation of such madness, apart from alcohol, seems to be that he was trying to provoke Custer into an impertinent response for which he could be severely punished.

July 9. Custer marched at the tail of the column with an air of nonchalance, which is to be expected. In a letter to Elizabeth he claimed that within forty-eight hours General Stanley apologized, saying: "I humbly beg your pardon, sir. . . ."

On August 15 a landmark known as Pompey's Pillar was sighted and here the Northern Pacific survey ended. The column turned around.

Four companies of cavalry were ordered back to Fort Rice. Custer himself was assigned to command six companies stationed at newly built Fort Abraham Lincoln a few miles upstream.

Elizabeth joined him there in November and on December 5 they celebrated his thirty-fourth birthday.

That winter in his Fort Lincoln study—Dante's famous warning *Lasciate Ogni Speranza, Voi Ch'entrate* posted above the door—he worked on magazine articles and finished his autobiographical narrative of life in Kansas and Oklahoma: "As I pen these lines," he wrote at the conclusion of *My Life on the Plains*,

I am in the midst of scenes of bustle and busy preparation attendant upon the organization and equipment of a large party for an important exploring expedition, on which I shall start before these pages reach the publishers' hands. During my absense I expect to visit a region of country as yet unseen by human eyes except those of the Indian—a country described by the latter as abounding in game of all varieties, rich in scientific interest, and of surpassing beauty in natural scenery. Bidding adieu to civilization for the next few months, I also now take leave of my readers. . . .

This was the Black Hills expedition. This time he would be in commmand, not subordinate to General Stanley or to anybody else. He by himself would run the show.

Luther North, employed as a scout, said they left Fort Lincoln with a sixteen-piece brass band mounted on white horses. It was the first and last expedition he was ever on in Indian country, North said, that took along a band. They started off to the tune of "Garry Owen," and every morning when they broke camp the band would serenade the troops for two or three miles, and just about every night Custer assembled the musicians at his tent for another concert. It sounds less like military reconnaissance than a summer excursion through the Catskills.

A feeling of disaster begins to charge the air. Electric clouds sizzle above the forbidding Dakota peaks while Custer's musicians on white horses play old favorites. Calamity Jane herself trailed the regiment, dressed in male clothing, covered with lice. John Burkman, who was Custer's orderly, said she did not smell good and usually was begging for a drink. The men avoided her, now and then giving her whisky in exchange for doing their laundry.

Custer and little brother Tom both enjoyed the Black Hills. Tom amused himself by pinning snakes to the ground with a forked stick. He liked to carry them some distance before turning them loose and it is said his horse objected violently when he tried to climb back in the saddle with a furious snake wrapped around one arm.

The general took a larger view of this region. He loved the fecundity of the earth. To Elizabeth he wrote that during one march every step was made "amidst flowers of the most exquisite colors & perfume." Troopers could lean down and pluck flowers without dismounting. The expedition's botanist, Professor A. B. Donaldson, who served also as correspondent for the St. Paul *Pioneer*, wrote that even the mule packers fashioned bouquets. Custer thought it a remarkable sight—this column of cavalrymen holding bouquets. In a dispatch to the Assistant Adjutant General, Department of Dakota, he notes that while seated at the mess table an officer called attention to the magnificent carpet beneath their feet and they decided to see how many different flowers they could pick without getting up. "Seven beautiful varieties were thus gathered."

Lt. Calhoun fairly exudes pleasure. "The air is serene and the sun is shining in all its glory. The birds are singing sweetly, warbling their sweet notes as they soar aloft. Nature seems to smile on our movement. Everything seems to encourage us onward."

But a small, sharp surprise awaited them. Two of Bloody Knife's scouts galloped up to report five Sioux lodges just ahead. Custer rode forward with E Company.

The Sioux, unaware of his presence, were going about their daily chores.

He sent an interpreter with a flag of truce into the village, then rode forward to talk. He learned that the wife of the head man was something of a celebrity—Red Cloud's daughter. He shook hands all around and assured the Sioux he had not come to molest them. He offered them food and invited them to visit the bluecoats. Bloody Knife's Rees, who had been anticipating a few easy scalps, were disappointed. Upon approaching the Sioux encampment they had unbraided their hair, rubbed vermilion on their faces, wrapped towels around their heads, and commenced a war song described as a dreary monotone, not especially frightening: "Um, ahaum, ahum, um um um ahaum Yah yah ahaum, yah yah . . ."

Presently the column entered another floral valley. Nobody could recall anything like it—not anything along the Yellowstone, not Yosemite, nothing in the valley of the Hudson or the Mohawk. One soldier remarked that although he had visited Central Park in New York City a thousand times, "its beauties will not compare with these."

After some entreaty the general consented to have this idyllic vale named in his honor: Custer Park.

Nearby stood a mountain named for General Harney and the expedition's principals resolved to climb it. They got almost to the top, at an estimated altitude of 7,500 feet. Professor Donaldson, meticulously scientific, reports that the rarefied atmosphere, the exertion, and the excitement drove Professor N. H. Winchell's pulse up to 136. Custer, too, was excited; his pulse rose to 112 and he celebrated by firing at distant cliffs. Apart from themselves, Donaldson comments, no human beings had climbed Harney Peak. Certainly no white man did, "and it is well known that the noble, the royal, the genuine North American Indian is one of the laziest mortals on earth."

They scribbled a message on a slip of paper which they rolled up and inserted in a copper cartridge. The cartridge was hammered flat and forced into a crevice. Sixty years later it was found. The paper had disappeared—nobody knows when, why, or how—but the message had been reported to the *Pioneer* by Donaldson:

Gen. G. A. Custer, Gen. G. A. Forsyth,
Col. Wm. Ludlow, W. H. Wood,
A. B. Donaldson, N. H. Winchell,
Script. July 31, 1874.

Mr. Wood, an engineer, recalled this trip during an interview in 1927. He said they rode as high as the horses could go, tethered them, and continued the climb on foot, all except Custer who forced his mount higher. On the return: "Custer's horse had a hard time getting down the steep peak—it was cruel, the horse's knees were bleeding. . . ."

This invasion of the sacred Black Hills by a creaking, jingling, clanking train of canvas-topped wagons and malodorous cavalrymen displeased the Sioux, not just that tiny community of five lodges but hundreds more who looked down from remote, pine-covered slopes. They already had announced their disapproval of visitors. Among the first whites to see these hills was a half-breed trapper named Hercule Levasseur. At that time—about 1855—the Sioux held no title except squatter's rights. Nevertheless they chopped off Hercule's hands and pulled out his tongue.

Some years later they had a legal claim. By virtue of the 1868 Laramie treaty: " . . . no persons except those designated herein . . . shall ever be permitted to pass over, settle upon, or reside in the territory described in this article." There could not be much question about those words, but the white tide of manifest destiny flowed westward.

"This abominable compact," cried the Yankton *Press and Dakotaian*, ". . . is now pleaded as a barrier to the improvement and development of one of the richest and most fertile sections in America. What shall be done with these Indian dogs in our manger? They will not dig gold or let others do it. . . ."

The government struggled against itself, troubled by conscience. There was the treaty, of course, in lucid English. Still, that mysterious wilderness demanded investigation. The government wanted especially to know more about aboriginal trails leading from the Yellowstone to the Missouri River agencies, and it wanted to locate a good spot for a fort—if a fort should be needed. Officially, therefore, Custer's purpose was to reconnoiter the Black Hills. Unofficially, and not altogether incidentally, he was looking for gold.

For a long time rumors had been percolating. The Jesuit missionary Father Pierre Jean De Smet thought there were mineral deposits in the hills. He himself had not been there, only close by, and he seems to have talked rather loosely about gold in other regions—Idaho, California, and elsewhere. But then, as now, the opinions of a cleric are discussed with respect.

John Burbank, a former Indian agent, reported seeing ore in the White River badlands, ore heavy with silver.

Crazy Hank Joplin told of meeting an Indian boy from the Bear Lodge Mountains who used gold-tipped arrows, so Hank and his partners went prospecting. They dug out $70,000 worth of gold, he said, but all were killed except himself. He could hardly talk about the experience.

In 1834 a bona fide strike may have been recorded. Seven miners from Laramie entered the hills. None returned, but years later a pathetic message was found scratched on both sides of a sandstone slab:

Came to these hills in 1833 seven of us De Lacompt Ezra Kind G. W. Wood T. Brown R Kent Wm King Indian Crow all ded but me Ezra Kind—Killed by Inds beyond the high hills got our gold June 1834

Got all the gold we could carry our ponys all got by the Indians I hav lost my gun and nothing to eat and Indians hunting me

A farmer near Kensington, Minnesota, once dug up a stone inscribed with medieval Scandinavian characters that told a somewhat similar story—a party of eight Goths and twenty-two Norwegians attacked by the red peril. For various reasons, including the fact that the farmer just happened to be a student of medieval runology, the Kensington stone has been rejected as fake. Similarly, Ezra Kind's horror story is suspect. The slab was discovered by one Louis Thoen, who just happened to be a stonemason.

In 1852, however, a party of thirty prospectors did venture into these sacred hills. Eight of them quickly departed; they had seen gold but also more Indian signs than they liked. The remaining prospectors vanished. What became of them has not been learned, except that in 1878 two skeletons were found near an old mine shaft. They lay behind a crude bulwark of rocks and branches, their bones scattered as though animals had eaten the flesh. One skull showed a bullet hole. The other man probably envied his partner because an iron arrowhead embedded in a thigh bone meant that he must have suffered until the Indians got around to finishing him. Inside the bulwark these men had constructed was the leather cover of a memorandum book. The pages were lost but on the cover was some writing, illegible except for "1 52"—which might originally have been "1852."

During the fall of 1863 a Mackinaw boat—the name goes back through Mackinaw Island to an Ojibwa word meaning big turtle—one of these boats en route from the Montana gold fields to civilization stopped at Fort Berthold. Aboard were seventeen men, one woman, and two children. Fred Gerard was shown that the boat had a false bottom, and concealed in this space were sacks of gold estimated to be worth $100,000. The men themselves wore belts packed with gold dust.

Considering the circumstances it sounds strange that they would reveal this, but they did, possibly because they wanted information from Gerard about their chances of continuing safely downstream. A party of Sioux happened to be in the area so he advised them to hang around Fort Berthold. They ignored his advice. Just north of the Heart River, which joins the Missouri at Bismarck, they were slaughtered. The sacks of gold and the men's belts were slashed open, the treasure poured on the sand. Some Rees who visited the site of the massacre carefully gathered a quantity of sand which they brought to Fort Berthold. Gerard bought two coffee pots full of it. This gold had not come from the Black Hills, but facts—however well documented—do not necessarily seem relevant. Here was gold, coffee pots loaded with gold-bearing sand. Who could say where it came from? From the Black Hills, most likely. Those who insisted it came from Montana were liars.

At about this time an escaped murderer named Toussaint Kensler, alias Tucson Kessler, made the first definite strike. He emerged from the back country with a fossilized skull and some goosequills packed with yellow dust. Like many another man, Toussaint should have kept his mouth shut because the sheriff jailed him again and this time the gallows prevailed. But before he expired Toussaint did the right thing: He said he had found this gold on a tributary of the south fork of the Cheyenne, and he drew a map. On the basis of his drawing it is obvious that he knew the region, but of his strike nothing else is recorded.

Still, men had seen those gleaming goosequills, and one could scarcely doubt the word of Father De Smet or agent Burbank.

And there were rumors without end. For instance, an Oglala hunting eagles in the Black Hills happened to see a badger digging a hole, and shot the badger, and when he went to pick up the carcass he saw the earth covered with gold nuggets. The Oglala filled a buckskin pouch with gold nuggets and started for Laramie where he meant to buy a horse, but along the way he told some Brulés. The Brulés got angry. They took the pouch and the Oglala's clothes and they beat him and threatened his life and killed his pony. They said the whites should never learn about this gold.

Custer understood that if his expedition verified such rumors there would be an immediate uncontrollable rush to the Black Hills. People already were talking, waiting for one positive sign. It had been said that in California men waded ankle-deep through gold, whereupon the forty-niners rushed west. In Colorado it was alleged that parties of miners slid down Pike's Peak on a harrow, each tooth gouging a curl of gold, and soon the east slope of the Rockies crawled with eighty thousand prospectors. So would hundreds and then thousands of people rush to the Black Hills.

A stampede of whites through Dakota Territory would bring war. The Sioux at first would defend the land by murdering isolated miners, next they would attack wagon trains. The United States would retaliate. Not much foresight was required to know this would happen. Custer understood this, but he did not formulate policy. He had been instructed to explore Paha Sapa. He wanted to do so and it is thought that he requested command of the expedition; but whether he commanded the troops or somebody else did, the provocative Black Hills were going to be studied.

On June 17 the Bismarck *Tribune* justified what was about to happen:

This is God's country. He peopled it with red men, and planted it with wild grasses, and permitted the white man to gain a foothold; and as the wild grasses disappear when the white clover gains a footing, so the Indian disappears before the advances of the white man.

Humanitarians may weep for poor Lo, and tell the wrongs he has suffered, but he is passing away. Their prayers, their entreaties, can not change the law of nature; can not arrest the causes which are carrying them on to their ultimate destiny—extinction.

The American people need the country the Indians now occupy; many of our people are out of employment; the masses need some new excitement. The war is over, and the era of railroad building has been brought to a termination by the greed of capitalists and the folly of the grangers; and depression prevails on every hand. An Indian war would do no harm, for it must come, sooner or later. . . .

With the expedition went two miners, Horatio Nelson Ross and William McKay, said to have been millionaires as many times as they had toes, who knew every promontory and gulch west of the Rockies—although nobody bothered to explain how an intimate knowledge of that distant region would be of much help in the Black Hills. Ross, as might be surmised from his illustrious name, was the more picturesque. There is one photograph of him with a long beard, wearing a tragic expression and what appears to be a Slavic peasant's shirt. He looks remarkably like Tolstoy except for the nose. Ross has a Gallic blade of a nose—a Charles de Gaulle nose.

These two experts had been enrolled in the scientific corps and whenever the column stopped they went to work. William Eleroy Curtis, an engaging literary stylist and the most vibrant writer among several journalists on this trip, attentively monitored their progress. Quartz rock had begun to show up in the eastern ranges and Curtis insists they saw mountains of it "as beautiful as the hills of a celestial city, white and red and green and yellow crystals that fell under the hammers blow into emeralds and rubies and opals. . . ."

Some weeks earlier, just before leaving Bismarck, he had posted a long dispatch to the New York *World* which concluded: "We are goading the Indians to madness by invading their hallowed grounds, and throwing open to them the avenues leading to a terrible revenge whose cost would far outweigh any scientific or political benefit possible to be extracted from such an expedition under the most favorable circumstances." He also mentioned a spectacular comet near the Big Dipper—a nebulous streak across the clear Dakota night—which Custer's Arikara guides believed would exert some influence, although they did not know whether this might be beneficial or malign. One argument maintained that it heralded the spirits of dead braves on the warpath, in which event Manitou must be on the side of the Sioux. Still, a comet indicated divine displeasure, so it might be construed as the bluecoats' ally.

Custer himself felt no premonitory apprehension. A comet was a comet, nothing else, and one day succeeded another while the exasperated Sioux kept their distance. Letters to his wife are cheerful, affectionate, bright with anecdotes reflecting his interest in just about everything. He addresses her as "My Sunbeam" and "My Sweet Rosebud."

A scout named Goose showed him a mysterious cave. Inscriptions, carvings, and drawings decorated the walls and lightning flashed across the roof. This cave extended for miles, said Goose, and it echoed with dreadful shrieks. Sometimes the carved figures shone as though rubbed with fire and the groans and shieks and howls grew louder. Sioux medicine men had tried to interpret the spirit-writing but could not, and wise men from other tribes had no better luck.

For a long time the Indians who lived in that area had regarded the cave as an unearthly place and had left offerings—bracelets, pipes, flints, beads. Other artifacts were noted during Custer's visit: a rusty knife blade, a shaving brush, an old flintlock horse pistol, a Canadian penny, a human skull with three holes in the forehead which regimental surgeons diagnosed from its frontal angle as the skull of a white man, and a gold ring inscribed *A.L.* This skull excited speculation. Three popular theories held that he must have been a sacrifice to the deity of the cave, a miner who died fighting for his life, or an early French trapper killed by a bison because the Indians called it The Place Where the Man Was Killed By a Bull.

Custer mentioned to his wife that among the various drawings of animals, birds, reptiles, and fish were prints of human hands and feet. "I think this was all the work of Indians at an early day, although I cannot satisfactorily account for the drawings of ships found there." Unimpressed by supernatural aspects, he named it Ludlow's Cave as a compliment to his topographical engineer, Capt. William Ludlow—who measured the cave and rudely destroyed Goose's theory that it extended for miles. Ludlow followed a steadily constricting passage some four hundred feet. Ghosts might proceed further, humans could not.

Then, after various officers and men carved their names in the sandy rock, the regiment continued rumbling, jingling, clattering, and creaking through Paha Sapa, alert for militant natives yet not particularly worried: twelve companies of cavalry and infantry, guides, scouts, interpreters, teamsters, a cannon, three Gatling guns, and more than one hundred bulky wagons—the fresh white canvas flapping and rocking like sails through dark green foliage. Meantime the hills resounded with the melodies of Hoffman and Flotow and various popular tunes as rendered by the Seventh Cavalry band.

Tom and the general enjoyed teasing kid brother Boston. This was Boston's first wilderness trip. Tom gave him a porous rock, saying it was sponge-stone and if submerged long enough in water it would become a very good sponge, so the greenhorn soaked his rock while Tom and the general in a nearby tent squeaked with laughter.

All of the Custers loved jokes, the more disrespectful the better. And because the general did not drink, the jokes he played on drunks might carry a sharp edge. He once ordered a big wooden box pegged upside down over a drunk who was lying on the ground and it is said that the man's frantic struggle to escape delighted him. Another drunk became the subject of a mock funeral. Games of this sort probably amused everybody except the victim because they reflected a fact thoroughly understood on the frontier: the indisputable, unwelcome fact that death might come visiting at any instant.

So, according to their dispositions, the men of the Seventh plucked flowers, played ball, joked, explored valleys and ridges, and listened to the band while squinting attentively at anything which might be a camouflaged Sioux.

The civilian engineer W. H. Wood recalled that while they were eating lunch—Custer, Wood, zoologist George Grinnell, and two or three other men—they saw what looked like a hawk chasing a pigeon. As the birds flew closer Grinnell identified the hawk as a peregrine falcon. Somebody else exclaimed that the quarry was a passenger pigeon, supposedly extinct. The pigeon flew straight toward them and settled on the ground underneath the belly of a horse where it rested for a few moments. Then it flew away, the falcon close behind. How this desperate little drama ended, they never knew.

A great white crane came sailing majestically into the valley. Custer halted the regiment, crept forward, and in the prose of Samuel J. Barrows reporting for the New York *Tribune*, "read the poor bird his death warrant." From tip to tip the wings measured almost seven feet. Not long after that an Indian caught a young crane which was destined for the expedition's Central Park collection. It lived just two days, apparently unable to stomach Army food. Grinnell mentions that the nestling's female parent was not seen, "but the male manifested much attachment for his young, and remained on the ground not far from the nest, croaking and displaying much anxiety. He finally was shot by General Custer."

The general also bagged a huge bear. There are two Illingworth photos of him posed behind the lunging carcass, flanked as usual by the devoted Bloody Knife, along with Capt. Ludlow and an enlisted man. In the second exposure Custer assumes a more aggressive stance while Ludlow is seated—perhaps at the general's suggestion. This bear always is identified as a grizzly, and Custer wrote to Elizabeth that he had experienced a hunter's greatest thrill: "I have killed my Grizzley."

Grinnell describes it as an old male whose canine teeth were mere stumps, many of the incisors gone, molars hardly visible above the gums. Pvt. Theodore Ewert, trumpeter of H Company, kept a diary of pickled observations, and in this diary Ewert writes that because Custer claimed the bear was a grizzly everybody else agreed. In fact, says the private, it was a cinnamon: "Such as he was, I never saw a larger; he was very old, his claws were worn. . . . General Custer, of course, wishes to magnify his discoveries to the fullest extent, but I cannot comprehend in what manner the species of a single bear is to add to, or detract from the importance of his work."

Along the Belle Fourche River they met a good Indian. Custer's ambulance driver, Fred "Antelope" Snow, recalled years later that the Indian had been lashed to a willow frame: "Tin cups, a small Tin Pail and a Canteen was suspended from the frame upon which the body was placed—the body was that of a young Brave—was wrapped in Gunny Sacks and tied with Shaggan-appi—or Raw-Hide thongs. From appearances he had been good but a short time."

So it is an instructive, pleasant trip for officers and for enlisted men lucky enough to attend them. The air is fragrant, valleys brim with flowers. Blueberries, cherries, and gooseberries grow everywhere. Masses of crystalized gypsum sparkle in the sun—Ludlow is shown an outcrop which the Indians have used for generations as a source of ornaments, splitting off fragments until they have carved a notch several feet deep.

Lt. Calhoun reflects upon these natural works, upon the conditions of mortal felicity, and God's ineffable scheme:

. . . Man is the promoter of earthly happiness. He is the divine instrument, pre-ordained from primitive existence to diffuse this beneficence upon the earth. Man is the noblest work of God. In this wild region man will ultimately be seen in the full enjoyment of true pleasure, in the possession of happiness obtained by honest labor. For the hives of industry will take the place of dirty wigwams. Civilization will ere long reign supreme and throw heathen barbarianism into oblivion. Seminaries of learning will raise their proud cupolas far above the canopy of Indian lodges, and Christian temples will elevate their lofty spires upward towards the azure sky while places of heathen mythology will sink to rise no more. This will be a period of true happiness.

Before long he continues with brisk efficiency: "Marched 14 3/10 miles—arrived at Camp No. 19, a delightful spring of cold water—sufficient for man or beast. Abundant quantity of wood. Private John Cunningham, Company H, 7th Cavalry, who has been sick for a few days past, died at 11 o'clock tonight." And with an eye to future business he notes that they had marched over some red clay which should make good bricks.

As for Pvt. Cunningham, he had indeed been sick for a few days—with diarrhea and pleurisy—but the contract doctor, S. J. Allen, would not excuse him from duty. Cunningham tried a second time to be excused. Again the doctor thought he was malingering. The next day Cunningham toppled off his horse. He was carried to an ambulance where he lay unconscious, exposed to the midsummer sun. Dr. Allen, when asked to inspect the patient, was too drunk to respond. Chief Medical Officer J. W. Williams was thereupon notified. He, too, was drunk, according to Ewert, but after being vigorously shaken and allowed some fifteen minutes to put his head in order he staggered as far as the ambulance where, with difficulty, he managed to climb the back steps, "looked at the dying man for a moment with a drunken stare, then staggered back to his tent, fell on his bed and slept."

Custer was notified. He sent for the medical men. Dr. Williams, upon being reawakened, was incoherent. Custer dismissed him. Dr. Allen, in slightly better shape, maintained that Pvt. Cunningham was not all that sick but consented to prescribe a few opium pills. At 11:25 P.M. the wretched private expired, and thereafter his fellow enlisted men referred to the doctors as Drunken Williams and Butcher Allen—whose opium prescription sounds a bit unusual. The customary treatment for just about every ailment in those knobby days was quinine, iodine, or epsom salts.

Ewert mentions that a hospital tent had been brought along but no sick man ever saw the inside of it; this tent served as a dining room for Custer and his staff. And the best ambulance was used to transport Custer's recent acquisitions which included—among other curiosities—two prairie owls, one hawk, several toads, three rattlesnakes, and a petrified tree trunk. Sick men therefore rode in jolting, rickety ambulances not much more comfortable than a buckboard wagon.

Obviously the color of the Black Hills varied, depending on a man's status in the regiment.

Inyan Kara, which sounds like a Turkish liqueur, was explored by the general on July 23. The name seems to be a corruption of Heéng-ya Ha-gá, which is Sioux for mountain goat. Inyan Kara rose well above six thousand feet and Custer, as usual, found this excursion stimulating. His second ranking officer, George Forsyth, climbed to the flinty summit with a hammer and chisel to engrave the date and Custer's name.

Not long afterward several members of the expedition were seated around a fire discussing the future of the Black Hills when Horatio Nelson Ross took a bottle of dust from his pocket and said, "I reckon the white people are coming, all right."

Grinnell said this dust was fine-grained with occasional nuggets about the size of a pinhead. "We turned the bottle round and round and by the light of the fire looked at the shining yellow mass. . . ."

At that moment the climactic battle became certain. The insistent rumors of half a century were verified.

"I haven't shown this to anybody but Charley," Ross continued, alluding to Lonesome Charley Reynolds. "If the boys knew we had got this, they'd throw away their rifles and begin to dig. Of course, I'll have to report it to the General. . . ."

William Eleroy Curtis, who talked with the miners, wrote that after having examined a streambed which yielded strong color they dug a hole, found what they wanted, and returned to camp with a trace of precious evidence wrapped in the leaf of an account book. The exact location of this strike was "near French Creek alongside the Chicago, Burlington and Quincy Railway," according to Mr. Cleophas O'Harra, who was guided there by Ross himself sometime around 1900. When O'Harra asked how much that first pinch of dust was worth, Ross answered: "About ten cents."

The dime's worth of dust was tested by all accepted folk methods: washed with acid, mixed with mercury, cut, chewed, and tasted.

Next morning at daybreak the discovery site was jammed with amateur prospectors carrying shovels, picks, axes, tent pins, bowie knives, pot hooks, kettles, cups, platters—anything that could lift dirt or hold dirt—and not many failed to find a little something: ". . . a few yellow particles clinging to a globule of mercury that rolled indifferently in and out of the sand. Officers and privates, mule-whackers and scientists, all met on a common level and the great equalizer was that insignificant yellow gold dust."

Who actually found it? Ross gets credit, but a journal kept by McKay includes this undated entry: "In the evening I took a pan, pick and shovel, and went out prospecting. The first panful was taken from the gravel and sand obtained in the bed of the creek; and on washing was found to contain from one and a half to two cents, which was the first gold found in the Black Hills." McKay moved downstream about twenty feet and tried again, panning three cents' worth. He then returned to headquarters where he showed the yellow grains to Custer and Forsyth. They examined the treasure with delight: "I never saw two better pleased generals in my life."

Regardless of who struck pay dirt first, the news would blossom and shower like a skyrocket.

An order from Custer, dated August 2, 1874, states that scout Charles Reynolds will carry dispatches to the commandant of Fort Laramie.

Lonesome Charley cleaned his rifle. He filled his cartridge belt. Out of leather and sponge he manufactured some footgear that would not make a sound or leave a distinct trail. He stuffed hardtack and bacon into a haversack, chose a good horse, strapped a blanket to the saddle, and said he was ready. He was given a canvas mail bag labeled by the regimental adjutant:

> Black Hills Express.
> Charley Reynolds, Manager.
> Connecting with
> All Points East, West,
> North, South.
> Cheap Rates; Quick Transit;
> Safe Passage.
> We are protected by the
> Seventh Cavalry.

It took him four nights to go ninety miles, hiding by day, and the midsummer badlands were so dry that he had to walk the last few miles because his horse collapsed. His tongue enlarged and by the time he reached Laramie he was unable to close his mouth.

Meanwhile, back in Paha Sapa, a Ree scout named Angry Bear had found gold "at a broken place . . . in a spring"—which sounds like the McKay-Ross excavation but must have been somewhere else. Angry Bear told his friends this yellow dust was good for trimming bridles, so a number of Rees visited the broken place. When they returned to camp their arms sparkled with gold. Custer asked where they had gotten it. They showed him. He posted guards around this spring, but he rewarded the scouts, although the Arikara narrative does not specify just how. Later he came to visit the scouts, bringing a cloth filled with gold. He explained to them that it was money and they should have some. As he said this he picked up and threw down gold by the handful.

Despite such excitement life went on very much the same. Calhoun wrote in his diary: "The men played the popular game of Base Ball."

Diarrhea, the regiment's worst enemy, continued its ugly work. Professor Donaldson recorded the end of Sgt. Charles Sempker: " 'Twas eight o'clock in the evening and the camp was all still; the deep blue sky was sprinkled with stars; the bright, full moon was pouring its flood of light over the plain; the noiseless zephry was floating by. The silence was broken by the mournful note of the bugle, calling us to the side of a grave, freshly made in the green turf."

And beneath this placid surface, like a trout in the shadows, hung a watchful presence. Scout Luther North recalled that when they got to the Little Missouri they saw an abandoned Indian camp—a big one—whereupon he remarked to Custer that it was just as well the Indians had moved along. Custer answered that with the Seventh Cavalry he could whip all the Indians in the northwest.

About one o'clock in the afternoon, August 30, they paused beside the Heart River, ten miles short of Fort Lincoln, to rest the horses and let the men fix coffee. Pickets were sent out to prevent anybody from going ahead. Pvt. Ewert thought this stop unnecessary: "*He* wanted to be the first. *His* was to be the honor. *He* wanted to surprise the people in the fort. *His*, and no other's voice, the one to proclaim: 'Here I am! The expedition is in safely! I have discovered gold! I am a big chief. Me big Inj--, no no, not Injun, but me big, big, big, well, big something! Here is George A. ready to have his noble brow entwined by laurels! Fetch on your wreaths, etc.' "

Ree scouts led the parade, wearing their best moccasins, leggings, and calico shirts. Next came the staff officers, the band, the trumpeters.

Women, children, and members of the garrison came running out of the fort.

The band struck up "Garry Owen."

As they rode past officers' quarters each officer dropped out to embrace his wife, then returned to his place in formation. Elizabeth appeared, hurrying toward Custer, but just as she got within catching distance she seemed to swoon. "A very pretty piece of byplay," comments Pvt. Ewert.

Everybody knew about the gold. Three weeks earlier the Bismarck *Tribune* had reported a bonanza in the Black Hills, predicting that the territory would become America's El Dorado.

The Chicago *Inter Ocean* editorialized that it would be a sin against the country and against the world if this region should remain unimproved, merely to provide hunting grounds for savages. The Sioux must leave their cherished hills:

Pleasant as be the pastures in which their children have sported, and the slopes that hold the bones of their dead, they must leave them for the land of the stranger, and stand not upon the order of their going. There is gold in the hills and rivers of the region, and the white man desires to take possession of it. What, to the roaming Yankee, are the links that bind the red man, to the home of his fathers. He is but an episode in the advance of the Caucasian. He must decrease that the new comers may grow in wealth. Happy for him the day when the last of his tribes shall fold his blankets around his shrunken limbs, and take his final sleep, to waken in the eyes of the Great Spirit.

On September 3 the *Press and Dakotaian* published a cautionary ad:

No sensible man will think of going to the Black Hills without first insuring his life. The Missouri Valley Life Insurance Co. of Leavenworth, Kan. offers peculiar advantages to such. For further particulars apply to Nathan Ford, Manager for Dakota.

The government not unexpectedly behaved like a twin-headed dinosaur: It attempted to stop miners from entering the Black Hills while at the same time following up Custer's report. Thus, in the spring of 1875 an eminent geologist, Walter P. Jenny, was dispatched with a military escort of four hundred troops to see what he could see. Jenny spent five months in the Sioux preserve. He found significant quantities of gold in gravel bars twenty miles northeast of Harney Peak. These deposits were "favorably situated," and he mentioned from his field camp that approximately two hundred prospectors had trailed him. There were a great many others he knew nothing about. Prospectors were streaming into the hills from every direction. Little more than a year later it would be commonplace wisdom to observe that those who dug for gold in Sioux territory had dug their hero's grave.

A year earlier Pvt. Ewert had written, with the taste of wormwood on his tongue: "Oh thou mighty and omnipotent, great and revered Almighty Dollar! Thou makest mankind corrupt and rotten! For thy smile men commit murder, sacrifice every noble feeling, cut the throat of father, mother, brother or sister to gain thee. Men lose their hope of heaven. . . ."

On November 3, after considering Jenny's report, President Grant discussed the matter with Crook, Sheridan, Indian Affairs Commissioner Edward P. Smith, Secretary of the Interior Zachariah Chandler, and Secretary of War William Belknap. We have no tapes of that meeting, but soon afterward the Army was instructed to let prospectors do as they pleased. If some should find their way to the Black Hills, General Sherman wrote, "I understand that the President and the Interior Dept will wink at it. . . ."

Inspector E. C. Watkins of the Indian Bureau submitted his opinion as to how the restless Sioux ought to be handled. Troops should be sent against them, preferably in winter, "and *whip* them into subjection."

On February 1, 1876, Secretary Chandler symbolically washed his hands. To Belknap he wrote:

Sir: On the 3rd December last I had the honor to address a communication to you relative to the hostile Sioux roaming in the Powder River country, under the leadership of Sitting Bull, informing you that I have directed couriers to be sent from each of the Sioux agencies, informing that chief that he must come in with his followers to one of the Sioux agencies, before the 31st ultimo, prepared to remain in peace near the agency, or he would be turned over to the War Department, and the Army be directed to compel him to comply with the orders of this Department.

The time given him in which to return to an agency having expired, and the advices received at the Indian Office being to the effect that Sitting Bull still refuses to comply with the directions of the Commissioner, the said Indians are hereby turned over to the War Department for such action on the part of the Army as you may deem proper under the circumstances.

I enclose copy of communication from the Commissioner of Indian Affairs, dated the 21st ultimo, recommending that hostilities be commenced.

Very respectfully, your obedient servant,

Z. Chandler,
Secretary.

Two days later Secretary Belknap replied in the courteous, logical, bureaucratic prose that inaugurates war:

Sir: Acknowledging the receipt of your letter of the 1st instant stating that the time given Sitting Bull and his followers to repair to an agency having expired, and this chief still refuses to comply with the directions of the Commissioner, and turning over the case to the War Department, in accordance with the recommendations of the Indian Bureau that hostilities be commenced against these Indians, I have the honor to inform you that the Adjutant-General has directed the General of the Army to take immediate measures to compel these Indians to remain upon their reservation, as requested by your department.

Very respectfully, your obedient servant.

W. W. Belknap
Secretary of War.

Five days later the Bismarck *Trib* reported that forty-seven teams loaded with provisions, passengers, and a steam sawmill had left for the promised land. Thirty more teams were expected to depart very soon with freight and passengers, including several families. "California Joe pilots the party assisted by Ed. Donahue and Tom Minton as scouts. . . . Fred Hollenbeck goes out with a herd of cows to start a dairy; Joe Pennell, Thomas Madden, Bob Roberts and others go as traders; O. Nickolson goes out with a stock of miners goods to locate and establish a wholesale and retail commission business. George Gibbs goes to start a blacksmith shop. . . ."

These were among the early gold bugs. Within two months there would be large parties—hundreds of adventurers traveling by boat and rail to Yankton, thence to Fort Pierre, and on to paradise. Wagon trains creaked through Sioux City day after day. It was commonly predicted that an army of fortune hunters would extend from the Black Hills to the Missouri River.

The first prospectors danced with delight. On May 17, the day Terry and Custer marched out of Fort Lincoln, a long letter from one Joseph G. Bemis appeared in the Fairbault *Republican*:

The miners are bringing in their bottles and buckskin pouches well filled with the yellow, and from the expression of their faces one would think they had been brought up on laughing gas. Improved claims are selling for two and three thousand dollars apiece, and everything is lovely except the accursed Indians. They seem to be trying to get a corner on horse-flesh, and so far, they are ahead.

On Friday the 14th inst., they attacked a party at Buffalo Gap . . . and at the same place, a man by the name of Woods, from this place, on his way to Spotted Tail Agency, lost his life, horse, saddle and scalp. On the same day a party of five persons were killed in Red Canyon, fifty miles south of here, on the Cheyenne road, and two others severely wounded. Among the killed were a Mr. Metz and wife, and Mrs. Mosby, (colored); did not get the names of the others. The women were ravished, then filled with arrows and bullets, and their brains beaten out.

Mr. Bemis discusses a few more atrocities, notes that a company is being organized to protect citizens, and proceeds to less significant matters, such as the fact that a horse thief has been caught: "Some fun for the vigilantes to-morrow. . . ."

Mr. Bemis soon writes again. The outbound stage was attacked, four passengers and the driver escaped by crawling several miles on hands and knees. Mr. Brown, the stagecoach agent, got a bullet just above the hip. He had been wearing a cartridge belt and the Indian bullet drove a cartridge into his side. He is not expected to recover.

A certain Mr. Allen came to town after six weeks of prospecting and his pockets bulged with gold dust. Mr. Allen joyously stayed overnight, he packed his mule, and he started out again next morning singing "Glory Hal-lelujah!" He was followed by three newcomers stocked with groceries who were caught by Indians before they had gone twenty miles. People in that vicinity heard shots but arrived too late. Indians had scalped two of the green-horns and helped themselves to such goods as they wanted, leaving the re-mainder a scrambled mess—oats, bacon, flour, coffee, sugar, dried fruit.

The road to Fort Laramie was alleged to be sprinkled with corpses and the editor of the *Wyoming Weekly Leader* threw a fit. In just about every issue, he said, they were compelled to detail the murder of citizens:

> . . . Day after day the telegraph brings to us the particulars of horrible atrocities committed upon the people of Wyoming and Dakota by the fiendish and blood-seeking Indians, whom the Government, under so-called treaty stipulations, is feeding and supporting with the utmost generous liberality. The very Indians who partake daily of the bounty of this great nation at their agency are found among the hordes who waylay the traveller to the mines, surprise the miner in his camp, and who now threaten to kill or drive out of the northern country the hardy pioneers and industrious miners who have reclaimed the northern country from the possession of the barbarians.

Standing Rock agent James McLaughlin commented in one official report not long before the Indian wars finally ended that the history of treaty-making with the Sioux was the history of treaty-making with all Indians. That is, treaties were made for the accommodation of whites. There could be no jus-tification for the natives' barbaric acts, he wrote, but they did what they did in the nature of reprisal: "That the Indian has not always discriminated be-tween the innocent and the guilty in taking his revenge is certain—else had there been no Minnesota massacre. If his sense of justice had led him to a fine discrimination in these matters, the red man would long ago have made an attack on the national Capitol."

The massacre to which he refers began on August 17, 1862, when Santees under Little Crow resolved to depopulate lower Minnesota and butchered 644 citizens before General Sibley could interfere. Fifty years of treaty-sign-ing had left the Sioux with one strip of land to call their own—ten miles wide, 150 miles long—and resentment enough to nourish them for a century. An-drew Myrick, a trader, was heard to remark just before the Santee explosion: "If they're hungry, let them eat grass." Myrick had not devised the land swin-dle, but as McLaughlin pointed out, Indians sometimes failed to discrimi-nate. When the soldiers located Myrick's body he had a mouthful of grass.

McLaughlin's sardonic appraisal reached Washington too late to be of use.

Whether his words might have affected government policy if he had expressed himself sooner is conjectural. Probably not. Not with gold in the Black Hills. Not with vast untilled plains beyond. Not with unlumbered forests. His indictment landed on the bureaucracy when it did with all the weight of thistledown, just as it would have landed sooner or later.

As Little Phil once remarked: "It is absurd to talk of keeping faith with Indians."

Fort Abraham Lincoln, Dakota Territory. May 17, 1876.

General Terry ordered the Seventh Cavalry to circle the parade ground: a maneuver intended to calm uneasy women and give married officers one more chance to say good-bye. The wives and children of Ree scouts wailed mournfully, which was the custom when Indians went to war. The wives of white soldiers probably looked as apprehensive as they felt, but white children tied handkerchiefs to sticks—pretending they were flags—and beat on tin pans and marched joyously beside their fathers. Custer, prancing ahead, wheeled his horse, bent down from the saddle to embrace his wife, and muttered, "Watch for our return, Bess." The terrible simplicity of his good-bye is like something out of Shakespeare.

Sitting Bull was thought to be encamped on or near the Little Bighorn, which flows northwest into the Bighorn, which flows north to the Yellowstone, which flows northeast to the Missouri. General Terry therefore decided to march west from Fort Lincoln until he intercepted the Yellowstone, follow the river upstream, locate the hostiles, and at that point determine how they should be approached.

A thick ground fog was beginning to evaporate when the column got under way, and by a rare meteorological phenomenon this army of soldiers, artillery, and white-hooded mule-drawn wagons—a caravan extending almost two miles—was ethereally reflected overhead. Elizabeth described it in *Boots and Saddles* as "a scene of wonder and beauty," yet she felt troubled; the sight of her husband leading his regiment across the sky left her ill at ease. The sun burning through the mist glinted on the weapons of departing soldiers: "The yellow, indicative of cavalrymen, outlined the accoutrements. . . ."

Custer's attitude may be deduced from the fact that he brought along four staghounds. His Fort Lincoln menagerie consisted of about forty dogs, a pelican, a porcupine that sometimes slept on the Custer marital bed, as well as various other wild or half-wild things, and he saw no reason to deprive himself of his pet staghounds until it was time to go to work.

A letter dated May 31, "Ten Miles West of the Little Missouri," mentions another trick played on kid brother Boston. All three Custers had been riding ahead of the army and while they were passing through a ravine Boston stopped to dislodge a pebble from his pony's shoe. The general and Tom kept going. As soon as they were out of sight they dismounted, scrambled up a bluff and peered over the edge. Down below was the kid. Custer snapped a shot over his head. Boston mistook it for a Sioux ambush, jumped on his pony and went galloping back for help.

If the Custer brothers were in high spirits, a good many enlisted men were not; like sailors of the Dark Ages whose captain ventured recklessly beyond the charts, they were being led through an increasingly dangerous wilderness. An occasional peg driven into the ground by Northern Pacific surveyors in 1873 was the only evidence that white men had visited this region.

On June 16 they reached the site of an Indian cemetery. Corpses lay on scaffolds and in trees. Lt. Edward Maguire noticed the body of an infant about ten months old, well preserved, which reminded him of an Egyptian mummy. He described it in an 1877 government report as though the army were a scientific expedition and himself an ethnologist: "The face had been painted red. The hands were closed and bent upward and backward on the arms. The feet were similarly bent backward on the legs. This was probably due to the wrappings of calico and buffalo skins. The whole body was covered with what appeared to be a salt of lime."

Near the confluence of the Tongue and the Yellowstone a warrior's scaffold—its vertical supports painted red and black to show that he had been unusually brave—was pulled down at Custer's direction. The remains were examined. A partly healed wound below the right shoulder indicated the probable cause of death. Officers and men were allowed to help themselves to the funeral equipment—beaded moccasins, rawhide bags, horn spoons—after which the stripped corpse was flung into the river by the black interpreter Isaiah Dorman. Ree scouts later observed Dorman fishing near this spot and concluded that he was using the flesh as bait.

Lt. Godfrey was bothered by this treatment of Sioux burials. Fifteen years afterward he wrote that Custer's troops would ride around exhibiting souvenirs as if they were trophies of valor, no more concerned by the desecration than if they had won prizes at a raffle. "Ten days later I saw the bodies of these same persons dead, naked, and mutilated."

At the mouth of the Tongue River where Miles City eventually would be built the troops found a skull beneath some charred wood. Nearby lay part of a cavalryman's uniform, recognizable as such by yellow piping on the tunic and a C on the overcoat buttons. Heavy sticks and clubs were scattered about. The Sioux evidently had beaten their victim before burning him. Custer paused to look at the bones, charred wood, and remnants of a uniform. He seems to have been disturbed, but did not speak. If he did, his words have been forgotten.

Farther upstream, at the confluence of the Yellowstone and Rosebud Creek, Boston wrote to their mother on June 21: "Armstrong, Tom and I pulled down an Indian grave the other day. Autie Reed got the bow with six arrows and a nice pair of moccasins which he intends taking home."

That night the senior officers met aboard the *Far West* to devise a plan of attack. They decided that the strongest and most flexible unit, Custer's Seventh, should ride south along Rosebud Creek to a position east of the Indians. Gibbon and Terry together would follow the Yellowstone to the Bighorn and go up the Bighorn to the Little Bighorn. The hostiles would be trapped.

Gibbon, writing for *American Catholic Quarterly* in 1877, explained that the Sioux could not move west because in this direction lived their mortal enemies, the Crows. Nor could they move north without confronting the Montana column, nor go east without doubling on their course—thus exposing themselves to attack from Gibbon and Terry as well as Custer. "They would, therefore, in all probability, go south; for, in addition to its being their natural and only practicable line of retreat, was the fact that in that direction lay the Big Horn range of mountains, in the fastnesses of which they would be comparatively secure, and could live on the game and wild berries which abounded there. But if, as we had good reason to expect, General Crook's column was somewhere in that direction, there was a third column against which the Indians incumbered with their families were liable to run."

Nobody on the *Far West* realized that Crook already had met the Sioux and had been forced to retreat.

The plan of attack seems to have been approved by all three senior officers, with disagreement limited to details. They concluded that because infantrymen would take longer to reach the battlefield—wherever it might be—Custer's Seventh should ride farther south than necessary. Gibbon is explicit: "Custer, instead of proceeding at once into the valley of the Little Big Horn, even should the trail lead there, should continue on up the Rosebud, get closer to the mountains, and then striking west, come down the valley of the Little Big Horn, 'feeling constantly to his left,' to be sure that the Indians had not already made their escape to the south and eastward."

Thus, God willing, they would meet again on June 26 or not long thereafter.

Scholars point out that whereas the Terry-Gibbon unit would be provisioned for about a week, Custer's regiment drew supplies for fifteen days. If Custer traveled thirty miles a day, which would not be excessive, he could descend to the middle of Wyoming and still get back to the Yellowstone. In other words, Terry had given him a loose rein. Almost certainly he was expected to locate the hostiles and herd them north until their path was blocked by Terry and Gibbon. June 26, therefore, might be construed not as the expected day of battle but the day on which Terry and Gibbon would be ready to shut the north gate. Then, as Custer arrived, the combined forces would count coup on Sitting Bull, Crazy Horse, Gall, Lame Deer, Two Moon, Little Wolf, Rain in the Face, Big Man, Hump, Spotted Eagle, Old Man Coyote, White Bull, He Dog, Crow King, and all the rest.

Some of Custer's troops suspected things might not go as scheduled because a number of them left instructions concerning the disposition of property. Captain Keogh, not a gloomy sort, approached an officer of the guard and asked for assistance in drawing up a will. Bloody Knife, who had been monitoring the countryside, appeared pessimistic. Lonesome Charley twice asked General Terry to release him from further service, but Terry persuaded him to continue. Custer must have been affected by these men whom he knew to be courageous. He himself may have foreseen death and the annihilation of his command. Terry and Gibbon walked with him to his tent after the last conference. Although it was midsummer there had been a hailstorm and as they walked side by side, their boots crunching the fresh hail, the two senior officers noted that he seemed apprehensive and easily irritated.

Grasshopper Jim Brisbin did not think Custer's regiment was strong enough; he urged that four companies of his own be added to the Seventh and respectfully asked Terry to go in command—which again implies that Custer was expected to meet the hostiles first. Terry rejected Brisbin's idea, saying Custer had been stung by Grant's treatment of him in Washington and needed a chance to vindicate himself with the Seventh Cavalry alone.

Years later Brisbin insisted that Custer knew the size of the hostile encampment. Scouts had estimated there must be three thousand fighting men in the village. "All this Custer knew," Brisbin wrote in a letter to Godfrey, "for I told him all about it, and cautioned him to be careful."

Brisbin felt so concerned that he asked General Terry a second time to go in command. Terry again rejected the idea, saying he had not had much experience fighting Indians. Besides, he added, Custer seemed positive that he could whip anything they met.

Brisbin said: "General, you have more sense in your little finger than Custer has in his whole body. You underrate your ability and overrate Custer's."

Terry laughed. He then suggested a compromise. "Go to Custer and offer him your cavalry, and if he says so, we will put the Montana battalion of the Second and Seventh together."

Brisbin asked if Terry would accept command of this combined force. Terry hesitated. Brisbin interrupted his thoughts: "You will pardon me, general, if I speak plainly, but my affection and respect for you, as well as the care of the lives of my men and officers always prompts me to do so in perilous times."

"I thank you," Terry replied, "and you may always speak plainly to me. . . ."

Brisbin then said he did not want his Montana battalion placed under Custer's command. If Terry would be in charge, all right. Otherwise he did not want his men attached to the Seventh.

"You do not seem to have confidence in Custer," said Terry.

"None in the world," said Brisbin.

"Well, speak to him anyway about going with him if you like, and see what he says."

"And if he thinks well of it, and the columns are united, you will go in command of both?"

"Yes," Terry said, "I will."

Brisbin approached Custer and offered his services, to which the Son of the Morning Star responded briskly that the Seventh could handle anything.

Brisbin said he was glad to hear this and walked away. Still worried, he suggested to Terry that Custer be given a battery of Gatling guns. Terry liked this idea, so Brisbin returned to Custer. How about some Gatling guns? Custer said all right, he would take them; but about an hour later he changed his mind, saying the gun carriages would impede his march. This was true. Each gun was hauled by four nags and very often it became necessary for soldiers to unhitch them and drag the guns by hand over some obstacle.

Even if Custer had accepted the Gatlings and managed to haul them up Rosebud Creek, across the divide, and down into the Little Bighorn Valley they would not have accomplished much. These weapons were invented in 1861 and had been very little improved since then. They frequently malfunctioned and the bullets that sprayed from six or ten barrels—depending on the model—would have been effective only against a massed attack, such as might be expected in Europe. British redcoats might march into the fire of Gatlings with heads up and arms swinging, but American Indians were less disciplined. Besides, the gun crews would have been knocked down like ducks in a shooting arcade. Each Gatling was mounted between two large wheels which lifted it so high off the ground that the gunners had to stand erect.

Gerard said he talked to Custer about these weapons during the march from Fort Lincoln. Custer planned to take them with his regiment because he thought they would make short work of the hostile village. Gerard told him Indians wouldn't stand around watching the Gatlings grind out shots. Take a twelve-pounder, Gerard advised. Throw some big shells at the village from a mile away.

Custer ignored this advice. At least there is nothing to suggest that he asked Terry for a cannon.

The Gatlings might inadvertently have saved him. These ponderous contrivances might have delayed the regiment, causing him to arrive more or less on schedule, in which case there would have been no last stand. The unified regiments of Terry, Gibbon, and Custer might have been forced to give up and withdraw, as Crook was forced to withdraw, but it is not likely they would have been slaughtered.

So the Gatlings accompanied General Terry all the way from Fort Lincoln to the Little Bighorn, and they did cause trouble. They were handled by a detachment of the Twentieth Infantry which found itself unable to keep up with the rest of the column.

If Custer had taken the brass Napoleon, though, the immortal Montana symphony might have ended on a different note. Exploding artillery shells make a prodigious noise and in the early days this noise alone was enough to terrify and demoralize militant Indians. Thirty years before the Little Bighorn when Col. Stephen Kearny wanted to intimidate a band of Arapahoes at Fort Laramie he delivered a threatening speech which he punctuated that night by firing a howitzer and a rocket. Many Arapahoes collapsed on the ground, says Francis Parkman, while others ran off screaming with amazement and terror.

By Custer's time the response might have been different. In 1870, for instance, when a delegation of Sioux visited Washington the Great Father's biggest guns were uncorked in an attempt to impress them. Sioux fighting men observed the bombardment without lifting an eyebrow. Still worse, before each explosion the squaws covered their ears. The government's *pièce de résistance* was a fifteen-inch coastal gun which sent a projectile ricocheting several miles down the Potomac. This caused some comment, as did the huge grains of powder. Otherwise the demonstration flopped. The coastal gun was a monstrous weapon, all the Sioux agreed, but nobody with any brains would sit on his pony in front of it.

Just why Custer disdained artillery is not known. The best explanation seems to be that he did not want anything impeding his march. No Gatlings. No howitzer. Lt. Bradley noted in his journal on June 21: ". . . it is understood that if Custer arrives first he is at liberty to attack at once if he deems prudent. We have little hope of being in at the death, as Custer will undoubtedly exert himself to the utmost to get there first and win all the laurels for himself and his regiment."

This determination to orchestrate a dramatic success for himself was thoroughly understood. On at least two occasions—at Fort Lincoln and at Young Man Butte—he told the Ree scouts that this campaign against the Sioux would be his last and he must win a great victory. Yet even a small victory, he told them, even if it were against only five tents of Sioux, would make him president.

Once while eating with a group of Mandans, Gros Ventres, and Rees he said through his interpreter: "When we return I will go back to Washington, and on my trip to Washington I shall take my brother here, Bloody Knife, with me. I shall remain at Washington and be the Great Father." He went on to say that Bloody Knife then would come home and live in a fine house and be in charge of all the work, and the other Indians would have papers made out for them so they would always have enough food.

Pvt. Peter Thompson said everybody knew Custer meant business, that he would move fast. A number of the men had served under him in Kansas and a very solemn feeling now settled upon them. Some of these veterans wedged their overcoats into the forks of cottonwood trees because they did not want to carry anything unnecessary. An overcoat weighed several pounds. "I kept mine," Thompson said, "as I had grave doubts of our ever returning that way. . . ."

On June 22 the Seventh passed in review before General Terry and Colonel Gibbon. Trumpets blared. Officers saluted. Ree scouts galloped back and forth singing their death songs. Pvt. Coleman wrote in his journal that Terry and Gibbon were highly pleased with the warlike appearance of officers and men, "Cartonly a fine boddy of Men."

Gibbon later remarked in a letter to General Terry: "So great was my fear that Custer's zeal would carry him forward too rapidly, that the last thing I said to him when bidding him good-by after his regiment had filed past you when starting on his march was, 'Now, Custer, don't be greedy, but wait for us.' He replied gaily as, with a wave of his hand, he dashed off. . . ."

It is unlikely that Gibbon expected this good advice to be followed. He had known Custer too long. He was an artillery instructor at West Point when Custer was a cadet. Nor is it probable that General Terry felt surprised by what happened. Twice during the march he threatened Custer with arrest for pacing ahead.

Still, despite this warning, despite Gibbon's last reminder, despite the plan, the ambitious young general hurried forward.

Grasshopper Jim was aboard the *Far West* on the night of the twenty-first. He wrote to Godfrey in 1892 that General Terry plotted Custer's line of march up Rosebud Creek with a row of pins stuck in a map, "and, being somewhat near-sighted as you know, Terry asked me to mark the line, and I did so with a blue pencil. Custer turned off that line of march from the Rosebud just twenty miles *short* of the end of the pins. . . ."

Two months after the battle Terry showed a Chicago *Times* correspondent a copy of the orders he had given Custer and stated that if Custer had lived he would have been court-martialed for disobedience.

Military strategists ever since then have argued about Terry's orders. Some argue that they were vague. That is, Terry gave Custer the freedom to do as he thought best. Others insist that Terry was specific. It is a matter of interpretation. As Robert Utley has pointed out, Terry expressed himself courteously, reflecting concern for his subordinate's injured pride as well as his realization that you do not send somebody into the wilderness with rigid instructions.

Benteen wrote to his wife from the banks of the Yellowstone that if Custer had followed orders, "the commands would have formed a junction exactly at the village, and have captured the whole outfit of teepees, etc. and probably any quantity of squaws, pappooses, etc. but Custer disobeyed orders from the fact of not wanting any other command—or body to have a finger in the pie—and thereby lost his life."

President Grant told a New York *Herald* reporter: "I regard Custer's massacre as a sacrifice of troops, brought on by Custer himself, that was wholly unnecessary—wholly unnecessary. He was not to have made the attack before effecting the junction with Terry and Gibbon."

So he obeyed or he disobeyed. It depends, like the blind men describing an elephant, on what part of the creature you touch.

If one wishes to argue that he disobeyed Terry, one might ask why.

Surely it was eagerness, founded upon a conviction that by himself he could disperse the Sioux, because he made no attempt to scout the region further south—unless Benteen's brief excursion may be so considered. Instead, he shortened the route by twenty miles, making certain that he would enter the valley alone.

But if he had obeyed and ridden much further south, what then?

Only a few days earlier the Indians had defeated Crook and they knew he retreated southward—a victory that excited them, gave them confidence. They did not expect Crook to try again, but he might. Which is to say, a column of bluecoats approaching from the south would quickly be detected. If the Indians then moved to attack, the battle would take place a number of miles up the valley and by the time General Terry arrived it is quite possible that all twelve companies of the Seventh Cavalry would have been destroyed.

If, instead, the Indians retreated from Custer they would have met Terry's relatively weak force and without doubt could have annihilated it. Then, as Mr. Ege suggests, the dreadful news might read:

TERRY-GIBBON COLUMN FALLS TO SAVAGES
AS CUSTER SEARCHES BIG HORN MOUNTAINS

About sunset on the evening of June 22, a few hours after leaving Terry and Gibbon, Custer summoned his officers. They squatted around his bed while he gave an uncharacteristic talk. He explained why he had refused the Gatling guns and four companies of Montana men, saying he felt confident they would meet no more than fifteen hundred warriors. Benteen spoke up, as usual. He did not care about the Gatlings but he did like the idea of another four companies. "I, for one, am very sorry you didn't take them," he said. "I think we will regret not having them."

Custer's attitude toward subordinates usually was brusque, even aggressive, according to Godfrey, but on this occasion he seemed subdued, almost conciliatory: "There was something akin to an appeal, as if depressed. . . ."

Godfrey returned to his bivouac with Lts. McIntosh and Wallace, and as they walked together Wallace said, "I believe General Custer is going to be killed." Godfrey asked why he thought so. Wallace answered that he had never heard the general talk like that.

Elizabeth clearly anticipated her husband's mood as the regiment moved up Rosebud Creek. In a letter to him dated June 21, which was returned unopened, she wrote: "I cannot but feel the greatest apprehension. . . ." Her anxiety must have increased when news arrived that the Sioux had stopped General Crook—which meant that instead of three armies converging on the hostiles there would be just two. Scouts immediately left Fort Lincoln in an effort to catch up with Terry because this news was important. They were too late.

If these scouts had located Terry before Custer started up Rosebud Creek, what then? Terry was a prudent man who seems to have let himself be seduced by Custer's bravado. If he had learned about Crook's defeat he probably would have asserted himself more than he did. Almost certainly he would have shortened the reins. He might have held the army together. He might have insisted that Custer accept Brisbin's Montana men—though even the addition of those companies might not have been enough. But one way or another, June 25 would not have unravelled as it did.

Something occult gathers inexplicably around this day. Charles Deland wrote in his exhaustive history of the Sioux: "Everywhere among the narratives of various writers and informants concerning this expedition and who were members thereof, this remarkable and prophetic fact of premonition of impending doom of the participants, is woven as if some spirit of evil were lingeringly but persistently hovering over camp and march as a kind of presiding genius."

Pvt. Thompson escaped death only because his horse gave out a few minutes before the hostiles discovered Custer's battalion. Thompson later described a dream he had on the night of June 24. He felt rather embarrassed about it, insisting he was too hard-headed to believe in black cats and such. He had lain down under a tree and was falling asleep when he dreamt that a detachment of soldiers including himself had been attacked. At this point Thompson woke up, but everybody around him was asleep, so he went back to sleep. His dream, though, instead of being disrupted, resumed its course, except that now he alone was the victim. An Indian came after him with an uplifted ax: "Just as the savage got close enough to me to strike I awoke only to find all vanish into thin air. But so profoundly had the dream impressed itself upon me that I could get no more sleep. Getting up I strolled through the camp looking at the horses and noting how poor and gaunt they were becoming. This was not to be wondered at when we take into account the long marches they had made. . . ."

Thompson's foreboding was shared by quite a few men during the march up Rosebud Creek, if not by all. Lt. Edgerly wrote to his wife several days after the battle that on the evening of the twenty-second, after listening to Custer's strange talk, some officers got together in his tent and sang for about an hour. Edgerly did not list the program, but a correspondent for the St. Paul *Pioneer* who accompanied these men through the Black Hills in '74 reported that Seventh Cavalry songbirds favored "Bonny Jean," "Fairy Bell," "Over the Sea," and "Lightly Row." These numbers probably were rendered in Edgerly's tent along with old favorites such as "Little Brown Jug," "Mollie Darling," "Captain Jinks," "Drill Ye Tarriers," "Dinah's Wedding," "The Man on the Flying Trapeze," and "Grandfather's Clock."

Lt. James Calhoun's wife—Margaret Emma Custer—had sent her husband a cake, apparently a large cake, because Calhoun announced during this melodious hour in Edgerly's tent that after the fight every officer was going to get a slice of it. She must have sent this cake by steamboat from Fort Lincoln to the Powder River base camp; there seems to be no other way he could have received it. Now, did Lieutenant Calhoun eat his cake at the Powder River depot while it was reasonably fresh, as a sensible man would? Of course not. Either he tied the cake to his saddle or he had it packed on a mule. One way or another he brought it to the Little Bighorn so that he and his merry comrades might celebrate the defeat of Sitting Bull.

No more is heard of Lieutenant Calhoun's cake. If it traveled on the pack train it may have been eaten by members of the Reno battalion during the two days they were surrounded; but if he attached it to his saddle it must have vanished from the battlefield, which suggests that a party of Sioux or Cheyennes found something quite unexpected. The image of half a dozen warriors with bloody hands squatting around the lieutenant's body while eating his cake is not easy to forget. He was known as the Adonis of the Seventh, handsomest man in the regiment, and he married the general's kid sister Maggie. He commanded L Company, which some analysts believe brought up the tail of the doomed battalion and was the first to fall.

The size of the hostile village seems to have worried Custer. Before leaving the Yellowstone he was told by Crow scouts that it was unusually large. Furthermore, he had reason to suspect that the modest estimates Terry got from headquarters might be inaccurate. In the first place, most Indians enjoyed visiting friends and relatives at agencies other than their own and sometimes visited for such a long time that it seemed advisable to enroll—"touch the pen"—in order to draw supplies. Thus, a single Indian might be listed at two or three or four agencies, which of course distorted the wasichu records. Custer had been around long enough to know this.

A more serious discrepancy occurred because many warriors had slipped away from the reservations to join Sitting Bull, although their absence was not reported by reservation agents. The reason these defectors went unreported was good old Yankee avarice: Agents profited according to the number of Indians on the reservation. Which is to say, an agent foolish enough to report a decrease in population was taking a bite out of his own paycheck.

Agent Howard of Spotted Tail agency had reported on April 1: "Very few, if any, of these Indians have been north this season, and I have heard of none who were in copartnership with those of the North."

Agent Hastings of Red Cloud agency: "I have experienced no difficulty whatever in taking the census, but have been somewhat delayed on account of the weather."

So it went. Falsified information trickled down through the bureaucracy, eventually reaching armies in the field, and Custer had been told to expect fifteen hundred warriors. Accordingly, this is what he told his subordinates, although the sense of depression they noted seems to reflect the gravity of his doubts.

After the battle, when Washington tried to figure out why Sheridan's plan did not work, a new census was ordered under Army supervision. Lo and behold! Instead of 9,610 Indians on the Spotted Tail Reservation there were 2,315. Instead of 12,873 at Red Cloud there were 4,760. At Cheyenne River: 2,280 instead of 7,586. At Standing Rock: 2,305 instead of 7,322.

One begins to sympathize with Reno gazing down from his hilltop upon an inconceivable agglutination of warriors: "I think we were fighting all the Sioux nation. . . ."

Benteen agreed: "They had little picnic parties of a regiment or two standing around in the bottom looking on. There was no place to put them. I think there were a couple of thousand around us, waiting for a place to shoot from."

How much quasi-official data reached Custer can only be surmised. On Christmas Eve, 1875, General Terry notified Division Headquarters: *Capt. Poland telegraphs that, although there is no game in the vicinity, the Indians at Standing Rock are selling all their hides for ammunition. . . .*

Custer probably read this telegram, or at least knew of it, and he must have known about two other telegrams from Terry to Sheridan.

March 24: *The most trustworthy scout on the Missouri recently in hostile camp reports not less than two thousand lodges and that the Indians are loaded down with ammunition.*

May 14: *It is represented that they have fifteen hundred lodges, are confident and intend making a stand.*

Custer's regiment moving south through the Rosebud Valley was greeted by those pleasant summer odors that had met General Crook a week before. Plum, crabapple, and the scent of wild roses permeated the smell of sweaty horses, leather, unwashed men, and alkaline dust.

Scouts picked up an Indian trail which they followed to the site of a recent encampment. There the remains of countless wickiups and lodge circles indicated a concentration of Sioux much larger than anyone had expected. The grass all around had been cropped by thousands of ponies, the earth was littered with droppings.

A rock carving near this encampment caused some discussion among the Rees, but at last Bloody Knife interpreted. On the rock were two bulls. One appeared to have been shot, the other struck by a lance. The smaller bull represented Custer with his army, therefore the larger must be the Dakotas. The message was this: *Do not follow the Dakotas into the Bighorn country to which they have gone, for they will turn and destroy you.* Bloody Knife and his associates were wrong in attributing this ideograph to Dakota Sioux because it was carved in prehistoric times, but that is not the point. Although the Rees may have been incompetent ethnologists, they understood what was about to happen.

One day before the battle Custer's troops saw a relatively fresh scalp mounted on a stick. It could not be identified but is thought to have come from the head of Pvt. Augustine Stoeker who, along with Pvt. Rahmeir and teamster Quinn, left Gibbon's camp without permission on May 23 to go hunting.

The same day Custer's men found this scalp on a stick they came upon a more troubling sight. Pvt. Coleman wrote:

Left Camp this morning at the usual hour the trail led up the Creek My Company B was in the advance after following the trail for four hours we Came to a Circular arbour about two hundred feet in Circumferance built with Crotches and strong Poles their was a tree in the Centar 35 feet high around which was pilled a number of Buffaloe heads this place was devoted to Religious Cermony Called the Sun dance usually practised by this tribe before going on the War Path. . . .

The Sun Dance—called Medicine Lodge by early fur traders—seems to have evolved during the eighteenth century among the Cheyennes, although they probably learned it from the Sutaio who either preceded them or joined them. It was held each summer when the tribes congregated in one huge circle with an opening toward the east. Here they appealed to the Great Mystery: Wakan Tanka.

This reverence for the east where the sun is born recurs again and again. Grinnell says that Indians would collect buffalo skulls and arrange them on the prairie in fantastic patterns dedicated to the sunrise. He himself saw an arrangement of sixty skulls painted with red and blue stripes and circles. They lay in five parallel rows, every skull facing east. Vestal says that when the Sioux found a buffalo skeleton somebody would dismount and turn the skull toward the east as a way of expressing gratitude to these animals whose flesh nourished them and whose hides kept them warm. Even in southwestern deserts, land of eternal sun, a hunter who killed a deer would turn its head toward the east.

The Sioux arbor usually was about 150 feet across with a twenty-foot pole in the middle from which dangled an array of rawhide or buffalo hair lariats. A medicine man, after having gashed a dancer's chest, would shove sticks beneath the muscles. These sticks would be attached to the dangling lariats and tightened until the brave was forced to stand on tiptoe, which might draw the chest muscles three or four inches out of his body. There were variations, more commendable because they were more agonizing. Sticks might be pushed through the dancer's cheeks just beneath his eyes or driven under the dense back muscles. However he was hooked up, he would be given an ornamental whistle to blow while he danced.

They would dance for hours, faces lifted to the sun. George Bent says it was customary for those undergoing this torture to give presents to spectators. Ordinarily they would give away ponies, but those who wanted to show off would give away everything, including their sisters.

It was a rite of initiation, a test of fortitude, and if the supplicant cried out or fainted he would be treated like a squaw for the rest of his life. The general and Elizabeth became acquainted with one of these wretched men. During his trial he had fainted and when he recovered he asked to be cut down. From that day on he wore a woman's garment and cooked meals. Warriors mocked him. Squaws refused to acknowledge his existence except when loading him with additional work. Wooden Leg, who calls this ritual the Great Medicine dance, never chose to participate, but his refusal was not interpreted as cowardice. Some of the most valiant warriors, including Crazy Horse, did not regard it as an essential certificate of manhood.

The ceremony seems unrelated to anything known among urban people, yet it is not quite that remote. Its foundation was dancing, which Col. Dodge notes is fundamental to religious observance everywhere. Even the most subdued forms of Christian worship involve rhythmic changes of posture—sitting, standing, kneeling—which are modifications of a primitive appetite for motion, perhaps a vestigial memory of the earliest hunters.

At any rate, the Sun Dance arbor found by Custer's scouts was several hundred yards west of the state highway that now parallels Rosebud Creek. The central cottonwood pole, the symbolic Enemy, was unusually large. Pvt. Coleman's estimate of thirty-five feet may have been conservative. Warriors celebrated for their courage had selected this tree and after striking it with coup sticks they chopped it down, assisted by a group of virgin women. The branches were trimmed and the log carried to the Unkpapa camp where it was painted: blue, green, yellow, red—each color to face the direction it represented: north, east, south, west. The log was then erected and to the top were bound offerings of tobacco, cherrywood sticks, a red robe, and two pieces of buffalo hide—one cut in the shape of this animal, the other in the shape of a man.

Only the Unkpapas participated. Among them was Sitting Bull. His hands and feet were stained red. Blue stripes—representing the sky—crossed his shoulders. Before joining the dance he sat on the ground with his back to the post while his adopted brother used an awl and a knife to cut fifty nubs of skin from each arm, beginning at the right wrist and mounting to the shoulder. This took about half an hour. As the skin was being removed he improvised a chant or a song, appealing to the omnipresent deity on behalf of his people.

An Unkpapa woman who witnessed this dance said that the others broke free or succumbed to pain, but Sitting Bull seemed unaware of blood trickling down his arms and breast and made no effort to tear himself loose. With his face absorbing the sun he danced continuously for two days and nights. On the morning of the third day he fainted or sank into a trance. When he revived he talked about a dream in which the Sioux killed enemy soldiers. He had watched these soldiers falling head downward toward the Dakota camp. Custer's scouts found this dream recorded on a smooth ridge of sand inside one of the sweat lodges: bluecoats plummeting toward an Indian village like so many grasshoppers.

The sense of the sand pictograph was perfectly clear to Custer's Ree and Crow scouts, but it is not known whether they guessed—or perhaps deduced from evidence incomprehensible to whites—that it represented a vision of Sitting Bull. If they did know the dreamer's identity they did not pass along the bad news to their flaxen-haired general.

In another sweat lodge they found, and explained to him, a rather depressing Sioux iconograph predicting victory: three red stones in a row. They also showed him a cairn of rocks with the skull of a buffalo bull on one side and the skull of a cow on the other, with a stick aimed at the cow. This meant the Sioux would fight like bulls and the whites would run like women.

A scout named Soldier came upon the site of a mystic ritual whose meaning was not so clear—the skin of a calf tied to four sticks thrust in the ground, accompanied by votive offerings. What could not be mistaken, however, was the confidence of these Indians.

Farther up Rosebud Creek the Indian trail was more than a mile wide, the earth so furrowed by thousands of travois poles that it resembled a plowed field.

Crow scouts found discarded trophies: scalps and beards of white men.

They showed these to Custer, who signaled that he had been sent by the Great Father in Washington to conquer these Sioux who were killing white people. He signaled that although he himself might be killed, the Sioux would feel his wrath. "I do not know whether I will pass through this battle, but if I live, I will recommend you boys and you will be leaders of the Crows."

Calamitous signs materialized, portents that disturbed superstitious soldiers as much as colored rocks and buffalo skulls troubled the scouts. Custer's swallowtail guidon was blown over by a gust of wind. Lt. Godfrey, who was nearby, picked it up and jammed the staff into the ground. Again the flag was blown over. "I then bored the staff into the ground where it would have the support of the sage-brush. This circumstance made no impression on me at the time, but after the battle an officer asked me if I remembered the incident; he had observed it, and regarded the fact of its falling to the rear as a bad omen, and felt sure we would suffer a defeat."

They camped for the last time on June 24.

Lonesome Charley distributed the contents of his haversack: shirts, tobacco, a sewing kit, whatever else he carried. Scout Billy Jackson said that some of the men refused to accept anything from Charley, while others took what he offered but only with reluctance. "We had little appetite for our coffee and hardtack. . . ."

Pvt. William Taylor of Moylan's A Company survived the next two days. Years later he corresponded with Elizabeth. He told her that when the frugal meal was finished he lay down for what he thought would be a night's rest. His company bivouacked near regimental headquarters and as he lay on the ground he could see General Custer sitting in front of a tent. Presently some officers arrived. Custer gave them instructions and they started to leave, but paused and sang "Annie Laurie," followed by "Little Footsteps Slow and Gentle," "The Good Bye at the Door," and "Doxology." After that—irreverently it seemed to Pvt. Taylor—they sang ". . . for he is a jolly good fellow that nobody can deny." The officers then said goodnight and separated. A deep quiet settled on the camp, interrupted only by the occasional stamp of a horse's hoof. Custer had issued orders on the twenty-second that trumpet calls should be discontinued and there should be no unnecessary noise, so it is odd that he permitted the lugubrious serenade.

At this meeting which Pvt. Taylor witnessed, Custer said he wanted to get as near the divide as possible before daylight. Therefore, instead of camping overnight, the march would be resumed.

About eleven o'clock they started up the long slope toward the ridge, and according to various memoirs the regiment produced an extraordinary racket. Godfrey said the clatter of horses' hooves and the rattle of equipment made it difficult to hear anything else. The night was so dark they had trouble following the trail. Now and then his men would stop to listen, "sometimes whistling or hallooing" until they got a response. Benteen followed the noise of a frying pan or a tin cup which kept banging against the saddle of a trooper in the company ahead. But the loudest noise came from pack train mules asserting their individuality with a concatenation of brays that could be heard for miles.

Even if the regiment had proceeded in absolute silence it might have been detected because an Indian with fingertips to the ground could pick up the rhythmic cadence of cavalry at a great distance. Messages coursing through the earth could be heard even by white men, blunted as their senses were by urban life. In November of 1876 when Ranald Mackenzie closed in on Dull Knife's village his scouts listened through the earth to a Cheyenne dance. One of these scouts nudged Capt. Bourke, "then pointed with his lips up the cañon in a way peculiar to savages. . . . We threw ourselves on the ground and then heard with startling distinctness the thumping of the drums . . ."

At about two-thirty in the morning one of the Crow scouts Lt. Bradley would meet far from the battlefield two days later—Hairy Moccasin—climbed a knoll from which he could look into the valley of the Little Bighorn. This knoll had been used as an observation post for years, perhaps for centuries, and Indians alluded to it as the crow's nest, referring not to that tribe but to the bird, probably because once upon a time a large nest could be seen. The ground beneath the pines was littered with agate and flint chips, the produce of generations of bored sentries who filled up the hours by making arrowheads.

At dawn Hairy Moccasin hooted softly and to his companions nearby the message could not be misunderstood. Once again the Rees began their death songs.

Lt. Varnum, in charge of these scouts, dispatched Red Star with a note to Custer. The regiment was then about ten miles east, breakfasting on coffee and bacon. The smoke of campfires could be seen from the knoll, which meant that any Sioux in the neighborhood also would see the smoke. Why Custer permitted these fires has not been explained.

Presently the regiment advanced, heralded by a rising dust cloud.

Custer himself reached the knoll sometime in midmorning. He did not climb to the top, but part way up he borrowed an old telescope belonging to one of the Crows. He was unable to see the village, possibly because the air had become less transparent. Nevertheless he accepted the word of Varnum's scouts and said the regiment would proceed, determine the exact location of the hostiles, and attack. This despite a warning from Mitch Bouyer that it was the largest gathering of Indians that he, Bouyer, had seen in more than thirty years.

In 1908, or shortly before, photographer Edward S. Curtis retraced the Seventh's route and climbed a knoll which he thought was the crow's nest. He got there in midafternoon when visibility was reduced by haze, yet he insisted he had a splendid view of the region and could distinguish cabins on the site of the 1876 village. Through a glass he could identify objects smaller than cabins and he was puzzled by Custer's inability to see much, despite the fact that Ree and Crow scouts reported the benchlands brown with ponies and so many teepees that the valley seemed to be draped in a white sheet.

One question asked by latter-day scholars concerns the knoll Curtis climbed, whether it was indeed the crow's nest. He might not have been where he thought he was. Still, he must have been close, just about the same distance from the encampment. Curtis' investigation, therefore, instead of resolving a small mystery has contributed to it, which often happens to Little Bighorn detectives.

Custer rode ahead of the column several times to look again, using an excellent pair of Austrian field glasses borrowed from DeRudio, and through them he was able to make out a few hazy patterns which the scouts assured him were pony herds. DeRudio said Custer never returned these glasses; he kept them, he carried them into the valley, and because they could not be found it must be assumed that a hostile warrior got them.

"Otoe Sioux! Otoe Sioux!" murmured the Rees when told about the decision to attack. Otoe Sioux. Plenty. Too many. Sioux everywhere.

Godfrey saw Custer with an interpreter and several Rees, including Bloody Knife, squatting in a circle. The Rees talked. They were disturbed. Custer looked serious but apparently was not listening. Bloody Knife at last said something, Godfrey did not know what, "that recalled the General from his reverie. . . ."

Meanwhile a sergeant and two troopers had gone back along the regiment's trail in search of several boxes of hard bread that had dropped off the pack train. This bread, if noticed by wandering hostiles, would of course betray the presence of soldiers. Why this bread was not picked up at once is incomprehensible, unless in the darkness it was not missed. Or it may never have been missed, because one report has the sergeant going back for some clothing that slipped off his saddle, at which time he noticed the bread.

Pvt. Coleman wrote in his diary on June 23:

We marched 8 miles and picquetted our horses without unsaddeling them and went to sleep several of the Companies lost suggar Bacon and Coffee we lost one Side of Bacon.

Coleman's dates are unreliable. He might have been referring to the bread-box incident. Regardless of the date, if what he says is true it would appear that the regiment stocked Rosebud Valley with quite a few edibles.

Whatever was lost, the sergeant surprised several Indians gathered around a box which one of them was trying to open with a hatchet. He and his troopers began shooting. The Indians hopped on their ponies and dashed away.

This incident concerning the lost bread often is used to justify Custer's hasty assault. No longer could he wait until Terry and Gibbon were positioned; by that time the Indians would have fled. Not until years later was it learned that the Indians who found this bread were not Sioux. They were Cheyennes under Little Wolf whose tiny band of seven lodges had been en route to the encampment. When they crossed the regiment's path they were more puzzled than alarmed. They could not believe that soldiers would attack such an enormous village. They followed at a discreet distance, keeping well hidden. After hearing gunfire they peeped over the divide. Everything looked all right so they came down from the hills cautiously, not sure what had happened, and were almost killed by furious Sans Arcs who accused them of having guided the soldiers. Thus the famous breadbox meant absolutely nothing. By the time Little Wolf's Cheyennes reached the village Custer was dead.

In 1939 an Oglala named Drags the Rope told a different story. Those who discovered the bread were Sioux, he claimed, and the one attempting to pry open the box was a ten-year-old nephew of Sitting Bull named Deeds. This boy was killed by the troopers. So said Drags the Rope.

Whatever the identity of these Indians—Sioux or Cheyenne—everybody assumed they were from the Little Bighorn camp, which meant that the regiment's presence would not be a secret much longer. Accordingly, if Custer wanted the advantage of surprise he must attack at once. Yet if he was concerned about being detected, why did he permit campfires that morning? Why did he allow whistling, hallooing, frying pans banging against saddles during the night march?

Perhaps he thought the hostiles could not escape, no matter what. Terry and Gibbon were up north, Crow territory lay to the west, while the Seventh Cavalry approached from the southeast. Before launching the attack he would send Major Reno to block the south while he himself swept down from the east. Where could the enemy go?

Or it may be that he meant to scare them, drive them north in the direction of Terry.

Or maybe, convinced of success, he felt indifferent. He never had known defeat.

In 1904 one survivor wrote to historian Brady: "From the hour we left the

Rosebud . . . his old-time restless energy had returned, and he seemed to think of nothing but to reach and strike the Indians."

Another described the anticipation: ". . . we moved along rapidly feeling that there was something ahead of us that we must see."

They traveled rapidly indeed. Sgt. Ryan stated in his memoirs that the fast gait loosened a number of packs, but instead of stopping to lash them securely in place the ropes were cut—undoubtedly at Custer's order—allowing this equipment to fall beside the trail.

So they came to the divide and passed over without hesitation.

Not long after this, about noon, Custer and the half-breed scout Mitch Bouyer exchanged a few words. Bouyer said they would find more Indians than they could handle. Custer said if he was afraid he could stay behind. Bouyer replied that he would go wherever Custer went, but if they did enter that valley neither of them would come out alive. Bloody Knife, who was present, understood this exchange; and by some accounts—which may or may not be true—after reflecting upon the situation for a moment he glanced up at the sun and signaled with his hands: "I shall not see you go down behind the hills tonight."

Scout Billy Jackson says it happened, and as he read Bloody Knife's hands: ". . . I almost choked. I felt that he knew his end was near, that there was no escaping it. I turned and looked the other way."

This was nine days before an important date, July 4, especially important in 1876 because of the centennial. It is known that Custer and several of his officers wanted to attend the opening of the Philadelphia Centennial Exposition—which some troopers thought was the reason he pressed forward. He and his friends would get to the fair on time if the power of the Sioux could be broken quickly. Such an explanation of the forced march, however absurd, might be true; but a less frivolous reason must not be overlooked. Not only was 1876 the centennial, it was an election year and the Democratic convention was just about to open in St. Louis. A messenger could ride from the Little Bighorn to the Bozeman telegraph office in two days, which meant that news of a victory would reach the delegates while presidential nominees were being selected.

At least that would be what Custer assumed. In fact the telegraph line, which stretched for miles through hostile territory, seems to have been temporarily *hors de combat*. A single Indian could break the wire at any moment so it should have been out of service practically all the time, but Elizabeth says Indians never molested the singing wire. One does not interfere with powerful medicine. Well, in the neighborhood of Bismarck and Fort Lincoln this might have been true, though not elsewhere. After raiding Julesburg in 1863 some ecstatic Cheyennes cavorted by the light of a telegraph pole bonfire, and George Bent says the poles occasionally were chopped down to make bonfires for scalp dances.

About the Bozeman telegraph line there are conflicting reports. Muggins Taylor reached Bozeman on July 3 with a dispatch from General Terry containing news of the disaster, but this news was bottled up, so to speak, for two days. The question is why. There is speculation that the wire might have been up while the operator was down. In other words, the telegrapher may have undertaken to celebrate Independence Day with such enthusiasm that he himself fell *hors de combat* not long after Muggins cantered out of the wilderness.

Capt. D. W. Benham, commanding Seventh Infantry at Fort Ellis, addressed the Assistant Adjutant General, Military Division of the Missouri, Chicago, Illinois, on July 5. A scout from General Terry's command had arrived at Fort Ellis with important dispatches for division headquarters. Capt. Benham personally took this material to the Bozeman telegraph office and was there informed that the line to Pleasant Valley was open:

> On the 4th of July I went to town to see if the telegrams above referred to had been sent and found the telegraph office closed.
>
> This afternoon on visiting Bozeman, I inquired if the telegrams left at the office on the 3rd had been sent and was informed that they had been forwarded by mail this morning.
>
> I deem this neglect of duty and criminal negligence on the part of the telegraph operator and report it accordingly.
>
> If telegraph rates are charged on the dispatches above referred to between Bozeman and Helena, the bill should be repudiated and proceedings instituted. . . .

In any case, the redoubtable Seventh, flanked by Crow and Arikara scouts, accompanied by a few civilians—mule packers, Lonesome Charley, kid brother Boston, nephew Armstrong "Autie" Reed, and correspondent Mark Kellogg who would describe the triumph—early Sunday afternoon, June 25, this undefeated regiment paused about twelve miles southeast of Sitting Bull's village to collect itself and hear the general's instructions. Counting Indian scouts, guides, and packers, Custer led approximately 675 men.

At this point he split the troops, a decision which has caused more argument among strategists than anything else the general ever did. Numerous explanations have been offered, the simplest being that he did not know just where the hostiles were. From the knoll he had been told where to look, but even through a telescope and/or DeRudio's field glasses he could not make out anything definite. Therefore it seemed logical to sweep the area by spreading his force.

It has also been suggested that he was a victim of West Point indoctrination. There he had studied European marshals who knew how to pinch an army at the waist or nail its feet to the ground while battering the head, and what succeeded in France or Russia or Poland or Italy ought to work equally well in Montana. After all, a similar approach succeeded in Oklahoma when he wiped out Black Kettle's village.

Pvt. Charles Windolph happened to be nearby and heard Benteen say: "Hadn't we better keep the regiment together, General? If this is as big a camp as they say, we'll need every man we have."

Custer replied: "You have your orders."

Those orders directed Benteen with three companies to search the badlands to their left. Reno with three companies would proceed down the valley, cross the Little Bighorn and attack. Custer himself with five companies would follow Reno, prepared to support the assault one way or another, depending on how things developed. Capt. McDougall with one company was ordered to stay behind with the slow, vulnerable pack train.

At just about this time the Crow scout Half Yellow Face—known also as Big Belly—may have echoed the grim premonition of Bloody Knife. "You and I," he said to Custer, "are both going home today by a road that we do not know." Half Yellow Face did not speak English and Custer did not speak Crow, which is why cautious historians doubt the story; but such a message may be expressed without words, and Custer did use sign language pretty well. Half Yellow Face might have delivered this prophecy, which Custer understood. If so, he ignored it. He had not traveled all the way from Bismarck to be dissuaded from his purpose by the gloomy demeanor of a painted savage.

That the Great Father in Washington was planning to disrupt the traditional pattern of Indian life seems to have been understood perfectly by these wild Sioux and Cheyennes. That being the case, they meant to resist. They would resist with utmost bitterness. "Custer's Indian scouts could smell all this on the prairie breeze," observed historian John Gray, "but were powerless to communicate their perceptions to insensitive and sometimes contemptuous soldier-whites."

Now, on the downward slope, in accordance with Custer's decision, the Seventh split into four parts.

Ree and Crow scouts ahead of the advancing troops discovered a lodge embellished with hieroglyphics. They stopped to investigate.

Inside this lodge on a scaffold lay the body of a Sans Arc, Old She-Bear, who had taken a bullet through the hips during the battle with Crook. He had been carried from the field still alive, but when it seemed he might be dying he was put down. He rested for several days, nursed by his wife and relatives. On the day before Custer's scouts found this lodge two of Old She-Bear's male relatives killed a badger, scooped out the entrails, and allowed the blood to congeal in the cavity until it formed a sanguine mirror which would reflect an image of the wounded man. Hassrick quoted Chief Arnold Iron Shell on this method of divination: "Should he see himself as he is, he knows he will die young. But if he sees himself as an old man with white hair, he cries 'Hye, hye' thanking the spirits. Now he knows he can risk getting many coup and will live long to die with a cane in his hand."

The wife and relatives of Old She-Bear noticed that he was dismayed by what he saw.

During the night he died. They dressed him in buckskin, painted his face red, and laid him on the scaffold. The widow gashed her legs and chopped off her braids. After leaving meat and soup beside the body, and painting the outside of the lodge with sacred symbols, they loaded their travois and continued downstream.

A Ree scout named Red Bear said that when he approached this lodge he saw other scouts striking it with their quirts, so he did the same. A scout named Red Feather went inside and drank the soup and ate some of the meat.

The Rees were still at this lodge when Custer arrived. He got very angry. He spoke to them mostly through signs: "I told you to dash on and stop for nothing. You have disobeyed me. Move to one side and let the soldiers pass you in the charge. If any man of you is not brave, I will take away his weapons and make a woman of him." One scout talked back. He told Custer that if he did the same thing to all of his soldiers it would take a long time. The other scouts laughed. Then they told Custer they were hungry for battle.

Benteen, following orders, had trotted off to the left with companies D, H, and K. The last he saw of Custer's battalion was Lt. Algernon Smith's gray horse company at a dead gallop.

During the 1879 inquiry into Reno's conduct Benteen testified that he did not think Custer had any plan. He said his orders were to go "valley hunting ad infinitum." He was sent off to look for Indians, pitch into them if they existed, and let Custer know. If no Indians cropped up in the first valley he should proceed to the next, to the next, and so on. He said he might have ridden all the way to Fort Benton. And if his three companies had been unlucky enough to meet a large force of Indians they would have been wiped out. "I understood it as a rather senseless order. . . ." He rode ten or fifteen miles in a southwesterly direction, uphill, downhill, uphill—"the horses were fast giving out"—but finally told himself that Indians were too smart to struggle across such rough country and it was time to turn around. He therefore gave the command "Right Oblique!" and angled toward the valley.

Reno said much the same: "There was no plan communicated to us; if one existed, the subordinate commanders did not know about it. . . . I do not think there was any plan."

Custer's logic is inscrutable. One military analyst said he seemed to reach decisions according to the striding of his mount. Very seldom did he discuss a problem with subordinates; he preferred to give orders.

Why he thought he could accomplish with a single regiment what would have been a difficult job for the entire army—why he thought he could pull it off is a puzzle that fascinates every student of this campaign. He had listened to knowledgeable scouts and he had read their faces. Bloody Knife understood beyond doubt that this would be the end of the trail. Mitch Bouyer, too, had made things quite clear. Maybe he felt no plan was necessary because of "Custer's luck." He was known to the public and to his officers as a lucky man. He himself alluded to it, not altogether as a joke. During the Civil War several horses were killed between his knees, yet he never was hurt. Bullets obligingly curled around him and always he seemed to be at the right place, at the right instant, to be noticed by superiors. Of course the gods must look upon him with approbation. If not, how could he have risen to such high rank with such ease?

Theodore Davis did not see much of Custer, but saw enough during the Hancock expedition to recognize a fatal weakness: "Endowed by nature with a confidence in himself which was never boastfully exploited, and a believer that the future would surely unfold a continuation of the successful past— Custer's luck, his talismanic guard was trusted by him all too blindly. . . ."

Crazy Horse called it something else. Crazy Horse tied a red-backed hawk on his head, wore magic pebbles, painted hailstones on his chest, and sprinkled his pony with dust, but it was all the same. Luck. Medicine. They were hatched in the same nest, these two.

Thus, chaperoned by Lady Luck, Custer advanced. At worst, by assaulting this congregation of feathered savages he would lose his life and the lives of everybody who followed him. A less disagreeable script included failure, accompanied by the humiliating necessity of defending himself until Gibbon and Terry arrived. But a third possibility must have obscured such lugubrious thoughts. This third possibility foresaw his regiment scattering the most dangerous horde of Indians ever gathered on the American continent. If that should be so, then he—George Armstrong Custer—would ride in triumph through the streets of Washington like Alexander through Persepolis.

Two or three decades after this resolute march Teddy Roosevelt would express the conviction of all *beau sabreurs*—himself, Custer, and the rest—when opposed by overwhelming force: "Far better it is to dare mighty things . . . than to take rank with those poor spirits who neither enjoy much nor suffer much, because they live in the gray twilight that knows not victory nor defeat." Given old Iron Butt's character, that must have been what he was thinking.

Just after his regiment left the Yellowstone he seemed less confident than usual; but then, as one survivor noted, his burning energy returned, he wanted only to reach and strike the Indians. They would start up like terrified quail. They would throw aside their buffalo robes and drop their horn spoons and knock over the kettles in a frantic effort to escape.

The last time any of the survivors saw him alive, with two or three questionable exceptions, was shortly after he turned up into the eastern hills. Reno's men in the valley saw him wave his hat, presumably to encourage them. Then he spurred his horse and rode out of sight.

That is the popular belief, one of the Little Bighorn's favorite snapshots. It may have happened. The trouble is, he would have been a long way from Reno's troops. Today if one stands where he is said to have been when he waved his hat—if one stands there looking into the valley it is easy to pick out cattle, people, and lesser creatures, provided one looks down at an acute angle. But the valley is wide and a century ago the river looped farther west than it does today and Reno's troops were beyond the river. From such a distance men with normal eyesight could make out a rider on the bluff. As for identifying him—maybe. A person can be recognized by the way he stands or moves, or by some other characteristic too subtle to be articulated, long before he comes close enough to be identified by his features; so perhaps Reno's troops did see Custer—although this excited man could have been Mitch Bouyer. The Crow scout Curly, interviewed again and again, told Walter Camp in 1908 that he and Bouyer looked down at Reno's command fighting in the valley and Two Bodies Bouyer began to shout and wave his hat.

The last wasichu to hear Custer's voice was an emigrant Italian trumpeter, Giovanni Martini, who died in Brooklyn in 1922. Martini—called John Martin—had not been in the States very long and did not speak much English. He probably enlisted because jobs were hard to get after the panic of 1873 when it was starve, stand in line for soup, or visit a recruiting depot. He once served as a drummer boy for Garibaldi, so the prospect of army life in America might not have seemed too frightening. Whatever his reason, the summer of '76 found him wearing a blue coat in the middle of Montana. He belonged to Benteen's H Company, but on that fateful day he had been detailed to serve as Custer's orderly.

Martini said Custer's battalion paused on the ridge for about ten minutes while officers studied the village through field glasses.

These tribes camped in six circles, each circle open to the east. Some Indians later insisted there were seven or eight circles, which would include a few Assiniboin, Brulé, and Santee lodges; but it is generally thought there were six self-governing tribes. At the extreme north, the direction in which they had been traveling, stood the Cheyenne circle. Southward from the Cheyennes along the west bank of the convoluted river stood the lodges of the Sans Arcs, Miniconjoux, Oglalas, Blackfeet, and Unkpapas.

From the appearance of the lodges Custer's Indian scouts could identify several of these camps, perhaps all of them. Sioux lodges were tall and narrow with a big flap opening at the top, whereas those of the Cheyennes were larger in circumference, shorter, with a small ventilating flap. Even among the Sioux there were differences. Santee lodges—for a reason now lost—were constructed with the poles upside down, butt-end up, and Custer's scouts knew that the Santees invariably camped beside the Unkpapas.

White officers may have perceived little more than one huge irregular village. Through field glasses they could make out women and children but no warriors, which was puzzling. They concluded that the warriors must be out hunting buffalo, there could be no other explanation. This was a nice surprise.

Custer said: "We will go down and make a crossing and capture the village."

It was thought that when the hunters got back they would be obliged to surrender, because if they started to fight they would be shooting at their own families. What Custer and his staff did not know was that the lodges were full of warriors who had stayed up half the night celebrating the victory over Crook. There was much dancing, scalp-dancing by some accounts, although one Cheyenne called it "entirely a social affair for young people."

So, anticipating a bloodless conquest, five companies of the Seventh started downhill.

A few minutes later Martini was dispatched with a message to Captain Benteen. Adjutant Cooke scribbled it on paper, probably because they mistrusted Martini's English:

Come on. Big village.
Be quick. Bring packs.

Custer had sent Benteen off to the left with vague instructions and could not possibly have known where he was at this time—whether he was within ten miles of the pack train—so it is odd that the message should be addressed to Benteen. McDougall had been detailed to escort the mules. If Custer wanted those ammunition packs in a hurry why did he not address a note to McDougall?

Anyway, Martini did as he was ordered, which is all he did. He met Benteen returning from an exploration of the badlands and delivered the note, but in response to Benteen's questions he gave the impression that Custer had things under control, and he neglected to say Reno was fighting for his life. He did, however, deliver to Benteen not only the written message but the text of a most astonishing remark. When Custer at last caught sight of the village—extending perhaps four miles—he studied the encampment through DeRudio's field glasses, then waved his hat to the troops and shouted: "Hurrah, boys, we've got them!" This is what the Italian trumpeter told Benteen the general said. Martini might have been mistaken, confused by a relatively unfamiliar language. If indeed Custer made such a remark after sighting the greatest concentration of militant Indians in the history of North America it sounds like a joke from an old vaudeville routine.

Lt. Edgerly testified that he heard Martini talking to Benteen's orderly. Martini was laughing and telling the orderly it was the biggest village he ever saw and they had caught the Indians off guard and Major Reno was charging and killing everybody. Captain Benteen, who could be less than gracious, subsequently referred to Martini as a "thick-headed, dull-witted Italian, just as much cut out for a cavalryman as he was for a King."

Martini's version of what occurred is quite different. He said he meant to tell Benteen about Reno being in action, but the captain never gave him a chance.

After showing Adjutant Cooke's note to Captain Weir, Benteen tucked it in his pocket. He must have realized at the time, or very soon, that it might become an important scrap of evidence. In a letter to his wife, dated July 4, he told her about this note, quoted it, and said: "I have the original, but it is badly torn and it should be preserved." During Reno's Court of Inquiry in 1879 he produced it, and some time afterward gave it to a friend in Philadelphia, who eventually sold it to a New Jersey collector—although not much of this was public knowledge. For about fifty years the note was presumed to have been lost, incinerated during a fire at Benteen's home. Not until the New Jersey collector's treasures went up for auction did the famous note reappear. An Army colonel learned about it and the slip of paper carrying that anxious message was obtained by the West Point library.

The last man to leave Custer's presence was Martini, but two men of C Company may have seen him from a distance after Martini galloped off with the note. Pvts. Peter Thompson and James Watson were observed climbing out of a ravine. Thompson explained after joining Reno's group on the hilltop that his horse had been unable to keep pace with the others. He said the animal was so exhausted that he dismounted and walked toward the developing battle. Along the way he met Watson whose horse also had played out. The two of them continued on foot. After many perilous adventures during which they resolved to infiltrate the encircling redskins and thus join their comrades at the Last Stand—adventures discredited by competent historians—they made their way to Reno's fortress.

Years later Thompson described his last view of the general:

> . . . it being a very hot day he was in his shirt sleeves; his buckskin pants tucked into his boots; his buckskin shirt fastened to the rear of his saddle; and a broad brimmed cream colored hat on his head, the brim of which was turned up on the right side and fastened by a small hook and eye to its crown. This gave him opportunity to sight his rifle while riding.

These two privates were enrolled in Tom Custer's company, which was annihilated, and they did join Reno's hilltop command. What is uncertain is how far they followed the general and why they turned around—whether their horses did indeed collapse, or whether they disliked the thought of following Custer to the end of the road.

Four Arikara scouts on a ridge east of the river said they could see trails left by Custer's battalion riding through high grass, and they came upon a soldier whose horse was down. The soldier was cursing, pounding the horse's head with his fists and kicking it under the belly. A little farther up the ridge they saw another soldier whose horse had fallen, and this one told them by sign language that he belonged to Custer's command.

Watson and Thompson were not the only men who failed to keep the deadly rendezvous. Quite a few soldiers assigned to Custer's battalion somehow appeared on Reno's hilltop, but with so many officers and non-commissioned officers dead it became impossible to learn why or when these men defected. For instance, twenty-four men from Capt. Yates' F Company joined Reno while the rest died with Custer. This is particularly strange. It might not be puzzling if Yates' company had formed the tail of the column because one man after another could lag behind and ease out of sight, but it appears that Yates may have been leading the way. Certainly he was not the last in line. How could twenty-four men desert in the shadow of old Iron Butt himself?

And had they stayed to fight—along with other defectors—might these companies have survived? Probably not.

Benteen has been criticized by some military analysts because he failed to obey instructions. He received the note, he read it, he thought enough of it to tuck it in a pocket, but he did not get the ammunition packs and rush forward to Custer's aid. Instead, as he approached the battleground after his scouting trip he saw Major Reno's demoralized men attempting to organize a defensive position on the bluff and he chose to join them. This decision assured Custer's death. It would seem, therefore, that Benteen must be condemned; yet if he had tried to carry out the order it is possible his three companies would have been hacked to pieces en route. Then Reno's weakened battalion surely would have collapsed, and when General Terry arrived he would count every single man of the Seventh Cavalry dead.

Benteen explained to the 1879 Court of Inquiry why he did what he did, and his reasoning is equally clear from subsequent remarks. He thought it impossible to obey; to do so would have been suicide. "We were at their hearths and homes," he said, referring to the Sioux, "their medicine was working well, and they were fighting for all the good God gives anyone to fight for."

An effort was made to reach Custer, although nobody knew exactly where he was. Captain Weir, enraged and disgusted by Reno's timidity, left the hilltop bunker without permission and, followed by an orderly, rode northward along the bluffs to see what he could see. Considering that these two men must have been visible to hundreds of Sioux it is surprising that they were not cut off and butchered.

Weir's lieutenant, Edgerly, thought the captain had obtained Reno's permission, so he ordered the entire company to mount. They, too, left the hilltop redoubt.

Weir's company was followed about ten minutes later by Benteen at the head of three companies. Other units came straggling after, apparently because Reno had lost control. Nobody knew just what to do. Reno was supposed to be in charge but Weir had ignored him, and Benteen—although nominally subordinate—became the actual commandant.

Reno partisans argue that he did not initiate a move to join Custer because this would have meant abandoning the wounded. In regard to this, Professor Stewart comments that the problem of wounded men was one for which no adequate provision could be made. In civilized warfare—an obviously contradictory phrase—wounded soldiers could be left in a field hospital which might be occupied by the enemy; but when fighting Indians this would be a death sentence. An Indian thought a battle was not finished until he or his opponent lay dead. The white man's concept of mercy struck him as not only peculiar but cowardly. So the presence of a few casualties could inhibit or paralyze the movement of an entire unit.

It has been argued that Reno might have protected these wounded men with Capt. McDougall's company which was guarding the pack train. Such a maneuver, of course, would further divide an already splintered regiment.

Was Reno mostly concerned about his own scalp? During the night of the twenty-fifth when it seemed the Indians had withdrawn, at least temporarily, he proposed to escape from the hilltop. When asked about the casualties he replied, according to Godfrey, that they must be left behind: "Benteen then told him he wouldn't do it. . . ."

Scholars who think Reno has been treated unfairly are quick to doubt Godfrey's statement. They suspect Godfrey might have invented this confrontation between the two senior officers. Fred Dustin wrote: "I cannot understand WHY an officer of Godfrey's standing should have given out this tale unless afflicted by senile dementia."

Godfrey did not make it up. Benteen wrote to ex-Private Theodore Goldin on January 6, 1892: "I expect Godfrey to say in his article that Reno recommended the abandonment of the wounded on the night of the 25th, and of 'skipping off' with those who could ride; well, so he did, to me, but I killed that proposition in the bud."

Was Benteen telling the truth? Did he himself invent this dialogue? Nobody will ever know.

Why did Reno mark time on the hill? Nobody knows.

It begins to sound like an existentialist movie.

What does seep through the malicious accusations and counter-accusations is that Reno was a not uncommon type of officer: obedient, brave enough, reasonably competent if a superior told him what to do. Left to himself, obliged to resolve some unanticipated difficulty, he might do nothing.

In any event, after Benteen headed north everybody else straggled the same direction, some afoot, carrying wounded friends in slings contrived from horse blankets—dismounted cavalrymen lurching along the ridge with a bloody comrade in the middle.

Just how far north the survivors of these seven companies marched is uncertain, partly because they had disintegrated into a mob of frightened, angry, irresolute, bewildered men held together spasmodically by a recollection of what they were, or were supposed to be, and by a realization that if they dispersed they would be chopped up like raw liver. They advanced—some advanced—more than a mile, which gave them an appalling view of the valley foaming with Sioux and Cheyennes, and they could see a cloud of smoke and dust about three miles farther north on the ridge, where by this time Custer, and every man with him, almost certainly was dead. The shots they could hear probably were made by excited warriors, boys, and old men blasting wasichu corpses.

Many years later Pvt. Edward Pigford of Capt. French's M Company said that he and two other soldiers advanced to a hill from which they actually saw the last stand. The soldiers with him were killed, Pigford said, and he himself was wounded. His story, like others of the genre, is not believed.

When it became apparent to the untidy Reno-Benteen mob that they were beginning to attract attention they retreated toward their first position on the bluff, but Indians caught up with them. Lt. Edgerly had dismounted and when he tried to get back on his horse it kept dancing aside—maybe because bullets were plopping into the dirt. Walter Camp, who interviewed Edgerly, said Indians got to within fifteen feet of him. Fifteen feet! An active man can jump fifteen feet. Allowing for exaggeration—say twenty, thirty, fifty feet— it sounds incredible. His orderly was holding the nervous animal while Edgerly tried to climb aboard and the orderly was smiling. Edgerly noticed this. Later he asked about it. The orderly said he could not help smiling because the Indian marksmanship was so bad.

This is preposterous. Indians a whoop and a jump away were trying unsuccessfully to kill the officer and his orderly thought it was funny.

Well, Edgerly and his bemused assistant escaped without being hit and as they retreated from this exposed position they passed Vincent Charley, the farrier of D Company. He had been shot through the hips. "He looked back at me and I told him to get into a hole and I would form a line and come back and save him."

Edgerly told Captain Weir about this wounded man and the promise to rescue him. Weir answered that he was sorry but they had been ordered to withdraw. Edgerly protested. Weir argued that they had no choice.

After the battle they discovered the farrier's body with a stick rammed down his throat.

Weir seems to have been emotionally ruined by the failure of this attempt to join Custer. He might have felt personally responsible, although it was not in any way his fault. He did everything he could, exceeding his authority to the point of disobedience.

When the Seventh Cavalry survivors were returning to Fort Lincoln the *Far West* stopped at Fort Buford where the Yellowstone enters the Missouri.

From this point most of the able-bodied men marched to Fort Lincoln, and because Major Reno remained aboard the *Far West* the command of this overland march devolved upon Captain Weir. Downstream at Fort Stevenson, where they halted one day for lunch, Weir entered the post. He did not come back, nor did any orders arrive from him until midafternoon when an orderly brought word that the regiment should bivouac two miles east of the fort.

That night, said Lt. E. A. Garlington, a number of officers were invited to supper at the fort, so they went, and stayed a long time. Not until early morning did Weir break up the party. He got into a wagon with a surgeon and some lieutenant identified only as "I." They were going to the regimental camp, but Weir disliked this lieutenant and not long after the wagon left Fort Stevenson he ordered the driver to stop, saying he would not ride with Lt. I. The surgeon objected to Weir's behavior, and the embarrassed lieutenant offered to walk to camp, but it did no good. Weir climbed out, saying he himself would walk. The night was dark and they quickly lost sight of him. They expected him to come back in a few minutes, but he did not, so they went looking for him. The lieutenant found him in a nearby stream. He had jumped in or had fallen in and had lost his hat and was swimming around. The lieutenant extended a hand but Weir refused it, saying he would drown before he would accept any favors. Only when the surgeon arrived would he permit himself to be helped out.

Next morning when the regiment continued its march to Fort Lincoln he rode in front, "a sorry spectacle." His clothes were wet and wrinkled and he wore a strange little narrow-brimmed hat which looked like a small boy's hat. The band of the hat was missing, giving it a sugarloaf shape. He rode a very handsome horse called Jake, and Garlington observes that on this occasion even Jake seemed humiliated by the appearance of his rider and commanding officer.

The column did not reach Fort Lincoln until the last of September or the first days of October. Weir immediately was ordered to New York on recruiting duty.

From St. Louis he wrote to Custer's widow: "You know I can't tell you now but will sometime tell it to you. . . . I have so much to tell you that I will tell you nothing now. . . ."

A month later he wrote to her from New York: "I know if we were all of us alone in the parlor, at night, the curtains all down and everybody else asleep, one or the other of you would make me tell you everything I know. . . ."

Such passages emanate like ectoplasm from a haunted mind.

Less than six months after the battle he died. He was thirty-eight. His physician told Elizabeth that when Weir arrived in New York he was depressed and nervous. He spent most of his time in one room, avoiding everybody. Toward the end he became so nervous that he was unable to swallow. Garlington said he died of pneumonia. Others ascribed his death to melancholia and congestion of the brain.

While responding to a number of questions posed by Colonel W. A. Graham, Godfrey described his first visit to the Custer battlefield. He seems to have been startled by the colors: "The marble white bodies, the somber brown of the dead horses . . . tufts of reddish brown grass on the almost ashy white soil. . . ." He observed that from a distance the stripped men resembled white boulders, and he heard Weir exclaim: "Oh, how white they look! How white!"

More than two hundred bodies and about seventy animal carcasses had been exposed to the June sun for two or three days when burial parties went to work. Pvts. Berry and Slaper remember being assigned to this duty on the twenty-seventh, Varnum went to work on the twenty-eighth, and there are reports of burial on the twenty-ninth. Soldiers detailed to hide the remains were overcome by nausea, vomiting and retching while they tried to dig graves, so the business was simplified. Bodies thought to be those of officers were nudged into shallow trenches. Each officer's name was written on a slip of paper which was inserted into an empty cartridge and the cartridge was hammered into the top of a stake or a length of lodge pole set beside the trench.

Those thought to be enlisted men were hastily concealed beneath sagebrush or a few shovels of dirt. Some attempt was made to identify them, although not much. Few could be recognized. Very often the features were distorted by fright or anguish. The faces of some had been pounded with clubs or stones until they were bloated masks of congealed blood encrusted with feeding insects. Pvt. Coleman, searching for a trooper he had known, said all were "horably mutilated." The rage of the Indians extended even to horses, which he found "cut and Sclashed." Pvt. Goldin said most of the corpses were so mortified they could not be handled; several times he watched members of a burial squad take hold of a man's arm only to have it slide away.

Lt. James Calhoun, Adonis of the Seventh and Custer's brother-in-law, was recognized by a distinctive dental filling. Capt. Moylan, who got a look at him during the burial, wrote to Maggie that neither his face nor his limbs had been disfigured. Perhaps. But it is more likely that Moylan was trying to comfort the widow.

Beyond doubt many corpses were abused, although some troopers who visited the field either did not notice this—which sounds impossible—or they justified it. Sgt. Knipe did not recall any scalped men and thought there had been no unnecessary disfiguration, just enough to kill the wounded: "What seemed to be a common method of doing this was to chop open the head across the forehead or across the eyes. . . ."

Pvt. Jacob Adam viewed the scene differently: "One dead body had one leg nicely cut off, as with a sharp knife, at the hip joint. It was done so carefully that the bowels had not come out. Bodies were mutilated in every conceivable way, some being set up on elbows and knees and the hind parts shot full of arrows. . . ."

Pvt. George Glease located the remains of his former bunkmate, Tom "Boss" Tweed, split up the crotch. One of Tweed's legs had been thrown across his shoulder. "He was shot with arrows in both eyes. A wounded horse lay near him groaning, and we knocked him in the head with a bloody ax. . . ."

These axes had been distributed by the government.

The mutilation of Custer's troops may be explained partly by the grief and bewilderment these Indians felt. They could not understand why soldiers pursued them when all they ever wanted was to be left alone so that they might live as they had lived for centuries: hunting, fishing, trailing the munificent buffalo. They failed to see why they should live in one place all year, why they should become farmers when they had been hunters. They did not see how the land could be divided, allotted, owned. They thought the earth was created for everybody, that it could not be appropriated by individuals or groups, and to destroy vegetation by plowing was to contradict the obvious plan of a supreme deity.

Wasichus, convinced of their status as the Almighty's Chosen, followed these people insistently—threatening, promising, smiling, cajoling—and far from the settlements Custer's regiment fell upon a summer camp. So the squaws, weeping for a dead husband or a dead brother or a son, hacked at naked white corpses with butcher knives and axes, lopped off fingers, hands, penises, and battered the skulls of dying cavalrymen with stone mallets.

Whittaker's famous biography of General Custer was produced with astonishing speed, and because the author kneels in perpetual adoration it is a silly tribute. Once in a while, however, a thought unfolds, and at such times his book becomes interesting. The abuse of corpses shocked him, forcing him to reflect. He observes that white men are not merely horrified but puzzled by such behavior, which almost never occurred during red-white battles of the eighteenth century, nor during the early part of the nineteenth.

> Catlin, Bonneville, Kendall, Lewis and Clark, and all those early voyagers who crossed the plains, down to the days of Fremont, record no such atrocities in their few contests with Indians, and leave, on the whole, a decidedly favorable impression of the savage character. At the present day, there is no doubt that such things are common, and the real reason is not far to seek, judging from the circumstances surrounding both periods. I am very strongly inclined to ascribe these mutilations to a mixture of *hatred* and *contempt*, produced by the different nature of the present contests from those waged up to the year 1850. In the past century in the woods, and up to 1850 on the plains, the Indians were principally fought by frontiersmen and veteran regulars, men of physical strength generally superior to the Indians, better shots, nearly as good riders, and their superiors in hand to hand fights. Above all things, savages respect physical prowess and courage, and there are strong indications that they were so proud to take the scalp of a brave white man, in the days when they respected him, that they scorned to otherwise mutilate his body when dead.
>
> Now the case is reversed. They know that, man to man, almost all the green recruits in the regular army *fear them*, and the frontiersmen they meet and mutilate are no longer brave *hunters*, but, in their eyes, despicable *tillers of the ground*. Hating and despising these men as cowards and plodders, yet finding themselves, slowly but surely, yielding to these loathed creatures, they take the same satisfaction in hacking them to pieces that many white men and boys do in beating a snake.

Tom Custer was treated with particular malevolence. He lay face down, bristling with arrows, the back of his skull smashed. His abdomen was slit both horizontally and vertically so the entrails emerged. His throat had been cut and the scalp almost completely ripped off, leaving just a few hairs at the nape of the neck. Interpreter Fred Gerard said an arrow had been shot into the top of his head with such force that it penetrated the brain and could not be pulled out. His decomposing features were unrecognizable, but one arm displayed a fancy tattoo of the American flag, the goddess of liberty, and his initials: TWC.

Sgt. Ryan said the skull was "crushed in as flat as a man's hand." Ryan guessed it might be the work of squaws, "as we found a number of stone mallets made from round stones covered with a rawhide handle. The Indians used these in camp for breaking buffalo bone to get the marrow out. . . ."

Godfrey wrote that when he looked down on the naked back of this man he suspected it might be Tom because they used to go swimming together and the form looked familiar.

McDougall said Tom was identified by a Civil War bullet scar on his left cheek and by "a split forefinger"—although he did not explain this curious injury.

Because Tom lay face down he may have been killed by a Cheyenne. George Bent states that it was bad luck to leave an enemy facing the sky. After a battle with Crows in 1865, he says, an old Cheyenne dismounted and turned the dead Crows over so they faced the ground. However, Bent also states that he had seen white men left just as they dropped, such was the bitterness his people felt against the whites.

Wooden Leg described a body that might have been Tom. This soldier fascinated the Indians because his breast and both arms were tattooed. They thought he might have been a soldier chief because of these marks—especially an eagle with outstretched wings—and because he had worn a buckskin suit. But this man's head was cut off, whereas Tom Custer, despite ferocious handling, had not been decapitated, so the wasichu wearing a painted eagle probably was somebody else.

Two other corpses attracted the Indians: Isaiah because of his black skin, and a soldier with gold spots on his teeth. "We did not understand how this metal got there," said Wooden Leg, "nor why it was there."

Downhill from Tom and the general lay Boston Custer, close to the body of his eighteen-year-old nephew, Harry Armstrong "Autie" Reed. Both young men had expected to watch their dashing relatives cut a swath through the infested valley like angels of God. Boston was stripped, except for white cotton socks. Godfrey observed that several bodies were partly dressed, wearing trousers or an undershirt or socks, but invariably the man's name had been cut from the cloth. These marked snippets could only have been regarded as Medicine, yet they do not seem to have been preserved like other charms.

An 1875 photograph of Boston shows a tubercular youth with pallid skin and prominent cheekbones. Excepting his color he could almost pass for Sioux. His lungs were weak and the family hoped that a season on the dry plains might improve his health, so he was employed as a civilian guide although he had never visited the region. He wrote to his mother on June 21 that he wanted to pick up a couple of Indian ponies and "a buffalo robe for Nev." Nev being another brother, Nevin, whose health seems to have been worse than his own. He did not know how many hostiles they would meet. Scouts who had seen trails left by their lodges thought there must be at least eight hundred. "But, be the number great or small, I hope I can truthfully say when I get back, that one or more were sent to the happy hunting-grounds."

Canadian W. W. Cooke, the general's adjutant, known to irreverent troopers as The Queen's Own, was scalped twice—the second scalp being one of his prodigiously long flowing sidewhiskers—Dundrearies they were called, after pompous Lord Dundreary in *Our American Cousin*, which was the comedy Lincoln went to see that night at Ford's theater.

A cavalryman at the Washita said Lt. Cooke vanished when the firing started and did not show up until the village was secure, but nothing substantiates this. Most reports describe him as reliable and brave. Custer praised his gallantry and habitually misspelled his name "Cook." In 1864 when he joined the American army some clerk wrote the name as it was pronounced and Cooke did not bother to have this mistake corrected until 1872. Obviously he did not much care. All the same it is odd. He must have noticed the misspelling quite often, yet never said a word.

He was deadly with a carbine or pistol; he and Capt. Thomas French probably were the best shots in the regiment. Cooke was also very fast afoot, which sounds irrelevant but is not. Athletic contests lighten the monotony of garrison life and men look upon athletes with more respect than women do, so the adjutant's speed undoubtedly strengthened his authority. And what a spectacle he must have been as he bounded across the prairie with those glossy black Dundrearies streaming in the breeze. He celebrated his thirtieth birthday in May of 1876, either at Fort Lincoln or en route to the end of the world. Years after the battle Walter Camp interviewed an Arikara named Kanauch or Hunach, who was shown photographs of various officers. He recognized most of them and talked about them, but when he saw Cooke's picture he kissed it, saying this man's very breath was kindness.

Wooden Leg, who sailed around the battlefield like a grasshopper, probably scalped Lt. Cooke's face. He said he noticed a dead soldier about thirty years old with a full mustache and a long beard growing from both cheeks. After telling a companion that this was a new kind of scalp he skinned one side of the man's face and tied the hair to an arrow shaft. Back in the village nobody paid much attention to this prize until his grandmother, who lived alone in a willow hut, asked what he had brought home. He offered it to her. Raw scalps customarily were turned over to women, who would prepare them for exhibit and sometimes sing of their champion's accomplishments while dancing with the scalps suspended from a pole, but Wooden Leg's grandmother did not like the look of this. She screamed.

They talked about it for a while. They also discussed what he had done on the battlefield. She thought his clothes—a Seventh Cavalry uniform—looked nice. Just which trooper gave up this uniform is not known, except that it could not have been Cooke, who was fairly large. Wooden Leg himself was big, well over six feet tall, and the uniform belonged to a smaller man.

Finally his grandmother accepted the scalp and carried it into her hut.

The next day, as Terry's army approached, the Sioux and Cheyennes dismantled their village and late that afternoon began traveling toward the Bighorn Mountains "in savage and majestic splendor," still hoping to escape the persistent bluecoats. The movement was rapid but orderly. They chose to avoid further conflict but they were not alarmed. In fact, a number of young braves wanted to stay around long enough to eliminate General Terry.

That night they rested for several hours without setting up their lodges.

At daylight they resumed traveling.

By the second night they were twenty miles south near the present town of Lodge Grass. Here the Cheyennes staged a victory celebration, although the important scalp dance did not take place until a few days later on the banks of Rosebud Creek. Various bands of Sioux danced with the Cheyennes, but Sitting Bull's Unkpapas did not because they thought it was too soon—a time for grief rather than rejoicing. No women took part in this celebration. Many of them could scarcely walk, having gashed their legs in mourning.

Quite a few women did participate in the scalp dance on Rosebud Creek, among them Wooden Leg's grandmother. She bragged about her grandson and waved the strange trophy, but afterward she flung it aside, as though troubled by such an unnatural scalp.

Cooke's right thigh had been punctured, which was how Sioux warriors marked a dead enemy—a fact Dr. Bell admittedly did not know when he analyzed the corpse of Sgt. Wyllyams near Fort Wallace. Some ethnologists believe it was traditional to pierce the left thigh. Left, right, no matter. Because one thigh was symbolically cut it appears that Cooke was killed by a Sioux who scalped him. Then Wooden Leg arrived.

Captain Myles Keogh had not been disfigured. He lay naked except for his socks, with a Catholic medal around his neck which usually is identified as an *Agnus Dei*, perhaps because Agnus Dei is a familiar phrase. Romantics describe it as a cross hanging from a golden chain. Almost certainly this medal was kept in a small leather purse or sheath and Keogh most likely wore it suspended by a leather thong or length of cord. It was the *Medaglia di Pro Petri Sede* awarded to him by Pope Pius IX for service with the Papal Army.

Captain Edward Luce does not think this medal was found on Keogh's body, but Lt. Godfrey—who was present—told artist E. S. Paxson in 1896 that it had not been removed. Trumpeter Martini, the last man to get out, insisted Benteen took the medal; but Martini did not care much for Benteen.

Certain historians provide Keogh with two medals: one around his neck, another in his pocket. This is conceivable because the pope awarded him, as a mark of special favor, the Cross of the Order of St. Gregory—which perhaps begot that romantic image of a cross suspended from a golden chain. Whatever the exact truth, most scholars agree that he had the pope's medal and that it prevented his corpse from being abused. Now this sounds illogical because there must have been no shortage of Catholics in a battalion sprinkled with Irish names, many of whom could have been wearing religious emblems; but the *Pro Petri Sede* was larger, more impressive. Then, too, he carried it in some sort of leather pouch just as Indians kept powerful tokens in leather bags.

They did take his custom-made English pistol, which turned up in Canada about a year later. Although the brave who owned the pistol would not sell it, at least four items belonging to Keogh have been recovered: his watch, his gauntlets, a photo of himself wearing the medal, and a blood-spotted photograph of Captain McDougall's sister.

Without doubt this man was created for the astonishment and delight of ladies; every picture of him projects a Mephistophelian sexuality. McDougall must have worried about his sister, and Benteen wrote to Mrs. Benteen while aboard the *Far West*:

My Frabbie Darling,
Just one month ago—today—at just about this time of day, Genl. Custer and his command commenced the attack. . . . I had a queer dream of Col. Keogh the night before last, 'twas that he would insist upon undressing in the room in which you were. I had to give him a "dressing" to cure him of the fancy. I rarely ever thought of the man—and 'tis queer I should have dreamt of him. We are steaming along very slowly. . . .

The Irish gallant may have excited ladies and given their husbands nightmares, but to most troopers he was a pain in the rump. Enlisted men describe him as drunken, insolent, and abusive. His swagger stick was a stout cane with a silver dog's head for a handle and he used it one way or another on subordinates who displeased him. He radiates a sense of electric violence which must have transmitted itself like a current because Keogh's I Company was known as the Wild I.

His circuitous but inevitable journey to the Little Bighorn began in southern Ireland on March 25, 1840. His family hated England with Catholic passion and Myles' favorite book is said to have been *Charles O'Malley, The Irish Dragoon*. Such a childhood may beget a pacifistic adult or a hotspur, but very seldom an adult insensible to military business.

Keogh could hardly wait to prove himself. After two years at St. Patrick's College he embarked for Africa as a soldier of fortune. Then the pope called upon Catholics everywhere to protect the Holy See and by August of 1860 Keogh was a second lieutenant at the pope's side. For gallantry against an overwhelming Piedmontese force he received the *Medaglia* which he carried ever afterward.

Because the Civil War promised excitement he emigrated to the United States, joined the Union volunteers, and again distinguished himself. Major General George Thomas, commandant of the Department of the Cumberland, wrote to General Halleck on April 25, 1865: "Major Keogh, Aide-de-Camp, to Major General Stoneman, went forward with a detachment of the 12th Kentucky Volunteer Cavalry—surprised and routed the rebels, near Salisbury,—killing 9 and capturing 68. Much credit is due Major Keogh. . . ." Demobilization left him unemployed, but soon he got back into uniform and by the summer of '66 he was a captain in the Regular Army. He missed the Washita because he had been assigned to General Sully's staff, so it was not until one Sunday in 1876 that he fulfilled the expectations of childhood.

The spot where he fell has been deduced from an 1877 photograph of a marker left by the burial party. The sergeants of his company lay near him, not far from a cluster of wild cherry bushes, and some historians theorize that a volley delivered by several Indians hiding in these bushes might have killed all of them at once.

Keogh and his horse Comanche probably were crippled by a single bullet. The reason for thinking so is that a bullet passed through Comanche, emerging at about the spot where a rider's knee would have been, and Keogh's left knee was shattered. Such a reconstruction is fragile, but there is also the testimony of a Sioux named Little Soldier who watched a bluecoat—thought to have been Keogh—kneeling and shooting from between the legs of a horse. This bluecoat died with the reins still clutched in one hand, a fact which may have prevented Indians from taking his horse. Little Soldier thought the wounded animal would recover, and he needed a horse, but he refused to touch one whose reins were held by a dead man.

Keogh has remained unsung by the public, although bits and pieces of evidence indicate that whatever his faults he must have been one of the Seventh's most redoubtable fighters. Years after the battle one of Gibbon's scouts named Will Logan insisted he had found Captain Keogh's body just outside a triangle of three war ponies. Logan described Keogh's death as it was described to him by various Indians. The wild Irishman was the last to fall. He stood alone, facing a charge: "pow-pow-pow-pow-pow-pow . . . came six lightning pistol shots from the triangle and six red warriors died in the air. . . . Like the flame of a coal blazed his eyes. His teeth glistened like a fighting grizzly. . . ." This is magnificent writing, of course, and Indian testimony does point to one wasichu of enormous courage—quite possibly the aggressive, rude, alcoholic, and somewhat melancholy soldier from suburban Limerick.

He or Major Alfred Gibbs suggested that the Seventh have its own band. Whoever came up with the idea, Custer approved—personally contributing $50 toward the cost of instruments—and it was either Keogh or Custer who proposed "Garry Owen" as the regimental marching tune.

"Garry Owen" is an old Irish quick-step that has been traced back to about 1800 and is known to have been used by several Irish regiments, including the Fifth Royal Lancers whose members regarded it as a suitable drinking song. Garryowen, being Gaelic for Owen's garden, is a suburb of Limerick and there, close by Keogh's birthplace, these rowdy lancers were stationed. Furthermore, Elizabeth said her husband first began humming and whistling the tune at Fort Riley not long after the Seventh was organized, and she thought Keogh had something to do with it. Still, when Custer was a boy he enjoyed the novels of one Charles Lever who often wrote about the Napoleonic wars. Among Mr. Lever's protagonists we find O'Malley, the dragoon who fascinated Keogh, but there is also *Jack Hinton, the Guardsman*—a favorite of young Custer—and in this dashing adventure a British regimental band strikes up "that well-remembered air." So a tiny knot remains to be untied.

However stirring "Garry Owen" might be if rendered with bagpipes and all, the lyrics evoke little else than the virginal camaraderie of pipe-smoking undergraduates worshipping the whiffenpoof:

> Let Bacchus' sons be not dismayed
> But join with me each jovial blade;
> Come booze and sing and lend your aid
> To help me with the chorus.
>   CHORUS
> Instead of Spa we'll drink down ale.
> And pay the reck'ning on the nail;
> No man for debt shall go to gaol
> From Garry Owen in glory.

There are at least four additional verses concerned with street brawls, stout hearts, shattering windows, chasing the sheriff, and otherwise extolling the masculinity of Garry Owen lancers. The poet Thomas Moore supplied fresh lyrics—smiling eyes, beams of joy, billows of woe, a green isle—and retitled it "The Daughters of Erin." Moore is celebrated for "The Harp That Once Through Tara's Halls" and "Believe Me, If All Those Endearing Young Charms," and at his best he is a fine romantic poet, but "The Daughters of Erin" is not among his best.

The last tune played by the regimental band for Custer's benefit was "Garry Owen." Excepting the indispensable buglers, all Seventh Cavalry musicians stayed at the Powder River Depot. They were posted on a knoll and when their comrades marched off to destiny they struck up that inspiriting tune, which brought a hearty cheer, said Pvt. Goldin: "its notes were still ringing in our ears as we left the river bottom and the band was lost to sight. . . ."

Keogh is remembered these days not because of a musical contribution, not for his gallantry, not for his sex appeal, but because of his horse Comanche, reputed to be the only survivor of the Little Bighorn.

Quite a few Seventh Cavalry mounts survived, probably more than a hundred. Indians caught the good ones and rode them as long as they lasted—which is to say, some of these big American horses adapted to the aboriginal way of life but others weakened and died because, unlike the tough little pintos, they were accustomed to grain and could not get through a Montana winter by nibbling willow bark and occasional tufts of brown grass. Gall said they were not worth much. Apart from these, the burial parties saw a number of Seventh Cavalry horses on the field. Most were so badly wounded that the troopers killed them, but some were unsaddled—if the saddle had not already been taken—and turned loose. One of these animals, a gray from E Company, followed Terry's column back down the valley to the *Far West*; it appeared to be terribly frightened and was last seen on the banks of the Yellowstone.

Then there was the bulldog. Custer's orderly, John Burkman, saw it trot off with the doomed companies. He whistled. The dog paid no attention. Two days later he saw it sniffing around the hillside. He did not know whose dog it was, but it must have accompanied the regiment from Fort Lincoln because it did not belong to the Indians. Wooden Leg saw it, although he does not mention the breed: "I did not see any other dog there. . . ."

On December 14, 1907, the magazine *Forest and Stream* published an article by one C. B. D. W. which concerns a greyhound supposedly given to Custer by Queen Victoria. "He was big in bone and muscle, with plenty of flesh and his tawny coat striped with black . . ." which makes the dog sound like a tiger. Anyway, outside of Fort Harker while the general was back east on unspecified business this greyhound was accidentally shot. The ball entered at the root of the tail, passed through the body, and emerged at the right shoulder. Obviously such a wound must be fatal. A bed of soft grass was prepared on flat stones beside a brook, there the dog was carried and left to die. Yet even as little Bob survived a picket pin through the head in Oklahoma, so Queen Victoria's greyhound survived this painful shot and two weeks after the accident came tottering back to the fort.

Then, in March of 1908, *Forest and Stream* printed a letter from Napoleon A. Comeau of Godbout, Quebec. Mr. Comeau said he had read with much interest the December article and wondered if this might be the dog he himself had seen at Fort Washakie in 1882. If so:

> . . . he bore a charmed life, because he and "Curly," a Crow Indian scout, were the only living beings that escaped in Custer's last fight with Sitting Bull, on the Little Big Horn River, on the 25th of June, 1876.
>
> Three days after the fight, when a scouting party reached the battle ground where Custer and the few survivors had made their last stand, the greyhound was found lying down near his dead master. A rifle bullet had struck him near the eye which made him blind on that side, but otherwise he was uninjured. He was taken good care of by the party and finally found a master in Lieut. R. E. Thompson, of the Sixth Infantry, who was stationed at Fort Washakie when I was there. It was the lieutenant himself who gave me the above details concerning the dog.

Mr. Comeau's greyhound tale is suspect. For one thing, he innocently repeats the Curly legend which is at best half-true. More significant, nobody else—not Lt. Bradley who was first on the field, not Benteen, not Reno, not one survivor of the fight, nor anybody from Terry's command—not one of them saw this greyhound.

Wooden Leg and Burkman, though, pretty well agree, and somehow a feeling of authenticity emanates from their statements. There does seem to have been a regimental dog alive on the field. A prominent Custer historian, John Carroll, states flatly: "I am convinced at least one dog belonging to Custer was on that field after the battle." One or more dogs and several wounded horses. Yet the legend persists of a lone survivor. Why? It is as reasonable to ask why the myth of Custer's long hair persists when there is no doubt that on the campaign his hair was short. He expected to be in the field several weeks and long hair collects dirt. On expeditions of this sort very few soldiers wore long hair. Nevertheless, at the climactic moment General Custer must have flowing locks.

So it is with Keogh's horse—the one survivor.

How Comanche got that name is uncertain, but on September 13, 1868, during a skirmish with Indians near the Cimarron—Luce identifies the site as Bluff Creek, Kansas—the horse was struck in the right hindquarter by an arrow. The shaft broke off and the wound went unnoticed until Keogh returned to camp, but during this fight or shortly afterward somebody named the horse. In a popular story by Margaret Leighton, which is reasonably factual, a trooper called McBane tells Keogh that he saw the arrow strike: "He sure squalled as loud as any of those Comanches. . . . I never heard a horse let out just that kind of holler. A sure enough Comanche yell." To which Keogh replies: "Comanche! That's the name for him."

He is described as a claybank sorrel, buckskin, light bay, mouse-colored, or dark cream with black mane and tail. The official Seventh Cavalry transcript of July 25, 1887, lists the horse as a bay, weight 925 pounds, height fifteen hands, date of birth probably 1862, and itemizes twelve scars caused by wounds.

Comanche had at least as many saviors as shades of color. Blacksmith Gustave Korn, who later became the animal's attendant, said he found Comanche on the battlefield bleeding from six wounds. Another trooper was about to cut the horse's throat when Korn dissuaded him.

Cpl. Henry Brinkerhoff saw Comanche in a clump of trees and was ordered to shoot him, but had not the heart to carry out this order when the horse whinnied.

Lt. Nolan saw Comanche in a ravine.

Capt. McDougall found him "sitting on his haunches, braced back on his forefeet," pocked with arrows and bullets, in very poor shape.

Major Peter Wey alleged that Comanche was standing: "The saddle had turned under his belly but the blanket and pad were missing."

Godfrey said Terry's men discovered him on the site of the Indian village: "McClernand, 2nd Cavalry, told me he saw some scouts assembled around a horse. . . ."

Seven grievous wounds he suffered, "each of which would have killed an ordinary horse," according to a nineteenth-century newspaper tribute. Almost all journalists wound him seven times, perhaps because seven is an esthetically pleasing number, or because it has mystic significance, although a book for bloodthirsty juveniles presents the poor beast skewered twenty-eight times.

No matter how many bullets and arrows pierced his hide, Comanche was hurt. Korn and some others got him to the river where they bathed him and dressed the wounds and led him ten or twelve miles to the *Far West* where Captain Marsh fixed up a stall between the rudders.

By the time the boat reached Fort Lincoln the horse could not walk, so they carried him to the stables in a wagon and there supported him with a sling. About a year later he had recovered enough that one of Col. Sturgis' daughters sometimes requisitioned him for a ride on the prairie. But then a major's daughter went for a ride, which enraged the colonel's daughter, and on April 10, 1878, Col. Sturgis issued General Orders No. 7, announcing in desiccated Army prose that because Comanche was "the only living representative of the bloody tragedy of the Little Big Horn, Montana, June 25, 1876, his kind treatment and comfort should be a matter of special pride and solicitude on the part of the 7th Cavalry, to the end that his life may be prolonged to the utmost limit." Sturgis went on to announce that henceforth: "He will not be ridden by any person whatever under any circumstances. . . ."

Thereafter, on ceremonial occasions, Comanche walked at the head of Keogh's old troop—draped in a black mourning net, a pair of cavalry boots slung across the saddle with the toes pointing backward.

He lived to be twenty-nine. He had been in good health until his attendant, Gustave Korn, was killed at Wounded Knee. After that, no matter what the new attendant did, Comanche grew increasingly morose. No longer did he root through garbage pails, which had been a special privilege and pleasure, and the beer he was issued at the enlisted men's canteen seemed to weaken him, so that he did nothing except lie gloomily in the barn or in a mud wallow.

Fifteen years after the Little Bighorn, Comanche moved on.

The regimental blacksmith, Samuel Winchester, was present and addressed this note to himself:

Fort Riley, Kansas, Nov. 7th, 1891—in memory of the old veteran horse who died at 1:30 o'clock with the colic in his stall while I had my hand on his pulse and looking him in the eye—this night long to be remembered.

The Seventh wanted to preserve him. A telegraphic inquiry went to naturalist L. L. Dyche at the University of Kansas. Dyche agreed to mount the remains for $400. He caught the train to Fort Riley and came back to Lawrence, where the university is located, with Comanche's hide and a load of bones.

The campus sprawls across a hill with the grandiose name of Mount Oread, and here Professor Dyche recreated the horse. He built a wooden frame to connect the skull, pelvis, and leg bones, padding this construction with excelsior, winding string around it to simulate musculature. He then applied a layer of clay and finally the brine-soaked hide, thickly dusted with arsenic to discourage pests. In the course of his work Dyche noticed that scar tissue had developed in seven places, which could explain why most histories say Comanche was wounded seven times. It is not known, however, just which of these injuries were sustained at the Little Bighorn. No doubt the Comanche arrow in the animal's flank had left a mark, and Dyche surmised that two growths of scar tissue might have been caused by the entrance and exit of one bullet through the neck. In other words, nobody can say how many times Comanche was hit by Sioux and Cheyenne arrows or bullets.

Dyche informed the regiment, when submitting his bill for taxidermy, that if they wished to donate Comanche to the University of Kansas there would be no charge. Transporting a stuffed horse would be awkward when the regiment moved, so the officers of the Seventh accepted this proposal.

Comanche was displayed at the Chicago Exposition of 1893, after which he returned to the university and stood in the natural history museum where passing students stroked his nose and plucked hairs from his tail until—somewhat bedraggled, looking more and more like an old brown rug—he was protected by a glass case.

Once in a while somebody tries to obtain custody, or at least borrow him. In 1939 the citizens of Hardin, Montana, asked that Comanche be transferred to a museum which was being built on the Custer Battlefield, but the Kansas legislature rejected this idea. In 1946 the hero of Bataan, General Jonathan Wainwright, wanted the horse returned to Fort Riley; but the university chancellor, Deane Malott, said no.

South Dakota Senator Francis Case tried in 1951. South Dakota was celebrating its seventy-fifth anniversary and wished to exhibit the horse. Chancellor Malott said no.

The World Publishing Company planned an autograph party for an author in Chicago and thought Comanche would add to the gala atmosphere. Chancellor Malott's response was predictable.

In 1953 the Kiwanis Club of Lewistown, Montana, made another pitch for the battlefield, claiming nobody in Kansas ever had heard of Comanche. Not true, replied the museum director, thousands of people come every year to look at him; whereupon Chancellor Murphy, picking up Malott's cudgel, said no to the Lewistown Kiwanis.

So, protected from moths and souvenir hunters by his humidity-controlled glass house, Comanche stands patiently upon Mount Oread, enduring generation after generation of undergraduate jokes. The other horses are gone and the mysterious yellow bulldog is gone, which means that in a sense the legend is true. Comanche alone survived.

Not one rider survived, military or civilian. Of the four Crows who directed Custer—Hairy Moccasin, Goes Ahead, White Man Runs Him, Curly—all thoughtfully withdrew when he gave permission. They had been employed to find the enemy, which they did; they hoped he would butcher the Sioux but doubted that he could, and saw no reason to commit suicide.

Excepting little brother Boston and nephew Autie Reed, the only excess baggage Custer carried from Fort Lincoln to the Little Bighorn was Bismarck *Tribune* correspondent Mark Kellogg.

There were not supposed to be any journalists. Sherman had wired Terry: "Advise Custer to be prudent, not to take along any newspapermen. . . ." Custer, however, ignored these disagreeable instructions and invited Clement Lounsberry, publisher of the *Tribune*. Lounsberry accepted but then his wife got sick, so Kellogg got the opportunity of a lifetime. His field dispatches would appear not only in the *Trib* but in the New York *Herald*.

Kellogg must have been surprised by this offer because he was not a full-time professional; he was a former telegrapher working that summer in a Bismarck law office and writing occasional newspaper articles under the pseudonym of "Frontier." The St. Paul *Daily Pioneer-Press* carried one of his stories on August 18, 1875, about a homesteader killed by Indians just outside Fort Lincoln. "Bah!" Frontier exclaimed, "I say, turn the dogs of war loose, and drive them off the face of the earth, if they do not behave themselves."

Aboard the *Far West* when the Seventh began its final march was Grasshopper Jim Brisbin, who also liked to write and who probably contributed this passage to a special report in the *Herald*:

> The very last one I saw at the mouth of the Rosebud was Mr. Kellogg, the *Herald* correspondent, who was mounted on a mule, with a pair of canvas saddle bags in which were stored paper and pencil, sugar, coffee and bacon sufficient to last 15 days. He sat on the right of General Gibbon, watching the review, and rode away with Custer, General Terry calling him back to say goodbye. I saw poor Kellogg on the boat the night before the troops marched, and he was busy until 12 o'clock writing up his despatches and getting his rations ready for the journey. At a little after midnight June 21, I went out on the deck of the steamer to smoke a cigar, and Kellogg came out a few minutes afterward and said he was through with his writing and ready for the forwarding on the morrow. He talked a long time about the campaign, and was full of hope they might during the coming march overhaul the Indians and have a good fight.

Kellogg appended a note to Lounsberry when forwarding these last dispatches to the *Trib*: "We leave the Rosebud to-morrow, and by the time this reaches you we will have met and fought the red devils, with what results remains to be seen. I go with Custer. . . ."

Gibbon, writing for *American Catholic Quarterly Review* in 1877, remarked that while exploring the ravine where E Company was wiped out he came upon a decomposing body in the high grass. It was not stripped, but had been scalped. One ear was gone. "The clothing was not that of a soldier, and, with the idea of identifying the remains, I caused one of the boots to be cut off and the stocking and drawers examined for a name. . . ." There was no name, but the boot had been patched in a curious way: reinforced by a leather band terminating in two straps which buckled together—apparently an attempt to tighten the instep. This boot was taken back to camp where somebody said it belonged to the journalist.

Kellogg is an indistinct figure. Until his death nobody paid much attention to him. He was about forty years old, youthful in appearance except that he wore spectacles and his hair was turning gray, a widower who smoked Bull Durham and enjoyed playing chess. Supposedly he had a brother in Chicago and two daughters attending college in Northfield, Minnesota. He is said to have preached a temperance lecture at the burial of a drunk.

Dying with Custer gave him a thimbleful of immortality. Historians began to study this faceless individual. Nobody could locate the Chicago brother. Northfield College registers from 1873 to 1876 disclosed no female students named Kellogg. He was said to have written sketches for *Harper's Weekly*. None could be found. A biographical tribute in the July 9 New York *Herald* mentioned that he had served as a telegrapher for the Army of the Potomac, but the National Archives contain no pay vouchers made out to him.

He rode away from Fort Lincoln with a pad of coarse gray paper, and with a diary which at some point he stowed on McDougall's pack train. An oilcloth satchel and this water-stained diary eventually were delivered to a Bismarck druggist with whom he played chess. The state historical society now owns them. Collapsible oilcloth nineteenth-century satchel containing a few personal items: wire spectacles, Bull Durham sack, one soft dark shirt—such was Kellogg's estate.

His notes cover a period from May 17 to June 9, from Fort Lincoln to the Powder. He logs the miles traveled each day, records the wind, snow, rain, clouds, wagon damage, antelope, General Terry's impatience. There is no insight, nothing memorable, nothing that sings in the mind. It is a pedestrian account kept by an ordinary man on a mule.

Whatever notes he took from June 10 until the end have been lost. It is alleged that sheets of paper were scattered in the grass near his body, which may or may not be true. In either event, Kellogg's value as a reporter seems to have concluded with those midnight messages written aboard the *Far West*— those and the determined little memo to his boss.

Had he gone with Reno or Benteen he might have survived and we would have a competent description of events, although not a classic. En route from Fort Lincoln he never chose the luminous detail. We learn less from Kellogg than from incidental revelations of the troopers preoccupied with that deadly business ahead. What he observed during those penultimate moments—the appearance of the valley, Reno's charge, Custer on the ridge—it is of course possible that this extraordinary pageant would have aroused him, although his pencil did not work six lines of magic between Bismarck and the Powder. A Blackfoot named Kill Eagle said that when the Indians splashed across the Little Bighorn they went like bees swarming from a hive, but such vibrant imagery never occurred to Kellogg.

Captain Charles King wrote that whatever is ornamental in warfare was left to the Indian, and those infuriated braves streaming out of the village must have been as ornamental as charcoal, buffalo blood, pigment, and feathers could make them. One Sioux wrapped himself in the pelt of a bear. Others rode naked, their skin smeared with medicine paint. Perhaps a dozen Cheyennes and forty or fifty Sioux wore bonnets with long trails. White Elk wore a famous headdress designed by his uncle—the brow embellished with dragonflies and butterflies, a forked-tail swallow sewn between a double row of eagle-down feathers at the trailing end. Sun Bear's bonnet was rudimentary and violent: a single horn projecting from his forehead.

Wooden Leg spent a long time getting ready. On the first day when he attacked Major Reno in the valley he wore a cloth shirt, beaded moccasins, and a pair of breeches given to him by a Sioux. A blue-black charcoal circle enclosed his face, the interior colored red and yellow—a design never to be altered—"done for me by Red Haired Bear at my first medicine making." His father urged him to hurry, but Wooden Leg studied himself in a mirror. He combed his hair. It should have been oiled and braided but his father kept insisting that he hurry, "so I just looped a buckskin thong about it and tied it close up against the back of my head, to float loose from there." On the second day it seemed to him that different clothes might be desirable. He discussed this with his father, who suggested the soldier uniform—even though the sleeves ended above his wrists and the trousers above his ankles. Thus dressed, wearing a big white hat captured during the Rosebud fight, seeing himself not at all as whites would see him, Wooden Leg went after Reno's forces trapped on the bluff.

Two years later General Nelson Miles marched up the Yellowstone valley to inspect the proposed route of a telegraph line. At the mouth of the Bighorn he found an encampment of Crows. They always had been friendly to whites and now that the whites had cleared this region of Sioux they were delighted to see Miles. They arranged a show for him. "I have often regretted that Frederic Remington was not with me," he said. "Their steeds were painted in most fantastic colors and decorated with spangles, colored horsehair, and hawks' feathers. They seemed as wild as their riders, racing, rearing, and plunging, yet controlled by the most expert horsemanship in the world. The warriors were painted and bedecked in every conceivable way, no two alike. Their war jackets were adorned with elk teeth, silver, mother-of-pearl, beads, and porcupine quills of the richest design and rarest workmanship. Some wore bear-claw necklaces, and human scalplocks dangled from their spears. Their eagle-feathered war bonnets waved in the air. . . ." So dazzled was Miles that he described this show in almost identical words in two memoirs published fourteen years apart. Never, he remarks with grave understatement, had he witnessed such a display. Yet the performance arranged by these Crows must have been a pale demonstration compared to the barbaric surge of Sioux and Cheyenne warriors.

Some of those Indians at the Little Bighorn may have been wearing silver medals commemorating the 1851 conference at Fort Laramie. These were distributed to influential chiefs. Embossed on one side was the head of President Millard Fillmore; on the reverse, clasped hands signifying peace and mutual trust. It is also possible that some of them wore British medallions which had been presented to Sioux chiefs in the name of King George III at the time of the American Revolution. These, of course, became important heirlooms and it is known that several were owned by tribal leaders as late as 1876. When Sitting Bull crossed the international boundary into Canada he was met by Inspector J. M. Walsh of the Mounted Police, who asked why he had come. Sitting Bull held up one or more of these old medals, saying, "We are British Indians. Our grandfathers were raised on British soil." So it may be, considering how much care these people devoted to their appearance, that half a dozen silver images of King George contributed to the spectacle.

For Custer's troops, locked inside a twisting circle, this show concluded as it did for those who watched the writhing hair of Medusa. It could have ended no other way because the Great Spirit rode with these Indians. Gall himself saw the Great Spirit riding on a coal-black pony.

How long it lasted, nobody knows. Not long. A cavalry regiment is neither trained nor provisioned to fight a sustained defensive battle. James Mannion, who claimed to be an eyewitness, said the general called upon a few survivors to follow him and managed to break through the howling savages, but upon discovering that only one Crow scout had escaped he gallantly reined up. The Crow, who understood that to return would mean death, seized the bridle of Custer's horse. Whereupon the fearless general laughed, "and, putting the reins of his horse between his teeth, with a revolver in each hand, he gave a wild cheer and dashed back through the hell of smoke and flying bullets. . . ."

Custer did pack two revolvers, and with a mouthful of reins it should be possible to emit a leathery cheer, so up to this point Mannion could be guilty of nothing worse than hyperbole; but for various reasons, including the fact that his credentials were not good, the story is suspect.

An old Cheyenne, who undoubtedly was present, told Frank Linderman in 1877 that the fight took about as long as it took the sun to travel the width of a lodge pole.

How thick is a lodge pole? Three inches, four inches, five inches.

How long does it take the sun to travel that far? Fifteen minutes. Twenty minutes.

The old Cheyenne peeled some twigs and stuck them into a mound of dirt. He arranged and rearranged them, apparently trying to remember how Custer's men were grouped. At last the twigs stood where he wanted them. But all at once he scooped them up, Linderman wrote, "and threw them spitefully away. 'Pooof!' he said, blowing upon his empty palms."

Dr. Marquis thought Linderman did not understand what this Cheyenne was saying. The fight lasted quite a while, as expressed by the old warrior's deliberate movements. The repeated realignment of twigs did not mean he had difficulty remembering; it meant that the soldiers changed position. Discarding the twigs violently meant they had thrown themselves away instead of fighting with courage. Blowing on the palms or spitting on the fingers indicated that the soldiers fought among themselves, which is to say they killed each other.

Gall said the fight took about half an hour. The bluecoats were dismounted, he said, when the Indians rode over them. Even if they had been mounted it would not have lasted much longer because the American horses were tired and hungry. They were so hungry that they cropped grass during the battle.

The last resistance may have been crushed by a squad of glory-hunting young braves who thought this was a memorable hour to die. The names of the Sioux have not been preserved, nor the names of all the Cheyennes, but among the latter were Little Whirlwind, Close Hand, Cut Belly, and Noisy Walking. Altogether there might have been twenty. A dance was given in their honor on the night before the battle—which shows that a visit from hostile bluecoats was anticipated—and the next morning they paraded through the village accompanied by old men who called for everybody to look at these boys because they would never be seen again. They were the last to enter the fight. Sioux heralds rode around telling the warriors to get ready for hand-to-hand fighting as soon as these boys led the way. At last they came riding up from the river toward the place where the museum is now located. It is said that some of them stampeded the gray horses of Lieutenant Smith's E Company while others charged up the slope toward Custer. A few terrified wasichus tried to escape by running along the ridge.

Fifty or sixty men died with Custer. It appears that several turned their horses loose, although why they did, if they did, has been argued for the past century. Others shot their horses to form a barricade, because a number of carcasses lay in a fairly symmetrical ring ten or fifteen yards across. Benteen testified that when he visited the field he saw "an arc of a circle of dead horses."

Companies C, E, F, I, and L had followed the general. They lay in five disorderly clusters, although toward the end—during those last moments—company structure began to disintegrate, with men fighting in smaller and smaller units, by fours and threes, in pairs, individually, so that bodies were scattered across the hillside and for hundreds of yards along the ridge. Still it can be seen that originally there had been five companies. From above, as one views the battlefield on the museum topographical map, they give the impression of being loosely arranged in the shape of a V—an arrowhead, if one chooses to see it like that—with General Custer at the northern point. Pointing slightly northwest, to be exact.

Because quite a few of the men who died with him belonged to Captain Yates' F Company, most scholars assume that he directed the operation while traveling with Yates. However, almost half of the officers from the entire battalion were found in this group, notably Tom Custer from C Company and Algernon Smith from E. This is puzzling. These officers should have stayed with their companies. Various theories have been proposed.

Charles Kuhlman suggested that Yates, Smith, and Tom Custer had assembled to hear the general's final instructions.

Dr. Marquis proposed that the general died early in the fight, whereupon Yates assumed command. Next in seniority was Captain Myles Keogh, yet he might have been killed right away, in which case Tom Custer would assume command. This sequence would explain Tom's presence. As for Lt. Smith, when E Company fell apart he might have escaped and made his way to field headquarters, which would be logical. But as Marquis himself points out, nobody knows when the general was killed.

Benteen's explanation was the simplest: absolute confusion.

As to the time of day, there are discrepancies. In Montana it could not have been much later than noon, although watches carried by soldiers registered midafternoon. Until 1894 there were no time zones; each settlement or village or fort correlated its clocks with a metropolis. Fort Lincoln operated on Chicago time.

Why was the Seventh Cavalry defeated? There must be almost as many theories as historians. Marquis suggests, along with inexperienced troops and misleading reports from Washington, a third reason which he labels "the rock-bottom cause"—a conviction held by Americans that Indians wanted nothing so much as a chance to capture people, palefaces especially, for the purpose of torture. This belief, he insists, founded upon some measure of truth, was deliberately exaggerated in order to create racial hatred that would excuse the encroachments of white men and justify the killing of redskins. "Every one of Custer's soldiers was saturated with that sort of education. For them, Indians were diabolical. On a critical day and at a critical moment, they became victims of this indoctrination."

If Marquis happens to be correct, and if soldiers of our explosive century are equally simple—nor does any sign point elsewhere—the implication transcends all boundaries of rational thought.

The last living bluecoat, according to Cheyenne memories, was a big officer with a curly mustache. Every wasichu appeared to be dead when this one gradually tried to sit up. He raised himself on his left elbow and with a pistol in his right hand he glared around. Squaws, boys, and old men who had been lacerating the bodies shrank away, thinking he had returned from the spirit world, but a Sioux warrior took the pistol out of his hand and shot him through the head. Then the others regained courage, they rushed forward and furiously stabbed the corpse. The identity of this officer has not been learned, only that he was a captain, because the Cheyennes said he wore two metal bars. This could have been Myles Keogh, although the description does not sound just right.

An Arapaho named Waterman also spoke of occasional movement among the dead, and whenever it happened the squaws would run away. Waterman did not know what the squaws were doing which caused these bodies to move. He did not look.

Disfigurement of the dead and dying sounds prehistoric, like a ritual in an Ice Age grotto, but one must be cautious while studying the past. Edgar Stewart points out that it is a mistake to impose the standards of one race upon another. Besides, we learn now and again of civilized contemporaries reverting to paleolithic behavior. As H. G. Wells wrote, if you make men sufficiently fearful or angry the hot red eyes of cavemen will glare out at you. On September 3, 1855, for instance, following an assault on a Brulé village north of the Platte, General Harney's soldiers gathered the pubic hair of dead squaws. A fourteen-year-old Sioux named Curly saw the mutilated genitals of these women, although what effect the sight had on this boy who later became known as Crazy Horse can only be imagined.

Then there was the giant Apache chief, Red Sleeves—Mangas Coloradas, or Mangus Colorado as frontier gringos improperly spelled it. "I want him dead or alive tomorrow morning," said General Joseph West to the guards. "Do you understand?" The guards understood. Late at night they heated their bayonets in a campfire and touched the prisoner's feet. Red Sleeves, wrapped in his blanket, told them he was not a child to be played with, so they lowered their muskets and shot him. Each guard then added two pistol shots just to be sure, and they reported the prisoner killed while attempting to escape. Next morning a certain John T. Wright, who wanted the chief's scalp, asked the camp cook, William Lallier, for a knife. Lallier offered a bowie knife. Wright took the scalp, wound the heavy black hair around the bloody skin and stuffed it in his pocket. Unidentified soldiers later cut off the entire head, which was boiled and shipped to the Smithsonian, and some time afterward the head was acquired by a phrenologist, Mr. O. S. Fowler.

Captain Jack, that volatile Modoc, seems to have been handled still more casually. After being hanged and buried, Jack was exhumed, embalmed, and exhibited at carnivals: admission ten cents.

How many instances of such sensibility one chooses to catalogue may be limited by the amount of time spent turning musty pages. During the seventeenth century, Robert Cavalier, Sieur de La Salle, came upon a wood plank near the ruins of Ft. Crèvecoeur deep in the wilderness of the New World, upon which a French deserter had printed:

NOUS SOMMES TOUS SAUVAGES

Years after the battle a number of Indians claimed that the soldiers became so terrified they dropped their guns. In fact, quite a few did drop their guns or throw them aside, although not necessarily in panic. The guns occasionally jammed because the soft copper shells—unlike hard brass—could be deformed by exploding powder, causing them to stick in the breech. Furthermore, troopers often carried loose ammunition in saddlebags where it was easily damaged. Another possible reason turned up when one of Reno's men talked with an ordnance officer. This officer subsequently wrote to the Chief of Ordnance that Custer's troops used ammunition belts made from scrap leather. The copper shells "thus had become covered with a coating of verdigris and extraneous matter, which had made it difficult to even put them in the chamber before the gun had been discharged at all. Upon discharge the verdigris and extraneous matter formed a cement which held the sides of the cartridge in place against the action of the ejector. . . ."

Whatever the cause, it could take some time to pry a deformed shell out of the breech, or one that had been cemented in place, which explains why troopers under attack occasionally threw aside their rifles. To the Indians it must have appeared that a soldier who did this was terrified—as of course he might have been—but at the same time he might have been enraged.

A letter from Reno to General S. V. Benét, dated July 11, 1876, states that an Indian scout—not identified—was hiding just outside the battle zone, close enough to see troopers working on their guns. Knives with broken blades were found beside several bodies, further proof that the Seventh had to fight more than one enemy.

Such men obviously did not lose their wits. Others did. It is usually assumed that Custer's regiment consisted of blue-jacketed wind-burned agate-eyed tobacco-chewing roosters who could live on sagebrush, alkali, and a little biscuit, who would gallop across the field of Armageddon without blinking. Partly this was true. But the Seventh also included unbaptized recruits—perhaps thirty percent—many of whom had not once fired a carbine. Senator Thomas Hart Benton, a Missourian who grew up close to the frontier, referred to these troops as "the sport of Indians." They could not even stay on a horse, he said, but rolled off like pumpkins. Yet such was their faith that most of these innocents thought a yelping mob of Sioux would retreat faster than the Red Sea when old Iron Butt charged. When this did not occur—when, in fact, their intrepid commandant tried to organize a defensive pattern—some of the recruits went bounding over the sagebrush like jackrabbits.

Red Horse, a Miniconjou chief, spoke of whites with contempt. He said many of them asked to be taken prisoner.

An Arapaho named Left Hand rode up to a soldier who simply held out his gun, which Left Hand accepted. Then a Sioux came along and stopped long enough to kill the coward.

"John" is said to have been the name ordinarily used by whites when addressing an Indian. One trooper was heard sobbing this name, as though it might save his life.

John! John! Oh, John!

The plea echoes horribly down a hundred years.

Indians reported many such instances of cowardice among Custer's troops but did not tell similar stories about Reno's battalion. Reno's men must have been terrified when they galloped out of the valley, plunged into the river, and scrambled up the bluff, yet it appears that not one became so crazed with fear that he shot himself or numbly surrendered his weapons.

Quite a few hostiles, among them the Unkpapa war chief Crow King, insisted that all the soldiers, including Custer's men, fought courageously as long as they lived. And the Oglala chief Low Dog said at a conference of government officials in 1881: "They came on us like a thunderbolt. I never before nor since saw men so brave and fearless. . . . No white man or Indian ever fought as bravely as Custer's men."

Perhaps. But it should be kept in mind that for years afterward these Indians told white journalists and politicians what they thought the whites wanted to hear. They believed, correctly or not, that if they said the wrong thing they would be punished; therefore it was advisable to praise Custer and his troops. Being realists, they knew that a wise prisoner does not anger his warden, and nothing infuriated whites more than allegations of cowardice or suicide at the Little Bighorn. Wooden Leg was challenged by another Cheyenne in 1906 to tell a white man—identified only as "Doctor Dixon"—that Custer killed himself. Wooden Leg refused. "Other Indians, at other times, had tried to tell of the soldiers killing themselves, but the white people listening always became angry and said the Indians were liars, so I thought it best to keep quiet."

This dread of punishment persisted for at least two generations. As late as 1926 a half-brother of Sitting Bull refused to attend the semi-centennial for fear of being hanged. And several years later Dr. Marquis, whom the Cheyennes liked and trusted, was shown a supply of guns they had kept hidden ever since 1876.

That Custer's elite regiment fell apart in a most unprofessional manner seems to be substantiated by the testimony of whites. The entire battleground was studied by officers from the Terry-Gibbon army and by survivors of the Reno-Benteen command in an effort to learn what happened. Capt. Myles Moylan said he could find no evidence of organized resistance anywhere on the ridge with the exception of Calhoun's L Company. DeRudio was surprised to see so few expended cartridges. Lt. Wallace also noted very few shells: piles of twenty-five or thirty at various places where Calhoun's men fought, otherwise not much indication of a battle.

Calhoun had kept a promise. On April 23, 1871, he wrote to Custer: "I have just received my commission as 1st Lt. in the 7th Cavalry, and it reminds me more vividly than ever how many, many times I am under obligations to you for your very great kindness to me in my troubles. I shall do my best to prove my gratitude. If the time comes you will not find me wanting. . . ."

Benteen could discern no organized line of defense. "You can take a handful of corn and scatter it over the floor. . . ." He said he examined the field carefully in an attempt to see how the battle was fought and concluded it had been a rout.

Custer's problem was compounded by the fact that several of his most experienced officers—among them two majors and four captains—were not with the regiment, having been temporarily assigned elsewhere. Some were in Philadelphia doing one thing or another in connection with the forthcoming centennial festivities. He had tried to get them reassigned to field duty, quite obviously because he suspected he would need dependable officers, but the Washington high command denied his requests.

Just what occurred can be deduced only from battlefield evidence and from what the Indians said later, but there is not much doubt that while certain units—such as Calhoun's—fought valiantly and intelligently, others did succumb to panic. This may have been what happened to Lt. Algernon Smith's E Company. It is thought that Indians stampeded most of E Company's horses by yelling and waving blankets. The dismounted troopers then ran downhill and slid into the ravine where their bodies were found.

Some military analysts view the matter differently. A charge by Lame White Man's Cheyennes may have forced Smith's men up the ravine or gully. However they got there, it was the end of the road.

Why Lt. Smith left his men, or they left him, could never be determined.

The hillside above this gully is irregular, spotted with small cactus and sage, and nothing suggests that the slope was forested a century ago. Which is to say, if the cavalrymen did lose their horses at this point they must have felt helplessly exposed and rushed toward the one place that might protect them. Yet the moment they skidded into the gully they were trapped. All they could do was hug the sides or crouch among bushes, look fearfully upward, and wait. A few tried to scramble up the south wall because the earth showed boot marks and furrows probably gouged by their fingers, but none of these tracks reached the surface.

An Unkpapa named Iron Hawk thought these soldiers were scared silly. Just above the ravine he attacked one who had managed to get on a horse. Iron Hawk put an arrow through him.

Most plains Indians could put an arrow entirely through a buffalo. One big, fleshy Gros Ventre claimed that when he was young he could drive an arrow into a buffalo so hard it would drop out the opposite side. Other Gros Ventres spoke of a warrior who killed three cows with a single arrow—the shaft passing through the first and so far into the body of the second that the blade projected enough to kill a third cow which bumped against it.

Capt. Philo Clark wrote in 1884: "The power of the bow may be better understood when I tell you that the most powerful Colt's revolver will not send a ball through a buffalo. I have seen a bow throw an arrow five hundred yards and have myself often discharged one entirely through a board one inch thick."

Col. Dodge did not think the bow all that strong. He calls it a short-distance weapon and says that although an arrow might travel two hundred yards it quickly lost strength. "Many stories are told of the ability of an Indian to throw an arrow through a buffalo, and one author claims to have himself sent an arrow completely through an inch board. I can only say, that with considerable knowledge of many tribes, I have never seen any such feats."

Concerning the speed with which arrows might be discharged, there is no disagreement. George Catlin watched a Mandan shoot so fast that an eighth arrow was en route before the first hit the ground. Dodge, the skeptic, said an Indian might grasp as many as ten arrows in his left hand and get rid of all ten before the first struck its target, each capable of inflicting a death wound at twenty or thirty yards. And because a quiver might hold quite a few arrows it is easy to understand why experienced frontiersmen avoided fighting Indians whenever possible, except on rainy days. Wet weather loosened the bow strings, which were made of animal tendon.

Just how far Iron Hawk's arrow traveled before spitting that unfortunate man from E Company we do not know. "I met a soldier on horseback," he remarked with Spartan brevity, "and I let him have it."

The impaled soldier screamed and clutched the saddle horn. Iron Hawk rode alongside and hit him in the neck with the bow, knocking him to the ground. Iron Hawk then jumped off his pony and beat the soldier to death: "I kept on beating him awhile after he was dead, and every time I hit him I said 'Hownh!' I was mad, because I was thinking of the women and little children. . . ." Those wasichus had come to the Little Bighorn looking for trouble, said Iron Hawk, and they got it.

One thing amused him. He saw two fat old women stripping a soldier who only pretended to be dead. After the squaws took the soldier's uniform they started to cut off his genitals, which made him jump up. He grabbed one squaw and swung her around while the other tried to stab him. Iron Hawk thought it was funny—a naked wasichu dancing with two fat old women.

Whether the men commanded by Lt. Smith lost their minds to fear, as Iron Hawk believed, or whether they tumbled into the gully through some persuasive logic of their own is a dark facet of the Little Bighorn enigma. Twenty-eight or twenty-nine bodies were discovered here, most of them apparently killed with stones or clubs. Yet again there are discrepancies. McDougall was ordered by Reno to bury the troops of E Company and McDougall said they were lying in a neat row, face down, each man shot in the side—not clubbed to death.

Trumpeter Martini, who saw these corpses, said quite a lot of paper money was torn up and sprinkled on the body of one sergeant. This sergeant had not been paid before leaving Fort Lincoln, nor had anybody else, not till the army was a full day's march beyond the fleshpots and saloons of Bismarck. It is a soldier's privilege to debauch himself as he pleases when off duty, but here the consequences would have been venereal disease and numerous desertions. So the affluent sergeant, loaded with pay like all the rest, and maybe something extra from card games along the route, lost his fortune in a Montana gully. Altogether how many greenbacks were torn to bits, carried off, or blown away, nobody knows.

"The soldiers had lots and lots of money," according to a Sioux named Paints Brown, "and we took it. We knew what the silver was, but the paper we didn't know. And the children played with it, they made little teepees out of it, and put about one hundred dollars in bills together and made toy shawls, and some of it was bloody."

Wandering Medicine, who was a boy in 1876, told of going through soldiers' pockets for green picture-paper which could be used as saddle blankets on mud ponies—a detail verified by Pvt. Charles Windolph, who said that in the spring of '77 while his company was exploring a deserted Indian camp he saw a five-dollar bill plastered on the back of a mud animal.

Not all of this wasichu money was wasted. Cheyenne warriors fashioned buckles out of coins, or bored holes in them to make hair ornaments and necklaces and decorations for the bridles of their ponies. And two sophisticated young Cheyennes spoke of loading saddlebags with money and hiding these bags very near a creek. "They rode up close to the rocks and stood on their horses and pushed the sacks in there. They might still be there some place," John Stands in Timber said, adding that he himself had once gone looking for those saddlebags.

One Cheyenne pulled a flat, round object out of a trooper's pocket. This thing was made of white metal and glass, with black marks under the glass, and was thought to be alive because of the noise it made. The Cheyennes decided this must be the soldier's medicine so the warrior kept it. But the next day it died. He threw it away—as far as possible.

Another Cheyenne found one of these, except that it made no noise and beneath the glass was a tiny fluttering arrow. If left alone the arrow would point down the valley. There were rumors of troops in that direction so they decided this thing might be used to locate soldiers.

Other Indians got binoculars, which they understood perfectly. They got flags, gloves, bullets, guns, and hats. Some of the older men took McClellan saddles.

I got coffee, an Indian would say.

I got tobacco.

I got a good knife.

Five companies had followed Long Hair, leaving plenty of useful objects on the hillside. Many things were buried. Squaws buried rings and trinkets of all sorts because they were frightened. "We had done more than we thought we ever could do," Paints Brown said, "and we knew that the whites were very strong and would punish us."

Custer's five companies had ridden north in column—two men abreast or four abreast, depending on the terrain. The last two companies, I and L, commanded by Myles Keogh and James Calhoun, might have been able to withdraw before the circle closed. The bodies of most of these men lay several hundred yards south of the others, as though a seam holding the battalion together had given way. For a while—a few moments—Keogh and Calhoun might have had a choice: to follow their commander, knowing almost certainly that they would be killed, or to retreat. By retreating in good order they probably could have withdrawn to Reno's hilltop.

If Keogh and Calhoun did have such an option they despised it.

Lt. Henry Harrington of Tom Custer's company may have gotten out. His body never was found. Indians said that a man on a sorrel horse raced back in the direction from which the troops had come; he was chased a long way by two Cheyennes and a Sioux and was hit between the shoulders and killed. This might have been Harrington. Or it is possible that he did escape, perhaps gravely wounded, and died some distance from the field.

He was one of those with premonitions. He had seen himself tied to a tree, surrounded by savages. He is said to have drawn a sketch of this which he mailed to a friend back east. That he would refrain from sending such a picture to his wife is understandable, yet she may have learned about it. She vanished for two years and was discovered in a small Texas town, apparently suffering from amnesia. Harrington's daughter, subsequently appointed by Herbert Hoover to the job of postmistress at West Point, said an attack of pneumonia restored her mother's mind. She knew who she was, although she could recall nothing about those years. "Several times," the daughter said, "we heard from Indians that a lady dressed in black had been seen on the battlefield."

Godfrey wrote to historian Brininstool in 1921 that a month after the battle Terry moved downstream to the mouth of Rosebud Creek, and here, according to rumors, a dead Seventh Cavalry mount lay on the south bank. Godfrey crossed the river to investigate. He saw the horse, shot in the forehead. It carried a halter, saddle, saddlebags, and a Seventh Cavalry grain bag full of oats strapped to the cantle. The saddlebags were empty. The rider's carbine, which he had been told was there, was missing. Godfrey could not learn anything else and he did not speculate on whether Harrington might have ridden this animal. It could have belonged to a deserter because the column passed through this area en route to the Little Bighorn and a few soldiers did take French leave.

Other possibilities turned up. Several years after the battle two Cheyennes noticed a skeleton about fifteen miles east of Custer ridge—perhaps the remains of a trooper who had been stripped and left for dead but who regained consciousness during the night and staggered away. Conceivably this was the lost lieutenant.

During the summer of 1928 a Crow named High Medicine Rock found a skeleton southeast of the battlefield with a slender iron arrowhead embedded in the neck vertebrae. The bones lay in a gully where they had been covered and uncovered season after season by wind, rain, and snow for half a century, so not much was left—fragments of cloth, a rotted leather gun scabbard. Nineteen empty shells and one loaded cartridge proved that he fought for his life. Lt. Harrington had worn white canvas trousers and a blue blouse, but there was not enough of this cloth to indicate whether it might have been his uniform. Because no positive identification could be made, the skeleton was buried in the battlefield cemetery and marked *Unknown*. Whoever he was, he almost got away.

It is said that Harrington's watch either was found or was bought from an Indian. Beyond that, nothing.

Another trooper unquestionably would have escaped if he had not lost his nerve. Several Indians saw him leap on a horse and start up a ravine. They chased him. As usual, there is very little agreement about who they were. Five Sioux according to one account: two Oglalas, two Unkpapas, one Brulé. According to a different memoir: two Cheyennes—Old Bear and Kills At Night—and an unnamed Sioux. No matter. The soldier had a fast horse and was leaving them behind so they began to drop out until he was followed by just one Indian, who for an unexplained reason did not carry either a bow or a rifle. This warrior, said to be an Unkpapa, was about to give up when the escaping soldier glanced backward, jerked out a pistol, and instead of shooting the unarmed pursuer shot himself in the head. The Unkpapa caught his horse and rode it for years afterward. He did not know just how far he chased the terrified soldier but he thought it might have been six or seven miles. The man's skeleton was not found. He wore chevrons, which of course eliminates Lt. Harrington.

The Crow woman, Pretty Shield, said that for a long time her people used to find the bodies of soldiers and dead Indians far from the Little Bighorn. "I remember that in the summer following the big fight my people found four blue soldiers together, one of them a chief, beyond Big-shoulder, on Bear-in-the-middle Creek. This is six miles from the fighting place. . . ."

Tom LeForge often camped in the vicinity of the battlefield, referring to it as his "summer-resort." He told Dr. Marquis about bones in the Rosebud Valley twenty-five miles distant. Ammunition belts, weapons, and rotted army clothes were scattered throughout the area. All of this, said LeForge, made it evident that a good many soldiers broke out of the trap. In an old blue blouse he once found a tintype of a young woman, which he kept. He did not report this, nor anything else he picked up. He said it wasn't expected. "I was at times with soldiers when discoveries were made. We merely looked, wondered, conjectured, and went on our way."

Of all those who claimed to have escaped—some historians dryly observe that there were more claimants than Custer had soldiers—of several hundred who reputedly survived the Last Stand, none is more often mentioned than the young Crow scout Curly. His miraculous escape was accomplished in various ways, such as eviscerating a dead horse and concealing himself within the cavity. Or he ducked into a ravine, arranged his hair in the Sioux style, snatched a blanket off a dead hostile, and slipped anonymously through the ring of fire. Curly did go with Custer and he did survive, but he did not accompany G. A. C. all the way. Nor was he expected to. The Rees and Crows had been employed to locate the Sioux, nothing else. They had not been hired to fight, although several did fight alongside Reno in the valley.

How far Curly traveled with the doomed men is uncertain. It appears that when he saw how things were developing he pulled off to the side. Mitch Bouyer may have advised him to leave. If you can get around the Sioux, Bouyer allegedly said to him, "go to the other soldiers (meaning Terry's men) and tell them that all are killed. That man (pointing to Custer) will stop at nothing. He is going to take us right into the village. . . . We have no chance at all."

Sometime after withdrawing from this party of the marching dead Curly met a Ree scout, Black Fox, and talked about provisions which the Seventh had abandoned on the trail. The two of them went back to this spot and presumably helped themselves. Curly then told Black Fox he was going home.

That might have been just what occurred, although Professor Stewart offers a slightly different scenario in which the two Indians pick up this food much earlier. Black Fox then vanishes. Curly returns to watch the battle from a distance. Convinced that the soldiers are losing, he decides it would be foolish to hang around.

Anyway, he was next seen on the bank of the Yellowstone across from a base hospital established by Terry. He asked in sign language for Gray Beard or No Hip-bone—Gibbon—and being informed that he had marched upstream Curly rode off.

Near the confluence of the Little Bighorn and the Bighorn the *Far West* was tied to a cottonwood. Hanson in his 1909 biography of Captain Grant Marsh, skipper of the *Far West*, describes this water as clean and cold, teeming with pike, salmon, and channel catfish. Several crew members therefore had cut willow poles and settled themselves for a pleasant morning. Captain Marsh, accompanied by his pilot, the engineer, and two U.S. Army officers, strolled off the boat not long after ten o'clock and selected a fishing spot close to a dense growth of willows. For the past couple of days there had been smoke on the southern horizon, which they attributed to Custer and Terry incinerating the hostile village. Now this smoke had blown away. The battle was over, the Sioux had been defeated, there was nothing to worry about. Still, they were very close to the willows. It would be easy for Indians to sneak up. They were discussing this when the willows quivered and a mounted warrior rode into view. The fishermen sprang to their feet, but the Indian lifted his carbine in a peaceful gesture. Then they noticed an erect scalplock which identified him as a Crow.

By other accounts, instead of lifting his carbine Curly held up both hands in a universally understood gesture, after which he hopped off his pony and began drawing pictures in the sand. He may have been waved aboard the steamboat and given a pencil so that he could draw more clearly.

Some say he lay prone on the deck, drew two concentric circles to convey the idea of men surrounded, and explained what had befallen them by seizing his own scalplock in one hand, encircling it with the other, and pretending to wrench it off. Nor was this enough: After pretending to scalp himself, Curly hooked the scalp to his belt and performed a war dance on the deck of the *Far West*. Such melodrama aside, there is little doubt that he emerged from the willows and tried to deliver a message. The whisky trader Coleman, who was present, said he saw Curly make the sleep sign, meaning death. But then several officers gathered around and he, Coleman, could not see what else Curly signaled.

George Morgan, a squaw man, probably translated some of what Curly said. One way or another his message seems to have been understood, although the men on the boat remained skeptical.

He had not claimed to be in the fight, yet the legend of his escape grew like a beanstalk. At first he denied the story, but when it became obvious that nothing he said would make much difference he stopped denying it; and after a number of years, realizing what the white men wanted to hear, he began to say yes, yes, it was true, he had been trapped with the general but escaped by galloping off with a blanket over his head. Few historians accept the tale of the blanket, and Rees who were interviewed a long time afterward said that when he came aboard the *Far West* he was wearing a black shirt, breechcloth, and moccasins. James Sipes, who was traveling on the *Far West* as a barber, told Walter Camp in 1909 that when Curly emerged from the willows his hair was not dressed in the usual Crow pompadour, he had three ponies, and he had a red Sioux blanket; but Sipes testified thirty-three years after the event, time enough for any man to rearrange the past.

The first Little Bighorn reunion occurred in 1886 and it sounds like quite a party. After being officially welcomed at Fort Custer the guests—at least the bluecoat guests—camped beside the river in tents furnished with every possible convenience, including whisky. Some of these officers got roundly drunk and for most of a week they wandered through the valley and across the ridge.

Many chiefs were there, shaking hands, talking sign language with old enemies such as Godfrey, Benteen, Edgerly, and McDougall. Sitting Bull did not attend because he was touring the East with Buffalo Bill's extravaganza, but Gall was an honored guest and he rejected with haughty contempt the myth of Curly's escape. It disgusted him. When he was introduced to Curly he said: "You have stated you were in this battle and that you got away. You were a coward and ran away before the battle began; if you hadn't you would not be here today."

Curly did not answer.

Gall turned away from him.

In another version of this meeting Gall said to the wretched Crow: "Where are your wings?"

"Wings!" Curly exclaimed. "What do you mean?"

"I mean," Gall said, "that nothing but a bird could have escaped after we surrounded the whites."

Inevitably a rumor developed that Custer, too, had escaped. It always happens. A hundred years after Lincoln's death a hole was cut in his casket and a man was appointed to peep inside, just to make sure. Old Mexican-Americans from Ruidoso to Clovis will tell you that Billy the Kid was seen long after Pat Garrett shot him in Maxwell's bedroom. John Kennedy never died but secretly was transported to a Caribbean island where he lived in seclusion, horribly disfigured. From legends do men draw ideas necessary to their existence, remarked Anatole France. If our heroes prove to be immortal, then so—perhaps—are we.

Thus it was alleged, and many believed, that the young general's body could not be found because he had not been killed. Some said he was captured by Cheyennes who nursed him back to health because they admired his bravery, after which he returned to civilization incognito. Others thought he broke away to the east, toward Rosebud Creek, and fled; and it was rumored that somebody who knew him had met him by accident, years afterward, on a street in New Orleans.

Before starting down the Little Bighorn Valley to the *Far West* with those who had survived, General Terry and Major Reno inspected the site of the village. They were shown the battered remains of the black white man Isaiah and the head of Bloody Knife. They also saw quite a lot of Indian household equipment, suggesting that the hostiles must have been frightened off—an incorrect deduction. Among these tribes it was customary either to destroy or abandon a lodge in which a relative had died and to distribute or throw away not only the deceased person's goods but also those of bereaved relatives, a practice that left a great many people destitute and littered the ground with useful and sometimes beautiful objects. The death of only a few warriors, therefore, could give an impression of hysterical flight.

Reno noted a "ghastly find," three lodge poles in the form of a triangle: ". . . on top of each were inverted camp kettles while below them, on the grass, were the heads of three men whom I recognized as belonging to my command. These heads had been severed from their trunks by some very sharp instrument, as the flesh was smoothly cut and they were placed within the triangle, facing one another, in a horrible sightless stare."

The head of a corporal from G Company was hidden beneath another kettle like a monstrous Easter egg.

Sgt. Knipe visited three burial lodges "full of dead Indians" wrapped in blankets and robes. He slit one of these bundles and discovered a string of scalps including those of four women, "with hair as long as my arm, two of them having red hair. It was a sight. I dropped them. . . ." He thought there must have been seventy-five corpses in these lodges, which sounds unlikely. When the Terry-Gibbon army passed through this encampment Lt. Charles Roe saw three lodges, perhaps the same ones, "shining white in the morning sun." Roe entered and found the interiors draped with black blankets. The bodies lay on truncated scaffolds, about a foot off the ground. Each was dressed in a war bonnet, thickly beaded shirt, leggings, and moccasins. How many he saw is not clear, but no more than a dozen.

Lt. Edgerly saw just two lodges, five bodies in one, six in the other. They had been richly dressed and ornamented and were tied to poles in a standing position. Outside lay eleven slaughtered ponies, each with its head pointing toward the center of the lodge. Edgerly does not say whether they were Sioux or Cheyenne, but they must have been Sioux because the Cheyennes placed their dead on travois and dragged them some distance from the battlefield. There they were hidden in gullies and covered with rocks to protect them from wolves and coyotes.

Ree scouts prowling through the debris came across a row of Dakotas lying on a blanket with their feet pointing toward a drum. The drum had been ritually slashed. They saw other Dakotas laid out on buffalo hides and pieces of canvas. These warriors had been dressed for burial in buckskin shirts, beads, and earrings, but Terry's men already had found them and had stolen everything. The Rees also saw the body of one Sioux still wearing his fine burial shirt, the shoulders marked with green paint, the red emblem of a secret society painted on his forehead. Young Hawk recognized this Sioux. His name was Chat-ka. He had been employed by the government and worked as a scout at Fort Lincoln.

Pvt. Coleman, too, looked around. He observed "all Kinds of Culinary and Mechanical Instruments," and better than anybody else he summarized the view:

Where the Village Stood and where the battle was fought is 24 miles from the big horn it is a lovely place the Valley is 1½ Miles brade and four miles long the River winding like a Snake and dotted with Islands thickly studded with timber the water Clear as Christal as it comes rushing from the Mountains Oh what a pittey that Such a loavely place should be the abode of such a band of blood thirsty demons. . . .

Capt. Walter Clifford, who commanded E Company of Gibbon's Seventh Infantry, seems to be meditating in chiaroscuro—his lucubration as febrile, morbid, and dolorous as anything fabricated by Edgar Allen Poe.

As the sun sinks from sight the listless breeze that has been lazily stirring dies away. The great round moon, bright as burnished silver, rolls slowly over our sorrowing heads. By its uncertain light a motionless black object can be seen at no great distance, which upon a nearer approach, proves to be a dead cavalry horse, and beside it the body of the rider, naked. Both are swollen almost to bursting. The legs of the horse are sticking straight out from the body, while the skin of the sleeping rider gleams in the moonlight like polished white marble. . . . Half fearfully I hasten to the river bank and listen to the sobbing gurgle of its waters as they hasten toward the busy east with their heart-breaking story. Even this mournful music is better than the stillness out yonder. But the polluted air is here also and one is forced to lie with face close to the water to be rid of the deadly poison that is permeating the clothing and filling the lungs with every respiration. A little delay on this death-stricken ground and we will remain forever. Let us hide our slain comrades from sight and resume, with quickened footsteps, our pursuit of their butchers. . . .

General Terry had not the slightest intention of pursuing those Indians but he did want to know where they were going, so he ordered Capt. Edward Ball at the head of one cavalry company to take a look. Ball followed the peripatetic village south toward the Bighorn Mountains for about twelve miles, at which point the trail divided. In both directions the air was smoky; the hostiles were setting the prairie afire as they withdrew. Capt. Ball turned east, and near the river he came upon something unexpected: a broad track leading north toward the now abandoned campsite. What this meant was that the signs Custer picked up on Rosebud Creek, extensive as they were, represented only part of the congregation. Custer's Ree and Crow scouts, gravely alarmed by the magnitude of the Rosebud trail, had not even suspected the existence of this additional party.

Lt. Varnum also followed a trail, a much smaller and less distinct trail—the one he thought Custer had taken after dividing the regiment. Along the way Varnum came to a hillside sprinkled with Indian medicine bags. This is a strange coincidence because it is known that on the evening before the fight Sitting Bull crossed the river and went up the slope where he sang a thunder song, smoked, and prayed for knowledge of things to come. He filled a number of buckskin pouches with tobacco and willow bark and fastened these offerings to sticks which he thrust into the ground. It appears, therefore, that the Seventh Cavalry rode directly through Sitting Bull's mystic arrangement.

The last of Custer's men probably were interred, or at least concealed, on June 28. Lt. McClernand noted in his journal that most of this day was occupied with burials, assisting wounded men from the bluff, and making litters.

About 6:30 P.M. they started for the mouth of the Little Bighorn, but litters were difficult to carry across such rough ground and by midnight they had marched less than five miles. The senior officers then resolved to try some other method. Gibbon suggested rafts because there was plenty of dry cottonwood along the river banks. Timber for these rafts had been selected when the order was canceled, presumably by Terry because nobody else outranked Gibbon. Rectangular frames were then constructed from saplings and lodge poles. Wounded horses were shot and skinned, their hides sliced into strips which were used to fashion a latticework within this frame. Blankets and robes were spread on the horsehide lattice.

Among the injured was a brevet sergeant, Michael Madden, who had been shot in the right leg while trying to get water from the river. Pvt. Peter Thompson made the same trip soon afterward and said that he was astonished to come upon a man sitting quietly on a mound of earth. "I was curious to know who he was," said Thompson. "I came up to him and saw that he had two camp kettles completely riddled with bullets. He had his gun in his hand and his eyes fixed on the grove of timber across the river, watching for the enemy. On looking him over, I could see the reason for his sitting and watching as he did. I discovered a pool of blood a short distance from him which had come from a terrible wound in his leg. It was impossible for him to move further. . . ." Thompson continued to the Little Bighorn with a kettle of his own and leaped off the bank, landing with a wild splash. "I depended on my ability to escape the bullets," he informs us, although he does not explain what sort of ability that might be. Bullets zipped into the water but this mysterious ability got him out with no holes in the kettle or in himself. Sgt. Madden, he noticed, was watching "with the greatest interest."

On the way back he offered Madden a drink, which was refused. This surprised Thompson because people who have lost a great deal of blood almost invariably are thirsty. Advising Madden "to be of good cheer," he continued uphill. One might think Sgt. Madden would respond to such pious encouragement with very little grace under these circumstances—seated beside the Little Bighorn in a steadily enlarging pool of his own blood—but Thompson says he replied cheerfully.

It is hard to believe any water carrier could survive such a trip. The Indians knew Reno's men were desperate and eventually must take a chance. This being the case, one would expect a platoon of red sharpshooters to hide on the west bank and knock off the waterboys like ducks, yet there seem to have been just two casualties: James Tanner of M Company killed, Madden seriously hurt.

Pvt. William Nugent tried it that night. As soon as he got to the river he dropped his canteens and fell face down for a gulp. Almost at once he felt a terrific blow on the forehead and when he touched the spot his hand came away slick with blood. A bullet had hit one of the canteen corks which flew up and caught him between the eyes—the only wound he suffered during six years of Indian warfare.

As for Madden, a rescue squad carried him back up the hill but his leg had been smashed in two places so Dr. Porter decided to amputate. There was no chloroform. The story repeated by one historian after another is that all Madden got to fortify himself was a drink of whisky. And when the job was done, they say, old Mike smacked his lips, told Dr. Porter to give him another drink and saw off the other leg. Pvt. William White happened to be nearby during the operation and does not think much of this picturesque story: "I helped in carrying the patient aside, for him to have a natural bodily discharge. He was weak, pale, very quiet, very serious in aspect. . . . There was no indication of his having had any whiskey." However, Madden did talk a little and he spoke with a peat moss brogue. When Pvt. Goldin asked how he was feeling he answered that he felt very bad, but added that he had been riding with the Seventh for quite a few years: ". . . and 'tis many a foine shindy we've had, too, but now I'm nothin' but a poor, damned wan-legged sojer."

Sgt. Madden's troubles were not over. An 1877 report in the Surgeon General's office notes that as Terry's caravan approached the *Far West*, "the leading mule of the litter bearing the amputated man knelt down and the patient rolled off. . . ." Why the mule knelt down is not explained. Concerning the patient, he was "uninjured."

A few other details about Madden's rough ride emerge from a 1909 letter to Walter Camp. Madden was dumped on a cactus when the reverent mule genuflected, but instead of fainting or dying as a normal person would, this tough turkey began to curse. His exact words probably were remembered for a while, although in deference to the manners of that era they were not recorded. Instead, we have a genteel circumlocution. We are told that his language "left no doubt that a considerable spark of vitality was still present."

If Madden had been carried on an Indian travois he would not have been dumped or rolled out of bed, nor would other injured men on hand-held or mule litters have suffered as much as they did; but nobody thought of emulating redskins, at least nobody with authority thought of it. A travois was simple to make: two lodgepoles crossed over a pony's withers or harnessed to its flanks, buffalo skins stretched between the poles. Many Indians told whites about how comfortable they were on travois, which rocked along gently, each shock absorbed by the long flexible poles. Ranald Mackenzie, more perceptive than most of his army colleagues, wrote that the travois exerted a beneficial effect due to the absence of jolting and because a passenger's head was higher than his body. Mackenzie's first observation certainly must be true, the second may or may not.

Terry's men had seen hundreds of travois, perhaps thousands, and could have made some, yet they did not. Why not? Maybe for the same reason that Sir John Franklin's explorers starved to death in the Arctic: They could not imagine themselves living like savages. So poor damned Mike was dumped on a cactus and nobody knows how much useless suffering other men endured.

Not only were litters—hand-held or mule-borne—unstable and uncomfortable, such transportation was preposterously inefficient. Pvt. White said that at first the carriers had to stop and rest every fifty yards. Then the number of carriers was doubled, each litter carried by alternating platoons of four. Thus, "out of the total aggregation of about seven hundred soldiers on that march there were more than four hundred on duty as walking carriers for the wounded men." White probably exaggerated or miscalculated. Capt. Clifford, who would be in a better position to know, states that twenty-one troopers had to be carried. The other wounded were able to ride, which means the column was not as vulnerable as White thought. Nevertheless, if Sioux and Cheyenne braves had again flooded the valley it might have been all up for the yellow-eyed wasichus.

They reached the Bighorn at an awkward spot, on a plateau, and for a while nobody could find a way down. But then fires were lighted in a gully and the column descended like figures in a medieval pageant.

The *Far West* was ready. Between the boilers and the stern an area of the deck had been converted into a hospital, the planks covered with fresh grass, tarpaulins spread over the grass to create one huge mattress. Wounded men were helped aboard just before sunrise on June 30, and presently the *Far West* went churning downstream.

Ree and Crow scouts also had been brought aboard but were given no medical treatment. *The Arikara Narrative* mentions this briefly, as though it were to be expected. A Ree named Goose had a bullet-mangled hand which by this time was swollen like a gourd. Nobody looked at it. Not one bluecoat inspected the hand as long as he was on the boat. Nor could a place be found for him on the mattress: "Young Hawk put Goose and his property near the wheel. . . ."

There is no more vivid chronicle of this trip from the battlefield to the Bighorn River than the diary of Pvt. Coleman. It was "a Melancholly Sight," he tells us:

> we have one Crow Indian Scout that Killed 7 Sioux and got their Scalps he was wounded five times and Strange to relate he is in a fairway to recover he rode along in silence Never Complaining the next bad Case was an Irish Mon Madden of K Company his leg was shot all whilst he was in the act of getting water for the Wounded when we were Correlled on the bluffs althow the litter he was on fell to the ground twice he never uttered a complaint we got to the boat at two A.M. of the 30th and put the wounded on board where the[y] were well taken Care of by the doctors we camped close by and lay down rapped our blankets around us and went to sleep not Caring for Sitting Bull or his Blood thirsty Wariors.

News traveled faster than the *Far West*. Vestal states that an Indian called Freighter reached Standing Rock with details of the battle long before any whites heard about it. These Standing Rock Indians refused to talk, but whites could tell from their attitude that something had occurred.

Two companies of the Seventh had been stationed at Fort Rice thirty miles below Bismarck and the women who were there evidently got some intimation of disaster on July 5. Several of them gathered at DeRudio's quarters. They lay on the floor all night. Next day when the mail was delivered each woman who got a letter from her husband looked first at the postmark to see if it was dated before or after June 25. Why these women chose the DeRudio house is not explained, nor what caused them such apprehension, although it is alleged that on July 5 a Fort Rice officer bought half a dozen arrows from a Sioux who told him they were pulled from the bodies of Custer's men. Whether these arrows were authentic souvenirs seems very doubtful, but the news did travel from Fort Rice to Bismarck, whereupon the *Tribune*—which had been expecting Mark Kellogg's dispatch—published a shocking extra.

So goes one version. Or maybe Bismarck heard about it via the *Far West*. Professor Stewart thinks crew members began telling stories as soon as the boat touched shore while Captain Marsh hurried to the telegraph office and operator J. M. Carnahan immediately went to work, "sending over the wire the news that was to confirm reports already circulating. . . ."

In brief, the catastrophic event seeped through by osmosis and nobody can say exactly when or where it first permeated.

The Bozeman *Times* and the Helena *Herald* both scooped the *Trib*, thanks to the furious ride of Muggins Taylor who reached Fort Ellis on July 3, but the Indians scooped everybody. By moccasin telegraph—mirror, smoke signal, courier—they told friends, relatives, and other interested natives throughout the area. Those around Fort Lincoln knew of it before the *Far West* tied up. Two Crow Indians, Horned Toad and Speckled Cock, appeared at Fort Lincoln nearly a week ahead of the boat. They described the battle, adding that Custer shot himself, whereupon Elizabeth—one of several wives listening to the story—shrieked and ran out of the room. David Humphreys Miller says this unpleasantness was suppressed by Army authorities. Other scholars doubt the incident.

On the evening of July 5, two or three hours before news reached Bismarck, a group of Fort Lincoln women gathered at the Custer home to sing hymns; but after the opening chords of "Nearer My God to Thee" they stopped, oppressed by a feeling of disaster. These women had planned to board the steamer *Josephine* next morning. The *Josephine* would be carrying mail and supplies upriver so they had decided to go along and give their husbands a surprise. They could have a picnic in the wilderness. But on the morning of the sixth the boat left without them. They seem to have sensed a calamity and chose to remain at the fort rather than spend several anxious days on the Yellowstone.

Later that morning Elizabeth was notified by a delegation consisting of Capt. William McCaskey, Lt. C. L. Gurley, Dr. Johnson Middleton, and two of the doctor's assistants—the presence of these last two indicating that hysteria was anticipated. They went to the back door of Custer's house. Elizabeth, wearing a dressing gown, received them in the parlor. It was a very hot day, but after getting the news she asked for a cloak to wear while she accompanied the delegation to the quarters of other widows.

"There was no fuss. We were soldiers' wives," she told an interviewer in 1927. "We women went to our homes as quickly as arrangements could be made. The Northern Pacific, to protect whose right of way my husband and his men had died, provided us with transport. . . ." Except for an official report she heard nothing from the War Department, and President Grant did not take formal notice of the tragedy—which troubled her. "President Roosevelt once said that General Custer's name was a shining light to all the youth of America. It was worth living on to hear a great President say that and to know that a great people think it."

In Elizabeth's hometown they got the news on July 4, according to a neighbor. "I was sitting upstairs by the window mending," she said in 1938:

> I saw father coming up the street, his coat off, his vest off, his hat in hand, waving a paper, the old *Tribune*. It was about eleven o'clock in the morning. He came in and called "Minnie! Minnie!" Minnie was not my name but father often called me by it. I flew downstairs for I knew something awful had happened. There he stood, white and chalky, with the paper shaking in his hands. "General Custer's entire Brigade has been wiped out," he gasped. "Think of it, Auttie, Lieutenant Calhoun, Ross, Tom, they're all gone!". . . . A great silence came over Monroe, then all the bells began to toll—church bells, firehouse bells, every bell in the town. To this day I never hear a bell toll that it does not bring back the memory. . . ."

In northern Wyoming, approximately one hundred miles south of the Little Bighorn, General Crook's Indian scouts learned about the fight within an hour or so—while Reno was battling to survive and furious squaws hacked at the bodies of Custer's five companies. Crook, who had been wandering around camp, paused to visit his Shoshone, Sioux, and Crow allies. These Indians liked Crook and trusted him so much that he had been given membership in the Soldier Lodge, a warrior fraternity. It is said that even the hostiles respected him because, unlike most whites, he never lied.

Now, observing the sullen scouts, he asked what was wrong but got no answer. He went back to his quarters and sent for the chief of scouts. Again he asked what was wrong, but could get no response. At last he invoked the Soldier Lodge. In the name of fraternal brotherhood, what was wrong? Then he was told. He asked for details. The chief of scouts either had none or refused to talk about it any more, but insisted there had been a fight between soldiers and Indians and the soldiers all were dead. Crook felt mystified. He never did learn how Indians could transmit information with such speed. Years later he told a journalist he did not think they did it with hand mirrors, smoke, or by nocturnal fire signals.

An 1894 biography of Frank "Grabber" Grouard tells a fantastic story which might explain how Crook's scouts knew about the battle. Grouard was looking for Indian signs on June 25 when he noticed smoke signals above the ridge that separates Rosebud Creek from the Little Bighorn. After reading the message he hurried back to camp and told some officers what he had learned. They laughed at him. The biography makes no mention of Grouard talking with Crook's Indian scouts, but if this much of the story is true he certainly would have discussed the matter with them.

Anyway, we are told, Grouard resolved to investigate. He saddled up and rode toward the signals. He got to the Rosebud divide about dark, struck the trail left by Custer's regiment, and followed it. An hour or two later he passed the hilltop where Reno's men were entrenched but never saw them. The night was cloudy, a few raindrops were falling. His horse balked at an object on the trail. Grouard dismounted. "I did not know what it was, so I commenced examining it, when I found that I had my hand on the head of a man who had been scalped."

He continued along the trail and guessed from the behavior of his horse that there were bodies in the darkness. He rode downhill, crossed the river, and rode up among the benchlands to the west, trying to find out where the Indians had gone. At dawn he realized they were moving south toward the Bighorn Mountains. He trailed them and caught up with an old man herding ponies. Grouard dressed like an Indian, he was very dark, and he spoke Sioux, but the suspicious old man wanted to know who he was. Grouard said he always had been called "Grabber"—whereupon the old man let out a yell, took two jumps crossing the river, and began shouting that soldiers had returned. Grouard laid the quirt to his horse and galloped off. Indians chased him forty miles to the Tongue River. Next day he got back to Crook's camp.

Such was the story he allegedly told his biographer, Joe DeBarthe. At first it sounds convincing. But then, why would Grouard identify himself to a hostile Sioux? This makes no sense. He was an experienced frontiersman, a professional scout, yet he went right past three hundred men and several hundred large animals on a hilltop. Which is to say, the longer one contemplates this adventure the more fabulous it becomes.

DeBarthe may have invented the whole thing. An employee at the Crow agency said a long time afterward that he was present during a quarrel between Grouard and DeBarthe when the scout complained about falsifications in the biography.

Capt. Bourke, Crook's intelligent and loyal adjutant, reported tersely: "Frank Grouard had made an inspection trip of the country . . . to determine the truth of reported smokes, but his trip failed to confirm the story." Bourke does not give the date of this trip. It could have been June 25, but might as easily have been two or three days later. The Indians set any number of grass fires when they withdrew, and on June 28 the debris they left at the Little Bighorn was set afire by General Terry.

Numerous questions curl around Mr. Grouard, which of course makes him a splendid bit player in this murky drama. He said he was born in the South Pacific, his father a missionary, his mother a Polynesian named Nahina—daughter of a high chief of the Paumoto Islands. The family moved to California in 1852, he said, where he was given to a couple named Pratt who later moved to Utah. Thus he reached the northwestern United States.

What has been more or less ascertained is that one day a swarthy individual dressed as an Indian, calling himself Frank Grouard, rode up to the Red Cloud agency, said he had been living among the Sioux for years and knew them well. There is no doubt that he did know them.

As to his heritage, some scholars think his parents were a Negro and an Indian, and that he was born along the upper Missouri. A Montana character named George "Clubfoot" Boyd sneered at all of Grouard's tales. Boyd said the exotic Sandwich Islander was nothing but a renegade horse thief. He stole a few government horses, Boyd said, and herded them to a Gros Ventre camp where he spent the winter, after which he stole some Gros Ventre ponies and moved in with the Assiniboines. Eventually he joined the Unkpapas where he managed to ingratiate himself with Sitting Bull. Rather than being employed by the government as a trustworthy scout, Clubfoot said, Grouard should be hanged.

Dr. John Gray concluded after quite a lot of research involving such arcane documents as a history of San Bernardino county, the eighth volume of a Mormon periodical titled *Heart Throbs of the West*, and the 1790 New Hampshire *Federal Census*, that the mysterious Mr. Grouard was, in fact, just what he claimed to be: half-Yankee, half-Polynesian.

Dr. Gray's letter of inquiry to the Mormon Historical Society brought back an excerpt from Mormon chronologies which revealed that Elder Benjamin Grouard, who had been "set apart" for missionary work in the South Seas, had married a native girl named Nahina. And a letter to an associate history professor at Utah State University brought a reference to the diary of Mrs. Addison Pratt. She, too, had gone to the South Seas where in 1850 she met Elder Grouard, Nahina, and their month-old son Frank. Two years later, evidently when the mission broke up, she was given custody of Elder Grouard's half-native child. The Pratts sailed to San Francisco and from there traveled to San Bernardino where they lived until 1858, at which time they were recalled to Utah. Seven years later Frank drove his foster mother to Salt Lake to visit Brigham Young, and just about here he vanishes. Mrs. Pratt's diary mentions in 1873 that she "desired to know the fate of my poor boy who had left me to go to Montana as a teamster. . . ."

Such details persuaded Dr. Gray that the mysterious Grabber must be telling the truth. If not, he was the world's greatest clairvoyant.

Whatever his parentage, however he got where he was, he established himself as a figure of some consequence in Dakota Territory.

Grabber sounds like a diminutive of the family name, but derives from his Sioux name, Standing Bear. In January of 1869 while working as a mail courier between Fort Hall and Fort Peck he was captured by Indians. Snow was blowing in his face, he could not see much, and the first thing he knew somebody hit him across the back and dragged him off his horse. He was a big man, weighing about 230 pounds. He had on a thick buffalo coat, mitts, leggings, and moccasins, and as he struggled with the Indians they thought he looked like a bear on its hind legs trying to hug the enemy.

There were at least a dozen Indians, so in spite of his efforts the struggle did not last long. They tied him up and he expected to be killed, but the leader of this party happened to be Sitting Bull, who decided to keep the prisoner alive. Sitting Bull later adopted him, perhaps because this gesture increased the medicine man's prestige, perhaps because of Grouard's complexion. The Sioux believed he was an Indian whom they had recaptured from the whites and it appears that Sitting Bull intended to hold him until he could recover his native language. And it is said that even though Grouard guided the bluecoats against them, Sitting Bull's nephews remembered him with affection and continued to insist he was an Indian. This last, if true, becomes hard to explain. Wasicun sapa Isaiah Dorman, the black white man, was treated with extreme cruelty because the Sioux judged him to be a traitor.

Today, so long after events, DeBarthe's concoctions can hardly be separated from what might be a variety of concoctions by Grouard himself. That nocturnal visit to the Custer abattoir is fraudulent, but who knows which man invented it?

Grouard's story of smoke signals sounds a bit more plausible, if not much. After all, to whom would the hostiles be signaling? Their camps lay close together. Nevertheless, he might have observed a pillar of smoke above the Little Bighorn.

Somehow, within hours, Crook's scouts did learn there had been a fight; of this there can be little doubt, and from their sullen demeanor it is evident that they knew they were on the losing team.

Lack of specific news began to make Crook nervous. On July 1, accompanied by a small escort, he rode high up into the Bighorn Mountains and looked around. Bourke went on this trip. Not even with the aid of powerful glasses could they detect the slightest trace of an army.

On July 6, increasingly restless, Crook ordered Grouard and Baptiste "Big Bat" Pourière to see what they could see. One day after leaving camp Grouard and Big Bat saw a great many Sioux. They returned with the utmost alacrity.

Crook did not move, except for occasional hunting and fishing excursions. On July 10 he was elk hunting when courier Ben Arnold arrived from Fort Fetterman with ugly news. Scouts promptly left camp, found Crook, and told him. The general did not say much, according to journalist Finerty, "but he kept up a big thinking."

Captain Anson Mills states that about June 30—an incorrect estimate, the actual date being July 12—he was commanding an outpost on lower Goose Creek when, just at sunrise, he observed three mounted men approaching whom he first mistook for Indians. They were white men riding mules: Pvts. James Bell, William Evans, and Benjamin Stewart of E Company, Seventh Infantry. Each man had a message from Terry sewn into his clothes, but one of them also carried a dispatch by hand. Mills states that this was given to him, and he in turn delivered it to Col. Royal who was temporarily in command because Crook once again had gone hunting. The information it contained, said Mills, "horrified the assembled officers."

Royal ordered Mills to carry the message to Crook. Mills located him eighteen miles up in the mountains: ". . . his pack mules loaded down with elk, deer and big horn sheep."

So the general seems to have learned little by little about his associates in Montana and it is no wonder he kept up a big thinking. He had spent three weeks comfortably encamped on Goose Creek. Ben Arnold called it "criminal inertia."

Col. Sturgis received no disturbing intimations of disaster; he got the news abruptly, like a slap in the face. When first notified at his St. Louis office where he had been assigned to superintend the Mounted Recruiting Service he displayed as much rage as grief. He likened Custer to a thief shot during a robbery, deserving no pity. He never had gotten along with his erratic subordinate so their immediate superior—Sheridan—had resolved the awkward relationship by giving Sturgis a desk and turning Custer loose in the field. This was just what Custer wanted and one might assume that Sturgis, who was fifty-four years old, probably had lost all desire to chase wild Indians. Not in the least. Sturgis resented this humiliating assignment.

Mutual antipathy does not explain the colonel's virulent response. More significant is the fact that the youngest officer of the regiment, Lt. Jack Sturgis, whose blood-soaked underwear had been picked up by Terry's men, was the colonel's son. Jack Sturgis was fresh from West Point. He had requested and had been granted a commission in his father's regiment.

His body could not be found. Such is the opinion of most scholars, although it has been said that his sister Ella—she who smote and devastated Major Reno—Ella visited the Little Bighorn in order to identify her brother's remains. And a photograph in the U.S. Signal Corps archives shows a heap of stones beside a crudely labeled board:

L' STURGIS
7th CAV JUNE, '76

Clearly this photo suggests that Jack was identified, but the stones were piled up and the board hastily lettered five years after the battle when his mother visited the field. She had not been informed that her son's body was missing and nobody had enough courage to tell her. After she went back east the cairn was torn apart, the board presumably tossed aside or burned.

Colonel Sturgis issued a more temperate statement when his passion subsided. Custer often wrote about Indian warfare, Sturgis remarked, and people who read these articles naturally supposed them to be a consequence of wide experience, but in fact, "his experience was exceedingly limited, and that he was overreached by Indian tactics, and hundreds of valuable lives sacrificed thereby, will astonish those alone who may have read his writings— not those who were best acquainted with him and knew the peculiarities of his character." True enough, yet rather presumptuous because Sturgis himself knew little about Indians, and as a military strategist his own record was less than distinguished. During the Civil War he performed well at South Mountain, Antietam, and Fredericksburg, but at Brice's Cross Roads he was chopped up by the Confederate general Nathan Bedford Forrest, losing his supply train and sixteen of his eighteen artillery pieces, even though he commanded more than twice as many soldiers as Forrest. A board of inquiry convened to study this disaster; it did not reprimand Sturgis, but his days as a field commandant were over. Thus, for more reasons than one, Col. Sturgis lived the good life in St. Louis and "awaited orders" while the fair-haired object of his contempt went Sioux-hunting.

Reaction throughout the country was no different in 1876 than it is today upon receipt of similar news: shock, followed by disbelief, fury, and a slavering appetite for revenge. The artist DeCost Smith commented some years afterward that, barring minor divagations, Sitting Bull's people were right and the United States government wrong. It was the government, not the Sioux, who broke treaties. There was gold in the Black Hills and the Northern Pacific Railroad must be built. Savages could not stand in the path of civilization. "It was the old argument of expediency; the shortest way out of a bad bargain. 'Barbarism,' and later 'fanaticism,' were traditional foes of 'civiliza-tion.' It was the detestable war cry of the Crusaders revamped for nineteenth-century needs, '*Dieu le veut. Guerre aux infidèles!*' . . ."

Volunteers popped up like daisies in April.

Salt Lake City promised twelve hundred.

Keokuk offered a staunch band of one hundred.

Sioux City, of all places, notified Washington that a thousand avengers would be ready within ten days.

Volunteers in faraway Virginia City, Nevada, were anxious to march.

In Springfield, Illinois, the Sherman Guards pronounced themselves alert, willing, and able.

Texas, armed to the hip, foamed at the mouth. Death to redskins! God wills it! Just give Texas a whack at those Sioux, begged the Galveston *Daily News*, "and there will be consternation and mourning in their wigwams be-fore many moons have passed."

"Killing a mess of Indians is the only recreation our frontier rangers want," yelped the Dallas *Daily Herald*.

"Texas deserves the honor of attempting to wipe out the Sioux . . ." bel-lowed the Austin *Daily State Gazette*.

Custer had been no favorite in the mossy South, certainly not in Texas, but he was American. More important, he was white.

"The North alone shall not mourn this gallant soldier," bayed the Rich-mond *Whig*. "He belongs to all the Saxon race; and when he carried his bold dragoons into the thickest of the last ambuscade, where his sun of life forever set, we behold in him the true spirit of that living chivalry which cannot die, but shall live forever to illustrate the pride, the glory, and the grandeur of our imperishable race."

Like cats hit with a spade, wits addled, state after state joined the national ululation. The Fort Smith, Arkansas, *Herald* yowled with inchoate desire that thousands of rebels would respond to any call. Tennessee sang to the moon, pledging the terrible swift might of the Jackson Guards, the Chicka-saw Guards, the ex-Confederate Irish Volunteers, and an unspecified Negro company. Ex-rebel General Jo Shelby of Missouri telegraphed Ulysses Grant for permission to enlist one thousand Indian fighters. Atlanta's Cle-burne Rifles yearned for retribution.

Newspaper editors printed violent letters. Mr. W. H. Eddys of Chicago addressed the *Tribune*: "In every case where an inoffensive citizen is slain, let 100 of these red brutes feel the power of a rope properly adjusted under their chins. . . ."

In New Rumley, Ohio, birthplace of the fallen hero, a group of schoolboys took an oath—"each with his right hand upraised over a McGuffey First

Reader"—to kill Sitting Bull on sight. Nine or ten years later Buffalo Bill introduced one of these dedicated avengers, William Markley, to the star of his Wild West show, namely Sitting Bull. How this confrontation ended we do not know, but Sitting Bull loved to shake hands, so it would be reasonable to assume that is how Mr. Markley consummated his boyhood oath.

The voices of a few reflective people could be heard amongst those of letter-writers, volunteers, and schoolboys in knickers, but not many. This was hardly a propitious moment for thought. Still, there were these few, because there always seem to be the uncommon few.

In Chicago, on the first Sunday after it became public knowledge, two weeks from the day Custer died, pastor D. J. Burrell asked from his pulpit who should be held responsible for an event so grim: "The history of our dealings with these Indian tribes from the very beginning is a record of fraud, and perjury, and uninterrupted injustice. We have made treaties, binding ourselves to the most solemn promises in the name of God, intending at that very time to hold these treaties light as air whenever our convenience should require them to be broken."

The London *Times*, commenting that this debacle would seem to America more like an insult than an injury, prophesied that the Indians would be driven backward to death or to yet more distant and barren reservations: "The conduct of the American Government towards the Indians of the Plains has been neither very kindly nor very wise. . . ."

As the *Times* shrewdly predicted, a way of life was ending. The Army regrouped—Sheridan reinforced Crook's paralyzed unit with ten companies under General Wesley Merritt—and once again a horde of angry wasichus picked up the trail of these obstreperous aborigines. Their approximate location was not hard to determine because they had set fire to the Bighorn timber. At night, says Bourke, the fire was quite beautiful, depicting the great line of foothills "in a tracery of gold."

Now the idea was for Crook to march northeast along Rosebud Creek, where the Indians should soon be, if they were not already there, while Terry and Gibbon would angle down from the Yellowstone. At some point they would slap the savages like a grizzly slapping trout. This time there would be no mistake.

General Terry headed south with sixteen hundred men.

Crook, guided by Ute and Shoshone scouts, started north with two thousand men. Among the paleface guides was none other than Buffalo Bill, who had closed his show at the Philadelphia Centennial Exposition, telling the audience his services were needed in the real West.

There was considerable enthusiasm among Crook's troops. Sgt. John Powers of the Fifth Cavalry, previously stationed at Fort Hays, wrote about this campaign to the Ellis County *Star* for the benefit of comrades still in Kansas. After joining Crook's army, he said, they got equipment for fifteen days on the trail. "We were, to believe all accounts, going right down into Mr. Sitting Bull's camp and eat him up without salt."

So away they went, General Crook commanding, General Merritt in charge of cavalry.

They left camp intending to have roast Sioux for supper, Powers wrote, "but after marching 30 miles in blinding dust we encamped on the Rosebud, six miles south of the place at which Crook had his battle in June last. We had to dispense with our roast Sioux, however, and fall back on fried bacon."

They saw many Dakota burials. Some of these were quite old, which made no difference to Shoshone and Ute scouts who prodded them with lances until bones came tumbling down accompanied by an occasional ax or bow or a nickel-plated revolver. But one of these scaffolds the Shoshones refused to touch, claiming it held bad medicine. Ute John, who had been baptized a Mormon numerous times, was not afraid. Bourke remarks parenthetically that Ute John was credited with having murdered his own grandmother and drunk her blood. He disdained speaking to any white man except General Crook about the problems of this expedition. "Hello, Cluke," Ute John would say, "how you gittin' on? Where you tink dem Clazy Hoss en Settin' Bull is now, Cluke?"

Nor could Ute John be intimidated by an ancient Sioux scaffold. He tore up this bad medicine burial and out scampered sixteen field mice.

So they proceed, warily, because from General Cluke on down everybody now had great respect for Clazy Hoss and Settin' Bull.

After a while the scouts reported a line of Indians ascending Rosebud Valley and just behind them the white canvas of a wagon train, meaning it must be Terry. Crook's Indians therefore prepared to welcome these allies—daubing their faces with mud, putting on war bonnets, prancing around, shaking lances and rifles—but this display of friendship alarmed the advancing Indians who mistook Crook's Shoshones and Utes for Sioux and began running away. Buffalo Bill then waved his hat and spurred forward.

How it looked from Terry's point of view is told best by LeForge, whose Crow scouts preceded the column. After sighting a dust cloud in the south they sent back word of approaching hostiles. The army quickly deployed. A fat newspaper reporter came hurrying up and galloped around the front lines, waving a rifle and declaring, "Boys, I'll be right with you in this fight!" LeForge remarks that his announcement did not increase the confidence of Terry's soldiers.

So the two paws of the grizzly met, except there was no trout.

As for the disposition of the Sioux, nobody could say. Generals Crook and Terry sat down on a strip of canvas, drank coffee, and talked about what to do. Bourke describes Terry as most charming and affable, a man who looked like a scholar, with kind blue eyes and a gentle face bronzed by sun, wind, and rain to the hue of an old sheepskin-covered Bible. The entire army felt proud of Terry, says Bourke; yet it is plain that in his own judgment General Crook was the significant commander, equaled only by Sheridan and Grant.

The Sioux had escaped northeast, all signs pointed that direction. The combined armies therefore pursued them across the Tongue, at which point the hostile trail evolved into three: one moving upstream, another downstream, while the main trail continued east toward the Powder. Here also were the skeletons of two prospectors who apparently had been caught and broiled alive. And here was a congregation of rattlesnakes which the Shoshones enthusiastically attacked with lances, shouting "Gott tammee you! Gott tammee you!"

Both armies followed the big trail east to the Powder, then veered north to the Yellowstone and their floating supply depot, the *Far West*. LeForge, Cody, and a Bannock scout named Buffalo Horn rode ahead. Although many trails could be seen, not an Indian was visible. On the banks of the Yellowstone, however, these riders observed "a broad patch of brassy, shimmering ground" which turned out to be thousands of bushels of corn. This corn had been transported upstream in sacks, unloaded, and left unguarded. The Indians who came across the deposit might have been puzzled, but only a fool rejects a gift. They dumped the grain, took the sacks, and went on their way.

Crook and Terry camped at the mouth of the Powder while supplies were distributed, and here they reorganized the plan of attack. Terry would pursue some hostiles who had crossed to the north side of the Yellowstone. Crook would follow the broad trail east because this large party of Sioux might be headed for the Black Hills, in which event quite a few prospectors were about to lose their scalps.

Crook's Utes and Shoshones thought it not only futile but dangerous to go chasing Sioux in the heart of Sioux country, so they departed. Terry's Crow scouts did not desert but they were getting restless and LeForge says they were allowed to return to the agency.

Late in August the columns separated.

Terry and Gibbon angled northeast, accompanied by Buffalo Bill, who seems to have been more or less swapped for five Rees. There were men in the command who did not consider this an advantageous trade. "When he joined us," one remarked many years later, "he was wearing all the accoutrements befitting a moving-picture scout. He had an entire suit of creamy buckskin, all beaded and fringed. A rich silk scarf encircled his neck and covered his shoulders. His headwear was a fine-quality big white hat having three or four eagle feathers standing up from its band."

Gibbon accepted him pleasantly, but was not much impressed. He turned Buffalo Bill over to Lt. Bradley, who had charge of civilian scouts.

"You'd better be careful of your clothing," Bradley said, "or it may get wet and dirty while you are with us."

How Buffalo Bill answered Lt. Bradley is not known.

His first assignment was to lead two enlisted men on a reconnaissance trip. They boarded a steamboat with their horses and went coasting out of sight. Two days later they returned on another boat. The celebrated scout and showman said they had scoured the territory for Indians. The enlisted men said privately that at Cody's order they disembarked on an island a few miles downstream and spent those days hiding in the brush.

Like Wild Bill Hickok, Buckskin Frank Leslie, Rowdy Joe Lowe, and other borderline personalities, Cody seems to have been a curious admixture of thespian and assassin. He had been working for General Merritt before the junction with Crook's forces, and on July 17 he killed a Cheyenne sub-chief named Hay-o-wai—Yellow Hair—commonly mistranslated as Yellow Hand and best known to Americans these days as a victim of Mr. Gary Cooper's deadly skill with six-gun and bowie knife. In this epic drama Mr. Cooper pretended to be Wild Bill, not Buffalo Bill, possibly because somebody in the studio got two screenplays mixed up and nobody knew the difference.

Whatever happened in Hollywood, it appears that in real life in the real West a band of about thirty Cheyennes was ambushed by four hundred troops of Merritt's Fifth Cavalry just above the Red Cloud agency. A signalman with the wagon train, who saw it, said that when Cody felt adequately positioned behind a small hill he shot a Cheyenne pony, after which he rode down the dismounted Indian, "soon had him killed and his scalp off." Buffalo Bill then held up the dripping topknot for everybody to see and proclaimed it the first scalp for Custer. He was tastefully dressed in a black velvet suit trimmed with silver and a red sash, and later he incorporated the death of Yellow Hand/ Yellow Hair into his show, an act which proved extremely popular.

Despite the services of this unusual scout, General Terry had not much luck flushing red men north of the Yellowstone.

General Crook, grimly pursuing the big trail east, had worse luck. He favored the idea of traveling light, unencumbered by wagon trains, which was one reason for his success against Indians all over the West, but this time he sliced it pretty thin. Rations gave out, soldiers began to eat their horses, and it rained. And rained. And rained. The troops got soggier and more distraught and soggier. This column of two thousand men became decidedly gloomy, says Bourke. They had not been able to change clothes since leaving Goose Creek a month before, now they were smeared with mud from top to bottom and the rain never never never stopped, and the best they had for supper was a sinewy strip of old Dobbin.

Crook kept going.

"So far the result of this expedition has been nothing but disaster, and a depletion of the public purse," wrote Pvt. Alfred McMackin to the *Star*. "The general supposition is that in order to draw the veil of obscurity over his being outgeneralled by Sitting Bull, and his signal failure to accomplish anything towards the defeat of the Indians, he conceived the brilliant idea of marching hither and thither. . . ."

The Indian trail bent south, unmistakably toward the Black Hills. Crook followed.

On September 7 a detachment of fifty mules and packers, escorted by 150 picked troops under the command of Capt. Anson Mills, was ordered ahead to look for food. Crook authorized the supply officer to buy up everything in the first town they reached—Deadwood or any other settlement.

Two days later a courier returned. Mills had struck a hostile village near a place called Slim Buttes.

Crook hurried forward and found Mills in control. A few Indians had been killed, the rest scattered, "several tons" of dried meat impounded, along with quite a bit of ammunition and other supplies which represented more of a loss to the reds than a gain to the whites. Of particular interest was a cavalry guidon "nearly new and torn from the staff," an officer's overcoat, a non-com's blouse, one of Myles Keogh's gloves, McClellan saddles, and some horses bearing the Seventh Cavalry brand.

The battle had not ended when Crook arrived. An unknown number of Indians had retreated to a gulch thickly forested with box elder. Interpreters creeping forward on hands and knees finally persuaded the squaws to give up, and Crook encouraged these women to tell the warriors that if they surrendered they would not be killed. At last the gulch emptied. Among those who came out was a mortally wounded chief. He had taken a load of buckshot in the stomach and his entrails were spilling from the wound. He gathered them up with his hands, walked to a campfire, and seated himself. Most of Crook's men at Slim Buttes thought this was American Horse, although Eleanor Hinman was told by Short Buffalo and by interpreter John Colhoff in 1930 that the man shot in the stomach was Iron Plume. American Horse, they insisted, was not captured. Whoever he was, he sat quietly near the fire with a stick between his teeth.

Adjutant Bourke discusses the evening meal—pony steak, buffalo tongue, berries—and remarks that a Sioux preparation of dried meat macerated with wild cherries and plums is nutritious and quite palatable, "cousin-german to our own plum pudding." He sounds bemused by the wounded captive, employing a poetic beat that perhaps was accidental: "In the drizzling rain of that night the soul of 'American Horse' took flight. . . ."

The death of this Sioux chief as reported by Bourke does not coincide with Dr. McGillycuddy's field diary for September 9: "I operated & tried to return intestines. He died at $4\frac{1}{2}$ p.m." But it was a dark, depressing day, scarcely distinguishable from night.

Regardless of the hour, regardless of this man's identity, his fortitude sounds unbelievable. Yet it was not uncommon among Indians; and most whites, after their first amazement, decided that the aborigine must be physiologically different. Colonel Dodge, with three decades of frontier experience, might be expected to display sharper insight than he did: "The tenacity of life of an Indian . . . indicates a nervous system so dull as to class him rather with brutes than with men." The shock of a bullet usually would paralyze so many nerves and muscles of a white man, said Dodge, that no matter where he was hit he would be knocked down. A red man, however, must be hit in the brain, heart, or spine. "I have myself seen an Indian go off with two bullets through his body, within an inch or two of the spine, the only effect of which was to cause him to change his gait from a run to a dignified walk."

Captain Philo Clark wrote that the small number killed during the Custer fight "is due to the fact that an Indian has a wonderful faculty of protecting himself, and unless he is shot through the brain, heart or back, there is no certainty at all about his dying, for since I have seen many Indians who have been shot in all manner of ways through the body and still enjoying excellent health, I have been convinced that of all animals they are superior in point of tenacity of life. . . ."

Finerty, who was with Crook at the Rosebud, said a hospital had been established beneath some trees near a sluggish creek and the surgeons wasted no time. Most of the wounded soldiers endured this treatment well enough, but an occasional groan or stifled shriek would tell where the knife or probe had touched a nerve. "The Indian wounded—some of them desperate cases— gave no indication of feeling, but submitted to be operated upon with the grim stolidity of their race."

George Catlin attended a Mandan ceremony much like the Sun Dance and sketched some braves who were being hooked to the apparatus. Several of them beckoned, pointing to their own faces: "I watched through all this hor- rid operation without being able to detect anything but the pleasantest smiles as they looked me in the eye, while I could hear the knife rip through the flesh, and feel enough of it to start uncontrollable tears down my cheeks."

A certain Mr. Cox watched the Flatheads torture a Blackfoot. Not only did the captive endure it without wincing, he taunted his captors, jeered at their best efforts, and told them they knew nothing about the business. While they were shortening his fingers a joint at a time he addressed a one-eyed Flathead as follows: "It was by my arrow that you lost your eye," whereupon the en- raged Flathead scooped out one of the Blackfoot's eyes with a knife and almost cut his nose in half. "I killed your brother, and I scalped your old fool of a father," said the Blackfoot to another, whereupon the second Flathead leaped forward, scalped him, and was about to stab him when the Flathead chief interfered. Says Mr. Cox: "The raw skull, bloody socket, and mutilated nose now presented an horrific appearance, but by no means changed his attitude of defiance." Then said the irrepressible Blackfoot to the chief: "It was I that made your wife a prisoner last fall; we put out her eyes; we tore out her tongue; we treated her like a dog. Forty of our young warriors . . ." At which point the Flathead chief shot him through the heart.

During the attack on Black Kettle's village in Oklahoma a number of chil- dren were shot by Custer's troops. Four or five days afterward those who survived were delivered to Camp Supply and their wounds treated. De- Benneville Keim was astonished. Not a single child made the slightest sound, "yet their distorted features, and the delirious glare of the eye, betrayed the physical anguish prevailing within their rigid exterior. During such painful operations as probing and cleansing the wounds the little sufferers placed their hands over their heads and closed their eyes, submitting without a murmur. One little girl, with a bullethole through her body on the left side, sat up as if in perfect health."

All of which implies superhuman courage, if not the dulled nervous system proposed by Col. Dodge. In fact, it probably was the result of training. Those who lived in a wild environment had to learn very early what every wild creature learns: Absolute silence and apparent unconcern, no matter how one has been hurt, might mean the difference between life and death.

The Sioux agent at Standing Rock, James McLaughlin, interpreted this legendary stoicism as shyness or a passion for secrecy. An Indian who suffered torture or the agony of a wound without making a sign was not oblivious, nor anxious to be thought so. It was just that he had too much regard for personal dignity to expose his feelings.

Henry David Thoreau at a somewhat earlier date also meditated upon this renunciation of the body. Jesuit priests, he says, while burning pagan Indians at the stake found themselves "quite balked" when the wretched victims suggested new methods of torture. "Being superior to physical suffering, it sometimes chanced that they were superior to any consolation which the missionaries could offer. . . ."

At any rate, Slim Buttes was the first victory—or act of retaliation—after the Little Bighorn. It was not pretty, not especially dramatic, not even very colorful. Gone were those ornamental days of 1812 and thereabouts with gold epaulettes, hussar helmets, vivid sashes, Trojan plumes. By the time of the Indian Wars if an American army could be regarded as picturesque it was because of a certain uncouth seediness, exemplified here by Crook himself. "This utterly unpretending party—" so Captain Charles King sketched him, "this undeniably shabby-looking man in a private soldier's light-blue overcoat, standing ankle-deep in mud in a far-gone pair of private soldier's boots. . . . The rain is dripping from the ragged edge of his old white felt hat and down over his untrimmed beard as he holds out his hand to greet, Indian fashion, the first squaw. . . ." Bourke sounds no more glamorous in an ancient hunting coat, "an indescribable pair of trousers, and a straw hat minus ribbon or binding, a brim ragged as the edge of a saw, and a crown without a thatch."

Such was the denouement of the first campaign to avenge General Custer: thirty-seven lodges captured at Slim Buttes. It has been estimated that during the Indian Wars the United States spent approximately a million dollars to kill each red man.

Sheridan disbanded this expedition in October of 1876, but still the natives were not where the government wanted them. All too many stayed away from their assigned reservations. Therefore a new campaign was devised to surprise, catch, and crush this independent opponent.

So, as the Canadian wind and snow came sweeping down, the Powder River Expedition got under way. This time, mostly at Crook's insistence, the army was led by Sioux and Cheyenne scouts recruited from various agencies. Crook wanted them not only to track their undomesticated relatives but for the psychological effect of their alliance with bluecoats. With them went other redskin scouts: Arapahoes, Shoshones, Bannocks, Pawnees, one Ute, and one Nez Perce.

The important battle of this campaign occurred on November 25 above Crazy Woman Creek near the Bighorn Mountains when Colonel Ranald Mackenzie hit the Cheyenne village of Dull Knife. This creek supposedly was named for a demented woman who lived by herself along its banks for many years and died there about 1850. However, the English word "crazy" does not fully translate the Cheyenne equivalent, which may indicate not only madness but promiscuity. That is, the outcast woman might not have been mad, just lascivious. The reason for the dual meaning of the Cheyenne word seems to be that in their eyes a woman who was not virtuous must be crazy—an opinion shared by most whites.

Mackenzie charged the village at dawn, awakening its inhabitants as briskly as Custer had awakened Black Kettle's village in 1868. Bourke said they wiped it from the face of the earth—more than two hundred lodges, each crammed with supplies. "The roar of the flames exasperated the fugitive Cheyennes to frenzy; they saw their homes disappearing in fire and smoke; they heard the dull thump, thump, of their own medicine drum, which had fallen into the hands of our Shoshones; and they listened to the plaintive drone of the sacred flageolets upon which the medicine men of the Pawnees were playing. . . ."

Mackenzie's raiders found numerous Seventh Cavalry artifacts—curry combs, shovels, axes, brushes, canteens, a notebook listing the best marksmen at every target practice held by Lt. McIntosh, and a sergeant's memorandum book containing this fearful entry: "Left Rosebud June 25th." The memo book had been embellished with drawings by a Cheyenne warrior to illustrate his most important feats, such as lancing a cavalryman who wore sergeant-major's chevrons—a drawing believed to represent the death of Sergeant-Major Kennedy who died with Elliott at the Washita. If so, the warrior must have been either a Southern Cheyenne or a northerner who happened to be visiting relatives when Custer attacked Black Kettle's village.

Troopers picked up wallets full of greenbacks, a letter addressed to a woman in the east—stamped, ready for mailing—and the hat of Sgt. William

Allen, I Company, Third Cavalry, who was killed June 17 during the Rose-bud fight. Also in Dull Knife's camp was a swallowtailed silk guidon bearing the regimental number and company letter. That is, it could be recognized as a Seventh Cavalry guidon although a squaw with an eye for unusual decor had turned it into a pillow case. Equally significant was Tom Custer's taffeta-lined jacket. And there were mattresses, indicating that the appearance on the frontier of such unimaginable equipment had created among these Indians a longing for new and exotic comforts.

Dull Knife punished neighborhood enemies as well as encroaching whites; Mackenzie's troops discovered a necklace of brown fingers, the arm of a squaw, and in a buckskin bag the right hands of twelve Indian babies.

On November 26 the column retreated from this devastated village. Bourke wrote that as soon as the troops were beyond rifle range two or three Cheyennes came back, sat down among the blackened ruins, and began to wail. Bourke thought they were no more afflicted than others of the tribe, but were symbolically representing them all. "Examples of just such Ceremonial Weeping I have seen at the Rosebud, at the Sun Dance and elsewhere. It was an observance known to the Hebrews, who, 'by the waters of Babylon' 'sat down and wept,' and to other nations."

That day the column marched just twelve miles. It was unusually cold and the wounded men needed attention. "The bodies of our dead, frozen hard, were slung over the backs of pack-mules, which at first were restive and frightened, but by the end of an hour or so had become reconciled to their ghastly cargoes."

During this fight the astounding vitality of aborigines was again noted. A Shoshone scout named Anzi got a bullet through the intestines and according to Mackenzie's surgeons was marked for death. There was no sense trying to save him. All they could do was give him a little morphine and as much whisky as he wanted, which was a lot. Bourke says the medical panniers were emptied "and the last drop poured into his mouth, to his inexpressible pleasure; but finding that no more was to come, with many an imprecation upon the 'Mellican Medicine-man,' he rolled out of his 'travois' and was assisted to the back of a pony which he rode all day. He basely went back on the doctors' predictions, returned with his people across the mountains, nearly two hundred miles of travel, and when I saw him at Fort Washakie, during the Nez Perce campaign in the following year, he was still living, although by no means, so his friends told me, the man he had been. . . ."

Wooden Leg missed this fight. He did not miss many but he missed this because everything appeared peaceful, which is to say boring, so he and nine companions decided to make war on the Crows—which seems to be what they did when nobody had a better idea. Just when they left Dull Knife's village is uncertain, probably a week or ten days before Mackenzie located it.

"As the snows of winter began to fall . . ." these ten ambitious young braves set out in a northwesterly direction looking for Crow scalps or horses. On the south bank of the Yellowstone they saw a Crow family—a man, his squaw, and some children traveling upstream with their one lodge—but decided not to harm them. The Crows never saw this Cheyenne war party.

The eleventh day of the trip found Wooden Leg and his companions near the site of the Little Bighorn battle. They thought they might as well look around. On a cool bright morning they walked across the field, leading their ponies, discussing those who had been killed, telling each other what they had done when the bluecoats attacked. Wind had swept away the snow to reveal a hillside littered with arrows and broken lances. They saw decayed horse carcasses. They saw mounds of sagebrush and dirt partly concealing the bodies of soldiers. Wooden Leg wanted cartridges because he had an army rifle. Near a dead horse he found a pasteboard box full. The box was rotten but the cartridges were good, they needed only to be wiped off, so he filled his belt and put the rest in his pocket. He found a soldier's jackknife. One of his friends picked up a Sioux sheathknife. Unused ammunition lay everywhere.

On Reno Hill they collected more ammunition. Then they crossed the river and Wooden Leg pointed out the place from which he had shot a man who tried to get water. This man's body fell into the stream. Wooden Leg took his rifle and some tobacco and metal money out of his pockets. The other Cheyennes laughed when he told them he had thrown away the green picture-paper.

Next morning they rode across the divide separating the Little Bighorn from Rosebud Creek, following a trail often used by Indians—the trail Custer himself had followed—and continued eastward to the Tongue. Below the mouth of Hanging Woman Creek they saw Indians coming down the valley on foot and wondered who they might be.

These walking Indians turned out to be their own people, cold and hungry, most of them without blankets or moccasins. Soldiers and Pawnees had fallen upon the village, they said, and burned everything. Many people were killed. Others froze to death while walking through the mountain snow. Pawnees captured three women and a boy. Now, they said, once again they were looking for the Oglalas under Crazy Horse.

Wooden Leg's veracity has been questioned on a few matters, such as the whisky-filled canteens, but this account of visiting the Custer battlefield in November of 1876 goes unchallenged. He and nine other young Cheyennes almost certainly were the first people to go back. Some wandering party of Sioux might have visited the field earlier, but if so they left no trace.

The first bluecoats to return were cavalrymen of the Seventh under Captain Henry Nowlan. They arrived in the summer of 1877 from newly built Fort Keogh at the junction of the Tongue and the Yellowstone. Followed by ox-drawn wagons carrying pine boxes they came to pick up what remained of Custer and fifteen officers. The valley had changed. In 1876 it was thick with dust, in some places several inches deep, but by 1877 grass grew as high as the riders' stirrups. One member of this party wrote that the knoll where Custer died was strewn with ivory horse bones, but all signs of corruption had disappeared—the only odor being that from shoals of wildflowers blooming in the valley.

Nowlan's detail collected the skeletons of enlisted men and dumped them in a pit near the summit of the ridge. A rock cairn was erected to mark the site, topped by a buffalo skull.

Because sixteen officers had died, and twelve of these were identified soon after the battle, it would be natural to suppose that Nowlan brought at least twelve coffins. For some reason he brought ten—possibly no more than seven. The family of Lt. John Crittenden had asked that he be buried on the field, which was done, after which the remnants of eleven men were placed in as many coffins as there were, and Nowlan returned with them to the mouth of the Little Bighorn where they were loaded aboard the steamboat *Fletcher*. Custer's adjutant, the Canadian W. W. Cooke, was shipped to Hamilton, Ontario. Most of the others went to Fort Leavenworth. Autie Reed and Boston Custer also were exhumed during the summer of 1877, at the direction of Reed's father, and were reburied in Monroe, Michigan.

That Lt. Crittenden was given a coffin must have been assumed, at least by his family; but in 1932 the War Department ordered him transferred to the battlefield cemetery. His decomposing bones were located three feet beneath the surface with no trace of a container.

Sgt. M. C. Caddle accompanied the Nowlan party. He belonged to Keogh's company but had been assigned to guard duty at the Powder River depot. Although he may have resented this ignominious job it saved his life. Caddle stated that when he arrived with Nowlan the skeletons of dead cavalrymen lay everywhere in plain sight. Tom LeForge, who scouted for Nowlan, already had visited the field several times: "Many a grinning skull, ribbed trunk, or detached limb bones I saw on top of the ground. . . ."

The historian Frank Linderman asked Pretty Shield if Custer's men had been buried. "I do not know, Sign-talker," she answered. "I do know that this country smelled of dead men for a whole summer after the fight, and that we moved away from here, because we could not stand it."

Such statements fail to agree with the Bismarck *Tribune* extra which assured a horrified public that all had been "decently interred."

It is probable that each man was covered up, although what was done beyond that remains conjectural. Rain, wind, and snow had worked on these graves. Vultures, ravens, wolves, and other scavengers had come to feed, and some of the identifying stakes might have been knocked over by animals tugging at the bodies. These stakes might have washed downslope or they could have been tumbled by wind from one corpse to another. Nowlan's crew had a difficult job.

After the general's bones were placed in a box somebody found the name of a corporal inside his disintegrating blouse. A nearby skeleton was then substituted for the first, and in Sgt. Caddle's judgment this time they got the right pieces. LeForge said Nowlan's men recovered nothing very palpable: one thigh bone and a skull attached to a ribcage. "Besides these, the quantity of cohering and transferable bodily substance was not enough to fill my hat." Scout George Herendeen said only a few small bones lay in Custer's grave—"a double handful." He thought the general's corpse had been torn apart by wolves.

Another witnesss, whose name is not given, said: "It was a disconcerting discovery to find that even the General could not be satisfactorily identified. . . ."

On July 28, at Fort Lincoln, Major Joseph Tilford wrote to Elizabeth that he had shipped the remains of her husband by U.S. Express to West Point in accordance with instructions from General Sheridan. Tilford enclosed a lock of Custer's hair in this letter to Elizabeth, mentioning that he had taken the liberty of keeping a few hairs for himself. Rumors of scattered bones had disturbed Elizabeth, as well as every other widow and relative of the dead cavalrymen. She is said to have felt reassured by this lock of hair from Tilford and regarded it as positive identification.

Sgt. John Ryan, who had charge of a three-man squad that buried Custer after the battle, also snipped a lock of his hair. So did Dr. Henry Porter, who managed to gather a bit of hair from each dead officer.

Human hair then possessed a cultural significance which it lacks today. Miniature pictures were created by combining various textures and colors. Men wore watch chains of braided hair. Women exchanged gifts made of hair. Two of Elizabeth's presents on her thirteenth birthday were a bracelet of her mother's hair with her father's hair in the clasp, and some of her aunt's hair braided into the shape of a heart.

On December 23, 1863, she wrote to her new husband: "Old fellow with the golden curls, save them from the barber's. When I'm old I'll have a wig made from them." So he did, and she did—although she did not wait until she was old. She wore this wig at least once to a Fort Lincoln dress ball and she probably wore it several times during amateur theatricals. Then one frigid night she awoke to a roaring noise in the chimney: "Women have such a rooted habit of smelling smoke and sending men on needless investigating trips in the dead of night that I tried to keep still for a few moments." Not for long. The ominous noise increased. She woke her husband, who dashed upstairs and found the room above them on fire. She heard a crash and was afraid he had been killed. Some insulating paper saturated with coal-oil had produced an explosive gas: ". . . the chimney had burst, the whole side of the room was blown out, and he was covered with plaster and surrounded with fallen bricks." A sentinel aroused the post. Men came running from every direction, but too late. The house burned. Nearly all of their possessions went up in smoke and sparks. What she most regretted was the loss of a collection of newspaper articles about her husband and the wig—the precious wig.

Custer also saved his mustache for Elizabeth. During the spring of 1864 he mailed it to her, a fact she mentioned in a letter to her parents. In that same letter she mentioned the story of a Confederate officer who gave some girl a lock of hair and asked her to deliver it to Mr. Lincoln, saying he would take dinner with the president in ten days. There was nothing more to the anecdote; Elizabeth knew her parents would understand. Today the meaning is not quite clear. The Confederate officer's boast or threat is plain enough, yet why should a lock of hair accompany the message?

Certain conventions were as grimly enforced then as now. A woman might spend half the day washing, brushing, arranging and rearranging her crowning glory, but a man who supervised the top of his head more than perfunctorily would risk speculative glances, and because of this G. A. C. drew attention to himself. He seems to have been fascinated and puzzled by his hair. He was labeled Fanny when he matriculated at West Point because of his pink-

and-white complexion and a head adorned with curls. He could not do anything about the skin but in an effort to look less feminine he clipped his hair short. Then he bought a toupee. Then he began to use a scented pomade which got him the name Cinnamon. By graduation day he was Curly—one of several names he never lost.

Had his complexion been coppery instead of wasichu pink he would have earned no such ridicule. Indians found nothing ludicrous about a man attending to his hair. Quite the opposite. They looked upon hair, male or female, with admiration and respect. A nineteenth-century trader, Henry Boller, speaks of seeing three Gros Ventre dandies "dressed and painted in the height of fashion, with bunches of shells surmounted with small scarlet feathers fastened to a lock of hair on each side of their foreheads. They wear false hair ornamented with spots of red and white clay. . . ." He describes Chief Four Bears as a tall, noble man whose black hair nearly swept the ground—"an ornamental appendage valued almost beyond price"—and there are reports of warriors with hair ten or fifteen feet long. Frank Linderman writes that a famous hank of Crow hair was examined by General Hugh Scott and Montana representative Scott Leavitt. He cites a letter to himself from Leavitt, dated June 10, 1931, on Congressional stationary: "As the hair was unrolled it was passed from hand to hand around the circle until its entire length was displayed, and Max Big Man measured it with his hands. The lock of hair measured seventy-six hands and the width of one of Big Man's fingers. This would prove it to be over twenty-five feet long. . . ."

Anyway, Elizabeth felt reassured by those curls Major Tilford sent, convinced they came from her husband's scalp and it seems unlikely she would be mistaken, so the general's bones might indeed be at rest where the government maintains they are. Benteen wrote with a quill dripping vinegar: "Cadets for ages to come will bow in humility at the Custer shrine at West Point. . . ."

The testimony of Caddle and LeForge about skeletons exposed on the battlefield was soon confirmed by other visitors. Late that summer eleven heads were collected and buried in a pit near the monument by a group of soldiers on a sightseeing trip; and trumpeter A. F. Mulford, assigned to a scouting expedition which stopped at the field, counted the remnants of eighteen men gathered in six heaps. Mulford said a length of lodge pole stood beside each pile of bones and on one of these hung a white sombrero with two bullet holes and a gash apparently made by an ax. Not far away he saw an ax with a dark stain on the rusty blade. He also saw the skeletons of four men and horses, "among the latter being the skeleton of the horse that Custer rode"— which is interesting, although he neglects to explain how Vic was identified.

His party camped on the site of the abandoned village. The weather was miserable and they were kept half awake by the howling of wolves searching out shreds of gristle adhering to bones. In the darkness one man felt something cold slither across his face and roused the camp with a cry of Snakes! It was a green lizard. There were dozens. Hundreds. By firelight the men rushed around slashing at them with sabers, and when the last one had been dismembered they tried again to sleep, but the creatures returned. It sounds like one of Goya's nightmares.

Newspapers reported that Terry's men burned everything the Indians left behind, everything belonging to Indians, whatever might conceivably have been owned or touched by a red, to the last moccasin. Not true, according to Mulford. Lodge poles stood as thick as aspens. The earth was carpeted with hides, robes, all sorts of equipage. He noticed a great quantity of leggings and thought the Indians must have discarded them in favor of socks or pants stripped from Custer's men.

General Terry did set much of the Indian camp afire, symbolically foretelling the next few years. White America's rage could not be checked after this blow to the elite Seventh. Indians who had been brutally treated in the past would suffer more, regardless of what they had or had not done. Those who never had stolen a mule or launched a single arrow at settlers would feel the government's wrath. Not until 1890 when Hotchkiss guns opened up at Wounded Knee and twenty-three troopers earned Medals of Honor—not until that ritualistic orgy would Anglo passion subside.

Two years after Mulford's visit a detachment of soldiers under Capt. George Sanderson dismantled the rock cairn, substituting a hollow pyramid of logs which they filled with horse bones. Then in 1881 the government began to recognize the significance of this battle. The field was cleaned up, human odds and ends were raked together and shoveled into a trench at the base of an eighteen-ton granite memorial inscribed with the names of those who died. The inscription contains several mistakes, which may be inevitable under the circumstances, but one or two are surprising. Custer's nephew, Armstrong "Autie" Reed, is listed as Arthur Reed, and Isaiah's last name has been omitted—which could be attributed to the fact that he was black.

On the slope below the monument is a small, neat museum exhibiting photographs, paintings, reproductions of famous paintings, and a topographical map of this bloody ground. There is also a bookshop, an unpublicized library in the basement, and a display of military artifacts—both red and white—in glass cases.

Capt. Bourke mentions a device used by Sioux warriors during the Rosebud fight, "a kind of tomahawk, with a handle eight feet long," and Sgt. Ryan describes an ax studded with half a dozen butcher knives. Neither of these grotesque implements can be seen, but the museum does have a Sioux knife-stick with triangular iron teeth which brings to mind those obsidian-edged maces used on the conquistadors by sixteenth-century Aztecs, and a brutally effective war club: an oval stone the size of a big fist wrapped in rawhide.

By comparison with these monstrous Sioux weapons, those of the Cheyenne seem graceful and delicate. Cheyenne braves did not care for eight-foot tomahawks, knife-sticks, or Pleistocene clubs; in addition to the bow-and-arrow, which was used by every tribe, Cheyennes carried long slender lances and small axes easy to manipulate with one hand.

A man fashioned his own arrows, their length equaling the length of his arm to the fingertips, and they could be identified by the way they were painted. Once upon a time every Cheyenne arrow was blue, paying homage to the blue of a certain lake in the Black Hills, although by the late nineteenth century this tradition had been discarded. In '76 a Cheyenne arrow could be recognized by three undulant lines flowing from the blade to the feathers, since it is not through straight lines but through undulations that one communicates with the presiding spirit. More interesting to Anglo eyes, however, was the significant difference between a hunting arrow and a war arrow. The blade of an arrow meant for *Pte* had narrow shoulders so it could be withdrawn from the carcass and used again; but the blade of an arrow used against man was short and broad, with hooked shoulders, making it difficult to extract.

A Cheyenne named Big Beaver fought the Seventh, and in a photograph taken fifty years after the battle he looks remarkably like President Lyndon Johnson wearing braids. His distinctive knife scabbard, embellished with four spots of paint, is on display. A green spot proves that Big Beaver struck the body of a Crow. Yellow signifies Shoshone, touched during another fight because no Shoshones accompanied Custer. Two red spots declare that he touched two white men.

Sioux and Arapahoes permitted four coups on an enemy, Cheyennes allowed three. The first could paint his face black, the color of death, with ashes and buffalo blood. The next was entitled to unbraid his hair, although he could not wear facial paint. So it went as the danger and honor decreased. One Cheyenne is said to have counted coup by lowering a rope until it touched a dead Shoshone at the base of a cliff. If there was an argument about who did or did not merit a coup, the contending warriors testified in the presence of a buffalo skull whose eye sockets had been stuffed with grass to assure impartiality.

Anglo-European decorations—stars, eagles, oak leaves, double bars, single bars, chevrons, emblems to indicate various degrees of heroism—all seem to parallel Indian symbolism. Hassrick was told by Sioux warriors that the first to touch an enemy could wear a golden eagle feather upright, the next wore an eagle feather tilted to the left, the next wore a feather horizontally, while the fourth might wear a buzzard feather dangling. A warrior who saved a friend's life might display a cross on his clothes, a double cross if the rescue was accomplished on horseback. Killing an enemy hand-to-hand entitled the victor to paint a red hand on his clothing or on his horse. Vertical stripes on leggings signified coups. A notched feather meant a wounded horse.

Alongside Big Beaver's knife scabbard is a mummified kingfisher in a leather pouch decorated with bright blue beads—a charm to insure the owner's survival because neither arrows nor bullets intercept the kingfisher's darting flight. White men also carried charms, usually religious tokens, but they were not so attractive. White men seldom wasted time on esthetics. Wasichu equipment, whether it belonged to an individual or to the government, remained functional. A flag might be ornamentally fringed and a soldier's trousers might have a colored stripe, but the Springfield rifles, Colt revolvers, sabers, cartridge cases, saddlebags—all such equipage was primarily utilitarian. The most engaging American relic is the lid of a metal cracker box subtly stained by a century of verdigris, labeled in the ornate calligraphic style of a more elegant age: *C. L. Woodman & Co., Chicago*. But none of the relics, Indian or Anglo, tells more about the ferocity of this battle than a slender notebook Tosh McIntosh carried in his breast pocket—one small, neat bullet hole through the binding.

Calhoun's saber, which he stored at the Powder River depot, now hangs in a glass case at the museum and except for a few nicks in the blade it looks new. Very little of Calhoun's property has been recovered. His brother, who was a soldier in the Department of the Platte, learned several years afterward that some Indians had a white man's watch. When he found out it was his brother's he bought it and sent it to Maggie. That the watch should have been recovered is surprising because after these mysterious objects quit making noise the Indians usually broke them apart in order to add the bright springs, screws, pointers, and crenulate wheels to their necklaces.

Side by side two Medals of Honor are suspended, the ribbons shabby and faded, awarded to men long forgotten by everybody except their descendants and students of the Little Bighorn. Windolph. Pym. The names sound curiously dated, yet it was not that long ago. Charles Windolph died at the age of ninety-eight in 1950, the last white survivor. He was a snowbird who deserted from the Second Infantry, reenlisting in the Seventh as Charles Wrangel. When unmasked he was allowed to take the oath again, this time as himself.

Several Indian participants outlived Windolph. The last two were Sitting Bull's deaf-mute son John, who died in May of 1955, and Dewey Beard— sometimes called Iron Hail—who died that November. The last witness, not a participant, probably was a Cheyenne named Charles Sitting Man who lived until 1961. So it is fairly recent, yet the Little Bighorn has become embedded in our nation's past like a flint arrowhead in a cottonwood tree.

Cyrus Brady got a letter in 1904 from Pvt. William Morris of Reno's M Company. After complaining about various details in one of Brady's historical essays, Morris added that he was much amused to learn of Windolph's medal. "I remember him as the tailor of 'H' troop, and have a distinct recollection of him coming into the field-hospital bent almost double and asking for treatment for a wound which, his appearance would suggest, was a mortal one, but which the surgeon found, on removing his trousers to be only a burn. The surgeon ordered him back to the line amid a shout of laughter. . . ."

Pvt. Jim Pym was different. In Miles City years after the battle somebody pulled a gun on him. Pym snatched it, threw it away, knocked the man down, kicked him, and told him to get out of town.

So there were the timorous and the dauntless, those as quick afoot as adjutant Cooke, others as lethargic as pokey Tosh McIntosh. A few like Lonesome Charley who never wasted a shot, others who fired at shadows.

Tacked up on the south wall of the museum is a faded Seventh Cavalry regimental standard which did not become a curtain in some aboriginal teepee only because it had been stowed on McDougall's pack train. The insignia, an eagle clutching in its talons a cluster of embroidered gold arrows sharper than lightning bolts, might be regarded as emblematic of the Seventh's electrifying commandant; and in a cabinet directly across the aisle, facing this tattered standard, hangs one of his elegant white buckskin suits. Like MacArthur with a crushed hat and corncob pipe, or Patton in a burnished steel helmet, he created an unforgettable image.

Captain William Ludlow, who had been acquainted with Custer since West Point, remarked that he never learned to spell the word "defeat." He knew nothing but success. He loved to take part in events, Ludlow commented, but was not much of a thinker, not much of a student. Custer's young brother Nevin disagreed. During one of many interviews Nevin talked about their school days. Tom, he said, raised hell. "Tom, he was always getting licked. Tom chewed tobacco, same as most of the boys did, but of course 'twasn't allowed in school. However, Tom couldn't let it alone, so he bored a hole in the school room floor with an augur to give him a place to spit. He tried to keep it covered with his foot. . . ." Unlike Tom, G. A. C. never raised hell. Old man Foster, the schoolteacher, was expected to give his pupils a treat at the start of each vacation, but he was stingy so one time they locked him out. When he tried to crawl through a window they threatened him with a heated coal shovel. "I guess we all got licked for that, except George. George wasn't in it. He was home studying. Always studying. . . ."

Everybody who knew him agreed that he was unnaturally energetic. He seems to have been created with a body immune to fatigue. On the Black Hills trip Ludlow often saw him grab an ax and go to work alongside the enlisted men, and he might be reading military reports or preserving a coyote by lamplight after everybody else in camp had fallen asleep. He was apt to exaggerate, Ludlow said, not from a wish to misrepresent, but because he saw things larger than they were. He had an exceptional memory: "He could recall in its proper order every detail of any action, no matter how remote, of which he was a participant."

This is an unexpected comment. It sounds incompatible with his reputation for impetuosity.

"I am not impetuous or impulsive," he himself said with evident peevishness. "I resent that. Everything that I have ever done has been the result of the study that I have made of imaginary military situations that might arise. When I became engaged in campaign or battle and a great emergency arose, everything that I had ever read or studied focused in my mind as if the situation were under a magnifying glass and my decision was the instantaneous result. My mind worked instantaneously, but always as the result of everything I had ever studied being brought to bear on the situation."

A sergeant carried his personal flag. No precise description of this flag exists, and because it was lost during the battle its dimensions are not known, nor the kind of fabric, nor if it had a fringe; it was a swallowtail design horizontally divided in two colors—red above, blue underneath—showing a brace of crossed white sabers.

This crossed-saber emblem appeared also on Custer's pocket watch, a handsome timepiece that floated around the western states for quite a while. Which Indian pulled it out of his pocket has never been learned, but in 1906 a Montana saloon keeper bought it from an unidentified Sioux and then lost it in a dice game to a traveling salesman who exhibited it for several years, after which it vanished but popped up in the hands of a California antique dealer called Wind River Bill, who sold it to somebody who sold it to somebody else who sold it to Mr. and Mrs. John Foote of Billings, Montana, who regarded it as one of the treasures in their "Treasures of the West" collection.

Mr. and Mrs. Foote eventually offered these western items to the city of Billings; but the Billings elders, wise with pecuniary wisdom, declined this gift because they did not want to allocate money for insurance. Now the collection is dispersed and old Iron Butt's watch has again dropped from sight, with many another curious relic. On the back of it, engraved above a brace of crossed sabers, is this legend:

TO GENERAL CUSTER
FROM THE MICHIGAN BRIGADE
'RIDE YOU WOLVERINES'

What a flamboyant, outrageous figure. What a sense of himself he had. He must have considered himself immortal, at least when his hair was long, as invincible as Beowulf or Siegfried or Harald Greatheart.

Apparently he thought his ancestors were English. He wrote to Elizabeth from New York in the spring of 1876 that he had received a letter from a gentleman of the same name who lived in the Orkneys, who believed they were from the same family and had traced it back to 1647 through Cusiter, Cursider, and Cursetter.

Cyrus Brady states without documentation that the *paterfamilias* in America was a Hessian officer captured at Saratoga in 1777. After being paroled, he decided to remain in the United States. This man in turn might be traced to a Paul Küster who was born at Hesse in 1630.

Without doubt the patronymic is Teutonic. A collateral descendant, Milo Custer, said that in various forms—Kuster, Coster, Cöster—the name is common to many Dutch, German, and American families. The earliest recorded usage seems to be Laurens Coster, "the reputed inventor of printing in Haarlem, Holland." Laurens Coster's birthdate is unknown but he died in 1440, so he and Gutenberg were contemporaries.

The first individual or family to use this name probably held office in a Dutch or German Catholic church during the Middle Ages because the English meaning is "sacristan." Milo Custer reports that in 1535 during the Inquisition one Pieter Koster, "a Mennonite preacher who had formerly been sacristan of what was then the Roman Catholic church of Oost Zaandam, Holland, was condemned by the Roman Catholic authorities and executed at Amsterdam because of his religious beliefs."

The first member of the family to reach America was a farmer and mason from Kaldenkirchen in the Rhineland, Paul Küster, who left the village of Crefeld in 1684 with his wife Gertrude and four children. They and twenty-eight other emigrant families settled, logically enough, at Germantown, Pennsylvania. Thus, a century and a half later, George Armstrong Custer was born in New Rumley, Ohio.

So he sprang from that race of blue-eyed long-nosed devils who once upon a time trotted arrogantly through cold black forests with the North Sea in their veins; and being who he was he must have felt their eyes on him as he galloped across the American prairie, strawberry curls flowing in the wind. Even his weapons—Remington sporting rifle with octagon barrel, two self-cocking ivory-handled Webley Bulldog pistols, a hunting knife in a beaded scabbard—everything about him contributed to the image. General George Armstrong Custer! Cöster! Kuester! His name reverberates like the clang of a sword.

When he was a child his father Emanuel dressed him in a velvet suit and took him to military drills. There, clutching a toy musket, he learned to execute the Scott manual of arms. War with Mexico was in the wind. Most citizens approved, but a few were dismayed. One day old Emanuel heard the boy repeat a school catechism: "My voice is for war!"

Just as it is no surprise to watch Myles Keogh recreate the militant life of his father, so it should not be surprising—given this childhood—to read what Custer wrote from Virginia in 1863: "Oh, could you but have seen some of the charges that were made! While thinking of them I cannot but exclaim 'Glorious War!'. . . I gave the command 'Forward!' And I never expect to see a prettier sight. I frequently turned in my saddle to see the glittering sabers. . . ."

Those words radiate from the mind of a bona fide nineteenth-century American romantic, cameo pink, nourished on sentiment, the immaculate product of his age. While helping to bury a Vermont soldier who had been shot through the heart he sympathized with the man's widow, and not wanting to reach into the dead man's pockets he slit them and removed a few personal items. "I then cut off a lock of his hair and gave them to a friend of his from the same town who promised to send them to his wife. As he lay there I thought of that poem: 'Let me kiss him for his mother . . .' and wished his mother were there to smooth his hair."

Today the pockets of slain soldiers are emptied and personal items delivered to next of kin, but slitting a pocket instead of unbuttoning it was a nineteenth-century delicacy. And in those genteel days Custer refrained from opening the letters of a defeated Confederate enemy, General Mumford, which quite possibly contained information of military significance. He did not even scan Mumford's letters; he tied them in a bundle, "neither reading them myself nor allowing others to do so."

Intimate correspondence might bring tears to his eyes, yet a blood-soaked field could leave him unaffected. At Bull Run in October of 1863 he enjoyed supper "under a stately oak that bears many a battle scar, surrounded by graves, many washed by rain so that skulls and skeletons are visible. . . . There is heavy firing to the left."

After every visit with his parents when the time came to say good-bye he would lose control. Elizabeth anticipated these lachrymose partings with dread. She would watch him follow his mother around, whispering to her, trying by any means to comfort her; and when he started to leave she would clutch at him, until finally, half insensate with grief, she would be led to her room. Custer himself would be sobbing when he left the house.

What is one expected to make of such a paradoxical figure?

Brian Dippie commented that between the last of the cavaliers and the glory-hunter a man waits to be discovered: "But the disputatious nature of almost all writing on Custer continues to cast an obscuring shadow."

"The day is almost done, when, look! heaven now defend him, the charm of his life is broken, for Custer has fallen; a bullet cleaves a pathway through his side, and as he falters another strikes his noble breast. Like a strong oak stricken by the lightning's bolt, shivering the mighty trunk and bending the writhing branches down close to the earth, so fell Custer; but like the reacting branches, he rises partly up again and striking out like a fatally wounded giant lays three more Indians dead. . . ." Thus the grand finale according to Mr. J. W. Buel, whose imaginative *Heroes of the Plains* graced the literary world in 1881. Rose-colored spectacles were the style in that era, whereas today the fashion might be called jaundice-yellow, but never mind. Since nobody truly knows what happened, Mr. Buel's vision of the last stand is as good as any.

Not one written description or painting can be regarded as authentic because not one of Reno's men saw it, and those Indians who did see Custer fall did not know who he was. At least it is unlikely that any of them knew. Afterward, when they found out about him, they told all sorts of stories.

Goes Ahead, Hairy Moccasin, and White Man Runs Him might have been the last to see General Custer. Photographer Edward Curtis states, apparently on the basis of what they told him, that at the start of the fight Custer and Mitch Bouyer were sitting down side by side while the general took long-range shots at the advancing enemy. Bouyer called to White Man Runs Him, who approached on hands and knees.

"You have done what you agreed to do—brought us to the Sioux camp," Bouyer said. "Now go back to the pack train and live."

The scouts thought this was a good idea. They were fired upon by Sioux as they rode away, but once out of danger they slowed down and watched. Custer was on horseback when they left. Other than that, they could provide no information.

White Man said they did return to the pack train as instructed and fought with Reno's troops until the sun went down. During the night, he said, they slipped away.

What is certain is that sometime after leaving Custer these three Crows traveled north, crossing the Bighorn at night or early next morning, no doubt looking back frequently to see if any Sioux were after them. And having crossed the river they paused to study several riders who were examining some equipment and the pony they abandoned on the east bank. Whether these riders were Sioux or came from Terry's army, they did not know. A blanket signaled friendship. They were not persuaded. They talked about this, built a fire to communicate by smoke, and finally approached the river where they recognized their brother scouts and Lt. Bradley. They did not mind talking across the water but they had seen plenty of Sioux and had no desire to visit the battlefield again. It seemed to them they would be better off at home so they continued westward. Their departure influenced other Crows; soldiers at the tail of the column saw Bradley's full complement of native scouts galloping west.

This seems to be what happened, although White Man said they met General Terry and told him about the disaster. General Terry was mad. The Crows told him their ponies' hooves were worn and asked permission to go home for fresh ponies. Terry answered: "Yes, you can go, but come back. Meanwhile I will travel up the river and see the dead soldiers." After that, according to White Man, he himself, together with Goes Ahead and Hairy Moccasin, proceeded to the Crow reservation.

If only they had hesitated at the rim of the battle. If they had lingered twenty minutes we would have the testimony of three eyewitnesses. Now we must depend on authors and artists, who are notoriously unreliable.

More painters and writers have converged on the Little Bighorn than on Gettysburg, which is puzzling. Erudite explanations compete with one another like professors at a cocktail party, yet none seems satisfactory. Robert Taft, for instance, observed that Custer entered Valhalla "with a drama and suddenness that left the nation shocked." True, but inadequate. One summer afternoon in 1628 the giant Swedish warship *Vasa*, newly christened, the pride of Gustav II, heeled over and went down in Stockholm harbor like a phantom disappearing before the astonished eyes of thousands of citizens, yet within a century, maybe less, this tragedy—even the ship's name—had been forgotten. So it appears that no matter how dramatic or abrupt or shocking the event, people do forget. Why, then, should the collapse of the Seventh Cavalry be almost as vivid today as it was in 1876? Nobody can be sure. We know only that it will be remembered as long as the nation lasts. The Little Bighorn has been stamped on America with the force of a prehistoric red handprint on a rock.

Because it was the greatest Indian victory, some say. Not true. In 1791 Chief Little Turtle's Miamis destroyed the army of General Arthur St. Clair, killing 632 soldiers—more than twice as many as Custer lost.

Because we are fascinated by battles in which one army is exterminated. Thermopylae. Roncesvalles. Khartoum. Davy Crockett's tiny garrison at the Alamo.

Because of the elemental contrast: fantastically painted redskins whirling in barbaric splendor around a disciplined unit of whites in uniform blue coats.

Because it exemplifies the subconscious combat between retiarius and secutor.

Because it recreates the mythic drama of sacrificial heroes in a foreign wilderness.

Because it is a classic morality play.

Because it nourishes the roots of this nation. Specifically, according to Professor Rosenburg, Custer meeting death at the Little Bighorn descends to some impalpable region of the American psyche, there to be united with those nameless impulses that stirred our grandfathers and theirs before them.

Because of Frederick Whittaker, perhaps, who did for the general what Ned Buntline did for Buffalo Bill. Some think such an advocate might be as necessary as the hero. Without Boswell, say, who would remember Dr. Johnson? Without Longfellow's nocturnal clippity-clop verse, who but a silversmith could identify Paul Revere? James Fenimore Cooper did a lot for Daniel Boone. Parson Weems polished up George Washington.

There are exceptions, notably Abe Lincoln. But he chanced to be president when a traumatic war erupted. If he had been twenty years younger or older he might be as obscure as Buchanan.

Whittaker ground out *A Complete Life of General Custer* and saw it published in December of 1876 while ravens and wolves picked through the butchered men's bones. He produced a general clad in unblemished armor and a villain to make the blood run cold—murderous Rain in the Face. Wicked politicians and jealous subordinate officers assisted the plot.

Elizabeth helped. *Boots and Saddles* revealed to America a superb horseman and sportsman, crack shot, affectionate husband, etc. What she wrote about her husband was not untrue; neither was it the truth. It is true that he loved birds. Once he altered the regimental line of march to avoid disturbing a meadowlark's nest, and when transferred to Dakota Territory from the South he brought along a mockingbird whose song delighted him. At the same time he could knock birds out of the sky with pleasure. In the Black Hills he shot that huge white crane for the satisfaction of measuring its wings.

Elizabeth saw him as a patron of the arts. At Fort Lincoln was a Swiss cavalryman who played the zither, who would be invited to Custer's home to play Tyrolean melodies while the general lounged on a bearskin rug.

She thought of her husband as a serious reader. When he left Fort Lincoln for the last time he was part-way through a three-volume novel titled *Her Dearest Foe* by a certain Mrs. Alexander, a book less memorable than one passage he marked: "I have faith in my own fortunes, and believe I shall conquer in the end."

So he appeared to the public, an American Siegfried, a warrior of matchless strength and purity.

Walt Whitman, obviously fascinated, worked at least as fast as Whittaker. One day after hearing about the tragedy he sent "From Far Dakota's Canyons" to the New York *Tribune*, which published it on July 10.

From far Dakota's canyons,
Land of the wild ravine, the dusky Sioux,
    the lonesome stretch, the silence,
Haply to-day a mournful wail, haply
    a trumpet-note for heroes. . . .

Whitman's music echoes faintly from those lines. Compared to most poetry evoked by Custer's demise the lines are not bad; compared to much of Whitman's other work they are not very good. If he had waited, as poets are supposed to do, recollecting in tranquility, he might have done better. Then again, it could have been worse. The significant thing, however, is not the quality of Whitman's tribute but his need to express what occurred on that lonesome stretch, just as painters from Des Moines to Stuttgart felt some urgent need to illustrate it.

If Robert E. Lee had gone down with the last of his butternut Confederates on a lush green Dixie hilltop he might have bathed the American psyche in such radiance that Custer would be no more than a pallid reflection. Even now we think about Lee with regret. His credentials were immaculate. He was a splendid man, everybody agrees. We could welcome him as the archetypal American hero; but quite sensibly he surrendered, while Grant, too embarrassed to accept his sword, waved it aside. The long war ended in mutual exhaustion, which is not especially dramatic.

The Revolution—our most spectacular event—does not play well on stage. Military giants of that era have winked out; with one or two exceptions it is hard to recall who they were. Maybe this is because Americans do not think much about their nation's past, only its future, and the future always has meant a mysterious, distant West—that menacing land designed for a saga as unmistakably as the constellation of traits in Custer destined him for a principal role. So he emerged as a demigod—Siegfried, Roland, Galahad— with eyes more blue than ice, and shining yellow hair; a demigod somewhat gelded, it is true, in deference to nineteenth-century taste. Thus the *Inter Ocean* correspondent, William Eleroy Curtis, wrote from Fort Lincoln:

> He is a great man—a noble man is General Custer, and one of whom most of the world—that part which does not know him—has a singularly wrong idea. I came here expecting to find a big-whiskered, swearing, ranting, drinking trooper, and I found instead a slender, quiet gentleman, with a face as fair as a girl's, and manners as gentle and courtly as the traditional prince. Hunting for the drunken raider, I found a literary gentleman. . . . He sat on a low stool by his desk, with a spelling-book in his hand; before him were two little girls, one white and the other colored, the children of his servants, whom he was affording the necessities denied by the lack of schools. . . . I have found that this has been his custom for several years, and all these little people of his household know of written words is what he has taught them.

Curtis hardly can summon praise enough. Never has he met a more courteous host, a more generous entertainer, a more urbane conversationalist. The general does not smoke: "One would know it from the clearness of his complexion and the pearly polish of his teeth." He is reputed to be the greatest sportsman, the finest shot, and so forth.

Then what, the correspondent rhetorically asks, are his vices?

"His soldiers will tell you he has none. . . ."

He was good copy. Dashing cavalry assaults contrasted wonderfully with the literate gentleman at home, his face as fair as any girl's, benevolently teaching the servants' children to read.

Whittaker wrote for *Galaxy* magazine, thoughtfully utilizing images appropriate to the publication, that history is like the sky at midnight. Regal stars are few, planets fewer, yet now and then a meteor flashes from the multitude, vanishing swiftly as it came, leaving behind a legend of light. "Who would not be Raphael the Divine, dead at thirty-seven, with no stain on his name, his life a story of perfect beauty?" Or the admirable Crichton, that embodiment of early success, dead at thirty-seven. Henry the Fifth, Alexander of Macedon, Titus, Bryon, Shelley, and in America the celebrated Joseph Rodman Drake—all died young, untarnished. The life of such a man might seem sad at its close, Whittaker reflects, yet in the grander scheme of the universe which recognizes death as a passage to illimitable freedom it is rounded and perfect. "Never was there life more rounded, complete, and symmetrical than that of George A. Custer, the favorite of fortune, the last cavalier. . . . To Custer alone was it given to join a romantic life of perfect success to a death of perfect heroism; to unite the splendors of Austerlitz and Thermopylae; to charge like Murat; to die like Leonidas."

Whittaker is only just getting warmed up, and sounds annoyed that McClellan did not stop a minie ball in the battle of Antietam. Had McClellan died there: ". . . what a heritage of fame would have been his!"

Thirty years later Custer continued to streak across the sky. Judge Richard Voorhees, who had known him, lifted great unleavened chunks of Whittaker's *Galaxy* article without a nod, playing the Austerlitz & Thermopylae theme with scarcely a variation. Judge Voorhees does omit the admirable Crichton but throws in Marshal Ney at Waterloo.

Infatuated biographers particularly liked to extol his marksmanship, revealing to the public a dead-eye who could drill a mosquito through the heart at three hundred yards, although Bloody Knife—an impertinent sort—used to say he could not hit a tent from inside. Well, Richard Anderson Roberts arrived at Fort Lincoln in March of 1876 as "Civilian Secretary" to Custer. Then Terry was put in charge of the expedition and Custer no longer rated a private secretary. Still, Roberts wanted to go along so he got a job as herder. Seventy miles short of the Little Bighorn his pony collapsed, a miserable stroke of luck which might have saved his life. All of which merely certifies Roberts as a witness. Many so-called witnesses to G. A. C.'s activities did not know the general and may never have come within miles of him. Roberts did know him and had plenty of chances to watch him handle a gun. He was, in Roberts' opinion, "the best shot with a Creedmore rifle in the Cavalry branch of the service, and I doubt if any other branch could produce his equal."

Custer practiced on targets outside Fort Lincoln. Roberts often watched him: "shooting under the greatest possible difficulties for a marksman, namely, a calm hazy atmosphere and a hot sun, besides these drawbacks his ungloved hands were covered, literally black, with mosquitos which you could see were filling themselves with his blood, but his nerve was so great and his will so strong that he never winced. . . ." Under these circumstances Roberts saw him hit the bull's eye ten out of ten at 500 yards, eight out of ten at 750, seven out of ten at 1,000 yards. If true, the Son of the Morning Star could have punched holes in James Fenimore Cooper's Natty Bumppo.

He himself modestly intimated that he had the eye of an eagle. While patrolling Oklahoma he and the twenty-year-old son of Satanta got into a friendly shooting match. Satanta's son was the best shot in the Kiowa tribe. Yet, said Custer, "my good fortune enabled me to make a better score . . ."

Contradicting such testimony is George Bird Grinnell who described an incident in the Black Hills. Scout Luther North, Custer, and Grinnell approached a pond where several half-grown ducks were paddling about. Custer dismounted, saying he would knock off their heads. Grinnell quietly signaled North to sit on the ground behind Custer. The general took aim and fired, but missed. North then blew off the head of a duck. Custer shot again and missed. North promptly blew off another head. Custer looked at North for a moment, then tried once more and missed. North decapitated a third duck, at which point an officer rode up to say their bullets were skipping across the water near the troops. "We had better stop shooting," Custer said, and got on his horse. The score—3–0 in favor of North—is convincing, yet even more so is the fact that Grinnell knew what to expect.

Despite his inability to cut off a duck's head, Custer must have been a pretty good shot. His physical coordination was superb, he loved weapons, used them constantly, and had been trained at West Point. If he was no match for professional hunters such as Lonesome Charley or the North brothers, undoubtedly he could shoot better than most of his men.

Erratic marksmanship could be blamed in part on the Spencer carbine. North said a man never could tell whether it would shoot straight or around a corner. During the Rosebud fight General Crook's troops burned up twenty-five thousand rounds of ammunition while killing approximately twenty-five Sioux, although the noise must have deafened a good many more. This inept fusillade—which earned Crook the soubriquet "Rosebud George"—is attributed to temperamental weapons in the hands of half-trained recruits. Very few soldiers knew how to sight and how to pull a trigger, North said. He watched a dozen antelope fly past one company. Everybody with a gun cut loose but not a single antelope was hit.

Custer probably never found out who organized that humiliating exhibition at the duck pond because two years later he invited Grinnell to join the Seventh on a trip to Montana. Grinnell was employed by the Peabody Museum and had quite a lot of work so he declined with regret. Had he been less conscientious he might have been riding alongside his good friend Charley Reynolds.

Anyway, the public loved to read about Custer, and what inspired millions of phlegmatic citizens to follow his picaresque adventures must have been what caused legions of journalists to describe him and as many artists to paint him. Indeed, the Last Stand has been resurrected so often that General Custer is beginning to rival Lazarus. Consider how many times the Seventh has been annihilated in prose, verse, and on canvas. Consider how many millions of plastic and painted lead troopers and Indians have been manufactured over how many generations. Given such statistics, old Iron Butt at the Little Bighorn must rank with Napoleon's retreat from Moscow, Hannibal crossing the Alps, and the charge of the Light Brigade.

Taft points out in *Artists and Illustrators of the Old West* that nearly all pictures of the disintegrating regiment are schlock. An esthete, if he does stoop to contemplate these works, "politely sniffs the tainted air. . . ." Nor does the historian waste time on them because they are, of course, imaginary. Thus it remains for the interested busybody with nothing much on his mind to evaluate them, if indeed they deserve evaluation.

Some are almost as familiar as Gilbert Stuart's Washington; they show up not only on calendars but on postcards, beer steins—on anything that might possibly be sold. Very few even approximate the truth. By now most people have learned that Custer's hair was clipped short, but again and again he is represented with flowing yellow locks. Nor did his men wear blue coats. On cool days they did, but on a hot day such as this particular June 25 a trooper took off his coat, rolled it up tight, and secured it to the saddle. Beneath the coat he would be wearing a coarse grey pullover shirt—although some men still wore white shirts issued during the Civil War while others wore the dark blue shirts which were just then being issued. Some might have been wearing checkered shirts they themselves had bought, the Army being less standardized than it is now. Then too, experienced campaigners often wore old clothes in the field. Hats, more than anything, reflected personal taste: straw hats, kepis, civilian felt hats, whatever. So, during the summer of 1876, Custer's regiment in Montana did not look much like those smartly dressed troopers on canvas.

Pictorially the Seventh was characteristic of that heterogeneous Anglo-Irish-German omnium-gatherum known as the United States Army—an army sometimes led by cripples and alcoholics, officers who would not be commissioned today or who would be removed from field service. General Oliver Howard, for instance, had just one arm. Gibbon and the myopic Terry both were hobbled by Civil War injuries. Grasshopper Jim Brisbin was rheumatic, frequently resorting to crutches and unable to mount a horse. Custer's nemesis, General David Stanley, was notoriously soused on the banks of the Yellowstone and elsewhere. Reno, Benteen, and countless others seldom were so impolite as to decline a flask. One gets an impression that half the wasichu commandants were physically limited and/or drunk, to say nothing of their wonderful neuroses and obsessions—Custer, for example, washing his hands again and again during the Civil War bloodbath. One can hardly avoid thinking of officers in more recent madhouses compulsively ticketing enemy corpses. Nothing changes. The basilisk may die, but another egg hatches.

In addition to senior officers such as these, various young men were in questionable shape. Godfrey, at that time a lieutenant, was rather deaf. Lt. John Crittenden, who transferred from the Twentieth Infantry and died on the ridge with Calhoun, was blind in one eye. Lt. Algernon Smith had been so shot up during the Civil War that he could not raise his left arm above the shoulder or put on his coat without help.

Artists who set out to recreate a unit of the nineteenth-century United States Army such as the Seventh Cavalry therefore had a problem. A short-haired general commanding what might be mistaken for a limping drunken mob of itinerant farmhands would be altogether unsatisfactory. What the public has a right to expect is a flaxen-haired saber-wielding general and his valiant troopers in neat blue uniforms trapped hopelessly within a constricting circle of muscular bronze savages wearing enormous feather bonnets while waving tomahawks. General James B. Fry had the right idea when he described a typical Cheyenne warrior: "The muscles under the bronze of his skin stood out like twisted wires. . . ." Unfortunately, as Grinnell pointed out, "Indians are notable for their smooth, rounded, small, and symmetrical limbs." Libbie Custer, too, not always the most acute observer, perceived the same thing at Fort Lincoln because she remarks on the unimpressive biceps of Sioux warriors, which she attributed to the fact that they did nothing except lie around while their squaws did all the work.

Adams, Becker, Eber, Elder, Hoskins, Leigh, Mulvany, Paxson, Ralston, Reusswig—artists throughout America and much of Europe were seduced by this treacherous, challenging subject.

An illustrator named William Cary scored first. His magnum opus titled "The Battle on the Little Big Horn River—the Death Struggle of General Custer" occupied a full page of the New York *Daily Graphic* on July 19, 1876, and for sheer compression it has yet to be surpassed. Desperate is the fray while smack in the middle stands Custer, eyes like a spaniel, one boot planted on the rump of a dead horse. With his left hand he fires a huge pistol and with his right he swings an uncommonly long saber. Indeed, so well situated is the hero that lines drawn diagonally through this picture intersect at his navel. Mr. Cary was no self-taught amateur.

Round and about our man gallop countless red devils, although in deference to the spectator none gallop between subject and audience. Several Indians are holding what could be mistaken for shepherd's crooks, although they actually represent one style of coup stick, and the Montana hills have been primed to explode. It is a marvelous picture, easy to ridicule because the artist unconsciously transformed drama into melodrama. At the same time, perhaps not in spite of his commercial training but because of it, his impression has lasted more than a century and will endure as long as the Little Bighorn is remembered. He created the prototype.

To say this is to suggest that Cary was a deeply intuitive artist. As a matter of fact, his seminal design could be only the result of circumstances. His was the first work to be seen by the public. Besides, how else could it be handled? Variations—and many artists have attempted new perspectives—do not show much originality. If, for instance, one sets out to represent a turkey— well, there is just so much one can do.

Brian Dippie remarks that even though modern realists pay attention to facts, which nineteenth-century romanticists did not, they still approach this subject in the spirit of the nineteenth century. Therefore the result must be anachronistic: correct to the tiniest button, yet permeated with values long lost.

Custer's Last Stand remains an inviolate myth. His bluecoats are glued to that ridge like toy soldiers in a diorama.

Whitman liked John Mulvany's work:

I sat for over an hour before the picture, completely absorbed in the first view. A vast canvas, I should say twenty or twenty-two feet by twelve, all crowded, and yet not crowded . . . swarms upon swarms of savage Sioux, in their war-bonnets, frantic, mostly on ponies, driving through the background, through the smoke, like a hurricane of demons. A dozen of the figures are wonderful. Altogether a Western, autochthonic phase of America, the frontiers, culminating typical, deadly, heroic to the uttermost; nothing in the books like it, nothing in Homer, nothing in Shakespeare; more grim and sublime than either, all native, all our own and all a fact. A great lot of muscular, tan-faced men brought to bay under terrible circumstances. Death ahold of them, yet every man undaunted, not one losing his head, wringing out every cent of the pay before they sell their lives.

. . . Two dead Indians, herculean, lie in the foreground clutching their Winchester rifles, very characteristic. The many soldiers, their faces and attitudes, the carbines, the broad-brimmed Western hats, the powder-smoke in puffs, the dying horses with their rolling eyes almost human in their agony, the clouds of war-bonneted Sioux in the background, the figures of Custer and Cook, with, indeed, the whole scene, inexpressible, dreadful, yet with an attraction and beauty that will remain forever. . . .

Whitman goes on to say that the painting has an ethic purpose as all great art must have, and he advised Mulvany to exhibit it in Paris because he felt sure the French would appreciate it. He seems to have had an artistic dispute with a certain Monsieur Crapeau, or was offended by an esthetic judgment of Crapeau, because he adds in a rather hurt tone: "I would like to show Messieur Crapeau that some things can be done in America as well as others."

Mulvany's monster cruised around the United States for ten or fifteen years and probably did reach Paris, but we do not know if M. Crapeau condescended to view it. Sometime after 1900 it was bought by Monsieur H. K. Heinz of Pittsburgh, and altogether earned a respectable amount for the artist. Very often such success evolves into a kind of insurance policy that matures, thereafter yielding dividends as well as guaranteeing the success of future work, but John Mulvany's bubble popped. He was reduced to painting portraits, so he drank a lot, or vice versa; and on May 22, 1906, he jumped into the East River. The New York *Times* reported that he had become "a ragged derelict, uncertain of a night's lodging or a day's food."

More esteemed than the Mulvany opus—indeed, the most popular of all Custer pictures—is an 1895 lithograph by Otto Becker, based on the work of Cassilly Adams, which hangs in thousands of saloons. With the exception of Stuart's Washington, no American picture has been reproduced more often. Millions of school children have gazed up at Washington enduring the discomfort of wooden teeth while millions of fathers have peered drunkenly at the other George battling a cloud of Sioux.

Although Becker started with Cassilly Adams, the finished product became very much his own. The original and Becker's litho both equip Custer with a sword, but in Adams' painting he uses it to thrust while in Becker's version he assumes his stance dead center and wields it like a flail. Becker eliminated two bathetic end panels which framed the drama like a medieval triptych: one showed Custer as a child pretending to be a soldier, titled "Coming Events Cast Their Shadows Before." The other, which had him expiring on a featureless prairie as the sun sinks in the west like a pumpkin, was titled with heavy emphasis: "Revered Even By His Savage Foes."

These two panels disappeared and were lost for nobody knows how many years until the Arizona Pioneers' Historical Society in conjunction with the Mountain Oyster Club arranged an exhibit of old-time saloon art. Naturally the Becker lithograph was included, and a newspaper item described the lost Adams panels. This information in the newspaper caused staff members of the historical society to remember a pair of crumbling brown canvases in the museum basement: One showed a boy playing soldier, the other a dying man on the prairie. Lo and behold!

Subsequent detective work revealed how these panels got to Arizona. The triptych's first home was a St. Louis saloon at Eighth and Olive which went broke in 1890, and among those left holding the bag was Anheuser-Busch. Adams' big painting being one of the major assets, Anheuser-Busch seized it, but in a fit of generosity Mr. Busch presented the work to the Seventh. Because of the Spanish-American war in 1898 the regiment moved from Fort Riley to Camp Grant, Arizona, and soon afterward Adams' triptych was dismantled, nobody knows why. The centerpiece—painted on a tent fly—turned up in the attic of a supply depot at Fort Bliss, Texas, in 1925. It then vanished, magically reappeared nine years later at Camp Grant, which had been abandoned, and was carried back to Fort Bliss where it hung in the officers' club until consumed by fire on June 13, 1946.

The side panels were found by Carl S. Gung'l, the caretaker of Camp Grant. Mr. Gung'l kept them on his ranch until 1944 when he gave them to the Arizona Pioneers. The society members did not know what they represented, nor did anybody else, and the basement seemed a good place to store them. There they rested until the Tucson exhibit of saloon art in 1967.

Eliminating these sentimental wings was Becker's most decided permutation, but he also reorganized the landscape, substituting a fairly accurate view of the Little Bighorn for a massive hill invented by Adams.

Concerning Indians, Becker was less exact. It is hard to guess what he had in mind. Obviously he did not know these people. Several of his braves are dressed like Apaches and one or two look like Aztecs carrying Zulu shields. In the foreground, however, whether it is technically correct or not, Becker provided an absolutely horrifying lesson in the art of scalping: A fierce black warrior with a knife between his teeth kneels on a cavalryman's back to peel away the top of his head, distorting the features until the Anglo face looks Oriental.

Lt. Varnum saw this lithograph and complained that there were too many war bonnets. He also said nobody wore gauntlets during hot weather—on June 25 they had been thrust into saddlebags. But he did not criticize the scalping, which implies that Becker's hideous vision must be accurate.

Fort Riley, Kansas, was the regiment's first home, so a copy of this grue-some and celebrated lithograph was presented to Governor Edmund Morrill, who turned it over to the Kansas State Historical Society. The brewer's name appeared beneath the picture but this did not trouble Kansas historians. They put General Custer and the Aztecs on display.

Then along came Blanche Boies, disciple of Carrie Nation.

On the morning of January 9, 1904, she entered the state house with a regulation woodcutter's ax hidden under a long cloak. She rode an elevator to the fifth floor, advanced upon the picture with its advertisement for beer, and did her duty. Mr. George Martin, Secretary of the historical society, alerted by the tinkle of shattering glass, rushed from his office and grappled with her. Secretary Martin is said to have cried out: "Such persons as you ought to be in the insane asylum!" He then told a janitor to call the cops.

After being escorted to a police station, Blanche faced a desk sergeant named Kenney. He knew her. Except for Mrs. Nation, Blanche was the state's most renowned prohibitionist. In 1902 she had horsewhipped the mayor of Topeka because she felt he was not enforcing the law against certain beverages.

While booking her, Sgt. Kenney asked her age.

Blanche responded crisply: "I'm over twenty-one."

Sgt. Kenney listed her age as twenty-two and charged her with malicious destruction of property.

Upon being bailed out by sympathizers, she produced a typewritten man-ifesto declaring that the advertisement of beer constituted an act of treason. Custer's struggle with the Sioux did not interest her. "I concluded to chop the name of the secesh firm off with no ill will toward the rest of the picture."

Two days after her release from jail an unknown vandal struck Becker's lithograph again. Blanche was suspected. A female answering her description had been observed lurking about the building.

On January 19 she appeared before Judge Zack Hazen who suspended sentence by reason of the fact that she already had served time for similar acts, which punishment having failed utterly to modify her behavior, additional punishment would be superfluous. Some exasperated authority then pre-ferred lunacy charges against her, perhaps at the behest of Secretary Martin, but the WCTU got her off. She was paroled on condition that she behave. This promise she gave grudgingly.

Promises are hard to keep and within a few months Blanche had smashed the window of a drugstore in Wichita, apparently because the merchandise offended her. She was therefore returned to Topeka as a parole violator, and according to the Topeka *Capital*: "She was given her old room at the county jail."

Her second assault on the lithograph was more successful than the first. Despite her professed lack of animosity toward the picture per se, she chopped out a big wedge-shaped section which included the general in fringed buckskin. Anheuser-Busch offered to replace the print, an offer Secretary Martin rather ungraciously declined, having had trouble enough. Some time later the society did accept a new print, but the members had been so intimidated that before exhibiting this copy they blacked out the brewer's name.

What afterward became of Kansas' No. 2 hatchet woman is not recorded.

Elk Eber could hardly have been more Germanic, despite his first name and a common belief that he was half-Indian. His mother was alleged to be a Sioux named Little Elk who watched the battle, joined Buffalo Bill's troupe, and toured Europe where she met Friedrich Wilhelm Eber—although in fact her maiden name was Eisele. His father was a wine merchant of Haardt where the artist was born on April 18, 1892. At an undetermined date young Wilhelm Emil exchanged his double-barreled Teutonic name for Elk, presumably to encourage the half-breed idea, but his soul remained Germanic; soon after painting General Custer he became a Nazi and devoted himself to *Deutschland über Alles*, and the perfect Aryan child—that little blond nightmare—was nourished by his chauvinistic posters. Now one may bite one's thumb at racist twaddle, indeed it might be obligatory, but artistically speaking Elk Eber did a respectable job on the Little Bighorn. Captain Edward Luce, who served in the Seventh Cavalry for three years and who was the battlefield's first superintendent, considered Eber's "Letzte Schlacht" to be among the most authentic representations.

Edgar Paxson's six-by-ten-foot panorama, which took twenty years to finish and holds so much paint that it weighs half a ton, must be the most thoroughly researched. Paxson was adept at sign language, as well as being able to speak several Indian dialects, and a number of surviving warriors led him around the field. Gall, Two Moon, Hump, Crow King, White Bull, and Crazy Horse all posed for him, according to his grandson. That Crazy Horse should pose for a picture is surprising, considering his obstinate refusal to be photographed—though there is a difference. Anyway, Paxson went after the subject with such industry that he might be called obsessive. He worked as hard as the great masters, and close inspection of his *chef-d'oeuvre* reveals a meticulous hand, together with a knowledge of anatomy and no small understanding of the various ways men react to their final hour.

Indian artists give the impression of being emotionally detached.

In a pictograph by an unidentified Sioux or Cheyenne, the artist looks down from infinitely high above and his swarming braves resemble ants scurrying about. There are no individuals. From the celestial viewpoint one man, regardless of color, could not be more important than the next.

Another noted the vast space beyond the battle. He drew both fights—Reno and Benteen trapped, Custer trapped far away—but he also drew the river with its tributary ravines, the lodges, the great surrounding space empty and white, as though snow covered the earth. He perceived no color. Not a drop of blood. No bright feathers. No blue coats.

Chief Red Horse filled up forty-one sheets of paper with pictographs. He showed Reno's troops in formation, each with a dangling saber—which means that by white men's logic his version is imaginary. None of these wasichus seem angry or distressed, at least not as whites are accustomed to seeing such emotions portrayed; they look interested, perhaps wondering why they have been skewered with arrows or have had a foot chopped off. Pieces of men are scattered everywhere. Bearded heads. A severed hand beside a hat. Most of the naked, dismembered torsos spout fountains of blood and have thick black marks representing cuts, yet the decapitated heads often smile. It is a view that could not be expressed by Anglo-Europeans. Academically trained white artists also represent Custer's troops being stabbed, brained, and scalped, but these paintings literally illustrate the emotions felt by dying men: incredulity, fright, rage, suffering, desperation. They seem half-consciously to celebrate the anguish of defeat. Never does the victim smile.

DeCost Smith, who worked in a one-room studio at the Standing Rock agency, probably understood the aboriginal point of view as well as a white man could. He says that an Indian of the northern plains is less apt to draw a thing as it appears to the eye than as he knows it to be—which might explain the nonexistent sabers drawn by Red Horse. Wasichus did sometimes carry sabers, they knew, as everybody knew, so that was that.

In earlier days, before they had a chance to study the paintings of Catlin, Bodmer, and the rest, Indian artists who represented a man on horseback would show both legs, as though he rode sidesaddle. Of course this did not look right, but after all a man has two legs. Much the same attitude made an Indian object to posing for a portrait in profile, which would deprive him of an eye, and might even account for his dislike of European style chiaroscuro which ignores certain details in spite of the fact that they exist. Smith complains that very often he was thwarted in attempts to paint three-quarters of an Indian's face by the subject persistently turning toward him.

A gunshot was represented by fan-shaped lines diverging from the muzzle, just as European artists tried to represent a shot, except that this symbol might appear without the gun—indicating that a shot had been fired at a certain time or place. Similarly, a club or a bow or a whip might be shown in contact with an enemy although the owner might be some distance away, meaning that this weapon did at one time strike the foe.

They had no concept of perspective and almost never attempted to foreshorten. In a trail of hoofprints passing out of sight the farthest would be as large as the closest for the very good reason that whether a horse is close to you or far away his hoofprints will be the same size.

The consequence of such logic to wasichu eyes is that Indian drawings and paintings look remarkably like newspaper comics, with the important difference that the Indian's purpose is not frivolous. Like the true artist of every age and every nation, he remains eminently concerned with what he represents; and we should be grateful, Mr. Smith observes, "that he does not make use of 'wham,' 'bam,' and 'awk,' nor put stars and exclamation points around the victim's head to indicate the force of a blow."

A Sioux calendar, or Winter Count, notes 1876 as *Pehin Hanska ktepi*—the year they killed Long Hair.

Colonel Richard Dodge, writing in the late nineteenth century, thought only one calendar existed, commencing with the first snowfall of 1799–1800: an expanding spiral of glyphs designating the memorable events of each successive year.

1: Thirty Sioux killed by Crow Indians.
2: Sioux afflicted with small-pox.
3: The Sioux stole a lot of horses that had shoes on,—the first they had ever seen.
4: The Sioux stole some "woolly horses" from the Crows.

5: Sioux had a grand "calumet dance," and then went to war.

6: Eight Sioux killed by Crows.

7: A Sioux killed an Arickaree as the latter was in the act of shooting an eagle.

Battles. Horse thieves. Plague of one sort or another. The Sioux who killed the Ree was himself killed by Rees. So it went, rather monotonously, concluding in 1870.

Dodge learned in 1877 that the Smithsonian had issued a pamphlet containing a Winter Count with interpretations. He got one, expecting something new, and was irritated to find precisely the same calendar. Later he heard that a Sioux chief had given an American doctor permission to copy a Winter Count, so Dodge wrote to the doctor, who sent him a copy. Same old calendar. Several times he heard of Winter Counts and always ran them down. Always it was the same chart. He concluded that it must be unique: ". . . the solitary effort to form a calendar ever made by the Plains Indians." He adds a bit sardonically that perhaps this is just as well, because none of the Indians he met could make any sense of it. Not once did he find an Indian who could interpret a single glyph. Indeed, none of them ever had heard of his calendar and seemed unable to grasp the idea, despite a careful explanation. He therefore decided that to the few individuals who had painted this spiral, and guarded it, the pictures must have had a special meaning, but to other Indians the Winter Count was merely a collection of senseless marks.

This is difficult to understand. The Indians with whom he spoke might have been feigning ignorance, yet other calendars did exist and could be interpreted, and quite a few whites with experience among Indians must have known this.

Such records would have been invaluable, Bruce Nelson wrote, "had the aborigines possessed any sense of historical values as we know them. But their sense of history was trivial, to say the least, and it is all too seldom that an event of more than passing interest emerges from the faded colors painted on the ancient buffalo hides." He cites as one example the Miniconjou year of 1796—the great event being a game of hoops-and-sticks during which a player named Penis was killed. How he got this name cannot be deduced from the calendar, but Penis was his name and he was killed while playing hoops-and-sticks. He had attacked two other players who responded by killing him, after which the game continued, using his corpse as a backstop. From then on the Miniconjoux identified 1796 as The-Year-When-the-Hoop-Rolled-against-Penis.

It is impossible even to guess how many Winter Counts exist. There are thought to be a good many in private collections, as well as in museums, and some might have been buried with their keepers—which sounds illogical, considering that their only purpose was to perpetuate tribal history. Alexis Praus in his discussion of an Unkpapa calendar owned by the Cranbrook Institute of Science refers to about a dozen.

Joseph White Bull, after conferring with old Miniconjoux noted for their memories, put together a tribal history extending from 1781 to 1932. That first year was remembered because many buffalo either froze to death or drowned, and warriors swam through the ice-filled Missouri to retrieve these floating carcasses. The following year an Englishman appeared and saw the Miniconjoux using stone knives. He went away but after a while came back with steel knives.

In 1804 a clown was killed. Clowns did everything backward. They behaved as foolishly as possible. In 1804 a clown led a charge against some unspecified enemy but shot his arrows straight up in the air. Then he stopped, turned around, and began shooting at his own people—first above their heads, then directly at relatives and friends. The enemy killed him.

In 1807 some white men hired an Indian to carry a book to other white men at trading posts. An Oglala named Red Dog carried it a long distance. Nobody knows what was in this book.

In 1817 a poor orphan boy without a bow joined warriors of his tribe who were chasing enemies. The Sioux hesitated when two of these enemies turned back to fight, but the orphan boy picked up a stick, rushed forward, and struck them both. This was so brave, according to White Bull, that the boy's tribe became known as Itazipdro, or Sans Arc. White Bull's explanation does not agree with the Unkpapa story about a hermaphrodite who advised his people to leave their bows and arrows on a hilltop, but after such a long time who knows the truth?

Not very often do these histories commemorate the same incident. One exception occurred in 1832 because of a brilliant meteor shower on November 12 which was noted around the world. Every Indian calendar mentions it as the winter of falling stars, easily depicted by a pattern of stars.

The year 1837 brought the steamboat *St. Peter's* with its deadly cargo of pox, shown on the Cranbrook chart by a single Indian wearing a spotted garment. Two years later the wretched Winkte, the hermaphrodite, killed himself/herself—although it is considered possible that this unhappy person may have been a transvestite. In either case, the Cranbrook chart illustrates suicide by hanging.

The year of Custer's defeat is not represented by a fight, as might be expected. Instead, Sitting Bull shakes hands with a uniformed white man. This could describe him entering Canada after the Little Bighorn and being greeted by a red-jacketed Mountie. A coup stick in the glyph might symbolize victory.

The leader of those bluecoats who were so thoroughly defeated in Montana seems to have been unknown to most Indians. It is true that at least one calendar does allude to him—*Pehin Hanska ktepi*—but others do not. Most of the Indians assumed that Three Stars Crook had returned. Only afterward, possibly because of an educated half-breed called Big Leggins, did they begin to understand that they had fought the Seventh Cavalry. At first this meant nothing. Not many of these Sioux and Northern Cheyennes knew anything about Custer.

Big Leggins' name among whites was John Bruguier or Brughière. His father Théophile was a French-Canadian trader with two Santee wives, Dawn and Blazing. They were sisters, daughters of a chief named War Eagle, and between them they filled the Bruguier lodge with thirteen children. John's mother was Dawn. He is said to have been a fearless young man with a good face, heavily built, very dark, and he must have been unusual because he was enrolled at the Christian Brothers college in St. Louis. After leaving college he went to work for his father. At Standing Rock on December 14, 1875, he got into a fight and clubbed one William McGee who died the next morning. McGee has been described as a quiet, industrious individual. Maybe so, but a post trader at Fort Lincoln testified that he could turn into a nasty drunk. The brawl apparently progressed like a minuet, step by step, with Johnny contributing to the rising ugliness; and in due time—June 13, 1898—he himself would be clubbed to death with a monkey wrench, which is a singular coincidence because victims of frontier violence customarily were shot or stabbed.

At any rate, knowing McGee was badly hurt, Johnny Bruguier took off. Where he went never has been learned, perhaps to the Black Hills, then farther west to Bighorn country; and whether or not he was responsible for telling the Sioux about Custer probably depends on the date of his arrival at Sitting Bull's camp. Dr. John Gray, who might be the foremost authority on this slice of western history, thinks he did not join the Sioux until late August.

Whenever it was, Big Leggins knew what to do upon reaching camp: he rode straight to Sitting Bull's lodge, presented his horse and gun, and addressed the medicine man as Brother. He could not have done anything more astute, which might be a tribute to his Catholic education. If he had not acted as he did he most likely would have been killed because he was trailed by a number of Sioux carrying weapons. These touchy people were so suspicious of a foreigner wearing wasichu clothes that they actually pulled up several pegs of Sitting Bull's lodge in order to raise the flap and peer inside. A long time afterward Johnny told his nephew that he did not know at what instant he might feel an arrow or a bullet.

Sitting Bull, having considered the state of his lodge and the presence of various neighbors contemplating his unexpected half-white guest, suggested that either they kill him or get him something to eat. So they decided to accept him, and because he wore cowboy chaps when he arrived they called him Big Leggins. And it is possible—perhaps not probable, yet possible—that when he noticed the 7 on several items of equipment captured by these Sioux at the Little Bighorn he told them which regiment they had defeated.

Wooden Leg, a Cheyenne, said his people learned about it from the Oglala Sioux, but he does not say how the Oglalas found out.

As for himself, a couple of days after the battle when the Indians camped near the present town of Lodge Grass he was stationed on a hill as a lookout. A Santee rode up, asking who he was. Wooden Leg replied that he was a Cheyenne. The Santee had tobacco so they smoked a while and the Santee then said: "I think the big chief of the soldiers we killed was named Long Hair. One of my people killed him. He has known Long Hair many years, and he is sure this was him. He could tell him by the long and wavy yellow hair."

Wooden Leg had never heard of Custer and the news seemed unimportant. He did not bother telling other Cheyennes. He himself had seen at least three dead soldiers with long, light-colored hair. One of them he had shot because he suspected the man was only pretending to be dead. There were no wounds on this soldier's body so Wooden Leg held the muzzle of his rifle against the man's head and put a bullet through it.

After a while, however, the news did seem important and many Indians claimed the distinction of having killed Long Hair, or were so credited by fellow tribesmen. Other Indians listened to such claims with amusement or scorn. Wooden Leg said these claimants were merely boasting, that there was no such talk immediately after the battle. He insisted that the few Southern Cheyennes and Sioux who had seen Custer at an earlier time did not know until weeks later that he was killed in this fight. At the time of the Little Bighorn, he said, most Indians did not even know the man existed.

Those most often mentioned in tribal folklore as having killed him are Hawk, Brave Bear, Flat Hip, Spotted Calf, Two Moon, Harshay Horse, an unidentified fifteen-year-old boy, and one of Sitting Bull's nephews—Joseph White Bull.

White Bull was a fearsome warrior, of this there can be no doubt. Kill-claims were discussed and resolved after each fight just as the claims of latter-day fighter pilots must be verified before those symbolic flags can be stenciled beside the cockpit, and at the Little Bighorn—despite the fact that he got a bullet in one ankle and his pony went down—this Miniconjou was credited with two kills, seven coups, and the capture of twelve American horses. He asserted that during the fight he grappled with a strong, yellow-haired soldier who almost bit off his nose. Finally, White Bull said, he managed to shoot the enemy with his own carbine. White Bull drew at least four pictures of the epic struggle. His claim is taken seriously by many historians. Others have said it gives off a suspicious odor.

The account proffered by an Arapaho named Waterman who rode with the Cheyennes is less dramatic. Waterman was dressed just as whites imagine an Indian on the warpath: breechcloth, beaded leggings, feathered bonnet. He had painted his face yellow and red and tied a deerskin pouch containing "a certain root" around his neck. Thus prepared, Waterman raced into battle and saw Custer at the top of the ridge on hands and knees: "He had been shot through the side and there was blood coming from his mouth. He seemed to be watching the Indians moving around him. Four soldiers were sitting up around him. . . ." This sounds right, although it might not have been acceptable to people of the nineteenth century. As to why an account of some historical event might be rejected by one generation only to be accepted later, nobody can say; but in the twentieth century Waterman's account seems more plausible than that of White Bull.

The Crow scout Curly reported, among a great variety of things, that just before his miraculous escape he watched Custer sink to a sitting position with a bullet in his side and then—struck by another bullet—fall backward. This, too, sounds convincing. But Curly also said he had fled to a butte east of the battleground from which point he observed Custer's death, and from which distance he could not have known Custer was hit in the side.

A number of Indians insisted Custer went down last, saber in hand, shot by Rain in the Face. He might possibly have gone down last, but not with saber in hand. As for Rain, he probably was in the fight. He could have shot Custer. There is no proof that he did, no proof that he didn't. Mathematically, considering how many shots were fired, it becomes most improbable.

Wasichus—especially those back east—were determined to find out which redskin had killed their hero, so they asked and they asked. The Indians got tired of this and at a 1909 council they resolved to end the matter. They themselves had no idea who killed him, but after discussing possible candidates they elected Chief Brave Bear of the Southern Cheyennes. He had been with Black Kettle at the Washita, he had been in the lodge when somebody dumped ashes on the general's boots, he had done his part at the Little Bighorn. Therefore he was as well qualified as any.

The socialistic tribesmen had another reason for doing what they did. Philadelphia millionaire Rodman Wanamaker had offered a reward for this nugget of information, the money to be distributed among those present at the council, and in 1909 many Indians were starving. So, they reasoned, if we produce a killer he will give us money to buy food for those who are hungry.

It is said that Brave Bear was not anxious to acknowledge this honor being urged upon him because he thought Mr. Wanamaker was planning to shoot him, but he gathered up his courage on behalf of his hungry people and stepped forward, thus solving the mystery.

Mr. Wanamaker of course was pleased, the hungry Indians were pleased, and Brave Bear was pleased when he realized that the wasichus only wanted to stare at him.

Yet the Bismarck *Tribune* had reported almost thirty years earlier that a trader bought from Chief Gall—"the worst Indian living"—an odd little matchbox-compass-whistle device that Custer carried in his pocket. How did this worst of all possible Indians get it? Gall could not have been Custer's angel of death. For one thing, he fought with a hatchet and beyond doubt Custer went down with a bullet in the side, another in the head. It has not even been determined whether the avenging angel was Sioux or Cheyenne, or perhaps a visiting Arapaho; but those five companies struck the Cheyenne end of the village so the odds increase that a Cheyenne bullet dropped him. Therefore, how does one explain a trinket from Custer's pocket in Gall's possession?

Finerty, who saw the chief several times and who could be quite blunt, called him "a restless vagabond, who looked like a horse-stealing gypsy, and was by repute a double-dealing, skulking rascal."

Lt. Godfrey—later a general—did not agree. He perceived Gall as a man of tremendous character, natural ability, and great common sense, a chief whose massive physiognomy reminded him of Daniel Webster.

Agent McLaughlin, who got to know him pretty well, regarded him as not only a crushing warrior but a persuasive councilor, the equal of such great Teton Sioux as Red Cloud and Spotted Tail. Physically, he was the most impressive man McLaughlin ever saw.

Elizabeth, despite the horror she felt, said almost the same thing: "Painful as it is for me to look upon the pictured face of an Indian, I never in my life dreamed there could be in all the tribes so fine a specimen of a warrior as Gall."

Most Unkpapas—at least those who talked to whites—considered him a peaceable sort who lost his temper that Sunday after Reno's troops shot two of his wives and three of his children. Gall thought they were killed by Ree scouts, a belief he could not possibly have verified. No matter who shot his women and children, the act turned his heart bad, as he confided to a journalist many years later, causing him to ride among the soldiers and split their heads with his hatchet. "I killed a great many;" he said.

His name in English is a literal translation of Pizi, given to him by his mother when she came upon him tasting the gall of a dead animal. But he was known also as Red Walker because his father once dressed him entirely in vermilion, with vermilion streamers, and paraded him for the admiration of guests. Sometime after that display, which must not have affected him as it would affect a Caucasian child, he became The Man Who Goes in the Middle. Just why he was called this is not clear, but he was proud of the name and probably earned it in battle.

He was not a hereditary chief. The family seems to have been undistinguished, and because his father died at an early age the boy was regarded more with sympathy than respect. So it appears that not through any legacy did he become a chieftain, but because he could feel within himself the seed of his own importance.

He was born somewhere along the Moreau River in South Dakota about the year 1840, perhaps the same year as Bloody Knife, possibly in the same village, and died in 1893 from a dose of patent medicine or bayonet wounds or from falling out of a wagon. And although it means nothing, he died on Custer's birthday: December 5. The general, had he been more discreet, would have turned fifty-four that year.

Even in pudgy middle age Gall was a man of such explosive strength that he fairly cracks the photographer's glass. Every plate reveals a leader of prodigious psychic and physical energy. Full-length photos make him look squat, with short bent legs and a torso the size of a beer keg. Twelve years after the great fight he stepped on a scale. He weighed 260 pounds. At the Little Bighorn with white stripes painted on his arms and a hatchet in one thick hand, in the fullness of manhood, he must have galloped through Custer's desperate troopers like a wolf through a flock of sheep.

McLaughlin asserts that at Standing Rock when Gall was no longer a young man he fell in love. Not only did he fall in love—this terrifying whirlwind—he blushingly admitted it to a reservation agent, which sounds preposterous. Nevertheless, McLaughlin asserts, those who know Indians will appreciate the literal truth of this. A Sioux chief "whose red skin was browned by the sun, who had painted his face every winter to keep the skin from chapping and painted it again in the summer to keep it from burning, blushed like a white-skinned girl."

The affair did not turn out happily. She who reduced the great Unkpapa to such an abysmal condition was, as not infrequently happens, somebody else's wife. McLaughlin discussed the matter with Gall and at last persuaded him to control himself.

"I have promised to go the white man's way and I stand by my word," Gall answered, "but I might not have promised if I thought my heart would sing again at the coming of a woman. I will pay the price of being as white men are."

After which they shook hands and Gall went away.

Billy Adams, who worked as a trader for Leighton, Jordan & Hedderich, used to haul beef to the prisoners of war at Fort Buford where he got to know Crow King, Low Dog, Sitting Bull, Rain in the Face, Gall, and other prominent Sioux. He did not think much of Sitting Bull, whom he describes as physically insignificant, bowlegged, with a suspicious, dishonest face. Snaky-eyed, says Billy, suspicious of everybody. Sitting Bull refused to drink coffee or eat his food until another Indian tasted it. But of Chief Gall he speaks with respect. Gall was outstanding. His sparkling black eyes revealed hostility bordering on wildness. No one could approach him without feeling the presence of a man of power and intelligence.

He visited Washington and while there was given money to spend as he wished. Later he was asked what he had seen and what he thought of Washington. "I went about your great city and saw many people," he replied. "Some had fine clothes and diamonds; others were barefoot and ragged. No money to get something to eat. They are beggars, and need your help more than the Indian does. I gave them the money you gave me. All people are alike among Indians. We feed our poor."

Late in life as Gall's features softened he is said to have looked less like Daniel Webster than Henry Ward Beecher.

Whatever his ethical nature as defined by whites, there could be no disagreement about his physique. In the winter of 1865–6 near Fort Berthold a detachment of soldiers tried to arrest him. The charge against him might or might not have been justified, but when soldiers approached his lodge—perhaps entering it—he slashed open the back and wriggled out. What he did not know was that some such escape attempt had been anticipated; a bluecoat stationed behind the lodge drove a bayonet through him. He was held like this, staked to the ground, until he fainted. The soldiers then marched off to inform their commandant that Gall was dead, whereupon a party was assigned to bring in the corpse. However, as the saying goes, the report of his death had been exaggerated. Gall woke up before these soldiers returned. He crawled into the woods where he hid until they stopped looking for him.

Maybe it did not happen quite like that. Some say Bloody Knife guided the soldiers and during the attempted arrest Gall was bayoneted more than once. Bloody Knife may have been just about to deliver the *coup de grace* with a double load of buckshot when the officer in charge, Lt. Bassett, knocked the shotgun aside. The blast dug a smoking hole in the earth a few inches from Gall's head. He already had been killed, or was breathing his last, the lieutenant thought. There was no reason to blast a corpse. So they left the bleeding man and rode off. Then Gall's people tied up his wounds, placed him on a travois and started at once for an Unkpapa village. There he recovered. Much later he showed Father De Smet the scars and boasted that seven white men had died because of the way he, Gall, was treated at Fort Berthold.

Vestal says a Two Kettle Sioux named Long Mandan brought the soldiers, and after the bayonet passed through Gall the soldier had to put one foot on his body in order to withdraw it. Gall feigned death while they kicked him, trampled him, stabbed him again and again. The Sioux themselves thought he was dead. They refused to touch his corpse. They dismantled their lodges and fled. Gall then staggered away through the falling snow and walked twenty miles to the lodge of a friend called Hairy Chin who saved his life. A year later one of the deep wounds was still suppurating. Crow Ghost, a son of Hairy Chin, was fifteen years old at this time and remembered that when Gall arrived his clothes were stiff with blood and bloody foam bubbled from his mouth, which meant the bayonet had pierced his lungs. Other Indians said he was bayoneted through the neck.

There are two accounts of Gall being shot. Lewis Crawford says Long Mandan slipped away to Fort Stevenson where he told the commandant, Colonel de Trobriand, that Gall was at Berthold. De Trobriand dispatched one hundred soldiers who reached Berthold at two in the morning. It must have been a moonlit night because a clerk at the fort was awakened by a noise, looked through field glasses, saw Gall's camp surrounded, and could hear an interpreter saying: "We want The Man Who Goes in the Middle." Gall then appeared at the entrance of his lodge and was shot with a revolver.

This is considered doubtful. A gunshot at night would arouse every Indian in the neighborhood, which the soldiers naturally would try to avoid.

Joseph Henry Taylor knew some of the participants. He said Gall had camped peaceably in the willows just south of Fort Berthold and when he stepped out of his lodge to meet the visitors he was shot, knocked down, and pinned to the ground by a bayonet through his breast. Blood gushed from the wound and from his mouth and nostrils—"he bled near a gallon." His life was saved not by Hairy Chin, but by some unidentified old woman.

Elsewhere it is stated that he was saved by a medicine man called Padanegricka.

Whether he owed his life also to Lt. Bassett, who kept Bloody Knife from filling him with buckshot, is questionable. The incident sounds too much like the story told by Col. de Trobriand: Bloody Knife hopped off his pony and was about to cut Sitting Bull's throat when ordered to cease and desist. It seems most improbable that Bloody Knife twice was prevented from killing a Sioux leader. One of these stories could be true, but which?

There is yet another version, a trifle shopworn, too vague for credibility, reported by the St. Paul *Pioneer Press* on July 18, 1886—which is to say, twenty years after the incident. Bluecoats from Fort Sully pursued and overtook Gall on the prairie. They pumped half a dozen bullets into him, followed by half a dozen bayonet thrusts. An unidentified corporal wanted to add a final thrust: "Let me give him one more punch, Lieutenant, just for luck." But the lieutenant said no and they rode away, whereupon "the wily redskin crawled off. . . ."

That Gall was bayoneted near Fort Berthold on a wintry night and recovered from one or more thrusts which would have killed an ordinary mortal, seems beyond dispute. He might also have been shot, but about this nobody can be sure. Too much snow has fallen. Anyway, according to what Vestal was told, from then on he hated whites and all the flattery they provided during his years on the reservation could not make up for this brutal indignity. "Some say he died from taking an overdose of Anti-fat, others because of a fall from a wagon. But the truth is, his wounds destroyed him, and he died regretting his half-hearted friendship for the white men."

Concerning Anti-fat, Gall did grow stout on reservation food; he worried about this and began to drink some sort of tonic recommended by a friend. He drank the prescribed amount for about a week, but then, seeing himself as fat as ever, he drank the entire bottle and collapsed. So it is said. If true, it sounds like a Chekov story.

One other preposterous detail about this fabulous warrior can be found in a 1907 letter from Major J. M. T. Partello to the photographer Barry. The major asks if Barry remembers Captain Clifford at Fort Buford, who had charge of Indian prisoners: "I used to play Mendelsohn's Wedding March for Gall on Capt. Clifford's piano. He always asked me to play that particular thing. . . ."

Vestal thought Gall died regretting his friendship for whites. Maybe.

Maybe not. In southern California at the Southwest Museum, at least a thousand miles from the battlefield, there is a large watercolor painted on muslin in 1898 by Chief Kicking Bear which graphically measures Gall's attitude. This painting was commissioned by Frederic Remington, but Remington never came back to get it so the artist sold it to an Indian agent.

Kicking Bear contemplates the Little Bighorn from high above, as a vulture might observe it, and on the diaphanous muslin field Custer's stricken soldiers look like dead brown sparrows—here and there the uncolored outline of a man to represent his departing spirit. Custer, dressed in buckskin, has lost his flat white hat and is shown with long hair, which is symbolically if not technically correct. A number of attractive horses may be seen—yellow, pink, and green horses. But most significant, in the center of this painting stand four important Sioux: Sitting Bull, Crazy Horse, Rain in the Face, and the artist himself. Chief Kicking Bear did not include Gall. Where Gall should stand there is a blank space, indicating that among these prominent men he alone softened his heart toward the enemy.

In that desolate land and lone,
Where the Big Horn and Yellowstone
    Roar down their mountain path,
By their fires the Sioux chiefs
Muttered their woes and griefs
    And the menace of their wrath.

"Revenge!" cried Rain-in-the-Face,
"Revenge upon all the race
    Of the White Chief with yellow hair!"
And the mountains dark and high
From their crags re-echoed the cry
    Of his anger and despair. . . .

Into the fatal snare
The White Chief with yellow hair
   And his three hundred men
Dashed headlong, sword in hand;
But of that gallant band
   Not one returned again. . . .

But the foemen fled in the night,
And Rain-in-the-Face, in his flight
   Uplifted high in air
As a ghastly trophy, bore
The brave heart, that beat no more,
   Of the White Chief with yellow hair.

Whose was the right and the wrong? . . .

Mr. Longfellow made so many mistakes that it becomes tedious to count coup on his doggerel. In the first place, it occurred not at the confluence of the Bighorn and Yellowstone but along the Little Bighorn, which is a tributary of the former. Nor do rivers in this part of Montana roar down mountain paths; they are shallow, reptilian rivers.

Next, it is most unlikely that Rain said such a thing. Nor are there any dark crags in this area.

Mr. Longfellow's third stanza characterizes the Indian village as being "silent as a dream," altogether quiet except for rushing water and "the blue-jay in the wood." In fact, there were thousands of Indians at this encampment, possibly fifteen thousand noisy Indians and nobody knows how many snarling dogs. So much for bluejays and a babbling brook.

The fourth stanza imagines Sitting Bull dressed in war paint and beads, waiting to ambush Custer like a bison among reeds—a peculiar simile because one does not ordinarily associate a bison with reeds. Nevertheless it evokes a dramatic image uniquely relevant to the American West. Just what Sitting Bull did wear that morning has been established from interviews with people who saw him. According to Vestal, he had on a smoke-tanned buckskin shirt embroidered with green porcupine quills, "with tassels of human hair on the long decorated shoulder straps." He wore moccasins, leggings, red breechcloth, and one eagle feather upright at the back of his head. His hair was braided. The braids, wrapped in otter fur, rested on his chest. At his belt in a black leather sheath studded with three rows of brass tacks hung a curved butcher knife.

Such specific information might not have been available to the poet, who therefore depended on a vague idea: "his war-paint and his beads." Although

imprecise descriptions seldom burn a place in memory, this is at least suggestive. However, Mr. Longfellow's "fatal snare" must be questioned. Gall
stated that the Indians waited for the bluecoats to trot into the parlor, whereupon they were gobbled up. This is not what Gall said, of course, but this was
the implication. He might have exaggerated. The Indians may not have been
so well prepared. Without doubt they knew a bluecoat column was approaching. Beyond that it becomes speculative.

The poet would have commander-in-chief Sitting Bull orchestrate a surprise counterattack by three thousand warriors. This is pure assumption.
Luther North, whose life was spent on the frontier, said that although the
chiefs were brave men and some were orators who could inspire enthusiasm
they could not give a command that would be obeyed, simply because Indians
had no military discipline. If a warrior felt like charging he would say: "I am
going!" And if others felt the same way they might follow him. But if Red
Cloud or Sitting Bull picked out a company of braves and ordered them to
charge the enemy at a specific time and place nobody would pay any attention.

Col. Dodge disagreed. He told of standing on a knoll overlooking the South
Platte where he witnessed "a drill of about a hundred warriors." Their commandant, a Sioux chief, sat on his pony for half an hour and directed these
troops by an occasional movement of his right arm. He later explained to
Dodge that he had been signaling with a mirror.

Scout George Herendeen insisted that he saw five chiefs at the Little Bighorn, each with a flag for his men to rally around: "Some of the flags were red,
others yellow, white and blue and one a black flag. All the chiefs handled their
warriors splendidly." Herendeen thought Sitting Bull was somewhere
nearby directing operations.

Agent McLaughlin did not think Sitting Bull even participated, saying
that he fled as soon as bullets came rattling through the lodge poles. "The
surprise created a panic in the heart, never very valorous of Sitting Bull." He
collected his wives and children, jumped on a pony and headed southwest.
He had traveled eight or ten miles when couriers from the village overtook
him to report the annihilation of Custer. "I have contended always that Sitting Bull was a physical coward. I know it from personal knowledge, also from
various incidents related of him, and from the attitude of contempt held toward him by the war-chiefs. But his medicine was great."

Regardless of Sitting Bull's presence or absence, regardless of the strategy
he did or did not contrive, there is no doubt that Custer tracked these temporarily peaceful tribes. He tracked them, following a plan drawn up by General
Terry, and it is clear that he meant to assault them. Instead of being am-

bushed, therefore, he must be likened to a hunter stepping into the jaws of his own trap.

As to the number of fighting men involved, Longfellow's figure of three thousand might be disputed, yet it seems not unreasonable. Estimates concerning the total number of Indians camped along the river begin at twenty-five hundred and end at twenty thousand—this latter being the estimate of Capt. Anson Mills who served with Crook. A year after the battle Lt. H. L. Scott visited the site and began counting circles where the lodges had stood, but gave up after counting fifteen hundred. These lodge circles, however, could be misleading because a family might decide to move, and move again, leaving two or three circles. In addition to lodges there were hundreds of wickiups—small brush shelters that blew apart soon after the inhabitants left. These were the homes of young warriors and at the north end of the village they were quite numerous.

The Indians themselves did not know. Gall, Flat Iron, Crazy Horse, Two Moon, Flying Hawk—they and many others were asked, but their estimates agree no better than those of whites. Besides, they did not consider it important. Very few Indians kept track of numbers above a thousand. They thought anybody who counted higher than that must be dishonest.

As for the number of soldiers, certain historians profess to know just how many followed the Son of the Morning Star into that arid cul-de-sac, but most will not cut it quite so fine. They say perhaps 220 or 225. Godfrey, who supervised much of the interment, counted 212 bodies, but several troopers were missing. Altogether, including those from Reno's command and some who later died of wounds, the total usually is fixed at about 265. In brief, these figures do not coincide with the poet's assertion that Custer led three hundred men.

Admittedly the poem does not flow as it should if "two hundred and twenty-five" is substituted, so the exaggeration might be justified as poetic license. However, Mr. Longfellow is unequivocally incorrect when he presumes that these doomed cavalrymen dashed headlong, swords in hand. They died fighting a defensive battle and none carried a sword.

Sabers had been issued, true, but they were cumbersome instruments, their principal value being psychological because most nineteenth-century Indians looked aghast at these long knives. So it has been argued that the Seventh ought to have carried sabers for the impression they made, if nothing else. Anyway, they were packed in wooden boxes and left at the Powder River depot. Lts. Edward Mathey and Charles DeRudio, neither of whom went with Custer, were the only members of the regiment who elected to keep their swords—for quite different reasons. Mathey stowed his on the pack train where it was readily accessible because he used it to kill snakes. He seems to have become the regimental expert, much in demand.

DeRudio's long knife vanished. *Hors de combat*: one saber. Property of First Lt. Carlo Camilius DeRudio, E Company.

Officially he belonged to E, which did follow Custer and fell apart in or near the big ravine, but DeRudio was lucky. On this expedition he served with A Company under Reno's command and thus managed to avoid contributing his name to the monument.

As to why he carried such an anachronistic weapon into battle—if indeed he did, and there is no evidence either way, only his assertion that he did; but assuming he did carry a saber, the explanation must be found in his patrician ancestry. He had something of a forked tongue—so numerous and dubious were his claims that unkind members of the Seventh called him Count No Account—but in fact he was a son of Count and Countess Aquila di Rudio; and Walter Camp, who interviewed him in 1910, was shown parchment records of the family dating back to 1680. Unquestionably this minor nobleman felt proud of his heritage and it may be that he did not feel well dressed without a saber.

Like quite a few men of the Seventh, his past life could be described as malodorous. On January 14, 1858, Emperor Louis Napoleon and his wife Eugénie arrived at the Paris Opera, escorted by a squadron of lancers. The crowd began to cheer, the orchestra inside the opera house struck up the "William Tell" overture, and three bombs met the royal procession. One horse was killed, two or three lancers were killed. Many people were hurt, including General Rogwet and two footmen. A piece of metal whistled through Louis Napoleon's hat. Eugénie was slightly cut on the left eyelid. Four men were arrested: chief terrorist Felice Orsini, Giuseppi Pieri, Antonio Gomez, and DeRudio—who claimed to be a Portuguese beer salesman named Da Selva. Gomez got off, the other three were commended to that surrealistic apparatus invented by Dr. Guillotin.

DeRudio at this time lived not in Paris but in East London and was married to an illiterate eighteen-year-old confectioner's assistant whom he had impregnated three years earlier. With the help of English political reformers, she may have delivered a petition on her husband's behalf to Empress Eugénie. Although this story has not been documented, what seems clear is that somebody spoke in his defense.

On March 12 at 5:30 P.M. the Procurer General received a warrant to execute the sentence pronounced by the Court of Assize upon conspirators Orsini and Pieri, which order was fulfilled two days later. Both terrorists lost their heads "with great bravery." DeRudio's sentence was commuted to life imprisonment on Devil's Island. There, in the fall of 1858, thirteen convicts—this extraordinary man among them—hollowed out a log and sailed to the British Guianas. From the Guianas he sailed by more conventional means to his good wife Eliza in London; and presently, as though to prove once again that nothing changes, he decided to make the lecture circuit. It seems, however, that nineteenth-century Englishmen were more discriminating than twentieth-century Americans because DeRudio's attempt to pump a fortune out of his murderous exploit did not succeed.

In 1864 he emigrated to the United States. He enlisted as a private in the Seventy-ninth Highlanders, this being a unit of New York volunteers; but what he wanted and felt entitled to was a commission. Once again somebody spoke up. He was discharged from the Seventy-ninth in order to accept a lieutenant's commission with the Second United States Colored Troops—a position few whites would accept. In January of 1866 he was mustered out, but by August of '67 he was again in uniform as a Regular Army lieutenant. Three weeks later this appointment was canceled because he failed a physical examination and because the War Department had learned about his activities in Paris.

Now, our government seldom holds a man's liabilities against him if he may be useful, as various Nazis discovered to their satisfaction and profit, so it came about that five weeks after declaring DeRudio unfit to wear the uniform of a United States Army officer the government restored his lieutenancy. On July 14, 1869, he was assigned to Custer's regiment.

Whether or not he waved a saber at the Little Bighorn, there can be no doubt that he liked the weapon. Along with the family parchment he showed Mr. Camp a gold-mounted saber—a gift from members of his company while the regiment was stationed in Kansas. Custer had rebuked him for accepting it. Custer told him it violated regulations and was prejudicial to good discipline, but apparently did not order him to return the present, so DeRudio hung on to it.

He is known to have carried a saber in the field on several occasions, despite ridicule. Evidently he would endure such remarks for the sake of tradition. Under the circumstances, then, if he did not leave his saber on the pack train, as Lt. Mathey did, he must have carried it into the valley. Chief Gall asserted during an interview that one soldier did have a sword.

There could have been a second long knife in this battle. An Oglala named Eagle Elk said another Sioux carried a saber captured during the Rosebud fight. So at most there were two, neither carried by Custer's men.

Nor did the Sioux flee in the night, as Mr. Longfellow contends in his seventh stanza; it has been well documented that they dismantled their lodges rapidly, yet without panic, and left the valley in late afternoon. As for Rain cutting out the general's heart, this is nonsense even though millions of Americans used to think he did, and many still do. The poem contains other mistakes, but enough is enough. By far the most egregious is Mr. Longfellow's charge that Rain fled the battlefield with General Custer's heart in his hand. During the late nineteenth century Rain in the Face was one of our most famous Indians—along with Pocahantas, Geronimo, and Sitting Bull—and he should not be slandered.

McLaughlin argues that it is impossible to render the soft Sioux syllables of this name into English, so any translation must be inadequate. Nevertheless, it seems to be literally correct. His mother left him outside the lodge one day while she was cooking lunch, when all at once "the thunder-bird settled in the limb of a nearby tree and a shower fell." Obviously this was a sign, thus the infant got his name. Now, that might be a true story. Who can prove it is not? But Rain loved to tell stories, and the more gullible his audience the better he liked it. He told Dr. Charles Eastman that he got the name after a fistfight with a Cheyenne boy when he was about ten years old. The Cheyenne boy bloodied his face and the blood streaked his facial paint just as if he had been caught in a storm.

Or maybe he got the name during a battle with Gros Ventres on a rainy day. He had painted his face to represent the sun half-visible on the horizon—half black, half red—but the rain streaked it.

No matter how he came by that name in childhood, it was so evocative that whites never called him anything else. Among the Sioux, however, he became known as Tok'-i'-tcu-wa, meaning He Who Takes the Enemy, or Enemy-Taker.

Some Indians believed he was miles away herding ponies at the time of the Little Bighorn fight, but others stated emphatically that he was one of Crow King's warriors who attacked from the southwest when Custer tried to ford the river, and they said that during this assault Rain's horse went down with a bullet through the head although he himself was not hurt. What he did next, nobody knows. He may have sent more than one wasichu to that great barracks in the sky; but he did not, despite Mr. Longfellow, flee at night holding aloft a ghastly trophy.

The curious aspect of this falsehood is why Longfellow misplaced Rain's animosity. It was not the general he hated so much as he hated Tom Custer. The reason for this dates back to 1874 when Rain was arrested and imprisoned on a charge of murdering a sutler named Balarian or Baliran and a veterinarian named Honsinger or Holzinger, both described as inoffensive, quiet, peaceable citizens. They had accompanied Stanley's 1873 Yellowstone expedition and imprudently wandered off to look for fossils, although they had been warned against this by Lonesome Charley.

Sgt. Ryan, who was with M Company guarding the wagon train, said the day was hot and he thought the vet and the sutler had gone to the river for a drink. Honsinger—"a very heavy man"—was riding a good bay horse while Baliran rode a black Mexican pony. Indians took both animals. The carcass of Honsinger's bay was discovered forty miles distant. Strips of meat had been sliced from one of the hindquarters, indicating that the bay's new owner probably rode it to death, after which several Indians helped themselves to steaks. Baliran's pony could not be found.

Honsinger may have been a quiet inoffensive citizen, but the sutler sounds like something else. This was a man who knew how to provide more than cold lemonade and fresh eggs. At one time he ran a gambling house in Memphis, and Benteen insists that on the Yellowstone trip he was in partnership with General Custer. He got the sutlership through Custer's influence and repaid his benefactor under the table. The partnership ended, according to Benteen, with Baliran losing his life and everything else, leaving a destitute widow and child.

Pvt. Windolph, interviewed sixty years after the incident, said the nature of their wounds proved that both men had been shot from the saddle. Elizabeth Custer, repeating what somebody told her, said the veterinarian was shot first and fell to the ground, whereupon the Indians pounded his head to jelly with a mallet. The sutler hid in some bushes. When he was found he held up one hand to signify peace and offered them his hat—that masculine symbol of authority—but they treated him with no more respect than they had treated the vet. Neither man, though, was scalped. Honsinger was bald and Baliran kept his hair cut disgustingly short.

An E Company bugler who witnessed the attack made this statement:

I saw Mr. Baliran the regimental sutler, and Mr. Honzinger, the veterinary surgeon, ride up to a large grove, a short distance up the river. I thought I would wait until the wagon train came in sight, so laid down near my horse and must have dropped into a light sleep, when suddenly I was startled by yells from the large grove. I jumped up and went out a few steps where I could see, when I was horrified to see a number of Indians killing Mr. Baliran and Mr. Honzinger. Mr. Baliran was running on foot and two Indians were shooting arrows into his back; Mr. Honzinger, also on foot, was running and a big Indian rode up and struck him over the head with the stock of his gun. When Mr. Baliran was found there was an arrow clear through his body and into the ground and he had hold of it with his right hand, his eyes open. . . .

Whatever the exact circumstances, Rain was overheard boasting that he had killed them. General Stanley was told about this and was shown a saddle, allegedly Honsinger's saddle, allegedly bought from Rain. Stanley therefore wrote to departmental headquarters, saying that if this Indian could be caught there would be no difficulty proving his guilt. "I respectfully advise that the arrest be entrusted to Lt. Col. G. A. Custer, with not less than 300 men."

Headquarters failed to respond.

Eight months later Rain showed up at the Standing Rock agency and this time the Army did go after him. Custer dispatched brother Tom and Capt. Yates with two companies of cavalry. They located the suspect in Baliran's store, of all places. Why Rain would enter the store of a man he claimed to have murdered seems beyond understanding, but he did.

According to Ryan this day was very cold, as cold as any he had experienced: 54 degrees below zero, two feet of snow on the ground. Lonesome Charley pointed out the suspect, Tom Custer sidled up, flung his arms around Rain, and wrestled him to the floor. "He was immediately handcuffed and taken out and put on one of our horses with his feet tied under the horse's belly. . . ." Rain seemed unable to realize that he was being arrested.

On the night of April 18, 1875, he escaped from the Fort Lincoln guardhouse. Just how he accomplished this remains a mystery. He told one brace of journalists that he was shackled to a grain thief—a white man—and after their escape the white man filed off the chains. What became of the white man, he did not know. He himself rejoined Gall and Sitting Bull, and he drew a picture of a bloody heart on a piece of buffalo skin which he sent to Tom Custer.

And the next time they met: "I got his heart."

He told photographer D. F. Barry something else. There were two thieves and as they crawled out of the guardhouse one of them beckoned. Rain followed. A guard ignored them; the guard went right on marching back and forth with his rifle on his shoulder. This does not sound plausible, but in fact may be reasonably close to the truth because the escapees were not pursued, nor was the guard punished for dereliction of duty—which argues that the whole thing must have been arranged.

Well then, one must ask why.

General Stanley thought Rain's guilt would be easy to prove. This was not so. There was very little evidence, if any. Rain's interminable boasting and a saddle which he allegedly sold. That was it. The Army may have decided the best way out of the mess was to make sure this objectionable Indian escaped.

Custer himself, though he ordered the arrest, may have suspected Rain was innocent because it is said that during the four months Rain was in jail the general and Elizabeth often came visiting. They treated him considerately and he became very fond of them. Possibly. But Captain Eli Huggins, who spoke pretty good Sioux, talked with this amiable warrior in 1880. Speaking of General Custer, Rain said: "He was a bad man and a liar and women and children slept better when they knew he was dead." And according to Capt. Huggins, Rain emphasized Custer's mendacity by making the forked-tongue sign, indicating with much vehemence that no friendship developed.

Probably he was lying when he talked about killing Baliran and Honsinger, although the boast nearly cost his life because several years after the great escape he was caught and jugged again. Same old charge: murdering the vet and the sutler. This time he ended up in a wasichu court, an unforgettable experience. In his defense it was argued that even if he did kill them—which was not admitted—these two men had accompanied United States soldiers through territory acknowledged by the government itself to be Indian hunting grounds. Which is to say, Baliran and Honsinger were part of an illegal expedition.

The Court agreed. Case dismissed.

It sounds like a legal nicety, the sort of business that enrages solid citizens, but the Court's scrupulous concern was justified. Subsequent investigation proved that the foolish fossil collectors almost certainly were killed by Cheyennes or Oglala Sioux, whereas Rain was an Unkpapa.

Just how he felt about the general is impossible to learn. On his deathbed in 1905, after being assured that the government would not now punish him for any of his misdeeds, he confessed to the missionary Mary Collins that during the famous battle he shot General Custer. Miss Collins had asked this question many times, but each time Rain insisted there was so much dust and smoke that nobody could say who killed Custer. On this occasion, as he lay dying, she knelt beside his bed. She held his hand and said to him: "Uncle, will you now tell me the truth for the sake of history?"

Rain lifted himself a little, looked earnestly into her eyes and said: "Yes, I killed him. I was so close to him that the powder from my gun blackened his face."

It was almost too much for the old man. His head sank back on the pillow.

Miss Collins waited until he revived. Then she began to read aloud from the Bible, among other comforting passages: "Though your sins be as scarlet they shall be white as snow. Though they be red like crimson they shall be as wool." She told him to be at peace because he and the other Indians were only defending themselves, and all men may do that. "I believe he told me the truth then," she wrote in answer to a letter from the artist DeCost Smith. "You would have believed it if you had seen him."

Mr. Smith might not have believed it. He knew more about people than she did. Furthermore, he had painted three portraits of Rain, he spoke Sioux easily, and during hours of conversation he had heard yet another account of Custer's demise from this accomplished storyteller: a Cheyenne named Hawk—Tce-tan'—fired the fatal shot.

Hawk and Rain looked almost alike that day. Both wore long bonnets but were otherwise naked except for breechcloth and moccasins. Their bodies were painted yellow and each carried a blue shield, although Rain emphasized that his shield was smaller, implying that he was the braver man. This resemblance, he said, might have caused people to think he killed the general, when in fact it was Hawk.

What about cutting out the heart of Long Hair's brother? Smith asked. People say you did that.

This question appeared to interest Rain very much, as though never in his life had he heard such an astonishing accusation, but he would neither affirm nor deny the truth of it.

Two months before his death he was visited by Dr. Eastman, himself a Sioux. Eastman found him lying on an iron bedstead in a log cabin, wrapped in a red blanket, alone except for an old dog at his feet. After they had talked a while Rain consented to discuss the past, saying he had reached the door of the spirit home and it was customary to retrace one's trail before leaving it. "Many lies have been told about me," he remarked. "Some say that I killed the chief, and others say that I cut the heart out of his brother, Tom Custer, because he had caused me to be imprisoned. Why, in that fight the excitement was so great that we scarcely recognized our nearest friends."

He said he had lived peaceably since coming to the reservation. He had not broken the Great Father's rules. "When we were conquered I remained silent, as a great warrior should." He died when he put down his weapons, he told Dr. Eastman. This was when the spirit departed, only the body lived on, and now the poor body was ready to lie down for the last time. "Ho, hechetu!—It is well."

However he might have felt about the general, there is no doubt he could do without Tom. He hated the man who physically arrested him and he did vow revenge. That he promised to extract Tom Custer's heart seems certain.

Elizabeth believed he did precisely what he vowed to do. In *Boots and*

Saddles she expressed herself passionately: "The vengeance of that incarnate fiend was concentrated on the man who had effected his capture. It was found on the battle-field that he had cut out the heart of that gallant, loyal, and lovable man, our brother Tom."

If Rain was aware of Elizabeth's animosity he did not respond to it, either through denunciation or by protesting his innocence. As years went by he would ask if she was still alive, and he wanted to know if she had acquired a new chief. His response to her uncontrolled hatred seems to have been altogether Christian.

Millions upon millions believed with Elizabeth that Rain did perform this odious surgery. Brigadier General Charles Roe, for example, who marched up the Little Bighorn as a second lieutenant with Terry and Gibbon, told the New York National Guard in 1904 that Tom's heart was plucked out: "A man's heart with a lariat tied to it, found in the village, might have been his."

All of this Mr. Longfellow revised by substituting the general for poor Tom. But why? Did he suspect the general's name would sell more copies? Whatever happened, his poem grossly misled the public.

Many poets have succumbed to the Little Bighorn's tumultuous music. Compare, for instance, the work of Mr. J. S. Carvell:

> The sun shone from an azure sky
>   On that eventful day,
> When Custer's band of troopers bold . . .

But of them all the most popular remains Mr. Longfellow with his inspired and erroneous image of Rain in the Face holding aloft a ghastly trophy while crying Revenge!

A meticulously composed photograph of Rain—Itiomagaju or I-to' ma-qa'-ju in Anglicized Sioux—wearing an immense feathered bonnet, grasping a ceremonial pipe in one hand and some sort of baton or coup stick in the other—this artful D. F. Barry picture reveals a fleshy, middle-aged personage who quite obviously would enjoy a drink with you in the neighborhood tavern.

He was indeed a congenial sort. At Standing Rock he grew fond of Barry, and when the photographer decided to move elsewhere Rain visited the studio to say good-bye. He took off his moccasins and handed them to Barry, saying that now his feet, like his heart, touched the ground.

He enjoyed visiting the painter DeCost Smith, who described him as a handsome young man with delicate features, not much more than a boy. He seems to have been nervous and demonstrative, in contrast to the stolid Sitting Bull. Smith thought him more quick-witted, although less sincere, but did not think Rain's facile wit indicated a higher grade of intelligence. Both of these Indians were convinced they would be assassinated and both are said by whites who knew them to have remained as vigilant as owls.

Sitting Bull's apprehension was not misplaced. The government thought he was encouraging Wovoka's ghost dancers, which may have been true; so, on December 15, 1890, forty-three Indian police—backed up by a detachment of one hundred soldiers and one or possibly two Hotchkiss guns—surrounded his cabin near Fort Yates. The show of force was designed to insure peace and the result was predictable. By the time it ended Sitting Bull and his young son Crow Foot lay dead, together with half a dozen police and about the same number of Sitting Bull's followers—probably including another of his sons named Blackbird—while the United States government had earned a further degree in militant stupidity.

According to Fletcher Johnson's 1891 biography, the medicine man was hustled out of his cabin by Lt. Bull Head and Sgt. Shaved Head. He protested this treatment, then called for help. There came a puff of smoke from beside a teepee, the crack of a Winchester. "The policeman at Sitting Bull's right, grasping the chief's bridle, reeled in the saddle, and, toppling over, was trampled under the hoofs of the ponies in the mad helter skelter of retreat from the village. . . ."

One of the soldiers told it differently. Bull Head approached Sitting Bull's cabin with a warrant for his arrest. When Sitting Bull cried out in alarm the lieutenant shot him:

> . . . the ball striking him in the breast over the left nipple, killing him instantly. While reeling Sitting Bull managed to draw a revolver, which exploded just as he fell, the ball entering Bull Head's thigh. One of the Indian policemen lifted Sitting Bull's scalp. The old chief's face was a sickening sight. An Indian battered his face into jelly after death with a plank. The few remaining hairs in his head were clipped off, and his moccasins and most of his clothing carried away for relics. Among his personal effects were letters from Mrs. Weldon, of New York, warning him to flee from the agency, as the Government was about to have him killed.

A Chicago *Tribune* correspondent wrote that a box supposedly containing his remains was dumped in an isolated grave and a guard stationed beside it, although in fact the body was taken to a military hospital for dissection. "It is an open secret that really the box did not contain the remains and that the guard was put on the grave as a blind. It is believed Sitting Bull's body is now in the dissecting-room, and that in time the skeleton will turn up either in the Government museum or some other place."

Perhaps it was necessary to kill him, Mr. Johnson comments, but those circumstances which required his death should only be regarded with national humiliation.

One of his nieces, Mrs. George Leonard of Wilmington, Delaware, had lived in Sioux territory during the Indian wars. When interviewed not long after the bungled arrest she said tearfully that her people had been robbed, ruined, and persecuted by whites, driven from lands that always had been their own, "and not content with this robbery they have now killed my uncle in cold blood."

Senator Sanders of Montana viewed the incident with characteristic wasichu levity: "I am in great distress of mind, my heart is bowed down with woe, because of the death of my fellow-being, Mr. S. Bull, formerly a resident of my State, but recently a sojourner in a neighboring territory. He has gone the way of all flesh, and there is other copper-colored flesh that would not go far astray if it followed him. . . ."

Buffalo Bill's wild west show featured some trained horses and Sitting Bull either was given one of these or had bought one. Various writers assert that during the attempt to arrest him the gunfire caused this animal to start performing: sitting back on its haunches, lifting one hoof, etc.

The government never clasped Rain in a deadly embrace, as it clasped Sitting Bull, Crazy Horse, Satanta, old Satank, Mangas Coloradas, and other prominent reds. The government ignored Rain during his latter years because he had no authority. Had the case been otherwise, he too might have communed with the Great Spirit before his appointed time. He probably did not understand this, but he did know that a wise man who enjoys life should behave cautiously in the presence of whites; so he conducted himself around them, even in the company of his good friend DeCost Smith. Often he visited Smith's studio and while there he always sat in the same place, near a corner where the artist's six-shooter hung on a nail. For quite some time, according to Smith, whenever he approached that part of the studio Rain would turn around uneasily.

He praised himself by comparing himself favorably to the old medicine man. He discovered that Sitting Bull was selling autographs, which filled him with contempt. Sitting Bull loved money while he, Rain, cared for nothing except his country, the land of the Sioux. Nevertheless he persuaded Smith to write his name in English and with Smith's help he learned to copy it, and some years later he was on Coney Island doing just what Sitting Bull had done.

He wanted to go to school. Several times he asked the missionary Mary Collins to intercede for him, saying he wanted his steps to go forward. "Let me go to school and learn, as a little child learns, to read and to write, so I may help my people."

There was talk of allowing him to matriculate at Hampton Institute. The *Atlantic Monthly* published an anguished nine-stanza poem by John Greenleaf Whittier in support of this idea.

The years are but half a score,
And the war-whoop sounds no more
    With the blast of bugles, where
Straight into a slaughter pen,
With his doomed three hundred men,
    Rode the chief with the yellow hair.

O Hampton, down by the sea!
What voice is beseeching thee
    For the scholar's lowliest place?
Can this be the voice of him
Who fought on the Big Horn's rim?
    Can this be Rain-in-the-Face?

His war paint is washed away . . .

Permission refused. The government thought Rain was too old to learn. Besides, it would cost $230 a year.

Smith was at first convinced that Rain did indeed want to study reading, writing, and arithmetic; so on behalf of the affable fox he wrote several letters which resulted in, as he put it, "a fairly voluminous correspondence leading to the final conclusion that what Rain in the Face really wished to do was to see the East, to verify with his own eyes the wonders related on their return by Sitting Bull and his companions, and as these Indians had been exhibited for an admission fee in the Eden Musée, and elsewhere, the laudable ambition of Rain in the Face resolved itself, in the last analysis, into a desire to join the show."

Agent McLaughlin, who understood him about as well as any white man could, wrote to General S. C. Armstrong at Hampton:

Yours of the 31st ultima and 1st inst., respectively, relative to "Rain in the Face," were duly received, and in reply would state that I doubt if he could be induced to remain at any school. . . . He has been importuning me for the past year to try and have some showman or museum engage him for exhibition and is exceedingly anxious to go on such a tour, as he is a little vain and somewhat inflated with his own importance. He is about 40 years old and is not thirsting for knowledge nor the desire to become a white man, but is otherwise well disposed. He is not a bad man in any sense, but on the contrary is rather intelligent, only inclined to be self-willed and a little obstinate. He was at one time a brave warrior of his tribe, but was never recognized as a chief of any prominence among his people and his present crippled condition leaves him without any following or influence. . . .

He may have been closer to fifty than forty at the time of McLaughlin's 1887 letter, perhaps in his early fifties. Certainly he was older than he looked, and Smith remarked that even with the best will in the world he could not have conformed to the discipline expected of Hampton students. This would have been asking too much. He could not be trained. One could as easily alter the veins of a leaf.

Three years after making a pitch to attend school he was stabbed by his wife. She had been in poor health, he was crippled and depressed because he thought he deserved to be famous, and out of this unsatisfactory situation—compounded by an inexplicable fit of jealousy—she whipped a knife. He seems to have been more embarrassed than hurt. They took him to the Fort Yates hospital and there, as Smith dryly observes, "knowing it was the strange custom of the white man to exact a penalty in such cases . . ." Rain asked agent McLaughlin to punish him, not his good wife, for the stabbing.

By 1893 things were looking up. His chief rival, Sitting Bull, had been assassinated, or was killed resisting arrest, however one chooses to interpret the business. In any event, thanks to the demise of Sitting Bull and to the popularity of Henry Wadsworth Longfellow's imaginative verse, to say nothing of more prosaic works, Rain had become the most celebrated survivor of the Little Bighorn. "I found him in that year the *pièce de résistance* in a side show on the Midway Plaisance, at the World's Fair. . . ."

Another unique attraction was Sitting Bull's cabin which had been dismantled, shipped from Fort Yates to Chicago, and reassembled. In this cabin the old medicine man had lived out his last years, in front of it he fell dead, and city folks paid to stare at the logs pocked with bullet holes.

Mr. Smith thought such an environment rather oppressive but Rain appeared cheerful, having only recently entered show business. From his seat on a platform he observed the crowd—a mass of wasichus gazing up at the dreadful savage who had eviscerated General Custer. Smith stood at the rear of this crowd. He was a short man, so for a while he went undiscovered, but

Rain eventually noticed him and beckoned. Smith pushed forward to the platform. They began to talk. Rain loved melons and one of the first things he asked was whether he could get melons in Chicago.

The last time Smith saw him was eight years later on Coney Island. They talked again, but Rain's voice was nearly inaudible and his face had lost its natural animation. He talked in senseless generalities about the Little Bighorn although Smith had not asked about it and they had gone over it many times in the past. Rain did not try to sell his old friend an autograph but he did beg a dollar. Smith noted that his autograph had changed. The capital letters were different, which meant that somebody else had been coaching him.

So, if he did not attend school, at least he was educated to this extent by whites; and by example they taught him to drink minnewaukan—the water of God. During his latter years he would take a drink or two or three or more upon occasion, any occasion. In 1894, he was interviewed by W. Kent Thomas with the help of minnewaukan—a not unfamiliar journalistic device, since it is known that the water of God encourages a man to speak.

How much of what Rain said under the influence is true, or partly true, nobody knows; and he, of course, has long since gone to hunt the white buffalo. But even if most of what he said during this interview is preposterous he cannot be dismissed as an alcoholic liar. Certain things about him have been verified, such as his astounding ability to ignore pain. He lived in a society whose fighting men were expected to endure just about anything, but Rain's capacity seems to have been remarkable. He volunteered for the excruciating torture of the Sun Dance not once but twice, a spectacle witnessed by Walter Gooding, a trader's employee at Standing Rock, in July of 1874. The first time Rain was strung up he dangled only a little while before his flesh gave way. Sitting Bull, who was in charge of the ceremony, did not think his courage had been adequately tested, whereupon Rain declared that nothing could cause him to flinch or cry out and he challenged Sitting Bull to try him further. Deep slits were then cut in the tough back muscles above his kidneys, a rawhide thong was pushed through these slits, and he was hoisted off the ground for another dance. He kicked and struggled for two days without being able to release himself and Sitting Bull eventually was convinced. He ordered buffalo skulls tied to the young warrior's legs and under the strain of additional weight the muscles tore loose.

That this did happen seems beyond doubt. Gooding's testimony is substantiated by Cyrus Brady, who states that there were hollows in Rain's back "big enough almost to take in a closed fist."

One might expect such a stoic to be uncommunicative, but he was as convivial as a man could be, and nothing pleased him more than talking about himself. Before revealing to journalist Thomas how he felt about the Custer brothers he confided that when he was a young buck he was very bad news indeed. All the Dakota girls admired him, he said, while other young bucks feared him. And the soldiers—Long Swords—they trembled at his approach. As for the Rees and Crows, every morning when they woke up they touched their hair to find out if it was where it belonged.

One night a girl dared him to kill a white man at Fort Lincoln. This was dangerous, but he did not want to be thought cowardly so he painted himself black, hopped on his pony, and rode to the fort. He had plenty of chances to kill a woodcutter or a Ree squaw, but he was after a Long Sword. At last he caught one, killed him, and cut the buttons off his uniform. He gave these buttons to the girl, who sewed them on her shawl.

Then he was asked—if indeed he was such a dangerous man—how it happened that Tom Custer, whom the Sioux called Little Hair, had managed to take him prisoner. What about this? Because Tom was not very big. Rain himself was still powerful at the age of sixty. He weighed almost two hundred pounds and he had a forty-six-inch chest.

Little Hair brought thirty soldiers, Rain said. That was how it happened.

By the Long Swords' count this was not exactly so. Two companies totaling seventy men had been detailed to arrest Rain, but just five were in Tom Custer's posse.

"He slipped up behind me like a squaw," Rain said, "when my back was turned." The soldiers jumped on him, thirty of them. Thirty men jumped on him and they did not let go until the jail door banged shut. "I told Little Hair that I would get away some time. . . . I would cut out his heart and eat it."

The next time they met was during the battle: "I shot him with my revolver. . . . I leaped from my pony and cut out his heart and bit a piece out of it and spit it in his face. I got back on my pony and rode off shaking it. I was satisfied and sick of fighting. . . ."

This 1894 interview appears to be the source of D. W. Bronson's 1907 account in *Overland Monthly*: "After he had killed Tom, he cut his heart out, and biting out a piece of it, spit it in the face of a wounded soldier who was lying nearby. He then rode away, waving what was left of Tom Custer's heart. . . ." The puzzling thing is why Mr. Bronson invented a nameless soldier who adds nothing whatever to the drama. It is also curious that Bronson, along with a great many other people, should uncritically accept this fabulous story, unless the idea of devouring an enemy's heart still sputters like a prehistoric torch in the human psyche.

Plenty Coups tasted a grizzly's heart when he was a boy, as boys of that tribe were expected to do, because in times of trouble it is good to say one has the heart of a grizzly, but not many instances of human heart-eating have been recorded. One authentic case is that of an Arikara named Bear's Ears who fell in love with somebody else's beloved. Bear's Ears tried to kill this rival, for which he was cast out of the tribe. The Rees and the Sioux were temporarily at peace so he joined the Sioux, and while living with them he chopped off two fingers of his left hand—such was his passion. Finally, in the last moon of the seventh year of exile, he chanced to meet his rival in the valley of the Cannonball River. There the gruesome deed was done. New York *Tribune* correspondent Samuel Barrows stated that the heart was broiled and that the vindictive lover had long hungered for this meal. Then, having eaten as much as he wanted, or could swallow, Bear's Ears returned to the Arikaras where he bragged about the exploit and became a hero. Why he should be allowed back and given this reception is not clear, but similar deportment is not unknown to the Anglo world. Concerning the light of his life, Wa-ka-ta-na, either she was unspeakably aroused by his concupiscence or fascinated by the horror of it all, because she married him.

William Curtis of the Chicago *Inter Ocean* encountered this mad lover at Fort Lincoln in 1874: "a rugged old man, with features black as a negro . . . clad in one of those uncouth stable frocks, a pair of cavalry pants, from which he had cut long strips under the thighs to give his limbs free motion, and a high crowned officer's hat, ornamented with plumes and bands of red flannel, from under which his long hair hung in a bushy mass." Curtis also met the creature who had inspired such lust: "Wa-ka-ta-na is a great, fleshy, dirty squaw, lugging water and building fires. . . ."

During the battle of the Little Bighorn, Rain said, he had not been afraid because he was wearing a weasel-tail charm—which he continued to wear during his years on the reservation. This charm worked pretty well, or perhaps not very well. A bullet caught him in the right leg just above the knee. He took a straight-edged razor from a dead soldier and tried to remove the bullet. He could not reach the bullet by slicing through the front of his leg so he reached around and began slashing at the back. He got the bullet, but he also mangled the tendons and walked on crutches for the rest of his life.

That was Rain's story. One of dozens, maybe hundreds. In fact, he was crippled while hunting buffalo in Canada four years after the Custer fight. His pony stumbled in a washout, his gun discharged accidentally and tore off a kneecap. It did not interfere with his ability to ride, but walking was difficult so he carried the crutches on his pony. After dismounting he would sometimes use them, at other times he preferred to hop.

Because he was lame he lost prestige among the Sioux, although not among wasichus—that strange race, in the words of Mr. Smith: "who while believing the tales of his horrid deeds were willing to treat him as a friend, shaking his hand and gazing in his face, while marveling at the mildness of his expression."

When he applied for a policeman's job at Standing Rock he was rejected because of the handicap. He was surprised and insulted. "Tell him to give me the name of any Indian he wants arrested," Rain said, referring to agent McLaughlin, "and I will go out and get him dead or alive."

"I believe that, all right," McLaughlin said upon receipt of this message, "but he will bring them all in dead."

When journalist Thomas asked him to name the Indian who had killed General Custer, Rain said he didn't know.

When asked why the general had not been scalped—if perhaps the Indians considered him too brave to be scalped—he said this was not the reason, but he did not know why Custer escaped scalping. Yellow Hair might have been lying under so many bodies that he was overlooked. The Americans went down like sheep, Rain said. It was as easy as killing sheep.

Traces of Fort Lincoln lie beneath the rectangular green surface of a state park within sight of Bismarck. Inconspicuous signs identify points of interest: granary, icehouse, teamsters' quarters, stables, commissary, barbershop, kitchens, parade ground, Officers' Row. Birds flutter from tree to tree as though looking for something that no longer exists while dandelions measure the wind. A peculiar ghostliness common to deserted military posts might explain why picnickers go elsewhere.

On a bluff overlooking Big Muddy to the east and not much except rolling emptiness in other directions stood Fort McKeen, incorrectly named for Colonel Henry Boyd McKean who died in the Civil War bloodletting at Cold Harbor. Construction of this fort, which housed the Sixth Infantry, began in June of '72 on the site of an ancient Anahaway village. Three tall gloomy wooden blockhouses extended the view. Rifle pits and a Gatling emplacement were dug on the western slope, which was considered the probable direction of attack. On November 19, 1872, the name officially changed to Fort Abraham Lincoln. Today nothing remains of this fort except skeletal outlines in the grass and a few weed-choked depressions on the slope, but in 1935 the blockhouses were reconstructed so that now a visitor can look through rifle slits and see almost exactly what those infantrymen saw at the time of the Indian Wars. The territory still looks ominous.

When Custer arrived in late summer of '73 after the Yellowstone expedition another post had been built on the adjacent plain. At first this was known simply as cavalry headquarters, then "Lincoln under the hill," but inherited the name Fort Abraham Lincoln when the infantry fort on the bluff was abandoned.

West of the parade ground stood Custer's home, flanked by those of subordinate officers. In February of 1874, after the fire which incinerated his wig, Custer's home was luxuriously rebuilt: a thirty-two-foot living room with a bay window, billiard room on the second floor, library, plenty of space to exhibit his gun collection and stuffed trophies. Behind the house were gardens, enclosed by a fence to keep out the dogs. At some later date a ballroom was added because the general and his lady liked to entertain. Elizabeth probably was responsible for the chandelier and a grand piano rented in St. Paul. It is said that the regimental blacksmith kept this piano in tune. Today on the site of the elegant home where Libbie and the general gave parties there are deep hollows in the earth and half-exposed flagstones.

Custer transplanted young cottonwoods from the river bank to Officers' Row and sowed grass on the parade ground, which improved the appearance of things somewhat, but not much else could be done. This was Dakota Territory. Summers were blistering, winters deadly. Only the giant Missouri with its serpentine tributaries kept the region from being uninhabitable. Fort Lincoln had not one cistern or well. Water wagons made daily trips to the river and by January the men might be forced to chop through five feet of ice. Then in summer the sky turned black with grasshoppers. Spring and fall could be pleasant, were it not for redskins. Fort Lincoln ladies enjoyed gathering crocuses on the slopes, but to do so without a heavy escort was worse than foolish.

Why a military post would be maintained on this flat is hard to understand because just to the west are some grassy hillocks—fine cover for prowling Indians. Logical quarters for the Seventh would seem to be the deserted fort on the bluff. But the cavalry post already was operational when the Sixth Infantry abandoned Fort McKeen, and climbing the bluff was wearisome. Besides, the invaluable river ran close by, and perhaps the regiment felt strong enough to repel surprise attacks. Then, too, guards could be stationed on the hills.

Through a winding ravine created by these hills, which resemble prodigious burial mounds, Custer led his troops westward in the spring of 1876.

U.S. highway 94 parallels his route to the Yellowstone and follows it almost exactly to the junction of Rosebud Creek where, on June 22, he waved goodbye to General Terry. At this point Montana 447 branches south and then southwest, occasionally angling across the creek, which means that a tourist has no trouble following the Seventh. What one encounters in this part of Montana is space. The yellow land goes on. On and on goes the land and still it goes on. Hills, gullies, sandstone buttes, burnt sienna earth tinted by coal. Now the valley widens, now it constricts, pine-darkened bluffs to either side, while the Rosebud trickles along—a brushy creek sometimes narrow enough to hop across.

Beyond Lame Deer, near the present town of Busby, Custer stopped on June 24. The approximate site of his final camp is marked by the Busby Post Office, G & J's store where a red-and-blue advertisement orders everybody to drink Pepsi-Cola.

A little beyond this sign one comes to a particularly unattractive stone-and-mortar mausoleum surrounded by a chicken-wire fence topped with barbs, constructed by Indian trader W. P. Moncure to hold the body of his friend Two Moon—not Two Moons. Two Moon, second moon of the year.

The trader built into this mausoleum a secret vault which held various relics: arrowheads, stone tools, a Seventh Cavalry gun, a primitive bullet mold and, among other items, a manila envelope. The vault, located behind a bronze plaque on the face of the cairn, is opened by pressing the bottom of the plaque and lifting outward, just as an overhead garage door is opened. One is then faced with a dusty, cobweb-shrouded glass plate.

In 1956, or perhaps somewhat earlier, a Billings newspaperwoman, Kathryn Wright, was permitted by the Cheyennes to see and photograph the relics, although she did not get to see what was in the manila envelope. It was her opinion, as well as the opinion of a prominent G. A. C. scholar, Dr. Charles Kuhlman, that this envelope might hold information of very considerable significance and should be opened sooner than the date specified by Moncure: June 25, 1986. This date does not sound correct. One assumes it should be 1976, a century after Custer's death, but is in fact half a century from the date Moncure sealed the vault.

Mrs. Wright, Paul Fickinger of the Indian Bureau, Kuhlman, and other inquisitive historians discussed with Cheyenne tribal authorities the idea of opening this envelope before 1986. Arrangements finally were made to open it in the spring of 1957. Measures were taken to prevent looting, after which Mrs. Wright published her story in the January issue of *Montana*; but before the vault with its mysterious envelope was to be officially opened it was opened unofficially by a party or parties unknown. Whatever was inside has now vanished.

Not far from the desecrated sepulchre is a gas station with a *Happy Motoring* sign. Beyond this landmark General Custer angled southwest toward the divide, while the present state highway continues due west—rising gently toward the ridge, curling and descending into the Little Bighorn Valley.

Indians knew it as the valley of greasy grass.

Greasy Grass is the usual translation, although there has been some quarreling about whether it ought not to be Rich Grass or perhaps Lodge Grass, these two expressions being very similar in the Crow language. However the name should be translated, Indians liked this valley and often camped here. Cottonwood trees beside the river provided not only firewood but a sort of ice cream—a frothy gelatin which accumulated when the bark was stripped off and the exposed trunk scraped. The larger the tree, according to Tom Le-Forge, the better the taste. This delicacy would keep for a week or so. "Buckets and cans would be filled and friends would be invited to partake. Lots of young fellows would treat their sweethearts by peeling the bark from a cottonwood tree."

Those cottonwoods long since have fallen and decayed but others grow nearby, and pleasant breezes still sweep the bluff where Reno's men held out. From this bluff things must look much the same as they did a century ago, though the river has changed—looping here where it coiled there. The Little Bighorn frequently changes course depending on the volume of water, which depends on the amount of snow in northern Wyoming, but it persists northwest toward the Bighorn. Willow trees, box elders, a variety of shrubs, and the everpresent cottonwoods seem to guide the river north.

Ex-Private Theodore Goldin, who revisited the scene in 1928, noticed that one thick stand of cottonwoods had been cut down, which in his judgment greatly affected the appearance of the valley. Still, the significant change has not been the river's course or a pattern of trees but the substitution of industrial life for aboriginal life. The valley used to be white with lodges while the benchlands as far as anybody could see were brown with Dakota and Cheyenne ponies. Not now. Gone is the sinuous continuity of primitive villages beside a coiling stream. Now, squinting down into the valley from Reno Point, one sees a vast green-and-black grid of mechanically cultivated farmland, the fulfillment of nineteenth-century America's belief in manifest destiny.

Our earliest prophet may have been George Catlin, who guessed the fatal charm of whisky and trinkets forty years before Sitting Bull met Custer; he spoke of voracious white men sweeping the streams and prairies all the way to the Pacific, "leaving the Indians to inhabit, and at last to starve upon, the dreary and solitary waste."

Three decades later an editorial in the Cheyenne *Daily Leader* argued with pious rhetoric that this region was destined to nourish the Anglo-Saxon race. Few editors have sliced closer to the bone: "The same inscrutable Arbiter that decreed the downfall of Rome has pronounced the doom of extinction upon the red men of America."

Judson Elliott Walker published a book on Custer's campaigns five years after the epic battle, and in chapter V, subtitled "A Careful Review of the Present Situation," he writes in a style that booms with mellifluous conceit, although in 1881 it might have sounded charitable and compassionate:

> Instead of hearing the oft-heard war-whoop and murderous yells of the hideous savages on the battle-field and the retort by our Gatling guns and musketry, and the loud cheering of our brave boys in blue, you will hear the persuasive eloquence of the kind-hearted theologian and the knightly young schoolmaster, pleading the cause of Christianity and education; and where Sitting Bull ofttimes held his medicine lodges and war dances on the banks of the Little Missouri and the Little Big Horn Rivers, for no other purpose only to strengthen and bolster up the heart of hundreds of Gall-hearted warriors, and urge them on to cold-blooded, heart-rending and blood-thirsty murders, you will see stately court-houses, with their benches occupied by the ablest jurists in the land to mete out justice, and members of the bar ably advocating and defending the cause of peace and good order.
>
> The energetic, sturdy, powerful and unconquerable Saxon race have decided that this country cannot afford to set aside an area the size of New York for the sustenance of a single chief and his hostile bands of warriors. . . .
>
> He, with his tribes and marauding bands of demoralized and half-starved followers, will be watched with vigilant eyes, but kindly cared for by the munificent agents of the Interior Department, assisted by a corps of large and open-hearted philanthropists, whose duties will not only in a measure be encouraged, but rigidly enforced by the authority of our powerful but ever humane and magnanimous government. . . .

The Crow medicine woman Pretty Shield thought differently. To her biographer, Frank Linderman, she said: "Ahh, my heart fell down when I began to see dead buffalo scattered all over our beautiful country, killed and skinned, and left to rot by white men. . . . The first I saw of this was in the Judith basin. The whole country there smelled of rotting meat. Even the flowers could not put down the bad smell. Our hearts were like stones. And yet nobody believed, even then, that the white man could kill *all* the buffalo. Since the beginning of things there had been so many! Even the Lacota, bad as their hearts were for us, would not do such a thing as this; nor the Cheyenne, nor the Arapahoe, nor the Pecunnie; and yet the white man did this, even when he did not want the meat."

Next the whites began fencing the plains, she said, and the Indians could not travel, although no longer was there a reason to travel. Then the ranchers began to shoot Indian ponies so their cattle and sheep might have all the grass. Ranchers paid three dollars for a pair of pony ears: "It was as though our horses, on our own lands, were wolves. . . ."

Thomas Henry Tibbles—editor, lecher, preacher, abolitionist, honorary member of the Omaha Soldier Lodge—Tibbles visited a band of Sioux huddled in leaky canvas tents near the Rosebud agency. They were not doing anything because there was nothing to do. Twenty years earlier he had known these people farther west, when they were strong and healthy. Now he found them weakened by this meaningless life. "I saw many of them covered with running sores, others with scrofula. . . . Many of the women here could not bear children after their twenty-fifth year. . . ."

General Sherman remarked in 1878 that western America had changed more in ten years than any other place on earth in fifty.

Little Phil Sheridan, noting that the aborigines had been content until the arrival of nineteenth-century progress "or whatever it may be called," went on thoughtfully: ". . . we took away their country and their means of support, broke up their mode of living, their habits of life, introduced disease and decay among them, and it was for this and against this that they made war. Could anyone expect less?" Sheridan's question is rhetorical, yet he seems to have been asking himself. Like other generals, bureaucrats, and private citizens who contribute to some irrevocable disaster, he wondered about it afterward.

What happened might be explained otherwise. The early Mandans, for instance, felt there was not only a benevolent spirit but an evil spirit which came to earth before the good spirit and whose strength was greater. However it came about, a way of life had been shattered. Plenty Coups during his address to the 1909 Little Bighorn assembly remarked that he could see as though in a vision the dying spark of Indian council fires, ashes cold and white. "I see no longer the curling smoke rising from our lodge poles. I hear no longer the songs of the women as they prepare the meal. The antelope have gone; the buffalo wallows are empty. Only the wail of the coyote is heard. The white man's medicine is stronger than ours. . . . We are like birds with a broken wing."

Well, these days a narrow asphalt trail outlines the dusty saucer where

Reno's men fought. Numbered posts erected by the government indicate where H Company dug a trench, where Jones and Meador were shot, where volunteers crept down a ravine for water, where Sioux and Cheyenne braves wriggled close enough to hurl clods of dirt at the beleaguered cavalrymen.

Within this depressed area at the top of the bluff Dr. Porter set up his hospital. Benteen described it as having sagebrush walls, an operating table made of sand, and the blue canopy of heaven for a roof. Visitors who stroll through the tousled grass and dry weeds will come upon a beer can or two winking in the Montana sun, cigarette butts, gum wrappers, little yellow Kodak boxes. There is also the chance of meeting a rattlesnake, which is why park rangers do not like visitors to leave the trail.

Just a few hundred yards north of this enclave General Custer looked down on Reno's troops fighting in the valley where the battle started, perhaps waved his buckskin hat to encourage them, and rode out of sight to the rhythmic thud of hooves, the creak of black leather, the clink and jangle of metal harness as the men of the Seventh obediently followed him two by two or four by four, depending on the terrain.

His orderly, John Burkman, said the regiment was excited on the morning of the twenty-fifth. The colors were flying, horses were dancing. Troopers laughed and joked, betting who would collect the most scalps. They told Burkman, who had been detailed to the pack train, that they would be back by noon ready for a good feed. Autie Reed, mounted on a horse beside his uncle Tom, was happy. He had never seen a fight with Indians. Burkman suggested that he stay behind. Autie pulled one foot out of a stirrup, gave him a friendly kick and said, "You're mad because you can't go along."

Burkman was holding the bridle of Custer's horse Vic when the general walked up.

"I ought to be goin' along," Burkman said.

Custer leaped into the saddle. Then he leaned down, put one hand on his orderly's shoulder and smiled. His mustache was so long that it nearly hid his mouth. "Your place is with McDougall and the pack train," Custer said. "But if we should have to send for more ammunition you can come in on the home stretch." Those were his last words to Burkman.

Two staghounds accompanied the regiment from Fort Lincoln. How far they went is a fine point to argue. Some historians think Custer left them at the Powder River depot, but years later Burkman insisted they traveled with the regiment up the Rosebud Valley and across the divide. When Custer split the Seventh into battalions and trotted off at the head of five companies Burkman held them by the collar. They whimpered and whined as they watched him ride out of sight.

Whether these dogs, Bleuch and Tuck, remained at the Powder River depot or spent a couple of unforgettable days on the hilltop with Reno's men, it is certain they went back to Bismarck—presumably aboard the *Far West*—and were delivered to Elizabeth. She did not keep them long. She asked "a gentleman of St. Paul," Mr. C. W. McIntyre, to find a home for them and the rest of Custer's pack. McIntyre tried to help by contacting the New York *Herald*. His letter was published on July 22 under the heading GENERAL CUSTER'S HOUNDS:

> . . . Our State laws forbid the running of deer with dogs; besides, the Indians shoot them, so that hounds are of no use here; but I have written Mrs. Custer to ship them all to me at once, as she wishes to leave the fort as soon as possible. Can you, to oblige Mrs. Custer, send me the names of some gentlemen who would like the dogs, and pay the express charges. . . .

At this point Custer's hounds vanish.

Burkman was not allowed to die with the man he worshipped and when it came time for the ultimate ceremony he was at work on Reno Hill—cleaning up, packing mules, helping in the construction of litters. When at last he got a chance to visit the battlefield all he saw was the grave.

He never got over this. As an eccentric, cranky old man he complained about it. Always, he felt, he had been left behind. He told his biographer that while he went about his duties on Reno Hill he kept wondering what would become of Bleuch and Tuck. He also thought about Lulu—another of Custer's dogs—and Lulu's pups which he had seen in their box after a blizzard, smothered, as though they were asleep. While chopping up a saddle so the Indians could not use it he thought about General Sheridan. Then he sat down to rest beside Custer's second horse, Dandy, and remembered that Custer had been planning to enter Dandy in a race when they got back from this campaign. Fifty years after the regiment left Fort Lincoln he could remember how Custer told the dogs good-bye. He saw Custer pat Tuck's head and heard him say, "Be a good dog. . . ." But hours later, miles from the fort, Bleuch and Tuck came racing toward the column, tongues lolling and tails wagging, so he let them stay.

Libbie rode with the regiment for a while and did not want to go back. Burkman said she clung to Custer with her arms tightly around his neck. There were tears in the general's eyes but he told her she was a soldier's wife and must return to the fort. He told her he would be there soon and they would have good times once again.

Custer argued with Godfrey about something—Burkman did not know what—on the night before the regiment started up Rosebud Creek. This argument put the general in a bad humor. He sat on the edge of his cot and frowned, ignoring the dogs, which was unusual. Once he called out: "John, I'm writing to Mrs. Custer. What shall I say for you?" The dogs had torn apart quite a few cats, which troubled Elizabeth, so Burkman responded by saying there were too many cats anyhow and Miss Libbie shouldn't worry about it. Custer laughed. Burkman tried to think of something else to make him laugh, but the night seemed heavy with foreboding. In front of each officer's tent a guard walked back and forth. The moon was down. Stars glittered among black clouds. Raindrops spattered against the tents. Burkman saw a light in the cabin of the *Far West* on the opposite side of the Yellowstone and thought some officers must be having a poker game. He said he could hear nothing except horses munching oats and the steady beat of Ree and Crow tomtoms.

Late that night Tuck stretched up his muzzle and began to howl. Indians and dogs were alike, Burkman said, in that they could smell death a long way off.

When the first streaks of light appeared in the sky he entered the tent to waken Custer and found him sitting up on the cot with a pen in his hand, fast asleep.

As they moved south the general often would ride ahead with a few members of his staff. On one of these trips they saw the paths of many travois poles in the dust. "We're close on their heels," he said, adding that there were more than he expected. The party dismounted to let their horses graze until the regiment caught up, and Custer lay beneath a tree staring at the sky.

Burkman saw him for the last time on June 25 as he galloped off with his bright red tie fluttering across his shoulder.

That night Sioux tomtoms reverberated through the Little Bighorn Valley. Otherwise, Burkman said, Reno Hill was quiet except for cottonwoods rustling in the breeze and a swishing noise from the river. Occasionally he stopped walking his post in order to listen because it seemed to him that he could hear voices and the crunch of hooves as Custer's men crept toward them in the darkness.

Burkman spent the last thirty years of his life in Billings, close to the fallen idol. Toward the end he became senile and one Friday morning was found dead on the porch of his boarding house with a smoking gun in one hand, a paper bag of candy in the other. His two important possessions were gold coins dated 1839 and 1876: the beginning and the end of a life which had more value than his own.

Today a narrow road undulates northward from Reno Hill to the site of the slaughter, past white marble tablets—one here, there another, a cluster in a gully, five on a knoll. These tablets have been placed where men are thought to have died. A few tablets have been situated where no remains could be found, but thick vegetation indicated that the soil was unnaturally fertilized. More often there were traces of a corpse, or a wooden stake left by the burial party; yet even this did not prove a man died there because Indians frequently amused themselves by roping enemies—alive or dead—and dragging them around, so a trooper might have been shot hundreds of yards from the place where his body was discovered.

Tourists seldom pause to read the inscriptions on these tablets, not after the first few, because they are almost all alike:

U.S. Soldier.
Unknown Soldier.
Unknown.
Unknown.
Unknown.
Unknown.

Debris still climbs to the surface. Heavy rains wash the side of a gully, exposing a rotten leather strap or a button. Twenty-eight years after the battle somebody found a boot marked *J D* with the bones of a foot inside. Workmen laying underground water pipes in 1932 turned up pieces of another soldier.

From Reno's fort to Custer's cul-de-sac is four miles plus 160 yards, as measured by Lt. Edward Maguire of General Terry's engineer corps. The distance corroborates Benteen's intuitive good sense. It seems doubtful that after receiving Custer's last urgent message he could have led three companies such a long way through a mob of infuriated Sioux. Even if he succeeded he would have arrived too late. Custer fell quickly. Throughout that first afternoon the besieged troopers on the hill heard occasional shots from somewhere down the valley, but no member of his star-crossed battalion could feel them.

These days the slope is quiet. Not many tourists congregate on Custer's ridge. They clog Yosemite and swarm at the lip of the Grand Canyon like colonies of iridescent beetles, but the Little Bighorn is a formidable drive from anywhere. Excepting Crow Agency, the nearest town is Hardin—fifteen miles northwest at the junction of the Little Bighorn and the Bighorn. Fifty miles beyond Hardin is Billings. From Billings to Great Falls or Butte is more than two hundred miles.

Strangely wrinkled umber hills half-enclose the site. If one overlooks highway I–90 and a spatter of rural buildings it might as well be Mongolia, there is such vast indifference beneath this bone-yellow sky. North of the battleground are a motel, coffee shop, gas pumps, and the Crow Agency rodeo stadium. To the east above a succession of waterless ravines the blunt brown Wolf Mountains slant toward nothing. Sixty or eighty miles south the snowy

Bighorns hang like a motionless cloud. And to the west—beyond Bozeman, very far west—one can make out the long rugged spine of the Rockies.

Imported pine trees and the deep luxuriant grass of Custer National Cemetery seem incongruous on this terra cotta hillside. Years ago there was thick vegetation, but sheepherders used the slope and sheep do not leave much, so any kind of moisture runs off quickly. Without irrigation this rectangular oasis would wither, the pines would shrivel. Every day the militant shadows of these pines travel across the graves of Major Reno, of the scout Curly, of Captain Fetterman who chased a band of Sioux away from Fort Kearny, and of many other soldiers.

The place where Custer died is surrounded by a black iron fence—an inclined plot whose midsummer custodians are grasshoppers, crickets, flies, and a few undistinguished little birds. Insects flicker across the weeds, except during hail-swept interludes, while a honey-warm sun pours down.

Pvt. Coleman wrote: "25th the sun rose this Morning with every appearance of it being verry hot . . ."

A month later Lt. Bradley wrote for the Helena *Herald*:

Probably never did hero who had fallen upon the field of battle appear so much to have died a natural death. His expression was rather that of a man who had fallen asleep and enjoyed peaceful dreams, than of one who had met his death amid such fearful scenes as that field had witnessed, the features being wholly without ghastliness or any impress of fear, horror or despair. . . .

Although Bradley was the first to look down upon the general he was soon followed by many others, and because their descriptions are so much alike it is possible to recreate the scene very much as it must have been. Gerard, for example, preceded the troops. "He found the naked bodies of two soldiers, one across the other, and Custer's naked body in a sitting posture between and leaning against them, his upper right arm along and on the topmost body, his right forearm and hand supporting his head in an inclining posture like one resting or asleep. . . ." Other reports indicate that Custer was seen with his right leg flung across a dead soldier, the heel resting on a horse carcass, the fingers of his right hand extended as though he had been holding a pistol—which suggests that someone lowered him from the upright posture noted by Gerard. But these discrepancies are slight.

He lay just south or southwest of the monument. He had been shot twice: in the left side beneath the heart and in the left temple. Either would have been fatal, but he probably was killed by the shot in the side because this wound was bloody. The hole in his temple was clean, a shot meant to guarantee that he was not feigning death. There was also a wound in his right forearm, but this might have been caused by the bullet emerging from his body. Benteen, who took a close look, did not think the wounds were caused by .45 caliber bullets, so it seems likely that he was hit the first time from some distance by a Henry rifle or a Winchester.

Sgt. Knipe said he lay across two or three dead soldiers with only a portion of his back touching the ground. Except for socks he had been undressed, as were the men around him. The bottom of one of his boots lay nearby, but the upper part was missing—which certainly means that a squaw sliced off the tops to make purses or moccasins. Knipe said he lay at the peak of the ridge, somewhat higher than the enclosed cluster of tablets. No matter. From within the black iron fence or from the peak of the ridge it is easy to imagine what he saw: an enormous village beside the Little Bighorn stretched out as though in subjugation at his feet.

With the possible exception of one fingertip, he had not been mutilated. So the public was told. But there are said to be unpublished letters detailing various disfigurements: thighs slashed to the bone, ears slit, arrows driven into the groin. Supposedly this information was withheld out of regard for Elizabeth, and even now may be too disagreeable for publication.

Why he escaped scalping has never been determined. For a long time many Americans thought he had earned this respect by his courage. Terry's men allegedly saw a mark on his cheeks, put there by an unidentified chief as a warning to the squaws that he should be left alone, but this appears to be no more than a white man's tale. Many Indians were consulted and their answers noted. From a warrior's point of view the Son of the Morning Star had an unattractive head. The hair was sparse because he was growing prematurely bald and what remained had been cut short. A number of braves might have inspected him and decided the hair was not worth keeping.

By one account he walked along the ridge carrying his white hat, leading his horse by the bridle, after everybody else was dead. Several Indians rose up and killed him but did not take the scalp, nor even touch the body, because they thought he was insane.

A Canadian identified as "Mr. Macdonald" said he had been told by Indians that Custer was not mutilated because of his buckskin suit; they mistook him for a hunter who was visiting the troops and was therefore innocent.

Lt. Col. William Bowen was told by Benteen that when Rain in the Face saw Custer's body he shook the right hand of the corpse and exclaimed, "My poor friend!" It was Rain, according to Col. Bowen, who saved Custer from further humiliation.

He is said to have shot himself, the ultimate proof of cowardice, and today many people believe it. That he did so can be verified by numerous testimonials. For instance, an army officer in Wyoming was told by an old Indian that he—the old Indian—was hiding in a buffalo wallow near the battlefield and saw Custer commit suicide. Buffalo seldom wallow on hillsides, but never mind. No powder burn was observed on his temple, but never mind. A right-handed man is not apt to shoot himself in the left temple, but never mind. These days it is stylish to denigrate the general, whose stock sells for nothing. Nineteenth-century Americans thought differently. At that time he was a cavalier without fear and beyond reproach.

Several facts can be sifted from the myth. There is no doubt that G. A. C. and his brother Tom were buried by Sgt. John Ryan of M Company, assisted by Corporals Harrison Davis and Frank Neeley and Private James H. Seaver. They dug a wide, shallow grave about eighteen inches deep at the foot of the knoll where the earth was soft and arranged the brothers side by side, covering their bodies with blankets and canvas tent sections. Dirt was shoveled over them and a travois found in the village was turned upside down on top, loaded with rocks and pegged to the ground. A large basket found with the travois may have been left on the grave to serve as a marker. Ryan is ambiguous about this, but states categorically that nobody else received such a fine burial. He states also that both bullets struck General Custer on the right side; however, testimony from men who examined the body more closely seems to indicate that on this point Ryan was mistaken.

Another point of dispute among scholars concerns the horse Vic, whether it was a stallion or a mare. Elizabeth, who saw the animal many times and should be considered an authority, alludes to it as a horse; yet old John Burkman years afterward persisted in calling Vic a mare: "Hadn't I orter know, Bud, seein' 's how I've curried her and trimmed her fetlocks and polished her hoofs time and time agin?"

Elizabeth said Vic was a Kentucky thoroughbred "found dead beside his devoted master." Well, just possibly Victor/Victoria emerged from the fight between the knees of a Santee Sioux named Walks Under the Ground—one of several Indians who claimed to have killed the soldier chief. Walks Under did come out with a blaze-faced sorrel, which properly describes the horse. By another account some unidentified Unkpapa recognized Vic among the captured animals and appropriated it. Still, the old Miniconjou known as Dewey Beard or Iron Hail, who lived almost forever—until 1955—Dewey Beard claimed to have seen a blaze-faced sorrel with white stockings tied by the reins to Custer's wrist, so maybe Elizabeth was right.

Col. Homer Wheeler and Capt. John Bourke visited the battlefield in 1877. Wheeler said they located the graves of General Custer and Tom, of Autie Reed, adjutant W. W. Cooke, and correspondent Mark Kellogg. Wheeler believed the remains of their horses lay nearby. He and Bourke cut off all four hooves of the animal supposedly ridden by Custer. Bourke had his pair turned into inkstands, one of which he donated to a museum in Philadelphia. Wheeler put his pair into a grain sack which was either lost or stolen while he was campaigning against the Nez Perces.

Lt. Edward McClernand, who arrived with Terry and Gibbon, was shown a dead horse lying about fifty yards from the last stand. Somebody told him this was Vic. From the position of the legs McClernand surmised that Vic must have been galloping, and because the head lay in the direction of the last stand it seemed to him that Custer would have been thrown to the ground, but got up and sprinted those last fifty yards in his boots: "I do not say that such was the case. . . ."

To these enigmas, and perhaps a grain sack stuffed with others, the general alone might provide answers.

Pvt. Coleman contemplated the horror on the ridge, and as usual he describes a scene more forcibly than his literate superiors. Now, he begins:

Comes the most heartrendering tale of all. as I have said before General Custer with five Companies went below the Village to Cut them off as he Supposed but instead he was Surrounded and all of them Killed to a Man 14 officers and 250 Men Their the Bravest General of Modder times met his death with his two Brothers Brotherinlaw and Nephew not 5 yards apart Surrounded by 42 Men of E Company. Oh what a slaughter how Manny homes are Made desolate by the Sad disaster eavery one of them were Scalped and otherwise Mutiliated but the General he lay with a smile on his face. . . .

All three bluecoat armies—Crook, Terry, Gibbon—were under surveillance by Sioux and Cheyennes. The Terry-Custer column might have been watched from the day it left Fort Lincoln, and there is no doubt that hostile scouts observed the *Far West* at the mouth of Rosebud Creek several days before the battle. They also reported soldiers traveling up the Rosebud; and on the morning of June 25, two or three hours before Custer crossed the fatal divide, it is almost certain they knew exactly where he was and the size of his regiment. The only thing that surprised them was the speed of his advance.

Not many Indians were alarmed. Just a few days earlier they had fought Three Stars Crook, and although they had defeated him there was a chance he might return. Yet they could not imagine that Crook, or any white general, would attack such a large camp. It is said that about noon of the twenty-fourth a Sans Arc herald went around crying: "Soldiers will be here tomorrow!" Nobody paid much attention.

A Cheyenne prophet named Box Elder saw the advancing regiment in a dream and when he awoke he tried to warn everybody, but other Cheyennes mocked him by howling—implying that he had gone mad and should be fed to the wolves.

A Miniconjou named Standing Bear went for a swim on the morning of the fight. When he got back to his lodge one of his uncles advised him to collect the horses right away because something might happen.

An Oglala named Joseph White Cow Bull slept late. When he got up he asked an old woman for breakfast and while he was eating she told him there would be a battle. "How do you know, grandmother?" he asked. She refused to talk about it. Not long after this he was visiting friends at the Cheyenne camp when they heard shots and saw dust in the air and an Oglala rode by calling out that soldiers had attacked the Unkpapa circle. Joseph and three Cheyenne friends were getting ready to join the Unkpapas when they saw Custer's battalion on the ridge, so instead of riding south they went east toward the river. An old warrior named Mad Wolf tried to stop them, saying there were too many bluecoats, but a Cheyenne—Bobtail Horse—replied: "Uncle, only the earth and the heavens last long." Joseph and his friends then continued east, all four singing their death songs.

Soldiers—pink and hairy—came riding down a coulee. Joseph noticed one in a big hat and a buckskin jacket who rode a blaze-faced sorrel with white stockings. Beside him rode a soldier with a flag. This man in buckskin looked across the river and shouted, which caused the bluecoats to charge. Joseph and the Cheyennes slid off their ponies and began to shoot. Bobtail Horse hit a soldier who fell out of the saddle into the water. Joseph hit the one in buckskin. He, too, fell out of the saddle and when this happened many soldiers reined up, gathering around him. After that it was difficult to see anything because other Indians were arriving and the air filled with smoke.

This story of four braves challenging Custer's battalion has been told various ways. They might have been searching the valley for injured warriors when Custer appeared on the ridge, so they splashed across a ford and rode some distance up Medicine Tail coulee before starting to fight.

Just what occurred is now forgotten, but almost certainly three or four young Indians did confront five picked companies of the elite Seventh—an act of suicidal defiance which may have affected Custer's battle plan. Not that they could intimidate him, but he had no way of knowing how many other hostiles lay in wait. Those four might have looked like decoys, so he withdrew.

How surprised the Indians were by almost simultaneous assaults on opposite ends of the village is impossible to say. Ten or fifteen thousand people had camped beside the river and there is no reason to suppose they would all agree. Most of them were startled and disconcerted. Others probably had been wondering if Crook would try again. Some must have realized it was not Crook's army. Some had heard about Custer and might have guessed this was his regiment.

Tribal leaders had talked about what to do if the camp was threatened. Their decision seems to have been that they would wait to see how the soldiers behaved.

Scouts watched the regiment cross the divide and later observed it separate into battalions. Gall himself watched Custer's five companies ride along the bluffs east of the river. He said they kicked up a lot of dust. They rode out of sight but soon reappeared. He said they were mounted on white horses, which must be an incorrect translation of his words, or else he was referring to Lt. Smith's gray horse company, or to the fact that among the grays and browns were a few white horses belonging to musicians who dismounted at the Powder River depot. Gall thought these soldiers looked nice, riding as if they were on parade. He and his Unkpapas continued to watch them, meanwhile rounding up the pony herd in case the bluecoats meant to cause trouble. He had no idea who was leading these men, or if they intended to start a fight.

In 1919 a Miniconjou, Feather Earring, said to General H. L. Scott: "If Custer had come up and talked with us, we had all agreed we would have surrendered and gone in with him." During subsequent conversations Feather Earring emphasized that if Custer had approached diplomatically the Indians would have gone back to the reservation. This was confirmed years later by other Indians. General Scott observed that such a method of dealing with the hostiles had not occurred to anybody.

The entire expedition might have been unnecessary. A Sioux chief whose name has been awkwardly translated as Pretty Voice Eagle spoke with Custer just before the army left Fort Lincoln. Whether this chief also spoke with General Terry is not clear, but he was very clear about the fact that he led a delegation of his people to Custer in an attempt to avoid a battle. He asked Custer to promise that he would not fight the Sioux. Custer promised.

> . . . and we asked him to raise his hand to God that he would not fight the Sioux, and he raised his hand. After he raised his hand to God that he would not fight the Sioux he asked me to go west with my delegation to see these roaming Sioux, and tell them to come back to the reservation, that he would give them food, horses, and clothing. After we got through talking, he soon left the agency, and we soon heard that he was fighting the Indians and that he and all his men were killed. If Custer had given us time we would have gone out ahead of him, but he did not give us time. If we had gone out ahead of Custer he would not have lost himself nor would his men have been killed. I did all I could to persuade the Ree scouts not to go. . . .

Capt. Bourke once remarked that some people learn quickly, others learn slowly, "preachers, school-teachers, and military people most slowly of all."

Many Indians at the Little Bighorn were so convinced of trouble that tribal leaders posted guards east of the river to prevent ambitious young men from riding out to locate the troops and drench themselves in glory by being the first to count coup. About sundown on the evening before the fight these guards made themselves visible on the ridge. Despite this warning, several braves sneaked across the river and got up into the hills. The next day they were riding around looking for soldiers when they heard the shots fired by Reno's troops in the valley.

Crazy Horse did not behave as usual. Ordinarily he was composed, even when battle was imminent, but it is said that this morning he rode back and forth, hurried into his lodge, and quickly reappeared with his medicine bag. After moistening one hand he dipped it in maroon pigment and printed a hand on each side of his pony's hips. On both sides of the neck he drew an arrow and a bloody scalp. All of which suggests intuitive knowledge of things to come, or else he had been talking with Oglala scouts who told him what to expect. Most Indians, however, seem to have felt secure in the belief that only a great fool would attack.

Low Dog thought it must be a false alarm when he heard about soldiers charging the Unkpapa circle.

Iron Thunder could not believe the truth until a few bullets whizzed by.

Chief Red Horse and several women felt so unconcerned that they were away from the village digging tipsina—wild turnip—a knobby root filled with starch, when they noticed a dust cloud and saw Reno's troops.

A female cousin of Sitting Bull, Pte-San-Waste-Win, usually translated as Mrs. Spotted Horn Bull, said that by the time the turnip diggers got back to the village everybody could see the flash of sabers, which is a puzzling remark. Not one cavalryman, with the possible exception of DeRudio, carried a saber. What she saw might have been sunlight glinting on gun barrels.

Rain in the Face had been invited to a feast. The guests were eating when they heard bluecoat guns, which did not sound like their own. Rain habitually carried a stone-headed war club, even to parties, but he rushed back to his lodge for a gun, his bow, and a quiver of arrows. Then he hopped on his pony and was about to ride south when he and his friends saw troops on the eastern ridge. While riding against these troops they discovered a young woman— Tashenamini, Moving Robe—riding with them. Her brother had been killed during the fight with Crook and now she was holding her brother's war staff above her head. Rain declared that she looked as pretty as a bird. "Behold, there is among us a young woman!" he called out, because this would make everybody brave. "Let no young man hide behind her garment!"

Custer's soldiers were almost surrounded by the time Rain got there. They had dismounted, he said, but climbed back on their horses, dismounted again, and split into several companies. They were shooting very fast. After a while some of them began riding toward Reno's troops, but Indians followed them like blackbirds following a hawk.

The Cheyenne chief Two Moon told Hamlin Garland in 1898 that he was trying to reassure a bunch of frightened women when Custer's men arrived, cloaked with dust: "While I was sitting on my horse I saw flags coming up over the hill to the east. . . ."

When it was all over Two Moon and four Sioux chiefs rode through the valley and across the hillside counting dead bluecoats. He explained through an interpreter, Wolf Voice, that one Indian carried a little bundle of sticks: "When we came to dead men, we took a little stick and gave it to another man, so we counted the dead. There were three hundred and eighty-eight." However, Two Moon told a different story sixteen years later. This time he said they went to the river to cut willow sticks. An Indian was assigned to throw down a stick beside each dead soldier, then the sticks were picked up and counted: "It was about six times we had to cut willow sticks, because we kept finding men all along the ridge. We counted four hundred and eighty-eight. . . ."

Either way the number has been inflated, but how to explain this seems impossible. As Robert Utley points out, meanings are difficult to convey from one language to another. "Testimony delivered from an aboriginal frame of reference risked serious distortion in the process."

Three hundred and eighty-eight. Four hundred and eighty-eight. What did Two Moon actually say? What did he mean?

In a communiqué from the north bank of the Yellowstone, dated July 9, 1876, General Terry wrote that two hundred sixty-eight officers, men, and civilians were killed, fifty-two wounded—which may or may not be accurate. Company rosters were kept by first sergeants and five of these sergeants— Edwin Bobo, James Butler, Frederick Hohmeyer, Michael Kenney, Frank Varden—died with Custer. When the bodies of these men were stripped the company rosters disappeared.

In 1927 a Northern Cheyenne woman, Kate Bighead, told Dr. Thomas Marquis about the battle. She spoke in sign language, which Marquis had learned while working as a government doctor on the Cheyenne reservation. He transcribed the story she delivered with her hands.

When she was young, she related, she lived with the southern branch of the tribe in Oklahoma. Early one morning during the winter of 1868, after a big storm, soldiers led by General Custer attacked Black Kettle's village on the Washita. She ran barefoot across the snow to escape being killed. Next spring, while the Cheyennes were camped on a branch of the Red River, General Custer returned. He smoked a peace pipe and said he would not fight any- more. The chiefs told him that if he broke this promise he surely would be killed, and they gave him the name Hi-es-tzie, which means Long Hair.

She saw him often, she told Dr. Marquis. One time the general came very close while she was mounting her pony and she looked at him. He had deep eyes and wavy red hair. He wore a buckskin suit with a big white hat. She was then twenty-two years old and she thought he was handsome. She admired him. All the Cheyenne women thought he was handsome.

She had a cousin, Me-o-tzi, who sometimes went riding with General Cus- ter. The Cheyennes were pleased that Me-o-tzi was important to him. Later, after he went away, quite a few young Cheyennes wanted to marry her but Me-o-tzi said General Custer was her husband. She told them he had prom- ised to come back for her. She waited seven years. During those years Kate Bighead joined the northern branch of the tribe so she did not know what happened when Me-o-tzi learned of Custer's death, but she was told that the girl gashed her legs and chopped off her hair.

Joseph White Cow Bull also gave an account of Me-o-tzi, which differed from the story told by Kate Bighead. According to Joseph, Me-o-tzi was at the Little Bighorn with her seven-year-old son—called Yellow Hair or Yellow Bird because of light streaks in his hair. Joseph said he knew her. In fact, he said, he was courting her.

This legend of Custer's child by a Cheyenne woman turns up again and again, like a will-o'-the-wisp at dusk, as though the Indians did not want their enemy absolutely eliminated, and it cannot be proved or disproved. Nor is it possible after such a long time to establish the presence or absence of Me-o-tzi at the Little Bighorn. This comely girl whose silken tresses, the general said, rivaled in color the blackness of a raven—was she in Oklahoma or with northern relatives in Montana? Kate Bighead told Dr. Marquis that about a year after the battle Me-o-tzi married a white man named Isaac. They had several children and Me-o-tzi died in Oklahoma in January of 1921, but among the Cheyennes her name lived on. One of Kate's granddaughters was called Me-o-tzi, and friends liked to tease this girl by saying she was Custer's Indian wife.

On the day of the battle Kate had gone to visit Miniconjou friends at the upper end of the camp. She found them bathing in the river. All at once two boys ran by shouting that soldiers were coming. Kate did not identify these boys, except as Sioux. They may have been grandsons of the Santee chief Inkpaduta—Scarlet Point—who was in his sixties or seventies and blind. An early history of Minnesota states that he was seventy-five at the time of the Little Bighorn, although Gall and Mazamane both said he was sixty-one. Whatever his age, he and two of his grandsons were fishing from the riverbank when Reno's battalion trotted down the valley. The boys might have rushed around trying to warn people before leading their grandfather back to the village. If so, these could have been the boys Kate mentioned.

Old Inkpaduta never did have good eyesight. In 1862 after the Minnnesota massacre he pointed out and ordered the murder of a man in a blue coat whom he took to be a ranking officer with General Sibley. The marked man was in fact a regimental surgeon. Anyway, despite age and blindness, Inkpaduta was a chief with authority. His Santees were among the first to challenge Reno; and this venomous old figurehead, exuding hatred for every white-skinned human on earth, may have been the dominant chief until Gall arrived.

As for Kate, terribly frightened, at first she tried to hide; but then she ran toward the Cheyenne circle more than a mile downstream. She ran by young men painting themselves for war, women hurriedly pulling down teepees and loading pack horses. She saw a woman screaming and jumping up and down because she could not find her child.

Later, when Custer's troops appeared, Kate asked her brother for a pony so she could cross the river to watch the fight and encourage their nephew, Noisy Walking. She wanted to sing strongheart songs for him. He had tied a red scarf around his neck to identify himself because he knew she would want to see how well he fought.

At the place where there is now a monument with an iron fence the soldiers got off their horses. This place had no trees, she told Dr. Marquis, and the smoke from the soldiers' guns showed exactly where they were. But they had trouble seeing the Indians because arrows do not make smoke and because arrows were shot high in the air instead of straight at the enemy. Thousands of arrows dropped from the sky, sticking in horses and in the backs of soldiers, and while the Indians shot arrows they crawled up gullies—getting closer and closer—because each one wanted to count coup on a living enemy.

After a while no more bullets came from that place. The Indians thought all of the soldiers were dead and began running toward them, but seven soldiers jumped up and ran downhill toward the river with Sioux and Cheyenne warriors chasing them. Kate did not know what happened to these soldiers. She heard afterward that they shot themselves, as did many who stayed on the ridge hiding behind dead horses. She watched one shoot himself by holding a revolver against his head. Then another did the same, and another. She watched several pairs of them shoot each other in the breast. She said that for a little while the Indians stayed where they were and just looked at these white men shooting each other. She thought the soldiers had gone crazy. She thought it was their punishment for attacking a peaceful village. One soldier sat on the ground and rubbed his head as if he could not understand what was happening. Three Sioux ran up to him. They stretched him out on his back. They did this slowly and she wondered what they would do next. Two of them held his arms while the third one cut off his head with a sheath knife.

When the battle ended she rode around looking for her nephew. Many soldiers were alive. Indians were cutting off their arms and legs.

She found her nephew in a gulch halfway to the river. He had been shot and stabbed. That night he died.

During the battle most of the women and children and old men watched from the benchlands to the west, ready to run away if the soldiers won, or come back to the village if the Indians won. It was hard to tell who was winning. They saw a band of riders cross the river and come toward them. These riders were dressed in blue and they were on American horses. The people watching from the benchlands thought these were soldiers. Women began screaming. Some fainted. Others started to run. One woman seized her two little boys and ran into a gully, but she was so excited that she picked them up by the feet and slung them across her shoulders upside down. After a while, though, everybody could see that the horsemen were their own warriors bringing the weapons and horses and clothing of dead soldiers.

Six Cheyennes were killed in this battle, Kate said, and twenty-four Sioux. More would have been killed if the soldiers had not gone crazy.

According to the Bismarck *Tribune* extra of July 6: "The Indian dead were great in number. . . . The Indians were severely punished." Reno opened the battle "most gallantly, driving back repeatedly the Indians who charged in their front. . . ." And from the bluff to which he had retreated, the hostile assaults "were each time repulsed with heavy slaughter." Lonesome Charley by himself wiped out a platoon: ". . . emptying several chambers of his revolver, each time bringing a red-skin before he was brought down—shot through the heart." None of this happened to be true, but the *Trib* was providing nourishment for the folks at home, which is necessary if citizens are to remain enthusiastic about a distant campaign.

Just how many Indians were killed at the Little Bighorn could no more be determined than the United States government could determine a century later how many Asiatics gave up the ghost in a remote jungle. Col. W. S. Nye noticed while interviewing old Indians how seldom they mentioned battle deaths. He thought this was not an attempt to deceive or to minimize losses, just that Indians had a tendency to report only what they themselves had seen or what they had been told by a relative. Then, too, they were reluctant to pronounce the names of dead men, a superstition which made Anglo scorekeeping difficult. Whatever the exact body count, it must have been shockingly low by wasichu standards.

David Humphreys Miller, who consulted dozens of old warriors, produced a list of thirty-two dead. Now that they are long gone, their exploits and even their personalities forgotten by all except a few descendants, their names would be meaningless if not for the images they evoke.

These were Cheyennes killed at the Little Bighorn: Black Cloud, Whirlwind, Left Hand, Owns-Red-Horse, Flying By, Mustache, Noisy Walking, Limber Bones, Hump Nose, Black Bear, Swift Cloud, Lame White Man.

Unkpapa Sioux: White Buffalo, Rectum, Hawk Man, Swift Bear, Red Face, Long Road.

Oglalas: White Eagle, Many Lice, Bad-Light-Hair, Young Skunk, Black White Man.

Sans Arcs: Two Bears, Standing Elk, Long Robe, Cloud Man, Elk Bear, Long Dog.

Miniconjoux: High Horse, Long Elk.

Two Kettle: Chased-by-Owls.

The most important Indian to be killed—a Southern Cheyenne chief, Lame White Man—was shot and scalped by a Sioux who mistook him for a Ree or a Crow. He may have been wearing a captured blue coat, a whim that cost his life, although his grandson John Stands in Timber said he was mistaken for a Custer scout because he rushed into battle without braiding his hair. He had been taking a sweat bath when Reno attacked and instead of dressing properly he wrapped a blanket around his waist, grabbed his moc-casins, a belt, and a gun.

Wooden Leg, that peripatetic fighter and raconteur, came across Lame White Man's half-hidden body and thought at first it must be a scalped Crow or Shoshone. But then he thought he recognized the form. "I backed away and went to find my brother. . . ." The two of them returned, got off their ponies, rolled the body on its back, and looked closely. They agreed it was Lame White Man—shot through the breast, stabbed many times. Other Cheyennes rode up. All agreed it was the chief. He had been killed and scalped by a Sioux. Because the Cheyennes did not know what to say about this accident they kept quiet.

So much gunsmoke and dust obscured the field it would have been hard to recognize one's best friend. An Arapaho named Left Hand came upon a wounded Indian—perhaps a Ree—whom he attacked with a lance as sharp as an arrow. The lance went clear through this enemy, who fell across a pile of dead soldiers: "Afterward I found out he was a Sioux, and the Sioux were going to kill me. . . ."

Hideous things appeared. Through the dust came a bloody Sioux, leaving the fight. Wooden Leg saw him walk toward a ravine. "He wabbled dizzily as he moved along. He fell down, got up, fell down again, got up again. As he passed near to where I was I saw that his whole lower jaw was shot away. The sight of him made me sick. I had to vomit. . . ."

On the second day, when the chiefs learned of more soldiers approaching, they decided to leave.

Late that afternoon the tribes began moving south. They traveled most of the night before stopping to rest. They went up the Little Bighorn, down the Rosebud, eastward to the Tongue, then farther east to the Powder.

Where the Sioux and Cheyennes separated is not known, probably some-where along the Powder. Before going their own ways they held a parade. They had a bugle, maybe more than one, and several warriors rode big gray horses which they had captured. They rode in a line, pretending to be Amer-ican cavalrymen. They wore Seventh Cavalry uniforms, except for boots and pants which they did not like. One warrior carried a guidon.

After this parade the Cheyennes continued north to the Yellowstone, which they called the Elk. Here they discovered the bodies of two Indians—an old Sioux and his squaw—huddled in some bushes as though they had been trying to hide. Around them were the tracks of metal-shod horses. The old man and the old woman had been shot in the back. The old man was scalped. Here, too, the Cheyennes discovered a cache of food: bacon, rice, beans, coffee, sugar, crackers, dried apples, and corn. A steamboat came up the river while they were helping themselves to food and several warriors shot at the boat just for fun. Kate Bighead told Dr. Marquis that months afterward, when they learned they had fought Custer, they joked about him, saying, "It is too bad we killed him, for it must have been him, our friend, who left all of the good food. . . ."

She might have seen Custer during the battle. She was not certain. She said two Southern Cheyenne women were at the Little Bighorn and when the fighting ended they went to the battlefield. They saw Custer. They knew him well. They had known him in Oklahoma. They recognized him even though his hair was short and his face was dirty. While they stood looking down at him a bunch of Sioux warriors came by and wanted to cut up his body, but these women made signs telling the warriors he was a relative. They did this because of Me-o-tzi. The Sioux then cut off one of his fingertips.

Kate said these two women punctured Custer's eardrums with a sewing awl. They did this to improve his hearing because he had not been able to hear what he was told in Oklahoma seven years before. When he smoked a pipe with Medicine Arrow and Little Robe they told him that if he broke his promise and again made war on the Cheyennes he would be killed. "Through almost sixty years," Kate signaled with her hands, "many a time I have thought of Hi-es-tzie as the handsome man I saw in the South. And I have often wondered if, when I was riding among the dead where he was lying, my pony may have kicked dirt upon his body."

BIBLIOGRAPHY

BIBLIOGRAPHY

University and civic libraries throughout the western states have graciously provided access to their collections during the course of this research, with the exception of the parochial Denver Public Library, which does not admit visitors. I would like to thank in particular the custodians of the Wyles Collection at the University of California at Santa Barbara, the Bancroft Library in Berkeley, the Special Collections department of the UCLA library, Brigham Young University, the Montana State Historical Society, the Billings Public Library, and the courteous staff of the battlefield museum.

I am indebted also to John M. Carroll and to Charles K. Mills for much informative correspondence.

ESC

Adams, Alexander B. *Sitting Bull*. New York, 1973.

Adams, Jacob. *A Story of the Custer Massacre*. Carey, Ohio, 1965.

Alfield, Philip L. "Major Reno and His Family in Illinois," *English Westerner's Brand Book*. April, 1971.

Allison, E. H. "Surrender of Sitting Bull," *South Dakota Historical Quarterly*. Vol. VI, 1912.

Allred, B. W., ed. *Great Western Indian Fights*. Lincoln, Nebraska, 1960.

Amaral, Anthony A. *Comanche*. Los Angeles, 1961.

Ambrose, Stephen E. *Crazy Horse and Custer*. Garden City, New York, 1975.

Andrist, Ralph K. *The Long Death*. New York, 1964.

Anglo, Michael. *Custer: Man & Myth*. London, 1976.

Bailey, John W. *Pacifying the Plains: General Alfred Terry and the Decline of the Sioux, 1866–1890*. Westport, Connecticut, 1979.

Barry, David F. *Indian Notes on the Custer Battle*. Edited by Usher L. Burdick. Baltimore, 1949.

Bates, Charles Francis. *Custer's Indian Battles*. Bronxville, New York, 1936.

Bell, Gordon & Beth L. "General Custer in North Dakota," *North Dakota History*. Vol. 31, No. 2, 1964.

Bell, William A. *New Tracks in North America*. London, 1869.

Benham, D. J. "The Sioux Warrior's Revenge," *The Canadian Magazine*. September, 1914.

Benteen, Frederick. *The Custer Fight*. Hollywood, California, 1933.

Berthrong, Donald J. *The Southern Cheyennes*. Norman, Oklahoma, 1963.

Billings (Montana) *Gazette*. May 15, 1932.

Bismarck (North Dakota) *Tribune*. July 6, 1876.

Blackburn, William. "History of Dakota," *South Dakota Historical Quarterly*. Vol. I, 1902.

du Bois, Charles. *Kick the Dead Lion*. Billings, Montana, 1954.

Boller, Henry A. *Among the Indians*. Lincoln, Nebraska, 1972.

Bookwalter, Thomas E. "The Custer Battle: An Aerial Analysis," *Chicago Westerner's Brand Book*. Vol. XXXIV, No. 2, 1977.

Bordeaux, William J. *Custer's Conqueror*. No city. No date.

Bourke, John G. *On the Border With Crook*. New York, 1891.

————*Mackenzie's Last Fight With the Cheyennes*. New York, 1966.

Bowen, William H. C. *Custer's Last Fight*. Caldwell, Idaho, 1935.

Boyes, W. *Custer's Black White Man*. Washington, D.C., 1972.

Brackett, William S. "Custer's Last Battle," *Montana Historical Society Contributions*. Vol. IV, 1903.

Bradley, James H. "Journal of Sioux Campaign of 1876," *Montana Historical Society Contributions*. Vol. II, 1896.

Brady, Cyrus Townsend. *Indian Fights and Fighters*. Lincoln, Nebraska, 1971.

————*Northwestern Fights and Fighters*. New York, 1907.

Briggs, Harold E. "The Black Hills Gold Rush," *North Dakota Historical Quarterly*. Vol. V, No. 2, 1931.

Brill, Charles J. *Conquest of the Southern Plains*. Millwood, New York, 1975.

Brininstool, E. A. *Troopers With Custer*. New York, 1952.

————"Chief Crazy Horse, His Career and Death," *Nebraska History*. Vol. XII, No. 1, 1929.

————*Fighting Indian Warriors*. Harrisburg, Pennsylvania, 1953.

Britt, Albert. *Great Indian Chiefs*. Freeport, New York, 1969.

————"Custer's Last Fight," *Pacific Historical Review*. Vol. XIII, 1944.

Bronson, D. W. "The Story of the Little Big Horn," *Overland Monthly*. January, 1907.

Brown, Barron. *Comanche*. Kansas City, Missouri, 1935.

Brown, Dee. *Bury My Heart At Wounded Knee*. New York, 1971.

Brown, Jesse & Willard, A. M. *The Black Hills Trails*. Rapid City, North Dakota, 1924.

Brown, Lisle G. "The Yellowstone Supply Depot," *North Dakota History*. Vol. 40, No. 1, 1973.

Burdick, Usher. *The Last Battle of the Sioux Nation*. Stevens Point, Wisconsin, 1929.

————*Tales From Buffalo Land*. Baltimore, 1940.

Burkey, Blaine. *Custer, Come at Once!* Hays, Kansas, 1976.

Byrne, P. E. *Soldiers of the Plains*. New York, 1926.

————"The Custer Myth," *North Dakota Historical Quarterly*. Vol. VI, No. 3, 1932.

Calhoun, James C. *With Custer in '74*. Edited by Lawrence Frost. Provo, Utah, 1979.

Camp, Walter. *Custer in '76*. Edited by Kenneth Hammer. Provo, Utah, 1976.

Campbell, Charles E. "Down Among the Red Men," *Kansas State Historical Collections*. Vol. XVII, 1926–28.

Capps, Benjamin. *The Scouts*. New York, 1975.

————— *The Indians*. New York, 1973.

Capron, Thaddeus. "The Indian Border War of 1876: Letters of Lt. Thaddeus Capron," *Journal of the Illinois State Historical Society*. Edited by Cynthia Capron. January, 1921.

Carriker, Robert C. *Fort Supply*. Norman, Oklahoma, 1970.

Carrington, Frances. *My Army Life and The Fort Phil Kearney Massacre*. Freeport, New York, 1971.

Carroll, John M., ed. *The Two Battles of the Little Big Horn*. New York, 1974.

————— *The Benteen-Goldin Letters on Custer and His Last Battle*. New York, 1974.

————— *Custer in Texas*. New York, 1975.

————— *Custer in the Civil War*. San Rafael, California, 1977.

————— "Sitting Bull," *Garry Owen 1976: Annual of the Little Bighorn Associates*. Seattle, 1977.

————— *A Potpourri of Custeriana*. No city. No date.

————— *Three Hits and a Miss!* No city. No date.

————— *Cavalry Scraps: The Writings of Frederick W. Benteen*. Athens, Georgia, 1979.

————— *The Court Martial of Frederick Benteen*. No city. 1981.

————— *D. F. Barry Correspondence at the Custer Battlefield*. No city. 1980.

————— *General Custer and the Battle of the Little Big Horn: The Federal View*. New Brunswick, New Jersey, 1976.

————— *4 on Custer*. No city. 1976.

————— *The Sand Creek Massacre*. New York, 1973.

————— *The Gibson and Edgerly Narratives*. Bryan, Texas, No date.

————— *The Lieutenant E. A. Garlington Narrative*. Bryan, Texas, 1978.

————— *The Sunshine Magazine Articles*. Bryan, Texas, 1979.

————— *Benteen's Footnotes to* Wild Life on the Plains and Horrors of Indian Warfare. Bryan, Texas, 1981.

————— *Seventh Cavalry Scrapbook*. Nos. 1–13. No date.

Carroll, Matthew. "Diary of Matthew Carroll," *Montana Historical Society Contributions*. Vol. II, 1896.

Carson, Kit. "Scalping of William Thompson," *The West*. Vol. 3, No. 2, 1965.

Catlin, George. *Letters and Notes on the North American Indians*. Edited by Michael M. Mooney. New York, 1975.

Chandler, Melbourne. *Of Garryowen in Glory*. Annandale, Virginia, 1960.

Chatfield, Harry. "Custer's Secret Romance," *The West*. Vol. 1, No. 3, 1964.

Coburn, Wallace David. "The Battle of the Little Big Horn," as told to Major Will A. Logan. *Montana*. Vol. VI, No. 3, 1956.

Coffeen, Herbert A. *The Custer Battle Book*. New York, 1964.

Cole, A. D. & Hencken, Jacqueline. *New Rumley: Birthplace of General Custer*. Strasburg, Ohio. No date.

Coleman, Thomas W. *I Buried Custer*. Edited by Bruce R. Liddic. College Station, Texas, 1979.

Connelley, William E. "The Treaty Held at Medicine Lodge," *Kansas State Histori-cal Collections*. Vol. XVII, 1928.

Conner, Daniel E. *Joseph Reddeford Walker and the Arizona Adventure*. Edited by Donald J. Berthrong & Odessa Davenport. Norman, Oklahoma, 1956.

Coughlan, T. M. *Varnum*. Edited by John M. Carroll. Bryan, Texas, 1980.

——— "Battle of the Little Big Horn," *Winners of the West*. Vol. XI, No. 4, 1934.

Cox, John E. *Five Years in the United States Army*. New York, 1973.

Crackel, Theodore J. "Custer's Kentucky: General George Armstrong Custer and Elizabethtown, Kentucky, 1871–1873," *Filson Club Historical Quarterly 48*. April, 1974.

Crawford, Lewis. *Rekindling Camp Fires: The Exploits of Ben Arnold*. Bismarck, North Dakota, 1926.

Creel, George. "To the Last Man," *Collier's*. January 22, 1927.

Curtis, Edward N. *The North American Indian*. New York, 1908.

Custer, Elizabeth. *Boots and Saddles*. New York, 1885.

——— *Following the Guidon*. New York, 1890.

——— *Tenting on the Plains*. New York, 1893.

Custer, George Armstrong. *My Life on the Plains*. Norman, Oklahoma, 1876, 1962.

——— "In Memoriam: Louis McLane Hamilton, Captain 7th U.S. Cavalry," *Chroni-cles of Oklahoma*. Vol. XLVI, No. 4, 1968–9.

Custer, Milo. *The Custer Families*. Bloomington, Illinois, 1912.

Dary, David. *Comanche*. Lawrence, Kansas, 1976.

Davis, Theodore. "A Summer on the Plains," *Harper's*. February, 1868.

——— "Henry M. Stanley's Indian Campaign in 1867," *The Westerner's Brand Book 1945–46*. Chicago, 1947.

——— "With Generals in Their Camp Homes: General George A. Custer," *The Westerner's Brand Book 1945–46*. Chicago, 1947.

De Barthe, Joe. *Life and Adventures of Frank Grouard*. Buffalo, Wyoming. No date.

Deex, Nelle. *Glory Trek*. New York, 1959.

Deland, Charles Edmund. "The Sioux Wars," *South Dakota Historical Collections*. Volume XV, 1930.

Dellenbaugh, Frederick. *George Armstrong Custer*. New York, 1926.

Dippie, Brian. "A Glance at Custer Humor," *Garry Owen 1976: Annual of the Little Bighorn Associates*. Seattle, 1977.

——— *Custer's Last Stand, The Anatomy of an American Myth*. Missoula, Montana, 1976.

——— "Southern Response to Custer's Last Stand," *Montana*. Vol. XXI, No. 2, 1971.

——— "The Custer Battle on Canvas: Reflections and Afterthoughts," *Montana*. Vol. XXIV, No. 1. 1974.

——— ed. *Nomad*. Austin, Texas, 1980.

Dixon, David. "A Scout with Custer: Edmund Guerrier on the Hancock Expedition of 1867," *Kansas History*. Vol. 4, No. 3, 1981.

Dixon, Joseph K. *The Vanishing Race*. New York, 1913.

Dobak, William A. "Yellow-Leg Journalists: Enlisted Men as Newspaper Report-ers," *Journal of the West*. Vol. VIII, No. 1, 1974.

Dodge, Richard I. *Our Wild Indians*. Hartford, Connecticut, 1883.

Donaldson, A. B. "The Black Hills Expedition," *South Dakota Historical Collections*. Vol. VII, 1914.

Donnelle, A. J. *Cyclorama of General Custer's Last Battle*. Boston, 1889.

Downey, Fairfax. *Indian-Fighting Army*. New York, 1941.

———— & Jacobsen, J. N. *The Red-Bluecoats*. Fort Collins, Colorado, 1973.

Dunn, J. P. *Massacres of the Mountains*. New York, 1886.

Dustin, Fred. *The Custer Tragedy*. Ann Arbor, Michigan, 1939.

Eastman, Charles. "Rain-in-the-Face, The Story of a Sioux Warrior," *The Outlook*. October 27, 1906.

Ediger, Theodore & Hoffman, Vinnie. "Some Reminiscences of the Battle of the Washita," *Chronicles of Oklahoma*. Vol. 33, No. 2, 1955.

Edmunds, R. David, ed. *American Indian Leaders*. Lincoln, Nebraska, 1980.

Ege, Robert. *Curse Not His Curls*. Fort Collins, Colorado, 1974.

———— *Settling the Dust*. Chinook, Montana, 1968.

Epple, Jess C. *Custer's Battle of the Washita*. Jericho, New York, 1970.

Evans, Harold C. "Custer's Last Fight," *Kansas Magazine*, 1938.

Ewers, John C. "Plains Indian Painting," *The American West*. Vol. 5, No. 2, 1968.

Ewert, Theodore. *Diary of the Black Hills Expedition of 1874*. Edited by John M. Carroll and Lawrence Frost. Piscataway, New Jersey, 1976.

Finerty, John F. *War-Path and Bivouac*. Norman, Oklahoma, 1961.

Fiske, Frank. *The Taming of the Sioux*. Bismarck, North Dakota, 1917.

Fougera, Katherine Gibson. *With Custer's Cavalry*. Caldwell, Idaho, 1942.

Fristad, Palma. "A Home for Custer's Seventh," *True West*. Vol. 9, No. 2, 1961.

Frost, Lawrence A. *General Custer's Libbie*. Seattle, 1976.

———— *Custer Legends*. Bowling Green, Ohio, 1981.

———— "Custer's Sabers—An Answer," *Little Bighorn Associates Research Review*. Vol. VIII, No. 3, 1981.

———— ed. *Some Observations on the Yellowstone Expedition, 1873*. Glendale, California, 1981.

———— *The Court-Martial of General George Armstrong Custer*. Norman, Oklahoma, 1968.

Garland, Hamlin. "General Custer's Last Fight as Seen by Two Moon," *McClure's Magazine*. September, 1898.

Garrett, Richard. *Famous Characters of the Wild West*. New York, 1975.

Gerber, Max E. "The Custer Expedition of 1874: A New Look," *North Dakota History*. Vol. 40, No. 1, 1973.

Gibbon, John. "Last Summer's Expedition Against the Sioux and its Great Catastrophe," *American Catholic Quarterly*. April & October, 1877.

Gibson, Francis. *The Battle of the Washita*. Edited by Edward S. Luce. Bryan, Texas. No date.

Gibson, Michael. *The American Indian*. New York, 1974.

Godfrey, Edward S. "Custer's Last Battle," *Century Magazine*. January, 1892.

———— "After the Custer Battle," edited by Albert J. Partoll. *Frontier and Midland*. Vol. XIX, No. 4, 1939.

———— "Battle of the Washita," *Winners of the West*. April 30 & May 30, 1929.

———— "Some Reminiscences, Including the Washita Battle, November 27, 1868," *The Cavalry Journal*. Vol. 37, No. 153, 1928.

Graham, W. A. *The Story of the Little Bighorn*. New York, 1926.

———— *The Custer Myth*. New York, 1953.

———— *Major Reno Vindicated*. Hollywood, California, 1935.

———— "Custer's Battle Flags," *Los Angeles Westerner's Brand Book*, 1950.

———— ed. *Abstract of the Official Proceedings of the Reno Court of Inquiry*. Harrisburg, Pennsylvania, 1954.

Gray, John S. *Centennial Campaign*. Fort Collins, Colorado, 1976.

———— "Last Rites for Lonesome Charley Reynolds," *Montana*. Vol. XIII, No. 3, 1963.

———— "Photos, Femurs and Fallacies," *Chicago Westerner's Brand Book*. Vol. XX, No. 6, 1963.

———— "Arikara Scouts With Custer,"*North Dakota Historical Quarterly*. Vol. 35, No. 2, 1968.

———— "What Made Johnnie Bruguier Run?"*Montana*. Vol. 14, No. 2, 1968.

———— "On the Trail of Lonesome Charley Reynolds," *Chicago Westerner's Brand Book*. Vol. 14, No. 8, 1957.

———— "Frank Grouard: Kanaka Scout or Mulatto Renegade," *Chicago Westerner's Brand Book*. Vol. 16, No. 8, 1959.

Greene, Jerome A. *Evidence and the Custer Enigma*. Reno, Nevada, 1973.

Grinnell, George Bird. *The Passing of the Great West*. New York, 1972.

———— *The Fighting Cheyennes*. New York, 1915.

———— *Two Great Scouts and Their Pawnee Battalion*. Lincoln, Nebraska, 1973.

Guthrie, John. "The Fetterman Massacre,"*Annals of Wyoming*. Vol. 9, No. 2, 1932.

Hahn, Mannel, ed. *The Westerner's Brand Book 1945–46*. Chicago, 1947.

Hammer, Kenneth. *Men With Custer*. Fort Collins, Colorado, 1972.

———— *The Glory March*. Monroe County, Michigan, 1980.

Hanson, Joseph Mills. *The Conquest of the Missouri: Being the Story of the Life and Exploits of Captain Grant Marsh*. Chicago, 1909.

Hassrick, Royal B. *The Sioux*. Norman, Oklahoma, 1964.

Hinman, Eleanor. "Oglala Sources on the Life of Crazy Horse," *Nebraska History*. Vol. 57, No. 1, 1976.

Hixon, John C. "Custer's 'Mysterious Mr. Kellogg' and The Diary of Mark Kellogg," *North Dakota History*. Vol. 17, No. 3, 1950.

Hockett, Mrs. C. W. *Some Monroe Memories*. Detroit, Michigan, 1939.

Hofling, Charles K. *Custer and the Little Big Horn: A Psychobiographical Inquiry*. Detroit, Michigan, 1981.

———— "George Custer: A Psychoanalytic Approach," *Montana*. Vol. XXI, No. 2, 1971.

Hoig, Stan. *The Sand Creek Massacre*. Norman, Oklahoma, 1961.

———— *The Battle of the Washita*. Garden City, New York, 1976.

Holley, Frances. *Once Their Home*. Chicago, 1892.

Hoopes, Alban W. *The Road to the Little Big Horn—and Beyond*. New York, 1975.

Horn, W. Donald, ed. *"Skinned": Delinquency Record of Cadet George Armstrong Custer, USMA Class of June 1861*. Short Hills, New Jersey, 1980.

Howard, James H., ed. *The Warrior Who Killed Custer*. Lincoln, Nebraska, 1968.

Howell, Edgar M. "Theodore R. Davis: Special Artist in the Indian Wars,"*Montana*. Vol. XV, No. 2, 1965.

Huggins, Eli L. "Custer and Rain in the Face,"*American Mercury*. November, 1926.

Hughes, Robert P. "The Campaign Against the Sioux in 1876,"*Journal of the Military Service Institute*. January, 1896.

Hunt, Frazier. *The Last of the Cavaliers*. New York, 1928.

Hutchins, James S. *Boots & Saddles at the Little Bighorn*. Fort Collins, Colorado, 1976.

Hutton, Paul A. "From the Little Bighorn to Little Big Man: The Changing Image of a Western Hero in Popular Culture," *Western Historical Quarterly*. Vol. VII, No. 1, 1976.

———— ed. *Custer and His Times*. El Paso, Texas, 1981.

Hyde, George E. *Life of George Bent*. Norman, Oklahoma, 1968.

———— *Spotted Tail's Folk, A History of the Brulé Sioux*. Norman, Oklahoma, 1961.

———— *Red Cloud's Folk, A History of the Oglala Sioux Indians*. Norman, Oklahoma, 1937.

Inman, Henry. "A Veteran War Horse," *Topeka Daily Capital*. Nov. 12, 1891.

Innis, Ben. *Bloody Knife!* Fort Collins, Colorado, 1973.

Isern, Thomas D. "Henry M. Stanley's Frontier Apprenticeship," *Montana*. Vol. XXVIII, No. 4, 1978.

Jackson, Donald. *Custer's Gold*. New Haven, Connecticut, 1966.

Jackson, Helen Hunt. *Century of Dishonor*. Minneapolis, 1964.

Jacob, Richard T. "Frontier Life in Oklahoma," *Chronicles of Oklahoma*. Vol. 2, No. 1, 1924.

Johnson, Barry C. "Custer, Reno, Merrill and the Lauffer Case," *English Westerners' Brand Book*. July and October, 1970.

———— *Case of Marcus A. Reno*. London, 1969.

Johnson, Roy P. "Jacob Horner of the 7th Cavalry," *North Dakota Historical Quarterly*. Vol. 16, No. 2, 1949.

Johnson, W. Fletcher. *Life of Sitting Bull*. No city. 1891.

Jones, Douglas C. *The Treaty of Medicine Lodge*. Norman, Oklahoma, 1966.

Josephy, Alvin M., Jr. *The Patriot Chiefs*. New York, 1961.

Judge, Bill. "The Custer Story," *True West*. September–October, 1963.

Kain, Robert C. *In the Valley of the Little Big Horn*. Newfane, Vermont, 1969.

Kanipe, Daniel. "A New Story of Custer's Last Battle," *Historical Society of Montana*. Vol. IV, 1903.

Keenen, Jerry. "Exploring the Black Hills: An Account of the Custer Expedition," *Journal of the West*. Vol. 6, No. 2, 1967.

Keim, DeB. Randolph. *Sheridan's Troopers on the Borders*. Philadelphia, 1885.

Kelly, Fanny. *My Captivity Among the Sioux Indians*. Secaucas, New Jersey, 1973.

Kennedy, John B. "A Soldier's Widow," *Collier's*. January 29, 1927.

Kidd, James H. *Historical Sketch of General Custer*. Monroe County, Michigan, 1978.

King, Charles. *Campaigning with Crook*. Norman, Oklahoma, 1964.

———— "Custer's Last Battle," *Harper's*. August, 1890.

Kinsley, D. A. *Favor the Bold*. New York, 1967.

Knight, Oliver. *Following the Indian Wars*. Norman, Oklahoma, 1960.

———— "Mark Kellogg Telegraphed For Custer's Rescue," *North Dakota Historical Society*. Vol. 27, No. 2, 1960.

Koury, Michael J. *To Consecrate This Ground*. Fort Collins, Colorado, 1978.
——ed. *Diaries of the Little Big Horn*. Bellevue, Nebraska, 1968.
Krause, Herbert and Olson, Gary D., eds. *Custer's Prelude to Glory*. Sioux Falls, South Dakota, 1974.
Kuhlman, Charles. *Did Custer Disobey Orders?* Harrisburg, Pennsylvania, 1957.
——*Legend into History*. Harrisburg, Pennsylvania, 1951.
Kurtz, Henry I. "Custer and the Indian Massacre, 1868," *History Today*. Vol. 18, No. 11.
Lane, Harrison. "Brush, Palette and the Battle of the Little Big Horn," *Montana*. Vol. XXIII, No. 3, 1973.
Larpenteur, Charles. *Forty Years a Fur Trader*. Edited by Elliott Coues. Minneapolis, 1962.
Larsen, Arthur J., ed. "The Black Hills Gold Rush: Letters from Men Who Participated," *North Dakota Historical Quarterly*. Vol. VI, No. 4, 1932.
Lavender, David. *Bent's Fort*. New York, 1954.
Leckie, William H. *The Military Conquest of the Southern Plains*. Norman, Oklahoma, 1963.
Libby, O. G., ed. "The Arikara Narrative," *North Dakota Historical Collections*. Vol. 6, 1920.
——"Biography of Old Settlers," *North Dakota Historical Society*. Vol. 1, 1908.
Liberty, Margot. *Cheyenne Memories*. New Haven, Connecticut, 1967.
—— ed. "Last Ghastly Moments at the Little Bighorn," told by John Stands in Timber. *American Heritage*, Vol. XVII, No. 3, 1966.
Linderman, Frank B. *Plenty-Coups: Chief of the Crows*. Lincoln, Nebraska, 1962.
——*Pretty-Shield: Medicine Woman of the Crows*. Lincoln, Nebraska, 1972.
Lockwood, John C. *Custer Fell First*. Edited by J. C. Ryan. San Antonio, 1966.
Longstreet, Stephen. *War Cries on Horseback*. New York, 1970.
Luce, Edward S. *Keogh, Comanche and Custer*. St. Louis, 1939.
——ed. "Our Last Camp on the Rosebud," *Montana*. Vol. II, No. 3, 1952.
——ed. "The Diary and Letters of Dr. James M. DeWolf," *North Dakota History*. Vol. 25, Nos. 2 & 3, 1958.
Luther, Tal. "Benteen, Reno and Custer," *The Trail Guide*. Vol. 5, No. 1, 1960.
Marquis, Thomas B. *Custer on the Little Bighorn*. Lodi, California, 1967.
——*Memoirs of a White Crow Indian*. New York, 1928.
——*Keep the Last Bullet For Yourself*. Algonac, Michigan, 1976.
——*Custer, Cavalry & Crows*. Fort Collins, Colorado, 1975.
——*Wooden Leg: A Warrior Who Fought Custer*. Lincoln, Nebraska, 1962.
Marshall, S. L. A. *Crimsoned Prairie*. New York, 1972.
Masters, Joseph G. *Shadows Fall Across the Little Horn*. Laramie, Wyoming, 1951.
Mattison, Ray H. *The Army Post on the Northern Plains, 1865–1885*. Gering, Nebraska, 1965.
McAndrews, Eugene, ed. "An Army Engineer's Journal of Custer's Black Hills Expedition," *Journal of the West*. Vol. XIII, No. 1, 1974.
McBlain, John F. "With Gibbon on the Sioux Campaign of 1876," *Journal of the U.S. Cavalry Association*. Vol. 9, No. 33, 1896.
McClernand, Edward J. *March of the Montana Column*. Edited by Robert Bruce. New York, 1927.

———— *With the Indian and the Buffalo in Montana*. Glendale, California, 1969.
McConnell, Ronald C. "Isaiah Dorman and the Custer Expedition," *Journal of Negro History*. Vol. XXXIII, July, 1948.
McFarling, Lloyd. *Exploring the Northern Plains, 1804–1876*. Caldwell, Idaho, 1955.
McLaird, James D. and Turchen, Lesta V. "Exploring the Black Hills, 1855–1875: Reports of the Government Expeditions," *South Dakota History*. Vol. 4, No. 3, 1974.
McLaughlin, James D. *My Friend the Indian*. Seattle, 1970.
McVey, Everett E. *The Crow Scout Who Killed Custer*. Billings, Montana, 1952.
Mears, David T. "Campaigning Against Crazy Horse," *Nebraska State Historical Society*. Vol. 15, 1907.
Mellor, William J. "The Military Investigation of Col. John M. Chivington Following the Sand Creek Massacre," *Chronicles of Oklahoma*. Vol. XVI, No. 4, 1938.
Mengel, Robert M. *Comanche: Silent Horse on a Silent Field*. Lawrence, Kansas, 1969.
Merington, Marguerite, ed. *The Custer Story*. New York, 1950.
Merkel, Charles E. *Unravelling the Custer Enigma*. Enterprise, Alabama, 1977.
Merrill, James M. *Spurs to Glory: The Story of the United States Cavalry*. Chicago, 1966.
Miles, Nelson. *Serving the Republic*. New York, 1911.
———— *Personal Recollections*. Chicago, 1897.
Millbrook, Minnie Dubbs. "The West Breaks in General Custer," *Kansas Historical Quarterly*. Vol. 36, No. 2, 1970.
———— "Custer's First Scout in the West," *Kansas Historical Quarterly*. Vol. 39, No. 1, 1973.
———— ed. "Mrs. General Custer at Fort Riley, 1866," *Kansas Historical Quarterly*. Vol. 40, No. 2, 1974.
Miller, David Humphreys. *Custer's Fall*. New York, 1957.
Mills, Anson. *My Story*. Washington, D.C., 1918.
Mills, Charles K. *A Mighty Afternoon*. Garden City, New York, 1980.
———— *Charles C. DeRudio*. Mattituck, New York, 1983.
Milner, Joe E. & Forrest, Earle R. *California Joe*. Caldwell, Idaho, 1935.
Monaghan, Jay. *Custer*. Boston, 1959.
———— ed. *The Book of the American West*. New York, 1963.
du Mont, John S. *Custer Battle Guns*. Fort Collins, Colorado, 1974.
Moore, Horace L. "The 19th Kansas Cavalry in the Washita Campaign," *Chronicles of Oklahoma*. Vol. 2, No. 4, 1924.
Mulford, A. F. *Fighting Indians in the 7th United States Cavalry*. Corning, New York, 1879.
Murphy, James P. "The Campaign of the Little Big Horn," *Infantry Journal*. Vol. 34, No. 6, 1929.
Murray, K. D. Iain. "Who Started Scalping?" *The West*. July, 1964.
Murray, Robert A. "The Custer Court Martial," *Annals of Wyoming*. October, 1964.
Myers, J. Jay. *Red Chiefs and White Challengers*. New York, 1971.
Myers, Rex C. "Montana Editors and the Custer Battle," *Montana*. Vol. XXVI, No. 2, 1976.

Nadeau, Remi. *Fort Laramie and the Sioux Indians*. Englewood Cliffs, New Jersey, 1967.

Neihardt, John G. *Black Elk Speaks*. Lincoln, Nebraska, 1961.

Nelson, Bruce. *Land of the Dacotahs*. Lincoln, Nebraska, 1964.

Nesbitt, Paul. "Battle of the Washita," *Chronicles of Oklahoma*. Vol. III, No. 1, 1924.

North, Luther. *Man of the Plains*. Edited by Donald F. Danker. Lincoln, Nebraska, 1961.

Noyes, Lee. "Major Marcus A. Reno at the Little Big Horn," *North Dakota History*. Vol. 28, No. 1, 1961.

Nye, Elwood. *Marching With Custer*. Glendale, California, 1964.

Nye, W. S. *Carbine and Lance*. Norman, Oklahoma, 1942.

——*Plains Indian Raiders*. Norman, Oklahoma, 1968.

O'Harra, Cleophas C. "Custer's Black Hills Expedition of 1874," *The Black Hills Engineer*. Vol. XVII, No. 4, 1929.

Olch, Peter D. "Medicine in the Indian-Fighting Army," *Journal of the West*. Vol. XXI, No. 3, 1982.

Olson, James C. *Red Cloud and the Sioux Problem*. Lincoln, Nebraska, 1965.

Overfield, Lloyd. *Official Documents of the Little Big Horn*. Glendale, California, 1971.

Paine, Lauran. *The General Custer Story*. London, 1960.

Palmer, Robert G. "The Death of Yellow Hair," *Denver Westerner's Brand Book 1963*. Denver, Colorado, 1964.

Parker, Watson. *Gold in the Black Hills*. Norman, Oklahoma, 1966.

Parkman, Francis. *The Oregon Trail*. New York, 1950.

——*La Salle and the Discovery of the Great West*. New York, 1963.

Paulding, Holmes Offley. *Surgeon's Diary With the Custer Relief Column*. Edited by W. Boyes. Washington, D.C., 1974.

Paxson, William Edgar. "Custer's Last Stand," *True West*. Sept.–Oct., 1968.

Peattie, Roderick. *The Black Hills*. New York, 1952.

Perkin, Robert L. "Chivington's Raid—a Black Day in Colorado," *Rocky Mountain News*. January 20, 1957.

Perrigo, Lynn I. "Major Hal Sayr's Diary of the Sand Creek Campaign," *Colorado Magazine*. Vol. XV, No. 2, 1938.

Pickard, Edwin. "I Rode With Custer," edited by Edgar Stewart. *Montana*. Vol. IV, No. 3, 1954.

Praus, Alexis. "The Sioux, 1798–1922: A Dakota Winter Count," *Cranbrook Institute of Science, Bulletin 44*. Bloomfield Hills, Michigan, 1962.

Remsburg, John E. & George J. *Charley Reynolds*. Kansas City, Missouri, 1931.

Reusswig, William. *A Picture Report of the Custer Fight*. New York, 1967.

Rexroth, Mary Collins. "Auntie May and Sitting Bull," *The West*. December, 1968.

Rickey, Don. *Forty Miles a Day on Beans and Hay*. Norman, Oklahoma, 1963.

—— "The Establishment of Custer Battlefield National Monument," *Journal of the West*. April, 1968.

Riggs, David F. *East of Gettysburg*. Bellevue, Nebraska, 1970.

Rister, Carl Coke. *Border Command, General Phil Sheridan in the West*. Norman, Oklahoma, 1944.

Roberts, Richard A. *Custer's Last Battle: Reminiscences of General Custer*. Monroe County, Michigan, 1978.

Robinson, Doane, ed. "Crazy Horse's Story of the Custer Battle," *South Dakota Historical Collections*. Vol. VI, 1912.

Roe, Charles F. *Custer's Last Battle*. New York, 1927.

Rosenberg, Bruce A. *Custer and the Epic of Defeat*. University Park, Pennsylvania, 1974.

Ross, Raymond J. "John A. Martin—Custer's Last Courier," *The West*. April, 1967.

Russell, Don. *Custer's Last*. Fort Worth, Texas, 1968.

——— "Those Long-Lost Custer Panels," *Pacific Historian*. Vol. XI, No. 4, 1967.

Ryan, John. *Ten Years With General Custer Among the American Indians*. Edited by John M. Carroll. Bryan, Texas, 1980.

Sandbertson, Delos G. "Scalped at the Washita," *Kansas Daily Tribune*. June 25, 1869.

Sandoz, Mari. *The Battle of the Little Bighorn*. New York, 1966.

——— *Crazy Horse*. New York, 1942.

——— *Cheyenne Autumn*. New York, 1953.

Saum, Lewis O. "Colonel Custer's Copperhead: The 'Mysterious' Mark Kellogg," *Montana*. Vol. XXVII, No. 4, 1978.

Schmitt, Martin F. & Brown, Dee. *Fighting Indians of the West*. New York, 1948.

——— ed. *General George Crook: His Autobiography*. Norman, Oklahoma, 1946.

Schneider, George A., ed. *The Freeman Journal*. San Rafael, California, 1977.

Schoenberger, Dale. "Custer's Scouts," *Montana*. Vol. XVI, No. 2, 1966.

——— "Charles DeRudio: European Assassin," *Little Bighorn Associates Research Review*. Vol. XIV, 1980.

Schultz, James. *Billy Jackson*. Springfield, Illinois, 1976.

Scott, Hugh L. *Some Memories of a Soldier*. New York, 1928.

Sievers, Michael. "Sands of Sand Creek Historiography," *Colorado Magazine*. Spring, 1972.

Smith, DeCost. *Indian Experiences*. Caldwell, Idaho, 1943.

Spotts, David L. *Campaigning with Custer and the Nineteenth Kansas Volunteer Cavalry*. New York, 1965.

Stallard, Patricia Y. *Glittering Misery*. San Rafael, California, 1978.

Stanley, Henry M. *My Early Travels and Adventures*. London, 1895.

Steckmesser, Kent Ladd. *The Western Hero in History and Legend*. Norman, Oklahoma, 1965.

Stewart, Edgar I. *Custer's Luck*. Norman, Oklahoma, 1955.

——— "A Psychiatric Approach to Custer: Some Reflections," *Montana*. Vol. XXI, No. 3, 1971.

——— "Which Indian Killed Custer," *Montana*. Vol. VIII, No. 3, 1958.

——— & Luce, Edward S. "The Reno Scout," *Montana*. Vol. X, No. 3, 1960.

Stewart, Miller J. "Army Laundresses: Ladies of the Soap Suds Row," *Nebraska History*. Vol. 61, No. 4, 1980.

Stewart, Edgar I. "Variations on a Minor Theme," *Montana*. Vol. I, No. 3, 1951.

Taft, Robert. *Artists and Illustrators of the Old West*. New York, 1953.

——— "The Pictorial Record of the Old West: Custer's Last Stand," *Kansas Historical Quarterly*. Vol. XIV, No. 4, 1946.

Tahan. "The Battle of the Washita," *Chronicles of Oklahoma*. Vol. VIII, No. 3, 1930.

Taunton, Francis B., ed. *Sidelights of the Sioux Wars*. London, 1967.

Taylor, Alfred A. "Medicine Lodge Peace Council," *Chronicles of Oklahoma*. Vol. 2, No. 2, 1924.

Taylor, Colin. *The Warriors of the Plains*. New York, 1975.

Taylor, Joseph Henry. *Sketches of Frontier and Indian Life*. Bismarck, North Dakota, 1897.

———*Kaleidoscopic Lives*. Washburn, North Dakota, 1902.

———"Bloody Knife and Gall," *North Dakota Historical Quarterly*. Vol. IV, No. 3, 1930.

Tebbell, John. *The Compact History of the Indian Wars*. New York, 1966.

Terrell, John Upton & Walton, George. *Faint the Trumpet Sounds*. New York, 1966.

Terry, Alfred H. *The Field Diary of General A. H. Terry*. Introduction by Michael J. Koury. Bellevue, Nebraska, 1970.

Thompson, Erwin N. "The Negro Soldiers on the Frontier: A Fort Davis Case Study," *Journal of the West*. Vol. VII, No. 2, 1968.

Thompson, Erwin N. "The Negro Soldiers on the Frontier: A Fort Davis Case Study," *Journal of the West*. Vol. VII, No. 2, 1968.

Thompson, Peter. *Narrative of the Little Bighorn Campaign*. Edited by Daniel O. Magnussen. Glendale, California, 1974.

Tibbles, Thomas Henry. *Buckskin and Blanket Days*. Garden City, New York, 1957.

Tillett, Leslie. *Wind on the Buffalo Grass*. New York, 1976.

de Trobriand, Philippe Régis. *Military Life in Dakota*. Translated and edited by Lucile M. Kane. St. Paul, Minnesota, 1951.

Turner, Don. *Custer's First Massacre: The Battle of the Washita*. Amarillo, Texas, 1968.

Upton, Richard, ed. *The Custer Adventure*. Fort Collins, Colorado, 1975.

Utley, Robert. *Custer and the Great Controversy*. Los Angeles, 1962.

———*Frontier Regulars*. New York, 1973.

———*Life in Custer's Cavalry*. New Haven, Connecticut, 1977.

———*Custer Battlefield*. Washington, D.C., 1969.

Van de Water, Frederic F. *The Glory Hunter*. New York, 1934.

Van Nuys, Maxwell. "Inkpaduta—the Scarlet Point," *The West*. June, 1967.

Vaughn, J. W. *Indian Fights: New Facts on Seven Encounters*. Norman, Oklahoma, 1966.

Vaughn, Robert. *Then and Now*. Minneapolis, 1913.

Vestal, Stanley. *Sitting Bull, Champion of the Sioux*. Norman, Oklahoma, 1957.

———*New Sources of Indian History*. Norman, Oklahoma, 1934.

———*Warpath*. Boston, 1934.

———*Warpath and Council Fire*. New York, 1948.

Victor, Frances. *Our Centennial Indian War and the Life of General Custer*. Hartford, Connecticut, 1879.

Voorhees, Richard M. "General George A. Custer," *Ohio Archaeological and Historical Quarterly*. Vol. XV, No. 2, 1906.

Wagner, Glendolin Damon. *Old Neutriment*. Boston, 1934.

Watson, Elmo Scott. "Echoes of the Custer Tragedy," *Winners of the West*. Vol. XII, No. 5, 1935.

Weems, John Edward. *Death Song*. Garden City, New York, 1976.

Wellman, Paul I. *The Indian Wars of the West*. Garden City, New York, 1954.

Wemett, W. M. "Custer's Expedition to the Black Hills in 1874," *North Dakota Historical Quarterly*. Vol. VI, No. 4, 1932.

Wheeler, Homer. *Buffalo Days*. Indianapolis, 1923.

Wheeler, Keith. *The Scouts*. Alexandria, Virginia, 1978.

Wheeler, Olin D. *Wonderland*. St. Paul, Minnesota, 1901.

White, Lonnie J. *Hostiles and Horse Soldiers: Indian Battles and Campaigns in the West*. Boulder, Colorado, 1972.

——— "The Hancock and Custer Expeditions of 1867," *Journal of the West*. Vol. V, No. 3, 1966.

——— "Winter Campaigning with Sheridan and Custer," *Journal of the West*. Vol. VI, No. 1, 1967.

Whittaker, Frederick. *A Complete Life of General George A. Custer*. New York, 1876.

——— "General George A. Custer," *Galaxy Magazine*. Vol. XXII, 1876.

Wilson, James Grant. "Two Modern Knights Errant," *Cosmopolitan*. July, 1891.

Wiltsey, Norman B. *Brave Warriors*. Caldwell, Idaho, 1963.

Windolph, Charles. *I Fought With Custer*. New York, 1953.

Wood, Norman B. *Lives of Famous Indian Chiefs*. Aurora, Illinois, 1906.

Wormser, Richard. *The Yellowlegs: The Story of the United States Cavalry*. Garden City, New York, 1966.

Wright, Kathryn. "Indian Trader's Cache," *Montana*. Vol. VIII, No. 3, 1958.

INDEX

Alexis, Grand Duke 207
Arikara 15

Barnitz, Capt. Albert 146, 149–150, 159–
  160, 185–186
Bent, George 64, 186
Benteen, Capt. Frederick 46, 53, 78, 125,
  205–206
  Civil War 31–32
  court-martial 34–39
  DeGress letter 197
  heritage 30–31
  kills Blue Horse 186
  route at battle 274–275, 281
Bighead, Kate 417–419, 422
"Big Leggens" Bruguier 372–373
Blackfeet 86–87
Black Hills 235–253
Black Kettle 163–164, 175–176, 182, 189–
  190, 274
black soldiers 124–126
Bloody Knife 12, 14–18, 265, 270, 272, 276,
  359, 378–379
Blynn, Clara 181–182, 198–199
"Bob" 182
Boies, Blanche 366–367
Bourke, Capt. John 69, 83–84, 92–93, 158,
  218, 337, 339–341, 415
Bouyer, Mitch 79–80, 269, 272, 276, 277
bow-and-arrow 309–310, 348
Bradley, Lt. James 1–4, 93–94, 96–98, 100,
  259, 335, 409
Brisbin, Maj. James 22–23, 256–257, 260,
  299
Brulé 85–86
Buffalo herds 135–141

Burkman, John 50, 405–407

"Calamity Jane" 236
calendar 369–371
Calhoun, Lt. James 237, 244–245, 262–263,
  286, 308–309, 349
"California Joe" 191–192
Catlin, George 133, 137–138, 141, 338, 402–
  403
Cheyenne 132–134, 172, 202–204
Chivington, Col. John 176–179
cholera 171
Cody, "Buffalo Bill" 332, 335–336, 393
Coleman, Pvt. Thomas 22, 59, 101, 265,
  270–271, 318–319, 323, 412
Collins, Mary 221, 389–390
"Comanche" 292–293, 296–298
conservation 138
Cooke, Lt. W. W. 278, 289–290
coups 348–349
Crazy Horse 62–75, 84–85, 266, 415
Crook, Gen. George 83, 325–326, 328–329,
  332–339
Crow 99–100
Curly 49–50, 314–316
Curtis, William Eleroy 17, 18, 241–242, 358,
  398
Custer, Boston 243, 254, 273, 288–289
Custer, Gen. George Armstrong
  ancestry 352–353
  Black Hills 235–253
  burial 345, 411
  Cheyenne child 201–202, 417–418
  Civil War 108–113
  court-martial 173–175
  death 373–375, 409–411

departs Fort Lincoln 253
exhumed 344
greyhound 294–295
horse "Vic" 411
hunting accident 141–142
Kansas 124, 126–127, 204–206
Kentucky 206–208
last message 278
marksmanship 359–360
marriage 113–115
musicians 103
"Nomad" 205
personal flag 351
route to battlefield 78–80, 264–279
"Son of the Morning Star" 184
taxidermy 232–233
Texas 119–124
water phobia 233
West Point 107
Yellowstone 232–235
Custer, Elizabeth 113–116, 120–122, 126–
    127, 324, 390–391, 405–407
Custer, Tom 236, 287–288, 343, 350, 390,
    397

Dakota Sioux 87
Davis, Theodore 135, 139, 276
De Rudio, Lt. Camilius 10, 22, 50, 383–385
desertion 149–152
de Trobriand, Col. Philippe Régis 208–212
dog-soldier 133–134
Dodge, Col. Richard 126, 135, 159, 310, 337,
    369–370, 382
Dorman, Isaiah 25–28, 254, 347
Dull Knife village 269, 340

Elliott, Maj. Joel 192–195

Fetterman massacre 128–132
Finerty, John F. 9, 217, 338
fireworks 182–183
flood 170–171
Fort Lincoln 253–254, 399–400
Fort McKenzie slaughter 63–64
Frett, John 50

Gall 316, 375–380
"Garry Owen" 293–294
Gatling guns 57, 257–259
Gerard, Fred 19–20, 24–25, 240, 257
Gibbon, Col. John 2, 93–94, 98–99, 255–
    256, 299–300
gold discovered 82, 239–241, 246–251
Grattan massacre 65–67
Grinnell, George Bird 243–244, 265, 360
Grouard, Frank 70–71, 73, 326–329

hair 344–346

Hancock expedition 132–148
Harrington, Lt. Henry 312
heart-eating 397–398
Henry, Col. Guy 90–92
Hickok, "Wild Bill" 133
Hyde, George 75, 84–85, 138, 214

Inkpaduta 219, 418
Iron Hawk 309–310

Joseph, Chief 82, 226
Joseph White Bull 371, 373–374

Kellogg, Mark 273, 299–301
Kelly, Fanny 94–97, 199
Keogh, Capt. Myles 290–294, 305
Keyserling, Count Hermann 220

Lincoln, Abe 115
Little Bighorn Battle
    art 362–369
    breadbox 270–271
    burials 285–286, 320
    Custer's route 264–279
    duration 302–303
    Indians killed 420–421
    Last Stand site 408–409
    monuments 407–408
    mythology 355–361
    national reaction 330–332
    number of Indians and soldiers 383
    officers exhumed 343–345
    panic 306–308
    Reno besieged 52–62, 76
    Reno Hill 404–405
    Reno skirmish 7–14
    soldiers killed 383
    survivors evacuated 320–323
Longfellow 380–391

McGillycuddy, Dr. Valentine 72, 192, 337
McIntosh, Lt. Donald 20–21
Mackenzie, Col. Ranald 340–341
McLaughlin, James 137, 222, 252–253, 375,
    382, 394–395, 399
Madden, Sgt. Mike 320–322
Mangas Coloradas 305–306
Marquis, Dr. Thomas 303, 304, 308, 417
Martini, Giovanni 277–280
Medicine Lodge conference 144–147
Me-o-tzi / Mo-nah-se-tah 200–202, 417–418
Miles, Gen. Nelson 216–217, 301–302
Mills, Anson 329, 336
Miniconjoux 86
Mosby's Rangers 14, 117–118
museum 347
mutilation 160–161, 285–286

Nash, Mrs. 156–157
news of battle 323–328
nomenclature 213–214
North, Luther 23, 236, 360

Oglala 86
oldest survivors 350

Parkman, Francis 135, 139–140
Plenty Coups 90–91, 233, 404
Powder River expedition 340
punishment 151–153

Rain in the Face 380–381, 386–399, 410, 416
Red Cloud 214
Ree 15
Reed, Harry Armstrong "Autie" 273, 288, 347, 405
Reno, Maj. Marcus
  ancestry 30–31
  and Ella Sturgis 44–47
  and Mrs. Bell 42–43
  Court of Inquiry 10–12
  court-martial 45–46
Reynolds, Lonesome Charley 18–20, 246–247, 268, 273, 360
Rosebud fight 88–92

sabers 383–384
Sand Creek 176
Sans Arcs 87, 371
Satank 145, 147–148
Satanta 143–146
scalping 162–167
Sheridan, Gen. Philip 82, 179–181, 253, 404
Sherman, Gen. Wm. Tecumseh 143–144, 149, 180
sign language 122–123, 161–162

Sitting Bull 87, 211–232, 377
  "Bison" 223–225
  British medals 302
  death 392
  dream 267
Slim Buttes battle 336–337, 339
smallpox 15–16
Smith, DeCost 217, 227–228, 330, 368, 390, 393
Stanley, Gen. David 234–236, 388
Stanley, Henry M. 133, 142–144, 166
stoicism 337–339
Sturgis, Lt. Jack 329–330
Sturgis, Col. Samuel 123, 329–330
Sun Dance 265–266

telegraph line 272–273
Terry, Gen. Alfred 145, 147, 253–261, 334–335
Terry-Custer army 100–101
Two Kettle 86
Two Moon sepulcher 401–402

Unkpapa 85–86
U.S. Indian policy 80–82, 143–144

Walker, Judson Elliott 221, 403
Wanamaker, Rodman 375
Washita battle 182–197
Weir, Capt. Thomas 281–285
whisky 49–52, 154
Whitman, Walt 357, 363–364
Whittaker, Frederick 287, 356–359
Wooden Leg 52, 85, 133, 214–215, 266, 289–290, 295, 301, 308, 341–342, 373, 421
Wyllyams, Sgt. Frederick 160–161

Yellowstone expedition 232–235
Young Hawk 28

Design by David Bullen
Typeset in Mergenthaler Imprint
by Wilsted & Taylor
Printed by Maple-Vail
on acid-free paper